"A groundbreaking compilation, this book offers a unique blend of theoretical and practical insights on climate litigation in the Global South. With a focus on vulnerabilities and intersectionality, the editors bring together a diverse range of voices to provide a framework for understanding the disproportionate impacts of climate change and the role of courts in addressing them. The book's contributors explore innovative ways litigation can be more responsive to the lived realities of affected communities, and relay novel perspectives and strategies rooted in local contexts. A significant contribution to the field of climate litigation, this volume reshapes how we think about climate justice and legal accountability in a rapidly changing world."

**Michael Burger**, *Executive Director of the Sabin Center for Climate Change Law, Columbia Law School*

# Climate Litigation and Vulnerabilities

This volume explores climate litigation as a means to tackle the rights and socio-ecological, intergenerational, gender, racial, and other justice implications of the ever-growing vulnerability to climate change, whilst critically engaging with the notions of vulnerability and intersectional climate justice.

With insightful analysis, thought-provoking case studies, and a global perspective, the collection illustrates the opportunities and pitfalls of litigation pursued by people from the Global South who face intersecting forms of oppression and marginalisation amidst the climate crisis. Contributors discuss litigation strategy, novel legal arguments, institutional barriers, and unique socio-ecological and political challenges in the Global South. Divided into two parts, the book recognises that climate change is an existential threat to humanity more frequently being tackled in courts worldwide. The first part exposes the limits of litigation as a mechanism for intersectional climate justice for vulnerable people in the Global South. The second part highlights innovations in climate litigation in pursuit of intersectional climate justice.

The book will be of interest to academics, researchers, and policymakers in the areas of human rights law, environmental law, climate law, Latin American studies, South Asian studies, and African studies.

**Maria Antonia Tigre** is the Director of Global Climate Change Litigation at the Sabin Center for Climate Change Law at Columbia Law School in New York, United States. She is originally from Brazil.

**Melanie Jean Murcott** is a South African intersectional climate justice scholar, and an Associate Professor at the Institute of Marine and Environmental Law at the University of Cape Town, South Africa.

**Susan Ann Samuel** is a lawyer in India and a PhD researcher at the University of Leeds – School of Politics and International Studies, United Kingdom.

## Routledge Studies in Law, Rights and Justice

Series Editor:

Chris Monaghan is the Head of Law and a Principal Lecturer in Law at the University of Worcester, and holds a PhD from the Dickson Poon School of Law at King's College London. He has published widely on aspects of public law.

*Routledge Studies in Law, Rights and Justice* seeks to publish leading monographs and edited collections that explore the interplay between rights and justice across different areas of law and legal practice. The series serves as a home for scholars working in areas such as human rights, social justice, constitutional justice, business and human rights, equality rights and civil justice. It encourages authors to address the theoretical and practical aspects of the application of rights, the achievability of justice in these uncertain times, and the methods available to individuals, organisations, and states to achieve justice. *Routledge Studies in Law, Rights and Justice* embraces both scholarship from a national and international viewpoint and encourages authors to explore rights and justice from a global perspective. It strives to break down existing disciplinary silos and encourage collaboration, which offers the opportunity to publish thought provoking, original and cutting-edge work. The aim is to foster debates, build bridges between different areas of scholarship, and encourage a wider perspective on the underlying issues that might limit the applicability of rights, or render justice difficult to achieve.

*Routledge Studies in Law, Rights and Justice* primarily consider rights and justice from a legal perspective, but does however, welcome submissions that take a broader view and engage with the wider socio-economic, political, and social context. The series editor is very keen to consider works by established and early-career academics, and submissions are encouraged from scholars based all around the world.

Titles in this series:

**Teaching of Rights and Justice in the Law School**
Challenges and Opportunities for Research Led Teaching
*Edited by Stephen Hurley and Chris Monaghan*

**Climate Litigation and Vulnerabilities**
Global South Perspectives
*Edited by Maria Antonia Tigre, Melanie Jean Murcott and Susan Ann Samuel*

# Climate Litigation and Vulnerabilities

## Global South Perspectives

Edited by Maria Antonia Tigre,
Melanie Jean Murcott and
Susan Ann Samuel

Routledge
Taylor & Francis Group
LONDON AND NEW YORK

First published 2025
by Routledge
4 Park Square, Milton Park, Abingdon, Oxon OX14 4RN

and by Routledge
605 Third Avenue, New York, NY 10158

*Routledge is an imprint of the Taylor & Francis Group, an informa business*



Funding: This work was supported by the UK Research and Innovation [grant number: MR/V021141/1].



*British Library Cataloguing-in-Publication Data*
A catalogue record for this book is available from the British Library

*Library of Congress Cataloging-in-Publication Data*
Names: Murcott, Melanie, editor. | Tigre, Maria Antonia, editor. | Samuel, Susan Ann, editor.
Title: Climate litigation and vulnerabilities : global south perspectives / edited by Melanie Jean Murcott, Maria Antonia Tigre, and Susan Ann Samuel.
Description: Abingdon, Oxon [UK] ; New York, NY : Routledge, 2025. | Series: Routledge studies in law, rights, and justice | Includes bibliographical references and index.
Identifiers: LCCN 2025006181 (print) | LCCN 2025006182 (ebook) | ISBN 9781032722863 (hardback) | ISBN 9781032747378 (paperback) | ISBN 9781003470632 (ebook)
Subjects: LCSH: Climatic changes—Law and legislation—Developing countries | Vulnerability (Personality trait)—Developing countries. | Environmental law, International.
Classification: LCC K3585.5 .C587 2025 (print) | LCC K3585.5 (ebook) | DDC 344/.124046—dc23/eng/20250212
LC record available at https://lccn.loc.gov/2025006181
LC ebook record available at https://lccn.loc.gov/2025006182

ISBN: 978-1-032-72286-3 (hbk)
ISBN: 978-1-032-74737-8 (pbk)
ISBN: 978-1-003-47063-2 (ebk)

DOI: 10.4324/9781003470632

Typeset in Times New Roman
by Apex CoVantage, LLC

*To the future generations who will inherit the world we shape today, and to those whose lives are already impacted by climate change, especially in the Global South. May this work contribute to a more just and resilient future.*

*For Nicholas, Theo, and Arthur – may you inherit a world that learns from the past and cherishes our planet.*

*With hope and dedication.*

# Contents

# Contributors

## Editors:

**Maria Antonia Tigre** is the Director of Global Climate Change Litigation at the Sabin Center for Climate Change Law at Columbia Law School in New York, United States. She is originally from Brazil.

**Melanie Jean Murcott** is a South African intersectional climate justice scholar and an associate professor at the Institute of Marine and Environmental Law at the University of Cape Town, South Africa.

**Susan Ann Samuel** is a lawyer in India and a PhD researcher at the University of Leeds – School of Politics and International Studies, United Kingdom.

## Authors:

**James Barrett** is an Australian legal practitioner with experience in native title, human rights, climate change advisory services, and cross-border disputes. He was educated at the Australian National University and Harvard University as a Fulbright scholar.

**Valeriana Augusta Broetto** is a PhD candidate in environmental science at the Institute of Energy and Environment of the University of São Paulo and a member of the South American Network for Environmental Migrations (RESAMA). She is originally from Brazil.

**Nina Burri** is a lecturer at the University of St. Gallen, Switzerland; counsel at RISE Attorneys at Law; and legal advisor on business and human rights for the Swiss development organisation HEKS/EPER. She regularly partners with lawyers and organisations from the Global South on human rights cases.

**Elisa Fiorini Beckhauser** is a PhD candidate in law and sustainability at the University of Salento and a researcher at the Euro-Mediterranean Center on Climate Change, Italy. She is originally from Brazil.

**Moushita Dutta** is a doctoral student at the Faculty of Law, McGill University, in Montreal, Canada. She is originally from India.

**Laura Duarte Reyes** is a senior legal advisor at the European Center for Constitutional and Human Rights (ECCHR), based in Berlin, Germany. She is originally from Colombia.

**Ayan Garg** is a fifth-year law student at the National Law University, Delhi. He is originally from India.

**Nitai Hinduja** is a fifth-year law student at the National Law University, Delhi, and a founding member of the Collective for Environmental Action. He is originally from India.

**Kanika Jamwal** is a PhD candidate at the Faculty of Law, National University of Singapore, Singapore. She is originally from India.

**Preetkiran Kaur** is a young professional at the Centre for Trade and Investment Law, established by the Ministry of Commerce and Industry, Government of India, in New Delhi. She is originally from India.

**Muhammed Tawfiq Ladan** is the director general/CEO of the Nigerian Institute of Advanced Legal Studies, Supreme Court Complex, Abuja/Akoka Campus, Lagos. He is a professor of law from Nigeria.

**Katherine Lofts** is a doctoral student in the Faculty of Law at McGill University in Montreal, Canada, and a research associate with the Canada Research Chair in Human Rights, Health, and the Environment.

**Nkiruka Chidia Maduekwe** is the Director General/CEO of the National Council on Climate Change, Abuja, Nigeria. She is an associate professor of law from Nigeria.

**Sathiabama S.** is a legal expert at the National Investigation Agency, Ministry of Home Affairs, New Delhi, India. She is originally from India.

**Vedavalli S.** is an assistant professor of law at the Tamil Nadu National Law University in Tiruchirappalli, India. She is originally from India.

**Thalia Viveros Uehara** is a postdoctoral researcher at the Department of Public Law and Governance at Tilburg University, Netherlands, and a senior research fellow at the Max Planck Institute for Comparative Public Law and International Law in Heidelberg, Germany. She is originally from Mexico.

# Foreword

## *Dina Lupin*

In 2020, while working as the Director of the Global Network for Human Rights and the Environment (GNHRE),[1] I was approached by Maria Antonia Tigre and Melanie Jean Murcott with an idea for a new and ambitious project. Over the previous few years, Tigre, in her work at the Sabin Center, had been carefully tracking emerging trends in climate litigation and the growing body of scholarship on that litigation. What was concerning to the editors of this volume was that there was a significant gap in the recognition of this scholarship: Very little attention was being paid to climate litigation in the Global South.

As discussed in the introduction to this book, Tigre, Murcott, and Ann Samuel recognise this as a product of two intersecting practices of injustice. This is, first of all, a climate injustice. Although Global South countries are, for the most part, the smallest contributors to global climate emissions, they suffer the worst of its consequences. As a result, these countries and their populations are all too often treated merely as the victims of climate change, whose salvation is thought to lie in the wealth, technology, and expertise of the Global North (a long-standing, colonial narrative). The struggles, initiatives, and solutions generated by the Global South go unseen and underappreciated.

Second, throughout this project, the editors have seen the absence of recognition of Global South voices in climate litigation scholarship as a practice of epistemic injustice – a failure to engage with the knowledge and expertise found in the Global South. As Tigre and Murcott have argued, knowledge produced in the Global South is given a particularly low status, seen always as particular and contextual, while research from the North is seen as timeless and universal.[2] Global South researchers are constantly called on to convince reviewers, editors, and publishers that their knowledge is relevant, useful, or sufficiently remarkable to be of interest to audiences in the North. Within academic research and scholarship, Global South scholars face significant obstacles to having their research published, and once published, they find that it is often simply ignored.

In addressing the epistemic injustice, by creating a platform for critical, reflective, and contextual research on climate litigation in the Global South by primarily Global South scholars, the editors of this book also seek to address the climate injustice. This book shines a bright light on the work that Global South activists and advocates are doing to address and respond to the climate crisis, but it also uncovers crucial lessons to be learnt from that work. Global South litigation is taking place in some of the most advanced legal systems in the world, but also in some of the most challenging contexts. Litigation in the Global South – its successes and failures – offers critical learning and insights for activists, lawyers, judges, and scholars all over the world, especially in the Global North.

The project – which has included not only this book but also a special collection of the *Journal of Human Rights Practice*, webinars and workshops, writing support and mentoring activities, and the compilation of two carefully researched and extensively annotated bibliographies of work on climate litigation and climate injustice – has been extraordinarily ambitious in both its breadth and its depth. It has powerfully demonstrated the intersection between climate and epistemic injustice and made apparent the extraordinary work of activists and scholars in the Global South.

## Notes

1 The Global Network for Human Rights and the Environment is a community of scholars, activists, practitioners, defenders, researchers, and policymakers working at the intersection of human rights and the environment. As a space for collaboration, learning, and resistant reimagining, we were incredibly excited to create a home for this critically important project.

2 Melanie Jean Murcott and Maria Antonia Tigre, 'Developments, Opportunities, and Complexities in Global South Climate Litigation: Introduction to the Special Collection' (2024) 16 *Journal of Human Rights Practice* 1.

# Acknowledgements

This project has been greatly enriched by the generous contributions and valuable insights shared by the editorial team during the closed workshop held on 26–27 January 2023. We would like to extend a heartfelt thank-you to Kim Bouwer, Michael Burger, Fernanda Cavedon-Capdeville, Erin Daly, Susan Elizabeth Farran, Tracy-Lynn Field, Giovanna Maria Frisso, Carlotta Garofalo, Dina Lupin, Stellina Jolly, Doug Kysar, Lea Main-Klingst, James May, Rohan Nanthakumar, Harj Narulla, Mayara Nunes Medeiros de Souza, Zaneta Sedilekova, Natalia Urzola, and Zunaida Moosa Wadiwala. Your input played a critical role in shaping this project, and we are deeply grateful for your thoughtful guidance.

Each contributing author showed incredible commitment to our vision of shining a light on Global South struggles for climate justice in the courts. We wish to acknowledge each author team for your wonderful contributions: Elisa Fiorini Beckhauser and Valeriana Augusta Broetto; Ayan Garg and Nitai Hinduja; Thalia Viveros Uehara, Moushita Dutta, and Katherine Lofts; Nina Burri and Laura Duarte Reyes; James Barrett, Preetkiran Kaur, Sathiabama S., and Vedavalli S.; Muhammed Tawfiq Ladan and Nkiruka Chidia Maduekwe; and Kanika Jamwal. Your collective voices are powerful and transformative as we confront intersectional injustice in a time of climate crisis.

We would also like to thank the anonymous peer reviewers, whose substantive feedback on each of the chapters significantly improved the work and enhanced its academic rigour. Your constructive critiques have been invaluable in elevating the overall quality of this project.

This work was supported by the UK Research and Innovation [grant number: MR/V021141/1], which empowered Susan Ann Samuel's involvement in the project during her complementary PhD studies. We are also grateful to the Worldwide Universities Network (WUN) for the research development grant awarded to enable collaboration among the University of Cape Town, University of Pretoria, University of Leeds, University of Southampton, and Columbia University, and the launch of this volume. We particularly appreciate the thoughtful input and contributions of Tafadzwa Mushonga, Richard Beardsworth, Viktoria Spaiser, and Dina Lupin, which were facilitated by the WUN grant. Funding from the University of Cape Town was also pivotal.

The second round of the project has been supported by an outstanding team, including Jemima Roe, Mathilde Knöfel, Şimal Efsane Erdoğan, Fezeka Ntsanwisi, and Danielle Yeatman. Your ongoing assistance and contributions are deeply appreciated, and your support continues to be crucial as we advance this vital work. We are also deeply grateful to the series editor, Chris Monaghan, for the incredibly valuable guidance and support throughout the writing and editing process.

We extend our heartfelt thanks to the Global Network for Human Rights and the Environment (GNHRE) for its ongoing support and partnership throughout this project. The collective expertise and collaboration within the GNHRE network have been integral, and we are profoundly grateful for your engagement. In particular, we are extremely grateful to Dina Lupin for championing this idea from the beginning, through her then role as director of GNHRE. This project would not have been possible without you.

Lastly, we acknowledge our families, partners, and friends, who have loved, nurtured, and supported us during this journey.

# Acronyms and abbreviations

## A

| | |
|---|---|
| **ACHPR** | African Charter on Human and Peoples' Rights |
| **AUD** | Australian dollars |

## C

| | |
|---|---|
| **CC** | Swiss Civil Code |
| **CCA** | Climate Change Act |
| **CCRI** | Children's Climate Risk Index |
| **CEC** | Central Empowered Committee |
| **CEDAW** | United Nations Convention on the Elimination of All Forms of Discrimination against Women |
| **$CO_2$** | carbon dioxide |
| **CRC** | United Nations Convention on the Rights of the Child |
| **CSO** | civil society organisation |

## E

| | |
|---|---|
| **ECCHR** | European Center for Constitutional and Human Rights |
| **ECHR** | European Court of Human Rights |
| **EIA** | environmental impact assessment |

## F

| | |
|---|---|
| **FAO** | Food and Agriculture Organisation |
| **FHC** | Federal High Court |
| **FIDA** | International Federation of Women Lawyers |
| **FMWR** | Federal Ministry of Water Resources (Nigeria) |
| **FPIC** | free, prior, and informed consent |
| **FREP** | Fundamental Rights (Enforcement Procedure) |

## G

| | |
|---|---|
| **GHG** | greenhouse gas |
| **GCF** | Green Climate Fund |
| **GNHRE** | Global Network for Human Rights and the Environment |
| **GW** | gigawatt |

## H

| | |
|---|---|
| **HRAEP** | human rights approach to environmental protection |

## I

| | |
|---|---|
| **IACtHR** | Inter-American Court of Human Rights |
| **ICCPR** | International Covenant on Civil and Political Rights |
| **ICESCR** | International Covenant on Economic, Social, and Cultural Rights |
| **ICJ** | International Court of Justice |
| **ICTs** | information and communications technologies |
| **INDC** | intended nationally determined contribution |
| **IPCC** | Intergovernmental Panel on Climate Change |
| **IRB** | institutional review board |
| **ITLOS** | International Tribunal for the Law of the Sea |

## K

| | |
|---|---|
| **KIADB** | Karnataka Industrial Areas Development Board |
| **km** | kilometres |

## M

| | |
|---|---|
| **MNES** | Ministry of Non-Conventional Energy Sources |
| **MNRE** | Ministry of New and Renewable Energy |
| **MoEFCC** | Ministry of Environment, Forest and Climate Change |
| **MW** | megawatt |

## N

| | |
|---|---|
| **NAP** | National Action Plan |
| **NAPCC** | National Action Plan on Climate Change of India |
| **NBWL** | Standing Committee of National Board for Wildlife |
| **NBS** | National Bureau of Statistics |
| **NDC** | nationally determined contribution |
| **NGN** | naira (Nigerian currency) |
| **NGO** | non-governmental organisation |
| **NGT** | National Green Tribunal of India |

| | |
|---|---|
| **NHRC** | National Human Rights Commission of Nigeria |
| **NIALS** | Nigerian Institute of Advanced Legal Studies |
| **NLAC** | new Latin American constitutionalism |
| **NOA** | National Orientation Agency |
| **NOC** | non-objection certificate |
| **NESREA Act** | National Environmental Standards and Regulations Enforcement Agency (Establishment) Act 2007 (Nigeria) |

## O

| | |
|---|---|
| **OECD** | Organisation for Economic Cooperation and Development |

## P

| | |
|---|---|
| **PIL** | public interest litigation |

## R

| | |
|---|---|
| **RVNL** | Rail Vikas Nigam Limited |

## S

| | |
|---|---|
| **SAN** | Senior Advocate of Nigeria |
| **SAPCC** | State Action Plans on Climate Change of India |
| **SAS** | South Asian states |
| **SDGs** | Sustainable Development Goals |
| **SEA** | Environmental Evaluation Service |
| **SPDC** | Shell Petroleum Development Company |
| **SPIDEL** | Section on Public Interest Litigation |

## U

| | |
|---|---|
| **UK** | United Kingdom |
| **UN** | United Nations |
| **UNEP** | United Nations Environmental Programme |
| **UNFCCC** | United Nations Framework Convention on Climate Change |
| **UNGA** | United Nations General Assembly |
| **UNICEF** | United Nations Children's Emergency Fund |
| **USA** | United States of America |

## W

| | |
|---|---|
| **WEP** | Women Environmental Programme |
| **WUN** | Worldwide Universities Network |

# Figures and tables

## Figures



## Tables

# Preface

## Confronting the Global South climate litigation 'visibility challenge'

Prominent climate law scholars lament the lack of visibility of Global South climate litigation in global climate law and governance discourse.[1] They argue that greater visibility could shine a light on 'the quest for climate justice for vulnerable communities and groups' as well as 'buttress understanding of whether the goals of the Paris Agreement are being met'.[2] The efforts of climate justice activists and litigators in the Global South to combat the human suffering and environmental destruction caused by climate change might also receive greater publicity, potentially attracting crucial donor funding to strengthen their important work. But how can this lack of visibility be addressed? One useful strategy is for scholars, legal practitioners, and activists from the Global South to build communities of practice that draw attention to climate justice advocacy by Global South interlocutors and produce scholarship that tests limited Global North narratives about climate litigation.[3] This volume embraces that strategy as part of a broader project in collaboration with the Global Network for Human Rights and the Environment (GNHRE), titled 'Climate Litigation in the Global South'.[4] Maria Antonia Tigre and Melanie Jean Murcott, established Global South voices in the field of climate law and governance, have led this GNHRE project since 2021, and Susan Ann Samuel joined in 2023 as an emerging scholar.[5]

Overall, by delving into the significance of climate litigation for vulnerable groups in the Global South, this volume pursues the goal of amplifying Global South perspectives of leading and emerging scholars, practitioners, and activists on how the courts can be used as a site of climate action to promote intersectional climate justice and address human rights violations linked to climate change. The volume advances epistemic justice by confronting some of the underlying causes of the lack of visibility of Global South climate litigation, including 'a lack of diversity among editorial boards and peer reviewers, language barriers, a lack of funding for open access publications, subscriptions, etc., and differences across academic (and legal) cultures'.[6] Cognisant of 'a model of gatekeeping, based on Northern (Anglophone) academic habits that ignore and belittle academic cultures elsewhere in the world', we have sought to disrupt the Global South's low level in hierarchies of knowledge.[7] However, doing so requires resources, particularly people's time, access to literature, and funding. Such resources are hard to come by but essential. For instance, they can help overcome the inequalities and asymmetries that the dominance of the English language in academia creates for those whose first language is not English.[8]

A research development grant from the Worldwide Universities Network (WUN) empowered us to appoint Fezeka Ntsanwisi as a junior research fellow at the University of Cape Town, who tirelessly conducted copy-editing on the contributions to this volume and offered her time and energy in other ways to advance our project. We are thankful that many other people generously volunteered their time, including an 'editorial team', comprising established scholars and respected practitioners in the field of climate change law and governance who provided mentorship and guidance to contributors during and following a closed workshop in January 2023;[9] Mathilde Knöfel, who provided research assistance; Şimal Efsane Erdoğan, who updated our project website; and Danielle Yeatman, who prepared a bibliography of sources related to climate vulnerability and provided editing support. We followed a double-blind peer-review process in editing this volume, approaching scholars and practitioners who kindly shared their expertise and showed an appreciation of the spirit and objects of our project in anonymously providing constructive and comprehensive input.

Each of the contributors to this volume demonstrated understanding and magnanimity as we sought to embrace epistemological diversity while navigating gatekeeping practices deeply entrenched in academia. One way in which epistemological diversity was embraced was by actively encouraging the citation of Global South scholarship in contributions. Problematically, when relatively well-resourced and established publications on the topic of climate litigation in the Global South overlook important Global South perspectives, particularly those of Black and Brown women, they unconsciously contribute to peripheralising these important voices. In other words, a failure to cite widely can itself operate as a form of epistemic injustice that entrenches existing hierarchies of knowledge. We do not mean to discount the challenges of keeping pace with the burgeoning body of climate litigation scholarship, or to suggest, in a high-handed manner, that we have been able to cite every relevant piece of scholarship in this volume. Instead, in the struggle for climate justice, we hope to encourage inclusivity and promote awareness of the politics of citation practices in knowledge production about climate litigation in the Global South.

Sadly, due to time and resource constraints, we were unable to include contributions from all the collaborators originally identified for participation. This limitation evidences the need for more resources to be directed toward knowledge production by Global South scholars, particularly emerging voices.

Our efforts have culminated in this volume, *Climate Litigation and Vulnerabilities: Global South Perspectives*, edited by three women from the Global South, with contributions from a team of 16 incredible scholars and/or legal practitioners, of which 13 are originally from the Global South. Four of the contributors are men, and the rest are women. Including the editors, five of the contributors to the volume are from Latin America, three are from Africa, eight are from Asia, while the remaining contributors are from various other parts of the world, including Canada, Switzerland, and Australia. In addition to our introduction and conclusion, the volume comprises nine chapters, divided into two parts: four chapters in the first part focus on the limitations of climate litigation when it comes to advancing intersectional climate justice for the Global South, and five chapters in the second part innovatively explore possibilities for the future of Global South climate litigation.

All chapters seek to fill a gap in vulnerability-centred analyses of climate litigation. They do so by bringing to the fore ways in which climate injustices converge along intersecting axes of race, age, location, gender, health, caste, class, ethnicity, and other social characteristics to render people particularly vulnerable to the causes and impacts of climate change. In other words, the volume frames climate litigation with reference to accounts of human suffering and the underlying causes of that suffering, drawing on intersectionality theory. However, rather than situating people in the Global South as passive victims of climate change, the volume brings to the fore their agency, particularly showcasing struggles of women, children, and Indigenous peoples in combatting the climate crisis in courts and other tribunals around the world. The volume disseminates original, scholarly research on the phenomenon of climate litigation, embedded in literature from diverse disciplines. Chapters illustrate both the realism and the optimism that the ongoing struggle for intersectional climate justice necessitates, with lessons for and from Nigeria, Bangladesh, India, Brazil, Colombia, Ecuador, the Pacific Islands, and beyond.

This volume was written primarily for an audience of academics, including in the fields of climate law, environmental law, human rights law, comparative constitutional law, and secondarily, for practising lawyers, government officials, judges, activists, and other participants in the global climate justice movement more broadly. Our hope is that the GNHRE project generally, and this volume in particular, will stimulate funding to support and empower more Global South–led research on climate action, including through multidisciplinary collaborations that can translate and render the findings of this and other climate litigation scholarship more accessible to lawyers, law, and policymakers, and the general public.

*Melanie Jean Murcott*
*Maria Antonia Tigre*
*Susan Ann Samuel*

## Notes

1 See, for example, Jolene Lin and Jacqueline Peel, *Litigating Change in the Global South* (Oxford University Press 2024) 51.
2 Lin and Peel (n 1) 17.
3 See, for example, Kim Bouwer, Uzuazo Etemire, Tracy-Lynn Field and Ademola Oluborode Jegede (eds), *Climate Litigation and Justice in Africa* (Bristol University Press 2024); Melanie Murcott and Maria Antonia Tigre, 'Developments, Opportunities, and Complexities in Global South Climate Litigation: Introduction to the Special Issue'

(2024) 16(1) *Journal of Human Rights Practice* 1, 6–8 <https://doi.org/10.1093/jhuman/huad070> accessed 31 January 2024.
4 GNHRE, 'Climate Litigation in the Global South Project' <https://gnhre.org/?page_id=14314> accessed 18 September 2024.
5 The outputs from the first round of our project were published as a special issue in the 16(1) *Journal of Human Rights Practice* (2024).
6 Murcott and Tigre (n 3) 4.
7 Murcott and Tigre (n 3) 3–4.
8 Murcott and Tigre (n 3) 4.
9 GNHRE, 'Editorial Team' <https://gnhre.org/?page_id=14332> accessed 18 September 2024.

# Introduction

## Linking Global South vulnerability, intersectionality, and climate litigation

*Melanie Jean Murcott, Maria Antonia Tigre, and Susan Ann Samuel*

### Introduction

In the first half of 2024 alone, the world saw floods in Afghanistan; heatwaves in Bangladesh; floods and landslides in Bolivia, Burundi, and the Philippines, and floods in Brazil, Ethiopia, Kenya, Papua New Guinea, Somalia, Tanzania, and Uganda.[1] A commonality is present in these events: Climate chaos disproportionately affects the lives and environments of people in the Global South, who have contributed the least to the climate crisis.[2] The economic costs are massive. Climate chaos is likely to push millions into poverty by the end of the century.[3] In the six months since the 28th Conference of the Parties (COP) to the United Nations Framework Convention on Climate Change (UNFCCC) in 2023 (COP28) alone, extreme weather events fuelled by human-induced climate change caused more than $41 billion in damage.[4] Meanwhile, many people affected by climate change, who are far from the political processes that take place each year at COP, have limited resources to defend themselves against the increasingly violent climate shifts.[5]

Yet in courtrooms worldwide, people – particularly those who are disproportionately vulnerable to climate change – along with lawyers and activists, have realised that their perspectives, stories, and voices can counteract the escalating threats they face. Climate litigation offers hope as people mobilise to pursue recognition, accountability, and change. Building on a burgeoning body of scholarship concerning courts as sites of contestation about the causes and impacts of climate change,[6] this volume focuses on the journey for climate justice through litigation advanced by people from the Global South.[7] The journey is fraught with complexities and limitations.[8] Among the many challenges identified in the literature, legal systems are often stretched thin, litigants have limited financial resources to bring cases and present the necessary evidence, and judges often lack capacity in climate law.[9] Still, the Global South is filled with success stories of climate litigation, both of communities mobilising and of courts accepting their claims of climate-related human rights violations. These stories illustrate both universal and particularised vulnerability[10] fundamentally shaped by climate change. Telling these stories promotes recognition of the struggles for climate justice[11] and shifts perceptions that people in the Global South are passive victims.[12] Recognition, in turn, presents an opportunity to respect, rather than romanticise, people's resilience and agency.[13]

DOI: 10.4324/9781003470632-1

For example, communities in Kenya affected by climate change–related flooding living on the shores of Lake Baringo sued the government for their failure to anticipate, prevent, or minimise the causes of climate change and mitigate its adverse impacts.[14] In Uganda, young people alleged that the government failed to mitigate loss and damage from extreme weather events and prevent environmental degradation for present and future generations.[15] In Nepal, a court halted the construction of a road due to its alleged impact on protected species and Nepal's obligation to mitigate climate change, preserving the park that would be damaged for present and future generations.[16] In the Philippines, the government agreed to settle a case and committed to ensuring proper legal responses to guarantee that the dangers of climate-related flooding were properly addressed.[17] In Colombia, inhabitants of a small town questioned the government's failure to provide an adequate water supply infrastructure when natural water reservoirs dried out due to climate change.[18] At the international and regional levels, countries from the Global South, most of them small island states, requested advisory opinions from the world's highest courts, the International Court of Justice (ICJ),[19] the International Tribunal for the Law of the Sea (ITLOS),[20] and the Inter-American Court of Human Rights (IACtHR),[21] asking them to clarify states' responsibilities for climate change.[22]

This small sample of cases shows the power of Global South actors to mobilise and confront the causes and impacts of climate change. Drawing on a broader sample of cases, this volume, *Climate Litigation and Vulnerabilities: Global South Perspectives*, brings together leading and new voices, mostly from the Global South, to unpack the evolving landscape of climate litigation in these regions. Part 1 of this volume, titled 'Exposing the Limits of Litigation as a Mechanism for Intersectional Climate Justice', includes four chapters, each offering a critical perspective on how climate litigation intersects with various forms of inequality and vulnerability in the Global South. Part 2, titled 'Innovative Litigation in Pursuit of Intersectional Climate Justice', explores diverse and groundbreaking legal strategies in climate litigation, focusing on elevating the voices and experiences of vulnerable and marginalised groups.

Our point of departure is that vulnerability to climate change is complex, and experienced universally, but also unevenly and acutely in the Global South.[23] While humanity's universal vulnerability to climate change is inherent insofar as humans exist in bodies susceptible to suffering,[24] many of the particularised experiences of vulnerability to climate change are socially constructed, illustrative of intersectional climate injustice, a concept we discuss later.[25] This vulnerability is inextricably intertwined with deeply entrenched, interlocking patterns of disadvantage shaped by colonisation, racial capitalism, patriarchy, and other oppressive systems.[26] Concurrently, those least responsible for climate change are disproportionately exposed to its devastating impacts,[27] while those most responsible – corporations and governments in the Global North – remain largely insulated from its impacts.[28]

Globally, vulnerability to the impacts of climate change is growing[29] and is an issue of life and death.[30] In 2023, the WHO reported that almost half of the world's population is acutely vulnerable to climate change.[31] Moreover, in vulnerable regions (largely in the Global South), 'the death rate from extreme weather events in the last decade – from around 2013 to 2023 – was 15 times higher than in less vulnerable ones'.[32]

In turn, climate science and key climate change laws have begun to acknowledge the links between climate change and vulnerability. For instance, the Intergovernmental Panel on Climate Change (IPCC) stated in 2022 that '[c]limate change is contributing to humanitarian crises where climate hazards interact with high vulnerability'.[33] Further, the IPCC emphasised that

> [v]ulnerability of ecosystems and people to climate change differs substantially among and within regions . . . driven by patterns of intersecting socioeconomic development, unsustainable ocean and land use, inequity, marginalization, historical and ongoing patterns of inequity such as colonialism, and governance.[34]

Against this background, the next part of this chapter engages more deeply with the concept of vulnerability and connects it to the concept of intersectional climate injustice. We do so to grapple with the value of these concepts in climate litigation analyses. We further justify the volume's focus on Indigenous peoples, women, and girls. We reflect on experiences of vulnerability in our home countries – Brazil, India, and South Africa – and consider how these experiences are illustrative of vulnerability and intersectional climate injustice. Thereafter, the chapter engages with the global phenomenon of climate litigation as a response to vulnerability and intersectional climate injustice. Lastly, we outline the structure of the volume and summarise the key insights on litigation as a mechanism available to confront vulnerability amidst the climate crisis in various parts of the Global South, particularly India,[35] Bangladesh,[36] Nigeria,[37] the Pacific Islands,[38] Indonesia,[39] and various countries in Latin America.[40]

## *Vulnerability*

*Vulnerability* stems from Latin origins, where the noun *vulnus* (meaning 'wound'), the verb *vulnerare* ('to wound'), and the Late Latin adjective *vulnerabilis* integrated into English as 'vulnerable' in the early 1960s.[41] Over time, since the late 1600s, the concept of vulnerability has undergone a transformation, expanding beyond mere physical susceptibility to include facets of psychological, moral, and spiritual anguish.[42] Lacking a precise definition, and often termed as 'complex',[43] the idea of vulnerability has experienced significant scholarly attention and growing incorporation across various disciplines.[44] It is now widely applied across various domains, including the medical sciences, sociology, psychology, development studies, climate science, engineering, human rights, disaster management, security, social risk, and public health, among others.[45]

How has vulnerability been understood in the context of a changing Earth system? Until the 1970s, environmental disasters were viewed in scholarly literature as 'natural events',[46] or 'acts of God'.[47] Little attention was given to human intervention or agency in mitigation, adaptation, or resilience; hazards and disasters were studied by geographers as 'physical' occurrences, leaving little space for the concept of vulnerability in their research.[48] Earth Day in 1970 was a catalyst for re-routing perceptions. A focus on human experiences of environmental problems thus gained traction in the environmental protection movement.[49]

Subsequently, global climate governance norms have emerged that recognise vulnerability to climate change. For example, the preamble of the 2015 Paris Agreement highlights the need for parties, when taking climate action, to

> respect, promote and consider their respective obligations on human rights, the right to health, the rights of indigenous peoples, local communities, migrants, children, persons with disabilities and people in vulnerable situations and the right to development, as well as gender equality, empowerment of women and intergenerational equity.

In addition to holding the increase in the global average temperature to well below 2 degrees Celsius, a core global goal of the Paris Agreement concerning adaptation is to strengthen resilience and reduce vulnerability to climate change.[50]

Scholars are increasingly recognising that the climate emergency is an 'act of man' and a distinct marker of the Anthropocene imagery.[51] Critical discourse on the Anthropocene imagery acknowledges universal exposure to environmental change but resists an undifferentiated view of humanity. An undifferentiated view obscures particularised experiences of suffering linked to 'the underlying social and economic drivers of anthropogenic Earth system disruption, including colonial conquest, imperial dispossession and the imposition of a global capitalist order that systematically abuses nature and exploits large segments of the world's population'.[52] Relatedly, nuanced understandings of vulnerability feature in modern climate change literature, recognising that exposure to climate harm and risk is not only universal but also 'determined by societal and economic preconditions that shape the way in which people are prepared for or respond'.[53]

In legal discourse, the notion of vulnerability has been unpacked as a heuristic in the context of the interpretation of human rights.[54] Kotzé argues that vulnerability invites an 'understanding of the vulnerability of the entire living order as a starting point to critique the epistemological closures and regulatory failures of the current human rights paradigm'.[55]

Other studies by legal scholars shed light on the diverse vulnerabilities and adaptive capacities of different demographic groups in the face of climate change. Jegede highlights the displacement of Indigenous peoples in Africa due to climate change and advocates for extending the Kampala Convention's protection to Indigenous populations.[56] Jamwal argues for including Indigenous peoples as 'expert' consultants in climate committees.[57] Samanta discusses the impact of environmental displacement on citizenship.[58] Nakayama looks into the need for preparation for climate migrations and how vulnerabilities can be reduced as well as addressed.[59] Krishnan explores gendered aspects of climate-induced displacement in India.[60]

Scholarship on the notion of vulnerability in the context of climate litigation is emerging.[61] For instance, Ohdedar points to how rights-based litigation in the Global South can confront structural vulnerability.[62] Fornalé explores how the international human rights framework takes into account vulnerability, within the lens of climate litigation at the international and domestic levels.[63] Sormunen discusses the need to rethink the available remedies in light of the climate crisis through a vulnerability approach.[64] Kelleher examines the issue of causation in rights-based climate litigation as a way to operationalise climate justice.[65]

A nascent body of literature engages with youth-focused climate litigation and youth-led movements, respectively, emphasising the role of children and future generations in promoting human rights–based approaches to climate change.[66] Similarly, scholars have started analysing the role of Indigenous peoples in climate litigation.[67] Batt considers how Indigenous knowledge is vulnerable to biopiracy and misappropriation and should be accorded due respect in climate litigation.[68] Feminist scholarship increasingly engages the links between litigation, vulnerability, and gender (in)justice.[69]

This volume deploys the notion both descriptively, to account for inherent and constructed vulnerability, and prescriptively, to advance appropriate legal responses, given that the ways in which societal or institutional arrangements cause, entrench, and heighten vulnerability to climate change.[70] In particular, this volume adds to the existing scholarship by exploring the potential of climate litigation to advance intersectional climate justice for people in the Global South in the face of vulnerability. We discuss the concept of intersectional climate justice next.

## *Intersectional climate justice*

Rooted in Black feminism and critical race theory,[71] intersectional understandings of climate (in)justice reveal how 'vulnerability to climate change impacts can be affected positively (through privilege) or negatively (through oppression) by many axes of difference at once'.[72] As Sultana argues, 'climate justice fundamentally is about paying attention to how climate change impacts people differently, unevenly, and disproportionately, as well as redressing the resultant injustices in fair and equitable ways'.[73] Intersectionality entails recognising 'the ways in which systems of inequality based on gender, race, ethnicity, sexual orientation, gender identity, disability, and other forms of discrimination "intersect" to create unique dynamics and effects'.[74] As we discuss further later on, adopting an intersectional approach, this volume aligns with the perspectives of climate justice scholars who highlight the connections (or intersections) among 'institutionalized dependence on fossil fuels, systematic disregard for human lives, racial discrepancy between those who have a say and those who fail pain'.[75] The starting point of these scholars is that justice entails an appreciation that every person has equal and inherent value, is entitled to the opportunity to have a decent life, and that we owe each other moral duties as a result.[76] Because climate change 'undermines indisputably basic needs, . . . kills,. . . inflicts disease [and] rips away livelihoods', 'the climate crisis constitutes a massive injustice'.[77] It is a form of environmental injustice. As Pettit puts it:

> [T]he climate justice message is that poor people have not been 'waiting for the science' on global warming. They have been living with it – and with many other forms of pollution and degradation – for many years, as 'social sinks' for the externalisation of environmental costs.[78]

According to Cripps, '[c]limate justice requires preventing that harm, making up for it as far as possible'.[79] Her scholarship embraces intersectionality theory, including by acknowledging that

> [c]limate change violates human rights. . . . But it doesn't violate them at random. Climate injustice feeds on existing violence and discrimination, on a history of rights abuses. Until we understand that, there is no prospect of climate justice.[80]

Contributions to this volume advance synergy among climate justice discourse and intersectionality theory to move beyond simplistic 'single-variable analyses of vulnerability and the resulting essentialism of inquiries focused on a single category'.[81] For instance, as Dutta and Lofts' chapter points out,

> there is now widespread recognition in the literature that gender, in conjunction with other intersecting social categories such as class, caste, race, disability, and sexuality, plays an important role in mediating both vulnerability to climate change impacts, as well as adaptive capacity.[82]

Intersectional analyses of climate injustice further reveal that 'while women in general find themselves frequently excluded from international climate policy-making, it is Indigenous women that experience this exclusion disproportionately'.[83] This is borne out, for example, by Duarte Reyes and Burri's discussion of the women of Pari Island, Indonesia, in this volume.[84] They highlight how, in the typical pattern of intersecting gender and climate injustice, women tend to be vested with disproportionate household responsibilities, including cleaning, collecting fuel and water, shopping for food, and cooking, and such tasks tend to become more labour-intensive because of disasters, heightening risks and experience of physical violence and leading to higher levels of mortality and morbidity among women.

Murcott has highlighted the value of courts adopting 'an intersectional, symbiotic approach to environmental and cultural rights protection and participation' in South African climate litigation led by Indigenous peoples.[85] As she points out, it can advance 'complementary norms of inclusion and equitable decision-making about the environment', which is 'important given that climate change represents an existential threat to indigenous peoples'.[86] Murcott's views are supported by various chapters in this volume, including that of Barrett, who highlights how the Torres Strait Islanders face becoming refugees in their own country given sea level rise and flooding, and that climate change is forcibly displacing their traditional culture of *Ailan Kastom*.[87] He comments on how climate litigation advanced by the Torres Strait Islanders has sought to introduce legally disruptive (novel) duties of care under Australian law, given their 'unique vulnerabilities' along multiple axes of oppression and marginalisation.

Chapters in this volume focus on litigation as a form of legal mobilisation by Indigenous peoples, women, and children in the Global South who face intersectional struggles for climate justice.[88] These groups emerged as an area of focus because they have been playing a remarkable role in advancing climate justice in courts worldwide.[89] One of this volume's goals is to shine a light on and strengthen these efforts. However, the focus on these groups should not be viewed as discounting constructed and particularised vulnerability along other axes of oppression, exclusion, and marginalisation that are heightened by the climate crisis. In our concluding chapter, we discuss the need for further climate litigation research adopting an intersectional climate justice lens in relation to disability, gender, race, caste, health conditions, age, migration, and other social conditions.[90] We note there that broadening the scope of the research on vulnerable populations, including by studying the adequacy of remedies and the implementation of decisions, is crucial to ensure that 'climate litigation more effectively responds to the diverse and pressing needs of those most at risk in the Global South'.[91] We also highlight the need for further research on climate litigation as a response to the vulnerability of more-than-human life. Further, our focus on the gendered impacts of climate change on women and girls should not be viewed as overlooking the reality that these impacts go further and include non-binary, gender-queer, bi-gender, gender-fluid, or male population groups, among others.[92]

## *Experiences of vulnerability and intersectional climate injustice in Brazil, India, and South Africa*

Whilst authoring and editing this volume, in our contexts – Brazil, India, and South Africa – we witnessed the devastating and unequal impacts of climate change. These climate impacts caused immense suffering, particularly for the most vulnerable in society, and for all other life with whom we share the Earth. This suffering brings to the fore the need for effective legal mechanisms to address intersectional climate injustice.

In April and May 2024, Rio Grande do Sul, a state in southern Brazil, experienced catastrophic floods that were among the most severe in recent memory. The flooding reached 478 cities and 90% of the state, an area equivalent to the United Kingdom. Over 183 people lost their lives, more than 640,000 properties were left without water, and 440,000 without electricity.[93] In total, 2.4 million people were affected.[94] The extreme weather event led to widespread destruction, displacing over 442,000 residents and straining local resources as communities struggled to respond with a damaged infrastructure.[95] The floods were exacerbated by unprecedented rainfall, with a third of the annual precipitation occurring in just ten days. The rain brought 14.2 trillion litres of water into the Guaíba Lake, a volume equivalent to almost half of the Itaipu Hydroelectric Plant's reservoir, the world's second-highest hydroelectric power plant.[96] The event was found to be unprecedented and extremely rare in the current climate, occurring once in a 100- to 250-year period, and very high uncertainty.[97] However, these 'extreme' and 'unprecedented' events have become increasingly common. This event occurred as the state was still recovering from an extratropical cyclone in September 2023, resulting in compounding impacts.[98] The 2024 floods were influenced by a heatwave in Brazil's central-western and southeastern regions, which caused a climatic imbalance and intensified rainfall in the south.

While Rio Grande do Sul is one of Brazil's wealthiest states, the recent floods have starkly highlighted the vulnerability of marginalised communities within its borders.[99] They have disproportionately impacted low-income groups, including Indigenous populations, riverbank dwellers, and small farming communities.[100] Reports indicate that at least 240 informal settlements, 80 Indigenous villages, and 40 predominantly *quilombola* (descendants of enslaved Africans) communities have suffered severe consequences.[101] While 90% of the state is affected by the floods, the poorest areas are among the hardest-hit.[102] These areas struggle with inadequate evacuation and relocation options, further deepening their vulnerability. The impact of climate change on these floods is evident not only in the sheer volume of rainfall but also in the vulnerability of the urban areas affected. Many cities in Rio Grande do Sul are not equipped to handle such extreme weather events due to poor urban planning, which often ignores local geography and environmental preservation. These vulnerable communities are often situated on hill slopes, riverbanks, and lakeshores, where housing is precarious and water management is lacking.[103] The occupation of flood-prone areas, particularly near rivers and lakes, has made these cities even more susceptible to flooding. The limited resources available to these communities significantly hinder their ability to cope with and recover from such extreme events, exacerbating the climate injustice they face.

The floods profoundly affected women, children, and older adults. Widespread school closures have impacted children's education.[104] Waterborne diseases have become a pressing concern.[105] Additionally, Rio Grande do Sul's status as home to Brazil's largest population of older adults adds another layer of complexity. Older adults face unique challenges during such disasters, including mobility issues, chronic illnesses, and a reluctance to evacuate, further highlighting the intersection of climate change and social vulnerabilities.[106] Furthermore, reports of gender-based violence against women and girls in shelters further contributed to a cycle of violence and vulnerability.[107] Intersectionality exposes how Black, Indigenous, *quilombola*, and older people, as well as the LGBTQ+ community, women, and people with disabilities, face heightened climate risks. Further, refugees from

Venezuela and Haiti – who had already fled their own countries and sought shelter in Brazil – are among those worst affected by the floods.[108]

In the summer of 2024, India experienced record-breaking heatwaves, with northern regions recording temperatures over 52.3 degrees Celsius (126 degrees Fahrenheit), resulting in more than 143 deaths.[109] Delhi alone has 33 million people, and the urban poor were affected the most, illustrative of intersectional climate injustice.[110] Simultaneously, Assam and Manipur faced devastating floods triggered by intense rainfall. People in Manipur are impacted by ethnic conflict and experienced the third-worst flooding since 1988.[111] Further, in late July, landslides in the district of Wayanad in Kerala caused by incessant rain claimed more than 230 lives,[112] displacing nearly 10,000 people[113] and destroying several villages – Punjirimattom, Mundakkai, Chooralmala, and Vellarimala.[114] The affected villages are located in remote, hilly terrains with limited infrastructure and emergency services. This geographical isolation results in delayed aid and minimal inclusion in disaster planning. Wayanad is home to particularly vulnerable groups: Indigenous people, the Adivasi, and tribes.[115] Roughly 31% of the Adivasi people who live in Kerala are based in Wayanad, according to the 2011 census. They are a particularly historically marginalised group, including through land dispossession, socio-economic pressures, and political manipulations.[116] Residing in ecologically fragile areas, they have livelihoods that depend heavily on agriculture and forestry, making them highly susceptible to environmental changes and disasters. Inherent and historically rooted injustices through the social norms of caste dynamics further intensify their vulnerability – with systemic discrimination limiting their access to resources, education, and political representation.[117] As Garg and Hinduja's chapter in this volume discusses, the colonial roots of *Adivasi* marginality are exacerbated by socio-economic and political dynamics, which the coloniality of the legal system has largely reinforced. The interlocking axes of oppression and marginalisation that the *Adivasi* experience hamper their ability to prepare for, respond to, and recover from climate-induced disasters, representing a vivid example of intersectional climate injustice.

On 15 July 2024, nearly 160,000 people were adversely affected by floods in and around Cape Town, South Africa, as around 47,663 structures were 'flooded or damaged during several days of extreme weather'.[118] While the research linking climate change to these particular floods is inconclusive, climate attribution science confirms that 'climate change has intensified extreme rainfall events'.[119] Most people worst affected by these floods are Black and live in shacks in informal settlements, a legacy of colonisation and apartheid spatial injustice.[120] The impacts of flooding in Cape Town include homelessness, loss of livelihoods, food and water insecurity, and disease.[121] They are felt most acutely by Black women, children, and elderly people who live below the poverty line,[122] illustrative of intersectional climate injustice.

These examples provide a glimpse into what is being felt by vulnerable people worldwide. Sadly, the devastation of climate change is widespread, and science shows it is set to worsen. They represent human faces and stories and families. With extremely diverse landscapes, cultures, languages, and ethnic groups, the vulnerability of people in Brazil, India, and South Africa to climate change is not only inherent to the human condition but also a product of historical legacies, literacy, the presence of communal tensions, gender disparities, economic inequalities, religion, caste, and more. These examples reinforce the need for the research conducted in this edited volume on vulnerability and intersectional climate injustice. Given the ways in which the climate crisis worsens existing vulnerabilities, next we consider litigation as a potential response.

## Litigating in response to climate vulnerabilities and injustice

Litigation in pursuit of climate change mitigation and adaptation measures, and to seek redress for loss and damage caused by climate change, has emerged as a potent strategy to combat injustice and foster greater ambition in climate action.[123] As a dynamic tool, climate litigation engages diverse stakeholders in the global effort to combat the climate crisis.[124] Through various legal avenues and strategies, climate litigation provides a means to challenge inadequate climate laws and policies and mobilise a more just and inclusive response to the climate crisis. This is so despite the limitations of litigation in general, and climate litigation in particular. The limitations include challenges in enforcing judgment,[125] restrictive standing rules,[126] the costs and time of litigating,[127] and the conservative nature of many legal systems around the world, rendering litigation ill-suited to combat the wicked problem of climate change absent legal disruption or transformation.[128]

Nevertheless, the IPCC has affirmed the influence of climate litigation on the outcome and ambition of climate governance, and as an avenue for actors to influence climate policy outside formal UNFCCC processes, such as the COP.[129] Indeed, since the early 2000s, climate litigation has expanded in numbers, geographical diversity, and scope.[130] At the end of 2024, the Sabin Center's Climate Litigation Databases encompassed 2,895 cases across 54 jurisdictions and 21 international or regional courts, quasi-judicial bodies, or other adjudicatory bodies.[131] In an analysis from April 2024, the Sabin Center identified that 8.3% of the cases arose in the Global South.[132] Such litigation is playing an important role in addressing the lack of international consensus on reducing greenhouse gas (GHG) emissions,[133] combatting developments authorised without climate change adaptation and mitigation measures having been properly considered,[134] compelling redress for human rights violations caused by the impacts of climate change,[135] granting rights to nature,[136] holding multinational corporations accountable for their contributions to the climate crisis,[137] and more.[138]

In many instances, climate litigation fills the void left by inadequate or inexistent laws and policies, pushing the boundaries of legal interpretation. For instance, South Africa provides an example of how climate litigation has compelled state actors to consider climate change in administrative decisions and be held accountable for planning choices that could worsen the causes or impacts of climate change.[139] Moreover, South Africa's climate litigation has emphasised the need for meaningful public participation in decision-making that affects the climate system.[140] In Brazil, a constitutional challenge brought by political parties pushed the boundaries of the interpretation of international climate law when the Brazilian Federal Supreme Court (STF) ruled that the Paris Agreement is considered a human rights treaty.[141] This precedent opens the door for a variety of stakeholders who are widely affected by the climate crisis to push for increased ambition in emissions reductions or the protection of essential carbon sinks.[142]

While the number and breadth of cases is significant, the growth of climate litigation only tells a part of the story. Importantly, climate litigation provides a platform to diversify voices and stakeholders involved in climate policy, advocating for a more inclusive agenda. Through public interest litigation, individuals – often those who do not get a seat at the table – can take steps to have their voices heard, rights protected, and ambitious climate laws and policies developed and implemented. Even unsuccessful cases can hold significance, contributing to the development of legal frameworks and ensuring the debate for further action persists. The role and limits of litigation in response to vulnerability amidst the climate crisis are the focus of this volume.

## Structure of the volume

Addressing narratives of climate litigation in the Global South and vulnerabilities, this volume is divided into two parts. Part 1, 'Exposing the Limits of Litigation as a Mechanism for Intersectional Climate Justice', highlights limits of climate litigation when it comes to addressing inherent and particularised vulnerabilities and intersectional climate injustices in the Global South. It exposes how legal frameworks in parts of Latin America and in India are not necessarily well-suited to delivering justice to marginalised communities, particularly Indigenous peoples, women, and those facing health crises. By highlighting how colonial legacies, extractivism, and inequality influence climate litigation, the chapters critique the ability of courts to remedy the vast injustices of climate change, particularly in regions with deeply embedded structural inequalities. At the same time, each of the chapters offers glimmers of hope, by demonstrating ways in which limits can be overcome or at least resisted.

Part 2, 'Innovative Litigation in Pursuit of Intersectional Climate Justice, adopts a more generally optimistic perspective, showcasing innovative legal strategies that seek to elevate vulnerable people's voices – especially those of women, children, and Indigenous peoples – given intersectional climate injustice in the Global South. From transnational cases to child-led initiatives, this section demonstrates how creative legal arguments and human rights–based approaches can be employed to disrupt legal systems and push for transformative change when traditional legal avenues fall short. Chapters explore transnational climate litigation, forum shopping, new procedural avenues for litigation, and the role of the precautionary principle. Elaborating on the vulnerability-centred lens outlined in this introduction, and recognising intersectional climate injustice, chapters seek to illuminate the potential of climate litigation as a form of transformative legal mobilisation, while also acknowledging the hurdles that must be overcome to ensure that legal actions are inclusive and equitable. Next, we discuss these two parts of the volume in more detail.

## Limitations of climate litigation in the Global South

Part 1 begins with a chapter by Beckhauser and Broetto, titled 'Facing Coloniality within Legal Systems: Indigenous Peoples in Latin American Climate Litigation'. Beckhauser and Broetto examine the role of coloniality in Latin American legal systems and its impact on Indigenous peoples' climate litigation efforts. Garg and Hinduja then explore the dynamics of wind energy projects and extractivism in India, reframing how climate litigation can address these issues in their chapter, titled 'Reframing Climate Change Litigation in the Global South: A Study of Wind Energy Projects and Extractivism in India'. In the third chapter, 'Addressing Health Crises through Courts? Understanding Inequality in Latin America's Climate Litigation', Uehara delves into the link between health crises and inequality in Latin America's climate litigation landscape. Finally, Dutta and Lofts analyse the inclusion of women and girls in India's climate adaptation policies, exploring the opportunities and challenges for future litigation in 'The Inclusion of Women and Girls in Climate Adaptation Policy in India: Opportunities and Challenges for Future Litigation'. Together, these chapters provide a comprehensive look at the limits and potential of litigation in advancing intersectional climate justice across different regions.

From a Latin American perspective, in Chapter 1, Beckhauser and Broetto engage with the coloniality of legal systems as a barrier to Indigenous peoples' participation in climate litigation. Chapter 1 therefore explores the deep-rooted colonial legacy within Latin America and its impact on climate litigation brought by Indigenous people. It examines how the coloniality of these legal frameworks continues to undermine Indigenous peoples, reinforcing vulnerabilities that make them disproportionately susceptible to the effects of climate change. The chapter highlights the tension between Western legal systems – rooted in colonialism – and Indigenous worldviews, particularly in the context of land stewardship and environmental protection. It argues that these legal systems, shaped by colonial ideals, often fail to fully address the unique vulnerabilities of Indigenous communities or respect their cosmological and legal interpretations.

At the same time, they demonstrate that Indigenous peoples' reliance on traditional knowledge and their intimate connection with ecosystems play a crucial role in biodiversity preservation and climate resilience. Focusing on two climate cases in Ecuador and Colombia, the chapter analyses how courts respond to Indigenous claims for justice. It assesses whether courts perpetuate colonial practices or embrace a decolonising approach that supports Indigenous perspectives. Through this analysis, the chapter reveals the legal and evidentiary challenges Indigenous peoples face in navigating legal systems that are not designed to accommodate their rights and cosmologies.

In Chapter 2, Garg and Hinduja illustrate how renewable energy projects inflict various harms on already-marginalised communities in India, such as exclusion, loss of livelihoods, and land dispossession. They expose these as harms caused by climate change, in that they represent a 'continuation of extractivism, albeit modified'. Yet climate litigation in India has not generally addressed these harms. Garg and Hinduja thus argue that climate litigation must be understood to include litigation instituted by vulnerable persons against climate adaptation and mitigation measures that heighten existing patterns of oppression, exclusion, and marginalisation. They draw on the experiences of communities resisting wind power projects in India to illustrate the need for climate litigation strategies imbued with an appreciation of extractivism theory.

Uehara exposes, in Chapter 3, how the intersection of health vulnerability with other forms of vulnerability to climate change has largely been overlooked in climate litigation in Latin America. Her chapter points out how social inequalities amplify exposure to ecological shifts. For instance:

> In Chile, warmer climates have been linked to the spread of vector-borne diseases, such as Chagas and dengue. The same is true in equatorial regions, like Colombia and Ecuador, due to El Niño and La Niña climatic phenomena. Climate change has been linked to mental health issues in Mexico, with longitudinal data projecting a 2.1% increase in suicide rates in some Mexican municipalities, attributed to heat-induced stress.

These shifts are experienced most acutely by those who are already vulnerable to climate change, including Indigenous peoples, due to existing patterns of exclusion, marginalisation, and oppression that influence who has access to healthcare.

Uehara emphasises the right to health as a crucial lens through which to understand climate-related health vulnerability. She illustrates how climate litigation in Latin America 'has only partially addressed vulnerable populations' lack of opportunities to prevent and treat climate-related and exacerbated health conditions'. She proposes 'a more comprehensive approach' in climate litigation that tackles the social dimensions of health vulnerability through community lawyering, fostering advocacy networks, progressive legal traditions, and judicial consideration of claimants' social contexts.

Chapter 4 reveals that, in India, climate litigation has not yet addressed the particularised vulnerabilities of women and girls to climate change. Moreover, climate law and policy in the country largely ignore the gendered impacts of climate change and the plight of women and girls in India. In this context, Dutta and Lofts explain how access to justice that empowers women to address environmental and social issues, human rights, and evolving climate change case law emerging from courts could facilitate such litigation. Dutta and Lofts argue thus:

> India's progressive constitutional framework and strong tradition of public interest litigation offer a promising foundation for advancing adaptation-related climate litigation to reduce the vulnerability of women and girls to climate change.

Overall, these chapters point to limits of litigation as a mechanism to address intersectional climate injustice experienced by Indigenous peoples and women. Nevertheless, they propose ways in which courts can enhance their role in facilitating climate justice. Further, Part 1 offers insights into the necessity of innovation in climate litigation strategy, thus setting the scene for Part 2 of the volume.

## Innovating climate litigation in the Global South

Part 2 includes five chapters highlighting specific cases and legal frameworks from different regions, all linked by a common pursuit of intersectional climate justice. Each chapter explains the methodology adopted for case selection. The first chapter of the second part, 'Elevating Women's Voices in Transnational Climate Litigation: The Case of *Asmania et al. v Holcim*', by Burri and Duarte Reyes, discusses the pivotal role of Indonesian women in transnational climate litigation, focusing on the high-profile case against Swiss-based cement company Holcim. The second chapter, 'Forum Shopping in Climate Litigation? Three Cases Involving the Torres Strait Islands', by Barrett, examines the potential of forum shopping in climate litigation through three landmark cases involving the Torres Strait Islanders at the domestic (Australia) and international level.

Next, 'Needs for Child-Led Climate Litigation in Bangladesh: Lessons from India and Pakistan', by Kaur, Sathiabama, and Vedavalli, emphasises the need for child-led climate litigation in Bangladesh while drawing lessons from India and Pakistan. In the fourth chapter, 'A Human Rights Approach to Environmental Protection (HRAEP) as a Tool for Fostering Climate Resilience for the Nigerian Woman', Ladan and Maduekwe present a human rights–based approach to environmental protection as a strategy for enhancing climate resilience among Nigerian women. Finally, 'A Litigation Strategy for Vulnerable Communities Pursuing Climate Litigation: The Indian Iteration of the Precautionary Principle and the Reversal of the Burden of Proof', by Jamwal, concludes this section by examining India's application of the precautionary principle and the reversal of the burden of proof, offering a litigation strategy tailored to the needs of vulnerable communities. Each chapter contributes to the broader conversation on how innovative legal tools can foster intersectional climate justice across various global contexts.

In Chapter 5, drawing on lessons from a case before the Swiss legal system instituted by people of Pari Island in Indonesia, *Asmania et al. v Holcim*, Burri and Duarte Reyes explore the possibilities of transnational litigation as a pathway to climate justice. They illustrate the value of intersectionality theory in developing innovative legal strategies that can overcome obstacles to access to justice and recognition of women who are leading climate justice movements in the Global South. For instance, they point to gender-sensitive interviews as one way to understand the lived realities of women and their communities in a time of climate change.

In Chapter 6, with reference to struggles for climate justice of the Torres Strait Islanders, Barrett defends the phenomenon of strategic forum shopping. He demonstrates how Indigenous peoples, as agents in their own cause, can instrumentalise their vulnerability to climate change in different ways to advance climate mitigation and adaptation efforts by choosing the right fora to litigate climate harms.

Kaur, Sathiabama, and Vedavalli engage with the need for child-led climate litigation in Bangladesh as a tool to build resilience against climate vulnerabilities of children in Chapter 7. They discuss the potential of such litigation with reference to human rights jurisprudence emerging from the Bangladeshi courts and lessons from child-led climate cases in India and Pakistan.

A human rights approach to environmental protection is explored in Chapter 8 to advance climate justice for the Nigerian woman, given the intersecting injustices she experiences. Ladan and Madukwe's chapter on this topic represents a first attempt to critically interrogate the practice and procedure of using Nigeria's Fundamental Rights (Enforcement Procedure) Rules 2009 as a tool for climate litigation, with a focus on the climate vulnerabilities of women in Nigeria.

In Chapter 9, Jamwal explains how vulnerable groups in India (and possibly beyond) could utilise the Indian Supreme Court's iteration of the precautionary principle. This iteration is particularly valuable for those with limited access to financial resources and scientific evidence. Jamwal explains:

> [A]s soon as the litigant can establish (1) the presence of scientifically uncertain and (2) justified concern(s) and (3) serious or irreversible harm, the [Indian Supreme Court] . . . presume[s] the presence of non-negligible risk of harm. Consequently, the burden of proof automatically shifts to the defendant. The defendant must then prove the absence of non-negligible risk.

Finally, the book ends with a conclusion, which points to recurring themes and lessons, gaps in our research, and a future research agenda. Ultimately, this volume reveals that litigation is plausible if there is insufficient mechanism to confront climate injustice. The power of this mechanism is strengthened by acknowledging the complexity of vulnerability and embracing intersectionality.

## Notes

1 Oli Pearce and Joe Ware, 'Climate Breakdown 2024: 6 Months of Climate Chaos Since COP28' (*Christian Aid*, 2024).
2 World Health Organisation (WHO), 'Climate Change' (12 October 2023) <https://www.who.int/news-room/fact-sheets/detail/climate-change-and-health> accessed 25 September 2024.
3 Andrea Willige, 'A Third of India's Economy Relies on Nature: Here's Why Corporates Need to Invest More in Natural Climate Solutions' (*World Economic Forum*, 5 August 2024)

<https://www.weforum.org/agenda/2024/08/india-economy-natural-climate-solutions/> accessed 25 September 2024; Emmanuel Skoufias, Mariano Rabassa and Sergio Olivieri, 'The Poverty Impacts of Climate Change: A Review of the Evidence' (2011) *Policy Research Working Paper No 5622* <https://elibrary.worldbank.org/doi/abs/10.1596/1813-9450-5622> accessed 17 August 2023. See generally, Susan Ann Samuel, 'Climate Justice and Capabilities Approach – A TWAIL Discourse: Redefining the Fourth Environmental Era' in Sumudu Atapattu, Freya Doughty-Wagner and Enéas Xavier (eds), *The Fourth Environmental Era: Climate Justice* (Vernon Press Forthcoming 2026).

4 Christian Aid (n 1).

5 Viktoria Spaiser, Nicole Nisbett and Cristina G Stefan, '"How Dare You?" – The Normative Challenge Posed by Fridays for Future' (2022) 1 *PLOS Climate* e0000053 <https://doi.org/10.1371/journal.pclm.0000053> accessed 24 October 2024. See further, Richard Beardsworth, '"Remember, Remember the Month of November": Ahead of COP29' (*Open Access Government*, 9 October 2024) <https://doi.org/10.56367/OAG-044-11158> accessed 22 October 2024; Richard Beardsworth, 'Climate Leadership and a Normative Framework for Political Action' (*Open Access Government,* 8 October 2021) <https://www.openaccessgovernment.org/climate-leadership-normative-framework-political-action/113753/> accessed 7 April 2023. See also Jamwal Chapter 9, p 272.

6 See, for example, César Rodríguez-Garavito (ed), *Litigating the Climate Emergency* (Cambridge University Press 2022); Kim Bouwer et al. (eds), *Climate Litigation and Justice in Africa* (Bristol University Press 2024).

7 We use the term 'Global South' normatively, as discussed in Melanie Murcott and Maria Antonia Tigre, 'Developments, Opportunities, and Complexities in Global South Climate Litigation: Introduction to the Special Issue' (2024) 16(1) *Journal of Human Rights Practice* 1, 6–8 <https://doi.org/10.1093/jhuman/huad070> accessed 31 January 2024. See also Jolene Lin and Jacqueline Peel, *Litigating Climate Change in the Global South* (Oxford University Press 2024) 6–10; Usha Natarajan, 'Environmental Justice in the Global South' in Carmen G Gonzalez, Sara L Seck and Sumudu A Atapattu (eds), *The Cambridge Handbook of Environmental Justice and Sustainable Development* (Cambridge University Press 2021); Antony Anghie, 'Rethinking International Law: A TWAIL Retrospective' (2023) 34 *European Journal of International Law* 7 <https://doi.org/10.1093/ejil/chad005> accessed 24 September 2024. See also Barrett, Chapter 6, p 193.

8 See, for example, Lisa Chamberlain and Melissa Fourie, 'Using Climate Litigation to Strengthen Advocacy Strategies: The Life After Coal Campaign in South Africa' (2024) 16(1) *Journal of Human Rights Practice* 248, 249 <https://doi.org/10.1093/jhuman/huad021> accessed 8 September 2023; Lisa Chamberlain, 'The Value of Litigation to Women Environmental Human Rights Defenders in South Africa' in Cathi Albertyn, Meghan Campbell, Helena Alviar García and Marta Rodriguez de Assis Machado (eds), *Feminist Frontiers in Climate Justice* (Edward Elgar 2023) 213, 214, 225–235; Bolanle Erinosho, 'Chapter 4: Climate Litigation: Access to Judicial Review in National Courts' in Francesco Sindico et al. (eds), *Research Handbook on Climate Change Litigation* (Edward Elgar 2024) 57–76; Joanna Setzer, Nicola Silbert and Lisa Vanhala, 'Chapter 13: The Effectiveness of Climate Change Litigation' in Francesco Sindico et al. (eds), *Research Handbook on Climate Change Litigation* (Edward Elgar 2024) 245–262; Lorena Zenteno Villa, 'Exploring Institutional Barriers to Effective Human Rights-Based Climate Litigation in Latin American Courts – Lessons from Chile and Ecuador' (2024) 16(1) *Journal of Human Rights Practice* 273 <https://doi.org/10.1093/jhuman/huad067> accessed 18 September 2024; Juan Auz, 'The Political Ecology of Climate Remedies in Latin America and the Caribbean: Comparing Compliance between National and Inter-American Litigation' (2024) 16(1) *Journal of Human Rights Practice* 182 <https://doi.org/10.1093/jhuman/huad057> accessed 18 September 2024;

Yusra Suedi and Marie Fall, 'Climate Change Litigation before the African Human Rights System: Prospects and Pitfalls' (2024) 16(1) *Journal of Human Rights Practice* 146 <https://doi.org/10.1093/jhuman/huad024> accessed 18 September 2024; Ademola Oluborode Jegede, 'Framing Climate Litigation in Individual Communications of the African Human Rights System: Claw-Backs and Substantive Divergences' (2024) 16(1) *Journal of Human Rights Practice* 107 <https://doi.org/10.1093/jhuman/huad018> accessed 18 September 2024; Maria Antonia Tigre, 'The "Fair Share" of Climate Mitigation: Can Litigation Increase National Ambition for Brazil?' (2024) 16(1) *Journal of Human Rights Practice* 25 <https://doi.org/10.1093/jhuman/huad032> accessed 18 September 2024; Conrado M Cornelius, 'What Might Future Rights-Based Climate Litigation Look Like in Indonesia? A Preliminary Analysis' (2024) 16(1) *Journal of Human Rights Practice* 285 <https://doi.org/10.1093/jhuman/huad064> accessed 18 September 2024; María Daniela de la Rosa Calderón, 'Rights-Based Climate Litigation in Colombia: An Assessment of Claims, Remedies, and Implementation' (2024) 16(1) *Journal of Human Rights Practice* 273 <https://doi.org/10.1093/jhuman/huad067> accessed 18 September 2024.

9 de la Rosa Calderón (n 8).

10 Lourdes Peroni and Alexander Timmer, 'Vulnerable Groups: The Promise of an Emerging Concept in European Human Rights Convention Law' (2013) 11(4) *ICON* 1056, 1058 <https://doi.org/10.1093/icon/mot042> accessed 24 October 2024.

11 Murcott and Tigre (n 7) 2–6.

12 See Barrett, Chapter 6, pp 193, 196–198, 203.

13 We acknowledge that simplistic understandings of *vulnerability* and *resilience* are insufficient in climate discourse, as discussed by Jessica Chaplain, 'Storytelling and Worldmaking Climate Justice Futures: Indigenous Climate Advocacy and Transnational Solidarity in UN Climate Conferences' (2024) 110(3) *Quarterly Journal of Speech* 370, 378 <https://doi.org/10.1080/00335630.2024.2315043> accessed 24 September 2024.

14 *Environment and Land Court (ELC) of Iten, Legal Advice Centre T/A Kituo cha Sheria et al. v Attorney General et al.* (2022) *ELC Petition No. 007 of 2022*, The Environment and Land Court of Iten (Kenya).

15 *Mbabazi et al. v The Attorney General and National Environmental Management Authority* Civil Suit No. 283 of 2012, High Court of Kampala (Uganda).

16 Interim Constitution of Nepal 2007, 13 April 2007, Article 35(5) (Nepal).

17 *Global Legal Action on Climate Change v The Philippines Government* (2010) Philippines Supreme Court (Philippines).

18 Decision T-218/17 of April 19, 2017, Constitutional Court (Colombia).

19 UN General Assembly, 'Request for an Advisory Opinion of the International Court of Justice on the Obligation of States in Respect of Climate Change' <https://climatecasechart.com/wp-content/uploads/non-us-case-documents/2023/20230301_18913_na.pdf> accessed 25 October 2024.

20 International Tribunal for the Law of the Sea, 'Request for an Advisory Opinion Submitted by the Commission of Small Island States on Climate Change and International Law' <https://www.itlos.org/fileadmin/itlos/documents/cases/31/Advisory_Opinion/C31_Adv_Op_21.05.2024_orig.pdf> accessed 25 October 2024.

21 'Request for an Advisory Opinion on the Climate Emergency and Human Rights Submitted to the Inter-American Court of Human Rights by the Republic of Colombia and the Republic of Chile' (9 January 2023) <https://www.corteidh.or.cr/docs/opiniones/soc_1_2023_en.pdf> accessed 12 August 2024.

22 See Maria Antonia Tigre, 'It is (Finally) Time for an Advisory Opinion on Climate Change: Challenges and Opportunities on a Trio of Initiatives' (2024) 17 *Charleston Law Review* 623 <https://scholarship.law.columbia.edu/sabin_climate_change/218> accessed 25 September 2024.

23 We draw on the work of Peroni and Timmer (n 10).

24 Peroni and Timmer (n 10) 1058–1059.
25 See, generally, Ana T Amorim-Maia, Isabelle Anguelovski, Eric Chu and James Connolly, 'Intersectional Climate Justice: A Conceptual Pathway for Bridging Adaptation Planning, Transformative Action, and Social Equity' (2022) 41 *Urban Climate* 1 <https://doi.org/10.1016/j.uclim.2021.101053> accessed 20 August 2024; Chaplain (n 13) 372.
26 Amorim-Maia et al. (n 25).
27 See, for example, Navroz K Dubash (ed), *India in a Warming World: Integrating Climate Change and Development* (Oxford University Press 2019).
28 Carmen Gonzalez, 'Racial Capitalism, Climate Justice, and Climate Displacement' (2021) 11(1) *Oñati Socio-Legal Series* 108, 113 <https://doi.org/10.35295/osls.iisl/0000-0000-0000-1137> accessed 23 September 2024; Melanie Murcott, Maria Antonia Tigre and Nesa Zimmermann, 'Transnational Insights for Climate Litigation at the European Court of Human Rights: A South-North Perspective in Pursuit of Climate Justice' (2023) 56 *VRÜ Verfassung und Recht in Übersee* 299, 302–304 <https://doi.org/10.5771/0506-7286-2023-2-299> accessed 24 September 2024; Melanie Murcott, *Transformative Environmental Constitutionalism* (Brill Nijhoff 2022) 5–7, 23–26.
29 Joern Birkman et al., 'Understanding Human Vulnerability to Climate Change: A Global Perspective on Index Validation for Adaptation Planning' (2022) 803 *Science of The Total Environment* <https://doi.org/10.1016/j.scitotenv.2021.150065> accessed 23 September 2024.
30 Prateek Chakraborty, '23 Dead in Uttarakhand, Himachal Cloudbursts, Several Highways Blocked' (*India Today*, 3 August 2024) <https://www.indiatoday.in/india/story/uttarakhand-himachal-pradesh-cloudbursts-landslides-kedarnath-pilgrims-rescued-iaf-choppers-drones-2576166-2024-08-03> accessed 25 September 2024.
31 WHO (n 2).
32 WHO (n 2).
33 IPCC, 'Summary for Policymakers in Climate Change 2022 – Impacts, Adaptation and Vulnerability: Working Group II Contribution to the Sixth Assessment Report of the Intergovernmental Panel on Climate Change' in HO Pörtner et al. (eds), (2022) 11 <https://www.ipcc.ch/report/ar6/wg2/downloads/report/IPCC_AR6_WGII_FullReport.pdf> accessed 8 October 2024.
34 IPCC (n 33) 12. A more universal understanding of *vulnerability* is reflected in the IPCC's definition of 'vulnerability', which conceptualises the term as 'the propensity to be adversely affected and encompasses a variety of concepts and elements, including sensitivity or susceptibility to harm and lack of capacity to cope or adapt' (p 5). This definition arguably obscures the underlying systemic and structural causes of peoples' vulnerability. The notion of 'resilience' is understood by the IPCC as 'the capacity of social, economic and ecosystems to cope with a hazardous event or trend or disturbance, responding or reorganising in ways that maintain their essential function, identity and structure as well as biodiversity in case of ecosystems while also maintaining the capacity for adaptation, learning and transformation' (p 7).
35 See Dutta and Lofts, Chapter 4, pp 143–145; Jamwal, Chapter 9; and Garg and Hinduja, Chapter 2, pp 78–81.
36 See Kaur, Sathiabama and Vedavalli, Chapter 7, pp 218–225.
37 See Ladan and Maduekwe, Chapter 8, pp 245–248.
38 See also Barrett, Chapter 6, pp 193–199.
39 See Burri and Duarte Reyes, Chapter 5, pp 164–165.
40 See Beckhauser and Broetto, Chapter 1, and Uehara Chapter 3.
41 Brian Stanley Turner, 'Vulnerability' in WA Darity (ed), *International Encyclopedia of the Social Sciences* (2nd edn, Vol. 8, Macmillan Reference 2008) 656–657 <http://philosociology.com/uploads/_philosociology.ir_international%20encyclopedia%20

of%20the%20social%20sciences_second%20edition_%20darity_5760%20pgs.pdf> accessed 21 April 2024.

42 Turner (n 41).

43 Benjamin Wisner, 'Vulnerability as Concept, Model, Metric, and Tool' (2016) *Oxford Research Encyclopedia of Natural Hazard Science* <https://oxfordre.com/naturalhazardscience/display/10.1093/acrefore/9780199389407.001.0001/acrefore-9780199389407-e-25> accessed 21 April 2024.

44 Doris Hanappi, Laura Bernardi and Dario Spini, 'Vulnerability as a Heuristic for Interdisciplinary Research: Assessing the Thematic and Methodological Structure of Empirical Life-Course Studies' (2015) 6(1) *Longitudinal and Life Course Studies* 59 <http://dx.doi.org/10.14301/llcs.v6i1.302> accessed 24 September 2024; Dario Spini et al., 'Vulnerability Across the Life Course: A Theoretical Framework and Research Directions' (2013) *Lives Working Paper No 2013/27*, 15 <https://www.researchgate.net/publication/305301274_Vulnerability_across_the_life_course_A_theoretical_framework_and_research_directions> accessed 24 October 2024. Klaus Armingeon and Giuliano Bonoli, *The Politics of Post-Industrial Welfare States: Adapting Post-War Social Policies to New Social Risks* (Routledge 2006). Martha Albertson Fineman, 'The Vulnerable Subject: Anchoring Equality in the Human Condition' (2008) 20(1) *Yale Journal of Law & Feminism* 1 <https://papers.ssrn.com/abstract=1131407> accessed 12 July 2023; Martha Albertson Fineman, 'The Vulnerable Subject: Anchoring Equality in the Human Condition' in Martha Albertson Fineman (ed), *Transcending the Boundaries of Law* (1st edn, Routledge-Cavendish 2010).

45 Wisner (n 43); Turner (n 41).

46 Wisner (n 43) 5.

47 See Ronald Perry, 'What is a Disaster?' in H Ridruquez, E Quarantelli and R Dynes (eds), *Handbook of Disaster Research* (1st edn, Springer 2006); Enrico L Quarantelli, 'Disaster Research: Socio-History of the Field' in Edgar F Borgatta and Rhonda JV Montgomery (eds), *Encyclopaedia of Sociology* (Macmillan Reference 2000) 681–688.

48 Riley E Dunlap, 'Environmental Sociology' in George Ritzer and J Michael Ryan (eds), *The Concise Encyclopaedia of Sociology* (Wiley-Blackwell 2011) 189–191.

49 Dunlap (n 48) 189.

50 Arts 2.1(b) read with 7.1. The Paris Agreement 2015 references vulnerability several other times, including in relation to food production systems and the 'particular vulnerability' of 'developing countries', for example, in the preamble, and Arts 6.6, 7.1, 7.2, 7.5, 7.6, 7.9, 9.4, 11.1.

51 Louis J Kotzé, 'The Anthropocene, Earth System Vulnerability and Socio-Ecological Injustice in an Age of Human Rights' (2019) 10 *Journal of Human Rights and the Environment* 62 <http://dx.doi.org/10.4337/jhre.2019.01.04> accessed 24 September 2024.

52 Gonzalez (n 28) 114. See also Murcott (n 28) 8–13.

53 Birkman et al. (n 29).

54 Martha Albertson Fineman and Laura Spitz, *Law, Vulnerability, and the Responsive State: Beyond Equality and Liberty* (Routledge 2023); Peroni and Timmer (n 10).

55 Kotzé (n 51) 64, referring to Martha Albertson Fineman, 'The Vulnerable Subject: Anchoring Equality in the Human Condition' (10 May 2008) <https://papers.ssrn.com/abstract=1131407> accessed 12 July 2023.

56 Ademola Oluborode Jegede, 'Rights Away from Home: Climate-Induced Displacement of Indigenous Peoples and the Extraterritorial Application of the Kampala Convention' (2016) 16 *African Human Rights Law Journal* 58 <http://dx.doi.org/10.17159/1996-2096/2016/v16n1a3> accessed 24 September 2024.

57 Kanika Jamwal, 'The Need to Include Indigenous Peoples as "Expert" Consultants in India's Apex Committee for Implementation of the Paris Agreement' (2021) 23(3) *Environmental Law Review* 203 <https://doi.org/10.1177/14614529211041723> accessed 24 September 2024.

58 Nabanita Samanta, 'Fragile Environment, Fractured Citizenship: Environmental Displacement and the Erosion of Citizenship' (2021) 12 *Jindal Global Law Review* 83 <https://doi.org/10.1007/s41020-021-00141-w> accessed 24 September 2024.
59 Nakayama M, Drinkall S and Sasaki D, 'Climate Change, Migration, and Vulnerability: Overview of the Special Issue' (2019) 14(9) *Journal of Disaster Research* 1246 <http://dx.doi.org/10.20965/jdr.2019.p1246> accessed 24 September.
60 Sneha Krishnan, 'Gender, Disasters and Climate: Case of Internal Displacement in Assam, India' (2022) 13(1) *Jindal Global Law Review* 87 <https://doi.org/10.1007/s41020-022-00163-y> accessed 24 September 2024.
61 See Melanie Murcott, 'Minding the Gap: The Constitutional Court's Jurisprudence Concerning the Environmental Right' (2023) 13 *Constitutional Court Review* 147, 148–150, 160–166 <https://doi.org/10.2989/CCR.2023.0007> accessed 24 September 2024; Murcott, Tigre and Zimmermann (n 28); Maria Antonia Tigre and Margaretha Wewerinke-Singh, 'Beyond the North–South Divide: Litigation's Role in Resolving Climate Change Loss and Damage Claims' (2023) 32 *Review of European, Comparative & International Environmental Law* 439 <https://doi.org/10.1111/reel.12517> accessed 24 September 2024; Maria Antonia Tigre, Natalia Urzola and Alexandra Goodman, 'Climate Litigation in Latin America: Is the Region Quietly Leading a Revolution?' (2023) 14 *Journal of Human Rights and the Environment* 67 <https://doi.org/10.4337/jhre.2023.01.04> accessed 24 September 2024; Milka Sormunen, 'Rethinking Effective Remedies to the Climate Crisis: A Vulnerability Theory Approach' (2023) 24 *Human Rights Review* 171 <https://doi.org/10.1007/s12142-023-00686-4> accessed 24 September 2024; Louis J Kotzé et al., 'Courts Climate Litigation and the Evolution of Earth System Law' (2024) 15(1) *Global Policy* 5 <https://doi.org/10.1111/1758-5899.13291> accessed 24 October 2024.
62 Birsha Ohdedar, 'Climate Adaptation, Vulnerability and Rights-Based Litigation: Broadening the Scope of Climate Litigation Using Political Ecology' (2022) 13 *Journal of Human Rights and the Environment* 137 <http://dx.doi.org/10.4337/jhre.2022.01.06> accessed 24 September 2024.
63 Elisa Fornalé, 'Vulnerability, Intertemporality, and Climate Litigation' (2023) 41(4) *Nordic Journal of Human Rights* 357 <https://doi.org/10.1080/18918131.2023.2225973> accessed 24 September 2024.
64 Sormunen (n 61).
65 Orla Kelleher, 'Incorporating Climate Justice into Legal Reasoning: Shifting Towards a Risk-Based Approach to Causation in Climate Litigation' (2022) 13(1) *Journal of Human Rights and the Environment* 290 <https://doi.org/10.4337/jhre.2022.01.12> accessed 24 September 2024.
66 Larissa Parker et al., 'When the Kids Put Climate Change on Trial: Youth-Focused Rights-Based Climate Litigation Around the World' (2022) 13 *Journal of Qualitative Research in Tourism* 64 <https://ssrn.com/abstract=3960982> accessed 24 September 2024; Giulia Gasparri et al., 'Children, Adolescents, and Youth Pioneering a Human Rights-Based Approach to Climate Change' (2021) 23 *Health and Human Rights* 95 <https://www.hhrjournal.org/2021/12/children-adolescents-and-youth-pioneering-a-human-rights-based-approach-to-climate-change/> accessed 24 September 2024; Susan Ann Samuel, '"Greening" International Law En Route to Agenda 2030: The Role of Youth in Enhancing the Soft Power of Climate Justice' (2023) *Yearbook of International Environmental Law* 3 <https://doi.org/10.1093/yiel/yvad064> accessed 24 September 2024; Thomas Elliott and Jennifer Earl, 'Organizing the Next Generation: Youth Engagement with Activism Inside and Outside of Organizations' (2018) 4 *Social Media + Society* 2056305117750722 <https://doi.org/10.1177/2056305117750722> accessed 24 September 2024; J Schnakenberg et al. (eds), 'Human Rights in the Face of Climate Crisis: A Youth Led Initiative to Bring Climate Justice to International Court of Justice' (July 2021) <https://static1.squarespace.com/static/5f063a0c8f53b604aed84729/t/638f9ee73dfbf63abd0cc021/1670356715298/Second+Edition+Legal+Report.pdf> accessed

25 October 2024; Sharon Buccino, 'Our Children's Future: Applying Intergenerational Equity to Public Land Management' (2020) 31 *Colorado Natural Resources, Energy & Environmental Law Review* 509 <https://www.colorado.edu/law/sites/default/files/attached-files/003_buccino_final_copy.pdf> accessed 24 September 2024 Environmental Law Review; Ziba Vaghri, 'Climate Change, An Unwelcome Legacy: The Need to Support Children's Rights to Participate in Global Conversations' (2018) 28 *Children, Youth and Environments* 104 <https://www.jstor.org/stable/10.7721/chilyoutenvi.28.1.0104> accessed 24 September 2024.

67 Maria Antonia Tigre, 'Climate Change and Indigenous Groups: The Rise of Indigenous Voices in Climate Litigation' (2022) 9(3) *E-Publica* 214 <https://scholarship.law.columbia.edu/sabin_climate_change/196> accessed 24 September 2024; Verity Thomson, 'Decolonization, Feminism, and Climate Change: A Commentary on "Misdzi Yikh v Canada"' 18 *McGill Journal of Sustainable Development Law* 157, 165 <https://search.informit.org/doi/abs/10.3316/informit.726493881327874> accessed 24 September 2024; Louise Du Toit, Caiphas Soyapi and Louis J Kotzé, 'David versus Goliath? Indigenous People, Carbon Majors and Climate Litigation in South Africa' (2024) 33 *RECIEL* 326 <https://doi.org/10.1111/reel.12534> accessed 24 September 2024, accessed 25 September 2024.

68 Fiona Batt, 'The Vulnerability of African Indigenous Peoples' Traditional Meteorological Knowledge in the Climate Change Debate' in Kim Bouwer et al. (eds), *Climate Litigation and Justice in Africa* (Bristol University Press 2024) 168–188.

69 See Cathi Albertyn, Meghan Campbell, Helena Alviar García and Marta Rodriguez de Assis Machado (eds), *Feminist Frontiers in Climate Justice* (Edward Elgar 2023); Natalia Urzola Gutiérrez, 'Gender in Climate Litigation in Latin America: Epistemic Justice Through a Feminist Lens' (2024) 16(1) *Journal of Human Rights Practice* 208 <https://doi.org/10.1093/jhuman/huad030> accessed 24 September 2024; Martha Rodriguez de Assis Machado, Denise Vitale and Danielle Hanna Rached, 'Indigenous Women Against Bolsonaro's Government in Brazil: Resisting Right-Wing Authoritarianism and Demanding Climate Justice' in C Albertyn et al. (eds), *Feminist Frontiers in Climate Justice* (Edward Elgar Publishing 2023); Susan Ann Samuel, 'Exploring the Scope of Ecofeminism in the Biodiversity-Climate Nexus' (*IUCN*, 10 April 2023) <https://www.iucn.org/story/202304/exploring-scope-ecofeminism-biodiversity-climate-nexus > accessed 15 April 2023.

70 See Peroni and Timmer (n 10) 1059 on the descriptive and prescriptive qualities of vulnerability.

71 Urzola Gutiérrez (n 69) 213–214.

72 Michael Mikulewicz et al. 'Intersectionality and Climate Justice: A Call for Synergy in Climate Change Scholarship' (2023) 32 *Environmental Politics* 1276–1277 <https://doi.org/10.1080/09644016.2023.2172869> accessed 24 September 2024.

73 Farhana Sultana, 'Critical Climate Justice' (2022) 188 *Geography Journal* 118 <https://doi.org/10.1111/geoj.12417> accessed 23 September 2024.

74 Centre for Intersectional Justice, 'What is Intersectionality? The Centre for Intersectional Justice' <https://sharing4good.org/article/what-intersectionality-center-intersectional-justice> accessed 22 October 2024.

75 Elizabeth Cripps, *What Climate Justice Means and Why We Should Care* (Bloomsbury 2022) 12–13. See also Gonzalez (n 28) 113; Murcott, Tigre and Zimmermann (n 28) 302–303. For a discussion of climate justice as a heterogenous term see Blanche Verlie, 'Climate Justice in More-than-Human Worlds' (2021) 31 *Environmental Politics* 297 <https://doi.org/10.1080/09644016.2021.1981081> accessed 23 September 2024.

76 Cripps (n 75) 17–20.

77 Cripps (n 75) 23.

78 Jethro Pettit, 'Climate Justice: A New Social Movement for Atmospheric Rights' (2009) 35(3) *IDS Bulletin Climate Change and Development* 102 <https://doi.org/10.1111/j.1759-5436.2004.tb00142.x> accessed 24 September 2024.

79 Cripps (n 75) 98.

80 Cripps (n 75) 71. See also Murcott, Tigre and Zimmermann (n 28) 303; Mikulewicz et al. (n 72) 1275.
81 Mikulewicz et al. (n 72) 1276.
82 See Dutta and Lofts, Chapter 4, p 137.
83 Mikulewicz et al. (n 72) 1276.
84 See Dutta and Lofts, Chapter 4.
85 Murcott (n 61) 160–162.
86 Murcott (n 61) 160–162.
87 See Barrett, Chapter 6, pp 193–195.
88 See also Maria Antonia Tigre, 'Litigation as an Avenue for Climate Justice: Addressing Vulnerabilities in Courts' in Sumudu Atapattu, Freya Doughty-Wagner and Enéas Xavier (eds), *The Fourth Environmental Era: Climate Justice* (Vernon Press Forthcoming 2026).
89 Child-led climate litigation includes *Sacchi et al. v Argentina* (2019) CRC/C/88/D/105/2019, UN Committee on the Rights of the Child; *Ridhima Pandey v Union of India et al.* (2019) 187/2017, National Green Tribunal (India); and *Rabab Ali v Federation of Pakistan et al.* (2016) ___ / I of 2016, Supreme Court of Pakistan (Pakistan). Women-led climate litigation includes: *Asmania et al. v Holcim* (2023) A1 2023 9, Cantonal Court Conciliation Authority Justice of the Peace of the Canton of Zug (Switzerland); *Verein Klimaseniorinnen Schweiz et al. v Switzerland* (2024) 53600/20, European Court of Human Rights; and *Herrera Carrion et al. v Ministry of the Environment et al.* (2021) 21201202000170, Corte Provincial de Justicia de Sucumbíos (Ecuador). Indigenous people–led litigation includes *Sustaining the Wild Coast NPC et al. v Minister of Mineral Resources and Energy et al.* (2021) (3491/2021) ZAECGHC 118 and ZAECMKHC 55, South African High Court (South Africa); *Billy v Australia* (2022) CCPR/C/135/D/3624/2019 and *Center for Social Justice v Ministry of the Environment et al.* (2016) T-622/16, Colombian Constitutional Court (Colombia).
90 See Tigre, Murcott, and Ann Samuel, Chapter 10.
91 Tigre, Murcott, and Ann Samuel, Chapter 10.
92 Urzola Gutiérrez (n 69) 210.
93 'Veja os números mais recentes das enchentes no RS nesta terça-fiera' (*Zero Hora*, 7 May 2024) <https://gauchazh.clicrbs.com.br/geral/noticia/2024/05/veja-os-numeros-mais-recentes-das-enchentes-no-rs-nesta-terca-feira-clvwaf-3cb000a0152rvvf5m36.html> accessed 24 September 2024.
94 'Defesa Civil atualiza balanço das enchentes no RS – 20/8' (*Governo do estado, Rio Grande do Sul*, 20 August 2024) <https://www.estado.rs.gov.br/defesa-civil-atualiza-balanco-das-enchentes-no-rs-20-8> accessed 24 October 2024.
95 '"Desperate" Rescues Under Way as Brazil Floods Kill 90, Displace Thousands' (*Aljazeera*, 7 May 2024) <https://www.aljazeera.com/news/2024/5/7/desperate-rescues-under-way-as-brazil-floods-kill-90-displace-thousands> accessed 19 October 2024.
96 Arthur Stabile, Paula Paiva Paulo, Gabriel Croquer e Poliana Casemiro 'Guaíba recebeu quase metade do volume de àgua de Itaipu em uma semana de chuvas, aponta instituto da UFRGS' (*Globo.com*, 10 May 2024). "Guaíba recebeu quase metade do volume de água de Itaipu em uma semana de chuvas, aponta instituto da UFRGS". g1.
97 Ben Clarke et al., 'Climate Change, El Niño and Infrastructure Failures Behind Massive Floods in Southern Brazil' (June 2024) <https://mcusercontent.com/854a9a3e09405d4ab19a4a9d5/files/5fd7d7a2-9d1f-6ca5-407f-cd3b8003d286/Scientific_report_Brazil_RS_floods_compressed.pdf> accessed 25 September 2024.
98 Clarke et al. (n 97).
99 Clarke et al. (n 97) 36.
100 Outra Saude, 'Health in Times of Climate Chaos: Floods in Rio Grande do Sul' (*Movimento dos Trabalhadores Rurais Sem Terra*, 20 May 2024) <https://mst.org.br/2024/05/20/health-in-times-of-climate-chaos-floods-in-rio-grande-do-sul/>

accessed 25 September 2024 and Andre Penner, 'Brazil's Rio Grande Do Sul Faces Economic Woes After Floods, and an Unclear Path to Rebuilding' (*U.S. News*, 23 May 2024) <https://www.usnews.com/news/world/articles/2024-05-23/brazils-rio-grande-do-sul-faces-economic-woes-after-floods-and-an-unclear-path-to-rebuilding> accessed 25 October 2024.

101 Vitor Abdala, 'Rains in Rio Grande do Sul Have Affected 8,000 Indigenous People' (*AgênciaBrasil*, 8 May 2024) <https://agenciabrasil.ebc.com.br/en/geral/noticia/2024-05/rains-rio-grande-do-sul-have-affected-8000-indigenous-people> accessed 25 September 2024 and Maria Tokarnia, 'Floods Have Affected 3,000 Health Care Units in Rio Grande do Sul' <https://agenciabrasil.ebc.com.br/en/geral/noticia/2024-05/floods-have-affected-3000-health-care-units-rio-grande-do-sul> accessed 25 September 2024.

102 'Núcleo Porto Alegre Analisa os Impactos das Enchentes na População Pobre e Negra do Rio Grande do Sul' (*Observatório das Metrópoles*, 23 May 2024) <https://www.observatoriodasmetropoles.net.br/nucleo-porto-alegre-analisa-os-impactos-das-enchentes-na-populacao-pobre-e-negra-do-rio-grande-do-sul/> accessed 25 September 2024.

103 Camilla Ghisleni, 'Floods in Rio Grande do Sul: The Tragedy of Non-Resilient Cities' (*Arch Daily*, 18 May 2024) <https://www.archdaily.com/1016509/floods-in-rio-grande-do-sul-the-tragedy-of-non-resilient-cities> accessed 25 September 2024.

104 'Brazil: Teachers and Educational Centres in Rio Grande do Sul Affected by Floods' (*Educaton International*, 15 May 2024) <https://www.ei-ie.org/en/item/28585:brazil-teachers-and-educational-centres-in-rio-grande-do-sul-affected-by-floods> accessed 25 September 2024.

105 O Globo, 'Enchentes no RS: Sobe para sete o Número de mortes por leptospirose' (*G1*, 29 May 2024) <https://oglobo.globo.com/brasil/sos-rio-grande-do-sul/noticia/2024/05/29/enchentes-no-rs-sobe-para-sete-o-numero-de-mortes-por-leptospirose.ghtml> accessed 25 September 2024.

106 Leandro Prazeres, João da Mata and Vinicius Lemos, 'O Drama dos Idosos nas Inundações do Rio Grande do Sul: "Paracem Deixados de Lado"' (*BBC News Brasil*, 20 May 2024) <https://www.bbc.com/portuguese/articles/ce550yrv3v7o> accessed 25 September 2024.

107 Ana Pimentel, 'Mulheres em Tempos de Crise: Uma Tragédia Dentro da Tragésia do RS' (*Lemonde Diplomatique Brasil,* 10 May 2024) <https://diplomatique.org.br/mulheres-tragedia-rio-grande-do-sul/> accessed 25 September 2024.

108 'ONU Reforça Proteção de Grupos Vulneráveis no Rio Grande do Sul' (*Nações Unidas*, 10 May 2024) <https://news.un.org/pt/story/2024/05/1831506> accessed 25 September 2024.

109 Vidya Krishnan, 'Climate Change Isn't India's Fault, But It is India's Responsibility' (*Harvard Public Health Magazine*, 16 July 2024) <https://harvardpublichealth.org/environmental-health/india-climate-change-perpetuates-injustices-against-vulnerable/> accessed 25 September 2024.

110 Vidya Krishnan, 'Climate Change Isn't India's Fault, but It is India's Responsibility' (*Harvard Public Health Magazine*, 16 July 2024) <https://harvardpublichealth.org/environmental-health/india-climate-change-perpetuates-injustices-against-vulnerable/> accessed 25 September 2024.

111 Robert Mizo, 'India's Climate Calamities' (*Toda Peace Institute,* 7 August 2024) <https://toda.org/global-outlook/2024/indias-climate-calamities.html> accessed 25 September 2024.

112 Government of India, 'Ministry of Home Affairs: Disaster Management Division. Situation Report Regarding Flood/Heavy Rainfall (12.08.2024)' (August 2024) <https://ndmindia.mha.gov.in/ndmi/viewUploadedDocument?uid=NEW2155> accessed 25 September 2024.

113 Aathira Perinchery, 'Nightmare in Wayanad: Torrential Rains Triggered Landslides But Climate Change May Not Be the Sole Culprit' (*The Wire*, 2024) <https://thewire.in/environment/nightmare-in-wayanad-torrential-rains-triggered-landslides-but-climate-change-may-not-be-the-sole-culprit> accessed 25 September 2024.

114 Parvathy Venukuttan, 'Wayanad Landslides Were Forecast Long Ago, Archives Reveal' (*Nature India*, 23 August 2024) <https://www.nature.com/articles/d44151-024-00133-4> accessed 22 October 2024.

115 The concepts of tribe, Adivasi, and Indigenous people are used interchangeably; see Jagannath Ambagudia and Virginius Xaxa, *Handbook of Tribal Politics in India* (1st edn, SAGE Publications 2021) 337.

116 Ambagudia and Xaxa (n 115).

117 Ambagudia and Xaxa (n 115).

118 'Citrusdal Cut Off, Nearly 160,000 Affected by Floods in Cape Town' (*TimesLive*, 15 July 2024) <https://www.timeslive.co.za/news/south-africa/2024-07-15-citrusdal-cut-off-nearly-160000-affected-by-floods-in-cape-town/> accessed 25 September 2024.

119 Sabina Abba Omar and Stefaan Conradie '"Cape Storms" – Climate Researchers Explain Cape Town's Recent Extreme Weather' (*The Conversation,* 30 May 2024) <https://theconversation.com/cape-of-storms-climate-researchers-explain-cape-towns-recent-extreme-weather-229012> accessed 13 September 2024.

120 Sandiso Phaliso, Ashraf Hendricks and Marecia Damons, 'Thousands of Homes Flooded as Violent Storm Batters Western Cape' (*GroundUp*, 9 July 2024) <https://groundup.org.za/article/thousands-of-homes-flooded-as-violent-storm-batters-western-cape/> accessed 25 September 2024.

121 Kaitano Dube, Godwell Nhamo and David Chikodzi, 'Flooding Trends and Their Impacts on Coastal Communities of Western Cape Province, South Africa' (2022) 87 *GeoJournal* 453 <https://doi.org/10.1007/s10708-021-10460-z> accessed 23 September 2024.

122 Niémah Davids, 'Women's Month: Floods Expose Plight, Pain of "Powerless" Khayelitsha Women' (*University of Cape Town News*, 7 August 2024) <https://www.news.uct.ac.za/article/-2024-08-07-womens-month-floods-expose-plight-pain-of-powerless-khayelitsha-women> accessed 23 September 2024.

123 See de la Rosa Calderón (n 8).

124 There is extensive debate concerning the kinds of cases that ought to be included within the meaning of 'climate litigation' (see, for instance, Jacqueline Peel and Jolene Lin, 'Transnational Climate Litigation: The Contribution of the Global South' (2019) 113 *American Journal of International Law* 19–30). This volume uses the term to refer to legal challenges brought before courts and similar tribunals that explicitly engage issues of law or fact concerning climate change science, adaptation or mitigation measures, and/or loss and damage (whether peripherally or centrally), aligned with the definition used by the *Sabin Center for Climate Change Law, Climate Change Litigation Databases: About* <https://climatecasechart.com/about/> accessed 15 September 2024. We recognise the limits of the scope of this conceptualisation. For instance, Tracy-Lynn Field, 'Towards a Risk-Thematic Approach for African Climate Litigation' in Kim Bouwer et al. (eds), *Climate Litigation and Justice in Africa* (Bristol University Press 2024) 15–42, argues that African climate litigation could usefully be viewed as encompassing cases that address climate change risks, such as water insecurity, food insecurity, ecosystem loss, drought, flooding, etc., even if *climate change* is not specifically mentioned. The development of an African database of cases concerning climate change risks on the continent could enhance studies such as the ones in this volume on the role of the courts and other tribunals in addressing vulnerabilities amidst the climate crisis in the Global South.

125 See, for example, Auz (n 8); de la Rosa Calderón (n 8).

126 See, for example, Daniel Armel Owona Mbarga, 'Climate Change Litigation in Civil Law African Countries: An Assessment of Barriers and Potentialities in Cameroon' in Kim Bouwer et al. (eds), *Climate Litigation and Justice in Africa* (Bristol University Press 2024) 102–122.

127 Ademola Oluborode Jegede, 'State Duty to "Protect" Rights and Legal Obstacles to Climate Litigation' in Kim Bouwer et al. (eds), *Climate Litigation and Justice in Africa* (Bristol University Press 2024) 48–49.

128 Zenteno Villa (n 8). On legal disruption and the wicked nature of climate change, see Elizabeth Fisher, Eloise Scotford and Emily Barritt, 'The Legally Disruptive Nature of Climate Change' (2017) 80 *Modern Law Review* 173 <https://www.jstor.org/stable/26646916> accessed 25 September 2024.

129 IPCC, 'Summary for Policymakers in Climate Change 2022 – Impacts, Adaptation and Vulnerability: Working Group II Contribution to the Sixth Assessment Report of the Intergovernmental Panel on Climate Change' in HO Pörtner et al. (eds), (2022) <https://www.ipcc.ch/report/ar6/wg2/downloads/report/IPCC_AR6_WGII_FullReport.pdf> accessed 8 October 2024. E Somanathan et al., 'Chapter 15 – National and Sub-National Policies and Institutions' in O Edenhofer et al. (eds), *Climate Change 2014: Mitigation of Climate Change, Contribution of Working Group III to the Fifth Assessment Report of the Intergovernmental Panel on Climate Change* (Cambridge University Press 2014). See further, Susan Ann Samuel, '"Greening" International Law en route to Agenda 2030: The Role of Youth in Enhancing the Soft Power of Climate Justice' (2022) 33 *Yearbook of International Environmental Law* 3 <https://doi.org/10.1093/yiel/yvad064> accessed 24 October 2024. Susan Ann Samuel, 'Rawls' Cake and Climate Governance: Relevance of "Our" Common Future Today' (2023) 17 *Carbon & Climate Law Review* 169 <https://doi.org/10.21552/cclr/2023/3/9> accessed 24 October 2024.

130 Michael Burger and Maria Antonia Tigre, 'Global Climate Litigation Report: 2023 Status Review' (*Sabin Center for Climate Change Law, Columbia Law School & United Nations Environment Programme*, July 2023). <https://scholarship.law.columbia.edu/sabin_climate_change/202> accessed 25 September 2024.

131 Maria Antonia Tigre and Margaret Barry, 'Climate Change in the Courts: A 2023 Retrospective' (*Sabin Center for Climate Change Law*, December 2023). <https://scholarship.law.columbia.edu/sabin_climate_change/212> accessed 25 October 2024.

132 Maria Antonia Tigre, 'Climate Litigation in the Global South: Mapping Report' (*Sabin Center for Climate Change Law, Columbia Law School*, 2024). <https://scholarship.law.columbia.edu/sabin_climate_change/230> accessed 25 September 2024.

133 See, for example, UN General Assembly, 'Request for an Advisory Opinion of the International Court of Justice on the Obligation of States in Respect of Climate Change' <https://climatecasechart.com/wp-content/uploads/non-us-case-documents/2023/20230301_18913_na.pdf> accessed 25 October 2024;
International Tribunal for the Law of the Sea, 'Request for an Advisory Opinion Submitted by the Commission of Small Island States on Climate Change and International Law' <https://www.itlos.org/fileadmin/itlos/documents/cases/31/Advisory_Opinion/C31_Adv_Op_21.05.2024_orig.pdf> accessed 25 October 2024, discussed in Tigre (n 8).

134 See, for example, *Saonu and Morobe Provincial Government v Minister for Environment and Conservation and Climate Change et al.* (2021), OS (JR) 35 of 2021, Court of Justice at Waigani (Papua New Guinea); *Mejillones Tourist Service Association et al. v Environmental Evaluation Service (SEA) of Antofagasta* (2021) 6930–2021 and 71.628–2021, Chilean Supreme Court of Justice (Chile); *Sustaining the Wild Coast NPC v Minister of Mineral Resources* (2022) ZAECMkHC 55, High Court (South Africa), discussed in Burger and Tigre (n 130) 47–49.

135 See, for example, *Billy v Australia* (2022) CCPR/C/135/D/3624/2019 and *Future Generations v Ministry of the Environment et al.* (2018) 11001 22 03 000 2018 00319 00, Colombian Supreme Court (Colombia), discussed in Urzola Gutiérrez (n 69).

136 See, for example, *Future Generations v Ministry of the Environment et al.* (2018) 11001 22 03 000 2018 00319 00, Colombian Supreme Court (Colombia); *Center for Social Justice Studies et al. v Presidency of the Republic et al.* (2016) T-622/16, Constitutional Court of Colombia (Colombia); *ONG Costa Legal et al. v Municipality of Florianópolis et al.* (2021) No. 5012843-56.2021.4.04.7200, 6th Federal Court of Florianópolis, Santa Catarina (Brazil), discussed in Fernanda de Salles Cavedon-Capdeville et al., 'An Ecocentric Perspective on Climate Litigation: Lessons from Latin America' (2024) 16 *Journal of Human Rights Practice* 89 <https://doi.org/10.1093/jhuman/huad031> accessed 30 October 2023.

137 See, for example, *In Re Greenpeace Southeast Asia et al.* (2015) CHR-NI-2016-0001, Commission on Human Rights (Philippines); *Conectas Direitos Humanos v BNDES and BNDESPar*, Ninth Federal Civil Court of the Federal District, ACP 1038657-42.2022.4.01.3400, 22 June 2022 (Brazil), discussed in Burger and Tigre (n 130) 50–59.

138 Maria Antonia Tigre, Lorena Zenteno, Marlies Hesselman, Natalia Urzola, Pedro Cisterna-Gaete and Riccardo Luporini, 'Just Transition Litigation in Latin America: An Initial Categorization of Climate Litigation Cases Amid the Energy Transition' (*Sabin Center for Climate Change Law*, January 2023). <https://scholarship.law.columbia.edu/sabin_climate_change/197/> accessed 23 October 2024. Natalia Urzola, Maria Antonia Tigre, Riccardo Luporini, Lorena Zenteno, Marlies Hesselman and Pedro Cisterna-Gaete, 'Just Transition Litigation in Latin America: Striking a Balance Between Economic Development and Environmental and Social Energy Justice' in Daniel Iglesias Márquez et al. (eds), *Legal Challenges at the End of the Fossil Fuel Era. Global Issues* (Palgrave Macmillan 2024) 151–186.

139 Melanie J Murcott and Clive Vinti, 'The Judge-Made "Duty" to Consider Climate Change in South Africa' (2024) 16(1) *Journal of Human Rights Practice* 125 <https://doi.org/10.1093/jhuman/huad069> accessed 7 September 2024.

140 See, for example, *Minister of Mineral Resources and Energy et al. v Sustaining the Wild Coast NPC et al.* [2024] ZASCA 84, Supreme Court of Appeal (South Africa) and the discussion of the High Court decisions in the same matter in Sandra Liebenberg, 'The Wild Coast Seismic Survey Judgments: A Case Study on Integrating the Principles of Sustainable Development in Law' in Mbuyiseli R Madlanga et al. (eds), *Enforcing Accountability, Consolidating Democracy and Compelling Sustainable Development in the 21*st *Century* (Juta and Company 2023) 17, 41; and Murcott (n 61) 160.

141 Maria Antonia Tigre and Joana Setzer, 'Human Rights and Climate Change for Climate Litigation in Brazil and Beyond: An Analysis of the Climate Fund Decision' (2023) 54 *Georgetown JIL* 593 <https://scholarship.law.columbia.edu/sabin_climate_change/219> accessed 25 September 2024; Danielle de Andrade Moreira, Ana Lucia B Nina, Carolina de Figueiredo Garrido and Maria Eduarda Segovia Barbosa Neves, 'Rights-Based Climate Litigation in Brazil: An Assessment of Constitutional Cases Before the Brazilian Supreme Court' (2024) 16 *Journal of Human Rights Practice* 47 <https://doi.org/10.1093/jhuman/huad023> accessed 25 September 2024; James R May, Marcelo Buzaglo Dantas and Luciana Bauer, 'Climate Rights in Brazil and the United States: A Convergence of Contrasts' (2024) 56(1) *Case Western Reserve Journal of International Law* 439 <https://scholarlycommons.law.case.edu/jil/vol56/iss1/19> accessed 24 October 2024.

142 Tigre (n 8).

## Bibliography

### *Books and book chapters*


Albertyn C, Campbell M, García HA and de Assis Machado MR (eds), *Feminist Frontiers in Climate Justice* (Edward Elgar 2023)

Ambagudia J and Xaxa V, 'Political Articulations of Adivasis in Kerala' in J Ambagudia and V Xaxa (eds), *Handbook of Tribal Politics in India* (1st edn, SAGE Publications 2021)

Ann Samuel S, 'Climate Justice and Capabilities Approach – A TWAIL Discourse: Redefining the Fourth Environmental Era' in S Atapattu, F Doughty-Wagner and E Xavier (eds), *The Fourth Environmental Era: Climate Justice* (Vernon Press Forthcoming 2024)

Armingeon K and Bonoli G, *The Politics of Post-Industrial Welfare States: Adapting Post-War Social Policies to New Social Risks* (Routledge 2006)

Batt F, 'The Vulnerability of African Indigenous Peoples' Traditional Meteorological Knowledge in the Climate Change Debate' in K Bouwer, U Etemire, TL Field and AO Jegede (eds), *Climate Litigation and Justice in South Africa* (Bristol University Press 2024)

Bouwer K, Etemire U, Field TL and Jegede AO, *Climate Litigation and Justice in Africa* (Bristol University Press 2024)

Chamberlain L, 'The Value of Litigation to Women Environmental Human Rights Defenders in South Africa' in C Albertyn, M Campbell, HA García and MR de Assis Machado (eds), *Feminist Frontiers in Climate Justice* (Edward Elgar 2023)

Cripps E, *What Climate Justice Means and Why We Should Care* (Bloomsbury 2022)

Dubash NK (ed), *India in a Warming World: Integrating Climate Change and Development* (Oxford University Press 2019)

Erinosho B, 'Climate Litigation: Access to Judicial Review in National Courts' in F Sindico, K McKenzie, G Medico-Colombo and L Wegener (eds), *Research Handbook on Climate Change Litigation* (Edward Elgar 2024)

Field TL, 'Towards a Risk-Thematic Approach for African Climate Litigation' in K Bouwer, U Etemire, TL Field and AO Jegede (eds), *Climate Litigation and Justice in Africa* (Bristol University Press 2024)

Fineman MA, 'The Vulnerable Subject: Anchoring Equality in the Human Condition' in M Albertson Fineman (ed), *Transcending the Boundaries of Law* (1st edn, Routledge-Cavendish 2010)

Fineman MA and Spitz L (eds), *Law, Vulnerability, and the Responsive State: Beyond Equality and Liberty* (Routledge 2023)

Jegede AO, 'State Duty to "Protect" Rights and Legal Obstacles to Climate Litigation' in K Bouwer, U Etemire, TL Field and AO Jegede (eds), *Climate Litigation and Justice in Africa* (Bristol University Press 2024)

Liebenberg S, 'The Wild Coast Seismic Survery Judgement: A Case Study on Integrating the Principles of Sustainable Development in Law' in MR Madlanga et al. (eds), *Enforcing Accountability Consolidating Democracry and Compelling Sustainable Development in the 21st Century* (1st edn, Juta and Company 2024)

Lin J and Peel J, *Litigating Climate Change in the Global South* (Oxford University Press 2024)

Martha Rodriguez de Assis M, Vitale D and Rached DH, 'Indigenous Women Against Bolsonaro's Government in Brazil: Resisting Right-Wing Authoritarianism and Demanding Climate Justice' in C Albertyn et al. (eds), *Feminist Frontiers in Climate Justice* (Edward Elgar Publishing 2023)

Mbarga DAO, 'Climate Change Litigation in Civil African Countries: An Assessment of Barriers and Potentialities in Cameroon' in K Bouwer, U Etemire, TL Field and AO Jegede (eds), *Climate Litigation and Justice in Africa* (Bristol University Press 2024)

Murcott MJ, *Transformative Environmental Constitutionalism* (Brill Nijhoff 2022)
Natarajan U, 'Environmental Justice in the Global South' in CG Gonzalez, SL Seck and SA Atapattu (eds), *The Cambridge Handbook of Environmental Justice and Sustainable Development* (Cambridge University Press 2021)
Perry RW, 'What is a Disaster?' in H Ridruquez, E Quarantelli and R Dynes (eds), *Handbook of Disaster Research* (1st edn, Springer 2006)
Quarantelli EL, 'Disaster Research: Socio-History of the Field' in Edgar F Borgatta and Rhonda JV Montgomery (eds), *Encyclopaedia of Sociology* (Macmillan Reference 2000)
Riley E and Dunlap RE, 'Environmental sociology' in G Ritzer and JM Ryan (eds), *The concise encyclopaedia of sociology* (Wiley-Blackwell 2011)
Rodríguez-Garavito C (ed), *Litigating the Climate Emergency* (Cambridge University Press 2022)
Setzer J, Silbert N and Vanhala L, 'The Effectiveness of Climate Change Litigation' in F Sindico, K McKenzie, G Medico-Colombo and L Wegener (eds), *Research Handbook on Climate Change Litigation* (Edward Elgar 2024)
Somanathan E et al., 'Chapter 15 – National and Sub-National Policies and Institutions' in O Edenhofer et al. (eds), *Climate Change 2014: Mitigation of Climate Change, Contribution of Working Group III to the Fifth Assessment Report of the Intergovernmental Panel on Climate Change* (Cambridge University Press 2014)
Tigre MA, 'Litigation as an Avenue for Climate Justice: Addressing Vulnerabilities in Courts' in Sumudu Atapattu, Freya Doughty-Wagner and Enéas Xavier (eds), *The Fourth Environmental Era: Climate Justice* (Vernon Press Forthcoming 2024)
Turner BS, 'Vulnerability' in *International Encyclopedia of the Social Sciences* (2nd edn, Macmillan Reference USA 2008)
Urzola N, Tigre MA, Luporini R, Zenteno L, Hesselman M and Cisterna-Gaete P, 'Just Transition Litigation in Latin America: Striking a Balance Between Economic Development and Environmental and Social Energy Justice' in DI Márquez, C Esteve-Jordá and BF Pérez (eds), *Legal Challenges at the End of the Fossil Fuel Era: Shaping a Just and Clean Energy Transition* (Springer Nature 2024)

## Cases

*Asmania et al. v Holcim* (2023) A1 2023 9, Cantonal Court of the Canton of Zug (Switzerland)
*Billy v Australia* (2022) CCPR/C/135/D/3624/2019, UN Human Rights Committee
*Center for Social Justice v Ministry of the Environment et al.* (2016) T-622/16, Colombian Constitutional Court (Colombia) (Atrato River Decision T-622)
*Conectas Direitos Humanos v BNDES and BNDESPar* (2022) ACP 1038657-42. 2022.4.01.3400, Ninth Federal Civil Court of the Federal District (Brazil)
*Environment and Land Court (ELC) of Iten, Legal Advice Centre T/A Kituo cha Sheria et al. v Attorney General et al.* (2022) ELC Petition No. 007 of 2022, The Environment and Land Court of Iten (Kenya)
*Future Generations v Ministry of the Environment et al.* (2018) 11001 22 03 000 2018 00319 00, Colombian Supreme Court (Colombia)
*Global Legal Action on Climate Change v The Philippines Government* (2010) Philippines Supreme Court (Philippines)
*Herrera Carrion et al. v Ministry of the Environment et al.* (2021) 21201202000170, Corte Provincial de Justicia de Sucumbíos (Ecuador)
*In Re Greenpeace Southeast Asia et al. v Chevron et al.* (2015) CHR-NI-2016-0001, Commission on Human Rights (Philippines)
*Mbabazi et al. v The Attorney General and National Environmental Management Authority* (2012) Civil Suit No. 238 of 2012, High Court of Kampala (Uganda)

*Mejillones Tourist Service Association et al. v Environmental Evaluation Service (SEA) of Antofagasta* (2021) 6930-2021 and 71.628-2021, Chilean Supreme Court of Justice (Chile)

*Minister of Mineral Resources and Energy et al. v Sustaining the Wild Coast NPC et al.* (2024) ZASCA 84, Supreme Court of Appeal (South Africa)

*ONG Costa Legal et al. v Municipality of Florianópolis et al.* (2021) No. 5012843-56.2021.4.04.7200, 6th Federal Court of Florianópolis, Santa Catarina (Brazil)

*Rabab Ali v Federation of Pakistan et al.* (2016) ___ / I of 2016, Supreme Court of Pakistan (Pakistan)

*Ridhima Pandey v Union of India et al.* (2019) 187/2017, National Green Tribunal (India) (Pandey or Ridhima)

*Sacchi et al. v Argentina* (2019) CRC/C/88/D/105/2019, UN Committee on the Rights of the Child

*Saonu and Morobe Provincial Government v Minister for Environment and Conservation and Climate Change et al.* (2021) OS (JR) 35 of 2021, Court of Justice at Waigani (Papua New Guinea)

*Sustaining the Wild Coast NPC v Minister of Mineral Resources* (2022) ZAECMkHC 55, High Court (South Africa)

*Verein Klimaseniorinnen Schweiz et al. v Switzerland* (2024) 53600/20, European Court of Human Rights

*Yánez González et al. v Alcaldía Municipal de Montería et al.* (2015) T-218/17, Colombian Constitutional Court (Colombia) (Decision T-218/17)

## Journal articles

Amorim-Maia AT, Anguelovski I, Chu E and Connolly J, 'Intersectional Climate Justice: A Conceptual Pathway for Bridging Adaptation Planning, Transformative Action, and Social Equity' (2022) 41 *Urban Climate* 1 <https://doi.org/10.1016/j.uclim.2021.101053> accessed 20 August 2024

Anghie A, 'Rethinking International Law: A TWAIL Retrospective' (2023) 34(1) *European Journal of International Law* 7 <https://doi.org/10.1093/ejil/chad005> accessed 24 September 2024

Ann Samuel S, '"Greening" International Law en route to Agenda 2030: The Role of Youth in Enhancing the Soft Power of Climate Justice' (2022) 33(1) *Yearbook of International Environmental Law* 3 <https://doi.org/10.1093/yiel/yvad064> accessed 24 October 2024

Ann Samuel S, 'Rawls' Cake and Climate Governance: Relevance of "Our" Common Future Today' (2023) 17(3) *Carbon & Climate Law Review* 169 <https://doi.org/10.21552/cclr/2023/3/9> accssed 24 October 2024

Auz J, 'The Political Ecology of Climate Remedies in Latin America and the Caribbean: Comparing Compliance between National and Inter-American Litigation' (2024) 16(1) *Journal of Human Rights Practice* 182 <https://doi.org/10.1093/jhuman/huad057> accessed 18 September 2024

Beardsworth R, '"Remember, Remember the Month of November": Ahead of COP29' (*Open Access Government*, 9 October 2024) <https://doi.org/10.56367/OAG-044-11158> accessed 22 October 2024

Birkmann J, Jamshed A, McMillan JM, Feldmeyer D, Totin E, Solecki W, Ibrahim ZZ, Roberts D, Kerr RB, Poertner HO, Pelling M, Djalante R, Garschagen M, Filho WL, Guha-Sapir D and Alegría A, 'Understanding Human Vulnerability to Climate Change: A Global Perspective on Index Validation for Adaptation Planning' (2022) 803 *Science of Total Environment* <https://doi.org/10.1016/j.scitotenv.2021.150065> accessed 23 September 2024

Buccino S, 'Our Children's Future: Applying Intergenerational Equity to Public Land Management' (2020) 31(3) *Colorado Natural Resources, Energy & Environmental Law Review* 509 <https://www.colorado.edu/law/sites/default/files/attached-files/003_buccino_final_copy.pdf> accessed 24 September 2024

Calderón MD, 'Rights-Based Climate Litigation in Colombia: An Assessment of Claims, Remedies, and Implementation' (2024) 16(1) *Journal of Human Rights Practice* 273 <https://doi.org/10.1093/jhuman/huad067> accessed 18 September 2024

Cavedon-Capdeville FS, Berros MV, Filpi H and Villavicencio-Calzadilla P, 'An Ecocentric Perspective on Climate Litigation: Lessons from Latin America' (2024) 16(1) *Journal of Human Rights Practice* 89 <https://doi.org/10.1093/jhuman/huad031> accessed 30 October 2023

Chakraborty P, '23 Dead in Uttarakhand, Himachal Cloudbursts, Several Highways Blocked' (*India Today*, 3 August 2024) <https://www.indiatoday.in/india/story/uttarakhand-himachal-pradesh-cloudbursts-landslides-kedarnath-pilgrims-rescued-iaf-choppers-drones-2576166-2024-08-03> accessed 25 September 2024

Chamberlain L and Fourie M, 'Using Climate Litigation to Strengthen Advocacy Strategies: The Life After Coal Campaign in South Africa' (2024) 16(1) *Journal of Human Rights Practice* 248 <https://doi.org/10.1093/jhuman/huad021> accessed 8 September 2024

Chaplain J, 'Storytelling and Worldmaking Climate Justice Futures: Indigenous Climate Advocacy and Transnational Solidarity in UN Climate Conferences' 110(3) *Quarterly Journal of Speech* 370 <https://doi.org/10.1080/00335630.2024.2315043> accessed 24 September 2024

Cornelius CM, 'What Might Future Rights-Based Climate Litigation Look Like in Indonesia? A Preliminary Analysis' (2024) 16(1) *Journal of Human Rights Practice* 285 <https://doi.org/10.1093/jhuman/huad064> accessed 18 September 2024

Du Toit L, Soyapi C and Kotzé LJ, 'David Versus Goliath? Indigenous People, Carbon Majors and Climate Litigation in South Africa' (2024) 33(2) *Review of European, Comparative & International Environmental Law* 326 <https://doi.org/10.1111/reel.12534> accessed 24 September 2024

Dube K, Nhamo G and Chikodzi D, 'Flooding Trends and their Impacts on Coastal Communities of Western Cape Province, South Africa' (2021) 87 *GeoJournal* 453 <https://doi.org/10.1007/s10708-021-10460-z> accessed 23 September 2024

Elliot T and Earl J, 'Organizing the Next Generation: Youth Engagement with Activism Inside and Outside of Organizations' (2018) 4(1) *Social Media + Society* <https://doi.org/10.1177/2056305117750722> accessed 24 September 2024

Fineman MA, 'The Vulnerability Subject: Anchoring Equality in the Human Condition' (2008) 20(1) *Yale Journal of Law & Feminism* <https://ssrn.com/abstract=1131407> accessed 12 July 2023

Fisher E, Scotford E and Barritt E, 'The Legally Disruptive Nature of Climate Change' (2017) 80(2) *The Modern Law Review* 173 <https://www.jstor.org/stable/26646916> accessed 25 September 2024

Fornalé E, 'Vulnerability, Intertemporality, and Climate Litigation' (2023) 41(4) *Nordic Journal of Human Rights* 357 <https://doi.org/10.1080/18918131.2023.2225973> accessed 24 September 2024

Gasparri G, Omrani OE, Hinton R, Imbago D, Lakhani H, Mohan A, Yeung W and Bustreo F, 'Children, Adolescents, and Youth Pioneering a Human Rights-Based Approach to Climate Change' (2021) 23(2) *Health and Human Rights Journal* 95 <https://www.hhrjournal.org/2021/12/children-adolescents-and-youth-pioneering-a-human-rights-based-approach-to-climate-change/> accessed 24 September 2024

Gonzalez CG, 'Racial Capitalism, Climate Justice, and Climate Displacement' (2021) 11(1) *Climate Justice in the Anthropocene* 108 <https://doi.org/10.35295/osls.iisl/0000-0000-0000-1137> accessed 23 September 2024

Hanappi D, Bernardi L and Spini D, 'Vulnerability as a Heuristic for Interdisciplinary Research: Assessing the Thematic and Methodological Structure of Empirical

Life-Course Studies' (2015) 6(1) *Longitudinal and Life Course Studies* 59 <http://dx.doi.org/10.14301/llcs.v6i1.302> accessed 24 September 2024

Jamwal K, 'The Need to Include Indigenous Peoples as "Expert" Consultants in India's Apex Committee for Implementation of the Paris Agreement' (2021) 23(3) *Environmental Law Review* 203 <https://doi.org/10.1177/14614529211041723> accessed 24 September 2024

Jegede AO, 'Rights Away From Home: Climate-Induced Displacement of Indigenous Peoples and the Extraterritorial Application of the Kampala Convention' (2016) 16(1) *African Human Rights Law Journal* 58 <http://dx.doi.org/10.17159/1996-2096/2016/v16n1a3> accessed 24 September 2024

Jegede AO, 'Framing Climate Litigation in Individual Communications of the African Human Rights System: Claw-Backs and Substantive Divergences' (2024) 16(1) *Journal of Human Rights Practice* 107 <https://doi.org/10.1093/jhuman/huad018> accessed 18 September 2024

Kelleher O, 'Incorporating Climate Justice into Legal Reasoning: Shifting Towards a Risk-Based Approach to Causation in Climate Litigation' (2022) 13(1) *Journal of Human Rights and the Environment* 290 <https://doi.org/10.4337/jhre.2022.01.12> accessed 24 September 2024

Kotzé LJ, 'The Anthropocene, Earth System Vulnerability and Socio-Ecological Injustice in an Age of Human Rights' (2019) 10(1) *Journal of Human Rights and the Environment* 85 <http://dx.doi.org/10.4337/jhre.2019.01.04> accessed 24 September 2024

Kotzé LJ, Mayer B, van Asselt H, Setzer J, Biermann F, Celis N, Adelman S, Lewis B, Kennedy A, Arling H and Peters B, 'Courts Climate Litigation and the Evolution of Earth System Law' (2024) 15(1) *Global Policy* 5 <https://doi.org/10.1111/1758-5899.13291> accessed 24 October 2024

Krishnan S, 'Gender, Disasters and Climate: Case of Internal Displacement in Assam, India' (2022) 13(1) *Jindal Global Law Review* 87 <https://doi.org/10.1007/s41020-022-00163-y> accessed 24 September 2024

May JR, Dantas MB and Bauer, L 'Climate Rights in Brazil and the United States: A Convergence of Contrasts' (2024) 56(1) *Case Western Reserve Journal of International Law* 439 <https://scholarlycommons.law.case.edu/jil/vol56/iss1/19> accessed 24 October 2024

Mikulewicz M, Caretta MA, Sultana F and Crawford NJW, 'Intersectionality & Climate Justice: A Call for Synergy in Climate Change Scholarship' (2023) 32(7) *Environmental Politics* 1275 <https://doi.org/10.1080/09644016.2023.2172869> accessed 24 September 2024

Moreira DA, Nina ALB, Garrido CF and Neves MESB, 'Rights-Based Climate Litigation in Brazil: An Assessment of Constitutional Cases Before the Brazilian Supreme Court' (2024) 16(1) *Journal of Human Rights Practice* 47 <https://doi.org/10.1093/jhuman/huad023> accessed 25 September 2024

Murcott MJ, 'Minding the Gap: The Constitutional Court's Jurisprudence Concerning the Environmental Right' (2023) 13 *Constitutional Court Review* 147 <https://doi.org/10.2989/CCR.2023.0007> accessed 24 September 2024

Murcott MJ and Tigre MA, 'Developments, Opportunities, and Complexities in Global South Climate Litigation: Introduction to the Special Collection' 16(1) *Journal of Human Rights Practice* 1 <https://doi.org/10.1093/jhuman/huad070> accessed 31 January 2024

Murcott MJ, Tigre MA and Zimmermann N, 'Transnational Insights for Climate Litigation at the European Court of Human Rights: A South-North Perspective in Pursuit of Climate Justice' (2023) 56 *Verfassung und Recht in Übersee* 299 <https://doi.org/10.5771/0506-7286-2023-2-299> accessed 24 September 2024

Murcott MJ and Vinti C, 'The Judge-Made "Duty" to Consider Climate Change in South Africa' (2024) 16(1) *Journal of Human Rights Practice* 125 <https://doi.org/10.1093/jhuman/huad069> accessed 7 September 2024

Nakayama M, Drinkall S and Sasaki D, 'Climate Change, Migration, and Vulnerability: Overview of the Special Issue' (2019) 14(9) *Journal of Disaster Research* 1246 <http://dx.doi.org/10.20965/jdr.2019.p1246> accessed 24 September

Ohdedar B, 'Climate Adaptation, Vulnerability, and Rights-Based Litigation: Broadening the Scope of Climate Litigation Using Political Ecology' (2022) 13(1) *Journal of Human Rights and the Environment* 137 <http://dx.doi.org/10.4337/jhre.2022.01.06> accessed 24 September 2024

Parker L, Mestre J, Jodoin S and Wewerinke-Singh M, 'When the Kids Put Climate Change on Trial: Youth-Focused Rights-Based Climate Litigation Around the World' (2022) 13(1) *Journal of Human Rights and the Environment* 64 <https://ssrn.com/abstract=3960982> accessed 24 September 2024

Peroni L and Timmer A, 'Vulnerable Groups: The Promise of an Emerging Concept in European Human Rights Convention Law' (2013) 11(4) *ICON* 1056 <https://doi.org/10.1093/icon/mot042> accessed 24 October 2024

Pettit J, 'Climate Justice: A New Social Movement for Atmospheric Rights' (2009) 35(3) *IDS Bulletin* 102 <https://doi.org/10.1111/j.1759-5436.2004.tb00142.x> accessed 24 September 2024

Samanta N, 'Fragile Environment, Fractured Citizenship: Environmental Displacement and the Erosion of Citizenship' (2021) 12 *Jindal Global Law Review* 83 <https://doi.org/10.1007/s41020-021-00141-w> accessed 24 September 2024

Sormunen M, 'Rethinking Effective Remedies to the Climate Crisis: A Vulnerability Theory Approach' (2023) 24 *Human Rights Review* 171 <https://doi.org/10.1007/s12142-023-00686-4> accessed 24 September 2024

Spaiser V, Nisbett N and Stefan CG, '"How Dare You?" – The Normative Challenge Posed by Fridays for Future' (2022) 1 *PLOS Climate* e0000053 <https://doi.org/10.1371/journal.pclm.0000053> accessed 24 October 2024

Spini D, Bernardi L and Oris M, 'Vulnerability Across the Life Course' (2017) 14(1) *Research in Human Development* 1 <https://doi.org/10.1080/15427609.2016.1268891> accessed 24 September 2024

Suedi Y and Fall M, 'Climate Change Litigation before the African Human Rights System: Prospects and Pitfalls' (2024) 16(1) *Journal of Human Rights Practice* 146 <https://doi.org/10.1093/jhuman/huad024> accessed 18 September 2024

Sultana F, 'Critical Climate Justice' (2021) 188(1) *The Geographical Journal* 118 <https://doi.org/10.1111/geoj.12417> accessed 23 September 2024

Thomson V, 'Decolonization, Feminism, and Climate Change: A Commentary on "Misdzi Yikh v Canada"' (2022) 18(2) *McGill Journal of Sustainable Development Law* 157 <https://search.informit.org/doi/abs/10.3316/informit.726493881327874> accessed 24 September 2024

Tigre MA, 'Climate Change and Indigenous Groups: The Rise of Indigenous Voices in Climate Litigation' (2022) 9(3) *E-Publica* 214 <https://scholarship.law.columbia.edu/sabin_climate_change/196> accessed 24 September 2024

Tigre MA, 'The "Fair Share" of Climate Mitigation: Can Litigation Increase National Ambition for Brazil?' (2024) 16(1) *Journal of Human Rights Practice* 25 <https://doi.org/10.1093/jhuman/huad032> accessed 18 September 2024

Tigre MA, 'It is (Finally) Time for an Advisory Opinion on Climate Change: Challenges and Opportunities on a Trio of Initiatives' (2024) 17 *Charleston Law Review* 623 <https://scholarship.law.columbia.edu/sabin_climate_change/218> accessed 25 September 2024

Tigre MA and Setzer J, 'Human Rights and Climate Change for Climate Litigation in Brazil and Beyond: An Analysis of the Climate Fund Decision' (2023) 54(4) *Georgetown Journal of International Law* 593 <https://scholarship.law.columbia.edu/sabin_climate_change/219> accessed 25 September 2024

Tigre MA, Urzola N and Goodman A, 'Climate Litigation in Latin America: Is the Region Quietly Leading a Revolution?' (2023) 14(1) *Journal of Human Rights and the Environment* 67 <https://doi.org/10.4337/jhre.2023.01.04> accessed 24 September 2024

Tigre MA and Wewerinke-Singh M, 'Beyond the North-South Divide: Litigation's Role in Resolving Climate Change Loss and Damage Claims' (2023) 32(3) *Review of*

*European, Comparative & International Environmental Law* 439 <https://doi.org/10.1111/reel.12517> accessed 24 September 2024

Urzola Gutiérrez N, 'Gender in Climate Litigation in Latin America: Epistemic Justice Through a Feminist Lens' (2024) 16(1) *Journal of Human Rights Practice* 208 <https://doi.org/10.1093/jhuman/huad030> accessed 24 September 2024

Vaghri Z, 'Climate Change, An Unwelcome Legacy: The Need to Support Children's Rights to Participate in Global Conversation' (2018) 28(1) *Children, Youth and Environments* 104 <https://www.jstor.org/stable/10.7721/chilyoutenvi.28.1.0104> accessed 24 September 2024

Verlie B, 'Climate Justice in More-Than-Human Worlds' (2021) 31(2) *Environmental Politics* 297 <https://doi.org/10.1080/09644016.2021.1981081> accessed 23 September 2024

Wisner B, 'Vulnerability as Concept, Model, Metric, and Tool' (2016) *Oxford Research Encyclopedia of Natural Hazard Science* <https://doi.org/10.1093/acrefore/9780199389407.013.25> accessed 21 April 2024

Zenteno Villa L, 'Exploring Institutional Barriers to Effective Human Rights-Based Climate Litigation in Latin American Courts – Lessons from Chile and Ecuador' (2024) 16(1) *Journal of Human Rights Practice* 273 <https://doi.org/10.1093/jhuman/huad067> accessed 18 September 2024

## Legislation

Interim Constitution of Nepal 2007, 13 April 2007

## Online sources

Abdala V, 'Rains in Rio Grande do Sul have Affected 8,000 Indigenous People' (*Agência Brasil*, 8 May 2024) <https://agenciabrasil.ebc.com.br/en/geral/noticia/2024-05/rains-rio-grande-do-sul-have-affected-8000-indigenous-people> accessed 25 September 2024

'About' (*Climate Change Litigation Database*) <https://climatecasechart.com/about/> accessed 15 September 2024

Ann Samuel S, 'Exploring the Scope of Ecofeminism in the Biodiversity-Climate Nexus' (*IUCN*, 10 April 2023) <https://www.iucn.org/story/202304/exploring-scope-ecofeminism-biodiversity-climate-nexus> accessed 15 April 2023

Associated Press, 'Brazil's Rio Grande Do Sul Faces Economic Woes After Floods, and an Unclear Path to Rebuilding' (*US News & World Report*, 23 May 2024) <https://www.usnews.com/news/world/articles/2024-05-23/brazils-rio-grande-do-sul-faces-economic-woes-after-floods-and-an-unclear-path-to-rebuilding> accessed 25 September 2024

Beardsworth R, 'Climate Leadership and a Normative Framework for Political Action' (*Open Access Government*, 8 October 2021) <https://www.openaccessgovernment.org/climate-leadership-normative-framework-political-action/113753/> accessed 7 April 2023

'Brazil: Teachers and Educational Centres in Rio Grande do Sul Affected by Floods' (*Educational International*, 15 May 2024) <https://www.ei-ie.org/en/item/28585:brazil-teachers-and-educational-centres-in-rio-grande-do-sul-affected-by-floods> accessed 25 September 2024

'Citrusdal Cut Off, Nearly 160,000 Affected by Floods in Cape Town' (*Times Live*, 15 July 2024) <https://www.timeslive.co.za/news/south-africa/2024-07-15-citrusdal-cut-off-nearly-160000-affected-by-floods-in-cape-town/> accessed 25 September 2024

'Climate Change' (*World Health Organization*, 12 October 2023) <https://www.who.int/news-room/fact-sheets/detail/climate-change-and-health> accessed 12 October 2023

Davids N, 'Women's Month: Floods Expose Plight, Pain of "Powerless" Khayelitsha Women' (*University of Cape Town News*, 7 August 2024) <https://www.news.uct.ac.za/article/-2024-08-07-womens-month-floods-expose-plight-pain-of-powerless-khayelitsha-women> accessed 23 September 2024

'Defesa Civil Atualiza Balanço das Enchentes no RS – 20/8' (*Governo do Estado*, 20 August 2024) <https://www.estado.rs.gov.br/defesa-civil-atualiza-balanco-das-enchentes-no-rs-20-8> accessed 24 September 2024

'"Desperate" Rescues Under Way as Brazil Floods Kill 90, Displace Thousands' (*Aljazeera*, 7 May 2024) <https://www.aljazeera.com/news/2024/5/7/desperate-rescues-under-way-as-brazil-floods-kill-90-displace-thousands> accessed 24 September 2024

Ghisleni C, 'Floods in Rio Grande do Sul: The Tragedy of Non-Resilient Cities' (*Arch Daily*, 18 May 2024) <https://www.archdaily.com/1016509/floods-in-rio-grande-do-sul-the-tragedy-of-non-resilient-cities> accessed 25 September 2024

Globo O, 'Enchentes no RS: Sobe para Sete o Número de Mortes por Leptospirose' (*G1*, 29 May 2024) <https://oglobo.globo.com/brasil/sos-rio-grande-do-sul/noticia/2024/05/29/enchentes-no-rs-sobe-para-sete-o-numero-de-mortes-por-leptospirose.ghtml> accessed 25 September 2024

International Tribunal for the Law of the Sea, 'Request for an Advisory Opinion Submitted by the Commission of Small Island States on Climate Change and International Law' <https://www.itlos.org/fileadmin/itlos/documents/cases/31/Advisory_Opinion/C31_Adv_Op_21.05.2024_orig.pdf> accessed 25 October 2024

Krishnan V, 'Climate Change isn't India's Fault, but It is India's Responsibility' (*Harvard Public Health Magazine*, 16 July 2024) <https://harvardpublichealth.org/environmental-health/india-climate-change-perpetuates-injustices-against-vulnerable/> accessed 25 September 2024

Mizo R, 'India's Climate Calamities' (*Toda Peace Institute*, 7 August 2024) <https://toda.org/global-outlook/2024/indias-climate-calamities.html> accessed 25 September 2024

'NúcleoPorto Alegre Analisa os Impactos das Enchentes na População Pobre e Negra do Rio Grande do Sul' (*Observatório das Metrópoles*, 23 May 2024) <https://www.observatoriodasmetropoles.net.br/nucleo-porto-alegre-analisa-os-impactos-das-enchentes-na-populacao-pobre-e-negra-do-rio-grande-do-sul/> accessed 25 September 2024

Omar SA and Conradie S, '"Cape of Storms" – Climate Researchers Explain Cape Town's Recent Extreme Weather' (*The Conversation*, 30 May 2024) <https://theconversation.com/cape-of-storms-climate-researchers-explain-cape-towns-recent-extreme-weather-229012> accessed 13 September 2024

'ONU Reforça Proteção de Grupos Vulneráveis no Rio Grande do Sul' (*Nações Unidas*, 10 May 2024) <https://news.un.org/pt/story/2024/05/1831506> access 25 September 2024

Penner A, 'Brazil's Rio Grande Do Sul Faces Economic Woes After Floods, and an Unclear Path to Rebuilding' (*U.S. News*, 23 May 2024) <https://www.usnews.com/news/world/articles/2024-05-23/brazils-rio-grande-do-sul-faces-economic-woes-after-floods-and-an-unclear-path-to-rebuilding> accessed 25 October 2024

Perinchery A, 'Nightmare in Wayanad: Torrential Rains Triggered Landslides But Climate Change May Not Be the Sole Culprit' (*The Wire*, 2024) <https://thewire.in/environment/nightmare-in-wayanad-torrential-rains-triggered-landslides-but-climate-change-may-not-be-the-sole-culprit> accessed 25 September 2024

Phaliso S, Hendricks A and Damons M, 'Thousands of Homes Flooded as Violent Storm Batters Western Cape' (*GroundUp*, 9 July 2024) <https://groundup.org.za/article/thousands-of-homes-flooded-as-violent-storm-batters-western-cape/> accessed 25 September 2024

Pimentel A, 'Mulheres em Tempos de Crise: Uma Tragédia Dentro da Tragédia do RS' (*Lemonde Diplomatique Brasil*, 10 May 2024) <https://diplomatique.org.br/mulheres-tragedia-rio-grande-do-sul/> access 25 September 2024

Prazeres L and Lemos JMV, 'O Drama dos Idosos nas Inundações do Rio Grande do Sul: "Parecem Deixados de Lado"' (*BBC News Brasil*, 20 May 2024) <https://www.bbc.com/portuguese/articles/ce550yrv3v7o> accessed 25 September 2024

Saude O, 'Health in Times of Climate Chaos: Floods in Rio Grande do Sul' (*Movimento dos trabalhadores rurais sem terra*, 20 May 2024) <https://mst.org.br/2024/05/20/health-in-times-of-climate-chaos-floods-in-rio-grande-do-sul/> accessed 25 September 2024

Stabile A, Paulo PP, Croquer G, Casemiro P and Paulo S, 'Guaíba Received Almost Half the Volume of Water from Itaipu in a Week of Rain, According to an Institute at UFRGS' (*G1*, 10 May 2024) <https://g1.globo.com/meio-ambiente/noticia/2024/05/10/guaiba-recebeu-quase-metade-do-volume-de-agua-de-itaipu-em-uma-semana-de-chuvas-aponta-instituto-da-ufrgs.ghtml> accessed 24 September 2024

Tokarnia M, 'Floods Have Affected 3,000 Health Care Units in Rio Grande do Sul' (*Agência Brasil*, 20 May 2024) <https://agenciabrasil.ebc.com.br/en/geral/noticia/2024-05/floods-have-affected-3000-health-care-units-rio-grande-do-sul> accessed 25 September 2024

UN General Assembly, 'Request for an Advisory Opinion of the International Court of Justice on the Obligation of States in Respect of Climate Change' <https://climatecasechart.com/wp-content/uploads/non-us-case-documents/2023/20230301_18913_na.pdf> accessed 25 October 2024

'Veja os Números Mais Recentes das Enchentes no RS Nesta Terça-feira' (*Zero Hora*, 5 July 2024) <https://gauchazh.clicrbs.com.br/geral/noticia/2024/05/veja-os-numeros-mais-recentes-das-enchentes-no-rs-nesta-terca-feira-clvwaf3cb000a0152rv-vf5m36.html> accessed 24 September 2024

Venukuttan P, 'Wayanad Landslides Were Forecast Long Ago, Archives Reveal' (*Nature India*, 23 August 2024) <https://www.nature.com/articles/d44151-024-00133-4> accessed 22 October 2024

Willige A, 'A Third of India's Economy Relies on Nature: Here's Why Corporates Need to Invest More in Natural Climate Solutions' (*World Economic Forum*, 5 August 2024) <https://www.weforum.org/agenda/2024/08/india-economy-natural-climate-solutions/> accessed 25 September 2024

## Reports

Burger M and Tigre MA, 'Global Climate Litigation Report: 2023 Status Review' (*Sabin Center for Climate Change Law, Columbia Law School & United Nations Environment Programme*, 2023) <https://scholarship.law.columbia.edu/sabin_climate_change/202> accessed 25 September 2024

Clarke B, Barnes C, Rodrigues R, Zachariah M, Alves LM, Haarsma R, Pinto I, Yang W, Vahlberg M, Vecchi G, Izquierdo K, Kimutai J, Otto F, Philip S, Kew S, Singh R, Biehl J and Mugge M, 'Climate Change, El Ninõ and Infrastructure Failures Behind Massive Floods in Southern Brazil' (June 2024) <https://doi.org/10.25561/111882> accessed 25 September 2024

Government of India, 'Ministry of Home Affairs: Disaster Management Division. Situation Report Regarding Flood/Heavy Rainfall (12.08.2024)' (August 2024) <https://ndmindia.mha.gov.in/ndmi/viewUploadedDocument?uid=NEW2155> accessed 25 September 2024

IPCC, 'Summary for Policymakers in Climate Change 2022 – Impacts, Adaptation and Vulnerability: Working Group II Contribution to the Sixth Assessment Report of the Intergovernmental Panel on Climate Change' in HO Pörtner et al. (eds), (2022) <https://www.ipcc.ch/report/ar6/wg2/downloads/report/IPCC_AR6_WGII_FullReport.pdf> accessed 8 October 2024

IPCC, 'Summary for Policymakers in Climate Change 2023: Synthesis Report, Contribution of Working Groups I, II and III to the Sixth Assessment Report of the Intergovernmental Panel on Climate Change' in Core Writing Team, H Lee and J Romero (eds), (2023) <https://www.ipcc.ch/report/ar6/syr/downloads/report/IPCC_AR6_SYR_FullVolume.pdf> accessed 8 October 2024

Pearce O and Ware J, 'Climate Breakdown 2024: 6 Months of Climate Chaos Since COP28' (*Christian Aid*, June 2024) <https://reliefweb.int/attachments/12b8a9b3-3a3c-47fa-aa2b-48ca5954e54a/Climate%20breakdown%202024.pdf> accessed 24 September 2024

Schnakenberg J et al. (eds), 'Human Rights in the Face of Climate Crisis: A Youth Led Initiative to Bring Climate Justice to International Court of Justice' (July 2021) <https://static1.squarespace.com/static/5f063a0c8f53b604aed84729/t/638f9ee73dfbf63abd0cc021/1670356715298/Second+Edition+Legal+Report.pdf> accessed 25 October 2024

Tigre MA, 'Climate Litigation in the Global South: Mapping Report' (*Sabin Center for Climate Change Law, Columbia Law School*, 2024) <https://scholarship.law.columbia.edu/sabin_climate_change/212> accessed 25 September 2024

Tigre MA and Barry M, 'Climate Change in the Courts: A 2023 Retrospective' (*Sabin Center for Climate Change Law*, December 2023). <https://scholarship.law.columbia.edu/sabin_climate_change/212> accessed 25 October 2024

Tigre MA, Zenteno L, Hesselman M, Urzola N, Cisterna-Gaete P and Luporini R, 'Just Transition Litigation in Latin America: An Initial Categorization of Climate Litigation Cases Amid the Energy Transition' (*Sabin Center for Climate Change Law*, 2023) <https://scholarship.law.columbia.edu/sabin_climate_change/197/> accessed 25 September 2024

### *Working papers*

Skoufias E, Rabassa M and Olivieri S, 'The Poverty Impacts of Climate Change: A Review of the Evidence' (2011) *Policy Research Working Paper 5622* <https://elibrary.worldbank.org/doi/abs/10.1596/1813-9450-5622> accessed 17 August 2023

Spini D et al., 'Vulnerability Across the Life Course: A Theoretical Framework and Research Directions' (2013) *Lives, Working Paper 2013/27*, 15 <https://www.researchgate.net/publication/305301274_Vulnerability_across_the_life_course_A_theoretical_framework_and_research_directions> accessed 24 October 2024

Part 1

# Exposing the limits of litigation as a mechanism for intersectional climate justice

Chapter 1

# Facing coloniality within legal systems

## Indigenous peoples in Latin American climate litigation

*Elisa Fiorini Beckhauser and Valeriana Augusta Broetto*

### Introduction

This chapter examines the interactions between the coloniality[1] of Latin American legal systems and the demands for climate justice advanced by Indigenous peoples in climate litigation. These legal systems originate from the colonial period[2] and may continue to reinforce a colonial rationale through the law and its institutions. Colonialism has been crucial in making Indigenous peoples vulnerable to climate change and other socio-ecological pressures. Currently, the historical failure of states to protect the interests of Indigenous peoples is aggravated by the urgency of the climate crisis. These groups have been advocating for their rights through different strategies of social mobilisation, such as protests to gain political attention. In addition to these tactics, the judiciary may represent a last stand[3] to guarantee Indigenous peoples' needs, the reason that some communities have been using courts as a way to safeguard their rights.[4] However, as colonial institutions,[5] courts might not be receptive to the claims of Indigenous peoples that are external to the positivist[6] legal order, that is, claims that translate interests and demands from ethnic communities – such as Indigenous, tribal, and Afro-Americans – that do not stem from Western worldviews.

Stemming from wildly different cultural frameworks and for a multitude of interests, European colonisers introduced their foreign laws and institutions in Latin America. This process of cultural assimilation excluded Indigenous peoples from the decision- and lawmaking processes and prohibited them from managing their lands through positive laws and institutions.[7] The absence of a fair intercultural dialogue in the legal arena facilitated land dispossession, natural resources exploitation, and the imposition of Western cultural values. Hence, law functioned as a central instrument of colonisation, universalising the interests of the coloniser and ensuring the continuance of the *status quo*.[8]

Despite the rupture with colonial administrations during independence processes, these legal dynamics persist[9] and sustain a new structure of colonialism, which continues to reproduce domination and inferiorisation towards racialised individuals and communities[10] and is key to climate change. The Intergovernmental Panel on Climate Change (IPCC) identifies colonialism as a driver of the

DOI: 10.4324/9781003470632-3

climate crisis, as it promotes historical patterns of inequity that severely impact Indigenous peoples.[11] The intersections between coloniality and climate change are thus a current justice issue in Latin America and elsewhere in the Global South, as Indigenous peoples and other groups seek to hold those responsible for climate change and its impacts accountable.

Ecosystems in Latin America play a crucial role in combating climate change, as the region is home to some of the most important biodiversity for the functioning of Earth systems.[12] Despite that, Latin American ecosystems are acutely vulnerable to climate-related risks, which reduce their resilience and intensify their vulnerability to climate change.[13] Loss of ecosystems has cascading and long-term impacts, especially on Indigenous peoples,[14] whose subsistence usually depends on the ecological integrity of their territories. Thus, Indigenous peoples are among the hardest-hit by climate change impacts.[15] Moreover, several Indigenous peoples' cultural, spiritual, and economic practices rely on their connection with their ancestral land, which often depend, in turn, on legal frameworks based on stewardship.[16] At the same time, Indigenous peoples and their traditional knowledge play a crucial role in climate mitigation and biodiversity preservation.[17] Despite being only 5% of the global population, their territories encompass 80% of the planet's biodiversity.[18] The historical struggle of Indigenous peoples to protect their lives and territories is part of a global effort to ensure the survival of humans and all living beings. As Marinete Almeida Costa, a leader of the Tucano people, has expressed, 'we don't fight just for ourselves, but for everyone – because the standing forest is life'.[19]

Legal frameworks play a pivotal role in this context, since the survival of these vulnerable groups within a context of extractivism and climate crisis depends on laws and institutions that recognise and protect their particular necessities and guarantee their rights. However, a colonial rationale within legal systems may undermine the state's capacity to address Indigenous peoples' vulnerability. Institutions and laws conceived under this rationale stem from a liberal conception of legal subjectivity characteristic of the Western[20] tradition, which is disconnected from the natural world and disembodied from its human interactions.[21] This abstract subject expects inaction from a minimal state. The rationalist disembodiment is inseparable from the exclusion of subjects who do not fit the standard. Similarly, these institutions apply laws that derive from rules and cultural assumptions external to Indigenous[22] cosmologies[23] – replicating a colonial model of imposing norms from outside, disregarding particular subjectivities.

This legal framework is also ill-suited to addressing the climate crisis, which requires the fulfilment of positive obligations by states that are failing to protect people from climate harm, particularly those most vulnerable. The lack of effective remedies against the climate crisis illustrates how societal structures can exacerbate vulnerability,[24] and how inadequate responses are deeply intertwined with the law's rational subject.[25] Indigenous peoples demand specific attention from governments, as climate change threatens their culturally differentiated livelihoods and lifestyle, a factor that is contributing to the rise of climate litigation cases.

Proceeding from the premise that vulnerability is not an inherent but rather an institutionally and systemically created or enhanced condition,[26] courts represent an opportunity to reduce this vulnerability. As mentioned earlier, vulnerable groups from Latin America once viewed courts as the last option for strengthening and recognising their fundamental rights.[27] However, judicial review has more recently assumed a central role in Latin American politics,[28] and courts are delivering disruptive rulings.[29] Nevertheless, given the persistence of coloniality within institutions, Indigenous peoples encounter challenges regarding, for instance, translating their demands into positive legal norms that do not encompass their cosmology and producing a solid set of evidence that supports their claims.

This chapter analyses two climate cases filed in Ecuador and Colombia by Indigenous peoples, to observe how courts can variously maintain a colonial rationale or advance Indigenous peoples' claims for climate justice. This analysis, based on a delimited and specific sample of cases, seeks to shed light on whether the judiciary may institutionally perpetuate the vulnerability of Indigenous peoples or adopt a decolonising posture that promotes the empowerment of these groups through the democratic framework of the rule of law. Furthermore, the analysis highlights how these Indigenous peoples are vindicating their interests within the legal order, legitimising their experiences of vulnerability from their discourses. Consequently, it reveals some of the primary constraints these communities face before adjudicatory bodies, which are the main avenue to protect their rights. Additionally, it sheds light on the posture of the judiciary in adjudication concerned with the highly interrelated vulnerabilities of Indigenous peoples and natural ecosystems, which enables the observation of whether national legal orders offer effective means to tackle vulnerabilities to climate change.

The cases were chosen to reflect Indigenous peoples' perspectives with as little interference from mediators as possible. Therefore, the selection excludes cases in which non-Indigenous actors, such as NGOs and representative institutions, were the only plaintiffs, even when dealing with the rights of Indigenous peoples. Cases in which Indigenous peoples were the only active party or co-plaintiffs were included in the scope of analysis. Thus, using the databases of the Sabin Center for Climate Change Law and of the Interamerican Association for Environmental Defense (the latter compiles specific climate cases from Latin America and the Caribbean), the chapter analyses two cases, one from Colombia and one from Ecuador: *Pushaina et al. v Carbones del Cerrejón Limited et. al.* (Colombia),[30] presented by representatives of the Wayúu Indigenous community, and *Baihua Caiga et. al. v PetroOriental SA*[31] (Ecuador), by representatives of the Waorani Indigenous community. In these lawsuits, Indigenous peoples are the only active parties or co-plaintiffs.

Along with the limited sample, several aspects may interfere with the evaluation of cases and, consequently, lead to different conclusions that do not derive from an analysis of the colonial frame. In general, the strategy adopted by the plaintiffs, as well as the availability of a favourable evidentiary and legislative set, may push the judgment of the claims and lead to more robust and favourable precedents for Indigenous peoples, while the lack of legally acceptable evidence and a legal system that does not recognise fundamental rights renders it more difficult to obtain a disruptive decision that advances climate justice. Beyond each decision's content, structural challenges regarding its enforcement remain a common scourge of the continent and yet another level of obstacle for the vulnerable people of the region. First, we briefly elaborate on how colonialism continues to influence Latin American legal systems. Then, we explore how Indigenous peoples in Latin America have made considerable efforts to ensure their rights through litigation, presenting a potentially decolonial counterpoint. Finally, we analyse two lawsuits that highlight the crucial connection between Indigenous communities, their territories, and ecosystems. The analysis of the cases aims to reflect the dynamics between the arguments and demands of Indigenous peoples and the judges' interpretations in the legal language and focuses on four elements: (1) the challenge to the licensed extractive activities; (2) the Indigenous plaintiffs' interpretations of human rights, rights of nature, and environmental impact assessment; (3) the causal link between fact and harm and evidence presented; and (4) the interpretation of the courts.

## Colonial roots in Latin American legal systems[32]

The vulnerability of Indigenous peoples to climate change impacts results from a historical colonisation process based on their dehumanisation and objectification due to ethnicity, indigeneity, and culture.[33] The classification of Indigenous peoples' bodies as inferior by the colonisers paved the way to a 'socially and legally acceptable' abyssal exclusion.[34] Although everyone is vulnerable to climate change,[35] communities in sacrifice zones are particularly susceptible to harm due to their subhuman condition.[36] These particular zones represent areas where the exploitation of racialised human beings intersects with the domination of nature.[37] In this sense, sacrifice zones are where extractive activities often take place, accompanied by environmental damages and severe human rights violations.[38] During the colonial period of Latin America, Indigenous peoples were dispossessed of their lands and deprived of spaces for social reproduction.[39] Indigenous peoples' cultures, cosmovision, and relationship with nature were considered subordinate to the former colonies.[40] Ultimately, colonisation took 'political territoriality' away from Indigenous peoples[41] and alienated their capacity to decide on their destinies.[42]

Colonialism was a form of domination and control related to the concept of power,[43] which involved a 'large-scale transfer of laws and legal institutions[44] from one society to another'.[45] The imposition of the conqueror's law inevitably replaced Indigenous law.[46] One of the long-range consequences of this replacement is the exploitation of natural resources to benefit the coloniser, which also made Indigenous peoples subjects of European monarchies.[47] Thus, the law was the main legitimising instrument that enabled domination, cultural transfer, and transformation of territories, ecosystems, and native populations' livelihoods.

Although the matrix of colonial power[48] transformed its initial structure of formal domination, its reasoning persists. Quijano and Ennis[49] point out that the relations of economic and political coloniality have not ended with colonialism as an explicit political order, since Western forms of domination continue to be reproduced by contemporary colonial structures and cultures.[50]

Coloniality is not just a question of subordination of other cultures to European culture; it is also the colonisation of the imaginary, replacing beliefs, ideas, and knowledge.[51] Building on the coloniality of power, the narrative control of the economy, authority, and nature often ensures the peripheralisation of regions that remain in a subjugated situation, even if they are no longer subject to a colonial administration.[52] Thus, the region's former colonies remain influenced by the metropolis through European institutions[53] conceived for other contexts and imported into Latin America.

Tapia[54] formulates the persistence of colonialism in terms of internal colonialism. For Latin America, this means the transformation of the region into partially extractivist societies,[55] with the incorporation of the exploitation of natural resources. Besides, internal colonialism reflects the governmental political structure not arising from within territories but being organised in modern elements imposed from outside.

The persistence of extractivism as the primary economic activity in Latin America has its roots in the colonial period.[56] It is a major source of Indigenous peoples' vulnerabilisation (including to climate change), as their livelihoods and identity survival rely on preserving their territories. Latin America, in general, is highly exposed to territorial reduction due to extractivism.[57] Extractive industries reproduce historical traces of environmental destruction, impose material domination, and act as a mechanism of neocolonial appropriation since they displace communities from their territories and prevent their ways of living by not considering them as people but as resources.[58] They are also a leading cause of climate change.

In the legal sphere, Bagni identifies a short circuit in the encounter of Indigenous cosmovisions and Western legal systems.[59] She argues that the Indigenous cosmovision is subsumed in a normative instrument (the Constitution), in a legal system (constitutionalism), and in a system of knowledge and normative production (the Western legal tradition). Despite intending to be open to legal pluralism, the Constitution remains imbricated in its cosmovision of origin – regarded as the only way of conceiving law and depicting the human–environment relationship. Thus, one may wonder whether legal systems are able to recognise non-Western cosmologies or whether colonial heritage is still dominant. This heritage is not the simple reproduction of colonial mechanisms but, rather, the complex devices that cover up coloniality, which in Latin American legal systems denotes that its laws and institutions have a 'living' colonial heritage. However, crucial advances in Latin American legal systems have been building greater autonomy and political and legal legitimacy for the region's Indigenous peoples. Constitutional reforms are a crucial driver for these changes, assembling a framework for deepening Indigenous autonomy to different extents.[60]

For example, following the International Labor Organization's 169th Convention from 1990,[61] many Latin American countries have adopted the right to free, prior, and informed consent (FPIC) in respect of development on ancestral lands. FPIC then became a resistance tool to tackle mining and extractive projects that loom over Indigenous communities.[62] Moreover, the recognition of the legal subjectivity of nature in the Constitution of Ecuador of 2008 also reinforces the rights of Indigenous peoples,[63] since it articulates the protection of their human rights with the rights of ecosystems. The Escazú Agreement, focused on procedural environmental rights, is another important legal tool since it can facilitate access to courts and reinforce the tradition of Indigenous litigation in environmental matters.

Thus, using 'coloniality' as an adjective to critically describe the heritage of legal systems emerging from colonisation does not imply a closed and immutable situation. The socio-legal contexts of Latin America are a dynamic and vivid reality. As such, they contend that there is a coexistence of forces between colonial heritage and innovative endeavours to empower Indigenous peoples through constitutional movements and the active role of the judiciary. Whether climate litigation can play a pivotal role in changing and decolonising[64] this reality (that is, incorporating Indigenous peoples' perspectives into the legal system) to advance climate justice depends on factors such as the capacity to translate Indigenous peoples' interests into the legal language and terms and on the interpretations of the courts. The next section explores the interaction between Indigenous peoples' demands and Latin American courts in climate litigation.

## Indigenous peoples' climate litigation in Latin America

Two associated factors contribute to the efforts of Indigenous peoples in Latin America to advance climate justice in the courts.[65] Firstly, constitutional reforms that occurred in Latin American countries since the 1980s[66] recognised social struggles, introduced new constitutional rights (especially environmental rights), and reinforced the role of the judicial review of politics.[67] Secondly, these changes were followed by the use of courts to enhance and reinterpret the rights of vulnerable groups.

Constitutional reforms enabled a shift in the use of courts, hitherto viewed as an obstacle to social change,[68] sustaining the power of elites and the *status quo*.[69] Following reforms, despite the colonial heritage of courts (as discussed earlier), marginalised groups have more readily resorted to these institutions to secure their rights.

In the context of climate change, several actors – such as NGOs, political parties, and individuals – in Latin America have used litigation to pursue climate action.[70] In the region, the leading characteristics of climate litigation are challenges to extractivism to protect the region's ecosystems and the use of rights-based arguments, mainly environmental rights recognised in constitutions.[71]

Climate litigation has been a tool of institutional resistance within this socio-political context for Indigenous people and other marginalised groups worldwide. Their claims are part of the Global South's trend of rights-based litigation,[72] which is particularly promising in the region because of (1) a multitude of constitutions recognising environmental rights[73] and the right to a healthy environment and, fewer, the rights of nature;[74] (2) the tradition of vindicating collective human rights in courts at national levels,[75] which now extends to vindicating climate issues;[76] and (3) the active role played by the Inter-American Court of Human Rights (IACtHR) concerning economic, social, cultural, and environmental rights.[77]

The IACtHR has linked human rights and the environment in disputes concerning the rights of traditional peoples to the demarcation of territories against authorisations for extractive activities. Indigenous peoples' demands have gradually inserted disruptive and structurally contesting claims[78] arising from the indivisible and collective nature of their rights.[79] In doing so, Indigenous peoples called into question the historical marginalisation and discrimination process they have been subjected to and challenged the hegemonic economic development model.[80]

Indigenous peoples' cases have contributed to creating jurisprudence that reinterprets the rights to property, life, physical integrity, and participation from an ecological perspective.[81] The link between environmental degradation and territorial rights lies in the integrity of ancestral land, which is an indispensable part of their way of life.[82] IACtHR jurisprudence has played a significant role in establishing the basis for the judicial defence of human rights.

Although based on constitutional rights, Indigenous peoples' claims frequently propose an interpretation of these rights from their own theoretical and conceptual lenses, which contrasts with a Western liberal understanding of rights.[83] Indigenous peoples' claims require an understanding of fundamental rights from the cultural logic of collective/communitarian subjects and comprehending the content (expressions and concepts) of rights from a biocentric epistemological referential.[84] Therefore, these cases present an opportunity to decolonise the legal framework, incorporating Indigenous peoples' perspectives and demands.[85] Such decolonisation is crucial for crafting holistic responses to the climate crisis that encompass vulnerable communities' knowledge, practices, and particular necessities according to their worldviews. Therefore, the cases shed light on how colonialism has shaped laws that have facilitated the climate crisis, in particular, through a liberal perspective that interprets territories and nature solely as a commodity to be exploited for profit.

Aside from the traditional challenges of litigation, such as costs and lengthy processes, Indigenous peoples face unique obstacles when presenting legal arguments. The next section shows that one of the barriers for Indigenous peoples is the comprehension of their demands by lawyers who translate their claims into the legal language and judges who analyse requests that stem from Indigenous peoples' ways of knowing, being, and reasoning. Even when courts rule in favour of Indigenous peoples' claims, Latin American countries struggle with enforcing decisions and adopting governance structures that engage Indigenous peoples as agents of change.[86]

These challenges relate to the persistence of a colonial rationale in Latin American legal systems, which may influence legal hermeneutics and the performance of institutions, conflicting with the non-Western rationalities brought up in Indigenous peoples' climate litigation.[87] The goals of plaintiffs (given their Indigenous cosmovisions) may be at odds with the capacity of the judiciary to respond meaningfully and effectively. This (in)capacity of adjudicatory bodies might relate to the claim (difficulty to fully understand the plaintiffs' reasoning) or the entire system (in enforcing the ruling while not respecting Indigenous demands and their participation in the governance of ecosystems within their territories, therefore embracing also the executive and the legislative branches).

Next, we discuss two climate cases filed by Indigenous peoples and explore whether the judiciary perpetuates their vulnerability in climate litigation or if it is open to adopting a decolonising posture that contributes to empowering this particular group.

## Case studies: engaging with Indigenous peoples' climate litigation and the role of the judiciary

The cases discussed in this section concerned the protection of ecosystems essential for the material and identity survival of Indigenous peoples in Latin America. They shed light on the dynamics between coloniality and Indigenous peoples' arguments. The judges' interpretations involve the essential links between communities, their territories, and ecosystems to reflect this relationship in legal language.

The Colombian case, *Wayúu Community*,[88] was filed by members of the Wayúu Indigenous community in 2015 before the Constitutional Court of Colombia. The Wayúu community is the largest ethnic community in a territory that crosses the Colombia–Venezuela border.[89] This community lives in La Guajira, a very hot and dry region that has been an intense area of conflict for environmental contamination and mining activities that affect the ecological structure of rivers.[90] The case concerned human rights violations caused by the diversion of the Bruno Stream for mining activities carried out by Carbones de Cerrejón Limited, a mining company. The invoked rights were health, water, food security, healthy environment, equality, identity, cultural diversity, and FPIC.

The Ecuadorian case, *Waorani Community*,[91] refers to human rights violations caused by gas flaring activities in the Ecuadorian Amazon carried out by an oil company. It was filed by members of the Waorani Indigenous community against PetroOriental S.A. in 2020. The Waorani are the most recently contacted of all Ecuadorian Indigenous peoples, and oil activities and road construction for this industry have severely impacted their lands and drastically affected the community and their water supply.[92]

In both cases, the engagement of women was central to safeguarding Indigenous peoples' self-determination and the protection of their territories in the face of climate change and extractive industries.[93]

*Table 1.1* Summary of the climate cases in Colombia and Ecuador

| *Case* | *Central argument* | *Outcome* |
|---|---|---|
| *Pushaina et al. v Carbones del Cerrejón Limited et. al.* (*Wayúu Community case*) | The community argued that a mining licence ignored the socio-environmental conditions of the territory and the particular relations between them, and the water bodies of La Guajira, violating fundamental rights. | The Colombian Constitutional Court ordered the production of a technical study to reassess the environmental viability of the detour, which remained unfinished as of February 2024. |
| *Baihua Caiga et al. v PetroOriental S.A* (*Waorani Community* case) | The community argued that gas flaring activities carried out by a company were a violation of the rights of nature and their constitutional rights. | The Family, Women, and Children Judicial Unit of Francisco de Orellana Canton denied the demand on the grounds that plaintiffs did not present enough evidence to support their claims.[94] |

Both cases concern extractive industries and the interaction between human rights and economic activities, a common feature of Latin American climate litigation. At the same time, these cases propose distinct perspectives of justice and vulnerability and ask for interpretations of human rights in the context of climate change that recognise Indigenous peoples' interests and particular needs. The plaintiffs claim protection of Indigenous peoples to seek recognition of their points of view, representing an opposition to the dominant (colonial) legal system. The following analysis discusses the main aspects of the cases. Eventual emphasis discrepancies in each case depend on the amount of content the lawsuit provides regarding each specific criterion.

## *Challenging previously licensed and authorised extractive activities*

Contesting environmental permits and the review process of projects with climate change implications is a consolidating global trend in climate litigation.[95] In both cases, Indigenous peoples and communities asked for the protection of their rights and the surrounding ecosystems in the face of legalised extractive practices that began with colonialism. The contested legality of the activities was a potential hurdle to the plaintiffs' claims, as they were challenging licensed and, therefore, potentially lawful activities.

In the *Wayúu Community* case, the plaintiffs challenged the licensed gas flaring activities of the company Carbones del Cerrejón Limited. The company argued that its activities were strictly within the parameters of the law, relying on licences obtained according to legal provisions.

In the *Waorani Community* case, the plaintiffs claimed that Ecuadorian authorities who had permitted gas flaring had not adequately addressed the proportionate responsibility of the company concerned, PetroOriental, for greenhouse gas (GHG) emissions. The plaintiffs argued that these emissions, in turn, contribute to global climate change and violate the rights of nature and the fundamental rights of the community (rights to an ecologically balanced and healthy environment, food, water, health, territory, life, and dignified life). They did not ask for the cessation of gas flaring activities but rather that gas flaring should occur observing the protection of their fundamental rights and the environment. The defence argued that gas flaring is (1) done in public interest, (2) legally regulated and licensed by the state, and (3) essential to the country's economy. The plaintiffs challenged a colonial and neocolonial vision of the law that privileges economic growth over Indigenous peoples' interests and rights, drawing on constitutional rights and values.

### *Indigenous peoples' interpretations of human rights violations, the rights of nature, and the environmental impact assessment*

The Indigenous peoples in both cases adopted rights-based arguments. They grounded their prayers for relief on the right to a healthy and ecologically balanced environment and other constitutionally protected rights, such as the right to life, health, food, and water.

However, the cases also discuss specific vulnerabilities of Indigenous peoples and distinct interpretations of justice. They contextualised their claims given their particular vulnerability to extractive practices and the corresponding impacts of climate change. Due to their culturally differentiated livelihoods and dependence on territories and ecosystems, these factors impact them more severely, and their human rights must be interpreted based on these differences. Thus, the cases integrate human rights and the rights of nature and concern the protection of the ecosystems involved, promoting an ecological perspective of human rights.[96]

The vital link between Indigenous cosmologies and ecosystems sheds light on another layer of vulnerability they face because of climate change. Besides the strong material impacts due to their dependence on natural resources, Indigenous peoples' cultural and spiritual practices are threatened by climate change. Since ancestral knowledge and traditional practices have been shaped according to long-term environmental conditions and natural cycles of ecosystems, the alteration of rainfall regimes or drought periods, for instance, weakens the socio-cultural tools that Indigenous peoples have to survive in their territories, as it diminishes the applicability of the knowledge developed so far. Short- and long-term risks linked to climate change increase the vulnerability of Indigenous peoples. There is an immediate threat of material survival that is linked to a permanent loss of socio-cultural heritage and ethnic identity.[97]

The *Wayúu Community* case[98] did not mention the rights of nature (which are not explicitly protected in the Colombian Constitution) but raised the interconnection between the plaintiffs' cosmology and the ecosystem. The community interprets the Bruno Stream as a 'living being'[99] responsible for shaping their cultural values based on the relationship with natural and spiritual resources directly dependent on it.

Given the formal recognition of the rights of nature in the Ecuadorian Constitution, the *Waorani Community* case articulated the fundamental rights of plaintiffs as connected to the rights of the ecosystems. It sought not only to repair environmental damage but also to protect the community's constitutional rights and the rights of nature, since ecological balance is fundamental to their survival. The constitutional recognition of the rights of nature was the main foundation of their claim. PetroOriental's activities, they claimed, violated these rights by breaking the vital cycles of nature, such as carbon cycles. The plaintiffs asserted that traditional food, loss of access to traditional medicine, and the obsolescence of ancestral practices are substantive content related to Indigenous cosmologies that human rights language must encompass.[100]

They claim to have seen their lifestyle altered by the loss of harmony with nature and by their livelihoods being threatened by climate change. This would ultimately violate their constitutional rights (to a healthy and ecologically balanced environment, food, water, health, having their territory, and life, from which derives the right to have a project of life). The plaintiffs also claim their right to have a project of life (that is, to plan a life as they want and need). In this context, the right to have a project of life requires interpretation from their particular necessities as Indigenous peoples.

In the *Wayúu Community* case, (in)justice narratives stem from granting permission to projects that have negative socio-environmental consequences for the Bruno Stream without consulting the affected communities, as the defendants used a restrictive interpretation to determine the affected areas considered in the environmental impact assessment (EIA). Through a holistic perspective of the ecosystem, the community argued that more than a physical subsistence, the stream represents cultural survival, as their culture has been shaped based on their relationship with natural and spiritual resources directly dependent on the stream. Thus, surviving as a Wayúu ethnic group meant merging the cosmology of the community with the adaptation of a physical territory that provided them with water sources.[101]

The connectivity of ecosystems is another topic strongly reinforced in the grounds of the *Wayúu Community* case. When discussing the stream's analysis perimeter in the EIA, the defendants applied a hydrogeological model examining the part of the stream limited to the area of the works. The plaintiffs and the scholars who conducted studies to help inform the court's decision stated that an ecosystem as complex as a river could not be understood simply in a linear water way, since 'the complexity of the stream implies its continuity'.[102] They argued that the study carried out by the defendants was not able to demonstrate the absence of impact on the stream, since 'in a watershed there are not only purely hydrological connections, but also biological and social linkages that can go in different directions vertically and horizontally'.[103] For this reason, the plaintiffs consider that the project affects not only the area of the river where the activities are carried out and the downstream but also all the other connections involved in the upstream ecosystem.

Highlighting that the stream cannot have an owner, the plaintiffs stated that the river has a 'free course' that reverberates in broader spaces, and elements that depend on it must be protected as a whole. In contrast, the EIA presented by the defendants did not approach the interrelationship of the detour area with the general watershed,[104] precisely because its basing model is not designed to represent the interrelationships existing within the ecosystem as understood by the Indigenous communities. Ultimately, the models used to conduct the EIA of the company did not adjust to reality according to Wayúu cosmology. For example, the analysis of water focuses on the supply for community consumption, ignoring regulation, stabilisation, maintenance, and cultural services that involve a more complex context of interrelationships.[105] In the *Waorani Community* case, the plaintiffs also indicated that the EIA studies did not highlight rights violations because they were not properly designed to do so.

As for the communities that should be consulted in the EIA process, two opposing epistemologies emerge – that of the Indigenous community (plaintiffs) and that of the government/developer (defendants) – in defining the criteria, parameters, and methodology to identify the potentially affected groups. In the *Wayúu Community* case, the plaintiffs noted that the affected communities could not be linearly defined as 'the ones by the riverside' (as stated by the defendant), since the Wayúu are semi-nomadic, with the grazing system and transfers that seasonally change – which renders more complex the causal chain of the affected community by dissociating physical proximity as a determining element for its characterisation. The study produced by the developer, Cerrejón, did not consider the totality of the links that Indigenous people have with the bodies of water.

Another aspect is the challenge of overcoming the economic language of the law, that is, the reduction of all environmental interventions and the compensation of damages in financial terms – which denotes a decolonial aspect. Monetary compensation for the plaintiffs for the loss of cultural supply of the ecosystem or the intergenerational relationships with the territory was not feasible for the Indigenous communities. There is a lack of a 'common denominator' between the conventional 'rational' legal institutes of redress and mechanisms of 'compensation' that meet the more-than-economic needs of Indigenous communities and make sense according to their cosmologies. Since the socio-ecological interactions of these populations with the territory and their livelihoods cannot be monetised, economic compensation for environmental damages does not restore the vital processes of communities or reduce their vulnerability, in contrast to large companies in the extractive and industrial sectors.

This argument is also introduced in the *Waorani Community* case, which claimed more than economic reparations for environmental and social damages. The plaintiffs argued that ancestral practices of the Indigenous communities associated with the ecosystems and territories were threatened or eliminated due to the gas flaring activities.

### *Evidence and the causal link*

In both cases, the plaintiffs had the challenge of producing enough evidence to trace the causal link between the alleged violations and the extractive activities. The use of current categories and the openness to new elements of the means of proof are essential to observe the challenges of transforming the orality, experience, and particularities of Indigenous communities into valid and accepted legal arguments and evidence that demonstrate the violation of the legal order by extractive activities and companies.

Making room for decolonial narratives and Indigenous cosmologies within hegemonic adjudicatory bodies means allowing more than the means of proof accepted as part of Western legal tradition and admitting that conflicting cosmologies can have the same level of legitimacy. The knowledge produced by a given human community comprises the interaction between their culture and the territory they inhabit over time. In this sense, culture brings together a system of codes for living in the world and is at the basis of Indigenous cosmologies (for example, in the case of some Indigenous peoples, it means living in harmonic interaction with ecosystems). The roots of dismissal of Indigenous ways of knowing in multiple spheres can be traced back to colonialism that categorised Indigenous knowledge systems as inferior to the Western epistemology.[106]

Thus, when courts handle Indigenous claims, there is a formal encounter between the Western legal systems' categories of what is accepted as evidence of a fact and what is offered as proof by Indigenous authors according to their cosmologies. For example, courts typically require peer-reviewed studies conducted with a precise methodology that is considered valid by modern scientific standards, while some Indigenous communities may rely on the empirical perception of their elders, rooted in ancestral knowledge, as evidence to support their claims.[107]

Although proving facts might seem an objective exercise, it is deeply tied to the subjects' underlying reasoning and worldview. In these cases, the court's decision has the power *de jure* over the knowledge bases on which Indigenous peoples build their narratives about the facts, legitimising it or not. Given the coloniality of power contained in this decision-making process, giving credibility to plural perceptions of facts and opening the possibility of building valid legal narratives through non-Western epistemologies may represent a decolonial path for decisions. It does not mean invalidating or not using scientific knowledge, but simply not assuming in advance that it is the only valid means of proof.

The *Wayúu Community* case opens a central debate on the role of the means of proof to prevent the cultural ethnocentrism that defines modern Western science as the only valid knowledge.[108] In the *Waorani Community* case, the plaintiffs made the case for a broader consideration of the means of proof, stating that courts must make room for traditional knowledge as evidence.[109] They argue that in the absence of scientific studies, the communities' testimonies based on ancestral knowledge are the only valid proof of changes in the cycles of nature. According to them, the Ecuadorian Constitution considers ancestral knowledge to be equivalent to scientific knowledge, and judges should enforce this.[110] The case highlights important considerations about access to justice for Indigenous peoples, as plaintiffs highlighted the power imbalance between Indigenous peoples and the defendants (a corporation and the state), which is amplified by the difficulty of enforcing their rights through the courts (not the battlefield they are used to) and the use of Spanish as the main language (not their native language).

### *The interpretations of the courts*

In the *Waorani Community* case, the court rejected the plaintiffs' claim. The court asserted that the evidence presented was insufficient and inadequate, failing to demonstrate the allegations and lacking public faith (such as non-official documents or lacking signatures). Furthermore, the court held that the plaintiffs did not prove a violation of the rights of nature or any derived constitutional rights.[111] In particular, the court considered that claims about PetroOriental's liability regarding climate change were generic and the cessation of the activities would not stop the problems raised, since it is a global problem.[112] As such, the court decided that the company could not be held liable, not even proportionally, for damages. In this way, the court refused to redress the unjust causes and impacts of climate change.

In the *Wayúu Community* case, the court requested a community-focused study to uncover the Indigenous communities' relationship with the ecosystem. Nevertheless, it did not recognise the violations of essential rights – such as FPIC – leaving a substantive gap by not stating peremptorily Indigenous participation in their territory as an integral element of their distinct identity.

Nevertheless, the court recognised that natural and social systems interact with each other, creating self-regulating contexts where physical processes occur on larger spatial and temporal scales. Against this backdrop, the court suggested updating EIA processes to include other elements. Firstly, EIA should consider the contextual conditions of the territory and adopt a systemic approach to the multiple elements that integrate the environment, including the complex and multidimensional relationships between them. Secondly, EIA should encompass intertemporal intercessions. This means considering the historical interventions carried out in the territory since they have a cumulative and residual effect that may weaken the ecosystems and diminish their resilience to human activity.

A decolonial element in the *Wayúu Community* case was the court's openness to non-Western (i.e. Indigenous ancestral) knowledge to understand what the Bruno Stream represents according to the subjects living in the territory. The judgment expresses that if the courts regard Indigenous peoples' knowledge as less valid than modern science, they deny their culture, 'and when you deny culture, you deny life'.[113] In this context, the judges stated that the Indigenous communities' intervention in the licensing process was vital to overcoming a unidimensional vision of the project's environmental effects. Thus, conceptualising the damage – and delimiting its extent – involves more than just objective data and becomes an ontological 'choice' since different cosmovisions lead to divergent conclusions. In the precise issue at stake, how water is interpreted changes the perception of damage and its scope.

Based on the complexity of the ecosystem's elements, the court concluded that the EIA study offered by the defendants as evidence provided uncertain and limited technical and legal guarantees for the protection of the Bruno Stream. The court acknowledged the need to consider more than the flow of water in the project, recognising that the ecosystem has other interactions.[114] The design proposed by Cerrejón did not consider all the impacts of the intervention. The shift, in this case, is the broad range of services implicated by an ecosystem, which consists not only of the material water supply but also of interrelational and cultural interactions with the subjects that co-create the ecosystem's context. One may observe a shared vulnerability of the Indigenous people and the ecosystem they inhabit to climate change. The court acknowledged the expressive fragility and deterioration of the Bruno Stream due to climate change events, which can strongly impact the Wayúu community because of its high dependence on and interconnection with the ecosystem. In this way, the court advanced climate justice.

The court asserted that studies[115] carried out in the lawsuit revealed that the Wayúu community has an intertemporal interpretation of their territory as the element which enables the continuity of their clan group and is linked to the community's spirituality. Since the territory is not physically delimited and the water is the source of life, these elements become a substrate for the continuity of ancestral knowledge.[116] This was a groundbreaking ruling in Latin America since, for the first time, ecosystem services–based approaches were used to protect the environmental rights of Indigenous communities.

However, tensions with other legal institutes and rights also appeared. In a dissenting vote of the *Wayúu Community* case, one judge emphasised that the decision of the Chamber disproportionately restricted the legitimately acquired contractual rights of the defendant.[117] The judge acknowledged that uncertainties about negative effects on the environment should be safeguarded by the rights of the Indigenous communities and the application of the precautionary principle. However, the dissenting vote argued the restriction of mining activities constituted a disproportionate measure against the company, violating the principle of legal certainty.

## Conclusion

The use of Indigenous peoples' climate litigation has proven to be a valuable tool for understanding these groups' specific needs, interests, and vulnerabilities. This chapter has examined the interactions between the colonial nature of legal systems and the demands made by Indigenous peoples in climate cases from Ecuador and Colombia. The imposition of European laws and legal institutions upon Indigenous territories and structures during the colonial period has had a lasting impact on

Latin American legal systems despite the subsequent independence processes in the region.

However, constitutional reforms in Latin American countries have acknowledged social struggles, introduced new environmental rights, and strengthened the role of judicial review of politics. As a result, marginalised groups have turned to the courts to advance and reinterpret their rights, despite the colonial legacy of the legal system. Indigenous peoples, in particular, have used climate litigation as a means of institutional resistance within the socio-political context, offering insights into their specific needs and vulnerabilities.

In the cases discussed, Indigenous peoples' claims have often sought to interpret fundamental rights according to their worldviews, providing an opportunity to decolonise the legal framework. However, the colonial influence in Latin American legal systems may affect legal interpretations and the performance of institutions, creating conflicts with the non-Western perspectives presented in Indigenous peoples' climate litigation. The cases analysed have shown that there is still a gap between the original goals of the plaintiffs based on their worldviews and the ability of the judiciary to respond to their claims.

Both cases challenge extractive practices that were licensed and authorised by the state, questioning (and, in the case of Colombia, achieving some legal changes) the rationale behind the EIA and arguing that despite the legality of the extractivist activities, they were violating their fundamental rights and the rights of the ecosystems. In this sense, these provisions usually rely on EIA. Still, the Indigenous communities note that the categories of the EIA do not catch holistic interactions within the ecosystem since their elements and criteria are not designed to do so.

In addition to rethinking the categories of EIA, the cases have also invited reinterpretations of human rights and the rights of nature. They both articulate the human rights of Indigenous communities and the interrelated rights of living beings and ecosystems. In the *Wayúu Community* case, the plaintiffs reason their rights from the notion of ecosystems, that is, conceiving human beings as ecological subjects constantly interacting and depending on a context they shape and through which they are also shaped. Indigenous plaintiffs finally argue that due to their culturally differentiated livelihoods and dependence on territories and ecosystems, their human rights must be interpreted based on these particularities. For example, in the *Waorani Community* case, plaintiffs refer to the right to access traditional food and medicine.

Finally, the cases have highlighted that the body of evidence must be reconsidered in terms of the categories pre-established by the law in force to make room for decolonial narratives within hegemonic adjudicatory bodies. This means allowing more than the established means of proof and admitting that scientific and ancestral knowledge can have the same level of legitimacy of scientific knowledge to influence the outcome of a judicial conflict.

In the *Waorani Community* case, the plaintiffs sought recognition of the violation of the rights of nature and the community's fundamental rights, using the testimonial and ancestral knowledge of their elders as evidence of the damage. The

Ecuadorian Constitution equates scientific knowledge with ancestral knowledge. The court, however, understood that the complainants did not demonstrate the fact or the damage since the testimonial based on ancestral knowledge was considered to be the community's perception and required an environmental study conducted according to modern scientific methods to demonstrate the damage.

On the other hand, in the *Wayúu Community* case, the court was open to ancestral knowledge, legitimising what the Bruno Stream represents to the subjects living in the territory. In this context, the judges stated that the Indigenous communities' intervention in the licensing process was vital to overcoming a unidimensional vision of the project's environmental effects. By doing so, the court faced a decolonial argument that underscored a historical process of marginalisation of Indigenous peoples and degradation of essential ecosystems and analysed categories, norms, and cultural logic linked to Indigenous legal systems.

In conclusion, the cases shed light on the contrast between the plaintiffs' demands and the judiciary's reasoning. Although there are institutional and epistemological challenges, courts in Latin America are an institutionalised route for vulnerable groups to protect their rights amidst the climate crisis. The *Waorani Community* case reveals that courts still face challenges in processing culturally differentiated claims. The *Wayúu Community* case demonstrates how courts can progressively promote the decolonisation of legal systems. The courts provide a forum to discuss and reinterpret rights from the perspectives of Indigenous peoples, who have historically been excluded from standard-setting processes within the democratic rule of law. In this way, courts present an opportunity to reduce their vulnerability, which is not an inherent but, rather, an institutionally and systemically created or enhanced condition.

Future research endeavours should continue to observe the evolution of climate cases proposed by Indigenous plaintiffs to gain a comprehensive understanding of the correlation between their demands and the judicial rationale. This will facilitate an expanded discourse based on an analysis that is currently limited in scope. Such an undertaking would be instrumental in determining whether the findings pertaining to colonial or decolonial judgments are incidental or indicative of a systematic trend.

## Notes

1 As a matter of conceptualisation, the authors use the word 'colonialism' to denote a political and economic relation in which the sovereignty of a nation or a people rests on the power of another nation, which makes such a nation an empire. The 'colonisation' is, therefore, the process of a foreign country taking political control of a dependent territory and its population. The term 'coloniality,' instead, refers to long-standing patterns of power that emerged as a result of colonialism but go beyond the limits of colonial administration, defining culture, labour, intersubjective relations, and knowledge production well beyond the strict limits of colonial administrations. Thus, *coloniality* are patterns of thought that are still involved in the structures of current societies and have been used to legitimise the exploitation of those considered as others. For further elaboration, see Walter Mignolo and Catherine Walsh, *On Decoloniality: Concepts,*

*Analytics, Praxis* (1st edn, Duke University Press 2018), and Nelson Maldonado-Torres, 'On the Coloniality of Being: Contributions to the Development of a Concept' (2007) 21(23) *Cultural Studies* <https://doi.org/10.1080/09502380601162548> accessed 20 April 2024.

2 This chapter assumes that the remnants of a colonial rationale, characterised by the imposition of external culture and order, continues to persist in Latin America, albeit through different channels. However, the colonial period referred to in the chapter spans from the arrival of Europeans, mainly Spanish and Portuguese, in the early 1500s to the onset of the formal independence processes of Latin American countries, which began around the 1800s. For an Indian perspective on the influence of coloniality in Indian climate litigation, see Garg and Hinduja, Chapter 2.

3 Cinnamon Piñon Carlarne, 'Climate Change, Human Rights, and the Rule of Law' (2021) 25(1) *Ohio State Legal Studies Research Paper No 591, 25 UCLA J Int'l L Foreign Aff* 11 <http://dx.doi.org/10.2139/ssrn.3761842> accessed 20 October 2023.

4 *Sawhoyamaxa Indigenous Community v Paraguay* (2006) Serie C 146, Interamerican Court of Human Rights; *Indigenous Communities of the Lhaka Honhat (Our Land) Association v. Argentina* (2020) Serie C 400, Interamerican Court of Human Rights; *Mayagna (Sumo) Awas Tingni Community v Nicaragua* (2001) Serie C 79, Interamerican Court of Human Rights; *Kichwa Indigenous People of Sarayaku v Ecuador* (2012) Serie C 245, Interamerican Court of Human Rights; *Kuna Indigenous People of Madungandí and the Emberá Indigenous People of Bayano and their members v Panama* (2014) Serie C 284, Interamerican Court of Human Rights; *Punta Piedra Garifuna Community and its members v Honduras* (2015) Serie C 304, Interamerican Court of Human Rights. For further information on the litigation of Indigenous peoples, see Fernanda de Salles Cavedon-Capdeville, 'Da Dimensão Ambiental à Ecologização dos Direitos Humanos: Aportes Jurisprudenciais' in José Rubens Morato Leite (ed), *A Ecologização do Direito Ambiental Vigente: rupturas necessárias* (1st edn, Lumen Juris 2020).

5 The adjective 'colonial' refers to institutions that were imported from the European society to Latin American territories during the colonial period.

6 The positivist represents the current and official legal order in force, regardless of ideals of justice, but the legitimacy for the imposition of violence. The 'positivist' then refers to what rights are (liberal tradition) and how they operate, what the categories of responsibility are, how legal concepts (such as harm, guilt, and victimhood) are signified, and how conflicts are resolved. In short, it is the idea of how the current legal system is organised and what categories it uses.

7 Colin Samson, *The Colonialism of Human Rights* (1st edn, Polity 2020); Catherine Lu, *Justice and Reconciliation in World Politics* (1st edn, Cambridge University Press 2017); Colin Samson and Carlos Gigoux, *Indigenous Peoples and Colonialism: Global Perspectives* (1st edn, Polity 2016); José Manuel Barreto (ed), *Human Rights from a Third World Perspective: Critique, History, and International Law* (1st edn, Cambridge Scholars Publishing 2013); Malcolm Ferdinand, *Decolonial Ecology: Thinking from the Caribbean World* (1st edn, Polity 2022).

8 Walter Mignolo, *Desobediencia Epistémica: Retórica de la Modernidad, Lógica de la Colonialidad y Gramática de la Descolonialidad* (1st edn, Ediciones del Signo 2010); Mohsen al Attar and Quintero Godínez, 'TWAIL Pedagogy: Un-Learning Colonial Ways of Teaching International Law' (*Opinio Juris*, 23 March 2023) <http://opiniojuris.org/2023/03/23/twail-pedagogy-un-learning-colonial-ways-of-teaching-international-law/> accessed 20 October 2023.

9 Aníbal Quijano asserts that all experiences, stories, resources, and cultural products have been articulated into a single global cultural order around European or Western hegemony. As part of the new pattern of global power, Europe concentrated under its hegemony the control of all forms of control over subjectivity, culture, and especially,

knowledge (production of knowledge). See Aníbal Quijano, 'Colonialidad del poder, eurocentrismo y América Latina' in Edgardo Lander (org), *La colonialidad del saber: eurocentrismo y ciencias sociales. Perspectivas Latinoamericanas* (1st edn, CLACSO 2020).

10 Samson (n 7). For insights on the connections between health crises and the climate crisis in Latin America, see Uehara, Chapter 3.

11 IPCC, 'Summary for Policymakers in Climate Change 2022 – Impacts, Adaptation and Vulnerability: Working Group II Contribution to the Sixth Assessment Report of the Intergovernmental Panel on Climate Change' in HO Pörtner et al. (eds), (2022) <https://www.ipcc.ch/report/ar6/wg2/downloads/report/IPCC_AR6_WGII_FullReport.pdf> accessed 11 November 2024.

12 OECD, 'Biodiversity Conservation and Sustainable Use in Latin America: Evidence from Environmental Performance Reviews' (*OECD Environmental Performance Reviews*, 2018) <https://doi.org/10.1787/9789264309630-en> accessed 19 September 2024.

13 OECD, 'Environment at a Glance in Latin America and the Caribbean: Spotlight on Climate Change' (*OECD*, 2023) <https://doi.org/10.1787/2431bd6c-en> accessed 19 September 2024.

14 IPCC, 'Summary for Policymakers in Climate Change 2023: Synthesis Report, Contribution of Working Groups I, II and III to the Sixth Assessment Report of the Intergovernmental Panel on Climate Change' in Core Writing Team, H Lee and J Romero (eds), (2023) <https://www.ipcc.ch/report/ar6/syr/downloads/report/IPCC_AR6_SYR_FullVolume.pdf> accessed 21 November 2024.

15 Yeter Ada Seko and Emre Basaran, 'Indigenous Peoples' Ways of Life Threatened by Climate Change' (2023) <https://www.aa.com.tr/en/environment/indigenous-peoples-ways-of-life-threatened-by-climate-change/2946035> accessed 23 February 2024. See also Murcott, Tigre and Ann Samuel, Introduction.

16 Sam Bookman, 'Indigenous Climate Litigation in Anglophone Settler-Colonial States' (2022)<https://verfassungsblog.de/indigenous-climate-litigation-in-anglophone-settler-colonial-states/> accessed 23 February 2024.

17 United Nations Development Programme, 'Climate, Peace and Security for Latin America and the Caribbean' (*UNDP*, 2021) <https://www.undp.org/sites/g/files/zskgke326/files/2023-08/guidance_note_climate_peace_security_in_lac.pdf> accessed 23 February 2024.

18 Australia State of the Environment, 'Indigenous Involvement' (2021) <https://soe.dcceew.gov.au/climate/management/national-and-international-frameworks#-cli-21-figure-21-indigenous-peoples-and-the-environment> accessed 23 February 2024.

19 MJ Altman, 'Meet 3 Women in Brazil Who are Protecting the Amazon Rain forest – and Indigenous Rights' (2023) <https://unfoundation.org/blog/post/meet-3-women-in-brazil-who-are-protecting-the-amazon-rainforest-and-indigenous-rights/> accessed 23 February 2024.

20 Scientific and technological innovations, as well as religious narratives, might have promoted anthropocentric approaches that set apart humans from their 'feelings of belonging to nature and fostered an indifference to the well-being of nonhuman organisms'. Bron Taylor, 'The Greening of Religion Hypothesis (Part One): From Lynn White, Jr and Claims that Religions can Promote Environmentally Destructive Attitudes and Behaviors to Assertions They are Becoming Environmentally Friendly' (2016) 10(3) *Journal for the Study of Religion Nature and Culture* <https://doi.org/10.1558/jsrnc.v10i3.29010> accessed 19 September 2024. These cultural transformations changed the Western view of humanity as a part of nature to viewing people as exploiters of it. See Maria Antonia Tigre, 'Exploring the Bedrock for Earth Jurisprudence' (2022) 22(2) *Rutgers J L & Religion* 223 <https://scholarship.law.columbia.edu/sabin_climate_change/188> accessed 22 February 2024.

21 Samson (n 7).
22 Samson (n 7).
23 The authors recognise that part of the literature criticises the use of the word 'cosmology' to describe complex categories of Indigenous philosophies, ontologies, and epistemologies. They also acknowledge that this word is not commonly used to describe similar categories in non-Indigenous cultures and Western society. Despite these criticisms, the authors chose to use the term 'cosmology' throughout the chapter because it is a well-known term and represents a worldview different from the Western one. For further elaboration on the issue, see Silvia Bagni, 'Diritti della natura nei nuovi costituzionalismi del Global South: riflessi sulla teoria dei formanti' (2023) 58 *DPCE Online* <http://dx.doi.org/10.57660/dpceonline.2023.1882> accessed 27 February 2024.
24 Milka Sormunen, 'Rethinking Effective Remedies to the Climate Crisis: A Vulnerability Theory Approach' (2023) 24 *Human Rights Review* <https://doi.org/10.1007/s12142-023-00686-4> accessed 20 October 2023.
25 Anna Grear, 'Deconstructing Anthropos: A Critical Legal Reflection on Anthropocentric Law and Anthropocene Humanity' (2015) 26 *Law Critique* <https://doi.org/10.1007/s10978-015-9161-0> accessed 20 October 2023.
26 Martha Fineman, 'Injury in the Unresponsive State: Writing the Vulnerable Subject into Neo-Liberal Legal Culture' in A Bloom, DM Engel and M McCann (eds), *Injury and Injustice: The Cultural Politics of Harm and Redress* (1st edn, Cambridge University Press 2018). See also Murcott, Tigre and Ann Samuel, Introduction.
27 Gretchen Helmke and Julio Ríos-Figueroa, 'Introduction' in Gretchen Helmke and Julio Ríos-Figueroa (eds), *Courts in Latin America* (1st edn, Cambridge University Press 2013); Rachel Sieder, Line Schjolden and Alan Angell, 'La Judicialización de la Política en América Latina' in Rachel Sieder, Line Scholden and Alan Angell (eds), *La Judicialización de la Política en América Latina* (1st edn, Editorial Universidad Externado de Colombia 2008); Carlarne (n 3); Javier Couso, 'The Changing Role of Law and Courts in Latin America: From an Obstacle to Social Change to a Tool of Social Equity' in Roberto Gargarella, Pilar Domingo and Theunis Roux (eds), *Courts and Social Transformation in New Democracies* (1st edn, Routledge 2016).
28 Teresa Kramarz, David Cosolo and Alejandro Rossi, 'Judicialization of Environmental Policy and the Crisis of Democratic Accountability' (2016) 34(1) *RPR* <https://doi.org/10.1111/ropr.12218> accessed 20 October.
29 Some important cases with a disruptive posture of the courts are at the national level; see *Center for Social Justice v Ministry of the Environment et al.* (2016) T-622/16, Colombian Constitutional Court (Colombia) (Atrato River Decision T-622); *Future Generations v Ministry of the Environment et al.* (2018) 11001 22 03 000 2018 00319 00, Colombian Supreme Court (Colombia) (Future Generations); *Herrera Carrion et al. v Ministry of the Environment et al.* (2021) 21201202000170, Corte Provincial de Justicia de Sucumbíos (Ecuador). See Uehara, Chapter 3, for insights on some of these cases. For the regional level, see A Request for an Advisory Opinion from the Inter-American Court of Human Rights Concerning the Interpretation of Article 1(1), 4(1) and 5(1) of the American Convention on Human Rights (OC 23/2017), issued by the Inter-American Court of Human Rights.
30 *Pushaina et al. v Carbones del Cerrejón Limited et al.* (2017) SU698/17, Colombian Constitutional Court (Colombia) (*Wayúu Community case*).
31 *Baihua Caiga et al. v PetroOriental SA* (2021) 22201202000469, Unidad Judicial de Familia, Mujer, Niñez y Adolescencia, Cantón Francisco de Orellana (Ecuador) (*Waorani Community case*).
32 This section briefly describes the colonial nature of current Latin American legal systems and the structural colonial factors of the law. For reasons of scope and length, it does not elaborate on legal institutes established during the colonial period, such as the

*mita* and the *encomienda* systems and the *terra nullius* concept, which symbolise the connection between Indigenous peoples and colonial legal structures. On the other hand, the authors acknowledge that legal institutes such as collective property; land tenure; free, prior, and informed consent; and plurinationalism have been essential for Indigenous peoples and the protection of their territories in the region.

33 Carmen Gonzalez, 'Racial Capitalism, Climate Justice, and Climate Displacement' (2021) 11(1) *Oñati Socio-Legal Series* <https://doi.org/10.35295/osls.iisl/0000-0000-0000-1137> accessed 20 October 2023. See also Murcott, Tigre and Ann Samuel Introduction.

34 Juanita Sundberg, 'Placing Race in Environmental Justice Research in Latin America' (2008) 21(7) *Society & Natural Resources* 570 <https://doi.org/10.1080/08941920802111538> accessed 20 October 2023.

35 Sormunen (n 24).

36 Gonzalez (n 33).

37 Gonzalez (n 33). See also the discussion of intersectional climate justice in Murcott, Tigre and Ann Samuel, 'Introduction', pp 5–10.

38 See n 55.

39 Lara Domínguez and Colin Luoma, 'Decolonising Conservation Policy: How Colonial Land and Conservation Ideologies Persist and Perpetuate Indigenous Injustices at the Expense of the Environment' (2020) 9(3) *Land* <https://doi.org/10.3390/land9030065> accessed 20 October 2023.

40 Juan Javier Rivera Andía and Cecilie Vindal Ødegaard, 'Introduction: Indigenous Peoples, Extractivism, and Turbulences in South America' in Juan Javier Rivera Andía and Cecilie Vindal Ødegaard (eds), *Indigenous Life Projects and Extractivism: Ethnographies from South America* (Palgrave Macmillan 2019).

41 CEPAL Comissão Econômica para a América Latina e o Caribe, 'Panorama Social da América Latina' (*CEPAL*, 2020) accessed September 2024.

42 Yrigoyen Fajardo, 'El Horizonte del Constitucionalismo Pluralista: del Multiculturalismo a la Descolonización' in César Rodriguez-Garavito (ed), *El Derecho en América Latina: los Retos del Siglo XXI* (Siglo XXI 2011).

43 Ronald Horvath, 'A Definition of Colonialism' (1972) 13(1) *Current Anthropology* <https://www.jstor.org/stable/2741072> accessed 13 August 2023.

44 The colonial laws reinforced other forms of domination as well, such as land grabbing, loss of life due to the introduction of diseases, and enslavement.

45 Bernard Cohn, 'Law and the Colonial State in India' in June Starr and Jane Collier (eds), *History and Power in the Study of Law: New Directions in Legal Anthropology* (Cornell University Press 1989).

46 John Schmidhauser, 'Legal Imperialism: Its Enduring Impact on Colonial and Post-Colonial Judicial Systems' (1992) 13(3) *International Political Science Review* <https://www.jstor.org/stable/1601479> accessed 13 August 2023.

47 John Schmidhauser, 'Legal Imperialism: Its Enduring Impact on Colonial and Post-Colonial Judicial Systems' (1992) 13(3) *International Political Science Review* <https://www.jstor.org/stable/1601479> accessed 13 August 2023.

48 Walter Mignolo, *The Idea of Latin America* (1st edn, Blackwell Publishing 2005).

49 Aníbal Quijano and Michael Ennis, 'Coloniality of Power, Eurocentrism, and Latin America' (2000) 1(3) *Nepantía* <https://edisciplinas.usp.br/pluginfile.php/347342/mod_resource/content/1/Quijano%20(2000)%20Colinality%20of%20power.pdf> accessed 20 October 2023.

50 Ramón Grosfoguel, 'Del "extractivismo económico" al "extractivismo epistémico" y "extractivismo ontológico": una forma destructiva de conocer, ser y estar en el mundo' (2016) 24 *Tabula Rasa* <https://www.revistatabularasa.org/numero24/del-extractivismo-economico-al-extractivismo-epistemico-y-extractivismo-ontologico-

una-forma-destructiva-de-conocer-ser-y-estar-en-el-mundo/> accessed 30 September 2023. See also Eugenio Zaffaroni, 'El Derecho Latinoamericano en la Fase Superior del Colonialismo' (2015) 7(2) *Passagens* <https://www.redalyc.org/pdf/3373/337338776002.pdf> accessed 12 August 2023; see also note n 5.

51 Aníbal Quijano, 'Colonialidad y Modernidad/Racionalidad' (1992) 13(29) *Perú Indígena* <https://www.lavaca.org/wp-content/uploads/2016/04/quijano.pdf> accessed 13 August 2023.

52 Luciana Ballestrin, 'América Latina e o Giro Decolonial' (2013) 11 *Rev Bras Ciência Política* <https://www.scielo.br/j/rbcpol/a/DxkN3kQ3XdYYPbwwXH55jhv/abstract/?lang=pt#> accessed 20 October 2023.

53 Despite many European countries having colonised Latin America, Spain and Portugal's influence was more significant in shaping the region's legal systems, especially of South American countries.

54 Luis Tapia, *Dialéctica del Colonialismo Interno* (1st edn, Traficantes de Sueños 2022).

55 Gudynas defines 'extractivism' as a type of high-volume extraction of natural resources which are essentially intended for export as raw materials in unprocessed form, or with minimal processing. Teijlingen observes that extractivist activities since colonisation have influenced the political, economic, environmental, social, and cultural dimensions of life in Latin American biomes. In this context, Tapia states that the continuation of colonialism is reflected in the organisation of a world system in which the production carried out by the formerly colonised countries is geared towards feeding consumption, production, and capitalist accumulation in other centres, notably Europe and North America. Thus, extractive production provides the manufacture of goods and industrial machinery in the new neo-colonial metropolises, which feed off the labour generated in the countries that continue to work for other societies. As a result, the economies of these countries are articulated in a subordinate and unequal way, which means that the wealth and value produced under these structures are transferred to these new metropolises of capitalism. Furthermore, Quijano explains that the colonial matrix of power has four interrelated domains, namely, the control of economy (land appropriation, exploitation of labour, control of natural resources), control of authority (institutions), control of gender and sexuality (family, education), and control of subjectivity and knowledge (epistemology and formation of subjectivity). In this sense, Mignolo asserts that extractivist societies are also featured by the coloniality of knowledge, in which there was the affirmation of a European 'zero point' of history and the silencing or relegation of other epistemologies as inferior. To conclude, Grosfoguel points out that all the 'extractivisms' conduct a process of reification and destruction in the subjectivity of non-European civilisations. These processes transform knowledge, forms of human existence, non-human life forms, and what exists in the ecological environment into 'objects' to be instrumentalised, with the purpose of extracting and exploiting them for one's own benefit. See Eduardo Gudynas, 'Extracciones, extractivismos y extrahecciones: un marco conceptual sobre la apropiación de los recursos naturales' (2013) 18 *Obervatorio del Desarrollo* 1; Karolien van Teijlingen, 'Mining Extraction in Latin America' in B Vinson (ed), *Oxford Bibliographies in Latin American Studies* (1st edn, Oxford University Press 2022); Luis Tapia, *Dialéctica del Colonialismo Interno* (1st edn, Traficantes de Sueños 2022); Quijano and Ennis (n 49); Walter D Mignolo, 'Introduction Coloniality of Power and De-Colonial Thinking' (2007) 21(2–3) *Cultural Studies* <https://doi.org/10.1080/09502380601162498> accessed 19 September 2024; Grosfoguel (n 50). Garg and Hinduja, Chapter 2, offer Indian insights on extractivism.

56 Henry Veltmeyer, 'Extractivism and Beyond: Latin America Debates' (2022) 11 *The Extractive Industries and Society* 101132.

57 Juan Auz, 'Litigios Climáticos Basados en los Derechos Humanos en América Latina' (*Fundación Heinrich Böll*, 26 April 2021) <https://co.boell.org/es/2021/04/26/litigios-climaticos-basados-en-los-derechos-humanos-en-america-latina> accessed 20 October 2023.
58 Grosfoguel (n 50).
59 Silvia Bagni, 'Diritti della natura nei nuovi costituzionalismi del Global South: riflessi sulla teoria dei formanti' (2023) 58 *DPCE Online* <http://dx.doi.org/10.57660/dpceonline.2023.1882> accessed 27 February 2024.
60 Fernanda de Salles Cavedon-Capdeville et al., 'An Ecocentric Perspective on Climate Litigation: Lessons from Latin America' (2023) *Journal of Human Rights Practice* <https://doi.org/10.1093/jhuman/huad031> accessed 20 February 2024.
61 International Labour Organization, 'C169 – Indigenous and Tribal Peoples Convention, 1989' <https://www.ilo.org/dyn/normlex/en/f?p=NORMLEXPUB:55:0::NO::P55_TYPE,P55_LANG,P55_DOCUMENT,P55_NODE:REV,en,C169,/Document> accessed 20 February 2024.
62 César Rodríguez Garavito and Carlos Baquero Díaz, 'The Right to Free, Prior, and Informed Consultation in Colombia: Advances and Setbacks' (2018) <www.ohchr.org/Documents/Issues/IPeoples/EMRIP/FPIC/GaravitoAndDiaz.pdf.> accessed 20 February 2024.
63 The new constitutions of Bolivia (2009) and Ecuador (2008) have recognised Indigenous grievances, such as legal pluralism, territorial autonomy and collective rights, and declaring the state to be intercultural and plurinational. The latter has also recognized the rights of nature, that is, the constitutional protection of the environment/*Pachamama*. See R Lalander, 'Rights of Nature and the Indigenous Peoples in Bolivia and Ecuador: A Straitjacket for Progressive Development Politics?' (2014) 3(2) *Iberoamerican Journal of Development Studies* <http://dx.doi.org/10.2139/ssrn.2554291> accessed 19 September 2024.
64 *Decolonisation* is understood as the emancipation of colonised subjects from structures of colonial or imperial domination. However, the process of decolonisation is far more complex and involves identifying the colonial structures and relationships, and it does not suffice to include the colonised subjects but precisely shift from a culture of exclusion and denial to making room for other epistemologies and ontologies within the societal structures. Power relations are a key factor for adjusting these structures. See D Temin 'A Decolonial Wrong Turn: Walter Mignolo's Epistemic Politics' (2024) *Constellations* <https://doi.org/10.1111/1467-8675.12744> accessed 20 April 2024; University of Essex, 'What is Colonialisation?' (2024) <https://library.essex.ac.uk/edi/whatisdecolonisation> accessed 20 April 2024.
65 See Charlotte Renglet, 'The Recognition of the Special Relationship of Indigenous Peoples with Their Environment Under International Law: A Potential Advantage in Climate Litigation?' (2022) 29(4) *International Journal on Minority and Group Rights* <https://brill.com/view/journals/ijgr/29/4/article-p720_006.xml> accessed 20 February 2024; Maria Antonia Tigre, 'Climate Change and Indigenous Groups: The Rise of Indigenous Voices in Climate Litigation' (2022) 9(3) *E-Publica* 214 <https://scholarship.law.columbia.edu/sabin_climate_change/196> accessed 20 February 2024; Giada GIacomini, 'Human Rights-Based Climate Litigation and Indigenous Peoples: Comparative Perspectives and New Trends for Climate Justice in Europe' (2023) <https://iris.uniroma1.it/handle/11573/1681551> accessed 20 February 2024; Giaga Giacomini, 'Human Rights-Based Climate Litigation and Indigenous Peoples: Critical Perspectives & Potential Venues for Redress in Europe' (2022) <https://iris.uniroma1.it/handle/11573/1615488> accessed 19 September 2024.
66 Chile (1980), Honduras (1982), El Salvador (1983), Guatemala (1985), Nicaragua (1987), and Brazil (1988). The 'New Latin American Constitutionalism' has as its core

constitutional exponents the Constitution of Venezuela (1999), but mainly the Constitutions of Ecuador (2008) and Bolivia (2009). See also Uehara, Chapter 3, n 21.

67 See Javier Couso, 'The Transformation of Constitutional Discourse and the Judicialization of Politics in Latina America' in Javier Couso, Alexandra Huneeus and Rachel Sieder (eds), *Cultures of Legality* (1st edn, Cambridge University Press 2010); Kramarz, Cosolo and Rossi (n 28); Sieder, Schjolden and Angell (n 27).

68 See Couso (n 27).

69 See Bruce Wilson, 'Enforcing Rights and Exercising an Accountability Function: Costa Rica's Constitutional Chamber of the Supreme Court' in Gretchen Helmke and Julio Ríos-Figueroa (eds), *Courts in Latin America* (1st edn, Cambridge University Press 2013); Ran Hirschl, 'The Political Origins of the New Constitutionalism' (2004) 11(1) *Indiana Journal of Global Legal Studies* <https://doi.org/10.2979/gls.2004.11.1.71> accessed 20 October 2023.

70 See also, Natalia Urzola Gutiérrez, 'Gender in Climate Litigation in Latin America: Epistemic Justice Through a Feminist Lens' (2023) 16(1) *Journal of Human Rights Practice* 208 <doi.org/10.1093/jhuman/huad030> accessed 20 February 2024; Gastón Medici-Colombo and Thays Ricarte, 'The Escazú Agreement Contribution to Environmental Justice in Latin America: An Exploratory Empirical Inquiry through the Lens of Climate Litigation' (2023) 16(1) *Journal of Human Rights Practice* 160 <doi.org/10.1093/jhuman/huad029> accessed 20 February 2024; Danielle de Andrade Moreira et al., 'Rights-Based Climate Litigation in Brazil: An Assessment of Constitutional Cases Before the Brazilian Supreme Court' (2023) 16(1) *Journal of Human Rights Practice* 27 <doi.org/10.1093/jhuman/huad023> accessed 20 February 2024; Délton Winter de Carvalho and Rafaela Santos Martins da Rosa, 'Climate Constitutionalism as a Foundation for Climate Litigation in Latin America' (2023) 16(1) *Journal of Human Rights Practice* 71 <doi.org/10.1093/jhuman/huad055> accessed 18 September 2024.

71 Auz (n 57); Maria Antonia Tigre, Natalia Urzola and Alexandra Goodman, 'Climate Litigation in Latin America: Is the Region Quietly Leading a Revolution?' (2023) 14(1) *Journal of Human Rights and the Environment* 67 <https://doi.org/10.4337/jhre.2023.01.04> accessed 30 September 2023; de Salles Cavedon-Capdeville et al. (n 60).

72 Joana Setzer and Lisa Benjamin, 'Climate Litigation in the Global South: Constraints and Innovations' (2019) *Transnational Environmental Law* <https://ssrn.com/abstract=3456330> accessed 20 October 2023; Jacqueline Peel and Jolene Lin, 'Transnational Climate Litigation: The Contribution of the Global South' (2019) 113 *American Journal of International Law* 679; César Rodríguez-Garavito, 'Human Rights: The Global South's Route to Climate Litigation' (2020) 114 *AJIL Unbound* 40; Jacqueline Peel and Hari Osofsky, 'Climate Change Litigation' (2020) 16 *Annual Review of Law and Social Science* 21 <https://www.annualreviews.org/doi/abs/10.1146/annurev-lawsocsci-022420-122936> accessed 20 October 2023. New literature has been exploring the trends and features of Global South climate litigation, notably Latin America and Africa. See Melanie Jean Murcott and Maria Antonia Tigre, 'Developments, Opportunities, and Complexities in Global South Climate Litigation: Introduction to the Special Collection' 16(1) *Journal of Human Rights Practice* 1 <https://doi.org/10.1093/jhuman/huad070> accessed 20 February 2024.

73 Almost all the constitutions of Latin American countries enshrine the right to a healthy environment, its derivations, or other substantive/procedural environmental rights provisions, except for Guatemala and Suriname.

74 Constitution of Ecuador (2008).

75 Carmen Gonzalez, 'Environmental Justice, Human Rights, and the Global South' (2015) 13(1) *Santa Clara J Int'LL* 151 <https://digitalcommons.law.scu.edu/scujil/vol13/iss1/8/> accessed 10 October 2023; James May and Erin Daly, 'Global Climate

Constitutionalism and Justice in the Courts' (2018) *Global Climate Constitutionalism* <https://papers.ssrn.com/sol3/papers.cfm?abstract_id=3251620> accessed 20 September 2023.

76 César Rodríguez-Garavito, *Litigating the Climate Emergency: How Human Rights, Courts, and Legal Mobilisation Can Bolster Climate Action* (1st edn, Cambridge University Press 2023); Juan Auz, 'Human Rights-Based Climate Litigation: A Latin American Cartography' (2022) 13(1) *Journal of Human Rights and the Environment* 114 <http://dx.doi.org/10.4337/jhre.2022.01.05> accessed 20 September 2023.

77 Juan Auz, 'The Political Ecology of Climate Remedies in Latin America and the Caribbean: Comparing Compliance between National and Inter-American Litigation' (2024) 16(1) *Journal of Human Rights Practice* 182 <https://doi.org/10.1093/jhuman/huad057> accessed 20 February 2024; Maria Antonia Tigre and Natalia Urzola, 'The 2017 Inter-American Court's Advisory Opinion: Changing the Paradigm for International Environmental Law in the Anthropocene' (2022) 12(1) *Journal of Human Rights and the Environment* 25 <https://doi.org/10.4337/jhre.2021.01.02> accessed 20 February 2024.

78 The reinterpretation of rights to (common) property, life, physical integrity, and public participation that, in Indigenous claims, are reformulated through an ecological perspective coming from Indigenous people's livelihoods. Specifically, they defend an inextricable connection between human rights and natural ecosystems – while the latter is a *conditio sine qua non* for realising rights. Thus, Indigenous peoples' claims in Latin America articulate traditional human rights with the specificities of the interrelatedness among culture, livelihoods, and the territory.

79 *Sawhoyamaxa Indigenous Community v Paraguay* [2006]; *Lagos del Campo v Peru* [1989]; *Lhaka Honhat Association v Argentin*a [2020]. About the latter lawsuit, see Maria Antonia Tigre, 'Indigenous Communities of the Lhaka Honhat (Our Land) Association v Argentina' (2021) 115(4) *American Journal of International Law* 706 <https://doi.org/10.1017/ajil.2021.47> accessed 20 February 2024.

80 Rachel Sieder, 'Pueblos Indígenas y Derecho en América Latina' in César Rodríguez-Garavito (ed), *El Derecho en América Latina: los Retos del Siglo XXI* (Siglo XXI 2011).

81 Fernanda de Salles Cavedon-Capdeville, 'Da Dimensão Ambiental à Ecologização dos Direitos Humanos: Aportes Jurisprudenciais' in José Rubens Morato Leite (ed), *A Ecologizaçao do Direito Ambiental Vigente: rupturas necessárias* (Lumen Juris 2020).

82 Pierre-Marie Dupuy and Jorge Viñuales, *International Environmental Law* (2nd edn, Cambridge University Press 2018).

83 See, for example, the case of the *Kichwa Indigenous People of Sarayaku v Ecuador* (2012) Serie C 245, Interamerican Court of Human Rights, where the Inter-American Court of Human Rights ruled against Ecuador for violating the rights of the Sarayaku by allowing the exploration and exploitation of oil in their ancestral lands. See also Mario Melo, 'Voices from the Jungle on the Witness Stand of the Inter-American Court of Human Rights' (2024) *SUR – International Journal on Human Rights* 283 <https://ssrn.com/abstract=2553347> accessed 19 September 2024, who makes the point that courts provide a 'forum where victims can make the moral weight of their words heard'.

84 Lynda Collins, *The Ecological Constitution: Reframing Environmental Law* (1st edn, Routledge 2022).

85 For example, the idea of collective property can be useful in rethinking the categories of the legal system, since the Western liberal concept of private property was imposed by force during colonial domination and led to a loss of the link between human subjects and the sustainable common use of the ecosystems of the territory – in a structure of colonial inhabitation. *Colonial inhabitation* refers to a singular conception regarding the existence of certain human beings on Earth (the colonists), of their relationships with

other humans (the non-colonists), and as well as of their ways of relating to nature and to the non-humans. The colonial inhabitation is (1) geographically subordinate to and ontologically dependent upon European inhabitation, (2) based on the exploitation of the land and nature for commercial purposes, and (3) grounded on the refusal of inhabiting the Earth with an other who is different from a 'self' in their appearance, their social affiliations, or their beliefs. Acts such as land grabbing and land clearing are at the very foundation of the colonial way of inhabiting the Earth, and for this reason, recognising Indigenous peoples' collective perspectives on the use and steward of a territory is central to decolonisation and tackling climate change. For further elaboration, see Malcolm Ferdinand, *Decolonial Ecology: Thinking from the Caribbean World* (1st edn, Polity 2022). According to this logic, it was precisely the possibility of extracting products for the enrichment of European colonisers that rendered Latin American territories inhabited.

86 See María Daniela de la Rosa Calderón, 'Rights-Based Climate Litigation in Colombia: An Assessment of Claims, Remedies, and Implementation' (2024) 16(1) *Journal of Human Rights Practice* 273 <https://doi.org/10.1093/jhuman/huad067> accessed 20 February 2024.

87 United Nations Environment Programme, 'Environmental Rule of Law: Tracking Progress and Charting Future Directions' (*UNEP*, 2023) <https://doi.org/10.59117/20.500.11822/43943> accessed 20 February 2024.

88 *Wayúu Community case* (n 30).

89 Hilary Rosenthal, 'People of Resilience Colombia's Wayúu Indigenous Community Confronts a Malnutrition Crisis Amid Covid-19' (*Human Rights Watch*) <https://www.hrw.org/video-photos/interactive/2020/08/13/people-resilience-colombias-wayuu-indigenous-community> accessed 28 February 2024.

90 Jacobo Ramirez, 'Wayúu Women Leading the Charge: Rethinking Green Energy Investments through a Decolonial Feminist Lens' (*Centre for Business and Development Studies*, 3 October 2023) <https://cbds.cbs.dk/wayuu-women-leading-the-charge-rethinking-green-energy-investments-through-a-decolonial-feminist-lens/> accessed 27 February 2024

91 *Waorani Community case* (n 31).

92 Amazon Frontlines, 'La nación Waorani' (*Amazon Frontiers*) <https://amazonfrontlines.org/es/partners/waorani-es/> accessed 28 February 2024.

93 Ramirez (n 90).

94 Unidad Judicial de Familia, Mujer, Niñez y Adolescencia, Cantón Francisco, primera instancia 22201202000469, [2021].

95 United Nations Environment Programme, 'Global Climate Litigation Report: 2023 Status Review' (*UN Environment Programme*, 2023) <https://wedocs.unep.org/bitstream/handle/20.500.11822/43008/global_climate_litigation_report_2023.pdf?sequence=3> accessed 19 September 2024.

96 Cavedon-Capdeville et al. (n 60).

97 For further information on the affection of climate change over Indigenous communities in Latin America and the Caribbean, please see Jakob Kronik and Dorte Verner, 'Indigenous Peoples and Climate Change in Latin America and the Caribbean' (2010) <https://documents1.worldbank.org/curated/en/654311468010837927/pdf/555400PUB0Indi1EPI1958810601PUBLIC1.pdf> accessed 17 May 2024.

98 *Wayúu Community case* (n 30) 48.

99 The term in Spanish used in the lawsuit is 'un ser viviente'; *Wayúu Community* case (n 30) 27.

100 *Waorani Community* case (n 31) 33.

101 *Wayúu Community* case (n 30) 31, [2].

102 *Wayúu Community* case (n 30) 69.

103 *Wayúu Community* case (n 30) 70.
104 *Wayúu Community* case (n 30) 81.
105 *Wayúu Community* case (n 30) 98.
106 Bagele Chilisa and David Denborough, 'Decolonising Research: An Interview with Bagele Chilisa' (2019) *International Journal of Narrative Therapy and Community Work* 12 <https://search.informit.org/doi/abs/10.3316/informit.290568258616957> accessed 19 September 2024.
107 See Sieder (n 80).
108 See *Wayúu Community* case (n 30) 88.
109 *Waorani Community* case (n 31) 28.
110 *Waorani Community* case (n 31) 29.
111 *Waorani Community* case (n 31) 30.
112 *Waorani Community* case (n 31) 26.
113 *Wayúu Community* case (n 30) 79, [1].
114 *Wayúu Community* case (n 30) 88, [2].
115 These studies were requested by the judges and presented as evidence in the case. Therefore, they were mentioned in the ruling but are not available online for consultation.
116 *Wayúu Community* case (n 30) 48.
117 *Waorani Community* case (n 31) 118, [3].

## Bibliography

### *Books*

Barreto JM (ed), *Human Rights from a Third World Perspective: Critique, History, and International Law* (1st edn, Cambridge Scholars Publishing 2013)

Cavedon-Capdeville FS, 'Da Dimensão Ambiental à Ecologização dos Direitos Humanos: Aportes Jurisprudenciais' in JRM Leite (ed), *A Ecologizaçao do Direito Ambiental Vigente: rupturas necessárias* (Lumen Juris 2020)

Cohn B, 'Law and the Colonial State in India' in J Starr and J Collier (eds), *History and Power in the Study of Law: New Directions in Legal Anthropology* (Cornell University Press 1989)

Collins L, *The Ecological Constitution: Reframing Environmental Law* (1st edn, Routledge 2021)

Couso J, 'The Transformation of Constitutional Discourse and the Judicialization of Politics in Latina America' in J Couso, A Huneeus and R Sieder, *Cultures of Legality* (1st edn, Cambridge University Press 2010)

Couso J, 'The Changing Role of Law and Courts in Latin America: From an Obstacle to Social Change to a Tool of Social Equity' in R Gargarella, P Domingo and T Roux (eds), *Courts and Social Transformation in New Democracies* (1st edn, Routledge 2016)

Dupuy PM and Viñuales J, *International Environmental Law* (2nd edn, Cambridge University Press 2018)

Fajardo Y, 'El Horizonte del Constitucionalismo Pluralista: del Multiculturalismo a la Descolonización' in C Rodriguez-Garavito (ed), *El Derecho en América Latina: los Retos del Siglo XXI* (Siglo XXI 2011)

Ferdinand M, *Decolonial Ecology: Thinking from the Caribbean World* (1st edn, Polity 2022)

Fineman M, 'Injury in the Unresponsive State: Writing the Vulnerable Subject into Neo-Liberal Legal Culture' in A Bloom, DM Engel and M McCann (eds), *Injury and Injustice: The Cultural Politics of Harm and Redress* (1st edn, Cambridge University Press 2018)

Helmke G and Ríos-Figueroa J, 'Introduction' in Gretchen Helmke and Julio Ríos-Figueroa (eds), *Courts in Latin America* (1st edn, Cambridge University Press 2013)
Lu C, *Justice and Reconciliation in World Politics* (1st edn, Cambridge University Press 2017)
Mignolo W, *The Idea of Latin America* (1st edn, Blackwell Publishing 2005)
Mignolo W, *Desobediencia Epistémica: Retórica de la Modernidad, Lógica de la Colonialidad y Gramática de la Descolonialidad* (1st edn, Ediciones del Signo 2010)
Mignolo W and Walsh C, *On Decoloniality: Concepts, Analytics, Praxis* (1st edn, Duke University Press 2018)
Quijano A, 'Colonialidad del poder, eurocentrismo y América Latina' in E Lander (org), *Cuestiones y Horizontes: De la Dependencia Histórico-Estructural a la Colonialidad/descolonialidad del* Poder (1st edn, CLACSO 2020)
Rivera Andía JR and Ødegaard CV, 'Introduction: Indigenous Peoples, Extractivism, and Turbulences in South America' in JJR Andía and CV Ødegaard (eds), *Indigenous Life Projects and Extractivism: Ethnographies from South America* (Palgrave Macmillan 2019)
Rodríguez-Garavito C, *Litigating the Climate Emergency: How Human Rights, Courts and Legal Mobilization Can Bolster Climate Action* (1st edn, Cambridge University Press 2023)
Samson C, *Gigoux C, Indigenous Peoples and Colonialism: Global Perspectives* (1st edn, Polity 2016)
Samson C, *The Colonialism of Human Rights* (1st edn, Polity 2020)
Sieder R, 'Pueblos Indígenas y Derecho en América Latina' in C Rodríguez-Garavito (ed), *El Derecho en América Latina: los Retos del Siglo XXI* (Siglo XXI 2011)
Sieder R, Schjolden L and Angell A, 'La Judicialización de la Política en América Latina' in R Sieder, L Scholden and A Angell (eds), *La Judicialización de la Política en América Latina* (1st edn, Editorial Universidad Externado de Colombia 2008)
Tapia L, *Dialéctica del Colonialismo Interno* (1st edn, Traficantes de Sueños 2022)
Teijlingen KM, 'Mining Extraction in Latin America' in B Vinson (ed), *Oxford Bibliographies in Latin American Studies* (Oxford University Press 2022)
Wilson B, 'Enforcing Rights and Exercising an Accountability Function: Costa Rica's Constitutional Chamber of the Supreme Court' in G Helmke and J Ríos-Figueroa (eds), *Courts in Latin America* (1st edn, Cambridge University Press 2013)

## Cases

*Baihua Caiga et al. v PetroOriental SA* (2021) 22201202000469, Unidad Judicial de Familia, Mujer, Niñez y Adolescencia, Cantón Francisco de Orellana (Ecuador) (*Waorani Community case*)
*Future Generations v Ministry of the Environment et al.* (2018) 11001 22 03 000 2018 00319 00, Colombian Supreme Court (Colombia) (*Future Generations*)
*Herrera Carrion et al. v Ministry of the Environment et al.* (2021) 21201202000170, Corte Provincial de Justicia de Sucumbíos (Ecuador)
*Indigenous Communities of the Lhaka Honhat (Our Land) Association v Argentina* [2018] Inter-American Court of Human Rights (2020)
*Inter-American Court of Human Rights*, Advisory Opinion No. 23/2017
*Kichwa Indigenous People of Sarayaku v Ecuador* (2012) Serie C 245, Interamerican Court of Human Rights
*Kuna Indigenous People of Madungandí and the Emberá Indigenous People of Bayano and their members v Panama* (2014) Serie C 284, Interamerican Court of Human Rights
*Lagos del Campo v Peru* (2017) Serie C 340, Interamerican Court of Human Rights
*Mayagna (Sumo) Awas Tingni Community v Nicaragua* (2001) Serie C 79, Interamerican Court of Human Rights

*Punta Piedra Garifuna Community and its members v Honduras* (2015) Serie C 304, Interamerican Court of Human Rights
*Pushaina et al. v Carbones del Cerrejón Limited et al.* (2017) SU698/17, Colombian Constitutional Court (Colombia) (*Wayúu Community case*)
*Sawhoyamaxa Indigenous Community v Paraguay* (2006) Serie C 146, Interamerican Court of Human Rights
Unidad Judicial de Familia, Mujer, Niñez y Adolescencia con sede en el Cantón Francisco, primera instancia 22201202000469, [2021]
*Xakmok Kasek Indigenous Community v Paraguay* (2010) Serie C 214, Interamerican Court of Human Rights
*Yakye Axa Indigenous Community v Paraguay* (2005) Serie C 125, Interamerican Court of Human Rights

## Conventions

Indigenous and Tribal Peoples Convention no 169 (International Labour Organisation 1989)

## Journal articles

Auz J, 'Human Rights-Based Climate Litigation: A Latin American Cartography' (2022) 13(1) *Journal of Human Rights and the Environment* 114 <https://papers.ssrn.com/sol3/papers.cfm?abstract_id=4037490> accessed 30 September 2023
Auz J, 'The Political Ecology of Climate Remedies in Latin America and the Caribbean: Comparing Compliance between National and Inter-American Litigation' (2024) 16(1) *Journal of Human Rights Practice* 182 <https://doi.org/10.1093/jhuman/huad057> accessed 20 February 2024
Bagni S, 'Diritti Della Natura nei Nuovi Costituzionalismi del Global South: Riflessi Sulla Teoria dei Formanti' (2023) 58(2) *DPCE Online* <http://dx.doi.org/10.57660/dpceonline.2023.1882> accessed 27 February 2024
Ballestrin L, 'América Latina e o Giro Decolonial' (2013) 11 *Rev Bras Ciência Política* <https://doi.org/10.1590/S0103-33522013000200004> accessed 20 October 2023
Carlarne CP, 'Climate Change, Human Rights, and the Rule of Law' (2021) 25(1) *UCLA Journal International Law and Foreign Affairs* 11 <http://dx.doi.org/10.2139/ssrn.3761842> accessed 20 October 2023
Carvalho DW and da Rosa RS, 'Climate Constitutionalism as a Foundation for Climate Litigation in Latin America' (2023) 16(1) *Journal of Human Rights Practice* 71 <doi.org/10.1093/jhuman/huad055> accessed 14 September 2024
Cavedon-Capdeville FS, Berros MV, Filpi H and Villavicencio-Calzadilla P, 'An Ecocentric Perspective on Climate Litigation: Lessons from Latin America' (2024) 16(1) *Journal of Human Rights Practice* 89 <https://doi.org/10.1093/jhuman/huad031> accessed 30 October 2023
Domínguez L and Luoma C, 'Decolonising Conservation Policy: How Colonial Land and Conservation Ideologies Persist and Perpetuate Indigenous Injustices at the Expense of the Environment' (2020) 9(3) *Land* 65 <https://doi.org/10.3390/land9030065> accessed 20 October 2023
Giacomini G, 'Human Rights-Based Climate Litigation and Indigenous Peoples: Critical Perspectives & Potential Venues for Redress in Europe' (2022) <https://iris.uniroma1.it/handle/11573/1615488> accessed 14 September 2024
Giacomini G, 'Human Rights-Based Climate Litigation and Indigenous Peoples: Comparative Perspectives and New Trends for Climate Justice in Europe' in I Alogna, C Billiet, M Fermeglia and A Holzhausen (eds), *Climate Change Litigation in Europe* (Intersentia 2023) ISBN 978-1-83970-385-0

Gonzalez CG, 'Environmental Justice, Human Rights, and the Global South' (2015) 13(1) *Santa Clara Journal of International Law* 151<https://digitalcommons.law.scu.edu/scujil/vol13/iss1/8/> accessed 10 October 2023

Gonzalez CG, 'Racial Capitalism, Climate Justice, and Climate Displacement' (2021) 11(1) *Oñati Socio-legal Series* 108 <https://doi.org/10.35295/osls.iisl/0000-0000-0000-1137> accessed 20 October 2023

Grear A, 'Deconstructing Anthropos: A Critical Legal Reflection on Anthropocentric Law and Anthropocene Humanity' (2015) 26 *Law Critique* 225 <https://doi.org/10.1007/s10978-015-9161-0> accessed 20 October 2023

Grosfoguel R, 'Del "Extractivismo Económico" al:Extractivismo Epistémico" y "Extractivismo Ontológico": Una Forma Destructiva de Conocer, ser y estar en el Mundo' (2016) 24 Tabula Rasa 123 <https://doi.org/10.25058/20112742.60> accessed 30 September 2023

Hirschl R, 'The Political Origins of the New Constitutionalism' (2004) 11(1) *Indiana Journal of Global Legal Studies* 71 <https://doi.org/10.2979/gls.2004.11.1.71> accessed 20 October 2023

Horvath R, 'A Definition of Colonialism' (1972) 13(1) *Current Anthropology* 45 <https://www.jstor.org/stable/2741072> accessed 13 August 2023

Kramarz T, Cosolo D and Rossi A, 'Judicialization of Environmental Policy and the Crisis of Democratic Accountability' (2016) 34(1) *Review of Policy Research* 31 <https://doi.org/10.1111/ropr.12218> accessed 20 October

Lalander R, 'Rights of Nature and the Indigenous Peoples in Bolivia and Ecuador: A Straitjacket for Progressive Development Politics?' (2014) 3(2) *Iberoamerican Journal of Development Studies* 148, <http://dx.doi.org/10.2139/ssrn.2554291> accessed 28 February 2024

Maldonado-Torres N, 'On the Coloniality of Being: Contributions to the Development of a Concept' (2007) 21(23) *Cultural Studies* 240 <http://dx.doi.org/10.1080/09502380601162548> accessed 20 April 2024

May J and Daly E, 'Global Climate Constitutionalism and Justice in the Courts' (2018) *Global Climate Constitutionalism* <https://papers.ssrn.com/sol3/papers.cfm?abstract_id=3251620> accessed 20 September 2023

Medici-Colombo G and Ricarte T, 'The Escazú Agreement Contribution to Environmental Justice in Latin America: An Exploratory Empirical Inquiry through the Lens of Climate Litigation' (2024) 16(1) *Journal of Human Rights Practice* 160 <doi.org/10.1093/jhuman/huad029> accessed 20 February 2024

Melo M, 'Voices from the Jungle on the Witness Status of the Inter-American Court of Human Rights' (2014) 11(20) *International Journal on Human Rights* 283 <https://ssrn.com/abstract=2553347> accessed 14 September 2024

Mignolo WD, 'Introduction: Coloniality of Power and De-Colonial Thinking' (2007) 21(2–3) *Cultural Studies* 155 <10.1080/09502380601162498> accessed 27 February 2024

Moreira DA, Nina ALB, Garrido CF and Neves ME, 'Rights-Based Climate Litigation in Brazil: An Assessment of Constitutional Cases Before the Brazilian Supreme Court' (2023) 16(1) *Journal of Human Rights Practice* 47 <doi.org/10.1093/jhuman/huad023> accessed 20 February 2024

Murcott MJ and Tigre MA, 'Developments, Opportunities, and Complexities in Global South Climate Litigation: Introduction to the Special Collection' (2024) 16(1) *Journal of Human Rights Practice* 1 <https://doi.org/10.1093/jhuman/huad070> accessed 14 September 2024

Peel J and Lin J, 'Transnational Climate Litigation: The Contribution of the Global South' (2019) 113(4) *American Journal of International Law* 679 <https://doi.org/10.1017/ajil.2019.48> accessed 14 September 2024

Peel J and Osofsky H, 'Climate Change Litigation' (2020) 16(1) *Annual Review of Law and Social Science* 21 <https://doi.org/10.1146/annurev-lawsocsci-022420-122936> accessed 20 October 2023

Quijano A, 'Colonialidad y Modernidad/Racionalidad' (1992) 13(29) *Perú Indígena* 11

Quijano A and Ennis M, 'Coloniality of Power, Eurocentrism, and Latin America' (2000) 1(3) *Nepantía* 533 <https://edisciplinas.usp.br/pluginfile.php/347342/mod_resource/content/1/Quijano%20(2000)%20Colinality%20of%20power.pdf> accessed 20 October 2023

Renglet C, 'The Recognition of the Special Relationship of Indigenous Peoples with their Environment under International Law: A Potential Advantage in Climate Litigation?' (2022) 29(4) *International Journal on Minority and Group Rights* 720 <https://doi.org/10.1163/15718115-bja10068> accessed 29 February 2024

Rodríguez-Garavito C, 'Human Rights: The Global South's Route to Climate Litigation' (2020) 114 *AJIL Unbound* 40 <https://doi.org/10.1017/aju.2020.4> accessed 14 September 2024

Rosa Calderón MD, 'Rights-Based Climate Litigation in Colombia: An Assessment of Claims, Remedies, and Implementation' (2024) 16(1) *Journal of Human Rights Practice* 273 <https://doi.org/10.1093/jhuman/huad067> accessed 20 February 2024

Schmidhauser J, 'Legal Imperialism: Its Enduring Impact on Colonial and Post-Colonial Judicial Systems' (1992) 13(3) *International Political Science Review* 321 <https://www.jstor.org/stable/1601479> accessed 13 August 2023

Setzer J and Benjamin L, 'Climate Litigation in the Global South: Constraints and Innovations' (2019) *Transnational Environmental Law* <https://ssrn.com/abstract=3456330> accessed 20 October 2023

Sormunen M, 'Rethinking Effective Remedies to the Climate Crisis: a Vulnerability Theory Approach' (2023) 24 *Human Rights Review* 171 <https://doi.org/10.1007/s12142-023-00686-4> accessed 20 October 2023

Sundberg J, 'Placing Race in Environmental Justice Research in Latin America' (2008) 21(7) *Society & Natural Resources* 569 <https://doi.org/10.1080/08941920802111538> accessed 20 October 2023

Taylor B, 'The Greening of Religion Hypothesis (Part One): From Lynn White, Jr and Claims that Religions Can Promote Environmentally Destructive Attitudes and Behaviors to Assertions They are Becoming Environmentally Friendly' (2016) 10(3) *Journal for the Study of Religion, Nature and Culture* 268 <https://doi.org/10.1558/jsrnc.v10i3.29010> accessed 13 September 2024

Temin DM, 'A Decolonial Wrong Turn: Walter Mignolo's Epistemic Politics' (2024) *Constellations* 1 <https://doi.org/10.1111/1467-8675.12744> accessed 20 April 2024

Tigre MA, 'Indigenous Communities of the Lhaka Honhat (Our Land) Association v Argentina' (2021) 115(4) *American Journal of International Law* 706 <https://doi.org/10.1017/ajil.2021.47> accessed 20 February 2024

Tigre MA, 'Climate Change and Indigenous Groups: The Rise of Indigenous Voices in Climate Litigation' (2022) 9(3) *E-Publica* 214 <https://scholarship.law.columbia.edu/sabin_climate_change/196> accessed 29 February 2024

Tigre MA, 'Exploring the Bedrock for Earth Jurisprudence' (2022) 22 *Rutgers JL & Religion* 223<https://scholarship.law.columbia.edu/sabin_climate_change/188> accessed 22 February 2024

Tigre MA and Urzola N, 'The 2017 Inter-American Court's Advisory Opinion: Changing the Paradigm for International Environmental Law in the Anthropocene' (2022) 12(1) *Journal of Human Rights and the Environment* 24 <https://doi.org/10.4337/jhre.2021.01.02> accessed 20 February 2024

Tigre MA, Urzola N and Goodman A, 'Climate Litigation in Latin America: Is the Region Quietly Leading a Revolution?' (2023) 14(1) *Journal of Human Rights and the Environment* 67 <https://doi.org/10.4337/jhre.2023.01.04> accessed 30 September 2023

Urzola Gutiérrez N, 'Gender in Climate Litigation in Latin America: Epistemic Justice Through a Feminist Lens' (2024) 16(1) *Journal of Human Rights Practice* 208 <doi.org/10.1093/jhuman/huad030> accessed 20 February 2024

Veltmeyer H, 'Extractivism and Beyond: Latin America Debates' (2022) 11 *The Extractive Industries and Society* <https://doi.org/10.1016/j.exis.2022.101132> accessed 14 September 2024

Zaffaroni E, 'El Derecho Latinoamericano en la Fase Superior del Colonialismo' (2015) 7(2) *Revista Internacional de História Política e Cultura Jurídica* 182 <https://www.redalyc.org/pdf/3373/337338776002.pdf> accessed 12 August 2023

## Legislation

The Bolivia (Plurinational State of) 2009 Constitution
The Constitution of Ecuador 2008

## Reports

Comissão Econômica para a América Latina e o Caribe, 'Panorama Social da América Latina' (*CEPAL*, 2020)

Forbes A, 'Guidance Note: Climate, Peace and Security in Latin America and the Caribbean' in *Climate, Peace and Security for Latin America and the Caribbean* (United Nations Development Programme, UNDP August 2021) <https://www.undp.org/sites/g/files/zskgke326/files/2023-08/guidance_note_climate_peace_security_in_lac.pdf> accessed 23 February 2024

Inter-American Court of Human Rights, The Environment and Human Rights (State Obligations in relation to the Environment in the Context of the Protection and Guarantee of the Rights to Life and to Personal Integrity: Interpretation and Scope of Articles 4(1) and 5(1) in relation to Articles 1(1) and 2 of the American Convention on Human Rights) (Advisory Opinion OC-23/17, 2017)

IPCC, 'Summary for Policymakers in Climate Change 2022 – Impacts, Adaptation and Vulnerability: Working Group II Contribution to the Sixth Assessment Report of the Intergovernmental Panel on Climate Change' in HO Pörtner et al. (eds), (2022) <https://www.ipcc.ch/report/ar6/wg2/downloads/report/IPCC_AR6_WGII_FullReport.pdf> accessed 21 November 2024

IPCC, 'Summary for Policymakers in Climate Change 2023: Synthesis Report, Contribution of Working Groups I, II and III to the Sixth Assessment Report of the Intergovernmental Panel on Climate Change' in Core Writing Team, H Lee and J Romero (eds), (2023) <https://www.ipcc.ch/report/ar6/syr/downloads/report/IPCC_AR6_SYR_FullVolume.pdf> accessed 11 November 2024

Kronik J and Verner D, 'Indigenous Peoples and Climate Change in Latin America and the Caribbean' (*The World Bank*, 2010) <https://documents1.worldbank.org/curated/en/654311468010837927/pdf/555400PUB0Indi1EPI1958810601PUBLIC1.pdf> accessed 17 May 2024

OECD, 'Biodiversity Conservation and Sustainable Use in Latin America: Evidence from Environmental Performance Reviews' (*OECD Publishing*, 2018) <https://doi.org/10.1787/9789264309630-en> accessed 19 September 2024

OECD, 'Environment at a Glance in Latin America and the Caribbean: Spotlight on Climate Change' (*OECD*, 2023) <https://doi.org/10.1787/2431bd6c-en> accessed 19 September 2024

United Nations Environment Programme, 'Environmental Rule of Law: Tracking Progress and Charting Future Directions' (2023) <https://doi.org/10.59117/20.500.11822/43943> accessed 20 February 2024

United Nations Environment Programme, 'Global Climate Litigation Report: 2023 Status Review Nairobi' (*Sabin Center for Climate Change Law*, 2023)

## Online sources

al Attar M and Godínez Q, 'TWAIL Pedagogy: Un-Learning Colonial Ways of Teaching International Law' (*Opinio Juris*, 23 March 2023) <http://opiniojuris.org/2023/03/23/

twail-pedagogy-un-learning-colonial-ways-of-teaching-international-law/> accessed 20 October 2023

Altman MJ, 'Meet 3 women in Brazil Who are Protecting the Amazon Rainforest – and Indigenous Rights' (*United Nations Foundation*, 7 March 2023) <https://unfoundation.org/blog/post/meet-3-women-in-brazil-who-are-protecting-the-amazon-rainforest-and-indigenous-rights/> accessed 23 February 2024

Auz J, 'Litigios Climáticos Basados en los Derechos Humanos en América Latina' (*Fundación Heinrich Böll*, 26 April 2021) <https://co.boell.org/es/2021/04/26/litigios-climaticos-basados-en-los-derechos-humanos-en-america-latina> accessed 20 October 2023

Bookman S, 'Indigenous Climate Litigation in Anglophone Settler-Colonial States' (*Verfassungsblog*, 25 March 2022) <https://verfassungsblog.de/indigenous-climate-litigation-in-anglophone-settler-colonial-states/> accessed 23 February 2024

Chilisa B and Denborough D, 'Decolonising Research: An Interview with Bagele Chilisa' (2012) *The International Journal of Narrative Therapy and Community Work* 12 <http://www.dulwichcentre.com.au/> accessed 14 September 2024

Gudynas E, 'Extracciones, Extractivismos y Extrahecciones: Un Marco Conceptual Sobre la Apropiación de los Recursos Naturales' (2013) 18 *Obesrvatorio del Desarrollo* <https://ambiental.net/wp-content/uploads/2015/12/GudynasApropiacionExtractivismoExtrahecciones OdeD2013.pdf> accessed 14 September 2024

'Indigenous Involvement' (*Australia State of the Environment*, 2021) <https://soe.dcceew.gov.au/climate/management/national-and-international-frameworks#-cli-21-figure-21-indigenous-peoples-and-the-environment> accessed 23 February 2024

'La nación Waorani' (*Amazon Frontlines*) <https://amazonfrontlines.org/es/partners/waorani-es/> accessed 28 February 2024

Ramirez J 'Wayúu Women Leading the Charge: Rethinking Green Energy Investments through a Decolonial Feminist Lens' (*Centre for Business and Development Studies*, 3 October 2023) <https://cbds.cbs.dk/wayuu-women-leading-the-charge-rethinking-green-energy-investments-through-a-decolonial-feminist-lens/> accessed 27 February 2024

Rodríguez-Garavito C and Díaz CB, 'The Right to Free, Prior, and Informed Consultation in Colombia: Advances and Setbacks' (2018) <https://www.ohchr.org/sites/default/files/Documents/Issues/IPeoples/EMRIP/FPIC/GaravitoAndDiaz.pdf> accessed 14 September 2024

Rosenthal H, 'People of Resilience Colombia's Wayúu Indigenous Community Confronts a Malnutrition Crisis Amid Covid-19' (*Human Rights Watch*) <https://www.hrw.org/video-photos/interactive/2020/08/13/people-resilience-colombias-wayuu-indigenous-community> accessed 28 February 2024

Seko YA and Basaran E, 'Indigenous Peoples' Ways of Life Threatened by Climate Change' (*Anadolu Ajansi*, 14 July 2023) <https://www.aa.com.tr/en/environment/indigenous-peoples-ways-of-life-threatened-by-climate-change/2946035> accessed 23 February 2024

University of Essex, 'What is Decolonisation?' (*University of Essex Library & Cultural Service*, 19 August 2024) <https://library.essex.ac.uk/edi/whatisdecolonisation> accessed 20 April 2024

Chapter 2

# Reframing climate change litigation in the Global South

## A study of wind energy projects and extractivism in India

*Ayan Garg and Nitai Hinduja*

### Introduction

With the evolving understanding of climate change vulnerability, which acknowledges the asymmetric social impacts of proposed solutions to climate change, climate litigation must also grow.[1] In this chapter, it is argued that a comprehensive understanding of climate litigation must include litigation by vulnerable persons challenging climate adaptation and mitigation measures that heighten existing patterns of oppression, exclusion, and marginalisation. Specifically, this chapter focuses on wind power projects in India and resistance from communities thereto. We locate such forms of resistance within the framework of climate litigation. This, we argue, allows for strategic legal interventions that recognise and draw legitimacy from histories of resistance.

This chapter is structured as follows: In the first part, the historical context and the theoretical framework are outlined, where the dominant narrative of wind energy as imperative to the Indian development project is traced in the context of extractivism theory. In the second part, the chapter explores how wind energy projects are developed in extractivist manners. Here, four case studies of local resistance movements to wind energy plants are discussed. These case studies were chosen to represent instances of sustained resistance to wind energy projects and were studied using primary litigation documents whenever available. They bring out the 'dark side' of wind energy: displacement, land ownership and forest rights violations, and social conflicts among tribal, rural, and marginalised communities. Within each case study, the role of litigation is analysed.

In its third part, the chapter discusses insights into possible litigation strategies emerging from these case studies. By assessing whether litigation is a viable tool for ensuring just transitions, the chapter attempts to provide an overview of litigation's strengths and weaknesses and argues for the inclusion of such just transition litigation into what has traditionally been classified as Indian climate litigation. A limited framing of climate change litigation that does not include litigation by marginalised communities challenging solutions to climate change implicitly upholds an oppressive and exclusionary narrative of development, heightening climate vulnerability. The fourth part concludes by proposing a framework for

DOI: 10.4324/9781003470632-4

understanding and conducting climate litigation. The proposed framework is, most importantly, anti-extractivist; it fundamentally rejects extractivism as a just, or even viable, mode of energy transition. Building on the critiques of extractivism advanced in earlier parts, it shows the importance of historic marginalisation, social position, and community identity in climate litigation and highlights the heterogeneity of actors and interests in Indian climate-related conflicts.

## Indian development and extractivism

In this section, we trace the evolution of the model of development in India. With this background, we explore the idea of extractivism and establish how development in India is rooted in extractivism, by viewing land and people as extractable commodities, to the benefit of capitalist exploitation by the elites in India. We then trace the development and narratives of renewable energy in India. In doing so, we question the predominantly positive and value-neutral narratives surrounding renewables in India and argue that renewable energy projects are intrinsically connected to extractivist development. We do so to argue that the harms so perpetuated ought to be recognised as those arising from climate change. This section hence attempts to unpack the incidence of the apparent contradiction, where solutions to climate change in themselves perpetuate asymmetric climate harm.

### *A history of Indian development*

For postcolonial India, the dominant paradigm of economic growth and development has been continually justified as a solution to structural and widespread poverty.[2] An example is the coal sector. Since the coal industry sought to be developed by post-colonial India and continues to be firmly established within the Indian energy economy, the sector is entrenched in systematic dispossession and extraction.[3] The coal industry was established at the cost of forests, treated as commodities to be exploited for the development of the nation. The tribes who are inherently connected to these forest lands also came to be perceived through the same lens of commodification, with widespread disregard for the customary rights of local communities, evidenced by the wide discretionary powers to forest officers to 'settle' such rights.[4] The government's claim of urbanisation as an end goal continued to be viewed as legitimate. However, the issue of systemic poverty remained largely unaddressed.[5] In short, the Indian government embraced environmental harm as necessary in the project to 'develop' and 'alleviate poverty'.[6]

Foundational postcolonial industrialisation has been the extraction of natural resources, in one form or another, through the appropriation of land. For instance, the draconian and colonial Land Acquisition Act of 1894 ignored the consent of those who were dispossessed, placed barriers in approaching courts for compensation, and functioned on a loose interpretation of public purpose. Such legislative tools have been central to industrialisation by providing mechanisms facilitating dispossession.[7] The continuing practice has legitimised a system of dispossession of land that ignores those at the margins of so-called 'development', both in terms of benefits and costs imposed.[8] This understanding of development has put in place a regime that takes away from those who do not reap its benefits.[9]

Parallels can be drawn between this understanding of development and structures of harm arising from neocolonialism. The imprint of neocolonial dependency of India is reflected in the Eurocentric form of development that was consistent with institutions such as the World Bank.[10] However, care must be taken in drawing conclusions from the effects of neocolonialism. Neocolonialism must be seen to play a role within the landscapes of different state, supra-state, and non-state actors and must not be used as a justification for displacing the culpability of the state in transposing and benefiting from these structures.[11]

## *Land and people as extractable commodities*

Extractivism theory considers the fundamental idea of nature as a commodity to be exploited, accumulated, and exported.[12] This drives social and economic instability and functions for the benefit of transnational corporations.[13] Extractivism theory also recognises the role played by the state in controlling natural resources, thereby facilitating extractivist activities, to the benefit of transnational corporations and the detriment of local communities.[14]

The centrality of the dispossession of land in developing India has been rooted in the framework of extractivism set in motion by colonial governance and oppression.[15] Land dispossession moves extractivism beyond the appropriation of other 'natural resources', encompassing livelihoods, cultural practices, and knowledge systems. Adopting an extractivism framework to understand dispossession constructs land and the people who live on it as natural resources, and thereby commodities exploited by the hegemony of transnational corporations.[16] Making this connection allows us to translate harm to the environment caused by extractivism into harm caused to people.

Viewing dispossession, land, and those who live on and from land as central objects of extractivism and development also helps us draw connections to the push in India toward renewable energy from around 2006.[17] It helps identify a continuity in processes of deprivation and dispossession from postcolonial development and examine the contemporary transition push towards renewable energy through the lens of the history of extractivism.[18] This construction is valuable because it allows one to challenge the dominant narrative of renewable energy (in the form and processes currently being employed in India as part of the energy transition)[19] as a shift from previous harmful practices and a positive step toward mitigating GHG emissions.

By demonstrating the continuation of extractivism, albeit modified, through the expansion of wind energy and other renewable sources of energy in India, we advance the proposition that the harms caused by renewable energy projects to local communities are harms caused by climate change. Framing renewable energy as straightforward solutions to mitigate climate change ignores the political economy of extractivism, within which these projects are located and whose legacies they advance.[20] We, therefore, argue that asymmetric harms arising from wind and other sustainable energy projects can be attributed to the commodification of both land and those who live on and from the land (very often Indigenous peoples) in an extractivist developmental regime.

### *Development of renewables*

India witnessed a significant push toward the development of renewable energy from 2006, when the Ministry of Non-Conventional Energy Sources (MNES) was renamed as the Ministry of New and Renewable Energy (MNRE).[21] The MNRE's mandate extended development research, incentive programs for states, and state nodal agencies, all of which played a pivotal role in the advancement of India's renewable energy industry.[22]

In India, coal and other conventional energy sources have dominated the energy mix.[23] In 2023, as much as 75.73% of India's energy production came from coal, with the total production of coal consistently rising during the previous three decades.[24] Given India's significant GHG emissions,[25] a question arises as to how the country will fulfil its climate mitigation obligations. The nature of this obligation is highly contested, especially when pitted against the 'right to develop'.[26] In India, climate mitigation has far-reaching implications, including for climate litigation strategy.[27]

Nevertheless, international and internal commitments mandating alternative energy sources to reduce GHG emissions have shifted the discourse concerning India's dependency on coal and other fossil fuels. These include developing alternative development pathways, infrastructure investments, employment restructuring, etc.[28]

India, from the time of MNRE's inception, has attempted to incentivise the rapid development of renewable energy sources, particularly solar and wind energy.[29] However, the far-reaching implications of renewable energy projects, especially for the communities affected in the regions where these projects are established, have been systematically ignored in light of ambitious and unchecked development goals.[30]

This lack of recognition is reflected in the foundation of the MNRE, as well as in its subsequent legislative and policy enactments. As an illustration, the MNRE's understanding of energy equity as part of its 'mission' is limited to per capita energy consumption, which ignores the intersecting social, economic, and cultural effects of large-scale infrastructure on local communities.[31]

The environmental impact assessment (EIA) regime in India, substantially flawed in itself (with reduced scrutiny of applications and activities, post facto clearances, curtailed public participation provisions, etc.),[32] creates an exception for certain renewable energy projects, such as hydroelectric power (up to 25 MW), etc., that fall under 'Category B2'. These projects are exempt from the need to undertake EIA public consultations before applying for environmental clearance, thereby creating a system in which preliminary assessments of a project's environmental impacts are not undertaken in consultation with interested and affected parties.[33] The increased burden of renewable energy projects on local communities is thus invisibilised. Some of the immediate impacts of such exemptions were exposed by the large fire at the Oil India Limited's Baghjan oilfield in 2020. The project expanded under the exemption without public hearing. The resultant fire endangered the biodiversity of the adjoining Dibru-Saikhowa National Park and led to the loss of two lives.[34]

Further, numerous policy instruments and guidelines which incentivise renewable energy projects, particularly wind energy, place only cursory obligations on project developers to check environmental acceptability.[35] These obligations are limited in scope, do not carry any compliance check mechanisms, and are in line with the rest of the policy framework on renewable energy, ignoring the significant impacts these projects tend to have on local communities. Policy instruments and academic literature about wind energy in India often consider resistance to land acquisition as a mere barrier to be overcome in the process of streamlining and incentivising the development of large-scale projects by private transnational developers.[36] This being the dominant narrative concerning the processes of developing renewable energy projects renders questions of possible harms to vulnerable groups unaddressed.

### *Lands for renewable energy projects*

The issues discussed earlier become even more important when we look at particular areas and lands that have been affected by the development of renewable projects. It is estimated that to achieve India's 175 GW target of renewable energy by 2022 (which has subsequently been increased to 500 GW by 2030),[37] 55,000 to 125,000 $km^2$ of land in India, including 6,700 to 11,900 $km^2$ of forest land, will be impacted.[38] As at 2013, 45% of India's installed wind power was already located in forest lands, with more than 3,900 ha of forest land, including those classified as ecologically sensitive, being diverted for the projects.[39] While wind projects in forest lands require forest clearance, the frequency and power dynamics involved in the process play a significant role in determining their ultimate outcomes, particularly for affected communities.

According to the 'Concept note for development of wind park/wind solar hybrid park' published by the MNRE in 2020,[40] most areas proposed by the MNRE for the development of wind energy projects lie in so-called 'Fifth Schedule states and forested areas'. These areas are primarily occupied by Adivasi communities (or Scheduled Tribes, per the Constitution of India), a blanket term to describe Indigenous peoples in India.[41]

These communities are primarily forest- and hill-dwelling and have faced deep histories of exploitation by the colonial and post-colonial states. The Constitution of India contains special provisions for the administration of areas inhabited by Scheduled Tribes under its Fifth and Sixth Schedule, alongside specific legislations to such effect. These provisions, incorporated after histories of political resistance, centre Indigenous peoples' autonomy in decision-making.[42] While their scant implementation reflects paternal trends of the Indian state,[43] their presence and operation are significant tools in securing tribal rights. Understanding these constitutional and legal safeguards is essential to recognise the specific violence of renewable energy development in India, which often involves large amounts of unchecked land acquisition by transnational corporations, as demonstrated by the cases of Kachchh, Attappady, and others, explored in the following text. Thinking of renewable energy simplistically, as an absolute good, and a shift from previous extractivist forms of energy generation is clearly flawed.[44] Land dispossession of vulnerable communities is central to the development of renewable energy. Dispossession in the context of renewable energy makes the issue more pervasive. The body of literature that criticises asymmetric dispossession in the context of traditional forms of energy (predominantly coal mining in India) is scarce when we speak about renewable energy.[45]

Instead, renewable energy projects are often portrayed as a break from previous forms of development.[46] They are wrongly treated as divorced from the deep political history associated with other developmental projects. The disconnect and supposed value neutrality of equally problematic renewable energy projects make their harms much less apparent. The positive framing of renewable energy by state functionaries,[47] alongside its developmental push, has mystified how these projects represent continuity in extractivism and dispossession. Importantly, this political disassociation has significant implications for the ability of mobilisation and litigation to draw from relevant political histories and stake their claims based on historical movements and resistance.

## Wind energy and extractivism: instances of just transition litigation in India

To demonstrate the omnipresence of the commodification of land and those who live on and from it in wind energy production and the continuation of harms associated with extractivism, we make three key assertions: First, we challenge the assumption of 'barrenness' of the lands where projects are located that justifies the construction of renewable energy projects. We demonstrate the flaw in such assumption, and how such classification is a political determination. Second, we examine the processes of land acquisition involved in the projects, particularly the sufficiency of and compliance with the legal framework. We show how such processes are intrinsic to commodification, justifying illegitimate acquisition. Third, we show that while renewable projects themselves may be different in nature from fossil fuel developments, associated activities intrinsically linked to the harms caused by renewable projects are equally prevalent.

These assertions are teased out with reference to litigation challenging renewable energy projects. Literature documenting litigation concerning renewable energy conflicts, while emerging through the recognition of human rights–based claims,[48] is nascent. The concept of 'just transition litigation' has emerged.[49] Just transition litigation, as a subset of climate litigation, encompasses 'lawsuits that raise questions over the justice and fairness of activities, policies or projects aimed at addressing climate change',[50] recognising that energy transitions may 'create new injustices and vulnerabilities, while also failing to address pre-existing structural drivers of injustice in energy markets and the wider socio-economy'.[51] Building on this literature, we highlight the importance of recognising the historicity of the nature of harms propagated by narratives of renewable energy. We show that the specific recognition of this continuity of harm plays an important role in litigation strategy, particularly in the precedential value this recognition holds.

### *Barrenness*

The locations of numerous renewable energy projects in India have been justified on the grounds that they convert previously 'barren' land into productive sources of green energy.[52] Moreover, the government has classified approximately 17% of India's land as 'wasteland'.[53]

Two points are important to note here. First, the classification of 'barren land' is very often false, with such classification being made on lands that are actively being used and lived on, including grasslands, shrublands, and pastures.[54] This misclassification, which inaccurately treats these lands as unproductive and unoccupied, arises as a result of administrative lapses, the uncertainty of certifying authorities, and other factors.[55] It also reflects a continuity of colonial systems that classified land as 'wasteland' not based on the value they provided to local communities but on their ability to generate revenue. Second, and more importantly, the rhetoric behind classification as a wasteland in India, and the Global South at large, must be seen as part of a political project toward a particular form of development.[56] In viewing these lands as waste, there is a concurrent depiction of the livelihoods that sustain on these lands as wasted.[57]

In the context of resistance towards solar plants in India, land acquisitions have become the focal point of local communities' concerns with transition measures. Increasingly large numbers of these concerns are taken to courts.[58] Similarly, a study of wind projects in Kachchh, which have been resisted through litigation in at least two cases, makes the impact of the barrenness argument clear. Kachchh, the largest district of India, is part of the western state of Gujarat. In 2023, after years of sustained ambition and attraction of foreign industries, Gujarat became the leading Indian state in terms of wind energy capacity.[59] For locals, the history of wind energy in Kachchh began in 2009, when developers began arriving in full earnest.[60] The windmills created a series of issues for the Kachchh locals: strewn debris, depleting groundwater, noise pollution, loss of local biodiversity, and loss of common land.[61] As such, these projects were met with consistent resistance, directed in particular towards the land acquisition that preceded their development.[62] The cases are discussed next.

#### Kasam Sidhiq Chuchiya v State of Gujarat *(Gujarat High Court)*

In 2018, Kasam Sidhiq Chuchiya, a Kachchh-based cattle farmer, filed a public interest litigation case at the Gujarat High Court challenging the allotment of *gauchar* lands (i.e. community lands meant for cattle grazing) to wind energy firms.[63] The applicant claimed that *gauchar* land – already in shortage in the village areas – could not be allocated for the purposes of constructing windmills as per previous court directions and due to the risk of local environmental harms.[64] The respondent wind energy firm disputed the claim that it had set up windmills on *gauchar* lands, claiming in its affidavit that '[this] claim is falsified on a bare reading of the allotment orders'.[65]

Since the case would turn on this question, the court began its inquiry by examining the impugned allotment orders. The following passage from an allotment order was found to be dispositive:

> The land in question is open, government vested, uneven and hilly on the site. It appears that the said land is not fit to keep reserve for the government or public purpose. As the land in question is hilly, it appears that it is not useful for farming or horticulture. Scattered thorny bushes and other bushes are there in the land in question. Timber would not be available, but firewood could be obtained. One point of land in question does not fall under the forest or grazing land. The land in question is not reserved for the public or any other purpose and it is not fit for the same.[66]

The court was deferential to the allotment order's characterisation of the land. Thus, the court held that the land at issue was not *gauchar*.[67] Here, two points are important: First, the official who found that the land is not fit for any public purpose ignored local knowledge about the land's value for grazing – surely an important public purpose for the inhabitant pastoral communities. Second, the court failed to inquire into the *fides* of the order, plausibly because the matter was not raised in the litigation.

To contextualise, it has been asserted by researchers that to secure land clearance for projects in Kachchh, wind companies' dedicated staff 'approach the local revenue department officials [and] mobilize their past experience . . . and personal connections with those who have the power to clear, sign, stamp and legalize the precious Non-Objection Certificate (NOC) and other papers'.[68] Indeed, even local residents question the neutrality of the process. For example, in one interview, a resident questioned how promulgation (the process by which land boundaries were redrawn, ostensibly using new technology) was only carried out in his home village of Sanganara and not done in nearby villages.[69] The implication was that promulgation was carried out purely to affect the necessary land transfer to the wind companies, and perhaps at their behest.

The court went on to hold that, even if *gauchar* land had indeed been utilised, 'still that by itself will not render the action or decision of the State Government to grant the necessary permission for setting up of Windmills in accordance with its policy [illegal]'.[70] This was based on its earlier decision in *Chaudhary Laxmanbhai Parthibhai v State of Gujarat*,[71] where the court found that the government was empowered to allocate *gauchar* land for suitable public purposes. Here, then, the court simultaneously accepted the development of wind energy and rejected the preservation of land for pastoralism as a valid public purpose. Pastoralism carries the colonial connotations of being backward and environmentally damaging.[72] The effect of the judgment and the allotment commodified not only the land but also the life and livelihoods connected to it, concurrently viewing them as 'wasted resources' that need to be converted to be made 'productive'. This understanding is akin to the rhetoric of extractivism.

## Shankarlal Gopalbhai Patel v Union of India *(National Green Tribunal)*

While the *Kasam Sidhiq Chuchiya* petition was based on the allocation of impugned *gauchar* lands, in *Shankarlal Gopalbhai Patel v Union of India*, the petitioner argued that windmills in and around the Sanganara village had been constructed on deemed forest land.[73] This case, therefore, challenged the allotment orders for having incorrectly identified the land as 'wasteland'.

The applicant, a pastoralist inhabitant of the village, argued that the State of Gujarat had failed to carry out an exercise of identifying deemed forest lands, as mandated by the Supreme Court in the landmark judgment of *T. N. Godavarman v Union of India*.[74] If the state had complied with this judgment, it would have found that the presence of the (sacred) thorny forests made the land a 'forest area'. In any case, the applicant further argued, in the absence of such an exercise having been undertaken when appropriate, the land ought to be 'deemed' as a forest area per the dictionary definition.

The Tribunal dismissed the applicant's argument. As the Gujarat High Court had done in the *gauchar* land case, it deferred to the official allotment order – which classified the land as 'barren and unused Government waste land [which] has hilly terrain, which cannot be used for agricultural or any other purpose'.[75] As for the fact that the state had not completed the exercise of identifying forest areas, the Tribunal again deferred to the state's submission that a Committee had been constituted in 2011 which had ruled Sanganara village as being outside the 'deemed forest' area.[76] Notably, despite the Committee having been set up 25 years after the Supreme Court judgment in *T. N. Godavarman v Union of India* and not having worked in any areas except Sanganara,[77] the Tribunal did not question the *fides* of this exercise of power. Finally, the official classification of wasteland was upheld, and the petitioners were denied the relief they sought.

The lands and livelihoods historically understood as wasted, and subsequently commodified, are intrinsically linked to social hierarchies (based on caste and other identity markers) and the livelihoods of Adivasi and Dalit communities.[78] The origins of the term 'wasteland' are reflective of this social hierarchy, given that it has been traced to the colonial conception of wilderness, not just of forested areas, but also of the inhabitants of those areas.[79] Notably, these lands are often 'common lands' that are utilised jointly by members of communities. Access and control over common lands through 'community forest rights' have been secured with forest-dwelling communities (including Adivasi) under the Forests Rights Act of 2006.[80] However, the processes of dispossession, particularly where mandatory consent requirements are ignored or watered down, undermine the value of these protections.[81]

## Land acquisition

The Land Acquisition Act of 2013, Forest Rights Act of 2006, and Panchayats Extension to Scheduled Areas Act of 1996 govern land acquisitions. These laws mandate consultation with and consent of forums known as Panchayats and Gram Sabhas when land is acquired by private individuals/corporations. These forums are the primary decision-making bodies constituted at local/village levels to enable democratic and participatory decision-making in India.

### *Andhra Lake Wind Farm*

In the case of the Andhra Lake Wind Farm in Maharashtra, since 2010, activists and local communities had opposed the setting up of the mega-project, sprawling over 14 villages and occupying almost 200 ac of reserved forest land.[82] It was found that the required Gram Sabha meetings for diversion of forest land under the Forest Rights Act were not conducted. Further, the authenticity of letters from Gram Sabhas authorising the diversion was questionable, with allegations being made of forged signatures.[83] Land acquisition was not the only issue: The activists also alleged that the companies were cutting down over 300,000 trees, in far excess of their permit to cut 26,615.[84] In public interest litigation filed by a social worker, Dr Dattatraya Kale, the Bombay High Court awarded a stay on all deforestation in 2010.[85] However, the case was closed in 2014 following Dr Kale's death.[86] The other issues associated with the project – land acquisition in particular – remain unlitigated.

The process of acquisition leads to a commodification of those who sustain the lands. This is a common occurrence, especially where smaller farmers, unaware of land prices, sell their lands at very low prices to middlemen, who later sell it at a much higher price to private corporations. This alienation of land, mostly agricultural and forest land, deprives people of long-term subsistence. Often, these sales are incentivised through the promises of future employment in developed renewable energy projects.[87] However, this employment is informal, temporary, and renders former pastoralists open to exploitation and plunder.[88]

### *Attappady*

Development in Attappady demonstrates how alienation of land is achieved through unscrupulous means and later justified through fake promises of employment or profit-sharing. In 2007, Sarjan Realities and Suzlon Energy began their operations in Attappady through leasing Adivasi land (totalling about 623 ac) in the Nilgiris Biosphere Reserve.[89] As the investigative journal *Tehelka* reported, this development was contentious:

> Kerala's Tribal Land Act, 1975 mandates that tribal land can only be sold to other tribals, that too under unavoidable circumstances. . . . The Supreme Court had asked the government to cancel all [sale] transactions after 1986, but the order was circumvented by convincing Adivasi people that the land is being taken on rent.[90]

In 2010, official inquiries reported that the companies were misrepresenting tribal lands as non-tribal, using fake documents, and misleading the Adivasi into thinking that the land would be used for widening village roads. In fact, many locals were still paying taxes under the false impression that the land was merely leased.

In 2011, the government, to pacify the situation following intense protests,[91] promised a portion of the wind plant's profit to the tribal families whose lands had been acquired. However, this plan received considerable criticism from various groups, including the Attappady Protection Council, since it would essentially deem the acquisitions as legitimate and retrospectively legalise them, and was ultimately dropped.[92] In 2014, the local Panchayats began approaching the Kerala High Court to demand a stay on the project and return of the land. In 2015, the court ordered the sealing of the wind farms and the removal of the turbines.[93]

*Suzlon Infrastructure Services Ltd v State of Kerala*[94] has been the only successful anti–wind project litigation in which the setting up of the projects was voided altogether. Notably, in 2017, another wind project at Attappady was announced. This time, the difference appears to be an upfront profit-sharing arrangement with the Adivasi whose lands are to be utilised.[95] While this is undoubtedly an outcome of the local communities' successful resistance to the previous wind energy project, whether it will be equitably implemented remains to be seen.

Further, within communities, the impact of the projects is caste-based and, therefore, asymmetric. This is particularly because the degree of representation that can be made and the subsequent benefits that can be accrued are a function of an individual/group's position in localised caste hierarchies.[96] The use of force, coercion, and caste-based atrocities in the aforementioned processes must be underscored. Private corporations systematically hire 'problem solvers' who use their caste positions and political connections to exploit vulnerable communities and coerce them into adopting favourable positions.[97] Further, these projects have been used as tools to exercise control over and subjugate minority groups by restricting access to land, controlling movement, and surveilling certain populations.[98] This, it has been argued, is a form of state-sponsored violence that effectively acts as a counterinsurgency mechanism.[99] Patterns of such violence are not limited to India but have been observed in other countries in the Global South.[100] Land and environment defenders have been documented to be at the receiving end of lethal violence. Notably,

36% of the killings in 2022 were of members of Indigenous communities and have also been linked to high-carbon-emitting industries across the Global South.[101]

Here, much like traditional extractivism, the identity of those who live on and from the land is seen as a commodity, naturally created by societal processes, and as a legitimate subject to be exploited.[102] While extractivism is seen as a phenomenon concentrated in the Global South, particular identities of individuals that have been historically marginalised, such as the Adivasi and the Dalit, effectively create a Global South within the Global South. Here, processes of extractivism that commodify and exploit these identities are fundamental in exacerbating asymmetric harm.

The idea of identities as commodities to be exploited is not novel.[103] It has been used within the extractivism theory when speaking of the processes of patriarchal oppression.[104] These processes dehumanise both land and women, particularly in the context of modern developmentalism.[105] These types of theoretical connections are important: They justify the extension of the extractivism framework to renewable energy projects.

Commodification, and its unjust impacts, have led activists to argue not just that land acquisition laws are violated by wind energy projects but that the laws *themselves* are violative of higher rights. In 2016, social activists in Udupi began raising concerns about the acquisition of 641 ac of village land by the Karnataka Industrial Area Development Board for Suzlon Energy, in huge excess of the publicly stated requirement of 150 ac.[106] Making matters worse was the fact that this land had been vacant and unused and was frequently transferred between companies at lucrative prices.[107]

In a public press conference, activists blamed the 'draconian' Karnataka Industrial Areas Development Act 1966, which enables land acquisition by state authorities for industrial and other developmental purposes. They further demanded *'land wapsi'* (i.e. return of lands) to the farming communities whose lands had been acquired,[108] and shared news of having lodged a claim with the Additional Chief Secretary of the Department of Industries and Commerce. However, they did not subsequently pursue these claims through litigation. One may speculate that the evidentiary burdens were an additional factor on top of usual reasons not to litigate. Here, the case would be that the Act itself was unconstitutional, and hence, land acquisition under it ought to be voided. This would entail a greatly heightened burden and standard of proof.

### *Activities associated with renewable energy projects*

The activities, raw materials, and infrastructure associated with renewable energy projects are largely the same as previously extractivist forms of energy production in India,[109] and elsewhere in the world. Renewable energy projects, therefore, give rise to another location of continuity of similar forms of harms.[110] While the activity itself may be different and not extractive in the sense of extraction of fossil fuels or minerals, it still requires large-scale infrastructure to be built.[111] These processes reflect a coercive 'physical un/re-making of spaces' that have been formally classified as wastelands but, as shown in the preceding text, are often sources of livelihood. This administrative act of classification in itself leads to an exacerbation of vulnerability of those that rely on them for their livelihoods, as discussed earlier. This is because it justifies the use of such land for 'more productive' infrastructure projects, thereby legitimising the act of extraction.

Examples of the harmful associated impacts of renewable energy projects include the acquisition of large parts of land for support infrastructure, including roads and transmission lines;[112] impacts on trees and other forms of biodiversity (which are integral to Adivasi lives); and depletion of groundwater and drinking water sources.[113]

Often, the developers of these projects justify the associated activities and infrastructure on the basis that they are 'co-benefits', in that it would improve the physical and social infrastructure in the area for enjoyment by local communities. However, in the absence of mandatory requirements, the infrastructure largely exists as empty promises or becomes a 'white elephant'.[114] Further, the infrastructure so developed is often reserved for the use of private companies, to the exclusion of communities in the area. This process renders both previously existing land and infrastructure, and subsequently built infrastructure, inaccessible to local communities. Therefore, these activities continue to extract from both land and communities to their exclusion, heightening their vulnerability to climate change.[115]

### *Green extractivism*

Traditionally, through the processes of extractivism, resources were extracted from the Global South and exported to nations in the Global North.[116] These processes have been mirrored to develop renewables in a slightly modified sense. The areas where renewable energy projects are concentrated see not a geographical export per se but, rather, a spatial and access-based export of community land and resources to private corporations,[117] who, while located in the Global South, can recreate the processes of Global North–South extraction due to the pervasiveness of hierarchies of finance, caste, power, etc.

'Green extractivism', a term coined post-2020, refers to an assemblage of practices and rhetoric which promote sustainability while legitimising and perpetuating the commodification of nature and extractivism.[118] As the risk of the transition to renewable energy turning into 'green extractivism' is being increasingly felt worldwide, reproducing historically uneven development, the effects of such development adversely impact already-vulnerable communities. Green extractivism thus has significant implications for the reproduction of historically continued social and economic vulnerabilities, as well as rural livelihoods.[119] Correspondingly, local communities and researchers are raising concerns about wind energy becoming a form of 'green extractivism' across jurisdictions.[120] These patterns of devaluation of economies and culture have been identified as entrenched to the processes of green extractivism.[121] Community ownership and recognition of resource sovereignty have been identified as central toward addressing the harms of green extractivism.[122] However, in most cases, power asymmetries either ignore or pervade such possible options, as has been demonstrated earlier. Resistance to green extractivism to prevent patterns of devaluation and commodification is becoming increasingly important.

Importantly, the fact that a shift to renewable energy is a required next step to mitigate climate change is not contested in this chapter. However, through examining the implications of such transitions and their politics in countries such as India, we centre the interests that ought to be protected and highlight those that are currently being served. An energy transition that mitigates certain future climate harms while exacerbating current vulnerabilities cannot be 'just'. It is with this in mind that we proceed to explore the role of litigation in enabling a truly just energy transition. While examining what this 'justness' means is beyond the scope of this chapter, we argue that a linkage between the political history of precarious development and renewable energy is required to politicise litigation. Politicised climate litigation in India can have fixed strategic goals and ideals, centred on minimisation of harm. This would also be in line with historical developmental litigation.

## Anti-extractivism litigation as climate litigation

While climate litigation in general, and the Global South climate litigation in particular, has gained much attention,[123] there persists a need to incorporate cases which are not argued on express climate grounds but still invisibly involve questions of climate justice within the scope of 'climate litigation'.[124] As noted previously, 'adaptation cases are often unnoticed because they are not directly argued on climate grounds, dealing with local developmental issues such as water access or land use'.[125]

Literature on Indian climate litigation – as well as Indian climate litigation itself – is relatively sparse.[126] Of the literature surveyed by the authors, almost none consider just transition litigation. Similarly, the Climate Change Litigation Database maintained by the Sabin Center for Climate Change Law lists zero just transition cases from India in its database.[127] As Bouwer notes, it is imperative to look at the 'multiple ways in which climate change issues might be present but invisible' in cases that are not 'overtly about climate change'.[128] Litigants in the cases surveyed in this chapter did not relate their actions to Indian climate change policy, and yet the judgments interacted with (and, in their own ways, shaped) it nonetheless. Ohdedar, in a survey of neglected Indian climate cases, finds that

> [l]itigation around land, credit, water rights, disaster management, and many other processes are . . . often the subject of smaller, more discrete disputes, void of climate language. Nevertheless, they still have an active role in shaping vulnerability and rights issues.[129]

In what follows, it is argued that considering cases against the development of wind energy projects is imperative for understanding and productively developing climate litigation. After providing an overview of the learnings from the cases discussed in this chapter, their relevance as 'climate cases' is discussed.

### What does wind energy litigation teach us?

At least three lessons emerge from the challenges to wind projects discussed in this chapter. The first is the importance of the petitioner's positionality. Under Indian law, both directly affected parties and publicly spirited individuals may oppose wind energy projects. However, the latter route – of cases being brought via public interest litigation – means that only concerns deemed important enough by the petitioner are litigated, as we saw in *Shri Dattatraya Kondaji Kale v Union of India*, where the petitioner focused on deforestation, ignoring issues of land acquisition. These concerns may not convey the full picture of extractivism and its impacts on local communities.

The former route, of directly affected parties initiating litigation, carries its own problems. The parties most often affected by wind energy projects are the Adivasi. These people tend to be unable to productively access the Indian judicial system. The 'constitutional estrangement' imposed upon and felt by the Adivasi towards the Indian state makes negotiation with state functionaries, including courts, complex.[130] Sharrif identifies at least four contributing factors behind this poor access to courts.[131] First, productive usage of Indian courts depends on knowledge of the Indian legal system and 'institutional skill',[132] which the Adivasi – due to their comparatively limited dealings with litigation – do not generally acquire.[133] Second, often being 'one-time users' of courts, the Adivasi cannot create leverageable personal contacts or networks in courts, which are indispensable for successfully navigating the Indian litigation system.[134] Third, language and literacy discrepancies create wariness of court hearings. Fourth, high costs bar litigation.[135] As Parmar puts it:

> Adivasi people [have to] save money for weeks before they can afford to forgo a day's wage and the bus fare to visit the nearest legal aid office. Sometimes, they decide to spend that money on buying rice instead, especially since they are repeatedly told that the law is "like that" and nothing can be done.[136]

This explains why the Adivasi often require affluent or resourceful persons, such as NGO workers or Panchayat heads, to file cases on their behalf.[137] The imbalance of power in these relationships, however, brings in the same issues as when a case is filed through public interest litigation.

Second, assuming that problems regarding petitioner identity are resolved, there are inherent issues with a judicial process in cases where knowledge and experiences are contested. A case transforms a 'real historical experience' into 'abstract legality',[138] and the judicial process can serve to filter out important experiences from the purview of the courts. For example, in Attappady, the Adivasi suspected that a gold rush was a motivating factor behind the choosing of their lands.[139] Such concerns were apparently not litigated, presumably due to the evidentiary issues associated with them.

More tangibly, judicial unwillingness or inability to give local knowledge their deserved weight is observed in the interpretation of land allotment or lease orders in India. In the Kachchh cases, no significance was given to concerns about the *fides* of the allotment order, since the findings of the authorities were deferred to.[140] As we have demonstrated, classifications of land are rarely objective or neutral. Courts, due to institutional design, do not supplant the state's characterisation of land with that of its inhabitants.

Third, the court's tendency to show deference to the state creates another concern in litigation. Courts usually go out of their way to emphasise that the development of wind energy is an important public purpose as determined by the government, while ignoring the extractivist implications of the development. This necessary deference to the executive in policy matters means that litigation can only go so far.[141] Ultimately, whether the emphasis on wind energy development could ever be meaningfully questioned by any court is doubtful, thus greatly limiting the scope of possible remedies.

## Conclusion

We have established how wind energy projects operate within an extractivist model of development which works through the silencing and marginalisation of the most vulnerable in the Global South. As such, we interrogate 'sustainable' wind in the context of a developing India, as a proposed solution to the multidimensional threats of climate change. Seeing renewable energy through the extractivism framework prevents simplistic conclusions that renewable energy is, in all situations, a legitimate form of climate change mitigation in terms of the Indian policy framework on renewables.[142] Our analysis problematises the unmoderated growth of renewable energy projects in India by pointing to the pervasive and structural harms that arise as a result. Pragmatically, our analysis hopes to facilitate more conscious policy and polity by providing critical insights about these projects.

Our chapter also illustrates the utility of extractivism theory in developing climate litigation strategies in countries such as India. Climate change litigation in India is an emerging phenomenon. Barring a few notable cases, much of the litigation has been on gaps in implementing climate change policies and environmental harm tangentially related to climate change. Furthermore, most mentions of climate change by Indian courts have been in the form of marginal discussions that are not directly related to litigation.[143] Hence, it would be fair to state that climate change litigation in India largely lacks a fixed teleological goal or a fixed set of objectives or principles that can be relied upon. Given the newness of climate change as a subject of litigation, it is largely ahistorical and apolitical. Further, given that direct litigation on climate change in India is lacking, there is a significant dearth of jurisprudence that can be relied on for any future climate litigation. This has had a direct impact on its effectiveness and ability to adequately redress asymmetric climate change harms.

We believe that by adopting extractivism theory and consequently recognising the deep history of extractivism in India, climate change resistance and litigation in India could more appropriately address the structural issues that drive asymmetric climate harm and vulnerability. Current forms of climate change litigation in India fail to do so given their apolitical and ahistorical nature. Asymmetric climate impacts can be understood only when due recognition is given to intersecting structures of power and dominance that pervade Indian history and are reflected in the literature on extractivism in India. In this manner, adopting the extractivism theory could legitimise climate change litigation in India as a political project with a clear and coherent goal.[144] Practically, this is a call for Indian climate actors giving greater heed to the concerns raised by the Adivasi and other marginalised groups in renewable energy projects. Activists could demand thorough protections for land and local ecology before projects are approved, lawyers could move courts into developing case law which recognises that renewable energy projects should not become extractivist themselves, and so forth.

Integrating the concept of extractivism into climate ligation in India, through petitions against renewable energy projects and their subsequent harms, could also allow for other strategic interventions. It could allow legal interventions based on legislation and judicial precedents that have historically provided communities with protection from extractivist activities. It could also provide grounds for climate change litigation to derive support and guidance from current environmental movements and resistance in India, which constantly takes issue with extractivist practices. Without this integration, climate litigation will remain limited, both conceptually and in its ability to allow tangible results for vulnerable groups. Adopting extractivism theory thus has significant importance in its potential to act as an organising force for the emergence of effective climate litigation in India in the face of climate vulnerability.

## Notes

1 Robin Leichenko and Julie A Silva, 'Climate Change and Poverty: Vulnerability, Impacts, and Alleviation Strategies' (2014) 5 *WIREs Climate Change* 539; Fraser Sugden and others, 'Agrarian Stress and Climate Change in the Eastern Gangetic Plains: Gendered Vulnerability in a Stratified Social Formation' (2014) 29 *Global Environmental Change* 258; Alex Arnall, Chris Hilson and Catriona McKinnon, 'Climate Displacement and Resettlement: The Importance of Claims-Making "from Below"' (2019) 19 *Climate Policy* 665. See also Murcott, Tigre and Ann Samuel Introduction.

2 P Chaudhuri, 'Changing Perceptions to Poverty in India: State and Poverty' (1993) 55 *Sankhyā: The Indian Journal of Statistics, Series B (1960–2002)* 317. For insights on the legacies of colonialism in Latin America, see Beckhauser and Broetto, Chapter 1, especially at n 55.

3 Kuntala Lahiri-Dutt, Radhika Balakrishnan and Nesar Ahmad, 'Land Acquisition and Dispossession: Private Coal Companies in Jharkhand' (2012) 47 *Economic & Political Weekly* 39.

4 Ruchira Talukdar and Priya Pillai, 'Countering the Coal Curse through Community Rights: Stopping Coal-Extraction through Forest Rights in Singrauli, Central India' (2022) 89 *Journal of Australian Political Economy* 90.

5 Devleena Ghosh, '"We Don't Want to Eat Coal": Development and Its Discontents in a Chhattisgarh District in India' (2016) 99 *Energy Policy* 252.

6 Sandeep Sengupta, 'Defending "Differentiation": India's Foreign Policy on Climate Change from Rio to Copenhagen' in Kanti P Bajpai and Harsh V Pant (eds), *India's Foreign Policy: A Reader* (1st edn, OUP 2013).

7 Mohammed Asif, 'Land Acquisition Act: Need for an Alternative Paradigm' (1999) 34 *Economic and Political Weekly* 1564.

8 Ramachandra Guha, 'Adivasi People, Naxalites and Indian Democracy' (2007) 42 *Economic and Political Weekly* 3305.

9 Michael Levien, *Dispossession without Development: Land Grabs in Neoliberal India* (OUP 2018).

10 John Brohman, 'Universalism, Eurocentrism, and Ideological Bias in Development Studies: From Modernisation to Neoliberalism' (1995) 16 *Third World Quarterly* 121.

11 Shalini Randeria, 'Glocalization of Law: Environmental Justice, World Bank, NGOs and the Cunning State in India' (2003) 51 *Current Sociology* 305.

12 Steffen Böhm and Maria Ceci Misoczky, 'Environment, Extractivism and the Delusions of Nature as Capital' in Raza A Mir, Hugh Willmott and Michelle Greenwood (eds), *The Routledge Companion to Philosophy in Organization Studies* (Routledge, Taylor & Francis Group 2016).

13 Alberto Acosta, 'Extractivism and Neoextractivism: Two Sides of the Same Curse' in Miriam Lang and Dunai Mokrani (eds), *Beyond Development: Alternative Visions from Latin America* (Rosa Luxemburg Foundation 2013).

14 Christopher W Chagnon et al., 'From Extractivism to Global Extractivism: The Evolution of an Organizing Concept' (2022) 49 *The Journal of Peasant Studies* 760. See also Beckhauser and Broetto, Chapter 1.

15 Natacha Rivi Bruna, 'Extractivism, Rural Livelihoods and Accumulation in a "Climate-Smart" World: The Rise of Green Extractivism' (PhD thesis, Erasmus University Rotterdam 2021) 240.

16 Kalyani Pricilla Arun and Soundiraraj Subbiah, 'Dispossession and Extractivism in the Life of the Marginalized: An Ecofeminist Reading of Mahasweta Devi's Witch' (2020) 36 *Asian Women* 45, 54.

17 Kripal Singh and others, 'India's Renewable Energy Research and Policies to Phase Down Coal: Success After Paris Agreement and Possibilities Post-Glasgow Climate Pact' (2023) 177 *Biomass and Bioenergy* 106944.

18 Hannes Warnecke-Berger, Hans-Jürgen Burchardt and Rachid Ouaissa, 'Natural Resources, Raw Materials, and Extractivism: The Dark Side of Sustainability' (*Extractivism.de*, 2022).

19 Suresh Lal S R and others, 'Advancements in Renewable Energy Transition in India: A Review' (2022) *Energy Sources, Part A: Recovery, Utilization, and Environmental Effects* 1; Arunabha Ghosh, 'Can India Become a Green Superpower?: The Stakes of the World's Most Important Energy Transition Essays' (2023) 102 *Foreign Affairs* 144.

20 Alexander Dunlap, 'The Structures of Conquest: Debating Extractivism(s), Infrastructures and Environmental Justice for Advancing Post-Development Pathways' (2023) *Revue internationale de politique de développement* <http://journals.openedition.org/poldev/5355> accessed 8 September 2024

21 Government of India, 'About Us | Ministry of New and Renewable Energy' <https://mnre.gov.in/about-department/introduction/> accessed 19 September 2024.

22 SC Bhattacharya and Chinmoy Jana, 'Renewable Energy in India: Historical Developments and Prospects' (2009) 34 *Energy* 981 <https://doi.org/10.1016/j.energy.2008.10.017> accessed 8 September 2024.

23 Ramchandra Pode, 'Addressing India's Energy Security and Options for Decreasing Energy Dependency' (2010) 14 *Renewable and Sustainable Energy Reviews* 3014 <https://doi.org/10.1016/j.rser.2010.07.007> accessed 8 September 2024.

24 Ministry of Statistics and Programme Implementation, 'Energy Statistics India 2023' (*Government of India*, 2023).

25 GHG Platform India, 'Analysis of Greenhouse Gas Emissions from 2005 to 2018' (2022) <https://www.ghgplatform-india.org/wp-content/uploads/2022/09/GHGPI_Trend-Analysis_2005-to-2018_India_Sep22.pdf> accessed 8 September 2024.

26 Kate Aronoff and others, 'A Reparative Politics for the Climate Crisis: A Roundtable' (2021) 68 *Dissent* 66; Michael Christopher Sardo, 'Responsibility for Climate Justice: Political Not Moral' (2023) 22 *European Journal of Political Theory* 26 <https://doi.org/10.1177/1474885120955l> accessed 8 September 2024.

27 Maria Antonia Tigre, 'The "Fair Share" of Climate Mitigation: Can Litigation Increase National Ambition for Brazil?' (2023) 16(1) *Journal of Human Rights Practice* 25 <https://doi.org/10.1093/jhuman/huad032>.

28 Navroz K Dubash and others, 'India and Climate Change: Evolving Ideas and Increasing Policy Engagement' (2018) 43 *Annual Review of Environment and Resources* 395 <https://doi.org/10.1146/annurev-environ-102017-025809> accessed 18 September 2024.

29 Abhishek Pratap, Priya Pillai and Arundhati Muthu, 'Powering Ahead: An Assessment of the Socio-Economic and Environmental Impacts of Large-Scale Renewables Energy Projects and an Examination of the Existing Regulatory Context' (*Heinrich Böll Stiftung*).

30 Chris Hesketh, 'Clean Development or the Development of Dispossession? The Political Economy of Wind Parks in Southern Mexico' (2022) 5 *Environment and Planning E: Nature and Space* 543, 544 <https://doi.org/10.1177/2514848621991764> accessed 8 September 2024.

31 'About the Ministry: Ministry of New and Renewable Energy, Government of India' <https://mnre.gov.in/the-ministry/what-does-the-ministry-do/> accessed 4 April 2024. For a discussion on intersectionality, see Murcott, Tigre, and Ann Samuel, 'Introduction', pp 5–10.

32 Urmila Jha-Thakur, 'Three Decades of EIA Reforms in India: Reflections on the Complexities of Simplifications' (2023) 41 *Impact Assessment and Project Appraisal* 244 <https://doi.org/10.1080/14615517.2023.2208397>; Manju Menon and Kanchi Kohli, 'Environment Impact Assessment in India: Contestations Over Regulating Development' in Philippe Cullet and Sujith Koonan (eds), *Research Handbook on Law, Environment and the Global South* (Edward Elgar Publishing 2019) <https://doi.org/10.4337/9781784717469.00035> accessed 20 May 2024.

33 Shibani Ghosh, 'EIA 2020: Two Steps Back . . .' (2020) *The India Forum* <https://www.theindiaforum.in/article/eia-2020-two-steps-back> accessed 20 May 2024.

34 Jayanta Kalita, 'Oil India Skipped Public Hearings Before Expanding Drilling in Assam's Baghjan' *The Wire* (21 June 2020) <https://thewire.in/environment/exclusive-oil-india-skipped-public-hearings-before-expanding-drilling-in-assams-baghjan> accessed 20 May 2024.

35 'Guidelines for Development of Onshore Wind Power Projects' (*Ministry of New and Renewable Energy, Government of India*, 2016) F. No. 66/183/2016-WE.

36 Ministry of New and Renewable Energy, 'Wind Overview' <https://mnre.gov.in/wind-overview/#:~:text=The%20Government%20is%20promoting%20wind,components%20of%20wind%20electric%20generators.> 20 May 2024; Abhishek Kumar, Divyanshi Pal, Sanjay Kumar Kar, Saroj Kumar Mishra and Rohit Bansal, 'An Overview of Wind Energy Development and Policy Initiatives in India' (2022) 24 *Clean Technologies and Environmental Policy* 1337; Ministry of New and Renewable Energy, 'Policy for Repowering of the Wind Power Projects' <https://cdnbbsr.s3waas.gov.in/s3716e1b8c6cd17b771da77391355749f3/uploads/2023/12/2023121318 74296229.pdf> accessed 26 April 2024.

37 Ministry of New and Renewable Energy, 'Renewable Energy in India' (*Press Information Bureau*, 9 September 2022) <https://pib.gov.in/FeaturesDeatils.aspx?NoteId=151141&ModuleId%20=%202> accessed 26 April 2024.
38 Joseph Kiesecker et al., 'Renewable Energy and Land Use in India: A Vision to Facilitate Sustainable Development' (2019) 12 *Sustainability* 281.
39 Chandra Bhushan and others, 'EIA Guidelines Wind Power Sector' (*Centre for Science and Environment*, 2013) <https://shaktifoundation.in/wp-content/uploads/2017/10/EIA-Guidelines-Wind-Power_1.pdf> accessed 26 April 2024.
40 Ministry of New & Renewable Energy, Government of India, 'Concept Note for Development of Wind Park/Wind Solar Hybrid Park' (2020) No 238/75/2017-Wind Office Memorandum.
41 S Faizi and Priya K Nair, 'Adivasis: The World's Largest Population of Indigenous People' (2016) 59 *Development* 350 <https://doi.org/10.1057/s41301-017-0115-8> accessed 26 April 2024.
42 Kamal Nayan Choubey, 'The State, Tribals and Law: The Politics behind the Enactment of PESA and FRA' (2016) 46 *Social Change* 355.
43 Nitai Hinduja, 'The Constitutional Imagination of Scheduled Tribes – Reflecting on State Violence and Inaction' (*NLSIR Online*, 25 June 2023) <https://www.nlsir.com/post/the-constitutional-imagination-of-scheduled-tribes-reflecting-on-state-violence-and-inaction> accessed 26 April 2024.
44 Hesketh (n 30).
45 Hesketh (n 30).
46 Subhashish Dey, Anduri Sreenivasulu, GTN Veerendra, K Venkateswara Rao and PSS Anjaneya Babu, 'Renewable Energy Present Status and Future Potentials in India: An Overview' (2022) 1 *Innovation and Green Development*.
47 Ministry of New and Renewable Energy (n 37).
48 Annalisa Savaresi and Joana Setzer, 'Rights-Based Litigation in the Climate Emergency: Mapping the Landscape and New Knowledge Frontiers' (2022) 13 *Journal of Human Rights and the Environment*.
49 Annalisa Savaresi and others, 'Just Transition Litigation: A New Knowledge Frontier' (2023) <https://dx.doi.org/10.2139/ssrn.4561679> accessed 26 April 2024; Maria Antonia Tigre, Lorena Zenteno, Marlies Hesselman, Natalia Urzola, Pedro Cisterna-Gaete and Riccardo Luporini, 'Just Transition Litigation in Latin America: An Initial Categorization of Climate Litigation Cases Amid the Energy Transition' (*Sabin Center for Climate Change Law*, January 2023) <https://scholarship.law.columbia.edu/sabin_climate_change/197/> accessed 26 April 2024.
50 Savaresi and others (n 49); Tigre et al. (n 49). For insights on climate litigation in India, see Dutta and Lofts, Chapter 4; Kaur, Sathiabama, and Vedavalli, Chapter 7; and Jamwal, Chapter 9.
51 Xinxin Wang and Kevin Lo, 'Just Transition: A Conceptual Review' (2021) 82 *Energy Research & Social Science* 102291 <https://doi.org/10.1016/j.erss.2021.102291> accessed 24 September 2024.
52 Pratap, Pillai and Muthu (n 29).
53 'Wastelands Atlas of India' (*National Remote Sensing Centre, Government of India*, 2019) <https://dolr.gov.in/en/documents/wasteland-atlas-of-india> accessed 24 September 2024.
54 Mahima Jain, 'In India, Grasslands are Classified as Wastelands That Have No Ecological Value' (*Scroll*, 10 December 2022) <https://scroll.in/article/1039213/in-india-grasslands-are-classified-as-wastelands-that-have-no-ecological-value> accessed 26 April 2024.
55 Heather P Bedi, '"Lead the District into the Light": Solar Energy Infrastructure Injustices in Kerala, India' (2019) 1 *Global Transitions* 181.

56 Carlos Tornel, 'Energy Justice in the Context of Green Extractivism: Perpetuating Ontological and Epistemological Violence in the Yucatan Peninsula' (2023) 30 *Journal of Political Ecology*.
57 Marco Armiero, *Wasteocene: Stories from the Global Dump* (1st edn, Cambridge University Press 2021).
58 As noted by Ohdedar, '[i]n recent years, the courts in India have seen numerous cases concerning land disputes that stem from renewable energy development. In one single state, Rajasthan, there have been at least 15 cases since 2011'. Birsha Ohdedar, 'Climate Adaptation, Vulnerability, and Rights Based Litigation: Broadening the Scope of Climate Litigation Using Political Ecology' (2022) 13(1) *Journal of Human Rights and the Environment* 137.
59 The Hindu, 'Gujarat Pips Tamil Nadu as the Leader in Wind Energy' (11 June 2023) <https://www.thehindubusinessline.com/economy/gujarat-pips-tamil-nadu-as-the-leader-in-wind-energy-capacity/article66957310.ece#:~:text=Gujarat%20has%20become%20the%20No,capacity%20was%20at%2010%2C125%20MW> accessed 26 April 2024.
60 For an investigative overview of the history and on-ground impacts of wind power plants in Kachchh, see Tabassum Barnagarwala and Vaishnavi Rathore, 'The Dark Side of Wind Energy Along Gujarat's Coast' (*Scroll*, 29 March 2023) <https://scroll.in/article/1046387/the-dark-side-of-wind-energy-along-gujarats-coast#:~:text=The%20wreckage%20of%20many%20turbines,to%20lie%20around%20in%20Lamba.=> accessed 26 April 2024.
61 See Barnagarwala and Rathore (n 60).
62 Damayantee Dhar, 'Protest Against Suzlon Windmills in Kutch Reignites' (*NewsClick*, 1 October 2021) <https://www.newsclick.in/Protest-Against-Suzlon-Windmills-Kutch-Reignites> accessed 26 April 2024.
63 *Kasam Sidhiq Chuchiya v State of Gujarat* (2021) C/WPPIL/122/2018 (Gujarat High Court).
64 *Kasam Sidhiq Chuchiya* (n 63) [2.1–2.4].
65 *Kasam Sidhiq Chuchiya* (n 63) [5].
66 *Kasam Sidhiq Chuchiya* (n 63) [7.2].
67 *Kasam Sidhiq Chuchiya* (n 63) [7.3].
68 David Singh, '"This is All Waste": Emptying, Cleaning and Clearing Land for Renewable Energy Dispossession in Borderland India' (2022) 30 *Contemporary South Asia* 402.
69 Ravleen Kaur, 'In Kachchh District, Locals are Resisting Wind Farms to Save a Unique Thorn Forest and Wildlife' (*Scroll*, 29 April 2022) <https://scroll.in/article/1021519/in-kachchh-district-locals-are-resisting-wind-farms-to-save-a-unique-thorn-forest-and-wildlife> accessed 14 May 2024.
70 *Kasam Sidhiq Chuchiya v State of Gujarat* (n 63) [7.7].
71 *Chaudhary Laxmanbhai Parthibhai v State of Gujarat* (2012) C/WPPIL/155/2011 Gujarat High Court (India).
72 Singh (n 68).
73 *Shankarlal Gopalbhai Patel v Union of India* (2023) OA/06/2020 (National Green Tribunal, Western Zone) [3].
74 *TN Godavarman v Union of India* (12 December 1996) WP(C)/202/1995 (Supreme Court) [144].
75 *Shankarlal Gopalbhai Patel* (n 73) [8].
76 *Shankarlal Gopalbhai Patel* (n 73)[16].
77 *Shankarlal Gopalbhai Patel* (n 73) [23].
78 Sarah Hilaly, 'Imagining Colonial Assam: The Figuring of "Wastelands" in Its Making' (2016) 51 *Economic and Political Weekly* 55 <https://www.jstor.org/stable/i40165981> accessed 23 September 2024.

79 Judy Whitehead, 'John Locke and the Governance of India's Landscape: The Category of Wasteland in Colonial Revenue and Forest Legislation' (2010) 45 *Economic and Political Weekly* 83.
80 Komali Yenneti and Rosie Day, 'Distributional Justice in Solar Energy Implementation in India: The Case of Charanka Solar Park' (2016) 46 *Journal of Rural Studies* 35.
81 Geetanjoy Sahu, 'FCR 2022: An Attempt to Subvert the Power of Gram Sabhas' (2023) 58 *Economic & Political Weekly* <https://www.epw.in/journal/2023/2/comment/fcr-2022-attempt-subvert-power-gram-sabhas.html> accessed 17 May 2024.
82 Amruta Byatnal, 'Green Energy Project Poses Threat to Wildlife in Maharashtra' (*The Hindu*, 9 April 2011) <https://www.thehindu.com/sci-tech/energy-and-environment/Green-energy-project-poses-threat-to-wildlife-in-Maharashtra/article14677164.ece> accessed 17 May 2024.
83 Pratap, Pillai and Muthu (n 29).
84 Kanchan Chaudhari, 'High Court Reprieve for Thousands of Trees' (*Hindustan Times*, 20 December 2010) <https://www.hindustantimes.com/mumbai/high-court-reprieve-for-thousands-of-trees/story-E1D0wK2JwTtcK2rSRHZo3I.html> accessed 17 May 2024.
85 *Shri Dattatraya Kondaji Kale v Union of India* (2010) PIL/223/2010 Bombay High Court (India).
86 Land Conflict Watch, 'Wind Farm in Western Ghats Poses Perennial Flooding Problem for Locals in Maharashtra' (2023) <https://www.landconflictwatch.org/conflicts/wind-farm-in-western-ghats-poses-perennial-flooding-problem-for-locals-in-maharashtra> accessed 17 May 2024.
87 Yenneti and Day (n 80).
88 Tornel (n 56).
89 Committee for Protection of Democratic Rights, 'Unclean Intrigues Behind Clean Energy: Dhule Adivasis' Glorious Struggle for Land Rights' (2007) <https://docs.wind-watch.org/adivasistruggle.html> accessed 17 May 2024.
90 Committee for Protection of Democratic Rights (n 89).
91 The Hindu, 'Tribes People Take Out March to Windmill Farm' (*The Hindu*, 15 November2010)<https://www.thehindu.com/news/national/kerala/Tribes-people-take-out-march-to-windmill-farm/article15689078.ece> accessed 11 June 2024.
92 Land Conflict Watch, 'Tribals Protest Against Illegal Windmill Farms in Attappady' (2017) <https://www.landconflictwatch.org/conflicts/windmills-on-tribals-land> accessed 17 May 2024.
93 KAShaji,'IllegallyErectedWindmillstobePulledDown'(*TheHindu*,22July2015)<https://www.thehindu.com/news/national/kerala/illegally-erected-windmills-to-be-pulled-down/article7450024.ece> accessed 11 July 2024.
94 *Suzlon Infrastructure Services Ltd v State of Kerala* (2010) W.P. (C) No. 34006/2010 Kerala High Court (India).
95 The New Indian Express, 'Attappadi Tribals to Get a Slice of NHPC Wind Farm's Profit Pie' (*The New Indian Express*, 3 April 2017) <https://www.newindianexpress.com/states/kerala/2017/Apr/03/attappadi-tribals-to-get-a-slice-of-nhpc-wind-farms-profit-pie–1589145.html> accessed 11 July 2024.
96 Komali Yenneti and Rosie Day, 'Procedural (in)Justice in the Implementation of Solar Energy: The Case of Charanaka Solar Park, Gujarat, India' (2015) 86 *Energy Policy* 664 <https://doi.org/10.1016/j.enpol.2015.08.019> accessed 11 July 2024.
97 Singh (n 68).
98 David Singh, 'When "Green" Becomes "Saffron": Wind Extraction, Border Surveillance, and Citizenship Regime at the Edge of the Indian State' (2023) 30 *Journal of Political Ecology* <https://doi.org/10.2458/jpe.5490> accessed 11 July 2024.
99 Singh (n 98).

100 Emmanuel Iniobong Archibong and Abiodun Paul Afolabi, 'From Colonial Exploitation to Renewable Transition: A Critical Analysis of Africa's Energy Paradigm' (2023) 7 *European Journal of Sustainable Development Research* em0236, 5.
101 'Standing Firm: The Land and Environmental Defenders on the Frontlines of the Climate Crisis' (*Global Witness Land and Environmental Defenders Campaign*, 2023) <https://www.globalwitness.org/en/campaigns/environmental-activists/land-and-environmental-defenders-annual-report-archive/> accessed 11 July 2024.
102 Hesketh (n 30) 550.
103 Julia C Morris, '(Im)Mobility Economies: Extractivism of the Refugee as a Human Commodity' (2023) *Revue internationale de politique de développement* <http://journals.openedition.org/poldev/5430>.
104 Charmaine Pereira and Dzodzi Tsikata, 'Contextualising Extractivism in Africa' (2021) 2 *Extractivism, Resistance, Alternatives* 14.
105 Arun and Subbiah (n 16).
106 Land Conflict Watch, 'Land Owners in Karnataka's Udupi Demand Return of Excess Land Acquired by KIADB' (*Land Conflict Watch*, 2017) <https://www.landconflictwatch.org/conflicts/windmills-in-sez> accessed 11 July 2024.
107 Mangalore Today, 'Social Activists Accuse Suzlon of Illegally Transferring 147 Acres Land to Another Firm' (*Mangalore Today*, 21 April 2016) <https://www.mangaloretoday.com/main/Social-activists-accuse-Suzlon-of-illegally-transferring-147-acres-land-to-another-firm.html> accessed 11 July 2024.
108 Mangalore Today (n 107).
109 Warnecke-Berger, Burchardt and Ouaissa (n 18).
110 Archibong and Afolabi (n 100).
111 Hesketh (n 30) 551.
112 Pratap, Pillai and Muthu (n 29).
113 Singh (n 68).
114 Yenneti and Day (n 80).
115 Pratap, Pillai and Muthu (n 29). See also Murcott, Tigre and Ann Samuel 'Introduction'.
116 Archibong and Afolabi (n 100).
117 Ashok Kumbamu, 'Bury My Heart in Bastar: Neoliberal Extractivism, the Oppressive State and the Maoist Revolution in India' (2018) 2 *Kairos: A Journal of Critical Symposium* 15 <https://kairostext.in/index.php/kairostext/article/view/36/27> accessed 11 July 2024.
118 Tornel (n 56) 1.
119 Bruna (n 15).
120 Bruna (n 15).
121 Jaume Franquesa, 'Wind Struggles: Grabbing Value and Cultivating Dignity in Southern Catalonia' (2022) 33 *Capitalism Nature Socialism* 18.
122 Cymene Howe and Dominic Boyer, 'Aeolian Extractivism and Community Wind in Southern Mexico' (2016) 28 *Public Culture* 215 <https://read.dukeupress.edu/public-culture/article/28/2%20(79)/215/85787/Aeolian-Extractivism-and-Community-Wind-in> accessed 11 July 2024.
123 For a small sample, see Joana Setzer and Lisa Benjamin, 'Climate Litigation in the Global South: Constraints and Innovations' (2019) 9 *Transnational Environmental Law* 77 <https://doi.org/10.1017/S2047102519000268>; Jacqueline Peel and Jolene Lin, 'Transnational Climate Litigation: The Contribution of the Global South' (2019) 113 *American Journal of International Law* 679.
124 Ohdedar (n 58). See also Murcott, Tigre and Ann Samuel, 'Introduction', n 124.
125 Ohdedar (n 58) 140. See also Joana Setzer and Lisa Benjamin (n 123) 60–61.
126 GN Gill and G Ramachandran, 'Sustainability Transformations, Environmental Rule of Law and the Indian Judiciary: Connecting the Dots through Climate Change Litigation' (2021) 23(3) *Environmental Law Review* 228–247; Shibani Ghosh, 'Litigating

Climate Claims in India' (2020) 114 *AJIL Unbound* 45; Lavanya Rajamani, 'Rights Based Climate Litigation in the Indian Courts: Potential, Prospects & Potential Problems' (2013) *Centre for Policy Research, Climate Initiative, Working Paper No 2013/1* <https://ssrn.com/abstract=2464927>; Ohdedar (n 58); Shibani Ghosh, 'Climate Litigation in India' in Francesco Sindico and Makane Moïse Mbengue (eds), *Comparative Climate Change Litigation: Beyond the Usual Suspects* (Springer 2021) 347. See also Dutta and Lofts Chapter 4, Kaur, Sathiabama and Vedavalli Chapter 7, and Jamwal Chapter 9.

127 'Climate Change Litigation Database' (*Sabin Center for Climate Change Law, India*) <https://climatecasechart.com/non-us-jurisdiction/india/> accessed 11 July 2024.

128 Kim Bouwer, 'The Unsexy Future of Climate Change Litigation' (2018) 30(3) *Journal of Environmental Law* 483.

129 Ohdedar (n 58) 10.

130 Kalpana Kannabiran, 'Constitution-as-Commons, Spatial Justice, and Estrangements in Adivasi India: The Continuing Legacy of Three Legal Cases' in Antje Linkenbach and Vidhu Verma (eds), *State, Law and Adivasi: Shifting Terrains of Exclusion* (SAGE 2022) 129; Kalpana Kannabiran, 'Constitutional Geographies and Cartographies of Impunity' (2016) 51(45) *Economic and Political Weekly* <https://www.epw.in/journal/2016/44-45/special-articles/constitutional-geographies-and-cartographies-impunity.html> accessed 11 July 2024.

131 Fauzia Shariff, 'Power Relations and Legal Pluralism: An Examination of 'Strategies of Struggles' Amongst the Santal Adivasi of India and Bangladesh' (2008) 40(57) *The Journal of Legal Pluralism and Unofficial Law* 1.

132 This is a term borrowed from Michael Anderson, 'Access to Justice and Legal Process: Making Legal Institutions Responsive to Poor People in LDCs' (2003) *Institute of Development Studies, Working Paper No 178/2003* <https://gsdrc.org/document-library/access-to-justice-and-legal-process-making-legal-institutions-responsive-to-poor-people-in-ldcs/>.

133 As Shariff (n 131) notes, while there are important differences in the levels of court-institutional knowledge among Adivasi groups, there is a uniformly identifiable gap between them and regular 'court-users'. See also Marc Galanter, 'Why the "Haves" Come Out Ahead: Speculations on the Limits of Legal Change' (1974) 9 *Law & Society Review* 95.

134 Shariff (n 131); on the importance of having personal contacts within courts, see Sumit Khanna, 'All Rise for Your Honour' (*Public Service Broadcasting Trust*, 2012) <https://psbt.org/films/all-rise-for-your-honour/> accessed 11 July 2024.

135 See also Kalpana Kannabiran et al., 'Legal Clinics and Adivasi Rights: Report of a National Workshop' (2012) 47(10) *Economic and Political Weekly* 21–24.

136 Pooja Parmar, *Indigeneity and Legal Pluralism in India: Claims, Histories, Meanings* (CUP 2015) 201.

137 This is a larger trend observed even during the famous anti-Coca-Cola struggle in Plachimada, where the Adivasi people who originally started the movement sat in protest while the Panchayat and other entities litigated. See Parmar (n 136) for an account of the movement.

138 Ranajit Guha, 'Chandra's Death' in Ranajit Guha (ed), *Subaltern Studies V: Writings on South Asian History and Society* (OUP 1987) 135.

139 KK Shahina, 'Windmills on Lush, Prime Forest Land, by Forging Papers and Conning Tribals' (2010) 7(27) *Tehelka Magazine* <https://assets-global.website-files.com/5d70c9269b8d7bd25d8b1696/5dc0014c375efbfa1d18dd1a_Windmill-attappady-Thehelka.pdf>.

140 See discussion on *Kasam Sidhiq Chuchiya v State of Gujarat* (n 63) and *Shankarlal Gopalbhai Patel* (n 73).

141 'Despite their "pro-environment" and "activist" reputation, Indian courts are often deferential to the executive on decisions on economic policy and infrastructure.' Shibani

Ghosh, 'Litigating Climate Claims in India' (2020) 114 *AJIL Unbound* 45. See also Beckhauser and Broetto, Chapter 1, on coloniality in legal systems in Latin America, where Indigenous peoples have experiences.

142 Tornel (n 56).

143 Shibani Ghosh, 'Climate Litigation in India' in Francesco Sindico and Makane Moïse Mbengue (eds), *Comparative Climate Change Litigation: Beyond the Usual Suspects* (Springer 2021).

144 Philip Hayward, 'Embodying the Anthropocene: Embattled Crustaceans, Extractivism, and Eco-Tourism on Christmas Island (Indian Ocean)' (2021) 16 *Island Studies Journal* 229, 246.

## Bibliography

### Books and chapters

Acosta A, 'Extractivism and Neoextractivism: Two Sides of the Same Curse' in M Lang and D Mokrani (eds), *Beyond Development: Alternative Visions from Latin America* (Rosa Luxemburg Foundation 2013)

Böhm S and Ceci Misoczky MC, 'Environment, Extractivism and the Delusions of Nature as Capital' in Raza A Mir, Hugh Willmott and Michelle Greenwood (eds), *The Routledge Companion to Philosophy in Organization Studies* (Routledge 2016)

Ghosh S, 'Climate Litigation in India' in F Sindico and MM Mbengue (eds), *Comparative Climate Change Litigation: Beyond the Usual Suspects* (Springer 2021)

Guha R, 'Chandra's Death' in Ranajit Guha (ed), *Subaltern Studies V: Writings on South Asian History and Society* (OUP 1987)

Kannabirān K, 'Constitution-as-Commons, Spatial Justice, and Estrangements in Adivasi India: The Continuing Legacy of Three Legal Cases' in A Linkenbach and V Verma (eds), *State, Law and Adivasi: Shifting Terrains of Exclusion* (SAGE 2022)

Levien M, *Dispossession without Development: Land Grabs in Neoliberal India* (OUP 2018)

Menon M and Kohli K, 'Environment Impact Assessment in India: Contestations over Regulating Development' in P Cullet and S Koonan (eds), *Research Handbook on Law, Environment and the Global South* (Edward Elgar Publishing 2019)

Parmar P, Indigeneity and Legal Pluralism in *India: Claims, Histories, Meanings* (CUP 2015)

Sengupta S, 'Defending "Differentiation": India's Foreign Policy on Climate Change from Rio to Copenhagen' in KP Bajpai and HV Pant (eds), *India's Foreign Policy: A Reader* (1st edn, OUP 2013)

Tigre MA, Zenteno L, Hesselman M, Urzola N, Cisterna-Gaete P and Luporini R, *Just Transition Litigation in Latin America: An Initial Categorization of Climate Litigation Cases Amid the Energy Transition* (Sabin Center for Climate Change Law 2023)

### Journal articles

Antonia Tigre M, 'The "Fair Share" of Climate Mitigation: Can Litigation Increase National Ambition for Brazil?' (2023) 16(1) *Journal of Human Rights Practice* 25 <https://doi.org/10.1093/jhuman/huad032> accessed 19 September 2024

Arnall A, Hilson C and McKinnon C, 'Climate Displacement and Resettlement: The Importance of Claims-Making "from Below"' (2019) 19(6) *Climate Policy* 665 <https://doi.org/10.1080/14693062.2019.1570065> accessed 19 September 2024

Arun KP and Subbiah S, 'Dispossession and Extractivism in the Life of the Marginalized: An Ecofeminist Reading of Mahasweta Devi's Witch' (2020) 36(1) *Asian Women* 45 <https://e-asianwomen.org/xml/23578/23578.pdf> accessed 20 September 2024

Bedi HP, '"Lead the District into the Light": Solar Energy Infrastructure Injustices in Kerala, India' (2019) 1 *Global Transitions* 181 <https://doi.org/10.1016/j.glt.2019.10.005> accessed 20 September 2024

Bhattacharya SC and Jana C, 'Renewable Energy in India: Historical Developments and Prospects' (2009) 34(8) *Energy* 981 <https://doi.org/10.1016/j.energy.2008.10.017> accessed 19 September 2024

Bouwer K, 'The Unsexy Future of Climate Change Litigation' (2018) 30(3) *Journal of Environmental Law* 483 <https://doi.org/10.1093/jel/eqy017> accessed 19 September 2024

Brohman J, 'Universalism, Eurocentrism, and Ideological Bias in Development Studies: From Modernisation to Neoliberalism' (1995) 16(1) *Third World Quarterly* 121 <https://library.fes.de/libalt/journals/swetsfulltext/14830998.pdf> accessed 19 September 2024

Chagnon CW, Durante F, Gills BK, Hagolani-Alboc SE, Hokkanen S, Kangasluoma SMJ, Konttinen H, Kröger, LaFluer W, Ollinaho O and Vuola MPS, 'From Extractivism to Global Extractivism: The Evolution of an Organizing Concept' (2022) 49 *The Journal of Peasant Studies* 760 <https://doi.org/10.1080/03066150.2022.2069015> accessed 19 September 2024

Choubey KN, 'The State, Tribals and Law: The Politics behind the Enactment of PESA and FRA' (2016) 46(3) *Social Change* 355 <https://doi.org/10.1177/0049085716654812> accessed 20 September 2024

Christopher Sardo MC, 'Responsibility for Climate Justice: Political Not Moral' (2023) 22(1) *European Journal of Political Theory* 26 <https://doi.org/10.1177/14748851209551> accessed 19 September 2024

Dubash KN, Khosla R, Kelkar U and Lele S, 'India and Climate Change: Evolving Ideas and Increasing Policy Engagement' (2018) 43 *Annual Review of Environment and Resources* 395 <https://doi.org/10.1146/annurev-environ-102017-025809> accessed 18 September 2024

Dunlap A, 'The Structures of Conquest: Debating Extractivism(s), Infrastructures and Environmental Justice for Advancing Post-Development Pathways' (2023) 16 *OpenEdition Journals* <http://journals.openedition.org/poldev/5355> accessed 19 September 2024

Faizi S and Nair PK, 'Adivasis: The World's Largest Population of Indigenous People' (2016) 59 *Development* 350 <https://doi.org/10.1057/s41301-017-0115-8> accessed 19 September 2024

Franquesa J, 'Wind Struggles: Grabbing Value and Cultivating Dignity in Southern Catalonia' (2022) 33(4) *Capitalism Nature Socialism* 18 <https://www.tandfonline.com/doi/full/10.1080/10455752.2022.2165259> accessed 19 September 2024

Galanter M, 'Why the "Haves" Come Out Ahead: Speculations on the Limits of Legal Change' (1974) 9(1) *Law & Society Review* 95 <https://doi.org/10.2307/3053023> accessed 19 September 2024

Ghosh D, '"We Don't Want to Eat Coal": Development and Its Discontents in a Chhattisgarh District in India' (2016) 99 *Energy Policy* 252 <https://doi.org/10.1016/j.enpol.2016.05.046> accessed 19 September 2024

Ghosh S, 'Litigating Climate Claims in India' (2020) 114 *AJIL Unbound* 45 <https://doi.org/10.1017/aju.2020.5> accessed 19 September 2024

Gill GN and Ramachandran G, 'Sustainability Transformations, Environmental Rule of Law and the Indian Judiciary: Connecting the Dots Through Climate Change Litigation' (2021) 23(3) *Environmental Law Review* 228–247 <https://doi.org/10.1177/14614529211031203> accessed 19 September 2024

Hayward P, 'Embodying the Anthropocene: Embattled Crustaceans, Extractivism, and Eco-Tourism on Christmas Island (Indian Ocean)' (2021) 16(1) *Island Studies Journal* 229 <https://doi.org/10.24043/isj.145> accessed 19 September 2024

Hesketh C, 'Clean Development or the Development of Dispossession? The Political Economy of Wind Parks in Southern Mexico' (2022) 5(2) *Environment and Planning E: Nature and Space* 543 <https://doi.org/10.1177/2514848621991764> accessed 8 September 2024

Hilaly S, 'Imagining Colonial Assam: The Figuring of "Wastelands" in Its Making' (2016) 51(3) *Economic and Political Weekly* 55 <https://www.jstor.org/stable/i40165981> accessed 19 September 2024

Howe C and Boyer D, 'Aeolian Extractivism and Community Wind in Southern Mexico' (2016) 28(2) *Public Culture* 215 <https://doi.org/10.1215/08992363-3427427> accessed 11 July 2024

Jha-Thakur U, 'Three Decades of EIA Reforms in India: Reflections on the Complexities of Simplifications' (2023) 41(3) *Impact Assessment and Project Appraisal* 244 <https://doi.org/10.1080/14615517.2023.2208397> accessed 19 September 2024

Kannabiran K, 'Constitutional Geographies and Cartographies of Impunity' (2016) 51(44–45) *Economic and Political Weekly* <https://www.epw.in/journal/2016/44-45/special-articles/constitutional-geographies-and-cartographies-impunity.html> accessed 11 July 2024

Kannabiran K, Gundimeda S, Gupta P and Vivek L, 'Legal Clinics and Adivasi Rights: Report of a National Workshop' (2012) 47(10) *Economic and Political Weekly* 21 <https://www.jstor.org/stable/41419926> accessed 19 September 2024

Kiesecker J, Baruch-Mordo S, Heiner M, Negandhi D, Oaklead J, Kennedy C and Chauhan P, 'Renewable Energy and Land Use in India: A Vision to Facilitate Sustainable Development' (2019) 12(1) *Sustainability* 281 <https://doi.org/10.3390/su12010281> accessed 19 September 2024

Kumar A, Pal D, Kar SK, Mishra SK and Bansal R, 'An Overview of Wind Energy Development and Policy Initiatives in India' (2022) 24 *Clean Technologies and Environmental Policy* 1337 <https://doi.org/10.1007/s10098-021-02248-z> accessed 19 September 2024

Kumbamu A, 'Bury My Heart in Bastar: Neoliberal Extractivism, the Oppressive State and the Maoist Revolution in India' (2018) 2(1) *Kairos: A Journal of Critical Symposium* 15 <https://kairostext.in/index.php/kairostext/article/view/36/27> 11 July 2024

Lahiri-Dutt K, Balakrishnan R and Ahmad N, 'Land Acquisition and Dispossession: Private Coal Companies in Jharkhand' (2012) 47(6) *Economic & Political Weekly* 39 <https://ssrn.com/abstract=2015125> accessed 19 September 2024

Lal S, Argunan P, Suryan A and Herbert J, 'Advancements in Renewable Energy Transition in India: A Review' (2022) *Energy Sources, Part A: Recovery, Utilization, and Environmental Effects* 1 <http://dx.doi.org/10.1080/15567036.2021.2024921> accessed 20 September 2024

Leichenko R and Silva JA, 'Climate Change and Poverty: Vulnerability, Impacts, and Alleviation Strategies' (2014) 5(4) *WIREs Climate Change* 539 <https://doi.org/10.1002/wcc.287> accessed 20 September 2024

Ohdedar B, 'Climate Adaptation, Vulnerability, and Rights Based Litigation: Broadening the Scope of Climate Litigation Using Political Ecology' (2022) 13(1) *Journal of Human Rights and the Environment* 137 <https://doi.org/10.4337/jhre.2022.01.06> accessed 20 September 2024

Peel J and Lin J, 'Transnational Climate Litigation: The Contribution of the Global South' (2019) 113(4) *American Journal of International Law* 679 <https://doi.org/10.1017/ajil.2019.48> accessed 20 September 2024

Pode R, 'Addressing India's Energy Security and Options for Decreasing Energy Dependency' (2010) 14(9) *Renewable and Sustainable Energy Reviews* 3014 <https://doi.org/10.1016/j.rser.2010.07.007> accessed 8 September 2024

Randeria S, 'Glocalization of Law: Environmental Justice, World Bank, NGOs and the Cunning State in India' (2003) 51(3–4) *Current Sociology* 305 <https://doi.org/10.1177/0011392103051003009> accessed 20 September 2024

Savaresi A and Setzer J, 'Rights-Based Litigation in the Climate Emergency: Mapping the Landscape and New Knowledge Frontiers' (2022) 13(1) *Journal of Human*

*Rights and the Environment* 7 <https://doi.org/10.4337/jhre.2022.01.01> accessed 20 September 2024

Savaresi A, Setzer J, Armeni C and Bouwer K, 'Just Transition Litigation: A New Knowledge Frontier' (2023) *SSRN Electronic Journal* <https://dx.doi.org/10.2139/ssrn.4561679> accessed 20 September 2024

Setzer J and Benjamin L, 'Climate Litigation in the Global South: Constraints and Innovations' (2019) 9(1) *Transnational Environmental Law* 77 <https://doi.org/10.1017/S2047102519000268> accessed 20 September 2024

Shahina KK, 'Windmills on Lush, Prime Forest Land, by Forging Papers and Conning Tribals' (2010) 7(27) *Tehelka Magazine* <https://assets-global.website-files.com/5d70c926 9b8d7bd25d8b1696/5dc0014c375efbfa1d18dd1a_Windmill-attappady-Thehelka.pdf> accessed 19 September 2024

Shariff F, 'Power Relations and Legal Pluralism: An Examination of "Strategies of Struggles" Amongst the Santal Adivasi of India and Bangladesh' (2008) 40(57) *The Journal of Legal Pluralism and Unofficial Law* 1 <https://doi.org/10.1080/07329113.2008.1075661 7> accessed 20 September 2024

Singh D, '"This is All Waste": Emptying, Cleaning and Clearing Land for Renewable Energy Dispossession in Borderland India' (2022) 30(3) *Contemporary South Asia* 402 <https://doi.org/10.1080/09584935.2022.2099812> accessed 26 April 2024

Singh D, 'When "Green" Becomes "Saffron": Wind Extraction, Border Surveillance, and Citizenship Regime at the Edge of the Indian State' (2023) 30(1) *Journal of Political Ecology* 765 <https://doi.org/10.2458/jpe.5490> accessed 11 July 2024

Singh K, Mena RS, Kumar S, Dhyani S, Sheoran S, Singh HM, Pathak VV, Khalid Z, Singh A, Chopra K, Bajar S, Ansari FA, Gupta SK, Varjani S, Kothari R, Tyagi VV, Singh B and Byun C, 'India's Renewable Energy Research and Policies to Phase down Coal: Success after Paris Agreement and Possibilities Post-Glasgow Climate Pact' (2023) 177 *Biomass and Bioenergy* 106944 <https://doi.org/10.1016/j.biombioe.2023.106944> accessed 20 September 2024

Sugden F, Maskey N, Clement F, Ramesh V, Philip A and Rai A, 'Agrarian Stress and Climate Change in the Eastern Gangetic Plains: Gendered Vulnerability in a Stratified Social Formation' (2014) 29 *Global Environmental Change* 258 <https://doi.org/10.1016/j.gloenvcha.2014.10.008> accessed 19 September 2024

Talukdar R and Pillai P, 'Countering the Coal Curse through Community Rights: Stopping Coal-Extraction through Forest Rights in Singrauli, Central India' (2022) 89 *Journal of Australian Political Economy* 90 <https://www.ppesydney.net/content/uploads/2022/07/5-Talukdar-Pillai.pdf> accessed 19 September 2024

Tornel C, 'Energy Justice in the Context of Green Extractivism: Perpetuating Ontological and Epistemological Violence in the Yucatan Peninsula' (2023) 30(1) *Journal of Political Ecology* <https://doi.org/10.2458/jpe.5485> accessed 19 September 2024

Wang X and Lo K, 'Just Transition: A Conceptual Review' (2021) 82 *Energy Research & Social Science* 102291 <https://doi.org/10.1016/j.erss.2021.102291> accessed 19 September 2024

Whitehead J, 'John Locke and the Governance of India's Landscape: The Category of Wasteland in Colonial Revenue and Forest Legislation' (2010) 45(50) *Economic and Political Weekly* 83 <https://www.jstor.org/stable/25764218> accessed 19 September 2024

Yenneti K and Day R, 'Procedural (in)Justice in the Implementation of Solar Energy: The Case of Charanaka Solar Park, Gujarat, India' (2015) 86 *Energy Policy* 664 <https://doi.org/10.1016/j.enpol.2015.08.019> accessed 11 July 2024

Yenneti K and Day R, 'Distributional Justice in Solar Energy Implementation in India: The Case of Charanka Solar Park' (2016) 46 *Journal of Rural Studies* 35 <https://doi.org/10.1016/j.jrurstud.2016.05.009> accessed 19 September 2024

### Cases

*Chaudhary Laxmanbhai Parthibhai v State of Gujarat* (2012) /WPPIL/155/2011, Gujarat High Court (India)

*Godavarman v Union of India* (1996) WP(C)/202/1995, Indian Supreme Court (India)

*Kasam Sidhiq Chuchiya v State of Gujarat* (2021) C/WPPIL/122/2018, Gujarat High Court (India)

*Shankarlal Gopalbhai Patel v Union of India* (2023) OA/06/2020, National Green Tribunal, Western Zone (India)

### Newspaper articles

Asif M, 'Land Acquisition Act: Need for an Alternative Paradigm' (*Economic and Political Weekly*, 19 June 1999) 1564

Sahu G, 'FCR 2022: An Attempt to Subvert the Power of Gram Sabhas' (*Economic & Political Weekly*, 15 February 2024) <https://www.epw.in/journal/2023/2/comment/fcr-2022-attempt-subvert-power-gram-sabhas.html> accessed 17 May 2024

### Notices

Ministry of New & Renewable Energy, Government of India, 'Concept Note for Development of Wind Park/Wind Solar Hybrid Park' (2020) No 238/75/2017-Wind Office Memorandum <https://solarquarter.com/wp-content/uploads/2020/11/concept-note.pdf> accessed 20 September 2024

Ministry of New & Renewable Energy, Government of India, 'Policy for Repowering of the Wind Power Projects' (2023) No 238/9/2018 <https://cdnbbsr.s3waas.gov.in/s3716e1b-8c6cd17b771da77391355749f3/uploads/2023/12/2023121318742962 29.pdf> accessed 26 April 2024

### Online sources

'About Us: Introduction' (*Ministry of New and Renewable Energy*) <https://mnre.gov.in/about-department/introduction/> accessed 4 April 2024

'All Rise for Your Honour by Sumit Khanna' (*Public Service Broadcasting Trust*, 2012) <https://psbt.org/films/all-rise-for-your-honour/> accessed 11 July 2024

Aronoff K, Kozul-Wright R, Rehman A, Riofrances T, Táíwò OO, 'A Reparative Politics for the Climate Crisis: A Roundtable' (*Dissent*, 2021) <https://www.dissentmagazine.org/article/a-reparative-politics-for-the-climate-crisis-a-roundtable/> accessed 8 September 2024

Balachandar G, 'Gujarat Pips Tamil Nadu as the Leader in Wind Energy Capacity' (*The Hindu Businessline*, 11 June 2023) <https://www.thehindubusinessline.com/economy/gujarat-pips-tamil-nadu-as-the-leader-in-wind-energy-capacity/article66957310.ece#:~:text=Gujarat%20has%20become%20the%20No,capacity%20was%20at%2010%2C125%20MW> accessed 26 April 2024

Barnagarwala T and Rathore V, 'The Dark Side of Wind Energy Along Gujarat's Coast' (*Scroll*, 29 March 2023) <https://scroll.in/article/1046387/the-dark-side-of-wind-energy-along-gujarats-coast#:~:text=The%20wreckage%20of%20many%20turbines,to%20lie%20around%20in%20Lamba.=> accessed 26 April 2024

Byatnal A, 'Green Energy Project Poses Threat to Wildlife in Maharashtra' (*The Hindu*, 9 April 2011) <https://www.thehindu.com/sci-tech/energy-and-environment/Green-energy-project-poses-threat-to-wildlife-in-Maharashtra/article14677164.ece> accessed 17 May 2024

Chaudhari K, 'High Court Reprieve for Thousands of Trees' (*Hindustan Times*, 20 December 2010) <https://www.hindustantimes.com/mumbai/high-court-reprieve-for-thousands-of-trees/story-E1D0wK2JwTtcK2rSRHZo3I.html> accessed 17 May 2024

Deepak CN, 'Land Owners in Karnataka's Udupi Demand Return of Excess Land Acquired by KIADB' (*Land Conflict Watch*, 18 October 2016) <https://www.landconflictwatch.org/conflicts/windmills-in-sez> accessed 11 July 2024

Dhar D, 'Protest Against Suzlon Windmills in Kutch Reignites' (*NewsClick*, 1 October 2021) <https://www.newsclick.in/Protest-Against-Suzlon-Windmills-Kutch-Reignites> accessed 26 April 2024

Ghorpade M, 'Wind Farm in Western Ghats Poses Perennial Flooding Problem for Locals in Maharashtra' (*Land Conflict Watch*, 24 May 2023) <https://www.landconflictwatch.org/conflicts/wind-farm-in-western-ghats-poses-perennial-flooding-problem-for-locals-in-maharashtra> accessed 20 September 2024

Ghosch S 'EIA 2020: Two Steps Back . . .' (*The India Forum*, 2 September 2020) <https://www.theindiaforum.in/article/eia-2020-two-steps-back> accessed 20 May 2024

Ghosh A, 'Can India Become a Green Superpower?: The Stakes of the World's Most Important Energy Transition Essays' (*Foreign Affairs*, 20 June 2023) <https://www.foreignaffairs.com/india/can-india-become-green-superpower> accessed 19 September 2024

Guha R, 'Adivasi People, Naxalites and Indian Democracy' (2007) 42(32) *Economic and Political Weekly* 3305 <https://www.epw.in/journal/2007/32/special-articles/adivasis-naxalites-and-indian-democracy.html> accessed 19 September 2024

Hinduja N, 'The Constitutional Imagination of Scheduled Tribes – Reflecting on State Violence and Inaction' (*NLSIR Online*, 25 June 2023) <https://www.nlsir.com/post/the-constitutional-imagination-of-scheduled-tribes-reflecting-on-state-violence-and-inaction> accessed 26 April 2024

Jain M, 'In India, Grasslands are Classified as Wastelands That Have No Ecological Value' (*Scroll*, 10 December 2022) <https://scroll.in/article/1039213/in-india-grasslands-are-classified-as-wastelands-that-have-no-ecological-value> accessed 26 April 2024

Kaur R, 'In Kachchh District, Locals are Resisting Wind Farms to Save a Unique Thorn Forest and Wildlife' (*Scroll*, 29 April 2022) <https://scroll.in/article/1021519/in-kachchh-district-locals-are-resisting-wind-farms-to-save-a-unique-thorn-forest-and-wildlife> accessed 14 May 2024

Ministry of New and Renewable Energy, 'Renewable Energy in India' (*Press Information Bureau*, 9 September 2022) <https://pib.gov.in/FeaturesDeatils.aspx?NoteId=151141&ModuleId%20=%202> accessed 26 April 2024

Ministry of New and Renewable Energy, 'Wind Overview' (*mnre.gov.in*) <https://mnre.gov.in/wind-overview/#:~:text=The%20Government%20is%20promoting%20wind,components%20of%20wind%20electric%20generators> accessed 20 May 2024

Satish A, 'Attappadi Tribals to Get a Slice of NHPC Wind Farm's Profit Pie' (*The New Indian Express*, 3 April 2017) <https://www.newindianexpress.com/states/kerala/2017/Apr/03/attappadi-tribals-to-get-a-slice-of-nhpc-wind-farms-profit-pie−1589145.html> accessed 11 July 2024

Shaji KA, 'Illegally Erected Windmills to be Pulled Down' (*The Hindu*, 22 July 2015) <https://www.thehindu.com/news/national/kerala/illegally-erected-windmills-to-be-pulled-down/article7450024.ece> accessed 11 July 2024

'Social Activists Accuse Suzlon of Illegally Transferring 147 Acres Land to Another Firm' (*Mangalore Today*, 21 April 2016) <https://www.mangaloretoday.com/main/Social-activists-accuse-Suzlon-of-illegally-transferring-147-acres-land-to-another-firm.html> accessed 11 July 2024

'Tribes People Take Out March to Windmill Farm' (*The Hindu*, 16 November 2010) <https://www.thehindu.com/news/national/kerala/Tribes-people-take-out-march-to-windmill-farm/article15689078.ece> accessed 11 June 2024

'Wastelands Atlas of India' (*National Remote Sensing Centre, Government of India*, 2019) <https://dolr.gov.in/en/documents/wasteland-atlas-of-india> accessed 19 September 2024

## Policy brief

Warnecke-Berger H, Burchardt H and Ouaissa R, 'Natural Resources, Raw Materials, and Extractivism: The Dark Side of Sustainability' (*Extractivism.de*, 2022)

## Reports

Bhushan C, Singh SK, Sambyal SS and Agrawal KK, 'EIA Guidelines Wind Power Sector' (*Centre for Science and Environment*, 2013) <https://shaktifoundation.in/wp-content/uploads/2017/10/EIA-Guidelines-Wind-Power_1.pdf> accessed 19 September 2024

Global Witness Land and Environmental Defenders Campaign, 'Standing Firm: The Land and Environmental Defenders on the Frontlines of the Climate Crisis' (September2023)<https://www.globalwitness.org/en/campaigns/environmental-activists/land-and-environmental-defenders-annual-report-archive/> accessed 19 September 2024

Ministry of Statistics and Programme Implementation, 'Energy Statistics India 2023' (*Government of India*, 2023) <https://www.mospi.gov.in/sites/default/files/publication_reports/Energy_Statistics_2023/Energy%20Statistics%20India%202023_07022024.pdf> accessed 20 September 2024

Pratap A, Pillai P and Muthu A, 'Powering Ahead: An Assessment of the Socio-Economic and Environmental Impacts of Large-Scale Renewables Energy Projects and an Examination of the Existing Regulatory Context' (*Asar Social Impact Advisors Pvt. Ltd.*, 2019)

Vasudha Foundation, 'Analysis of Greenhouse Gas Emissions from 2005 to 2018' (*GHG Platform India*, 2022) <https://www.ghgplatform-india.org/wp-content/uploads/2022/09/GHGPI_Trend-Analysis_2005-to-2018_India_Sep22.pdf> accessed 19 September 2024

## Thesis

Rivi Bruna N, 'Extractivism, Rural Livelihoods and Accumulation in a "Climate-Smart" World: The Rise of Green Extractivism' (PhD thesis, Erasmus University Rotterdam 2021)

## Working papers

Anderson M, 'Access to Justice and Legal Process: Making Legal Institutions Responsive to Poor People in LDCs' (2003) *Institute of Development Studies, Working Paper 178/2003* <https://gsdrc.org/document-library/access-to-justice-and-legal-process-making-legal-institutions-responsive-to-poor-people-in-ldcs/> accessed 19 September 2024

Rajamani L, 'Rights Based Climate Litigation in the Indian Courts: Potential, Prospects & Potential Problems' (2013) *Centre for Policy Research, Climate Initiative, Working Paper 2013/1* <https://ssrn.com/abstract=2464927> accessed 20 September 2024

## Other

'About the Ministry: Ministry of New and Renewable Energy, Government of India' (*mnre.gov.in*) <https://mnre.gov.in/the-ministry/what-does-the-ministry-do/>

'Guidelines for Development of Onshore Wind Power Projects' (*Ministry of New and Renewable Energy, Government of India*, 2016) F. No. 66/183/2016-WE

Chapter 3

# Addressing health crises through courts? Understanding inequality in Latin America's climate litigation

*Thalia Viveros Uehara*

## Introduction

Climate change has increased the incidence of diseases – like malaria, dengue fever, and Chagas disease – and already caused hundreds of thousands of deaths.[1] While everyone can be affected by these alarming impacts, not all population groups are *equally* vulnerable.[2] Those who, in addition to being exposed to changing climatic patterns, lack access to services and infrastructure for preventing, treating, and addressing the resulting effects bear the brunt of the adverse health consequences of climate change.[3] This heightened vulnerability is particularly evident among populations experiencing poverty and social exclusion.[4] The urgent coupling of such pressing issues – the severity of climate change and precarious opportunities for healthcare – compounds climate change into health crises.

The implications of such heightened vulnerability for climate lawsuits have garnered attention in climate litigation scholarship. Some emphasise the sharp global disparities in vulnerability, showing a clear divide in litigation grounds and goals between the Global North and South.[5] Others explore how power relations, institutions, and broader structures of exclusion mediate the localised effects of climate change in the Global South and their manifestation in climate litigation.[6] Despite progress towards an increasingly nuanced understanding of the socio-ecological relationships underlying climate vulnerability,[7] climate litigation scholarship lacks answers to critical questions about *how* and *why* these relationships surface in litigation and, crucially, their implications for the process. Addressing this gap, this chapter explores *how* complex forms of health vulnerability emerge and are addressed through climate litigation, and *why* courts' approaches toward responding to climate-induced health crises are comprehensive or not. It expands in two directions that complement existing climate litigation scholarship. First, it transcends a doctrinal approach by analysing how socio-political factors, as they are manifested in the profiles, legal opportunity structures, and resources of both claimants and judges, influence the course and outcomes of litigation.[8] Second, it places emphasis on the right to health as a crucial lens through which to understand more granularly the social dimension of climate-related health vulnerability.[9] This scrutiny leverages epistemological insights from scholarship on social rights litigation in Latin America.[10] In particular, Gloppen's analytical framework is used

DOI: 10.4324/9781003470632-5

to elucidate how the 'input' and 'output' dynamics of the litigation process relate to broader socio-political contexts and influence the outcomes of lawsuits.[11] Input dynamics occur during the formation of claims, influencing the likelihood of rights claims reaching courts and involving factors like the profile of claimants and their legal representatives, legal opportunities structures, and resources.[12] Discerning *who* litigates or *whose realities are represented* is relevant as it reflects underlying power relations between legal professionals and the claimant affected communities they represent.[13] Environmental and social justice scholarship increasingly scrutinises these interactions, highlighting how practitioners and NGOs involved in litigation face the risk of excluding the knowledge, experiences, and needs of frontline and marginalised claimants.[14]

Output dynamics take place at the adjudication stage, affecting how judges handle health rights claims.[15] These dynamics comprise the courts' opportunity structures, resources, and political contexts.[16] Studies on Latin American judiciaries have illuminated how judicial independence and authority impact the adjudication of social rights.[17]

## Methodology and structure

The inquiry into how socio-political contexts are expressed through the 'input' and 'output' dynamics of the litigation process, and how these dynamics influence the outcomes of lawsuits, requires a method capable of discerning 'real-world' context–agent interactions preceding the construction of texts.[18] Therefore, this chapter applies a contextual analysis to case law and draws on interviews with claimants' legal representatives and judges to explore the socio-political *rationale* influencing their behaviour.[19] It examines five constitutional climate lawsuits across Chile, Colombia, Ecuador, and Mexico. These case studies were selected because they (1) leverage the available constitutional proceeding, (2) invoke the right to health, and (3) have been adjudicated successfully (in favour of claimants seeking to advance climate action). Further selection criteria relate to these cases' socio-legal settings within a 'most similar' and 'most different' systems comparative design.[20] That is, the countries where the lawsuits were filed share common challenges: They all grapple with social justice concerns leading to uneven vulnerability to climate change across different population segments and exhibit traits of the so-called new Latin American constitutionalism (NLAC).[21] At the same time, these countries exhibit differences in their constitutional justice systems, particularly concerning their proclivity toward enforcing social rights. In particular, Colombia and Ecuador have made strides in judicialising health rights,[22] while constitutional adjudication in Chile and Mexico has taken a more conservative approach to addressing health challenges experienced by socially excluded individuals.[23]

Semi-structured and informal interviews for this study were conducted with claimants' legal representatives, judges, and experts across the five case studies. The semi-structured interviews followed a rubric of questions (**Table 3.1**) based on Gloppen's analytical framework, while the informal interviews explored the broader socio-political contexts and opportunity structures influencing how climate

*Table 3.1* Interview schedule

| | *Claimants' legal representatives* | *Judges* | *Experts* |
|---|---|---|---|
| 1. Experience on research topic | How were you involved in [case name and number]? Could you please share what brought you there? | How were you involved in [case name and number]? Could you please share what brought you there? | In which capacity have you followed the [case name and number]? Could you please share what brought you there? |
| 2. Profiles (knowledge, references, possibilities, and constraints) | Which social challenges do you experience? Are poverty and access to healthcare issues that concern you directly?<br>Do you self-describe as a population group living in vulnerable conditions? Which one? Why?<br>How have such circumstances played into the case?<br>Were you assisted by for-profit lawyers, Global North or South non-profit organisations? How?<br>Are you related with other civil society actors/social movements fighting against climate change? How? | Could you please share your professional background? How does it relate to climate change?<br>The intersections between human rights and climate change law began materialising just recently; how does this knowledge permeate into the court's work?<br>How does the court inform itself on climate change, its relationship with health and poverty generally? What references does it use to inform its work?<br>In your view, how does law address the relationship between climate change and health? How does human rights law address this link particularly?<br>Are human rights and climate change law concerned with poverty? If so, how?<br>What are the opportunities and limits at the legal, institutional, and broader national levels that the judiciaries confront to address the connection between climate change, health, and poverty? | Could you please share your professional background? How does it relate to climate litigation?<br>The intersections between human rights and climate change law began materialising just recently; how does this knowledge permeate into the case?<br>How did the plaintiffs and court inform themselves on climate change, its relationship with health and poverty generally? What references did they use to inform their claims and judgment?<br>In your view, how does the case address the relationship between climate change and health? How does human rights law address this link particularly?<br>Is the case concerned with poverty? If so, how?<br>What are the opportunities and limits at the legal, institutional, and broader national levels that the plaintiffs and judiciaries confront to address the connection between climate change, health, and poverty? |

(*Continued*)

*Table 3.1* (Continued)

| | *Claimants' legal representatives* | *Judges* | *Experts* |
|---|---|---|---|
| 3. Opportunity structures | Why did you choose this type of legal action over other strategies?<br>Was this judicial pathway accessible for you in terms of procedural requirements? How?<br>Was the court physically accessible?<br>Is this type of legal action the best suited to address the linkage between climate change, health, and poverty? Why? If not, which action would it be? | Why was this type of legal action better suited over other strategies?<br>Is this type of legal action the best suited to address the linkage between climate change, health, and poverty? Why? If not, which action would it be?<br>Was this judicial pathway accessible for claimants in terms of procedural requirements? How? | Why was this type of legal action better suited over other strategies?<br>Is this type of legal action the best suited to address the linkage between climate change, health, and poverty? Why? If not, which action would it be?<br>Was this judicial pathway accessible for claimants in terms of procedural requirements? How? |
| 4. Accessibility and resources | What type of economic, knowledge, and organisational resources did you need to file the claim? How did you get these resources?<br>What resources do you wish you had for the case? Why? | Is the court physically and economically accessible for population groups living in poverty?<br>What are the resources (economic, human, material) you count with to focus on the study of the case?<br>What are the resources you count with (and also that you wish you counted with) for analysing the existing and emergent health concerns of vulnerable populations in relation to climate change? | Is the court physically and economically accessible for population groups living in poverty?<br>What are the resources (economic, human, material) that plaintiffs and judges count with to focus on the study of the case?<br>What are the resources both actors count with (and also wish they counted with) for analysing the existing and emergent health concerns of vulnerable populations in relation to climate change? |

*(Continued)*

*Table 3.1* (Continued)

| | *Claimants' legal representatives* | *Judges* | *Experts* |
|---|---|---|---|
| 5. Motives, objectives, and arguments | What motivated you to file the claim?<br>What did you seek through the lawsuit?<br>How did health concerns factor into your motivation and objectives?<br>How do you connect climate change with such health concerns?<br>Did you seek access to healthy environmental conditions and/or access to healthcare services?<br>How are such health concerns? Are they collective or personal, tangible or projected? | How did you frame the health–climate change nexus in the case? Why? (Did you address it as a personal or collective issue?)<br>What motivated you to frame it in such a sense?<br>Would you consider that such a frame could be argued differently, in a way that better addresses the linkage between climate change, health, and poverty?<br>What should be the objective of rights-based climate lawsuits that rely on the right to health? | How does the case frame the health–climate change nexus? Why? (Was it addressed as a personal or collective issue?)<br>What were the motives of claimants and judges to frame the nexus in such a sense?<br>Would you consider that such a frame could be argued differently, in a way that better addresses the linkage between climate change, health, and poverty?<br>What should be the objective of rights-based climate lawsuits that rely on the right to health? |
| 6. Legal bases | Why did you invoke the right to health in your argumentation?<br>Where did you ground such a claim on the right to health?<br>How did the right to health play into the course of the lawsuit?<br>How did you juxtapose the right to health with climate change law? Why? | Did you draw on the right to health and climate change law? How?<br>Where did you ground such arguments legally?<br>How do the right to health and climate change law overlap in such judicial reasoning?<br>Are there ways in which their overlap could better address the linkage between climate change, health, and poverty? | Did the case draw on the right to health and climate change law? How?<br>Where were such arguments legally grounded?<br>How do the right to health and climate change law overlap in such judicial reasoning?<br>Are there ways in which their overlap could better address the linkage between climate change, health, and poverty? |

litigation addressed health crises. Recruitment of 15 potential participants – one claimants' legal representative, one judge, and one expert for each of the five case studies – began in October 2022, involving written invitations sent via email and third-party contacts. Eleven participants agreed to take part in the semi-structured interviews, which were conducted in Spanish via Zoom over six months, from October 2022 to March 2023. **Table 3.2** displays these participants, anonymised for confidentiality purposes. Five academic experts were also informally interviewed during the same period at academic conferences.

To adhere to ethical principles for studies involving human participants, the research underwent review and approval by the University of Massachusetts Boston's IRB. The IRB confirmed that the study posed minimal risks and approved it on 25 October 2022 (IRB ID Number 3325). Informed consent was obtained from all participants prior to the interviews. Additionally, reflexivity was a cornerstone of this research, particularly given the intricate socio-political landscapes where the author was an 'outsider'. Embracing this perspective, the author took on the role of a 'facilitator' of knowledge rather than claiming expertise in any specific geographical or disciplinary context. This approach nurtured multi-perspective and interdisciplinary exchanges, giving equal weight to the experiences of those involved in the analysed cases.

The focus of the chapter is not intended to be broadly generalisable. However, by examining both the input and output dynamics of each lawsuit and projecting these onto similar and differing socio-political *milieus*, the research offers a more nuanced and textured understanding of two angles rarely explored in climate litigation scholarship: the exclusive focus on health and the comprehension of *why* courts' responses to climate-induced health crises are either comprehensive

*Table 3.2* List of participants in semi-structured interviews per case study

| *Case study* | *Participant* | *Date of interview* |
|---|---|---|
| *Mejillones Tourist Service Association et al. v Environmental Evaluation Service (SEA) of Antofagasta* (Chile) | Interviewee 1 (claimants' legal representative)<br>Interviewee 2 (claimants' legal representative)<br>Interviewee 3 (expert) | 15 November 2022<br>5 December 2022<br>6 December 2022 |
| *Future Generations v Ministry of the Environment et al.* (Colombia) | Interviewee 4 (claimants' legal representative) | 29 November 2022 |
| *Center for Social Justice v Ministry of the Environment et al.* (Colombia) | Interviewee 5 (claimants' legal representative)<br>Interviewee 6 (judge) | 18 January 2023<br>2 February 2023 |
| *Herrera Carrion et al. v Ministry of the Environment et al.* (Ecuador) | Interviewee 7 (claimants' legal representative)<br>Interviewee 8 (expert) | 17 November 2022<br>3 December 2022 |
| *Greenpeace Mexico v Ministry of Energy et al.* (Mexico) | Interviewee 9 (judge)<br>Interviewee 10 (claimants' legal representative)<br>Interviewee 11 (expert) | 11 November 2022<br>17 March 2023<br>13 March 2023 |

or lacking. Embracing such an epistemological horizon, the chapter proceeds as follows: The next section first delineates the concept of health crises in relation to vulnerability and provides an overview of the inequality contexts underlying them in the selected lawsuits. It then scrutinises the input and output dynamics of these cases through contextual analysis and insights gained from interviews. The chapter subsequently discusses the implications of the cases' socio-political contexts on the suitability of the judicial pathway to address health crises. Finally, it concludes that, while health crises do indeed emerge in both claimants' arguments and judges' rulings to varying degrees, they have only been partially addressed through this judicial avenue. Reversing this scenario appears more feasible through community lawyering, the fostering of advocacy networks, progressive legal traditions, and independent judges, who consider claimants' social contexts.

## Health crises in Latin America's climate litigation

Health vulnerability to climate change spans across two equally critical dimensions: ecological and social. The ecological dimension pertains to environmental determinants of health, with the global temperature increase driving climatic events that adversely impact health. The social dimension involves the lack of infrastructure and opportunities necessary to counter such impacts, including disparities in access to quality healthcare.[24] This chapter identifies the intertwining of both dimensions in Chile, Colombia, Ecuador, and Mexico as constitutive of health crises. Firstly, in the four countries, present and projected health consequences correlate with shifting climatic patterns.[25] In Chile, warmer climates have been linked to the spread of vector-borne diseases, such as Chagas and dengue.[26] The same is true in equatorial regions, like Colombia and Ecuador, due to El Niño and La Niña climatic phenomena.[27] Climate change has been linked to mental health issues in Mexico, with longitudinal data projecting a 2.1% increase in suicide rates in some Mexican municipalities, attributed to heat-induced stress.[28]

Secondly, social inequalities play a pernicious role in amplifying current and anticipated health consequences of climate change.[29] Although Chile, Colombia, Ecuador, and Mexico have experienced improvements in healthcare coverage over the past decades,[30] persistent disparities in income, education, and rural–urban factors continue to affect the quality and accessibility of healthcare.[31] The Chilean health system arguably displays a pro-rich bias in the utilisation of public services.[32] In Colombia, Indigenous and Afro-descendant children are at a higher risk of stunting and wasting due to considerable disparities in care access.[33] Similar patterns are evident in regions of Ecuador, such as the Amazon, central Andean highlands, and north-central coastal areas, which are predominantly inhabited by Indigenous, Afro-Ecuadorian, and Montubio populations.[34] In Mexico, residents of low-income neighbourhoods and informal settlements, often situated in areas prone to recurrent flooding,[35] typically lack access to healthcare resources for risk reduction, exacerbating their vulnerability to climate change impacts.[36]

Specifically, the social dimension of health crises, which is closely linked to poverty and social exclusion, reflects the experiences of populations at the lowest tier of the inequality ladder. This inequality is a well-known challenge across Latin America.[37] In response, many countries of the region underwent significant constitutional reconfigurations during the 1980s and the 1990s, collectively known as the NLAC.[38] Crucially, the NLAC has empowered the judiciary to drive social change through two main avenues. Firstly, it enabled courts to interpret fundamental rights through the international human rights framework.[39] Secondly, it introduced constitutional protections that consist of swift judicial procedures, allowing marginalised groups to directly assert their rights in national courts.[40] For example, Chile's 1980 Constitution established the *recurso de protección* (protection action) under Article 20.[41] Similarly, Colombia's 1991 Constitution introduced the *tutela* action in Article 86,[42] Ecuador's 2008 Constitution enshrines the protection action in Article 88,[43] while Mexico's 1917 Constitution includes the *amparo*, which underwent significant reforms in 2011 and 2013 to expand its scope and streamline the process.[44] All these mechanisms provide valuable means of accessing justice across the four countries. They differ, however, in their specific procedural requirements, standing criteria, and scope of redress, as summarised in **Table 3.3**.

Given the avenues for social change through the courts opened by the NLAC, the widespread use of constitutional protection actions in the surge of climate change lawsuits across the four countries is unsurprising.[45] As illustrated in **Figure 3.1**, as of October 2023, Mexico has the highest number of constitutional climate lawsuits, followed by Colombia, Chile, and Ecuador. Within this *corpus* of cases, this chapter selects one case each from Chile, Ecuador, and Mexico, and two cases from Colombia, based on the criteria outlined in the previous section. The relevant information of each of these selected case studies is presented in **Table 3.4**.

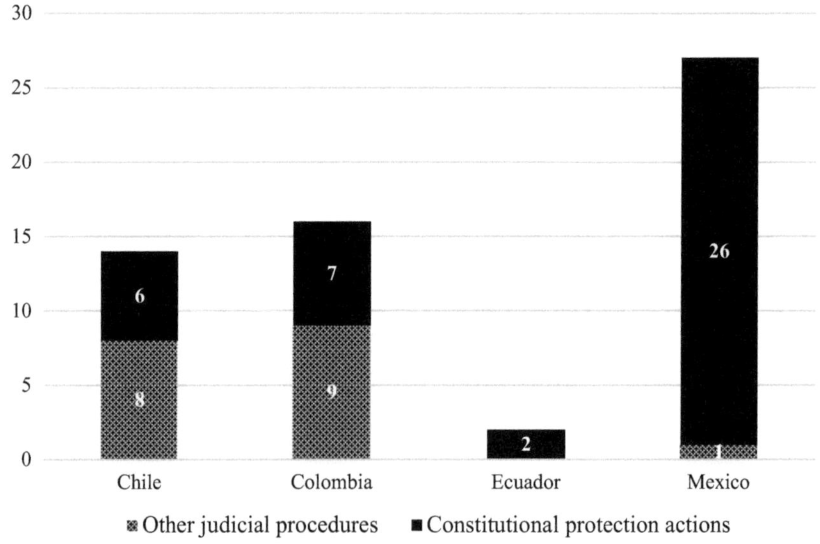


*Figure 3.1* Number of constitutional protection actions among the total number of climate cases filed in Chile, Colombia, Ecuador, and Mexico as of October 2023.

*Source:*[46]

*Table 3.3* Overview of constitutional protection actions in Chile, Colombia, Ecuador, and Mexico

| *Country* | *Protection action* | *Constitutional provision* | *Relevant standing and procedural requirements* | *Scope of redress measures* |
|---|---|---|---|---|
| Chile | *Recurso de protección* | Article 20 of the 1980 Constitution | Petitioner must be an affected party; can be filed by the person or someone on their behalf; must specify the legal rights or guarantees infringed | Declaration of rights, prevention and/or cessation of harmful actions |
| Colombia | *Acción de tutela* | Article 86 of the 1991 Constitution | Petitioner must be an affected party; immediate protection required; can be filed directly or through a representative; applicable when no other means of judicial defence available or as a temporary measure | Protection of fundamental rights, restoration of the violated right, and adoption of necessary reparation measures |
| Ecuador | *Acción de protección* | Article 88 of the 2008 Constitution | Petitioner must be a person, group, or community whose rights have been violated or are at risk; must be filed within 30 days from the violation; can be presented to any jurisdictional authority | Declaration of rights, suspension of harmful actions, restoration of the violated right, and adoption of necessary reparation measures |
| Mexico | *Juicio de Amparo* | Articles 103 and 107 of the 1917 Constitution | Petitioner must be an aggrieved party; can be filed against acts of authority that violate individual guarantees; must be filed within 15 days from notification of the act; must exhaust prior remedies | Declaration of rights, prevention and/or cessation of harmful acts or omissions, restoration of the situation (whenever possible) |

*Table 3.4* Overview of case studies

| *Country* | *Case* | *Summary* | *Adjudicating court* | *Type of action* | *Area of law* |
|---|---|---|---|---|---|
| Chile | *Mejillones Tourist Service Association et al. v Environmental Evaluation Service (SEA) of Antofagasta*[47] | In September 2021, the Mejillones Tourist Services Association and other organisations challenged the Antofagasta Environmental Assessment Service's rejection of climate change variables in the revision of the environmental assessment resolution of a thermoelectric power plant. The court of appeals rejected the claim on procedural grounds, but the Chilean Supreme Court overruled it on 19 April 2022. The ruling orders the inclusion of climate change variables in the review process of the environmental authorisation. | Supreme Court of Justice | *Protección* action | Constitutional |
| Colombia | *Future Generations v Ministry of the Environment et al.*[48] | In January 2018, a group of children and youth sued several government agencies for their failure to reduce deforestation in the Colombian Amazon. A lower court ruled against the youth claimants. However, in April 2018, the Supreme Court reversed the lower court's decision and ordered the government to formulate and implement action plans to address deforestation in the Amazon. | Supreme Court of Justice | *Tutela* action | Constitutional |

(*Continued*)

*Table 3.4* (Continued)

| *Country* | *Case* | *Summary* | *Adjudicating court* | *Type of action* | *Area of law* |
|---|---|---|---|---|---|
| Colombia | *Centre for Social Justice v Ministry of the Environment et al.*[49] | In January 2015, Indigenous and Afro-descendent communities sued governmental authorities for failing to prevent the pollution of the Atrato River. In October 2015, the Constitutional Court reversed the lower court's decision, which denied the claimants' petition. The higher court recognised the Atrato River as a subject of rights and ordered the government to decontaminate the river and eradicate illegal mining. | Constitutional Court | *Tutela* action | Constitutional |
| Ecuador | *Herrera Carrion et al. v Ministry of the Environment et al.*[50] | In February 2020, a group of girls filed a constitutional injunction against the government of Ecuador for authorising gas flaring, which causes severe impacts on the environment and people's health. In July 2021, the Court of Justice of the Sucumbíos Province reversed the court's dismissal of the case at first instance and mandated the government to update the plan for the gradual and progressive elimination of the gas flares. | Court of Justice of the Sucumbíos Province | *Protección* action | Constitutional |
| Mexico | *Greenpeace Mexico v Ministry of Energy et al.*[51] | In May 2020, Greenpeace Mexico filed a lawsuit against the Mexican government, challenging the constitutionality of two electricity-sector policies that would limit renewable energies. In November 2020, the court ruled in favour of the claimants. | Second District Court | *Amparo* | Constitutional |

### *Overview of the inequality evident from the cases*

Health crises arise in different ways in the claimants' legal arguments and the corresponding judicial decisions, mirroring the inequality of the contexts in which litigation unfolds. In some cases, the claimants' legal arguments encompassed solely ecological concerns, while in others, they navigate both the social and ecological challenges that constitute health crises. *Mejillones Tourist Service Association et al.* (Chile) and *Greenpeace Mexico* (Mexico) exemplify the former group of cases. *Centre for Social Justice* (Colombia), *Herrera Carrion et al.* (Ecuador), and *Future Generations* (Colombia) exemplify the latter.

In 2021, a group of residents from the Mejillones commune, situated over 1,400 km north of the Chilean capital, Santiago, filed a constitutional protection action against the Environmental Service of the Antofagasta Region. They challenged the approval of the environmental assessment for the *Angamos* power plant, arguing that the emissions generated would contribute to climate change, consequently increasing health risks for the commune due to the projection of more frequent heatwaves.[52] The claimants demanded that the defendant re-evaluate the power plant's environmental assessment, taking into account its impacts on broader environmental variables, such as atmospheric impacts, pH, temperature, and sediment levels.[53]

Further north on the American continent, in 2020, Greenpeace Mexico filed an *amparo* against Mexico's legislative and executive branches for enacting an agreement on the national electric system that favoured fossil fuels.[54] Greenpeace contended that the climate change–inducing and polluting emissions resulting from the carbon-based energy production encouraged by the disputed agreement were linked to health risks, such as respiratory and cardiovascular diseases.[55] Consequently, the organisation sought to have the agreement declared void.[56]

The Chilean Supreme Court and a district judge in Mexico upheld the remedies sought by the claimants. The former directed the Environmental Service of the Antofagasta Region to consider additional environmental impacts in the assessment of the *Angamos* power plant,[57] while the latter invalidated Mexico's executive agreement that encouraged fossil fuel–based energy production.[58] By reducing emissions that contribute to climate change and thereby curbing global temperature rises, the outcomes of litigation are anticipated to broadly improve health. In essence, these measures should prevent further warming for all, benefitting both litigants and non-litigants, regardless of their vulnerability. However, for historically marginalised groups in Chile and Mexico, who face significant barriers to healthcare access, these benefits are likely to provide only partial relief. Focusing solely on the ecological dimension of health vulnerability, the measures arising from this legal argumentation and reasoning do not establish the necessary social infrastructure to treat ongoing health conditions arising from or exacerbated by climate change.

The *Centre for Social Justice* (Colombia), *Herrera Carrion et al.* (Ecuador), and *Future Generations* (Colombia) navigate *both* the social and ecological challenges that constitute health crises. In January 2015, Paimadó's community leader denounced the severe health consequences of new and unknown diseases affecting children and women in the Chocó department of Colombia.[59] He was among the claimants of a *tutela* action filed by ethnic communities in the Chocó department against various Colombian government entities for failing to prevent Atrato River pollution in the face of changing climate conditions (*Centre for Social Justice*).[60] A few years later, Carlos and Rosa, pseudonyms for two children hailing from the Bolívar and Cauca departments in Colombia, recounted their struggles with atopic dermatitis and fever exacerbated by rising temperatures, which significantly impacted their daily lives.[61] These children, along with other young activists, took the Colombian government to the Supreme Court in 2018, accusing several of its agencies of not sufficiently addressing deforestation in the Amazon rainforest (*Future Generations*).[62]

Not far away, just over 800 km south of Colombia's capital city of Bogotá, in February 2020, Sofia (a pseudonym), an 8-year-old from the province of Orellana in Ecuador, joined forces with eight other girls of similar age to file a constitutional protection action against multiple Ecuadorian government ministries, including the Ministry of the Environment.[63] The case, known as *Herrera Carrion et al.*, was presented before the Cantonal Judge of Lago Agrio in the Ecuadorian oil-rich province of Sucumbíos. Sofia's primary objective was to remove gas flares from her community, as she lived in constant fear of developing cancer, much like her mother had.[64]

These three lawsuits depict how climate change and health concerns weave into on-the-ground social realities. The claimants navigate both the social and ecological dimensions that constitute health crises to varying extents, evident in their motives and the remedies they seek. For example, *integral* to their concerns regarding climate change, Colombia's ethnic communities decried that the emergence of new diseases aggravated their *already*-precarious socio-economic situation due to the absence of healthcare access.[65] Consequently, they requested that the Constitutional Court issue 'structural redress measures to address the grave health, socio-environmental, ecological, and humanitarian crises' they are experiencing in the Atrato River Basin, highlighting the lack of an adequate healthcare system as a major contributing factor to these crises.[66] Similarly, the girls in the Ecuadorian case highlighted the financial and logistical barriers faced by those already sick, who must travel long distances to Quito for medical care, only to find they lack the resources for medicines and lodging.[67] Given this social context, they sought access to healthcare for diseases related to air pollution caused by the climate change–inducing gas flares, which they lacked.[68] In contrast to both the *Centre for Social Justice* and *Herrera Carrion et al.*, the claimants in *Future Generations* did not include any requests for medical treatment of their atopic dermatitis and fever, which they claimed to be exacerbated by climate change. Instead, they solely demanded that the Colombian government create an action plan to reduce deforestation in the Amazon.[69]

In adjudicating these three lawsuits, the courts recognised that the claimants' right to health, among others, had been violated and thus ordered redress measures along the dimensions of vulnerability that the claimants highlighted[70] – albeit not in the breadth claimants sought. In *Centre for Social Justice* and *Herrera Carrion et al.*, the Constitutional Court of Colombia and the Court of Justice of Sucumbíos Province in Ecuador mandated an end to illegal mining and gas flaring, respectively.[71] Furthermore, these courts required the Ministries of Health in each country to investigate the adverse health effects denounced by the claimants.[72] However, such measures, while considering the claimants' health concerns, fell short of meeting their requests for further redress in relation to their lack of healthcare. In *Future Generations*, the Supreme Court of Colombia ordered the government, in collaboration with relevant stakeholders, to establish an intergenerational pact aimed at reducing deforestation, thereby contributing to the prevention of the increase in global temperature[73] – which claimants highlighted as the primary driver of their health conditions.

Discerning whether courts can serve as a venue for the most affected populations to fully realise their right to health depends on having a clearer understanding of *why* climate cases have not comprehensively addressed the social dimensions of health vulnerability, even when claimants sought such remedies. The following section offers a contextual analysis of each case, incorporating the experience from involved parties.

## The input dynamics: the claimants and formation of climate-related health claims

### *Claimants' profiles and opportunity structures*

In the cases reviewed, the involvement of both international and domestic civil society organisations with professional expertise, acting either as representatives or as claimants themselves, was a common feature – as widely noted already in climate litigation literature.[74] These organisations' areas of work and lawyering methodologies appeared to significantly influence the legal framing of claimants' health vulnerabilities. Specifically, top-down cause lawyering tended to prioritise ecological concerns within the legal strategy. In contrast, bottom-up participatory lawyering not only considered ecological challenges but also demonstrated deep engagement with the social realities of the communities they represented, thereby incorporating these elements into the legal strategy.

*Greenpeace Mexico* and Colombia's *Future Generations* depict a top-down lawyering methodology. In these instances, professionals from international and domestic organisations working from the countries' capitals, respectively, responded to environmentally detrimental junctural circumstances by engineering legal arguments that did not fully factor in local social concerns and realities. These legal experts strategically used the right to health as a tool to bolster legal claims, employing science-based arguments to connect health to climate change within the framework of global environmental movements. For example, in *Future*

*Generations*, while children and youth – a demographic afforded special protection – were the plaintiffs, the legal strategy overlooked whether they had access to medical care to overcome the health conditions they claimed to be experiencing.[75] Instead, it aligned with a transnational green advocacy narrative for the rights of future generations,[76] viewing health as primarily influenced by global climate change and neglecting the more localised social determinants that are equally constitutive of health crises.

In the *Centre for Social Justice* and *Herrera Carrion*, the claimants' legal representatives devised strategies that integrated both ecological and social dimensions of the claimants' vulnerabilities, notably including the lack of healthcare access.[77] This approach was rooted in the institutional ethos of the organisations involved, for which collaboration with the communities – involving deep engagement with local cultures and concerns – was essential.[78] Guided by this commitment, claimants' lawyers sought to balance the claimants' actual experiences and the agenda of the organisations.[79] They facilitated a co-creation process that considered the real-life impacts on the communities within the framework of available legal opportunities.[80] This approach led to the development of arguments that reflected the claimants' prolonged suffering due to the dual pressures of changing climatic conditions and the state's neglect of healthcare services, while also assessing the likelihood of legal success in court.

In the four countries studied, constitutional proceedings aim, at least on paper,[81] for more expedited processing and openness to all affected citizens compared to popular actions in Colombia[82] and Mexico[83] or Chile's specialised environmental tribunals,[84] which entail longer durations and stricter legal standing rules. However, all interviewed claimants noted that bringing a constitutional protection action was still a 'bumpy road' in practice,[85] especially as defendants involved politically and technically powerful actors, such as national governments and transnational corporations. This required claimants to articulate their arguments in a professionalised vernacular and gather substantial evidence. Consequently, the involvement of civil society organisations was therefore pivotal in facilitating this pathway to justice.

### *Resources and claims formation*

The five cases reflect the mechanics of the NLAC, particularly in how claimants based their legal arguments on international human rights standards. This strategic use of international norms was facilitated by the countries' constitutional provisions that allow national courts to directly interpret these norms into cases through the block of constitutionality.[86] Pertaining to the right to health, the invoked standards included the International Covenant on Economic, Social, and Cultural Rights (ICESCR); General Comment 14 on the right to health; Article 10 of the Protocol of San Salvador; and inter-American standards such as the Advisory Opinion 23/2017 on the environment and human rights.[87] While these norms offer a comprehensive framework encompassing both the ecological and social dimensions of health vulnerability,[88] claimants tailored the use of the right to health based on the legal opportunities available within each country's legal system. For example, in Chile and Mexico, comprehensive redress along various social and ecological aspects is less common due to the formalistic traditions of these countries' constitutional justice systems.[89] In contrast, in Colombia, the *tutela* action enables a broader range of redress measures, including integral reparations.[90]

Besides utilising the human rights framework as a legal tool, claimants also leveraged it as a social language.[91] Particularly, by framing their concerns in terms of the right to health, claimants from the *Centre for Social Justice*, *Herrera Carrion et al.*, and the *Mejillones Tourist Service Association* were able to align with broader national networks of actors. These networks proved to be valuable resources for advancing a more comprehensive understanding of health crises in courts through the submission of *amicus curiae* briefs. The *Centre for Social Justice* benefited from 17 such briefs from academic institutions and advocacy organisations.[92] Additionally, trust and community resilience emerged within these networks, which interviewed claimants' legal representatives and an expert deemed essential for standing up against powerful defendants.[93]

In summary, the analysis of the five cases elucidates a link between the claimants' profiles, legal opportunity structures, and resources, and how they articulate their health vulnerabilities in court. Legal expertise is essential to embark on the judicial pathway against powerful opponents, making the involvement of professional civil society organisations crucial. The methodologies these organisations adopt influence their advocacy for health rights and the pursued remedies. Notably, participatory lawyering approaches were instrumental in bringing the social dimension of health vulnerability to the attention of the courts, as was the submission of *amicus* briefs by the networks these claimants developed.

## The output dynamics: adjudicating health in climate litigation

### *Judges' opportunity structures and resources*

Three cases were adjudicated by the high courts of Chile and Colombia – the Supreme Court of Justice in both countries, along with Colombia's Constitutional Court – while two cases were decided by lower courts, specifically Ecuador's Court of Justice in Sucumbíos Province and Mexico's Second District Court. Notably, all cases except the one in Mexico underwent multiple appellate stages. This progression to advanced stages of judicial review demonstrates that the cases were ultimately adjudicated by specialised courts endowed with extensive technical expertise. Contrary to appearing as an anomaly, Mexico's Second District Court on Administrative Matters, although a first-instance court, has been specifically established as a specialised forum since 2013. It is tasked with adjudicating complex issues related to telecommunications and energy policy, including regulatory compliance, licensing, and competition.[94]

Interviewed judges and experts across the five case studies highlighted the critical role of technical expertise in interpreting the nexus between international human rights standards and climate change law.[95] Particularly, for them, scientific evidence, notably from the Intergovernmental Panel on Climate Change (IPCC), acts as a consistent bridge between both fields of law.[96] This evidence reached the courts primarily through two pathways. First, it was introduced via document submissions by judges' clerks, by claimants, and through *amicus curiae* briefs from supporting organisations. In *Centre for Social Justice* and *Herrera Carrion et al.*, whose judgments most comprehensively addressed health crises, the courts benefited from multiple *amicus curiae* submissions that underscored concerns about climate change and the precarious healthcare conditions affecting the claimants. Second, uniquely in the case of Colombia's Constitutional Court, evidence was gathered through direct on-site evaluations of affected areas. This court's decision to conduct an on-site inspection in the Atrato River basin was pivotal. It provided the justices with first-hand knowledge of the living conditions and potential pollution impacts on the fundamental rights of these communities, thereby laying before the justices the intertwined ecological and social issues at stake.[97]

Another determinant for the cases' outcomes was the countries' legal culture. Actors involved in the litigation processes of *Mejillones Tourist Service Association* and *Greenpeace Mexico* perceived the existence of a 'formalistic legal tradition' in the Chilean and Mexican constitutional justice systems, which prevented judicial reasoning from extending beyond well-established national jurisprudence.[98] This reluctance to embrace legal innovations stands in contrast to the well-known openness of Colombian constitutional justice and the progressive impetus embedded in the Ecuadorian constitutional system, as reflected in its 2008 Constitution.[99] However, even in the cases from these latter countries (*Centre for Social Justice* and *Herrera Carrion and et al.*), whose judgments most comprehensively addressed health crises (as earlier described), redress measures did not extend far enough to mandate the state to fulfil its duty of ensuring quality and resilient healthcare, even at the most basic level. An exploration of the political contexts of these cases, discussed next, offers some explanations for this observation.

### Judicial independence and political contexts

The adjudication of *Centre for Social Justice* and *Herrera Carrion et al.* faced challenges that tested the autonomy and authority of the courts, ultimately appearing to impact the judicial outcomes. In Ecuador, Interviewees 7 and 8 reported allegations that federal agency representatives subtly pressured the judges. They noted that these officials warned courts that rulings unfavourable to the government could deplete the country's funds for essential social services, by either driving away wealthy oil corporations or mandating costly compensation for affected regions. To counter this, both interviewees emphasised the importance of the judges' ties to the impacted regions: In their view, judges who lived in the affected areas were perceived as more empathetic to the severe health issues faced by the petitioners and, therefore, more likely to rule in favour of their protection.

In Colombia, interviewees perceived that presidential interference was not a restraint in the work of the Supreme and Constitutional Courts.[100] Despite this, the well-known proactive and consequential stance of the latter has prompted various interest groups to seek reforms that would reduce its authority.[101] Within this context, the interviewed judge asserted that the Constitutional Court has been cautious, ensuring that its decisions do not overstep the jurisdiction of other government branches and are unanimously adopted to bolster legitimacy.[102] This consideration is visible in the remedies prescribed in *Centre for Social Justice*. The court's orders were deliberately broad, granting the executive branch considerable discretion in their implementation and thus respecting the separation of powers. Instead of mandating specific and costly measures, like the provision of healthcare, the court advocated for 'progressivity' and financial planning in the remedies.[103] These included health assessments of affected communities and the establishment of baseline indicators,[104] demonstrating a balanced approach to addressing the concerns.

In Chile and Mexico, interview data did not reveal interference from the countries' executive branches in the work of the adjudicating courts. The rulings in the *Mejillones Tourist Service Association* and *Greenpeace Mexico* attest to these courts' autonomy as they challenged powerful actors, namely, corporate interests and state actions, respectively. As a high court in Chile and a highly specialised court in Mexico, they possess resources that potentially enable them to better navigate adverse circumstances compared to local first-instance courts. Nonetheless, for reasons of scope and length, this analysis did not investigate the experiences of lower courts, nor did it examine cases with negative outcomes. Including such cases could have offered a more insightful sample for exploring the contextual factors that hinder courts from countering the growing pro–fossil fuel stance of governments, particularly in Mexico. In this country, according to interviewees,[105] the current federal administration has not only pursued policies favouring fossil fuels but also allegedly attempted to undermine the judiciary's autonomy. This has further exacerbated the challenges the courts face in upholding environmental protection and the rule of law.

In summary, the output dynamics of adjudicating health in climate litigation across the discussed cases reveal intricate interconnections among judges' opportunity structures, available resources, and prevailing political contexts. The courts' legal expertise and access to scientific evidence were pivotal in facilitating interpretations of international human rights and climate law that were attuned to the claimants' alleged contexts. Additionally, as the pursuit of *ad hoc* remedies for health crises was perceived as requiring innovation, it was significantly influenced by each country's legal culture. However, even in more progressive traditions, such as those in Colombia and Ecuador, the possibility of issuing such comprehensive remedies was restricted, respectively, by the perceived need to preserve judicial legitimacy and interference by the executive power.

## Discussion: health crises in the hands of courts

This chapter has grappled with how the inequality contexts that underlie the ecological and social dimensions of health vulnerability manifest in climate litigation. In particular, the study reveals that although the health consequences of climate change are by no means isolated from these countries' social challenges, health crises reflect only partially in the judicial arena. Out of the five cases analysed, two – *Centre for Social Justice* and *Herrera Carrion et al.* – epitomise how frontline communities, affected by harsh climatic conditions and climate change–inducing pollution, concurrently suffer from inadequate healthcare access, thereby exacerbating their detrimental health conditions. Yet though the judgments recognise the claimants' precarious socio-economic conditions, the redress measures did not go far enough to compel the state to ensure quality and resilient healthcare at even the most basic level.

While it is unrealistic to expect uniform emphasis on social inequalities in every case, particularly in democratic societies where multiple interests coexist, such limited visibility of health crises in the courts raises important questions. A crucial one concerns the ability of climate litigation to deliver justice for those at the lowest end of the inequality spectrum. Given the *corpus juris* that the NLAC has facilitated, which even heralds new frontiers for climate constitutionalism and access to justice in Latin America,[106] the question of *why* claimants and courts have not framed or addressed these health crises in a manner that reflects the lived concerns of affected communities arises. Indeed, a deeper examination of the socio-political factors that underpin climate lawsuits, viewed through the lens of the input and output dynamics of the litigation process, suggests that this partial emergence of health crises is far from coincidental.

In concordance with environmental and social justice scholarship, as well as climate studies in Latin America,[107] this research illustrates the double-edged nature of civil society organisations' involvement in legal strategising. While essential for countering the technical and political prowess of defendants, it risks overshadowing the localised voices, knowledge, and concerns of the communities these organisations aim to represent. The comparative examination of Colombia and Ecuador versus Chile and Mexico further illuminates this point. Legal arguments collaboratively crafted with community input tend to deliver more comprehensive narratives and remedial requests to the courts. Conversely, top-down lawyering methodologies relegate the social dimension of health issues to the periphery of global green advocacy, often overlooking the nuanced socio-economic challenges faced by plaintiffs, such as limited access to healthcare.

Furthermore, the use of the right to health by claimants transcended its legal value, serving also as a social language that helped them foster networks instrumental in providing a more comprehensive understanding of health crises to the courts through *amicus curiae* briefs. Such networks also expanded the claimants' support base, which proved crucial for standing up against powerful defendants. Scholarship on rights legal mobilisation suggests that these support structures are a key factor in the transformative impact of litigation. Sandra Botero, Daniel Brinks, and Ezequiel Gonzalez-Ocantos highlight their significance in enabling the implementation of judicial decisions,[108] while, similarly, Armin von Bogdandy and René Urueña underline their role in the broader impact of judicial decisions on the ground.[109] Equally significant is the observation that pursuing legal actions within more progressive constitutional frameworks, such as those in Colombia and Ecuador, appears to expand the legal imagination of professionals crafting the legal strategy. These frameworks reveal new possibilities, enabling legal strategists to incorporate the underlying social dimensions associated with health crises into their climate litigation strategies.

This chapter's insights on the output dynamics of the litigation process have shown how the courts' legal expertise, evidence analysis methods, legal culture, and independence are equally vital for their understanding of health crises. Where judges' training enables them to dissect scientific knowledge and connect it with international human rights standards, climate change law, and the social contexts of claimants, the most comprehensive outcomes were achieved. The involvement of *amicus curiae* from various organisations and the unique practice of conducting on-site inspections by Colombia's Constitutional Court have proven valuable for enhancing judges' understanding of claimants' health concerns. Additionally, differences in legal cultures have been decisive. In Chile and Mexico, the judiciary appeared reluctant to embrace innovative interpretations that address the ecological and social dimensions of health crises. In contrast, courts in Colombia and Ecuador pursued a more comprehensive approach yet refrained from extending their efforts further to maintain legitimacy by not interfering with executive powers.

## Concluding remarks

The faith vested in the judiciaries to confront climate change through recent and expanding litigation wavers between what is desirable and what is feasible. Health, epitomising the human face of climate change, arguably justifies bridging these two cognitive horizons. If it is desirable for courts to deliver justice to individuals whose health is most compromised by the dual crises of rising global temperatures and social exclusion, this chapter has revealed that this possibility is not yet being fully realised. Addressing health crises through the judicial pathway, at least for now, remains a challenge. Building on climate litigation scholarship, which demands attention to the specific weight of social exclusion markers and costs in remedial approaches,[110] this chapter has highlighted that bridging the gap between what is desirable and what is feasible requires more than conventional legal expertise. Support from civil society organisations employing participatory lawyering seems pivotal for integrating the situated realities of frontline affected communities into legal strategies. Ideally, such cases should then be adjudicated within a framework of progressive legal tradition by judges who not only understand human rights and climate change law and can interpret scientific data but also are deeply considerate of the social contexts of the claimants. Moreover, these judges must have the structures in place to withstand political interference.

It ultimately falls upon the litigants and the courts to either maintain the status-quo partial visibility of what the climate change–health nexus encompasses or to expand their horizons to meet the challenges posed by climate change and structural exclusion. Particularly in Latin America and other climate-vulnerable regions, where the entanglement of these increasingly complex challenges continually redefines the 'new desirable', attaining climate justice through the courts requires nothing less than a reciprocal reconfiguration of what is deemed the 'new possible'.

## Notes

1 Edwin J Castellanos et al., 'Central and South America' in Hans-Otto Pörtner et al. (eds), *Climate Change 2022: Impacts, Adaptation, and Vulnerability: Contribution of Working Group II to the Sixth Assessment Report of the Intergovernmental Panel on Climate Change* (CUP 2022) 1691; Graciela O Magrin et al., 'Central and South America' in Vicente R Barros et al. (eds), *Climate Change 2014: Impacts, Adaptation, and Vulnerability: Part B: Regional Aspects: Contribution of Working Group II to the Fifth Assessment Report of the Intergovernmental Panel on Climate Change* (CUP 2014) 1535.

2 Louis J Kotzé, 'The Anthropocene, Earth System Vulnerability and Socio-Ecological Injustice in an Age of Human Rights' (2019) 10(1) *Journal of Human Rights and the Environment* 62, 68.

3 Anthony J McMichael and Elisabeth Lindgren, 'Climate Change: Present and Future Risks to Health, and Necessary Responses' (2011) 270 *Journal of Internal Medicine* 401, 410; Linda Rudolph and Solange Gould, 'Climate Change and Health Inequities: A Framework for Action' (2015) 81 *Annals of Global Health* 432, 433.

4 Luke Parry et al., 'The (in)Visible Health Risks of Climate Change' (2019) 241 *Social Science & Medicine* 112448. For a detailed discussion on vulnerability see Murcott, Tigre and Ann Samuel, Introduction, pp 1–3.

5 Jacqueline Peel and Jolene Lin, 'Transnational Climate Litigation: The Contribution of the Global South' (2019) 113(4) *American Journal of International Law* 679; Joana Setzer and Lisa Benjamin, 'Climate Litigation in the Global South: Constraints and Innovations' (2020) 9(1) *Transnational Environmental Law* 77.

6 For example, Birsha Ohdedar examines the multiscale social and ecological factors that drive climate vulnerability in India, reflecting these in climate litigation; see Birsha Ohdedar, 'Climate Adaptation, Vulnerability and Rights-Based Litigation: Broadening the Scope of Climate Litigation Using Political Ecology' (2022) 13 *Journal of Human Rights and the Environment* 137. Similarly, Tracy-Lynn Field sheds light on the spatial and temporal specificity of impacts in Africa through a climate-risk approach in the scholarly categorisation of climate litigation; see Tracy-Lynn Field, 'Towards a Risk-Thematic Approach for African Climate Litigation' in Kim Bouwer et al. (eds), *Climate Litigation and Justice in Africa* (Bristol University Press 2024) 16. Natalia Urzola explores the gendered power dynamics that mediate knowledge production in

climate litigation; see Natalia Urzola Gutiérrez, 'Gender in Climate Litigation in Latin America: Epistemic Justice Through a Feminist Lens' (2024) 16(1) *Journal of Human Rights Practice* 208.

7 See, for example, Milka Sormunen, 'Rethinking Effective Remedies to the Climate Crisis: A Vulnerability Theory Approach' (2023) 24 *Human Rights Review* 171.

8 This chapter, however, does not focus on the stages following adjudication, namely, implementation and compliance with judgements. For an analysis of compliance in climate litigation in Latin America, refer to Juan Auz, 'The Political Ecology of Climate Remedies in Latin America and the Caribbean: Comparing Compliance between National and Inter-American Litigation' (2024) 16(1) *Journal of Human Rights Practice* 184.

9 The social dimension is primarily understood as access to life-sustaining services; specific markers of structural exclusion were, for now, left out of the analysis. For a more detailed analysis of how marginalisation based on gender dynamics plays out in climate litigation, see Urzola Gutiérrez (n 6).

10 For notable examples, see Varun Gauri and Daniel M Brinks (eds), *Courting Social Justice: Judicial Enforcement of Social and Economic Rights in the Developing World* (CUP 2008); Malcolm Langford, 'Domestic Adjudication and Economic, Social and Cultural Rights: A Socio-Legal Review' (2009) 11 *SUR-Int'l J on Hum Rts* 91; Alicia E Yamin and Siri Gloppen (eds), *Litigating Health Rights: Can Courts Bring More Justice to Health?* (HUP 2011).

11 See, specifically, Siri Gloppen, 'Litigation as a Strategy to Hold Governments Accountable for Implementing the Right to Health' (2008) 10 *Health and Human Rights* 21, 25. However, the conceptualisation of this framework originates from earlier works, particularly regarding the factors that influence judges' opportunity structures and the potential of courts to amplify the voices of people in poverty, as developed, respectively, in Siri Gloppen et al. (eds), *Democratization and the Judiciary: The Accountability Function of Courts in New Democracies* (Frank Cass 2004); Roberto Gargarella et al. (eds), *Courts and Social Transformation in New Democracies: An Institutional Voice for the Poor?* (Ashgate 2006).

12 Gargarella et al. (n 11).

13 Camila Bustos, 'Movement Lawyering in the Time of the Climate Crisis' (2022) 39(1) *Pace Environmental Law Review* 1, 26; Benjamin Hoffman and Marissa Vahlsing, 'Collaborative Lawyering in Transnational Human Rights Advocacy' (2014) 21 *Clinical Law Review* 255, 264; Stephen Meili, 'Latin American Cause-Lawyering Networks' in Austin Sarat and Stuart Scheingold (eds), *Cause Lawyering and the State in a Global Era* (Oxford University Press 2001) 307, 321.

14 See, generally, Matt Baillie Smith and Katy Jenkins, 'Disconnections and Exclusions: Professionalization, Cosmopolitanism and (Global?) Civil Society' (2011) 11 *Global Networks* 160; Emilie Dupuits et al., 'Scaling Up But Losing Out? Water Commons' Dilemmas between Transnational Movements and Grassroots Struggles in Latin America' (2020) 172 *Ecological Economics* 106625. See also Murcott, Tigre and Ann Samuel, Introduction.

15 Gloppen (n 11).

16 Gloppen (n 11).

17 See, generally, Sandra Botero, Daniel Brinks and Ezequiel Gonzalez-Ocantos, 'Working in New Political Spaces: The Checkered History of Latin American Judicialization' in Daniel M Brinks, Ezequiel A Gonzalez-Ocantos and Sandra Botero (eds), *The Limits of Judicialization: From Progress to Backlash in Latin America* (CUP 2022); Daniel M Brinks and Abby Blass, *The DNA of Constitutional Justice in Latin America. Politics, Governance, and Judicial Design, Comparative Constitutional Law and Policy* (CUP 2018).

18 Malcolm Langford, 'Interdisciplinarity and Multimethod Research' in Bård A Andreassen, Hans-Otto Sano and Siobhán McInerney-Lankford (eds), *Research Methods in Human Rights: A Handbook* (Edward Elgar Publishing 2017) 183.
19 See, generally, Urszula Jaremba and Elaine Mak, 'Interviewing Judges in the Transnational Context' (2014) 2014(5) *Law and Method*; Philip Selznick, 'Law in Context' Revisited' (2003) 30(2) *Journal of Law and Society* 177. For insights on the colonial rationale of Latin American legal systems, see Beckhauser and Broetto, Chapter 1.
20 Bård A Andreassen, 'Comparative Analyses of Human Rights Performance' in Bård A Andreassen, Hans-Otto Sano and Siobhán McInerney-Lankford (eds), *Research Methods in Human Rights: A Handbook* (Edward Elgar Publishing 2017) 222, 244.
21 Castellanos et al. (n 1) 1691; Magrin et al. (n 1) 1535. For a general overview on the NLAC, see Armin von Bogdandy, 'Ius Constitutionale Commune en América Latina: Observations on Transformative Constitutionalism' in Armin von Bogdandy et al. (eds), *Transformative Constitutionalism in Latin America: The Emergence of a New Ius Commune* (OUP 2017) 33; Javier A Couso, 'The Changing Role of Law and Courts in Latin America: From an Obstacle to Social Change to a Tool of Social Equity' in Roberto Gargarella, Domingo Pilar and Roux Theunis (eds), *Courts and Social Transformation in New Democracies* (Ashgate Publishing Limited 2006) 65. For an analysis of Latin American constitutionalism in the development of climate-related normative precepts, see Délton Winter de Carvalho and Rafaela Santos Martins da Rosa, 'Climate Constitutionalism as a Foundation for Climate Litigation in Latin America' (2024) 16(1) *Journal of Human Rights Practice* 71.
22 For example, in *Osorio Palacio et al. v Colpatria EPS et al.* (2008) T-760/08, Colombia's Constitutional Court addressed 22 individual *tutelas* and mandating structural reforms in the health system. These reforms led to the 2015 Statutory Framework Law that enshrines the right to health at the core of the healthcare system. For an in-depth commentary of this and other illustrative cases, see Óscar Parra-Vera, 'The Protection of Social Rights' in Juan F Gonzalez-Bertomeu and Roberto Gargarella (eds), *The Latin American Casebook: Courts, Constitutions, and Rights* (Routledge 2016) 150; Alicia E Yamin, 'The Right to Health: The Potential and Limits of Catalysing Systemic Change through the Courts' in Conrado Hübner Mendes, Roberto Gargarella and Sebastián Guidi (eds), *The Oxford Handbook of Constitutional Law in Latin America* (OUP 2022) 767. In *Asanza Reyes et al. v Dr. Chiriboga and the Public Health Ministry of Ecuador* (2016) 074-16-SIS-CC, Ecuador's Constitutional Court ordered the provision of health services and the delivery of medications as measures of comprehensive reparation for a group of children diagnosed with a rare disease who sought protection of their right to health. For further discussion, see Pamela Aguirre Castro and Pablo Alarcón Peña, 'El estándar de la reparación integral en la jurisprudencia de la Corte Constitucional' (2018) *Foro: Revista de Derecho* 121, 138. See also the cases discussed in Beckhauser and Broetto Chapter 1.
23 Regarding the conservative culture in Chile's constitutional adjudication, see Javier Couso and Lisa Hilbink, 'From Quietism to Incipient Activism: The Institutional and Ideological Roots of Rights Adjudication in Chile' in Gretchen Helmke and Julio Rios-Figueroa (eds), *Courts in Latin America* (CUP 2011) 99; Siri Gloppen et al., *Courts and Power in Latin America and Africa* (Palgrave Macmillan 2010) 59. On Mexico's formalistic style in constitutional adjudication, see Roberto Lara Chagoyán, *El constitucionalismo mexicano en transformación: Avances y retrocesos* (Instituto de Estudios Constitucionales del Estado de Querétaro 2020) 65; Francisca Pou Giménez, 'The Constitution of Mexico' in Conrado Hübner Mendes, Roberto Gargarella and Sebastián Guidi (eds), *The Oxford Handbook of Constitutional Law in Latin America* (OUP 2022) 224.

24 McMichael and Lindgren (n 3); Rudolph and Gould (n 3).
25 Castellanos et al. (n 1) 1691, Magrin et al. (n 1) 1535.
26 Paulina Pino et al., 'Chile Confronts Its Environmental Health Future After 25 Years of Accelerated Growth' (2015) 81 *Annals of Global Health* 354, 362.
27 Castellanos et al. (n 1) 1702; Magrin et al. (n 1) 1535.
28 Marshall Burke et al., 'Higher Temperatures Increase Suicide Rates in the United States and Mexico' (2018) 8 *Nature Climate Change* 723.
29 Parry et al. (n 4). For a discussion of the health impacts of climate change for children in Bangladesh, see Kaur, Sathiabama and Vedavalli Chapter 7.
30 Pan American Health Organization and World Health Organization, *Health in the Americas. Summary: Regional Outlook and Country Profiles* (PAHO 2017) 112.
31 Castellanos et al. (n 1) 1715.
32 Pamela Bernales-Baksai, 'Tackling Segmentation to Advance Universal Health Coverage: Analysis of Policy Architectures of Health Care in Chile and Uruguay' (2020) 19 *International Journal for Equity in Health* 106, 107.
33 Lucrecia Mena-Meléndez, 'Ethnoracial Child Health Inequalities in Latin America: Multilevel Evidence from Bolivia, Colombia, Guatemala, and Peru' (2020) 12 *SSM – Population Health* 100673, 7.
34 Andrés Peralta et al., 'Developing a Deprivation Index to Study Geographical Health Inequalities in Ecuador' (2019) 53 *Revista de Saúde Pública* 97, 10.
35 Jeffrey A Hicke et al., 'North America' in Hans-Otto Pörtner et al. (eds), *Climate Change 2022: Impacts, Adaptation and Vulnerability. Contribution of Working Group II to the Sixth Assessment Report of the Intergovernmental Panel on Climate Change* (CUP 2022) 1953.
36 Paty Romero-Lankao et al., 'Scale, Urban Risk and Adaptation Capacity in Neighbourhoods of Latin American Cities' (2014) 42 *Habitat International* 224, 228.
37 Parry et al. (n 4).
38 Bogdandy (n 21) 33; Couso (n 21) 65. For an exploration of the role of constitutionalism in effecting societal change in response to socio-ecological challenges beyond Latin America, see Melanie Murcott, *Transformative Environmental Constitutionalism* (Brill Nijhoff 2022).
39 Bogdandy (n 21) 33; Couso and Hilbink (n 23) 65; for an analysis of the prominent role of domestic courts in Latin America in implementing the Escazú Agreement, see Gastón Medici-Colombo and Thays Ricarte, 'The Escazú Agreement Contribution to Environmental Justice in Latin America: An Exploratory Empirical Inquiry through the Lens of Climate Litigation' (2024) 16(1) *Journal of Human Rights Practice* 1, 11.
40 Bogdandy (n 21) 33; Couso and Hilbink (n 23) 65.
41 Domingo Lovera Parmo, 'Chile' in Conrado Hübner Mendes, Roberto Gargarella and Sebastián Guidi (eds), *The Oxford Handbook of Constitutional Law in Latin America* (OUP 2022) 94.
42 Rodrigo Uprimny Yepes and Luz María Sánchez Duque, 'Constitución de 1991, justicia constitucional y cambio democrático: un balance dos décadas después' (2012) 71 *Cahiers des Amériques latines* 33, 37.
43 Daniela Salazar, 'The Constitutional History of Ecuador: Twenty Constitutions and Counting' in Conrado Hübner Mendes, Roberto Gargarella and Sebastián Guidi (eds), *The Oxford Handbook of Constitutional Law in Latin America* (OUP 2022) 199.
44 Giménez (n 23) 223.
45 de Carvalho and da Rosa (n 21) 4.
46 According to the author's database, which compiles data from the following sources: Asociación Interamericana para la Defensa del Ambiente, 'Plataforma de Litigio Climático para América Latina y el Caribe' <https://litigioclimatico.com/es/

sobre-la-plataforma> accessed 15 June 2022; The Sabin Centre for Climate Change Law at Columbia Law School, 'US Climate Change Litigation Database' <http://climatecasechart.com/climate-change-litigation/about/> accessed 31 October 2023.

47 *Mejillones Tourist Service Association et al. v Environmental Evaluation Service (SEA) of Antofagasta* (2021) 6930–2021 and 71.628–2021, Chilean Supreme Court of Justice (Chile) (*Mejillones Tourist Service Association et al*)

48 *Future Generations v Ministry of the Environment et al.* (2018) 11001 22 03 000 2018 00319 00, Colombian Supreme Court (Colombia) (*Future Generations*).

49 *Center for Social Justice v Ministry of the Environment et al.* (2016) T-622/16, Colombian Constitutional Court (Colombia) (*Atrato River Decision T-622*).

50 *Herrera Carrion et al. v Ministry of the Environment et al.* (2021) 21201202000170, Corte Provincial de Justicia de Sucumbíos (Ecuador).

51 *Greenpeace Mexico v Ministry of Energy et al.* (2020) 104/2020, Second District Court of Mexico (Mexico) (*Greenpeace Mexico*).

52 *Mejillones Tourist Service Association et al. v Environmental Evaluation Service (SEA) of Antofagasta* (2021) 6930–2021 and 71.628–2021, Chilean Supreme Court of Justice (Chile) (*Mejillones Tourist Service Association et al*) 42.

53 *Mejillones Tourist Service Association et al. v Environmental Evaluation Service (SEA) of Antofagasta* (2021) 6930–2021 and 71.628–2021, Chilean Supreme Court of Justice (Chile) (*Mejillones Tourist Service Association et al*) 51.

54 *Greenpeace Mexico v Ministry of Energy et al.* (2020) 104/2020, Second District Court of Mexico (Mexico) (*Greenpeace Mexico*) 2.

55 *Greenpeace Mexico v Ministry of Energy et al.* (2020) 104/2020, Second District Court of Mexico (Mexico) (*Greenpeace Mexico*) 59.

56 *Greenpeace Mexico v Ministry of Energy et al.* (2020) 104/2020, Second District Court of Mexico (Mexico) (*Greenpeace Mexico*) 70.

57 *Mejillones Tourist Service Association et al. v Environmental Evaluation Service (SEA) of Antofagasta* (2021) 6930–2021 and 71.628–2021, Chilean Supreme Court of Justice (Chile) (*Mejillones Tourist Service Association et al*) 20.

58 *Greenpeace Mexico v Ministry of Energy et al.* (2020) 104/2020, Second District Court of Mexico (Mexico) (*Greenpeace Mexico*) 199.

59 *Center for Social Justice v Ministry of the Environment et al.* (2016) T-622/16, Colombian Constitutional Court (Colombia) (*Atrato River Decision T-622*) 298.

60 *Center for Social Justice v Ministry of the Environment et al.* (2016) T-622/16, Colombian Constitutional Court (Colombia) (*Atrato River Decision T-622*) 298.

61 *Future Generations v Ministry of the Environment et al.* (2018) 11001 22 03 000 2018 00319 00, Colombian Supreme Court (Colombia) (*Future Generations*) 107.

62 *Future Generations v Ministry of the Environment et al.* (2018) 11001 22 03 000 2018 00319 00, Colombian Supreme Court (Colombia) (*Future Generations*) 107.

63 *Herrera Carrion et al. v Ministry of the Environment et al.* (2021) 21201202000170, Corte Provincial de Justicia de Sucumbíos (Ecuador), [4.2]. For a discussion on child-led litigation focused on India, Pakistan, and Bangladesh, see Kaur, Sathiabama and Vedavalli, Chapter 7.

64 *Herrera Carrion et al. v Ministry of the Environment et al.* (2021) 21201202000170, Corte Provincial de Justicia de Sucumbíos (Ecuador), [6.1.6].

65 *Center for Social Justice v Ministry of the Environment et al.* (2016) T-622/16, Colombian Constitutional Court (Colombia) (*Atrato River Decision T-622*) 304.

66 *Center for Social Justice v Ministry of the Environment et al.* (2016) T-622/16, Colombian Constitutional Court (Colombia) (*Atrato River Decision T-622*) 15.

67 *Herrera Carrion et al. v Ministry of the Environment et al.* (2021) 21201202000170, Corte Provincial de Justicia de Sucumbíos (Ecuador), [7.1.1].

68 *Herrera Carrion et al. v Ministry of the Environment et al.* (2021) 2120120200170, Corte Provincial de Justicia de Sucumbíos (Ecuador), [5.1].
69 *Future Generations v Ministry of the Environment et al.* (2018) 11001 22 03 000 2018 00319 00, Colombian Supreme Court (Colombia) (*Future Generations*) 4.
70 *Center for Social Justice v Ministry of the Environment et al.* (2016) T-622/16, Colombian Constitutional Court (Colombia) (*Atrato River Decision T-622*) 167; *Future Generations v Ministry of the Environment et al.* (2018) 11001 22 03 000 2018 00319 00, Colombian Supreme Court (Colombia) (*Future Generations*) 39; *Herrera Carrion et al.* (n 65), [VII].
71 *Center for Social Justice v Ministry of the Environment et al.* (2016) T-622/16, Colombian Constitutional Court (Colombia) (Atrato River Decision T-622) 170; *Herrera Carrion et al. v Ministry of the Environment et al.* (2021) 2120120200170, Corte Provincial de Justicia de Sucumbíos (Ecuador), [VII.1].
72 *Center for Social Justice v Ministry of the Environment et al.* (2016) T-622/16, Colombian Constitutional Court (Colombia) (*Atrato River Decision T-622*) 170; *Herrera Carrion et al. v Ministry of the Environment et al.* (2021) 2120120200170, Corte Provincial de Justicia de Sucumbíos (Ecuador), [VII.5].
73 *Future Generations v Ministry of the Environment et al.* (2018) 11001 22 03 000 2018 00319 00, Colombian Supreme Court (Colombia) (*Future Generations*) 48.
74 Juan Auz, 'Human Rights-Based Climate Litigation: A Latin American Cartography' (2022) 13 *Journal of Human Rights and the Environment* 114, 115; Peel and Lin (n 5) 685; Setzer and Benjamin (n 5) 82. For further insights on lawyering methodologies in Global South climate litigation, see, especially, Burri and Duarte Reyes, Chapter 5; Barrett, Chapter 6; Ladan and Maduekwe, Chapter 8; and Jamwal, Chapter 9.
75 *See Herrera Carrion et al.* (n 63).
76 Elizabeth Donger, 'Children and Youth in Strategic Climate Litigation: Advancing Rights through Legal Argument and Legal Mobilization' (2022) 11(2) *Transnational Environmental Law* 263, 272.
77 Interviewees 5 and 7.
78 Interviewees 5 and 7.
79 Interviewees 5 and 7.
80 Interviewees 5 and 7.
81 Bogdandy (n 21) 33; Couso and Hilbink (n 23) 65.
82 Pursuant to Article 88 of the Colombian Constitution, popular actions are a constitutional mechanism for the protection of collective rights related to public health, the environment, and other rights.
83 Popular complaints in Mexico are an administrative complaint procedure enshrined in Article 189 of the General Law on Ecological Balance and Environmental Protection. Any person or organisation can file this complaint with the Federal Environmental Protection Agency if they believe any act or omission has caused damage to the environment.
84 For an overview of the implementation of Chile's Law 20.600/2012, which created environmental tribunals, see Carolina Riquelme Salazar, 'Los Tribunales Ambientales en Chile. ¿Un avance hacia la implementación del derecho de acceso a la justicia ambiental?' (2013) 4(1) *Revista Catalana de Dret Ambiental* 1. On the suitability of the constitutional protection action in Chile's climate litigation, see Pilar Moraga Sariego, 'Climate Change Litigation in Chile: Between the Constitutional and the Environmental Jurisdiction Path' in Francesco Sindico and Makane Moïse Mbengue (eds), *Comparative Climate Change Litigation: Beyond the Usual Suspects* (Springer International Publishing 2021) 292.
85 Interviewees 1, 2, 5, 7, and 8.

86 Manuel E Góngora-Mera, 'The Block of Constitutionality as the Doctrinal Pivot of a Ius Commune' in Armin von Bogdandy et al. (eds), *Transformative Constitutionalism in Latin America: The Emergence of a New Ius Commune* (OUP 2017) 235; de Carvalho and da Rosa (n 21) 6.

87 United Nations General Assembly, International Covenant on Economic, Social, and Cultural Rights (adopted 16 December 1966, entered into force 3 January 1976) 993 UNTS 3; UN Committee on Economic, Social and Cultural Rights, 'General Comment No. 14: The Right to the Highest Attainable Standard of Health (Art 12)' (11 August 2000) E/C.12/2000/4; Organization of American States, Additional Protocol to the American Convention on Human Rights in the area of Economic, Social, and Cultural Rights 'Protocol of San Salvador' (adopted 17 November 1988, entered into force 16 November 1999) OAS Treaty Series No. 69, Article 10; Inter-American Court of Human Rights, 'Advisory Opinion OC-23/17 on Environment and Human Rights' (15 November 2017) Series A No. 23.

88 Thalia Viveros-Uehara, 'Litigating Climate Justice: The Right to Health and Vulnerable Populations in Latin America' (2023) 56 *VRÜ Verfassung und Recht in Übersee* 321, 332.

89 Redress measures in Chile and Mexico have declarative and concrete *inter partes* effects; they do not encompass integral reparation measures. See Humberto Nogueira Alcalá, 'La acción constitucional de protección en Chile y la acción constitucional de amparo en México' (2010) 16(1) *Ius et Praxis* 219, 271.

90 See, generally, Débora Guerra Moreno, Liliana Damaris Pabón Giraldo and Diana María Ramírez Carvajal, 'La reparación integral como principio prevalente en la responsabilidad del estado. Una visión a partir de la jurisprudencia de la Corte Constitucional y del Consejo de Estado Colombiano' (2020) 28 *Revista republicana* 59.

91 Armin von Bogdandy and René Urueña, 'Comunidades de práctica y constitucionalismo transformador en América Latina' in Armin von Bogdandy (ed), *Transformaciones del derecho público: fenómenos internacionales, supranacionales y nacionales* (Instituto Max Planck de Derecho Público Comparado y Derecho Internacional Público 2020) 137.

92 *Center for Social Justice v Ministry of the Environment et al.* (2016) T-622/16, Colombian Constitutional Court (Colombia) (*Atrato River Decision T-622*) 21.

93 Interviewees 1, 2, 5, 7, and 8.

94 Consejo de la Judicatura Federal, 'Acuerdo General 22/2013 del Pleno del Consejo de la Judicatura Federal' (*Diario Oficial de la Federación*, 9 August 2013).

95 Interviewees 3, 4, 6, 8, 9, and 11.

96 Interviewees 3, 4, 6, 8, 9, and 11. See IPCC, Summary for Policymakers in Climate Change 2022 – Impacts, Adaptation and Vulnerability: Working Group II Contribution to the Sixth Assessment Report of the Intergovernmental Panel on Climate Change' in HO Pörtner et al. (eds), (2022) <https://www.ipcc.ch/report/ar6/wg2/downloads/report/IPCC_AR6_WGII_FullReport.pdf> accessed 21 November 2024.

97 *Center for Social Justice v Ministry of the Environment et al.* (2016) T-622/16, Colombian Constitutional Court (Colombia) (*Atrato River Decision T-622*) 225.

98 On Chile's and Mexico's conservative style in constitutional adjudication, see Jaremba and Mak (n 19).

99 Regarding the receptiveness of Colombian and Ecuadorian courts for adjudicating social rights, see Brinks and Blass (n 17) 36 and Langford (n 18).

100 Interviewees 5 and 6.

101 Juan Carlos Rodríguez-Raga, 'Strategic Deference in the Colombian Constitutional Court, 1992–2006' in Gretchen Helmke and Julio Rios-Figueroa (eds), *Courts in Latin*

*America* (1st edn, Cambridge University Press 2011) 86; Uprimny Yepes and Sánchez Duque (n 42) 50.

102 Interviewee 6.

103 *Center for Social Justice v Ministry of the Environment et al.* (2016) T-622/16, Colombian Constitutional Court (Colombia) (*Atrato River Decision T-622*) 171.

104 *Center for Social Justice v Ministry of the Environment et al.* (2016) T-622/16, Colombian Constitutional Court (Colombia) (*Atrato River Decision T-622*) 170.

105 Interviewees 10 and 11.

106 Medici-Colombo and Ricarte (n 39) 2; de Carvalho and da Rosa (n 21) 4; Thalia Viveros-Uehara, 'The Fundamental Rights to Life and Health in Climate Litigation' (2022) 9 *e-Publica* 147, 153.

107 See n 13 and n 14.

108 Botero et al. (n 17).

109 Armin von Bogdandy and René Urueña, 'Introducing Compliance as a Transformative Process. The Bright Side of a Dismal Record' in Armin von Bogdandy et al. (eds), *The Impact of the Inter-American Human Rights System: Transformations on the Ground* (OUP 2024) 29.

110 Auz (n 8); Urzola Gutiérrez (n 6).

## Bibliography

### *Books and book chapters*

Andreassen BA, 'Comparative Analyses of Human Rights Performance' in BA Andreassen, H-O Sano and S McInerney-Lankford (eds), *Research Methods in Human Rights: A Handbook* (Edward Elgar Publishing 2017)

Bogdandy AV, 'Ius Constitutionale Commune en América Latina: Observations on Transformative Constitutionalism' in AV Bogdandy, EF Mac-Gregor, MM Antoniazzi, F Piovesan and X Soley (eds), *Transformative Constitutionalism in Latin America: The Emergence of a New Ius Commune* (OUP 2017)

Bogdandy AV and Urueña R, 'Comunidades de práctica y constitucionalismo transformador en América Latina' in AV Bogdandy (ed), *Transformaciones del derecho público: fenómenos internacionales, supranacionales y nacionales* (Instituto Max Planck de Derecho Público Comparado y Derecho Internacional Público 2020)

Botero S, Brinks DM and Gonzalez-Ocantos EA, 'Working in New Political Spaces: The Checkered History of Latin American Judicialization' in DM Brinks, EA Gonzalez-Ocantos and S Botero (eds), *The Limits of Judicialization: From Progress to Backlash in Latin America* (CUP 2022)

Bouwer K, Etemire U, Field TL and Jegede A (eds), *Climate Litigation and Justice in Africa* (Bristol University Press 2024)

Brinks DM and Blass A, *The DNA of Constitutional Justice in Latin America* (CUP 2018)

Chagoyán RL, *El Constitucionalismo mexicano en transformación: Avances y retrocesos* (Instituto de Estudios Constitucionales del Estado de Querétaro 2020)

Couso J and Hilbink L, 'From Quietism to Incipient Activism: The Institutional and Ideological Roots of Rights Adjudication in Chile' in G Helmke and J Rios-Figueroa (eds), *Courts in Latin America* (CUP 2011)

Gargarella R, Pilar D and Theunis R (eds), *Courts and Social Transformation in New Democracies: An Institutional Voice for the Poor?* (Routledge 2006)

Gargarella R and Roux T, 'The Changing Role of Law and Courts in Latin America: From an Obstacle to Social Change to a Tool of Social Equity' in R Gargarella, D Pilar and R

Theunis (eds), *Courts and Social Transformation in New Democracies: An Institutional Voice for the Poor?* (Routledge 2006)
Gauri V and Brinks DM (eds), *Courting Social Justice: Judicial Enforcement of Social and Economic Rights in the Developing World* (CUP 2008)
Giménez FP, 'The Constitution of Mexico' in CH Mendes, R Gargarella and S Guidi (eds), *The Oxford Handbook of Constitutional Law in Latin America* (OUP 2022)
Gloppen S, Gargarella R and Skaar E (eds), *Democratization and the Judiciary: The Accountability Function of Courts in New Democracies* (Frank Cass 2004)
Gloppen S, Wilson BM, Gargarella R, Skaar E and Kinander, *Courts and Power in Latin America and Africa* (Palgrave Macmillan 2010)
Góngora-Mera ME, 'The Block of Constitutionality as the Doctrinal Pivot of a Ius Commune' in AV Bogdandy, EF Mac-Gregor, MM Antoniazzi, F Piovesan and X Soley (eds), *Transformative Constitutionalism in Latin America: The Emergence of a New Ius Commune* (OUP 2017)
Hammergren L, *Envisioning Reform: Conceptual and Practical Obstacles to Improving Judicial Performance in Latin America* (Pennsylvania State University Press 2007)
Meili S, 'Latin American Cause-Lawyering Networks' in A Sarat and S Scheingold (eds), *Cause Lawyering and the State in a Global Era* (Oxford Academic 2001)
Mendes CH, Gargarella R and Guidi S (eds), *The Oxford Handbook of Constitutional Law in Latin America* (OUP 2022)
Murcott M, *Transformative Environmental Constitutionalism* (Brill Nijhoff 2022)
Parra-Vera Ó, 'The Protection of Social Rights' in JF Gonzalez-Bertomeu and R Gargarella (eds), *The Latin American Casebook: Courts, Constitutions, and Rights* (Routledge 2016)
Rodríguez-Raga JC, 'Strategic Deference in the Colombian Constitutional Court, 1992–2006' in G Helmke and J Rios-Figueroa (eds), *Courts in Latin America* (1st edn, Cambridge University Press 2011)
Salazar D, 'The Constitutional History of Ecuador: Twenty Constitutions and Counting' in C Hübner Mendes, R Gargarella and S Guidi (eds), *The Oxford Handbook of Constitutional Law in Latin America* (OUP 2022)
Sarat A and Scheingold S (eds), *The Worlds Cause Lawyers Make: Structure and Agency in Legal Practice* (Stanford University Press 2005)
Sariego PM, 'Climate Change Litigation in Chile: Between the Constitutional and the Environmental Jurisdiction Path' in F Sindico and MM Mbengue (eds), *Comparative Climate Change Litigation: Beyond the Usual Suspects* (Springer International Publishing 2021)
Yamin AE 'The Right to Health: The Potential and Limits of Catalysing Systemic Change through the Courts' in CH Mendes, R Gargarella and S Guidi (eds), *The Oxford Handbook of Constitutional Law in Latin America* (OUP 2022)
Yamin AE and Gloppen S (eds), *Litigating Health Rights: Can Courts Bring More Justice to Health?* (HUP 2011)

## Journal articles

Aguirre Castro P and Alarcón Peña P, 'El Estándar de la Reparación Integral en la Jurisprudencia de la Corte Constitucional' (2018) 30 *Foro: Revista de Derecho* 121 <https://doi.org/10.32719/26312484.2018.30.8> accessed 19 September 2024
Alcalá HN, 'La Acción Constitucional de Protección en Chile y la Acción Constitucional de Amparo en México' (2010) 16(1) *Ius et Praxis* 219 <http://dx.doi.org/10.4067/S0718-00122010000100009> accessed 19 September 2024
Auz J, 'Human Rights-Based Climate Litigation: A Latin American Cartography' (2022) 13(1) *Journal of Human Rights and the Environment* 114 <https://doi.org/10.4337/jhre.2022.01.05> accessed 19 September 2024

Auz J, 'The Political Ecology of Climate Remedies in Latin America and the Caribbean: Comparing Compliance between National and Inter-American Litigation' (2024) 16(1) *Journal of Human Rights Practice* 182 <https://doi.org/10.1093/jhuman/huad057> accessed 19 September 2024

Bernales-Baksai P, 'Tackling Segmentation to Advance Universal Health Coverage: Analysis of Policy Architectures of Health Care in Chile and Uruguay' (2020) 19 *International Journal for Equity in Health* 106 <https://doi.org/10.1186/s12939-020-01176-6> accessed 19 September 2024

Burke M, González F, Baylis P, Heft-Neal S, Baysan C, Basu S and Hsiang S, 'Higher Temperatures Increase Suicide Rates in the United States and Mexico' (2018) 8 *Nature Climate Change* 723 <https://doi.org/10.1038/s41558-018-0222-x> accessed 19 September 2024

Bustos C, 'Movement Lawyering in the Time of the Climate Crisis' (2022) 39 *Pace Environmental Law Review* 1 <https://doi.org/10.58948/0738-6206.1854> accessed 19 September 2024

Donger E, 'Children and Youth in Strategic Climate Litigation: Advancing Rights through Legal Argument and Legal Mobilization' (2022) 11(2) *Transnational Environmental Law* 263 <https://doi.org/10.1017/S2047102522000218> accessed 19 September 2024

Dupuits E, Baud M, Boelens R and Castro F, 'Scaling Up But Losing Out? Water Commons' Dilemmas between Transnational Movements and Grassroots Struggles in Latin America' (2020) 172(2) *Ecological Economics* 106625 <http://dx.doi.org/10.1016/j.ecolecon.2020.106625> accessed 19 September 2024

Gloppen S, 'Litigation as a Strategy to Hold Governments Accountable for Implementing the Right to Health' (2008) 10(2) *Health and Human Rights* 21 <https://pubmed.ncbi.nlm.nih.gov/20845857/> accessed 19 September 2024

Guerra Moreno D, Pabón Giraldo LD, Ramírez Carvajal DM, 'La reparación integral como principio prevalente en la responsabilidad del estado. Una visión a partir de la jurisprudencia de la Corte Constitucional y del Consejo de Estado Colombiano' (2020) 28 *Revista Republicana* 59 <https://ojs.urepublicana.edu.co/index.php/revistarepublicana/article/view/608> accessed 19 September 2024

Gutiérrez NU, 'Gender in Climate Litigation in Latin America: Epistemic Justice Through a Feminist Lens' (2024) 16(1) *Journal of Human Rights Practice* 208 <https://doi.org/10.1093/jhuman/huad030> accessed 19 September 2024

Hoffman B and Vahlsing M, 'Collaborative Lawyering in Transnational Human Rights Advocacy' (2014) 21 *Clinical Law Review* 255 <https://ssrn.com/abstract=2642928> accessed 19 September 2024

Jaremba U and Mak E, 'Interviewing Judges in the Transnational Context' (2014) *Law and Method* <https://doi.org/10.5553/REM/.000003> accessed 19 September 2024

Kotzé L, 'The Anthropocene, Earth System Vulnerability and Socio-Ecological Injustice in an Age of Human Rights' (2019) 10(1) *Journal of Human Rights and the Environment* 62 <http://dx.doi.org/10.4337/jhre.2019.01.04> accessed 19 September 2024

Langford M, 'Domestic Adjudication and Economic, Social and Cultural Rights: A Socio-Legal Review' (2009) 6(11) *Sur International Journal of Human Rights* 91 <https://ssrn.com/abstract=1706762> accessed 19 September 2024

McMichael AJ and Lindgren E, 'Climate Change: Present and Future Risks to Health, and Necessary Responses' (2011) 270(5) *Journal of Internal Medicine* 401 <https://doi.org/10.1111/j.1365-2796.2011.02415.x> accessed 19 September 2024

Medici-Colombo G and Ricarte T, 'The Escazú Agreement Contribution to Environmental Justice in Latin America: An Exploratory Empirical Inquiry through the Lens of Climate Litigation' (2023) 16(1) *Journal of Human Rights Practice* <http://dx.doi.org/10.1093/jhuman/huad029> accessed 19 September 2024

Mena-Meléndez L, 'Ethnoracial Child Health Inequalities in Latin America: Multilevel Evidence from Bolivia, Colombia, Guatemala, and Peru' (2020) 12 *SSM – Population Health* 100673 <https://doi.org/10.1016/j.ssmph.2020.100673> accessed 19 September 2024

Ohdedar B, 'Climate Adaptation, Vulnerability and Rights-Based Litigation: Broadening the Scope of Climate Litigation Using Political Ecology' (2022) 13(1) *Journal of Human Rights and the Environment* 137 <http://dx.doi.org/10.4337/jhre.2022.01.06> accessed 19 September 2024

Parry L, Radel C, Adamo SB, Clark N, Counterman M, Flores-Yeffal N, Pons D, Romero-Lankao P and Vargo J, 'The (In)Visible Health Risks of Climate Change' (2019) 241 *Social Science & Medicine* 112448 <https://doi.org/10.1016/j.socscimed.2019.112448> accessed 19 September 2024

Peel J and Lin J, 'Transnational Climate Litigation: The Contribution of the Global South' (2019) 113(4) *American Journal of International Law* 679 <https://doi.org/10.1017/ajil.2019.48> accessed 19 September 2024

Peralta A, Espinel-Flores V, Gotsens M, Pérez G, Benach J and Marí-Dell'Olmo, 'Developing a Deprivation Index to Study Geographical Health Inequalities in Ecuador' (2019) 28(53) *Revista de Saúde Pública* 97 <https://doi.org/10.11606/s1518-8787.2019053001410> accessed 19 September 2024

Pino P, Iglesias V, Garreaud R, Cortés S, Canals M, Folch W, Burgos S, Levy K and Naeher LP, 'Chile Confronts Its Environmental Health Future After 25 Years of Accelerated Growth' (2015) 81(3) *Annals of Global Health* 354 <https://doi.org/10.1016/j.aogh.2015.06.008> accessed 19 September 2024

Romero-Lankao P, Hughes S, Qin H, Hardoy J, Rosas-Huerta A, Borquez R and Lampis A, 'Scale, Urban Risk and Adaptation Capacity in Neighbourhoods of Latin American Cities' (2014) 42 *Habitat International* 224 <https://doi.org/10.1016/j.habitatint.2013.12.008> accessed 19 September 2024

Rudolph L and Gould S, 'Climate Change and Health Inequities: A Framework for Action' (2015) 81(3) *Annals of Global Health* 432 <http://dx.doi.org/10.1016/j.aogh.2015.06.003> accessed 19 2024

Salazar CR, 'Los Tribunales Ambientales en Chile. ¿Un Avance Hacia la Implementación del Derecho de Acceso a la Justicia Ambiental?' (2013) 4(1) *Revista Catalana de Dret Ambiental* 1 <http://dx.doi.org/10.17345/1335> accessed 19 September 2024

Selznick P, '"Law in Context" Revisited' (2003) 30(2) *Journal of Law and Society* 177 <https://www.jstor.org/stable/1410767> accessed 19 September 2024

Setzer J and Benjamin L, 'Climate Litigation in the Global South: Constraints and Innovations' (2020) 9(1) *Transnational Environmental Law* 77 <https://ssrn.com/abstract=3456330> accessed 19 September 2024

Smith MB and Jenkins K, 'Disconnections and Exclusions: Professionalization, Cosmopolitanism and (Global?) Civil Society' (2011) 11(2) *Global Networks* 160 <http://dx.doi.org/10.1111/j.1471-0374.2011.00317.x> accessed 19 September 2024

Sormunen M, 'Rethinking Effective Remedies to the Climate Crisis: A Vulnerability Theory Approach' (2023) 24 *Human Rights Review* 171 <https://doi.org/10.1007/s12142-023-00686-4> accessed 19 September 2024

Uehara TV, 'The Fundamental Rights to Life and Health in Climate Litigation' (2022) 9(3) *e-Publica* 147 <https://e-publica.pt/article/57632-the-fundamental-rights-to-life-and-health-in-climate-litigation-insights-from-latin-america> accessed 19 September 2024

Uehara TV, 'Litigating Climate Justice: The Right to Health and Vulnerable Populations in Latin America' (2023) 56 *VRÜ Verfassung und Recht in Übersee* 321 <https://ssrn.com/abstract=4405980> accessed 19 September 2024

Uprimny R and Duque LMS, 'Constitución de 1991, Justicia Constitucional y Cambio Democrático: Un Balance dos Décadas Después' (2012) 71(71) *Cahiers des Amériques Latines* 33 <http://dx.doi.org/10.4000/cal.2663> accessed 19 September 2024

Winter de Carvalho D and Martins da Rosa RS, 'Climate Constitutionalism as a Foundation for Climate Litigation in Latin America' (2023) 16(1) *Journal of Human Rights Practice* <http://dx.doi.org/10.1093/jhuman/huad055> accessed 19 September 2024

## Cases

*Center for Social Justice v Ministry of the Environment et al.* (2016) T-622/16, Colombian Constitutional Court (Colombia) (*Atrato River Decision T-622*)

*Future Generations v Ministry of the Environment et al.* (2018) 11001 22 03 000 2018 00319 00, Colombian Supreme Court (Colombia) (*Future Generations*)

*Greenpeace Mexico v Ministry of Energy et al.* (2020) 104/2020, Second District Court of Mexico (Mexico) (*Greenpeace Mexico*)

*Herrera Carrion et al. v Ministry of the Environment et al.* (2021) 21201202000170, Corte Provincial de Justicia de Sucumbíos (Ecuador)

Inter-American Court of Human Rights, 'Advisory Opinion OC-23/17 on Environment and Human Rights' (15 November 2017) Series A No. 23

*Mejillones Tourist Service Association et al. v Environmental Evaluation Service (SEA) of Antofagasta* (2021) 6930-2021 and 71.628-2021, Chilean Supreme Court of Justice (Chile) (*Mejillones Tourist Service Association et al*)

## International instruments

Organization of American States, Additional Protocol to the American Convention on Human Rights in the area of Economic, Social, and Cultural Rights 'Protocol of San Salvador' (adopted 17 November 1988, entered into force 16 November 1999) OAS Treaty Series No. 69, art 10

UN Committee on Economic, Social and Cultural Rights, 'General Comment No. 14: The Right to the Highest Attainable Standard of Health (Art 12)' (11 August 2000) E/C.12/2000/4

United Nations General Assembly, International Covenant on Economic, Social, and Cultural Rights (adopted 16 December 1966, entered into force 3 January 1976) 993 UNTS 3

## Online sources

'Litigio Climático para América Latina y el Caribe' (*Plataforma de Litigio Climático para América latina y el Caribe*) <https://litigioclimatico.com/es/sobre-la-plataforma> accessed 15 June 2022

'USClimate Change Litigation Database' (*The Sabin Centre for Climate Change Law at Columbia Law School*) <http://climatecasechart.com/climate-change-litigation/about/> accessed 31 October 2023

## Reports

IPCC, 'Summary for Policymakers in Climate Change 2022 – Impacts, Adaptation and Vulnerability: Working Group II Contribution to the Sixth Assessment Report of the Intergovernmental Panel on Climate Change' in HO Pörtner et al. (eds), (2022) <https://www.ipcc.ch/report/ar6/wg2/downloads/report/IPCC_AR6_WGII_FullReport.pdf> accessed 21 November 2024

Magrin GO et al., *Climate Change 2014: Impacts, Adaptation, and Vulnerability: Part B: Regional Aspects: Contribution of Working Group II to the Fifth Assessment Report of the Intergovernmental Panel on Climate Change*, VR Barros et al. (eds), (CUP 2014)

Pan American Health Organization, 'Health in the Americas+, 2017 Edition. Summary: Regional Outlook and Country Profiles' (*PAHO*, 2017)

### *Research papers*

Consejo de la Judicatura Federal, 'Acuerdo General 22/2013 del Pleno del Consejo de la Judicatura Federal' (*Diario Oficial de la Federación*, 9 August 2013)

Langford M, 'Interdisciplinarity and Multimethod Research' in BA Andreassen, HO Sano and S McInerney-Lankford (eds), *Research Methods in Human Rights: A Handbook, University of Oslo Faculty of Law Research Paper 2016–30* (Edward Elgar Publishing Forthcoming 2017) 8 <https://ssrn.com/abstract=2854037> accessed 19 September 2024

Chapter 4

# The inclusion of women and girls in climate adaptation policy in India

## Opportunities and challenges for future litigation

*Moushita Dutta and Katherine Lofts*

### Introduction

India is one of the countries most affected by climate change globally,[1] and women and girls in India are particularly vulnerable to the impacts of the changing climate.[2] Indeed, there is now widespread recognition in the literature that gender, in conjunction with other intersecting social categories, such as class, caste, race, disability, and sexuality, plays an important role in mediating both vulnerability to climate change impacts as well as adaptive capacity.[3] Yet in India, climate adaptation policies adopted at the national and subnational levels – namely, the National Action Plan for Climate Change (NAPCC)[4] and the State Action Plans for Climate Change (SAPCC)[5] – have unevenly addressed gender and largely fail to operationalise the consideration of gender in tangible and transformative ways.[6] Moreover, as Singh, Solomon, and Rao point out, these policy documents tend to equate gender with women – an 'artificially homogenous' and often essentialist category that obscures the implications of intersecting identities and power dynamics and overlooks the potential vulnerabilities of people of all genders.[7] While our analysis also focuses on women and girls as a lens through which to approach the need for more effective and inclusive adaptation measures in pursuit of gender justice, we recognise that these categories are heterogeneous and that discussions of vulnerability and adaptive capacity are multidimensional in nature.

The failure to sufficiently include and operationalise gender considerations in adaptation measures in India is a missed opportunity to enhance the resilience of women and girls; it also threatens their enjoyment of a wide range of human rights, including socio-economic and equality rights. Nevertheless, the issue of women's and girls' rights in the context of adaptation to climate change has yet to be brought before the Indian courts. We argue that there is an opportunity to bring a novel climate case addressing the failure of current Indian climate adaptation policies to prevent and mitigate harm to women and girls. Although India lacks legally binding climate legislation, the country has a progressive body of constitutional environmental, social, and equality rights provisions and jurisprudence that could provide a strong foundation for rights-based adaptation litigation, facilitated by a flexible procedural regime for public interest litigation. Moreover, the Supreme

DOI: 10.4324/9781003470632-6

Court's 2024 decision in *Ranjitsinh et al. v Union of India* on the recognition of the right to equality in the context of climate change, as well as the right to be free from the adverse effects of climate change, holds a great deal of promise for future litigation.[8]

The chapter proceeds as follows: First, the chapter examines how women and girls have been included and excluded in climate change adaptation policies in India at the national and subnational levels. Second, the chapter explores two key aspects of India's legal framework – access to justice for public interest litigation on environmental and social matters and a strong constitutional human rights framework – that could underpin adaptation-related climate litigation to reduce the vulnerability of women and girls to adverse climate impacts. This section also surveys the current state of climate litigation in India. Finally, the chapter discusses further considerations for adaptation-related climate litigation focused on women and girls in India.

## The inclusion and exclusion of women and girls in Indian climate adaptation policy at the national and subnational levels

Women and girls are disproportionately impacted by climate change, particularly in lower-income countries.[9] These disproportionate impacts stem in large part from 'socially constructed gender roles [that] give rise to different tasks and identities'[10] and affect a range of human rights, including the rights to life, health, food and water, sanitation, housing, education, and work.[11] For example, women are more likely to live in poverty and often have primary responsibility for household food security and water management.[12] Climate change–induced environmental degradation can make these tasks more challenging.[13] Women are also more likely to experience displacement, violence, and health problems due to climate-related disasters.[14]

The impacts of climate change on women and girls in India have been well-documented.[15] For example, climate change has led to irregular monsoons, resulting in water scarcity in many parts of India.[16] Women, who are often primarily responsible for fetching water for their households, bear the brunt of this increasing water stress.[17] Unpredictable weather patterns, droughts, and floods have led to a decline in agricultural productivity and an increase in food insecurity, both of which disproportionately affect women and children[18] and contribute to their malnutrition.[19] In India, as with other countries, climate change also threatens to widen existing gender-based health disparities.[20]

The increased vulnerability of women and girls to climate change can be understood as a function of their exposure, sensitivity, and adaptive capacity.[21] In the Indian context, this vulnerability is affected by the interaction of a range of social, economic, political, institutional, and technological factors, including pre-existing gender inequalities, prevalent social norms, and limited access to resources, education, and decision-making power.[22] Critically, the vulnerability of women and girls in India is also impacted by the intersection of other social categories, such as race, class, caste, disability, and sexuality, which interact with gender to shape individuals' experiences and access to power and other types of resources.[23]

Nevertheless, India has failed to address gender in climate change adaptation policies adequately at the national level.[24] Women and girls are not specifically mentioned in the country's nationally determined contribution (NDC).[25] The 2008 NAPCC – India's national strategy outlining existing and future policies and programmes to address climate mitigation and adaptation – only briefly addresses the disproportionate impact of climate change on women, noting that consequences such as water scarcity and malnutrition 'would add to deprivations that women already encounter'.[26] The NAPCC thus advises that 'in each of the adaptation programmes, special attention should be paid to the aspects of gender';[27] however, no additional attention is given to mitigating these risks in the remainder of the document.[28]

At the subnational level, progress on integrating gender considerations into climate policies has also been uneven. In 2012, the Ministry of Environment, Forest, and Climate Change directed all states to incorporate gender into their SAPCCs.[29] While a number of states have complied with this directive and included some form of gender-based approach to their SAPCC, others have yet to complete this task. Indeed, of the 28 states with functioning SAPCCs, only 17 (just over 60%) explicitly include the terms 'gender' or 'women'.[30]

Those states that address gender in their SAPCC do so to varying extents. In their analysis of gender inclusion in SAPCCs, Singh, Solomon, and Rao note that amongst those SAPCCs that mention *gender*, women are most commonly framed in passive terms, 'as highly and disproportionately vulnerable to climate change risks and impacts'.[31] Some of these policies recognise the role of structural gender inequalities in shaping this vulnerability.[32] For example, the SAPCCs of Rajasthan and Tamil Nadu discuss women and children's increased vulnerability to climate change in terms of pre-existing developmental deficits, such as poor health, literacy levels, and livelihood factors.[33] The SAPCC of Gujarat discusses how women's assigned social roles and existing social and economic inequalities create increased vulnerability.[34]

Other SAPCCs recognise that women's roles within various sectors may be impacted by climate change. For example, the SAPCCs of Bihar and Chhattisgarh recognise the role of women in agriculture and provide for the inclusion of gender-specific planning and interventions.[35] Similarly, the SAPCCs of Tamil Nadu, Rajasthan, Punjab, and Jharkhand contain some targeted initiatives for addressing women's needs in sectors primarily dependent on the female labour force. Tamil Nadu's SAPCC recognises the importance of women workers in the state's dairy sector and includes capacity-building programmes for them, while Punjab's SAPCC includes capacity-building programmes for women farmworkers and other rural women.[36] Other SAPCCs noting the gendered division of labour report that 'women are vulnerable due to reproductive tasks including additional burdens of care that potentially have negative effects on women's own health'.[37]

Some SAPCCs have also included the development and financing of capacity-building programmes to enhance the adaptive capacity of women. In this regard, Kerala, Odisha, and Gujarat have undertaken gender mainstreaming initiatives in their climate policies for sectors such as agriculture and forestry. The SAPCC of Uttarakhand goes further, recognising women as crucial and active agents in the adaptation process and its outcomes and prescribing departmental efforts for gender mainstreaming.[38] It also encourages efforts to include women in climate change decision-making and implementation efforts.[39] Finally, in 2018, Kerala became the first Indian state to adopt a separate gender-focused state action plan intended to govern the gendered aspects of climate change, in addition to its SAPCC.[40]

Despite these elements of inclusion, the majority of SAPCCs fail to recognise the intersectional nature of climate vulnerability and overlook the heterogeneity within women's experiences.[41] Moreover, the majority of attempts at gender mainstreaming in the SAPCCs are superficial. Singh, Solomon, and Rao note that the SAPCCs 'tend to report existing development projects aimed at women rather than a reconsideration of existing policies to make them transformative'.[42] Most lack 'a clear articulation of how they will address gendered vulnerabilities or enable gender-responsive climate action', and while they 'use language to signal recognition of gendered vulnerability', this language is seldom translated into actual policy approaches.[43] Thus, the majority of SAPCCs fail to outline any systematic or concrete plans to identify and address the gender-based gaps in climate adaptation, including risk assessment, specific measures to reduce exposure and sensitivity to climate impacts or bolster adaptive capacity, or greater inclusion and participation of women in policy- and decision-making.

The failure of the majority of Indian states to consider gender in their budgeting for climate change is an illustrative example.[44] Climate budgeting is an area that has gained prominence in recent years for its role in mainstreaming climate adaptation expenditure within the public financial expenditure systems.[45] Within the broader practice of climate budgeting, 'gender budgeting' for adaptation is an emerging practice relating to the allocation of a portion of climate adaptation funds towards meeting women's needs and priorities in that sector. Though some Indian states such as Maharashtra, Odisha, and Kerala have initiated steps to incorporate climate budgeting within state budgeting systems in some form, they have not done so in a gender-responsive manner.[46] To date, only Uttarakhand and Madhya Pradesh have adopted gender-based adaptation budgets.[47]

The implementation of gender-responsive measures also remains a key policy concern. Studies have found that while SAPCCs offer considerable potential to address gender-based vulnerabilities and strengthen adaptive capacity, they face critical implementation challenges, including inadequate leadership, institutional barriers, and resource constraints.[48] In addition, SAPCCs are under the jurisdiction of states, which have limited capacities and often lack strong climate institutions at the local level.[49] Such shortcomings cause states to develop weak and inadequate climate plans in the first place – a situation compounded by implementation hurdles leading to poor outcomes.[50]

Overall, gender considerations have been unevenly and insufficiently included, operationalised, and implemented in most climate adaptation plans across India. The remainder of the chapter explores the prospects of adaptation and gender-focused climate litigation as a means of addressing these failures and reducing the vulnerability of women and girls to adverse climate impacts.

## The legal foundation for adaptation-related climate litigation to reduce the vulnerability of women and girls in India

The following sections examine key aspects of India's legal framework that could underpin adaptation-related climate litigation to reduce the vulnerability of women and girls to adverse climate impacts – namely, easy access to justice for public interest litigation on environmental and social matters, a strong constitutional human rights framework, and a developing body of climate change jurisprudence.

### *Access to justice for public interest litigation*

Public interest litigation (PIL) in India provides a flexible procedural regime that has allowed for the realisation and enforcement of constitutional rights, including socio-economic and environmental rights.[51] Through PIL writ petitions to the Supreme Court and state high courts for the violation of their fundamental rights, citizens have brought cases on a range of subjects affecting their fundamental rights as individuals, as well as on behalf of society more broadly.[52] Indeed, as a critical feature of constitutional litigation in India, PIL is intended to provide 'access to justice to all societal constituents' by relaxing the rules of standing to enable matters of public interest to be brought before the court by those who are not directly involved in the case, such as members of the public or non-governmental organisations (NGOs).[53] The judiciary has also sought to overcome evidentiary challenges for PIL plaintiffs and to assist in finding suitable remedies. In this way, PIL has been framed as a 'collaborative and cooperative project in which all concerned parties should work together to realise the human rights of disadvantaged sections of society'.[54] It provides an avenue for those seeking justice in the public interest and for those who would otherwise find it difficult to access the court due to poverty or other forms of marginalisation. PIL could thus be a particularly useful tool for petitioners seeking to bring adaptation-related climate litigation on behalf of women and girls.

India's National Green Tribunal (NGT) also facilitates improved access to environmental justice. The NGT was established under the National Green Tribunal Act of 2010 for the speedy and effective disposal of all cases related to environmental protection and all matters involving environmental disputes.[55] It was developed as a specialised body to ensure that environmental justice is accessible to all and to provide momentum for environmental litigation to grow.[56] In addition, commentators have noted that the NGT serves additional roles and functions beyond those described in the National Green Tribunal Act, including 'dispensing environmental justice, evolving environmental jurisprudence, and promoting discourse and awareness on environmental issues'.[57] Considering the NGT's wide scope and progressive record, and in conjunction with PIL, its strategic utilisation could be an advantageous forum for adjudicating matters pertaining to the adaptation of vulnerable individuals and groups.

### *Constitutional framework*

#### *Environmental and socio-economic rights under the right to life and liberty*

The right to life and liberty under Article 21 of the Constitution of India (Constitution) has been interpreted expansively by the Supreme Court to confer a wide range of rights (including socio-economic and environmental rights) that can be enforced through the courts against the government. It states that '[n]o person shall be deprived of his life or personal liberty except according to procedure established by law'.[58] Section III of the Constitution, which enshrines fundamental rights and provides for the protection of life and personal liberty, has been widely interpreted by the Supreme Court to include within its scope a variety of other human rights to promote and ensure freedom, justice, and peace.[59] This includes the right to live with human dignity, the right to a clean environment, the right to pollution-free air and water, the right to health, the right to shelter, the right to livelihood, and the right to social security and protection of family, among a host of other rights.[60]

The breadth of interpretation of Article 21 has potentially significant implications for climate change litigation. First, the Supreme Court's and several high courts' recognition of the right to a clean and pollution-free environment as an integral part of the 'right to life'[61] provides a clear hook for litigants seeking to challenge the government's climate record.[62] For example, a series of cases have found that any disturbance to the basic environmental elements – namely, air, water, and soil – would be hazardous to life within the meaning of Article 21.[63] The court in *Subhash Kumar v The State of Bihar*[64] observed that a pollution-free environment is integral to the right to a healthy life and human dignity. The range of precedents linking environmental harms to the violation of Article 21 – including multiple instances where courts have *suo moto* taken cognisance of environmental matters to prevent damage and remedy environmental harms[65] – shows promise for claims addressing the mitigation of and adaptation to increasingly hostile environmental conditions due to climate change.

Secondly, the courts' willingness to read a range of socio-economic rights into Article 21 may also provide an opportunity for litigants seeking to address the underlying determinants of climate change vulnerability and adaptive capacity. The courts' approach aligns with an understanding of climate change adaptation that acknowledges adaptive capacity as linked to a complex mix of social, economic, political, and biophysical factors. Several scholars emphasise that effective approaches to climate change adaptation must take into account systemic inequalities that affect an individual's ability to cope with various climate impacts.[66] Enhancing the adaptive capacity of women and girls thus implicates a range of other factors relating to their vulnerability and resilience, including indicators as diverse as literacy rates, political rights, caloric intake, and access to sanitation.[67]

Some scholars have argued that it may be apposite to broaden the scope of what has traditionally been classified as 'climate litigation', targeting the diverse factors that lead to climate vulnerability and expanding opportunities for strategic interventions.[68] For example, in the Indian context, Ohdedar has identified cases addressing drought, land conflict, and agrarian debt as potentially profoundly impacting climate vulnerability, adaptation, and rights despite not being expressly argued on climate grounds.[69] The broad interpretation given to rights under Article 21 by the courts thus offers many potential avenues, as the fulfilment of human rights can ultimately serve to reduce vulnerability and bolster adaptive capacity.

### *Constitutional provisions on gender equality*

The Constitution contains provisions that directly obligate the state to ensure gender equality, which could be mobilised in relation to unequal climate adaptation provisions. For instance, Articles 14 and 15 provide for equality before the law, equal protection of the law, and prohibition of discrimination on the grounds of sex, respectively.[70] Article 15(3) empowers the state to make exceptions or special provisions for women and children, supporting equality and non-discrimination for women on social, political, and economic grounds.[71] Article 21 has also been invoked in several matters relating to women's rights to divorce, safe abortions, and protection from violence.[72] These constitutional provisions can serve as important tools for raising gender equality concerns in relation to India's climate adaptation policies.

Tackling gender discrimination in climate adaptation policies will also require courts to recognise indirect discrimination and substantive equality to harness the full potential of India's constitutional provisions on gender equality. The reasoning of the Indian Supreme Court in *Lt. Col Nitisha v Union of India* (*Nitisha*)[73] provides important insights into how this can be done. In *Nitisha*, the court invoked Articles 14 and 15(1) of the Constitution to recognise indirect discrimination and its role in pursuing substantive equality.[74] To reach its decision, the court specifically considered women's social, economic, and political exclusion in the context of disadvantage and how such exclusion prevents women from functioning as economic actors.[75] Moreover, the court underlined how patterns of indirect discrimination resulting from exclusion contribute to the subordination of a disadvantaged group and the validation of an unjust status quo.[76]

The legal reasoning in *Nitisha* has important implications for gender-based climate adaptation litigation in India because it recognises that indirect discrimination and the role of substantive equality are firmly grounded in Indian constitutional jurisprudence.[77] While *Nitisha* lacks coherence in certain respects, it can nevertheless serve as a critical tool to pursue claims of indirect discrimination against women and girls in Indian climate adaptation policy.[78]

### *Current climate litigation landscape in India: cases against the state*

Domestic climate litigation in India is nascent, with only 12 climate-focused cases decided to date, primarily focused on mitigation.[79] This situation mirrors the trend seen globally. Although climate litigation has become an increasingly prominent strategy for addressing the climate emergency in the Global South,[80] the vast majority of climate change–related legal cases have focused on mitigation rather than adaptation.[81]

India's best-known case is *Ridhima Pandey v Union of India* (*Pandey*),[82] which a 9-year-old girl brought before the NGT. Pandey's petition challenged the government over climate inaction on three principal grounds. First, she challenged the government's non-implementation of existing environmental legislation, leading to the intensification of the climate crisis in the country.[83] Second, she sought judicial intervention to direct the government to adopt 'science-based' actions to reduce and minimise the adverse impacts of climate change.[84] By invoking the principles of sustainable development, precaution, and intergenerational equity, Pandey's petition argued that existing governmental climate policies fail to take into account the future of the country's youth, who constitute the most vulnerable class in the context of climate change. Third, she challenged the failure of the government to implement the country's obligations under the Paris Agreement by not enacting the necessary domestic legislation to address climate change concerns.[85]

The *Pandey* case was a turning point for climate litigation in India because it raised the question of the legally binding effect of India's international climate commitments before the judiciary.[86] The petition also sought climate justice for children as a vulnerable demographic that is disproportionately affected by the adverse effects of climate change.[87] Nevertheless, the NGT's final order did not engage with the many important climate change concerns raised by the petition; rather, it dismissed the matter without addressing the implementation of environmental legislation or the question of intergenerational equity and young people's vulnerability to climate change. On the question of non-implementation of India's obligations under the Paris Agreement, the NGT held that 'there is no reason to presume that the Paris Agreement and other international protocols are not reflected in the policies of the government or are not taken into consideration in granting environmental clearances'.[88]

In most other climate-related cases in India, the NGT has also avoided actively addressing the question of climate change policy. For example, in *Gaurav Bansal v Union of India*,[89] the petitioner requested judicial intervention to address the issue of the non-implementation of the NAPCC, including orders from the NGT to the central and state governments showing the steps taken by them to implement the NAPCC.[90] Instead of delving into the question of the NAPCC's implementation, the NGT disposed of the matter by directing the concerned state governments to comply with the directions of the Union Ministry of Environment, Forests, and Climate Change.[91] However, the NGT allowed the petitioner to file a separate and more specific petition for violating the NAPCC and its consequences.[92]

The Supreme Court has been receptive to climate concerns raised in the case of *Hanuman Laxman Aroskar v Union of India* (*Hanuman*).[93] Here, the petitioner challenged the government's approval for an airport construction project in the state of Goa. The Supreme Court suspended the approval on the grounds that the statutory process for granting the approval was not followed properly.[94] Of particular relevance to future climate litigation, the Supreme Court relied upon international climate agreements, such as the Paris Agreement and the Sustainable Development Goals (SDGs), to arrive at its determination. The court cited the Paris Agreement and India's NDC as crucial aspects of India's environmental rule of law.[95] The Paris Agreement and the SDGs could serve as a hook for future adaptation-related climate litigation, as both address adaptation directly and recognise the role of gender equality and women's empowerment in strengthening resilience.

In 2024, in *Ranjitsinh*,[96] the Supreme Court recognised the right to be free from the adverse effects of climate change within the ambit of the fundamental rights enshrined under the Constitution. The court noted that Articles 14 and 21 of the Indian Constitution are the sources of this right and stated that the government must acknowledge the same in undertaking climate actions.[97] In so doing, the judgment provided a detailed discussion of the linkages between human rights and climate change[98] and the applicability of climate change–related obligations and principles under international law, stating:

> It is imperative for states like India, to uphold their obligations under international law, including their responsibilities to mitigate greenhouse gas emissions, adapt to climate impacts, and protect the fundamental rights of all individuals to live in a healthy and sustainable environment.[99]

Notably, the court also found that the equality rights of women and girls are implicated by the state's climate-related actions, noting:

> Unequal energy access disproportionately affects women and girls due to their gender roles and responsibilities, such as through time spent on domestic chores and unpaid care work. Women in many developing countries spend, on average, 1.4 hours a day collecting fuelwood and four hours cooking, in addition to other household tasks that could be supported by energy access. The importance of prioritising clean energy initiatives to ensure environmental sustainability and uphold human rights obligations cannot be understated.[100]

The judgment thus paves the way for future climate litigation in India due to its strong endorsement of fundamental rights as the legal basis for claims for protection from the adverse effects of climate change.[101] In the context of prospective adaptation-focused climate litigation relating to women and girls, the judgment provides an opening for judicial intervention to enforce positive state obligations that prohibit discrimination and support the right to equality for women and girls in climate action.

## Considerations for adaptation-related climate change litigation focused on women and girls in India

As argued earlier, the Indian legal landscape includes strong procedural, constitutional, and jurisprudential elements that could help ground future litigation focused on reducing the vulnerability of women and girls in the context of climate change adaptation. Nevertheless, clear obstacles remain.

Firstly, international norms on adaptation are generally less cogent than those for mitigation.[102] As Luporini points out, 'the international provisions on adaptation are still largely vague and with unclear legal value'.[103] The lack of strong international norms 'corresponds with overall legally weak and fragmented adaptation norms at the domestic level'.[104] This is true in India, where adaptation is addressed through policy documents in the form of heterogeneous 'action plans' which lack uniform content or quality. Adaptation is also addressed through a vast array of sectoral regulations rather than through a legally binding adaptation law.

Nevertheless, as described earlier, the Supreme Court has recognised the role of international climate and sustainable development obligations and principles in both *Hanuman* and *Ranjitsinh*. Moreover, in considering the development of a potential adaptation case, petitioners could also draw on the Pakistani case *Leghari v Federation of Pakistan*,[105] one of the few successful rights-based adaptation cases decided globally to date. In *Leghari*, the Lahore High Court drew on both domestic and international legal principles, such as inter-generational equity, the precautionary principle, and the public trust doctrine, finding that the government's failure to implement its climate mitigation and adaptation targets violated the right to life under Article 9 of Pakistan's Constitution.[106]

On the other hand, in the context of climate change adaptation, human rights– and constitutional rights–based arguments can permit litigants to bypass some of the obstacles posed by mitigation cases.[107] States have positive obligations under human rights law to protect and fulfil human rights by taking appropriate steps, such as adopting adaptation measures to counteract the adverse effects of climate change. These obligations require action to prevent or reduce human rights interference caused by climate change, regardless of the state's contribution to the problem. Thus, unlike mitigation, adaptation cases do not face significant obstacles of causation and attribution, making it clear that the responsibility for adaptation lies primarily with the territorial state. Therefore, there are significant opportunities for adaptation-related climate litigation based on the relatively straightforward nature of a state's human rights obligations in this context.

A related challenge is the lack of precise metrics for adaptation, making adaptation 'successes' and 'failures' difficult to quantify.[108] In the Indian context, the vast majority of SAPCCs fail to include targets or indicators relating to women's and girls' adaptation.[109] India also lacks sex- and gender-disaggregated data on climate risks at both the federal and state levels, resulting in a dearth of information concerning how gender and gender inequalities affect women's experiences of climate change and their adaptive capacity.[110] As a result, policymakers lack a strong evidence base upon which to develop gender-responsive adaptation policies, and potential litigants might subsequently face challenges in building a legal case. On the other hand, the government's failure to collect data and set gender-related adaptation targets could become part of a challenge before the courts.

Given the normative uncertainty around climate change adaptation and the challenges with its measurement, it may also be useful to direct attention to types of claims that '[broaden] the scope of "climate litigation" by incorporating smaller, more discrete cases' that may not be framed expressly in terms of climate change or adaptation but which nevertheless may provide opportunities to address the structural causes of vulnerability.[111] Many aspects of adaptation are addressed in various regulations across different sectors rather than incorporated into climate adaptation laws or policies as such.[112] Beyond cases explicitly invoking climate change, these other types of claims can significantly impact the adaptive capacity of women and girls.

Finally, it may be necessary to sensitise judges on the issues of gender inequality, non-discrimination, and the intersectional nature of vulnerability in the domain of climate policy to challenge stereotypes and frame women and girls as agents of climate change adaptation, rather than simply as victims.[113] In 2021, the Indian Supreme Court ordered mandatory gender sensitisation for Indian lawyers and judges to curb decisions influenced by gender biases and patriarchal norms.[114] In 2023, the Supreme Court published the *Handbook on Combating Gender Stereotypes*.[115] While these efforts are particularly pertinent to cases of sexual assault and domestic violence, they nonetheless have implications for how judges understand issues of gender framing and equality more broadly and may also have a positive impact on the adjudication of gender-related climate matters. To this end, it is crucial to draw links between the types of attitudes and structural harms that underpin sexual and gender-based violence and how adaptation measures (or the lack thereof) may affect the vulnerability of women and girls to climate change.

## Conclusion

In India and throughout the Global South, climate litigation is bringing the climate emergency into the courts. As climate change intensifies, climate litigation is expected to expand and further impact climate law and policymaking.[116] As this chapter has discussed, there are significant gaps in India's current climate adaptation policies concerning the intersection of gender, climate change vulnerability, and adaptive capacity.

The omission of comprehensive gender considerations in adaptation plans not only represents a missed opportunity to enhance the resilience of women and girls but also poses a threat to their socio-economic and equality rights. Despite this, the issue of gendered vulnerabilities in climate adaptation has not yet been robustly addressed through judicial means in India. The nascent state of climate litigation in the country, with its predominant focus on mitigation rather than adaptation, underscores the need for a paradigm shift towards addressing adaptation issues through legal avenues. To this end, India's progressive constitutional framework, coupled with a robust tradition of public interest litigation, offers a promising pathway for advancing adaptation-related climate litigation to reduce the vulnerability of women and girls to the climate crisis. We argue that the evolving jurisprudence, which in 2024, acknowledged environmental and equality rights in the context of climate change, provides a foundation for novel litigation efforts.

Future efforts should focus on leveraging this legal framework to bring forward strategic litigation that both seeks redress for the current inadequacies in adaptation policies and strives to embed gender-sensitive approaches within the broader climate adaptation agenda. Such litigation could play a crucial role in driving policy reform and ensuring that adaptation measures are inclusive, equitable, and effective in safeguarding rights and enhancing the resilience of all vulnerable groups, particularly women and girls.

Addressing these critical gaps through targeted legal action can pave the way for more inclusive and transformative climate adaptation strategies. This approach will not only mitigate the adverse impacts of climate change on vulnerable populations but can also contribute to realising a more just and equitable society in the face of the escalating climate crisis.

## Notes

1 David Eckstein, Vera Kunzel and Laura Schafer, 'Global Climate Risk Index 2021: Who Suffers most from Extreme Weather Events? Weather-Related Loss Events in 2019 and 2000–2019' (2021)' (*Germanwatch*, January 2021) <https://www.germanwatch.org/en/19777> accessed 8 September 2024.
2 SS Yadav and Rattan Lal, 'Vulnerability of Women to Climate Change in Arid and Semi-Arid Regions: The Case of India and South Asia (2018) 149(1) *J Arid Env* 4, 5–6; Aditi Madan and Arjun Dubey, 'The Gendered Impact of Heatwaves and Water Crisis in India' (*Observer Research Foundation,* 2 May 2024) <https://www.orfonline.org/expert-speak/the-gendered-impact-of-heatwaves-and-water-crisis-in-india> accessed 20 May 2024.
3 C Singh, D Soloman and N Rao, 'How Does Climate Change Adaptation Policy in India Consider Gender? An Analysis of 28 State Action Plans' (2021) 21 *J Climate Policy* 958. For discussion on vulnerability and intersectional climate injustice, see Murcott, Tigre and Ann Samuel Chapter 1.
4 Government of India, 'National Action Plan on Climate Change' (2008) <https://archivepmo.nic.in/drmanmohansingh/climate_change_english.pdf> accessed 10 April 2023.
5 See Oxford Policy Management, 'India's State Action Plans on Climate Change: Towards Meaningful Action' <https://www.opml.co.uk/files/Publications/corporate-publications/briefing-notes/id-state-action-plan-climate-india.pdf> accessed 26 September 2024.
6 Singh, Solomon and Rao (n 3) 968.

7 Singh, Solomon and Rao (n 3) 962; see also Maureen Fordham, 'Gender, Sexuality and Disaster' in Ben Wisner, JC Gaillard and Ilan Kelman (eds), *Handbook of Hazards and Disaster Risk Reduction* (Routledge 2012).

8 *Ranjitsinh et al. v Union of India* (2024) SC 2024 INC 280, Indian Supreme Court (India) (*Ranjitsinh*); Lavanya Rajamani, 'Rights Based Climate Litigation in the Indian Courts: Potential, Prospects and Potential Problems' (2013) *Centre for Policy Research Climate Initiative Working Paper No 2013/1* <https://cprindia.org/system/tdf/working_papers/Working%20paper%202013_LRajamani_Climate%20Litigation_5.pdf> accessed 3 January 2023; Rajamani (n 8) 8; Gitanjali N Gill, 'Environmental Standards and Right to Life in India: Regulatory Framework and Judicial Enterprise' in Stephen J Turner et al. (eds), *Environmental Rights: Development of Standards* (CUP 2019) 222, 223–225.

9 Mayesha Alam, Rukmani Bhatia and Briana Mawby, 'Women and Climate Change: Impact and Agency in Human Rights, Security, and Economic Development' (2015) <https://giwps.georgetown.edu/wp-content/uploads/2017/09/Women-and-Climate-Change.pdf> accessed 16 September 2024; Susana Borras, 'Climate Migration, Gender and Poverty' in Jordi Jaria Manzana and Susana Boras (eds), *Research Handbook on Global Climate Constitutionalism* (Edward Elgar Publishing 2019) 220; UN Women, 'The Impact of Climate Change on Women and Girls in the Pacific' (2020) <https://asiapacific.unwomen.org/en/digital-library/publications/2020/08/the-impact-of-climate-change-on-women-and-girls-in-the-pacific> accessed 9 April 2023> accessed 9 April 2023. Duarte Reyes, Chapter 5, pp. 166–168; and Ladan and Madukwe, Chapter 8, pp. 242–245.

10 Lena Bendlin, 'Women's Human Rights in a Changing Climate: Highlighting the Distributive Effects of Climate Policies' 27(4) *Cambridge Rev Int Affairs* 680, 681.

11 Ryan Jeremiah D Quan, 'Securing Women's Rights amid the Changing Climate' (2015) 60(1) *Ateneo LJ* 98, 103–104.

12 Food and Agriculture Organization, 'The State of Food and Agriculture: Women in Agriculture, Closing the Gender Gap for Development' (*FAO*, 2011) <https://www.fao.org/4/i2050e/i2050e.pdf> accessed 16 September 2024.

13 Food and Agriculture Organization (n 12).

14 UN Women, 'Gender and Climate Change: Overview' (2015) <https://www.unwomen.org/en/news/in-focus/climate-change> accessed 9 April 2023; Elaine Enarson and PG Dhar Chakrabarti, *Women, Gender and Disaster: Global Issues and Initiatives* (Sage Publications 2009).

15 For example, see Nitya Rao et al., 'Gendered Vulnerabilities to Climate Change: Insights from the Semi-Arid Regions of Africa and Asia' (2019) 11(1) *Climate and Development* 14–26; Alam, Bhatia and Mawby (n 9); Borras (n 9) 220; UN Women (n 9); Stellina Jolly and KS Roshan Menon, 'Climate Change, Disasters, and Gender Resilience: A Legal Analysis from India' (2019) 61(4) *Journal of the Indian Law Institute* 420. For insight on how climate change impacts women in Nigeria, see Ladan and Maduekwe, Chapter 8, pp. 242 and 244–245, and for insight on how climate change impacts women in the Pari Islands of Indonesia, see Buri and Duarte Reyes, Chapter 5, pp. 164 and 165–167.

16 Rajat K Chakraborti, Jagjit Kaur and Harpreet Kaur, 'Water Shortage Challenges and a Way Forward in India' (2019) 111(5) *Journal AWWA* 42.

17 Aayushee Swaraj and Basant Maheshwari, 'Understanding the Role of Groundwater in the Lives of Rural Women in India' (2022) 8(2) *World Water Policy* <https://doi.org/10.1002/wwp2.12085> accessed 8 September 2024; Nandita Singh and Om Prakash Singh, 'Climate Change, Water and Gender: Impact and Adaptation in North-Eastern Hills of India' (2015) 58(3) *International Social Work* <https://doi.org/10.1177/0020872814556826> accessed 8 September 2024.

18 Chetan Choithani, 'Gendered Livelihoods: Migrating Men, Left-Behind Women and Household Food Security in India' (2019) 27(3) *Gender, Place and Culture A Journal of*

*Feminist Geography* <http://dx.doi.org/10.1080/0966369X.2019.1681366> accessed 8 September 2024; Srinivasa Rao et al., 'Climate Resilient Villages for Sustainable Food Security in Tropical India: Concept, Process, Technologies, Institutions, and Impacts' (2016) 140 *Advances in Agronomy* <https://doi.org/10.1016/bs.agron.2016.06.003> accessed 8 September 2024; Yadav and Lal (n 2) 5.

19 Sangram Kishor Patel et al., 'Climate Change and Women in South Asia: A Review and Future Policy Implications' (2020) 17(2) *World Journal of Science, Technology and Sustainable Development* 145.

20 Cecelia Sorensen et al., 'Climate Change and Women's Health: Impacts and Opportunities in India' (2018) 10(2) *Geohealth* 283.

21 Kimberley Thomas et al., 'Explaining Differential Vulnerability to Climate Change: A Social Science Review' (2018) 10(2) *WIREs Climate Change* e565.

22 Birsha Ohdedar, 'Climate Adaptation, Vulnerability, and Rights-Based Litigation: Broadening the Scope of Climate Litigation using Political Ecology' (2022) 13(1) *Journal of Human Rights and the Environment* 137; UN Women, 'Gender and Climate Change: Overview' (2015) <https://www.unwomen.org/en/news/in-focus/climate-change> accessed 9 April 2023; UN Women, 'Facts and Figures' (2012) <https://www.unwomen.org/en/news/in-focus/commission-on-the-status> accessed 9 April 2023; Sangram Kishor Patel et al., 'Climate Change and Women in South Asia: A Review and Future Policy Implications' (2020) 17(2) *World Journal of Science, Technology and Sustainable Development* 145; Jolly and Roshan Menon (n 15) 421–422.

23 NS Ray-Bennett, 'The Influence of Caste, Class and Gender in Surviving Multiple Disasters: A Case Study from Orissa' (2009) 8(1) *India Environmental Hazards* 5; Ayesha Qaisrani and Samvia Batool, 'Vulnerabilities of Rural Women to Climate Extremes: A Case of Semi-Arid Districts in Pakistan' in Asha Hans et al. (eds), *Engendering Climate Change – Learnings from South Asia* (Routledge 2021) 19; Karen Morrow, 'Integrating Gender Issues into the Global Climate Change Regime' in Susan Buckingham and Virginie Le Masson (eds), *Understanding Climate Change through Gender Relations* (Routledge 2017) 31; Margaret Alston, 'Introducing Gender and Climate Change: Research, Policy and Action' in Margaret Alston and Kerry Whittenbury (eds), *Research, Action and Policy: Addressing the Gendered Impacts of Climate Change* (Springer 2013) 3.

24 Jolly and Roshan Menon (n 15) 425–429; Divya Pradeep and KC Adaina, 'G20 Called for Gender Inclusive Climate Action: Is it Another Empty Rhetoric in India's Context' (*The Wire,* 23 September 2023) <https://thewire.in/women/g20-called-for-gender-inclusive-climate-action-is-it-another-empty-rhetoric-in-indias-context> accessed 13 October 2023.

25 Ministry of Environment, Forests and Climate Change (MoEFCC), 'India's Intended Nationally Determined Contribution: Working towards Climate Justice' (2015) 1–38 <https://faolex.fao.org/docs/pdf/ind188478.pdf> accessed 17 September 2024.

26 Government of India, 'National Action Plan on Climate Change' (2008) <https://archivepmo.nic.in/drmanmohansingh/climate_change_english.pdf> accessed 10 April 2023.

27 Government of India (n 26).

28 Government of India (n 26).

29 Chandni Singh et al., 'How Does Climate Adaptation Policy in India Consider Gender? An Analysis of 28 State Action Plans' (*University of East Anglia Digital Depository*) <https://core.ac.uk/reader/457751320> accessed 17 April 2023.

30 Singh et al. (n 29).

31 Singh, Solomon and Rao (n 3) 964.

32 Singh, Solomon and Rao (n 3) 966.

33 Singh, Solomon and Rao (n 3) 968.

34 Singh, Solomon and Rao (n 3) 968; Government of Rajasthan, 'Rajasthan State Action Plan on Climate Change' (2014) <moef.gov.in/wp-content/uploads/2017/09/

Rajasthan.pdf> accessed 15 April 2023; Government of Tamil Nadu, 'Tamil Nadu State Action Plan on Climate Change' (2013) <https://cag.gov.in/uploads/media/tamil-nadu-climate-change-action-plan–20200726073516.pdf> accessed 15 April 2023; Government of Gujarat, 'Gujarat State Action Plan on Climate Change' (2014) <https://moef.gov.in/wp-content/uploads/2017/08/Gujarat-SAPCC.pdf> accessed 15 April 2023.

35 Singh and Singh (n 17); Government of Bihar, 'Bihar State Action Plan on Climate Change' (2015) <moef.gov.in/wp-content/uploads/2017/08/Bihar-State-Action-Plan-on-Climate-Change–2.pdf> accessed 15 April 2023; Government of Chhattisgarh, 'Chhattisgarh State Action Plan on Climate Change' (2013) <moef.gov.in/wp-content/uploads/2017/08/Chhattisgarh.pdf> accessed 15 April 2023.

36 Government of Tamil Nadu, 'Tamil Nadu State Action Plan on Climate Change' (2013) <https://cag.gov.in/uploads/media/tamil-nadu-climate-change-action-plan–20200726073516.pdf> accessed 16 April 2023; Government of Punjab, 'Punjab State Action Plan on Climate Action' (2014) <moef.gov.in/wp-content/uploads/2017/09/Punjab.pdf> accessed 21 April 2023.

37 Singh, Solomon and Rao (n 3) 966.

38 Government of Uttarakhand, 'Uttarakhand Action Plan on Climate Change' (2014) <moef.gov.in/wp-content/uploads/2017/08/Uttarakhand-SAPCC.pdf> accessed 21 April 2023.

39 Singh and Singh (n 17).

40 India Environment Portal, 'Gender Inclusive State Action Plan for Climate Change (SAPCC) Kerala' (*India Environment Portal*, 1 December 2018) <http://www.indiaenvironmentportal.org.in/content/461498/gender-inclusive-state-action-plan-for-climate-change-sapcc-kerala/> accessed 1 May 2023.

41 Singh, Solomon and Rao (n 3) 969.

42 Singh, Solomon and Rao (n 3) 968.

43 Singh, Solomon and Rao (n 3) 970.

44 Nikhila Menon, 'Mainstreaming Gender in India's Climate Smart Agriculture Policy' (*East Asia Forum*, 30 July 2019) <https://www.eastasiaforum.org/2019/07/30/mainstreaming-gender-in-indias-climate-smart-agriculture-policy/> accessed 13 October 2023; Somiha Chatterjee, 'Why Gender Matters: Climate Change and Agriculture in India' (*Social and Political Research Foundation,* 2021) <https://sprf.in/wp-content/uploads/2021/03/SPRF-2021_Gender-Agriculture-and-Climate_IB_Final.pdf> accessed 13 October 2023.

45 Gopalika Arora, 'Climate Budgeting: Unlocking the Potential of India's Fiscal Policies on Climate Action' (*Observer Research Foundation*, 26 April 2023) <https://www.orfonline.org/expert-speak/climate-budgeting/> accessed 3 June 2023.

46 Arjun Malhotra, 'Mainstreaming Climate Change in India through Climate Budgeting' (*The Bastion India*, 19 October 2020) <https://thebastion.co.in/politics-and/mainstreaming-climate-change-in-india-through-climate-budgeting/> accessed 3 June 2023.

47 Alternative Futures et al., 'Policy Brief – Climate Change Adaptation in Four Indian States: The Missing Gender Budgets' (2014) <https://www.cbgaindia.org/wp-content/uploads/2017/03/Climate-Change-Adaptation-and-Gender-Budgeting-Policy-Brief.pdf> accessed 24 April 2023.

48 Elizabeth Gogoi, 'India's State Action Plans on Climate Change: Towards Meaningful Action' (*Oxford Policy Management*, 2017) <https://www.opml.co.uk/files/Publications/corporate-publications/briefing-notes/id-state-action-plan-climate-india.pdf?noredirect=1> accessed 6 June 2023; Ashish Chaturvedi et al., 'State Action Plans on Climate Change Need Upscaling and Capacity Enhancement' (*Down to Earth,* 18 September 2019) <https://www.downtoearth.org.in/blog/climate-change/state-action-plans-on-climate-change-need-upscaling-and-capacity-enhancement-66796> accessed 6 June 2023.

49 G Dhanapal et al., 'Barriers and Opportunities in Achieving Climate and Sustainable Development Goals in India: A Multilevel Analysis' (2023) 20(1) *Journal of Integrative Environmental Sciences* 1.
50 Navroz K Dubash and Anu Jogesh, 'From Margins to Mainstream? State Climate Change Planning in India' (2014) 49(48) *Economic and Political Weekly* 86.
51 Ashok H Desai and S Muralidhar, 'Public Interest Litigation: Potential and Problems' in BN Kirpal et al. (eds), *Supreme But Not Infallible: Essays in Honour of the Supreme Court of India* (Oxford University Press 2000) 159; Eeshan Chaturvedi, 'Climate Change Litigation: Indian Perspective' (2021) 22(8) *German Law Review* 1459.
52 Mahima Jain, 'In India, Grasslands are Classified as Wastelands That Have No Ecological Value' (*Scroll*, 10 December 2022) 1372 <https://scroll.in/article/1039213/in-india-grasslands-are-classified-as-wastelands-that-have-no-ecological-value> accessed 26 April 2024.
53 Surya Deva, 'Public Interest Litigation in India: A Critical Review' (2009) 1(1) *Civil Justice Quarterly* 21.
54 Deva (n 53) 25–26.
55 National Green Tribunal, 'About Us – National Green Tribunal' <https://www.greentribunal.gov.in/about-us> accessed 4 June 2023.
56 Sairam Bhat and Lianne D'Souza, 'A Tribunal in Trouble' (*Centre for Environmental Law, Education, Research and Advocacy Publication,* 1 September 2020) <https://ceerapub.nls.ac.in/a-tribunal-in-trouble/> accessed 6 June 2023.
57 Neethi Varadaraja Rao, Varsha Bhaskaran and Harini Nagendra, 'Can Green Tribunals Help to Resist Neo-Liberalism in Environmental Governance – The Case of India' (2023) 131 *Land Use Policy* 1, 2.
58 The Constitution of India 1950, Article 21.
59 Jain (n 52) 1188.
60 See *Maneka Gandhi v Union of India* (1978) AIR 597, Indian Supreme Court (India); *Coralie v Union Territory of Delhi* (1981) 1981 AIR 1981, Indian Supreme Court (India); *Mehta v Union of India* (1988) SC 1037, Indian Supreme Court (India); *Subhash Kumar v State of Bihar* (1991) 1991 AIR 420, Indian Supreme Court; *State of Punjab v MS Chawla* (1997) AIR 1997 SC 1225, Indian Supreme Court (India); *Avas Vikas Parishad v Friends Co. Housing Society* (1996) AIR 1996 SC 114, Indian Supreme Court (India); *Calcutta Electricity Supply Corporation (India) Ltd v Subhash Chandra Bose* (1992) AIR 1992 573, Indian Supreme Court (India).
61 Jain (n 52) 1125.
62 Naveen Sukumaran, 'Climate Change and Indian Courts: Are We on the Right Track?' (2022) 7(1) *VBCL Law Review* 81; Shibani Ghosh, 'Climate Litigation in India' in F Sindico and MM Mbengue (eds), *Comparative Climate Change Litigation: Beyond the Usual Suspects* (Springer 2021); Erika McDonald, 'The Judicial Activism of Inaction: India's National Green Tribunal and the Reeducation of U.S. Jurists' (2020) 25(1) *UCLA Journal International Law and Foreign Affairs* 159.
63 Jain (n 52) 1173.
64 *Subhash Kumar v State of Bihar* (1991) 1991 AIR 420, Indian Supreme Court (India).
65 See *Mehta v Kamal Nath* (1997) 1 SCC 388, Indian Supreme Court (India); *Mahesh R Desai v Union of India* (1988) W.P. 989, Indian Supreme Court (India).
66 Benjamin K Sovacool, Björn-Ola Linnér and Michael E Goodsite, 'The Political Economy of Climate Adaptation' (2015) 5(7) *Nature Climate Change* 616–618; W Neil Adger, 'Vulnerability' (2006) 16(3) *Global Environmental Change* 268–281; Jonathan Ensor et al., 'A Rights-Based Perspective on Adaptive Capacity' (2015) 31 *Global Environmental Change* 38–49.
67 Nick Brooks, W Neil Adger and P Mick Kelly, 'The Determinants of Vulnerability and Adaptive Capacity at the National Level and the Implications for Adaptation' (2005) 15(2) *Global Environmental Change* 151.

68 Ohdedar (n 22); Kim Bouwer, 'The Unsexy Future of Climate Change Litigation' (2018) 30 *Journal of Environmental Law* 483.
69 Ohdedar (n 22).
70 The Constitution of India 1950, Arts 14 and 15.
71 The Constitution of India, Article 15(3).
72 The Constitution of India 1950, Article 21.
73 *Lt. Col Nitisha v Union of India* (2021) W.P. 1109/2020, Indian Supreme Court (India).
74 Vandita Khanna, 'Indirect Discrimination and Substantive Equality in Nitisha: Easier Said Than Done Under Indian Constitutional Jurisprudence' (2022) 22(1) *Int J Discrimination & L* 74, 75.
75 Khanna (n 74) 78.
76 Khanna (n 74) 78.
77 Khanna (n 74) 82.
78 Khanna (n 74) 74–75.
79 UN Environment Programme and Sabin Centre for Climate Change Law, 'Global Climate Litigation Report: 2023 Status Review' (2023) <https://wedocs.unep.org/bitstream/handle/20.500.11822/43008/global_climate_litigation_report_2023.pdf?sequence=3> accessed 7 October 2023. See also the discussions on Indian climate litigation in Garg and Hinduja, Chapter 2; Kaur, Sathiabama, and Vedavalli, Chapter 7; and Jamwal, Chapter 9.
80 Joana Setzer and Lisa Benjamin, 'Climate Litigation in the Global South: Constraints and Innovations' (2019) 9 *Transnational Environmental Law* 77; Jacqueline Peel and Jolene Lin, 'Transnational Climate Litigation: The Contribution of the Global South' (2019) 113 *American Journal of International Law* 679.
81 Riccardo Luporini, 'Strategic Litigation as a Tool to Advance Climate Change Adaptation? Challenges and Prospects' (2021) 4(1) *Yearbook of International Disaster Law* 202.
82 *Pandey v Union of India and another* (2019) 187/2017, National Green Tribunal (India) (*Pandey*). See also the discussion of *Pandey* in Kaur, Sathiabama and Vedavalli Chapter 7.
83 *Pandey* (n 82).
84 *Pandey* (n 82).
85 *Pandey* (n 82).
86 Nikita Pattajoshi, 'Riddhima Pandey v. Union of India' (2019) 6(1) *J Env L Pol & Dev* 83.
87 *Pandey* (n 82) 25.
88 *Pandey* (n 82).
89 *Gaurav Bansal v Union of India* (2014) 498/2014, National Green Tribunal (India).
90 *Gaurav Bansal* (n 89).
91 *Gaurav Bansal* (n 89).
92 *Gaurav Bansal* (n 89).
93 *Hanuman Laxman Aroskar v Union of India* (2019) SC/0444/2019, Indian Supreme Court (India) (*Hanuman*).
94 *Hanuman Laxman Aroskar* (n 93).
95 *Hanuman Laxman Aroskar* (n 93).
96 *Ranjitsinh et al.* (n 8).
97 Free Law India, 'Supreme Court Recognises the Right to be Free from the Adverse Effects of Climate Change as a Distinct Right' (*Free Law India,* 10 April 2024) <https://www.freelaw.in/legalnews/Supreme-Court-recognizes-the-Right-to-be-Free-from-the-Adverse-Effects-of-Climate-Change-as-a-Distinct-Right> accessed 21 May 2024.
98 Parul Kumar and Abhyaraj Naik, 'India's Constitutional Climate Rights: Examining the Significance of MK Ranjit Singh for Climate Litigation in India' (*Verfassungsblog,*

25 April 2024) <https://verfassungsblog.de/indias-new-constitutional-climate-right/> accessed 21 May 2024.

99 *Ranjitsinh et al.* (n 8) [35].

100 *Ranjitsinh et al.* (n 8) [34].

101 Satyajit Sarna, 'A Tale of Two Climate Change Verdicts, and What They Mean' (*The Times of India,* 13 April 2024) <https://timesofindia.indiatimes.com/blogs/toi-edit-page/a-tale-of-two-climate-change-verdicts-and-what-they-mean/> accessed 21 May 2024.

102 Sarna (n 101).

103 Sarna (n 101).

104 Sarna (n 101).

105 *Leghari v Federation of Pakistan* (2015) W.P. 25501/201, Lahore High Court (Pakistan).

106 *Leghari* (n 105).

107 Luporini (n 81) 11.

108 Luporini (n 81) 9.

109 Singh et al. (n 29).

110 Sorensen et al. (n 20); Ministry of Women and Child Development, 'Report of the High Level Committee on the Status of Women – Vol. 4' (*Government of India,* June 2015) <https://wcd.nic.in/sites/default/files/Vol%204.pdf> accessed 17 June 2023.

111 Ministry of Women and Child Development (n 110).

112 Luporini (n 81) 8.

113 Harsh Mahaseth and Aditi Mishra, 'Indian Courts Need to be Gender Sensitised' (*The Leaflet,* 2 February 2021) <https://theleaflet.in/indian-courts-need-to-be-gender-sensitised/> accessed 10 June 2023; Climate Justice for Women and Girls: A Rule of Law Approach to Feminist Climate Action, 'Enhancing Women's Rights to Land and Other Resources' (*International Development Law Organisation,* 2022) <https://issuu.com/idlonews/docs/a_rule_of_law_approach_to_feminist_climate_action/s/15173386> accessed 17 September 2024.

114 Tanishka Goswami, 'Data Story: SC Mandated Gender Sensitisation for Judges, But Who Followed It?' (*Youth Ki Awaz,* 15 February 2022) <https://www.youthkiawaaz.com/2022/02/gender-sensitise-training-module-court-judiciary-legal-survey-data/> accessed 10 June 2023.

115 R Mihir, 'Supreme Court Handbook on Gender Stereotypes, Progressive, But will the Law Catch Up?' (*Supreme Court Observer,* 19 August 2023) <https://www.scobserver.in/journal/supreme-court-handbook-on-gender-stereotypes-progressive-but-will-the-law-catch-up/> accessed 21 May 2024.

116 Elizabeth Donger, 'Children and Youth in Strategic Climate Litigation: Advancing Rights through Legal Argument and Legal Mobilization' (2022) 11(2) *Transnational Environmental Law* 263.

## Bibliography

### *Books and book chapters*

Alston M, 'Introducing Gender and Climate Change: Research, Policy and Action' in M Alston and K Whittenbury (eds), *Research, Action and Policy: Addressing the Gendered Impacts of Climate Change* (Springer 2013)

Auz J, 'Two Reputed Allies: Reconciling Climate Justice and Litigation in the Global South' in C Rodríguez-Garavito (ed), *Litigating the Climate Emergency: How Human Rights, Courts, and Legal Mobilization Can Bolster Climate Action* (Cambridge University Press 2022)

Boele-Woelki K and Arroyo DPF (eds), *Ius Comparatum – Global Studies in Comparative Law* (Springer 2015)
Borras S, 'Climate Migration, Gender and Poverty' in Jordi Jaria-Manzana and Susana Borras (eds), *Research Handbook on Global Climate Constitutionalism* (Edward Elgar Publishing 2019)
Desai AH and Muralidhar S, 'Public Interest Litigation: Potential and Problems' in BN Kirpal, AH Desai, G Subramanian, R Dhavan and R Ramchandran (eds), *Supreme But Not Infallible: Essays in Honour of the Supreme Court of India* (Oxford University Press 2001)
Enarson E and DharChakrabarti PG, *Women, Gender and Disaster: Global Issues and Initiatives* (Sage Publications 2009)
Fordham M, 'Gender, Sexuality and Disaster' in B Wisner, JC Gaillard and I Kelman, (eds), *Handbook of Hazards and Disaster Risk Reduction* (Routledge 2012)
Ghosh S, 'Climate Litigation in India' in Francesco Sindico and Makane Moise Mbengue (eds), *Comparative Climate Litigation: Beyond the Usual Suspects* (Springer 2021)
Gill GN, 'Environmental Standards and Right to Life in India: Regulatory Framework and Judicial Enterprise' in SJ Turner, DL Shelton, J Razzaque, O McIntyre and JR May (eds), *Environmental Rights: The Development of Standards* (Cambridge University Press 2019)
Jain MP, *Indian Constitutional Law* (LexisNexis 2016)
MacGregor S, 'Moving Beyond Impacts: More Answers to the "Gender and Climate Change" Question' in Susan Buckingham and Virginie Le Masson (eds), *Understanding Climate Change through Gender Relations* (Routledge 2017)
Morrow K, 'Integrating Gender Issues into the Global Climate Change Regime' in S Buckingham and V Le Masson (eds), *Understanding Climate Change through Gender Relations* (Routledge 2017)
Qaisrani A and Batool S, 'Vulnerabilities of Rural Women to Climate Extremes: A Case of Semi-Arid Districts in Pakistan' in A Hans, N Rao, A Prakash and A Patel (eds), *Engendering Climate Change: Learnings from South Asia* (Routledge 2021)
Singh MP, *VN Shukla's Constitution of India* (Eastern Book Company 2010)

## Briefing papers

Eckstein D, Kunzel V and Schafer L, 'Global Climate Risk Index 2021: Who Suffers Most from Extreme Weather Events? Weather-Related Loss Events in 2019 and 2000–2019' (2021) *Germanwatch* <http://www.germanwatch.org/en/cri> accessed 8 September 2024

## Cases

*Avas Vikas Parishad v Friends Co. Housing Society* (1996) AIR 1996 SC 114, Indian Supreme Court (India)
*Calcutta Electricity Supply Corporation (India) Ltd v Subhash Chandra Bose* (1992) AIR 1992 573, Indian Supreme Court (India)
*Coralie v Union Territory of Delhi* (1981) 1981 AIR 1981, Indian Supreme Court (India)
*Gaurav Bansal v Union of India* (2014) 498/2014, National Green Tribunal (India)
*Hanuman Laxman Aroskar v Union of India* (2019) SC/0444/2019, Indian Supreme Court (India)
*Leghari v Federation of Pakistan* (2015) W.P. 25501/201, Lahore High Court (Pakistan)
*Lt. Col Nitisha v Union of India* (2021) W.P. 1109/2020, Indian Supreme Court (India)
*Mahesh R Desai v Union of India* (1988) W.P. 989, Indian Supreme Court (India)
*Maneka Gandhi v Union of India* (1978) 1978 AIR 597, Indian Supreme Court (India)
*Mehta v Kamal Nath* (1997) 1 SCC 388, Indian Supreme Court (India)

*Mehta v Union of India* (1988) 1988 SC 1037, Indian Supreme Court (India)
*Ranjitsinh et al. v Union of India* (2024) SC 2024 INC 280, Indian Supreme Court (India)
*Ridhima Pandey v Union of India and Another* (2019) 187/2017, National Green Tribunal (India)
*State of Punjab v Chawla* (1997) AIR 1997 SC 1225, Indian Supreme Court (India)
*Subhash Kumar v The State of Bihar* (1991) 1991 AIR 420, Indian Supreme Court (India)

## Conference papers

Malla SP, 'Upholding Women's Rights through Litigation' (*45th Session of United Nations Commission on the Status of Women, New York*, March 2010) <https://www.un.org/womenwatch/daw/beijing15/interactive_panel_III/Sapana%20Pradhan%20Malla%20paper.pdf> accessed 10 September 2024
Ministry of Women and Child Development, 'Report of the High Level Committee on the Status of Women-Vol 4' (*Government of India*, June 2015) <https://wcd.nic.in/sites/default/files/Vol%204.pdf> accessed 17 June 2023

## Journal articles

Adger WN, 'Vulnerability' (2006) 16(3) *Global Environmental Change* 268 <https://doi.org/10.1016/j.gloenvcha.2006.02.006> accessed 9 September 2024
Bahr CC and others, 'Klima Seniorinnen: Lessons from the Swiss Senior Women's Case for Future Climate Litigation' (2018) 9(2) *J Hum Rts & Env't* 194 <http://dx.doi.org/10.4337/jhre.2018.02.04> accessed 17 September 2024
Bendlin L, 'Women's Human Rights in a Changing Climate: Highlighting the Distributive Effects of Climate Policies' 27(4) *Cambridge Review of International Affairs* 680 <https://doi.org/10.1080/09557571.2014.960507> accessed 8 September 2024
Bouwer K, 'The Unsexy Future of Climate Change Litigation' (2018) 30(3) *Journal of Environmental Law* 483 <https://doi.org/10.1093/jel/eqy017> accessed 9 September 2024
Brooks N, Adger WN and Kelly PM, 'The Determinants of Vulnerability and Adaptive Capacity at the National Level and the Implications for Adaptation' (2005) 15(2) *Global Environmental Change* 151 <https://doi.org/10.1016/j.gloenvcha.2004.12.006> accessed 9 September 2024
Chakraborti R and Kaur J, 'Water Shortage Challenges and a Way Forward in India' 111(5) *American Water Works Association* 42 <http://dx.doi.org/10.1002/awwa.1289> accessed 8 September 2024
Chaturvedi E, 'Climate Change Litigation: Indian Perspective' (2021) 22(8) *German Law Journal* 1459 <https://doi.org/10.1017/glj.2021.85> accessed 8 September 2024
Choithani C, 'Gendered Livelihoods: Migrating Men, Left-Behind Women and Household Food Security in India' (2019) 27(3) *Gender, Place and Culture A Journal of Feminist Geography* 1373 <http://dx.doi.org/10.1080/0966369X.2019.1681366> accessed 8 September 2024
Deva S, 'Public Interest Litigation in India: A Critical Review' (2009) 28(1) *Civil Justice Quarterly Issue* 19 <https://ssrn.com/abstract=1424236> accessed 8 September 2024
Dhanapal G, Gupta D and Prakash A, 'Barriers and Opportunities in Achieving Climate and Sustainable Development Goals in India: A Multilevel Analysis' (2023) 20(1) *Journal of Integrative Environmental Sciences* 1 <https://doi.org/10.1080/1943815X.2022.2163665> accessed 8 September 2024
Donger E, 'Children and Youth in Strategic Climate Litigation: Advancing Rights through Legal Argument and Legal Mobilization' (2022) 11(2) *Transnational Environmental Law* 263 <https://doi.org/10.1017/S2047102522000218> accessed 9 September 2024

Ensor JE, Park SE, Hoddy ET and Ratner BD, 'A Rights-Based Perspective on Adaptive Capacity' (2015) 31 *Global Environmental Change* 38 <https://doi.org/10.1016/j.gloenvcha.2014.12.005> accessed 9 September 2024

Gill GN and Ramachandran G, 'Sustainability Transformations, Environmental Rule of Law and the Indian Judiciary: Connecting the Dots through Climate Change Litigation' (2021) 23(3) *Environmental Law Review* 228 <https://doi.org/10.1177/14614529211031203> accessed 10 September 2024

Iyengar S and others, 'Selectively Assertive: Interventions of India's Supreme Court to Enforce Environmental Laws' (2019) 11(24) *Sustainability* 7234 <https://doi.org/10.3390/su11247234> accessed 10 September 2024

Jolly S and Menon RKS, 'Climate Change, Disasters, and Gender Resilience: A Legal Analysis from India' (2019) 61(4) *Journal of the Indian Law Institute* 420

Khanna V, 'Indirect Discrimination and Substantive Equality in Nitisha: Easier Said than Done Under Indian Constitutional Jurisprudence (2022) 22(1) *International Journal of Discrimination and the Law* 74 <https://doi.org/10.1177/13582291211062363> accessed 9 September 2024

Lin J, 'Litigating Climate Change in Asia' (2014) 4(1–2) *Climate Law* 140 <https://doi.org/10.1163/18786561-00402012> accessed 17 September 2024

Luporini R, 'Strategic Litigation as a Tool to Advance Climate Change Adaptation? Challenges and Prospects' (2022) *Yearbook of International Disaster Law* <https://ssrn.com/abstract=4247167> accessed 9 September 2024

McDonald E, 'The Judicial Activism of Inaction: India's National Green Tribunal and the Reeducation of U.S. Jurists' (2020) 25(1) *UCLA Journal of International Law and Foreign Affairs* 159 <https://escholarship.org/uc/item/85n9v6k3> accessed 9 September 2024

Ohdedar B, 'Climate Adaptation, Vulnerability, and Rights-Based Litigation: Broadening the Scope of Climate Litigation Using Political Ecology' (2022) 13(1) *Journal of Human Rights and the Environment* 137 <http://dx.doi.org/10.4337/jhre.2022.01.06> accessed 8 September 2024

Patel SK, Agrawal G, Mathew B, Patel S, Mohanty B and Singh A, 'Climate Change and Women in South Asia: A Review and Future Policy Implications' (2020) 17(2) *World Journal of Science, Technology and Sustainable Development* 145

Pattajoshi N, 'Ridhima Pandey v Union of India: The Onset of Climate Change Litigation in India' (2019) 6(1) *NLS Journal on Environmental Law, Policy and Development*

Peel J and Lin J, 'Transnational Climate Litigation: The Contribution of the Global South' (2019) 113(4) *American Journal of International Law* 679 <https://doi.org/10.1017/ajil.2019.48> accessed 9 September 2024

Peel J and Osofsky HM, 'A Rights Turn in Climate Change Litigation?' (2018) 7(1) *Transnational Environmental Law* 37 <https://doi.org/10.1017/S2047102517000292> accessed 10 September 2024

Quan RJD, 'Securing Women's Right Amind the Changing Climate' (2015) 60(98) *Ateneo Law Journal* 99

Rao NV, Bhaskaran V and Nagendra H, 'Can Green Tribunals Help to Resist Neo-Liberalism in Environmental Governance – The Case of India' (2023) 131 *Land Use Policy* <https://doi.org/10.1016/j.landusepol.2023.106739> accessed 8 September 2024

Rao NV, Lawson ET, Raditloaneng WN, Solomon D and Angula MN, 'Gendered Vulnerabilities to Climate Change: Insights from the Semi-Arid Regions of Africa and Asia' (2019) 11(1) *Climate and Development* 14 <https://doi.org/10.1080/17565529.2017.1372266> accessed 8 September 2024

Rao S, Gopinath K, Prasad J, Prasannakumar and Singh A, 'Climate Resilient Villages for Sustainable Food Security in Tropical India: Concept, Process, Technologies, Institutions, and Impacts' (2016) 140 *Advances in Agronomy* 101 <https://doi.org/10.1016/bs.agron.2016.06.003> accessed 8 September 2024

Ray-Bennett NS, 'The Influence of Caste, Class and Gender in Surviving Multiple Disasters: A Case Study from Orissa, India' (2009) 8(1) *Environmental Hazards* 5 <https://doi.org/10.3763/ehaz.2009.0001> accessed 8 September 2024

Setzer J and Benjamin L, 'Climate Litigation in the Global South: Constraints and Innovations' (2019) 9(1) *Transnational Environmental Law* 77 <https://doi.org/10.1017/S2047102519000268> accessed 9 September 2024

Singh C, Soloman D and Rao N, 'How Does Climate Change Adaptation Policy in India Consider Gender? An Analysis of 28 State Action Plans' (2021) 21(7) *Climate Policy* 958 <https://doi.org/10.1080/14693062.2021.1953434> accessed 8 September 2024

Singh N and Singh OP, 'Climate Change, Water and Gender: Impact and Adaptation in North-Eastern Hills of India' (2015) 58(3) *International Social Work* 375 <https://doi.org/10.1177/0020872814556826> accessed 8 September 2024

Sorensen C, Saunik S, Sehgal M, Tewary A, Govindan M, Lemery J and Balbus J, 'Climate Change and Women's Health: Impacts and Opportunities in India' (2018) 2(10) *Geohealth* 283 <https://doi.org/10.1029/2018GH000163> accessed 8 September 2024

Sovacool BK, Linnér BO and Goodsite ME, 'The Political Economy of Climate Adaptation' (2015) 5(7) *Nature Climate Change* 616 <http://dx.doi.org/10.1038/nclimate2665> accessed 9 September 2024

Sukumaran N, 'Climate Change and Indian Courts: Are We on the Right Track' (2022) 7(1) *VBCL Law Review* 81 <https://ssrn.com/abstract=4315975> accessed 9 September 2024

Swaraj A and Maheshwari B, 'Understanding the Role of Groundwater in the Lives of Rural Women in India' (2022) 8(2) *World Water Policy* 116 <https://doi.org/10.1002/wwp2.12085> accessed 8 September 2024

Thomas K, Hardy RD, Lazrus H, Mendez M, Orlove B, Rivera-Collazo I, Roberts JT, Rockman M, Warner BP and Winthrop R, 'Explaining Differential Vulnerability to Climate Change: A Social Science Review' (2018) 10(2) *Wiley Interdisciplinary Reviews Climate Change* e565 <https://doi.org/10.1002/wcc.565> accessed 8 September 2024

Yadav S S and Rattan Lal, 'Vulnerability of Women to Climate Change in Arid and Semi-Arid Regions: The Case of India and South Asia' (2018) 149(1) *Journal of Arid Environments* 4 <http://dx.doi.org/10.1016/j.jaridenv.2017.08.001> accessed 8 September 2024

## *Online sources*

Arora G, 'Climate Budgeting: Unlocking the Potential of India's Fiscal Policies on Climate Action' (*Observer Research Foundation*, 26 April 2023) <https://www.orfonline.org/expert-speak/climate-budgeting/> accessed 3 June 2023

Bhat S and D'Souza L, 'A Tribunal in Trouble?' (*National Law School of India University*, 1 September 2020) <https://ceerapub.nls.ac.in/a-tribunal-in-trouble/> accessed 6 June 2023

Chaturvedi A, Rattani V and Awasthi K, 'State Action Plans on Climate Change Need Upscaling and Capacity Enhancement' (*Down to Earth*, 18 September 2019) <https://www.downtoearth.org.in/blog/climate-change/state-action-plans-on-climate-change-need-upscaling-and-capacity-enhancement-66796> accessed 6 June 2023

Dahiya Y, 'Poor Implementation of Environmental Laws in India' (*Ipleaders*, 3 August 2018) <https://blog.ipleaders.in/poor-implementation-environmental-laws/> accessed 15 June 2023

'Facts and Figures' (*UN Women*, 2012) <https://www.unwomen.org/en/news/in-focus/commission-on-the-status-of-women-2012/facts-and-figures> accessed 9 April 2023

'Gender Inclusive State Action Plan for Climate Change (SAPCC) Kerala' (*India Environment Portal*, 1 December 2018) <http://www.indiaenvironmentportal.org.in/content/461498/gender-inclusive-state-action-plan-for-climate-change-sapcc-kerala/> accessed 1 May 2023

Goswami T, 'Data Story: SC Mandated Gender Sensitisation for Judges, But Who Followed It?' (*Youth Ki Awaz*, 15 February 2022) <https://www.youthkiawaaz.com/2022/02/gender-sensitise-training-module-court-judiciary-legal-survey-data/> accessed 10 June 2023

Kumar P and Naik A, 'India's New Constitutional Climate Right: Examining the Significance of MK Ranjitsinh and Others v Union of India and Others for Climate Litigation in India' (*Verfassungsblog*, 25 April 2024) <https://verfassungsblog.de/indias-new-constitutional-climate-right/> accessed 21 May 2024

Madan A and Dubey A, 'The Gendered Impact of Heatwaves and Water Crisis in India' (*Observer Research Foundation*, 2 May 2024) <https://www.orfonline.org/expert-speak/the-gendered-impact-of-heatwaves-and-water-crisis-in-india> accessed 20 May 2024

Mahaseth H and A Mishra, 'Indian Courts Need to be Gender Sensitised' (*The Leaflet*, 2 February 2021) <https://theleaflet.in/indian-courts-need-to-be-gender-sensitised/> accessed 10 June 2023

Malhotra A, 'Mainstreaming Climate Change in India through Climate Budgeting' (*The Bastion India*, 19 October 2020) <https://thebastion.co.in/politics-and/mainstreaming-climate-change-in-india-through-climate-budgeting/> accessed 3 June 2023

Menon N, 'Mainstreaming Gender in India's Climate-Smart Agriculture Policy' (*East Asia Forum*, 30 July 2019) <https://eastasiaforum.org/2019/07/30/mainstreaming-gender-in-indias-climate-smart-agriculture-policy/> accessed 8 September 2024

Mihir R, 'Supreme Court Handbook on Gender Stereotypes: Progressive, But will the Law Catch Up?' (*Supreme Court Observer*, 19 August 2023) <https://www.scobserver.in/journal/supreme-court-handbook-on-gender-stereotypes-progressive-but-will-the-law-catch-up/> accessed 21 May 2024

'No Govt. Mechanism to Implement Court Orders' (*The Hindu*, 3 December 2020) <https://www.thehindu.com/news/national/karnataka/no-govt-mechanism-to-implement-courts-orders/article33235504.ece> accessed 12 June 2023

Park A, 'How Climate Change Exacerbates Gender Inequality Across the Globe' (*Time*, 26 November 2019) <https://time.com/5738322/climate-change-gender-inequality/> accessed 4 April 2023

Pathak S, 'Role of Indian Legal System in Protecting Gender Equality' (*India Legal Live*, 8 July 2022) <https://www.indialegallive.com/laws-research-indepth/role-of-indian-legal-system-in-protecting-gender-equality/> accessed 11 April 2023

Pradeep D and Adaina KC, 'G20 Called for Gender Inclusive Climate Action: Is It Another Empty Rhetoric in India's Context' (*The Wire*, 23 September 2023) <https://thewire.in/women/g20-called-for-gender-inclusive-climate-action-is-it-another-empty-rhetoric-in-indias-context> accessed 13 October 2023

Sarna S, 'A Tale of Two Climate Change Verdicts, and What They Mean' (*Times of India*, 13 April 2024) <https://timesofindia.indiatimes.com/blogs/toi-edit-page/a-tale-of-two-climate-change-verdicts-and-what-they-mean/> accessed 21 May 2024

Singh C, 'How is India Mainstreaming Gender in Climate Change Adaptation?' (*Question of Cities*, 8 September 2023) <https://questionofcities.org/how-is-india-mainstreaming-gender-in-climate-change-adaptation/> accessed 21 May 2024

'Supreme Court Recognizes the Right to be Free from the Adverse Effects of Climate Change as a Distinct Right' (*Free Law*, 10 April 2024) <https://www.freelaw.in/legal-news/Supreme-Court-recognizes-the-Right-to-be-Free-from-the-Adverse-Effects-of-Climate-Change-as-a-Distinct-Right> accessed 21 May 2024

UNWomen, 'Gender and Climate Change: Overview' (2015) <https://www.unwomen.org/en/news/in-focus/climate-change> accessed 9 April 2023

## Reports

Alam M, Bhatia R and Mawby B, 'Women and Climate Change: Impact and Agency in Human Rights, Security, and Economic Development' (*Georgetown Institute for Women, Peace and Security*, 2015)

Chatterjee S, 'Why Gender Matters: Climate Change and Agriculture in India' (*Social & Political Research Foundation*, 2021) <https://sprf.in/wp-content/uploads/2021/03/SPRF-2021_Gender-Agriculture-and-Climate_IB_Final.pdf> accessed 13 October 2023

Dubash NK and Jogesh A, 'From Margins to Mainstream? State Climate Change Planning in India as a "Door Opener" to a Sustainable Future' (*Climate Initiative, Research Report*, 2014) <https://dx.doi.org/10.2139/ssrn.2474518> accessed 8 September 2024

Food and Agriculture Organization, 'The State of Food and Agriculture: Women in Agriculture, Closing the Gender Gap for Development' (*FAO*, 2011) <https://www.fao.org/4/i2050e/i2050e.pdf> accessed 16 September 2024

'Global Climate Litigation Report: 2023 Status Review' (*United Nations Environment Programme*, 2023) <https://doi.org/10.59117/20.500.11822/43008> accessed 7 October 2023

Gogoi E, 'India's State Action Plans on Climate Change: Towards Meaningful Action' (*Oxford Policy Management*, 2017) <https://www.opml.co.uk/files/Publications/corporate-publications/briefing-notes/id-state-action-plan-climate-india.pdf?noredirect=1> accessed 6 June 2023

Government of Bihar, 'Bihar State Action Plan on Climate Change' (2015) <https://faolex.fao.org/docs/pdf/ind194002.pdf> accessed 15 April 2023

Government of Chhattisgarh, 'Chhattisgarh State Action Plan on Climate Change' (2013) <https://cgclimatechange.com/wp-content/uploads/2018/04/CGSAPCC.pdf moef.gov.in/wp-content/uploads/2017/08/Chhattisgarh.pdf> accessed 15 April 2023

Government of Gujarat, 'Gujarat State Action Plan on Climate Change' (2014) <https://moef.gov.in/wp-content/uploads/2017/08/Gujarat-SAPCC.pdf> accessed 15 April 2023

Government of India, 'National Action Plan on Climate Change' (2008). <https://archivepmo.nic.in/drmanmohansingh/climate_change_english.pdf> accessed 10 April 2023

Jerath N, Ladhar S, Kaur S, Sharma V, Saile P, Tripathi P, Bhattacharya S and Parwana HK, 'Punjab State Action Plan on Climate Change' (*Punjab State Council for Science and Technology and GIZ*, 2014) <https://moef.gov.in/uploads/2017/09/Punjab.pdf> accessed 10 September 2024

National Disaster Management Authority, 'National Disaster Management Plan' (*Government of India, Ministry of Home Affairs*, 2016) <https://ndma.gov.in/sites/default/files/PDF/ndmp–2019.pdf> accessed 10 September 2024

National Human Rights Commission India, 'Women's Rights in India: An Analytical Study of The United Nations Convention on the Elimination of All Forms of Discrimination against Women (CEDAW) and The Indian Constitution, Legislations, Schemes, Policies & Judgements' (*Research Division, National Human Rights Commission, India*, 2021) <https://nhrc.nic.in/sites/default/files/Women%E2%80%99s%20Rights%20in%20India%20complete_compressed.pdf> accessed 5 April 2023

Oxford Policy Management, 'India's State Action Plans on Climate Change: Towards Meaningful Action' <https://www.opml.co.uk/files/Publications/corporate-publications/briefing-notes/id-state-action-plan-climate-india.pdf> accessed 26 September 2024

'Rajasthan State Action Plan on Climate Change' (*Government of Rajasthan*, 2014) <https://environment.rajasthan.gov.in/content/dam/environment/RPCB/Reports%20n%20Papers/ClimateChange_09_04_2012.pdf> accessed 10 September 2024

'Tamil Nadu State Action Plan on Climate Change (Draft)' (*Government of Tamil Nadu*, 2013) <https://cag.gov.in/uploads/media/tamil-nadu-climate-change-action-plan–20200726073516.pdf> accessed 10 September 2024

'Uttarakhand Action Plan on Climate Change' (*Government of Uttarakhand*, 2014) <https://forest.uk.gov.in/uploads/climate_change_information/1616764235.pdf> accessed 21 April 2023

## *Guidelines*

National Disaster Management Authority, 'National Disaster Management Guidelines' (*Government of India*, 2007) <https://nidm.gov.in/PDF/guidelines/sdmp.pdf> accessed 10 September 2024

### Policy documents and briefs

International Development Law Organization, 'Enhancing Women's Rights to Land and Other Resources' in *Climate Justice for Women and Girls: A Rule of Law Approach to Feminist Climate Action* (International Development Law Organization 2022) <https://www.idlo.int/publications/climate-justice-women-and-girls-rule-law-approach-feminist-climate-action> accessed 9 September 2024

Kapoor A, Shrivastava S and Panda GR, 'Climate Change Adaptation in Four Indian States: The Missing Gender Budgets' (*Alternative Futures and Centre for Budget and Governance Accountability*, 2014) <https://www.cbgaindia.org/wp-content/uploads/2017/03/Climate-Change-Adaptation-and-Gender-Budgeting-Policy-Brief.pdf> accessed 24 April 2023

Ministry of Women and Child Development, 'National Policy for Women 2016: Articulating a Vision for Empowerment of Women (Draft)' (*Government of India*, 2016) <https://judicialacademy.nic.in/sites/default/files/1464237598_draft%20national%20policy%20for%20women%202016.pdf> accessed 10 September 2024

National Disaster Management Authority, 'National Policy on Disaster Management' (*Government of India, Ministry of Home Affairs*, 2009) <http://wbdmd.gov.in/writereaddata/ndm_policy2009.pdf> accessed 10 September 2024

Sinha D, Mehta D, Rana E and Kuriakose S, 'Research Findings: Courting the Environment: Implementation of Environmental Judgments' (*Vidhi Centre for Legal Policy*, 2021) <https://vidhilegalpolicy.in/wp-content/uploads/2021/04/Courting-the-Environment-Full-Report.pdf> accessed 15 June 2023

### Working papers

Rajamani L, 'Rights Based Climate Litigation in the Indian Courts: Potential, Prospects and Potential Problems' (2013) *Centre for Policy Research Climate Initiative Working Paper 2013/1*, <https://cprindia.org/system/tdf/working_papers/Working%20paper%202013_LRajamani_Climate%20Litigation_5.pdf> accessed 3 January 2023

UN Women, 'The Impact of Climate Change on Women and Girls in the Pacific' (2020) <https://asiapacific.unwomen.org/en/digital-library/publications/2020/08/the-impact-of-climate-change-on-women-and-girls-in-the-pacific> accessed 9 April 2023

### Other

'A Comprehensive Guide to Women's Legal Rights' (*Majlis Legal Center*, 2018) <https://www.iitk.ac.in/wc/data/Majlis_Legal-rights-of-women.pdf> accessed 5 April 2023

WEDO, 'Factsheet: Climate Change and Women' (2008) <https://wedo.org/wp-content/uploads/CCWOMENFactsheet-final.pdf> accessed 9 April 2023

# Part 2

# Innovative litigation in pursuit of intersectional climate justice

Chapter 5

# Elevating women's voices in transnational climate litigation

## The case of *Asmania et al. v Holcim*

*Nina Burri and Laura Duarte Reyes*

### Introduction

This chapter explores the challenges and opportunities related to the inclusion of women[1] – and, more specifically, fisherwomen – communities in transnational climate litigation[2] from a practitioner's point of view. It does so by discussing *Asmania et al. v Holcim* (*Asmania*),[3] a climate case filed by four Indonesian plaintiffs against a multinational corporation in a Swiss court under Swiss law.

Although climate litigation is on the rise,[4] civil law cases focusing on adaptation and loss and damage have been launched rarely, and even fewer times have women acted as plaintiffs.[5] This might stem from the fact that civil cases generally face severe procedural hurdles and factual and contextual limitations.[6] *Asmania* is, therefore, an exception in the landscape of climate litigation and a good example for showcasing why the involvement of women is critical for catalysing intersectional transformative climate action and the quest for community-based climate adaptation solutions.

To this end, the chapter first discusses the factual aspects of *Asmania* by presenting the background of the litigation. Secondly, it discusses how an intersectional approach can prove key to understanding how differentiated impacts of climate change on women shape, and are shaped by, the complex power dynamics of existing systems of inequality and oppression. Against this backdrop, the chapter looks at the gendered impacts of climate change on the Indonesian island of Pari and how women on the island have collectively responded. Thirdly, the chapter explains how listening to community demands in Pari, specifically from women, exposed the importance of adaptation measures and non-financial damages. Finally, the chapter describes how incorporating the Indonesian reality into the Swiss civil law framework discloses new gender-sensitive challenges that are disadvantageous for women.

The authors, who have been closely involved in the campaign 'Call for Climate Justice'[7] in support of *Asmania*, have analysed information gathered in several individual and group interviews conducted by them or their colleagues on the island of Pari, as well as the evidence presented in the legal proceedings in Switzerland.

DOI: 10.4324/9781003470632-8

## Background of the litigation: *Asmania et al. v Holcim*

### *Climate change impacts on Pari Island*

Pari is a small island in the Indonesian Western Pacific Ocean located about 40 km from Jakarta, the capital of Indonesia. The island is 2.6 km long and measures approximately 430 m at its widest point. At its highest point in altitude, Pari's elevation measures 1.5 m.[8] About 1,500 inhabitants live permanently on the island. Its geographic location, size, and elevation make the island particularly vulnerable to the effects of climate change.

Due to climate change–induced sea level rise, small islands and low-lying coasts are particularly exposed to cascading and mutually reinforcing impacts, such as loss of coastal ecosystems and ecosystem services, salinisation of groundwater, flooding, or damage to coastal infrastructures.[9] These impacts, in turn, affect the health, food, water security, as well as traditions and cultural values of humans living in such areas.[10] Indonesia is exceptionally affected by these impacts due to its geographic location and many coastlines.[11]

These impacts are already severely felt on Pari Island. With increasing intensity and regularity, parts of the island are flooded by the sea.[12] Sometimes, the water stays on the island for up to one week before flowing back into the sea, which forces some inhabitants to move to other places. Other inhabitants sleep with water under their beds and raise their beds with a handful of stones.[13] The floods cause damage to houses and other infrastructure and pollute freshwater wells. Tourism, which is, besides fishery, the main source of income for the islanders, is highly affected by these developments.[14]

A study by German climate scientists analysing the attribution of the floods on Pari Island and the related impacts to climate change draws a daunting outlook for the island's future. The study asserts that the mean sea level will continue to rise for the next centuries.[15] This rise will lead to an increase in extreme water levels, and thus more frequent and intense floods.[16] This makes it almost certain that human-induced global warming and the associated sea level rise will lead to more future climate change–related impacts and damages on Pari.[17] Yet the extent of these impacts and damages depends largely on how much the Earth warms in the years to come.

### *Litigation filed in Switzerland*

Facing these increasingly challenging threats to their livelihoods, four inhabitants of Pari Island – Asmania, Arif Pujanto, Mustaqfirin, and Edi Mulyono – took legal action. They filed a lawsuit against the world's biggest cement manufacturer, the multinational corporation Holcim Ltd (Holcim), demanding climate justice.[18] Holcim is a public limited company with subsidiaries in 70 countries, headquartered in the city of Zug, Switzerland.[19] The Holcim Group operates 266 cement and grinding plants worldwide and is on the list of the so-called carbon majors, which constitute the 107 companies that have contributed most to climate change.[20] According to an analysis conducted by attribution scientist Richard Heede, Holcim and its predecessor, Lafarge, have produced 7.26 Gt (billion tons) of cement from 1950 to 2021, which caused an estimated 7.15 Gt$CO_2$ emissions (scopes 1, 2, and 3).[21] This result amounts to 0.42% of all global industrial emissions from 1751 to 2021.[22]

The plaintiffs demand Holcim to (1) reduce the emissions of the whole group in accordance with the 1.5 degrees Celsius limit defined in the Paris Agreement (mitigation),[23] (2) contribute to the costs of local flood prevention measures and water distilleries (adaptation), and (3) compensate them for financial and non-financial damages they have already suffered, as well as for future impending damages (loss and damages).[24] This holistic approach of the claim includes both a historical dimension of accountability for past contributions to climate change–induced loss and damages and a forward-looking dimension of accountability for future effects of greenhouse gas emissions. Yet the plaintiffs demand from Holcim solely the share of 0.42% of all costs of the damages, in line with the contribution of Holcim to all industrial emissions from 1751 to 2021.[25] Their requests are based on a classic tort claim under Swiss civil law for compensation of financial and non-financial harm and, for the emission reduction and the flood prevention measures, on a violation of their personality rights.[26]

In July 2022, the plaintiffs filed a conciliation request to the conciliation authority in Zug, where the Holcim Group is registered. The conciliation meeting between the parties failed in October 2022, which led the plaintiffs to file a complaint to the district court (Kantonsgericht) of Zug in January 2023. In October 2023, the plaintiffs received a first favourable decision from the court. Contrary to the arguments brought forward by Holcim, the judge granted the plaintiffs legal aid.[27] That means that the state covers the costs of their lawyer as well as the court fees and that they are exempt from paying a deposit for the fees of Holcim's lawyers. The legal action of the four islanders of Pari is backed by the 'Call for Climate Justice'[28] campaign supported by three non-governmental organisations (NGOs),[29] highlighting not only the wider topics of climate justice and loss and damages but also the role of the cement industry in the context of climate change.[30]

## Getting the full picture through the lens of intersectionality

The situation on Pari Island is not exceptional. Human-induced climate change is increasingly causing weather and climate extremes around the world.[31] This has resulted in extensive adverse impacts and related losses and damages to humans and nature, which, in turn, have exacerbated existing inequalities and created new vulnerabilities.[32] All this is aggravated by historic marginalisation linked to gender, ethnicity, disability, age, economic poverty, and historical and ongoing patterns of inequity, such as colonialism.[33]

There is consensus on the fact that the adverse impacts of climate change affect women differently than other population groups.[34] Women also constitute most of the world's poor and often depend directly on ecosystems at risk as their primary source of food and income, which aggravates their exposure.[35] Nevertheless, not all women are equally affected by climate change. A series of contextual factors and power structures exacerbate the vulnerability to climate change impacts of particular groups of women and determines their ability to adapt to them.[36]

In order to better understand this convergence, intersectionality, as an analytical tool, sheds light on how social identities, such as race, age, gender, class, religion, geography, and mental health, among others, intersect with one another and interact with power structures to create and reinforce power, disparity, and discrimination.[37] In turn, this understanding can uncover emancipatory pathways for women in the face of climate change, as it sheds light on the agency that women may (or may not) be able to exercise in climate adaptation or mitigation processes.

While it is outside the scope of this chapter to do an intersectional analysis of the *Asmania* case, the authors refer to the main factors intersecting the lives of the women of Pari island, especially those politically active in the defence of their island.

### *Multi-layered gendered impacts of climate change*

The gendered impacts of climate change appear in various ways, yet it is important to note that 'gendered' impacts are too often solely understood as impacts of climate change on women. This understanding falls short of the multifaceted gender dimensions of humans, including, for instance, non-binary, gender-queer, bi-gender, gender-fluid, or male population groups, to name just a few.[38] However, since the impact of local women in Pari on the presented case study was the most influential, this chapter focuses on the 'gendered' impacts on women.

For instance, in rural and agriculture-dependent areas, women tend to be vested with disproportionate household responsibilities, including cleaning, collecting fuel and water, shopping for food, and cooking. Following disasters and extreme weather events, such tasks become more labour-intensive, decreasing women's ability to achieve economic autonomy and heightening the risks and experiences of physical violence.[39] This exposure results in higher levels of mortality and morbidity among women in situations of disaster and extreme weather events.[40] These risks are further exacerbated by failures to engage in gender-responsive disaster planning, implementation, and information sharing, which neglect the specific needs of diverse groups of women.[41]

Similarly, as climate change negatively affects the availability, accessibility, consumption, and production of food,[42] it multiplies the risk of women facing food insecurity. Women are often the first in the family to skip meals or abstain from eating during times of scarcity.[43] This has negative impacts on their health, even more so for pregnant and breastfeeding women. Climate change further reduces the availability of clean water in terms of its quality and quantity. As women are often primarily responsible for water collection, a lack of access or longer distances to clean water worsens their situation.[44] In turn, women's inability to meet family or household expectations exposes them to violence, recrimination, or punishment.[45] This disproportionate pressure on women to support their families may also affect women's mental health.[46] In times of crisis, this can cause stress-related disorders or even depression, especially if there is no prospect of an amelioration of the situation in the future. For Indigenous women and girls who have a special connection to the territories they live on and cultivate, these impacts are even more severe.[47]

Women not only tend to lack equal access to environmental and climate information but also are often excluded from participation in environmental, climate, and disaster risk decision-making processes, and from access to justice and effective remedies when their rights are threatened or violated.[48] This systematic under-representation of women inhibits climate action and further exacerbates harm, even more so as the needs of Black, rural, and Indigenous women have been highly disregarded in the context of global climate measures (both in the design and implementation phases).[49] This reality reflects that climate change mitigation, adaptation, and financing for loss and damages have mainly focused on male livelihoods, neglecting the usually unpaid responsibilities fulfilled by women.[50]

### *Intersectionality and women's agency in the face of the climate crisis*

Understanding the differentiated impacts of climate change and how they interact with the multiple social identities of women is crucial to address their needs in the face of the climate crisis effectively.[51] Failing to consider the inequalities and power relations at play when assessing these impacts has led to a disproportionate focus on vulnerability in current debates, which is often associated with victimhood and passiveness, disregarding agency and empowerment as a crucial part of adaptation and mitigation strategies.[52]

Empowerment is linked to the ability to make meaningful choices by those previously denied this capacity.[53] However, for empowerment to take place, the exercise of the ability to choose must be carried out in ways that do not merely reproduce but, indeed, actively challenge the structures of inequality in their society.[54] The capacity to make such choices requires not only control and access to resources (for instance, land, education, healthcare, financial assets, or services) but also a process in which women see themselves as having the capacity and the right to participate and exert influence.[55]

In the context of climate change, the ability of women to choose the ways in which their society will adapt to the challenges posed by the crisis entails the participation of women in decision-making at all levels (community, local, national, and international). But simply 'adding women' to the table does not equal empowerment.[56] This requires, for instance, addressing structural gender inequality with respect to information-sharing and knowledge.[57] Consequently, all attempts to actively include women in climate action (either in litigation, policy formulation, or implementation) must guarantee that women's participation is not nominal or tokenistic.

Succeeding in meaningful inclusion would not only empower women but also boost the general struggle against climate change as more comprehensive solutions emerge. As an example, the prominent role of women in the aftermath of natural disasters, and in the implementation of climate adaptation measures, has been increasingly recognised.[58] Women and women-led organisations are often the first responders during a crisis. Thanks to their strong local networks, they can identify the most vulnerable in need of assistance.[59] Furthermore, the participation of women's organisations in local decision-making on climate change adaptation has proven to be essential to ensure that the socio-economic needs of all members of their communities are included. This is because women's perspectives often include consideration and awareness of their immediate family and surrounding community.[60] In this sense, women's differentiated views and perspectives can inform more holistic, effective, and transformative climate action, including litigation pathways. Similarly, an intersectional approach can show how power structures and categorisations can be reinforced, but also challenged and renegotiated.[61]

### *Gendered climate impacts on Pari Island and the women's collective response*

The risks mentioned at the beginning of this chapter are particularly high for women living in small island developing states. These women are exposed to extreme hazards, such as rising sea levels, intensifying natural disasters, and the destruction of natural ecosystems on which their primary income depends, as the example of Pari shows.[62]

Many women on Pari Island have traditionally worked as fisherwomen and seaweed cultivators to provide for their families. Water pollution around the Thousand Islands coastal area, changes in currents and sea temperature, combined with recurrent flooding have led to a significant decline in fish availability and have made seaweed farming unviable, affecting major sources of women's income.[63] After a decline in their harvest during the past years, in 2023, two of the plaintiffs stated that for the first time the local seaweed harvest was completely ruined because of the high temperature of the sea, which hinders the natural growth of the plants.[64] Faced with these challenges, during the last decade, many women have turned away from fishing and seaweed cultivation, venturing into tourism, cooking for tourists, renting bicycles, or working in homestays and shops.[65] All these alternatives are currently threatened by the impacts of flooding on tourism on Pari Island.

The aftermath of each flooding event involves an extensive clean-up process to eliminate seawater and waste that has entered houses, shops, and public spaces. This task is taken on primarily by women, who, in the face of a flood and its aftermath, have to not only ensure the physical safety of their children but also provide them and their families healthy food (including safe drinking water). Yet after most of the floods, men would not bring income home from fishery and tourists would cancel their trips, leaving women without income and the necessary cash to buy fresh food. Various women described this overall situation as a 'double burden' for the women of the community.[66] This situation has affected not only the financial stability and economic advancement of women on Pari but also their mental health. Many women worry about their future, their physical safety, the safety of their loved ones, and the livelihoods of the whole island community.[67]

The community of Pari is battling these effects through collective action.[68] A group of women founded a female collective called *Perempuan Pejuang Pulau Pari* (Women's Group of Pari Island), which carries out various community activities.[69] The women's collective manages a beach at the eastern tip of the island, which includes regular cleaning and caretaking of the facilities and the local ecosystem, for example, cutting trees which are dying from the augmenting salinisation of the soil due to rising sea levels. The group further cultivates communal gardens, where they grow different types of vegetables. Yet due to recent floods, the group had to change the location of this communal garden twice in the last three years. Many of its members are worried because the sandy land and the availability of fresh water on the limited territory of the island leave them not many alternative spaces to cultivate in the future.[70] This threatens the local food supply of fresh fruit and vegetables, which is next to the loss of income and the salinisation of groundwater, one of the most concerning consequences of flooding for the inhabitants.

The women's group further undertakes massive adaptation efforts to protect the island from the impacts of flooding by planting mangroves on a large scale.[71] The group cultivates mangrove seedlings, sells them to tourists and school classes, and assists them in planting. This sensitises the visitors to the collective struggle to respond to climate change. These seedlings and their growth are then systematically monitored and documented. Yet the women stated that their efforts do not suffice to protect the island, because the seedlings need many years to grow to a size big enough to grant protection to the shores; thus, a larger quantity of seedlings is needed.[72]

## The impact of women's voices on the legal design of the case

Having discussed the multi-layered systems of oppression that shape how women on Pari experience the impacts of climate change and how they might exercise their agency, this section highlights the challenges of capturing these multidimensional realities in fact-finding and fitting them into the pre-framed procedural framework of a civil suit in the Swiss legal system. It firstly shows how the women of Pari were vital in determining the legal design of the case. Secondly, the section discusses how some norms of the Swiss legal framework are disadvantageous for women's participation in transnational climate litigation and thereby add additional layers of discrimination.

### *The influence of women's participation in the fact-finding process*

During the fact-finding process in preparation for the 'Call for Climate Justice' campaign and, ultimately, the legal case, several individual and group interviews were conducted.[73] The outcome of the interviews on the impacts of the floods on the island and community life varied substantially when women were involved, either as interviewers or respondents. A salient trend was that when men were interviewed, conversations circled mainly around damages to property and the impacts on fishing. Conversely, when the interviews involved predominantly women, more facets of the impacts on the island emerged, including impacts on food and water security, as well as on children and the mental well-being of the community at large. In addition, several women demonstrated a better understanding of household finances and how the floods had affected this aspect of their family life than their male partners. For instance, while one of the male plaintiffs explained how the water well in his house was regularly flooded by seawater and how much it cost them to supplement the family with distilled water, the women who were interviewed explained how the water system on the island functioned and how many of the wells were at risk. The women further elaborated on how the floods affect not only their financial stability and economic advancement but also their mental health. Children cannot go to school after each flood, as the floods start mostly during the night and scare them, so they can't sleep.[74] Similarly, the women expressed concerns not only for their physical safety and that of their children and neighbours but also where they themselves and their families would live in the future, as many coral reef islands like Pari are likely to become uninhabitable by 2050.[75]

Furthermore, a group interview with the local women's group, with the support of female interpreters, confirmed the aforementioned individual impacts on a larger scale. A more comprehensive image of the collective social support system on the island emerged. For example, whenever a family would not have enough savings for food due to a flood or lack of fishery income, others would support them. Or when the house of one family is flooded, others help bridge the challenges and support renovating potential damages. As a last resort, women would borrow money to cover their daily needs and the educational expenses of their older children who moved to neighbouring islands after primary school to continue their education.[76]

It became evident how religious practices on the island can impact women's participation. Most of the inhabitants of the island of Pari practice Islam. Therefore, at special times of the year, like the holy month of Ramadan, women have additional domestic responsibilities, such as preparing the food for the fast-breaking meal, *Itfar*. These responsibilities made it difficult for women to participate in community meetings to strategise around the island's climate struggle if they were held before sunset. Hence, finding times compatible with women's responsibilities on the island played an essential role in engaging in conversations with women and actively listening to their differentiated experiences and needs.

Along these lines, the perspectives of the women of Pari proved to be highly influential in the demands of the public campaign and the legal case. The inclusion of female perspectives, both from interviewers and from interviewees, in the fact-finding and decision-making was crucial not only for capturing a differentiated and holistic picture of different human rights implications of the floods but also for including demands for adaptation measures into the litigation strategy. Women advocated for building longer and higher gabion seawalls (traditional seawalls, called '*bronjongs*') and planting mangroves to protect the island. In addition, in terms of adapting to the threat to the island's groundwater, the women brought forward the need for each family to have its own water distillery to provide safe drinking water.[77]

## *Fitting the reality of Pari Island into Eurocentric legal concepts*

Before diving into the material and procedural obstacles of the litigation, two introductory questions should be answered: First, how can such a claim be filed in Switzerland? Second, what is the material legal basis for this transnational loss and damage claim?

Whenever launching transnational litigation, the choice of forum is crucial. To access Swiss jurisdiction for loss and damages, the facts of a civil matter must be 'international' and have a link to Switzerland.[78] Such 'internationality' can be caused by a contractual or non-contractual relationship among parties in different countries or by events that take place outside the Swiss territory with a connection to Switzerland.[79] There is no contractual relationship between the plaintiffs and Holcim (nor has there ever been one). Hence, the only option for a forum is a non-contractual relationship with a connection to Switzerland. But one might ask, How is the damage of the fishers on Pari Island linked to Switzerland?

In Swiss law, potential doors to access a forum are claims of unjust enrichment or classical tort claims.[80] As for tort cases, an asset (both financial and non-financial in nature) affiliated to an individual person, and so-called 'absolute rights', must be violated or endangered. Under such absolute rights fall different kinds of property rights (material and immaterial property rights, for example, patents and authorship) and personality rights.[81] Pure financial damages can only be claimed if there is an additional legal norm which protects financial assets from specific behaviour, for example, criminal norms for fraud or theft.[82]

Hence, to launch transnational litigation in a Swiss court, victims of climate-related loss and damage need to claim a violation of their property or of their personality rights caused by an action of a person or entity based in Switzerland. Yet these legal notions, as well as the procedural rules for claiming them, are at least partially disadvantageous for women, as we show next.

### *The patriarchy of property rights*

The first known transnational climate case against a polluter launched in the Global North, *Luciano Lliuya v RWE*, is based on an infringement of property rights.[83] In this case, a Peruvian farmer, Saúl Luciano Lliuya, argues that his property is threatened by the impacts of climate change, and that RWE, a major German coal producer, is partially responsible for this threat. To substantiate his claim, Lliuya argues that he and RWE live in a neighbourly relationship and that RWE's emissions, therefore, affect his property, despite RWE's headquarters being located in Germany, more than 10,000 km from his house in the Peruvian Andes.[84] While the case was rejected in the first instance, in the second instance, the Higher Regional Court of Hamm foreshadowed in November 2017 that due to the cross-border effects of greenhouse gas emissions, such a kind of global neighbourly relationship might fall under a provision of the German Civil Code and that property rights might be applicable in this situation.[85] This preliminary decision already broke a legal paradigm.[86]

However, property rights might not be an avenue open to many women on the front line of the climate crisis living predominantly in the Global South.[87] This is because women do not own as much land and assets as men on a global scale. Due to legal, cultural, and economic barriers, only 20% of the world's land is owned by women.[88] In many countries, a woman's ability to inherit land is restricted by discriminatory land, succession, civil, customary, religious, and family laws.[89] For instance, 76 states do not have laws granting women equal rights to property and inheritance.[90] The land and property rights of Indigenous and rural women often rely on community-based tenure systems that are under-recognised and insecure.[91] As a consequence, rural women are also disproportionately affected by land grabs.[92] These patriarchal-designed property cycles make it difficult for women to access fertile land and agricultural extension services.[93] In addition to limited land ownership, the land owned by women tends to be smaller than men's, inferior in quality, and usually more exposed to flooding, erosion, and other adverse climatic effects.[94] Consequently, requiring a property right to have legal standing as a plaintiff in a transnational claim is a systemic disadvantage for women.

As for the women of Pari, many of them co-own assets with their husbands (for example, their family houses and fish farms). However, the property rights on the island have been historically contested since the country's independence from the Netherlands.[95] Although a decision of the Indonesian Ombudsmen acknowledged the property rights of the islanders, some inhabitants have been left without formal property titles.[96] Furthermore, many women are personally and professionally active on territories that are not legally owned by or assigned to them, such as the communal gardens they use for cultivation and the beach at the eastern tip of the island which they operate as a women's collective. Consequently, the damages to communal gardens, the installations of the women's group at the beach, the coastal habitat, and the freshly planted mangroves were not included in the compensation claim in the *Asmania* case, despite being of high financial value and importance to the women of the island. The same is true for the general damages to the ecosystems of the island which lack a formalised asset link to one or various persons.

### *The door opener of personality rights*

As mentioned previously, the second legal basis for transnational climate litigation under Swiss law are so-called 'personality rights'. Unlike property rights, personality rights offer a much broader angle of women's participation in transnational litigation. Therefore, personality rights were used as the legal basis for the claims of the Indonesian plaintiffs in the *Asmania* case.[97]

The notion of the protection of personality is codified in the Swiss Civil Code (CC) and traditionally applied in cases of invasive journalism that might affect the reputation or right to privacy of the subject of the media reports.[98] Article 28 of the CC states that '[a]ny person whose personality rights are unlawfully infringed may petition the court for protection against all those causing the infringement'.

An infringement is unlawful if it is not justified by the consent of the person whose rights are violated, by an overriding private or public interest, or by the law.[99] Yet while not widely known or applied in practice, the protection of personality rights has a much broader scope than the protection from aggressive media reporting. Essentially, it is the realisation of the horizontal effects of human rights, meaning, the materialisation of human rights among private individuals and entities. These horizontal effects of human rights stem from the state's duty to protect human rights from infringements by third parties. Article 28 of the CC fulfils this purpose by protecting the personality of persons from infringement by others.[100]

As a result of humans having a wide set of rights, the notion of personality rights is broad. According to legal scholarship, the legal definition of 'personality' consists of numerous facets which should be interpreted by legal notions (rights) ascribed to a person. Scholars list, for instance, (1) physical areas of protection, such as the right to life, physical integrity, sexual freedom, bodily self-determination, or personal freedom; (2) psychological areas of protection, such as one's emotional life and mental integrity or the right to relationship and respect for loved ones; or (3) social spheres of protection, such as the right to one's image, voice, and words, the right to informational self-determination, the right to respect intimacy and privacy, and the protection of economic advancement.[101]

When a violation of anyone's personality rights occurs, the affected person may petition the court for protection against all those causing or contributing to the infringement. This differs from the traditional causality criterion in tort law, as minor contributions are also sufficient to be held legally responsible for violating personality rights. When claiming such a violation, affected persons may ask the court to (1) prohibit the threatened infringement, (2) order that an existing infringement cease, or (3) declare that an infringement is unlawful if it continues to have an offensive effect.[102] Suppose a claimant has suffered financial damage or mental harm due to the violation of his or her personality rights and wants to request financial compensation. In that case, the Swiss Civil Code refers to the general clauses for ex-contractual tort claims and just satisfaction, referred to as the 'law of delict'.[103]

With this wide angle, personality rights offer much more legal ground for claims of women to participate in litigation than property rights. For instance, the disproportionate climate change impacts on women in the areas of physical safety, mental health, and food (in)security all fit into this notion. Applying this concept, the plaintiffs argue in the complaint that the climate change impacts on Pari violate and further threaten their personality rights in all areas of protection, physical, psychological, and social, which ultimately hinders their personal freedom, economic advancement, and mental well-being. For one of the plaintiffs, a violation of his physical safety is claimed because his house is regularly flooded during the night while electric appliances are connected to the grid, which poses a severe safety hazard for him and his family.[104]

This argumentation is crucial in the context of climate justice as it opens the litigation door to many individuals and vulnerable groups impacted by climate change who tend not to have contractual relationships with the biggest polluters. It is even more interesting considering the landmark judgment by the Grand Chamber of the ECtHR in the case of *Klimaseniorinnen v Switzerland*, as Article 8 of the European Convention on Human Rights, and its interpretation by the ECtHR, must also flow into the domestic interpretation of personality rights in the context of climate change.[105]

Although health and physical integrity are a facet of a person's personality rights, the literature does not name any eco-dimension of personality rights. This might change considering the case law of the European Court of Human Rights reading this dimension into other human rights and with the emerging right to a clean, healthy, and sustainable environment, which Switzerland has not only recognised but also heavily supported in the process of codification in the United Nations (UN) system.[106]

### *Procedural obstacles as door stoppers*

One of the hurdles of civil litigation in Switzerland and other jurisdictions is the burden of proof of the claimant, combined with a relatively high threshold of the duty to substantiate the claim. In the Swiss judicial system, this duty to substantiate means that an assertion of fact does not have to contain all details.[107] It is sufficient if the facts, which are to be subsumed under the standards supporting the claim, are asserted in their essential features or outlined in a manner corresponding to the customs of life.[108] In tort claims, the assertion of facts traditionally heavily relies on documentary evidence. For example, bills and bank statements are used as evidence of financial transactions or debts. Tax declarations and salary statements can be proof of wealth and income. Medical documentation, advisory opinions, and health insurance statements can serve as evidence of health issues. This practice relies heavily, as the Swiss Federal Supreme Court states, 'in a manner corresponding to the customs of life'[109] in Switzerland or other economies in the Global North.

The community on Pari Island, on the other hand, primarily does business in an informal economy, meaning that most transactions of finances and goods are executed in cash based on oral agreements, without a paper trail. Freshly bought fish is sold directly at the harbour or to neighbours. Mangrove seedlings are produced in local gardens and sold to tourists without receipts. Tourists pay for their accommodation in cash without any formal proof of purchase. Furthermore, the inhabitants of Pari are exempt from paying income or wealth taxes, which leaves them without any formal tax statement issued by an official state authority.[110] This informality is not unusual in the Global South, as 2 billion people (roughly 61% of the global employed population) earn their living in the informal economy.[111] Out of this 61% of the global employed population, women are more exposed to informal employment in sub-Saharan African countries, Southern Asia, and Latin American countries. Female labour force participation is low in many countries, and women are predominantly responsible for guaranteeing a family's access to food and water.[112]

Furthermore, on a global scale, women do not have the same access to information and communication technologies (ICTs) as men.[113] Therefore, they benefit less from the emerging field of scanning and advanced photograph applications on mobile phones and computers, which simplify the documentation of evidence and financial transactions and assets. Although women often have the best overview of their family's financial situation,[114] the high procedural threshold for its substantiation often poses a major hurdle for female plaintiffs from the most vulnerable communities in the Global South. In the *Asmania* case, Asmania, the leader of the local women's group, is one of the plaintiffs, who, unlike most women in the community, has a bank account, which facilitated the documentation of her financial situation.[115] For many other women, however, the evidentiary requirements of the Swiss judicial system could act as an insurmountable obstacle.

## Conclusion

This chapter aimed at understanding how the women of Pari have influenced the building of the legal case of *Asmania* in the wider context of women participation in transnational climate litigation. The chapter first showed how climate change has different impacts on women but that not all women are affected equally. It described how understanding and considering the power dynamics and systems of oppression that traverse the lives of women in the context of climate change are a critical resource for catalysing effective and transformative climate action, including litigation. The chapter then turned to the example of the women of Pari and showed how they carry a double burden when dealing with the impacts of climate change on the island. When preparing the litigation, due to their special exposure, the voices of the Pari women were immensely important for unveiling the multifaceted impacts of climate change – especially regarding non-financial damages – not only on women but also in the broader community. Gender-sensitive interviews proved to be a crucial tool for capturing the full picture of damages. Then, the chapter outlined the vital role of the women of Pari when developing solutions and concrete suggestions for adaptation measures at the local level. Their ideas flowed directly into the legal design of the complaint against Holcim. Lastly, the chapter looked at the Swiss legal system. The example of the *Asmania* case showed how certain legal norms, which heavily determine access and success of civil loss and damage claims, mirror a Western and patriarchal-dominated world. By design, the Swiss legal system forms another disadvantageous layer for women's participation in transnational litigation.

In light of these, when dealing with climate litigation, an intersectional approach by practitioners is key to cast light on new and existing linkages and positions that can facilitate alliances between voices that are usually marginalised in the negotiations between the most dominant stakeholders in the climate arena.[116] This becomes increasingly important in transnational litigation, as legal norms and procedures in some countries might inadequately reflect societies from outside their jurisdiction and thereby foster disadvantages for vulnerable groups. A failure to address these dynamics actively might lead to litigation and litigators being closed off to and not driven by the demands of the individuals and communities they are representing – including the differentiated demands of the individual members within the communities.[117] However, when local communities, particularly women, like in the case of the Pari islanders, are effectively involved in transnational climate litigation, the law can be used as a tool not only to obtain redress but also to give voice to their demands and their differentiated experiences of climate change impacts in a political and legal arena that would otherwise be inaccessible to them.[118]

Along these lines, recognising women's leadership in climate struggles should be acknowledged and promoted. The chapter has shown that women, like Asmania, who lead such cases are not mere heroes. Asmania is a leader in her community and most probably inspirational for other women. However, people like Asmania need the right structural conditions to execute their agency. A critical intersectional approach in this context moves away from a reductionist narrative; instead, it critically assesses and addresses how power relations and social inequalities interfere with the ability of women to exercise their agency.[119]

Understanding these processes and dynamics helps develop alternative climate actions, including litigation processes that not only address the differentiated impacts of climate change on women but also do so from an intersectional and community-based perspective and approach.

Ultimately, only by listening to and elevating the voices of women and girls on the front line of the climate crisis will the goal of achieving systemic and empowering transformation be possible.

## Notes

1 Whenever this text uses to the term 'women', it refers to both women and girls.

2 For the purpose of this chapter, 'transnational *corporate* climate litigation' is understood as cases of plaintiffs who aim to hold parent companies liable in the jurisdictions of their headquarters for climate-related harms that have occurred in other jurisdictions. The term 'transnational climate litigation' also involves legal actions against governments which have a cross-border component.

3 *Asmania et al. v Holcim* (2022) A1 2023 9, Justice of the Peace of the Canton of Zug (Switzerland) (*Asmania*); for more background of the case, see the website of the supporting campaign HEKS, 'Call for Climate Justice' (*Call for Climate Justice*) <https://callforclimatejustice.org/en/the-case> accessed 2 May 2024.

4 See Joane Setzer and Catherine Higham, 'Global Trends in Climate Change Litigation: 2023 Snapshot' (*Grantham Research Institute on Climate Change and the Environment*, 2023) <https://www.lse.ac.uk/granthaminstitute/wp-content/uploads/2023/06/Global_trends_in_climate_change_litigation_2023_snapshot.pdf> accessed 1 September 2024;

Michael Burger and Maria Antonia Tigre, 'Global Climate Litigation Report: 2023 Status Review' (*Sabin Center for Climate Change Law*, 2023) <https://scholarship.law.columbia.edu/sabin_climate_change/202/> accessed 2 September 2024; see also *Lliuya v RWE* (2017) 2 O 285/15, Oberlandesgericht Hamm (Germany) (*Lliuya*).

5 For an overview of tort climate litigation, see Laura A Duarte Reyes and Nina Burri, 'Transnational Corporate Liability in the Era of Loss and Damages: The Case of Asmania et al. vs Holcim' in Stefano Zirulia, Lidia Sandrini and Cesare Pitea (eds), *What Future for Environmental and Climate Litigation? Exploring the Added Value of a Multidisciplinary Approach from International, Private and Criminal Law Perspectives* (Milano University Press 2024); Maria Antonia Tigre and Margaretha Wewerinke-Singh, 'Beyond the North-South Divide: Litigation's Role in Resolving Climate Change Loss and Damage Claims' (2023) 32(2) *RECIEL* <https://onlinelibrary.wiley.com/doi/epdf/10.1111/reel.12517> accessed 2 September 2024.

6 See Duarte Reyes and Burri (n 5). For a discussion of attribution and causation, see John McClure et al., 'Attributions for Extreme Weather Events: Science and the People' (2022) 174 *Climatic Change* 22; F Otto et al., 'Causality and the Fate of Climate Litigation: The Role of the Social Superstructure Narrative' (2022) 13(5) *Global Policy* 736; Rupert F Stuart-Smith et al., 'Attribution Science and Litigation: Facilitating Effective Legal Arguments and Strategies to Manage Climate Change Damages' (2021) <https://www.smithschool.ox.ac.uk/sites/default/files/2022-03/attribution-science-and-litigation.pdf> accessed 2 May 2024; RF Stuart-Smith et al., 'Filling the Evidentiary Gap in Climate Litigation' (2021) 11 *Nature Climate Change* 651.

7 See HEKS (n 3).

8 See Jochen Hinkel et al., 'Heutige und zukünftige Auswirkungen des Klimawandels und Meeresspiegelanstiegs auf der Insel Pari' (2023) *GCF Working Paper* <https://zenodo.org/record/7566046> accessed 2 May 2024; Walhi, 'The Impacts of Climate Change on the Island of Pari' (*Walhi*, 2022); *Asmania* (n 3), [42].

9 IPCC, 'Chapter 12' in *Climate Change 2021: The Physical Science Basis. Contribution of Working Group I to the Sixth Assessment Report of the Intergovernmental Panel on Climate Change* (2021) 1786 <https://www.ipcc.ch/report/ar6/wg1/downloads/report/IPCC_AR6_WGI_FullReport_small.pdf> accessed 2 September 2024; IPCC, 'Summary for Policymakers in Climate Change 2022 – Impacts, Adaptation and Vulnerability: Working Group II Contribution to the Sixth Assessment Report of the Intergovernmental Panel on Climate Change' in HO Pörtner et al. (eds), (2022) <https://www.ipcc.ch/report/ar6/wg2/downloads/report/IPCC_AR6_WGII_FullReport.pdf> accessed 21 November 2024.

10 IPCC, 'Summary for Policymakers 2022' (n 9) B.4.2, B.4.3, B.5.2, figures SPM.2, SPM.3.

11 The World Bank Group, 'Indonesia, Climate Change Overview' (*World Bank Climate Change Knowledge Portal*, 2020) <https://climateknowledgeportal.worldbank.org/country/indonesia?fbclid=IwAR15fRpwkzJuhQ2nGZamVYiUofeEO5uN4KLp8v99a7XEaCQSAVBz4bMo90s> accessed 2 May 2024; The World Bank Group and Asian Development Bank, 'Climate Risk Profile: Indonesia' (2021) 2, 16–17, Table 7 <https://www.adb.org/sites/default/files/publication/700411/climate-risk-country-profile-indonesia.pdf> accessed 8 September 2024.

12 *Asmania* (n 3), [66ff].

13 See *Asmania* (n 3) and oral testimony by Asmania during her visit to Switzerland in June 2023.

14 Testimonies of the plaintiffs presented in *Asmania* (n 3); Walhi (n 8) 6ff; see also Fadli Gaper, 'Warga Pulau Pari Terdampak Banjir Rob, Holcim Digugat' (*KBR Indonesia*, 21 September 2022) <https://kbr.id/nasional/09-2022/warga-pulau-pari-terdampak-banjir-rob-holcim-digugat/109571.html> accessed 2 May 2024; Peter Jeung, 'Four Indonesians Take Swiss Cement Giant to Court Over Climate' (*Al Jazeera*, 1 February 2023)

<https://www.aljazeera.com/news/2023/2/1/four-indonesians-take-swiss-cement-giant-to-court-over-climate> accessed 2 May 2024; Matthias Müller, 'Ein Paradies zerrt Holcim vor Gericht' (*Neue Zürcher Zeitung*, 2 February 2023) 22 <https://callforclimatejustice.org/wp-content/uploads/Seiten_22_23_Neue_Zuercher_Zeitung_2023-02-02.pdf> accessed 2 May 2024. For a detailed analysis of the attribution of these impacts to climate change see Hinkel et al. (n 8).

15 Hinkel et al. (n 8) 32. See also Barrett Chapter 6, pp 193–195.

16 See Hinkel et al. (n 8); Makan A Karegar et al., 'Nuisance Flooding and Relative Sea-Level Rise: the Importance of Present-Day Land Motion' (2017) 7 *Scientific Reports* 1; IPCC, 'Climate Change 2021' (n 9) 1786; see also Sean Vitousek et al., 'Doubling of Coastal Flooding Frequency within Decades Due to Sea-Level Rise' (2017) 7 *Scientific Reports* 1.

17 Hinkel et al. (n 8); see also Karegar et al. (n 16); IPCC, 'Climate Change 2021' (n 9) 1786; Vitousek et al. (n 16).

18 *Asmania* (n 3).

19 The group was created after the merger of the companies Holcim Ltd and Lafarge in 2015.

20 See Paul Griffin, Richard Heede and Ian van der Vlugt, 'The Carbon Majors Database – Methodology Report 2017' (*CDP*, 2017).

21 Of this total, scope 1 operational emissions account for 5.33 GtCO2 (74.6%), scope 2 emissions 0.40 GtCO2 (5.5%), and scope 3 indirect emissions 1.42 GtCO2 (19.8 per cemt); Richard Heede, 'Carbon History of Holcim Ltd: Carbon Dioxide Emissions 1950–2021' (*Climate Accountability Institute,* 2022) <https://callforclimatejustice.org/wp-content/uploads/Heede-Report.pdf> accessed 2 May 2024.

22 Heede (n 21) 24. These calculations do not include other anthropogenic sources of greenhouse gases, such as non-$CO_2$ gases (nitrous oxide, various methane sources, F-gases), and non-energy $CO_2$, such as from land use, deforestation, agriculture, animal husbandry, etc. See all the reports available at Holcim, 'Sustainability Reports' (*Holcim*, 2023) <https://www.holcim.com/sustainability/esg/sustainability-reports> accessed 2 May 2024. For the majority of the subsidiaries listed in the consolidated report, the defendant holds a 100% stake.

23 When describing the gap between Holcim's current strategy and the necessary reduction pathways to reach 1.5 degrees Celsius, the plaintiffs refer to the analysis done by HEKS, 'Holcim's Climate Strategy: Too Little – Too Late' (*HEKS*, 2023) <https://callforclimate-justice.org/wp-content/uploads/HEKS-EPER_Climate-Analysis_Summary_EN_DEF.pdf> accessed 2 May 2024.

24 *Asmania* (n 3); 'Rechtsbegehren 1–5', 3–4.

25 *Asmania* (n 3), 'Rechtsbegehren 2–5', 3–4.

26 For a more detailed analysis, see heading titled 'The patriarchy of property' in the following text.

27 *Asmania* (n 3).

28 See HEKS (n 3). For an analysis of this campaign from a political science perspective, see Anya Mayaputri, Gracia Paramitha and Nurul Isnaeni, 'The Island's Call for Justice: NGO Advocacy in the Climate Litigation Case of Pari Island in Indonesia' (2024) 56 *Technium Social Sciences Journal* 282.

29 The three NGOs are the Swiss Church Aid HEKS/EPER, the German organisation European Center for Constitutional and Human Rights (ECCHR), and the Indonesian environmental organisation Walhi.

30 The industry as a whole emitted an estimated total of up to 8% of global $CO_2$ emissions by 2022. See Robbie M Andrew, 'Global CO2 Emissions from Cement Production, 1928–2018' (2019) 11 *Earth System Science Data* 1675, 1676.

31 For a comprehensive overview, see IPCC, 'Summary for Policymakers 2022' (n 9).

32 Following Shellae Versey's definition, *vulnerability* is understood as 'a state when experiencing harm from a hazardous event has high probability, and recovery time is

lengthy'. See H Shellae Versey, 'Missing Pieces in the Discussion on Climate Change and Risk: Intersectionality and Compounded Vulnerability' (2021) 8 *Policy Insights from the Behavioral and Brain Sciences* 67, 68.

33 IPCC, 'Summary for Policymakers 2022' (n 9) A.2., C.5. See also Murcott, Tigre and Ann Samuel 'Introduction', pp 2–5.

34 UNHRC, 'Report of the Office of the United Nations High Commissioner for Human Rights, Analytical Study on Gender-Responsive Climate Action for the Full and Effective Enjoyment of the Rights of Women to the Human Rights Council' (UN doc A/HRC/41/26, 2019); UNHRC, 'Report of the Special Rapporteur on the Issue of Human Rights Obligations Relating to the Enjoyment of a Safe, Clean, Healthy and Sustainable Environment, David R Boyd' (UN doc A/HRC/52/33, 2023) [34]; ECOSOC, 'Report of the UN Secretary-General on Achieving Gender Equality and the Empowerment of All Women and Girls in the Context of Climate Change, Environmental and Disaster Risk Reduction Policies and Programs, Presented to the Commission on the Status of Women' (UN doc E/CN.6/2022/3, 2022); OHCHR, 'Analytical Study on Gender-Responsive Climate Action for the Full and Effective Enjoyment of the Rights of Women' (UN doc A/HRC/41/26, 2019); UNHRC, 'Report of the Office of the United Nations High Commissioner for Human Rights on the Summary of the Panel Discussion on Women's Rights and Climate Change: Climate Action, Good Practices and Lessons Learned' (UN doc A/HRC/42/26, 2018); CEDAW, 'General Recommendation No. 37 (2018) on the Gender-Related Dimensions of Disaster Risk Reduction in the Context of Climate Change' (CEDAW/C/GC/37, 2018).

35 UNHRC, 'Analytical Study' (n 34).

36 Ana T Amorim-Maia et al., 'Intersectional Climate Justice: A Conceptual Pathway for Bridging Adaptation Planning, Transformative Action, and Social Equity' (2022) 41 *Urban Climate* 101053. See also Dutta and Lofts, Chapter 4, pp 137–138, for an Indian perspective on gendered vulnerability to climate change, and Ladan and Maduekwe, Chapter 8, pp 240–242, for a Nigerian perspective.

37 In this chapter, the authors address the notion of intersectionality with a focus on human–human relationships. Relations of power can be found in all relations from institutional practices to individual actions and human–nature power dynamics. For a more detailed discussion of different intersectionality approaches, see Angela Hefti, 'Intersectional Victims as Agents of Change in International Human Rights-Based Climate Litigation' (2024) 0 *Transnational Environmental Law* 1 (on the recent climate cases before the European Court of Human Rights); Natalia Urzola Gutiérrez, 'Gender in Climate Litigation in Latin America: Epistemic Justice Through a Feminist Lens' (2024) 16(1) *Journal of Human Rights Practice* 208 (for an overview of the gender-specific context in Latin American and litigation); Amorim-Maia et al. (n 36) (with a focus on adaptation planning and action); Michael Mikulewicz et al., 'Intersectionality and Climate Justice: A Call for Synergy in Climate Change Scholarship' (2023) 32(7) *Environmental Politics* 1276 (for linking intersectionality to climate justice); Shellae Versey (n 32) 68 (with a perspective from the discipline of psychology). See also Murcott, Tigre and Ann Samuel, 'Introduction'.

38 See Urzola Gutiérrez (n 37) 210.

39 UNHRC, 'Report of the Special Rapporteur on Violence Against Women and Girls, Its Causes and Consequences, in the Context of the Climate Crisis, Including Environmental Degradation and Related Disaster Risk Mitigation and Response, Reem Alsalem' (UN doc A/77/136, 2022).

40 CEDAW (n 34) [4]; E Neumayer and T Plümper, 'The Gendered Nature of Natural Disasters: The Impact of Catastrophic Events on the Gender Gap in Life Expectancy, 1981–2002' (2007) 97 *Annals of the Association of American Geographers* 551; UNHRC, 'Summary Panel Discussion' (n 34) [11]; UNHRC, 'Report of David R Boyd' (n 34).

41 CEDAW (n 34) [4], [6].

42 UNHRC, 'Analytical Study' (n 34) [6].
43 Global Gender and Climate Alliance, 'Gender and Climate Change: A Closer Look at Existing Evidence' (2016) <https://wedo.org/wp-content/uploads/2016/11/GGCA-RP-FINAL.pdf> accessed 2 May 2024.
44 UNHRC, 'Report of David R Boyd' (n 34), [17f]; UNHRC, 'Analytical Study' (n 34) [9]; UNHRC, 'Summary Panel Discussion' (n 34) [1], [5].
45 UNHRC, 'Report of David R Boyd' (n 34) [17f]; UNHRC, 'Analytical Study' (n 34) [9]; UNHRC, 'Summary Panel Discussion' (n 34), [1], [5].
46 Kim R Van Daalen et al., 'Extreme Events and Gender-Based Violence: A Mixed-Methods Systematic Review' (2022) 6 *The Lancet Planetary Health* 504; Gender and Alliance (n 43).
47 UNHRC, 'Report of David R Boyd' (n 34) [83].
48 See for many UNHRC, 'Report of David R Boyd' (n 34) [34]; UNHRC 'Analytical Study' (n 34), [12].
49 See, for an overview, UNFCCC, 'Synthesis Report by the Secretariat on the Differentiated Impacts of Climate Change on Women and Men; the Integration of Gender Considerations in Climate Policies, Plans and Actions; and Progress in Enhancing Gender Balance in National Climate Delegations' (UN doc FCCC/SBI/2019/INF.8, 2019), [46ff] <https://unfccc.int/sites/default/files/resource/sbi2019_inf8.pdf> accessed 2 May 2024.
50 UNHRC, 'Report of the Special Rapporteur (Reem Alsalem)' (n 39).
51 See Versey (n 32) 67 and Murcott, Tigre and Ann Samuel Introduction, pp 6–11.
52 Houria Djoudi et al., 'Beyond Dichotomies: Gender and Intersecting Inequalities in Climate Change Studies' (2016) 45 *Ambio* 248, 251; Urzola Gutiérrez (n 37) 4.
53 Naila Kabeer, 'Economic Pathways to Women's Empowerment and Active Citizenship: What Does The Evidence From Bangladesh Tell Us?' (2017) 53 *The Journal of Development Studies* 649.
54 Kabeer (n 53).
55 A Cornwall, 'Women's Empowerment: What Works?' (2016) 28 *Journal of International Development* 342.
56 UNFCCC (n 49) [30ff].
57 UNFCCC (n 49) [30ff]. See also Lisa Chamberlain, 'The Value of Litigation to Women Environmental Human Rights Defenders in South Africa' in Cathi Albertyn et al. (eds), *Feminist Frontiers in Climate Justice* (Edward Elgar Publishing 2023) 213 ff, for insight on the experience of the use of litigation by women impacted by mining in South Africa. See also Ladan and Maduekwe, Chapter 8, pp 240–242, and Dutta and Lofts, Chapter 4, pp 137–140 (on gender inequality).
58 M Picard, 'Beyond Vulnerability to Gender Equality and Women's Empowerment and Leadership in Disaster Risk Reduction: Critical Actions for the United Nations System' (2021) <https://caribbean.eclac.org/publications/beyond-vulnerability-gender-equality-and-womens-empowerment-and-leadership-disaster> accessed 2 May 2024.
59 Picard (n 58).
60 Picard (n 58).
61 Anna Kaijser and Annica Kronsell, 'Climate Change through the Lens of Intersectionality' (2014) 23(3) *Environmental Politics* 417. See also Uehara, Chapter 3, pp xx–xx.
62 UNFCCC (n 49), [13ff]; see also UNHRC, 'Report of the Special Rapporteur (Reem Alsalem)' (n 39) [6] and [61].
63 Walhi (n 8) 13.
64 See Walhi (n 8) 13 and information provided by the plaintiffs during their visit to Switzerland in June 2023, supported with visual documentation.
65 See Walhi (n 8) 12f.
66 Wahli (n 8) 12.
67 *Asmania* (n 3) [72–75], [88], [100–104], [114–119].
68 This sub-chapter is based on information gathered in various individual and collective interviews conducted by the authors on Pari Island. Furthermore, see Walhi (n 8) 3f, 12f.

69 Bincang Perempuan, 'Perempuan Pulau Pari Mengeluh Sulitnya Menjaga Laut dan Pesisir' (*Bincang Perempuan*, 10 November 2023) <https://bincangperempuan.com/perempuan-pulau-pari-mengeluh-sulitnya-menjaga-laut-dan-pesisir/.> accessed 2 May 2024.
70 Perempuan (n 69); *Asmania* (n 3), [102], [114].
71 See, for example, 'Indonesians Sue Swiss Firm Over Climate Change' (*Deutsche Welle*, 2 February 2023) <https://www.youtube.com/watch?v=yJKXmPFz4a4&ab_channel=DWNews> accessed 2 May 2024; 'Inselbewohner verklagen Weltkonzern' (*ARD Weltspiegel*, 24 September 2023) <https://www.ardmediathek.de/video/weltspiegel/indonesien-inselbewohner-verklagen-weltkonzern/das-erste/Y3Jp-ZDovL2Rhc2Vyc3RlLmRlL3dlbHRzcGllZ2VsLzQyYWYwMzc3LTZjN-DUtNDg0Zi1iODk1LWRjODQ0NDE3OGRmZQ#:~:text=Vier%20Bewohner%20der%20Insel%20Pari,f%C3%BCr%20den%20steigenden%20Meeresspiegel%20ver-antwortlich> accessed 2 May 2024.
72 *Asmania* (n 3) [72], [214].
73 See HEKS (n 3); Walhi (n 8) 3f; see also evidence offered in *Asmania* (n 3).
74 Testimony of Asmania provided in June 2023 during her visit in Switzerland; *Asmania* (n 3); Walhi (n 8) 8ff; HEKS, 'Asmanias Kampf für Klimagerechtigkeit' (*HEKS Blog*, 2023) <https://www.heks.ch/blog/asmanias-kampf-fuer-klimagerechtigkeit> accessed 2 May 2024.
75 Hinkel et al. (n 8) 20.
76 Walhi (n 8); interviews conducted by the authors on Pari in April 2022.
77 *Asmania* (n 3) [205].
78 See 'Federal Act on Private International Law' <https://www.fedlex.admin.ch/eli/cc/1988/1776_1776_1776/de> accessed 2 May 2024 (PILA).
79 For instance, see Article 113 of PILA to determine when a characteristic obligation of a contract is to be performed in Switzerland. Article 3 of PILA further offers the exceptional forum in Switzerland if proceedings abroad are impossible or cannot reasonably be required and when the case has a 'sufficient' connection to Switzerland.
80 See PILA, Articles 127 and 129.
81 M Kessler, 'Artikel 41' in H-U Vogt et al. (eds), *Basler Kommentar Obligationenrecht I* (Basel 2019), N 31ff.
82 Kessler (n 81) N 8, 12f.
83 *Lliuya* (n 4).
84 *Lliuya* (n 4) 2–3, 25–31; see also N Walker-Crawford, 'Climate Change in the Courtroom: An Anthropology of Neighborly Relations' (2023) 23 *Anthropological Theory* 76.
85 Oberlandesgericht Hamm, *Lliuya vs RWE*, Hinweis-und Beweisbeschluss of 30 November 2017; Oberlandesgericht Hamm, *Lliuya vs RWE*, Oral Hearing of 17 November 2017. For the oral arguments of the judge, see Germanwatch, '§1004 – Global Neighbourhood' (*The Climate Case – Saúl vs. RWE*, 2023) <https://rwe.climatecase.org/en/legal#neighbourhood> accessed 2 May 2024.
86 Duarte Reyes and Burri (n 5).
87 The authors acknowledge the limitations attached to referring to the Global South as a reduced and heterogeneous reality, which leaves out important considerations of the complicated roles played by developing and developed nations in the context of climate change. Nevertheless, Jacqueline Peel and Jolene Lin contend that 'there is still value in the Global South grouping as the basis for an analysis of transnational climate litigation, not least because it is these countries – situated in Asia, the Pacific, Africa and Latin America – that are among the most vulnerable to impacts from climate change'. See Benjamin J Richardson et al., 'Introduction: Climate Law and Developing Countries' in Benjamin J Richardson, Yves Le Bouthillier, Heather McLeod-Kilmurray and Stepan Wood (eds), *Introduction: Climate Law and Developing Countries – Legal and Policy Challenges for the World Economy* (Edward Elgar Publishing 2009) 1, 5–6; J Peel and J Lin, 'Transnational Climate Litigation: The Contribution of the Global South' (2019) 113 *AJIL* 4, 679–726.

88 UNHRC, 'Report of David R Boyd' (n 34) [21].
89 UNHRC, 'Report of David R Boyd' (n 34) [76].
90 UNHRC, 'Report of David R Boyd' (n 34) [76].
91 UNHRC, 'Report of David R Boyd' (n 34) [21] and [25]; see also UNHRC, 'Analytical Study' (n 34) [8].
92 UNHRC, 'Report of David R Boyd' (n 34) [26].
93 UNHRC, 'Analytical Study' (n 34) [8].
94 UNHRC, 'Report of David R Boyd' (n 34) [25].
95 Martini Martini and Efridani Lubis, 'Analisis Yuridis Peralihan Tanah Girik Ke Hak Guna Usaha Berdasarkan Itikad Tidak Baik Di Pulau Pari Kepulauan Seribu DKI Jakarta' (2021) 7(1) *Veritas* 547632.
96 'Press Release: Ombudsman Temukan Maladministrasi dalam Penerbitan 62 SHM dan 14 SHGB di Pulau Pari' (2018) <https://ombudsman.go.id/artikel/r/artikel – press-release – ombudsman-temukan-maladministrasi-dalam-penerbitan-62-shm-dan-14-shgb-di-pulau-pari-> accessed 2 May 2024.
97 *Asmania* (n 3) [228ff].
98 See arts 28ff of 'Swiss Civil Code' <https://www.fedlex.admin.ch/eli/cc/24/233_245_233/de> accessed 2 May 2024 (CC).
99 See CC (n 98) Article 28 [2].
100 For an overview, see A Meili, 'Article 28' in T Geiser and C Fountoulakis (eds), *Basler Kommentar Schweizerisches Zivilgesetzbuch I* (Schulthess 2022); see also C Kirchschläger, 'Articles 28/28a' in W Fischer and T Luterbacher (eds), *Kommentar zu den schweizerischen Haftpflichtbestimmungen* (Dike Publishing 2016).
101 See Meili (n 100) N 17 and 37; Kirchschläger (n 100) N 9ff. The wide scope resembles the approach of the European Court of Human Rights (ECtHR) in the interpretation of Article 8 of the Convention.
102 See CC (n 98) Article 28a.
103 See Article 41 of the Swiss Code of Obligations (CO) for financial tort claims, and Article 49 CO for just satisfaction for mental harm. Article 41 CO reads: 'Any person who unlawfully causes loss or damage to another, whether wilfully or negligently, is obliged to provide compensation.' Further, specific tort rules are available for product liability, consumer credits, or the sale of travel packages, among others.
104 *Asmania* (n 3) [232–243].
105 The Grand Chamber found that Article 8 also encompasses a right for individual effective protection (by the state authorities) from the serious adverse effects of climate change on their lives, health, well-being, and quality of life. ECtHR, *Verein Klimaseniorinnen Schweiz et al. v Switzerland* (2024) 53600/20, European Court of Human Rights.
106 UNHRC, 'The Human Right to a Safe, Clean, Healthy and Sustainable Environment' (UN doc A/HRC/48/L.23/Rev.1, 2021); UNGA, 'The Human Right to a Clean, Healthy and Sustainable Environment' (UN doc A/76/L.75, 2022); The Federal Council, 'Switzerland's Contribution to Recognising the Human Right to a Clean, Healthy and Sustainable Environment' <https://www.admin.ch/gov/en/start/dokumentation/medienmitteilungen.msg-id–89824.html> accessed 28 July 2022.
107 Swiss Federal Court, BGer 4A_443/2017 of 30 April 2018, E 2.1 and E 4.1.
108 Swiss Federal Court, BGer 4A_443/2017 of 30 April 2018, E 2.1 and E 4.1.
109 Swiss Federal Court, BGer 4A_443/2017 of 30 April 2018, E 2.1.
110 *Asmania* (n 3) [324].
111 Florence Bonnet, Joann Vanek and Marty Chen, 'Women and Men in the Informal Economy – A Statistical Brief' (*WIEGO*, January 2019) 1 <https://www.wiego.org/sites/default/files/publications/files/Women%20and%20Men%20in%20the%20Informal%20Economy%20-%20A%20Statistical%20Brief%20-%20for%20web.pdf>

accessed 16 September 2024. This 61% amounts to approximately 2 billion people aged 15 or older. The proportion of informal employment varies in different regions, whereby the vast majority stems from Africa, Asia and the Pacific, and the Arab states. See also International Labour Office, 'Women and Men in the Informal Economy: A Statistical Picture' (*International Labour Office – Geneva,* 2018) 13 <https://www.ilo.org/sites/default/files/wcmsp5/groups/public/@dgreports/@dcomm/documents/publication/wcms_626831.pdf> accessed 16 September 2024.

112 International Labour Office (n 111) 21.

113 See, for example, Xin Pei and Arul Chib, 'Beyond the Gender (Dis)Empowerment Dichotomy: The Mobile Phone as Social Catalyst for Gender Transformation in the Global South' (2020) 23(3) *New Media & Society* 578. For a good overview on positive economic and social effects as well as disadvantages of access of women to ICT, see Kelly H Summers et al., 'Mobile Phones and Women's Empowerment in Maasai Communities: How Men Shape Women's Social Relations and Access to Phones' (2020) 77 *Journal of Rural Studies* 126.

114 See previous page, f.

115 *Asmania* (n 3), [325ff].

116 See similar: Kaijser and Kronsell (n 61) 419.

117 Nani Jansen Reventlow, 'Building Systemic Justice: Reflections on Using the Master's Tools to Fight for Communities' Rights' (*SystemicJustice*, 18 May 2022) <https://www.nanijansen.org/blog/building-systemic-justice/> accessed 2 May 2024.

118 Duerte Reyes and Burri (n 5).

119 Amorim-Maia et al. (n 36); UNHRC, 'Report of David R Boyd' (n 34).

## Bibliography

### *Books and book chapters*

Chamberlain L, 'The Value of Litigation to Women Environmental Human Rights Defenders in South Africa' in C Albertyn, M Campbell, HA García, S Fredman and M Rodriguez de Assis Machado (eds), *Feminist Frontiers in Climate Justice* (Edward Elgar Publishing 2023)

Duarte Reyes LA and Burri N, 'Transnational Corporate Liability in the Era of Loss and Damages: The Case of Asmania et al. v Holcim' in C Pitea, L Sandrini and S Zirulia (eds), *What Future for Environmental and Climate Litigation? Exploring the Added Value of a Multidisciplinary Approach from International, Private and Criminal Law Perspectives* (University Press 2024)

*International Labour Office Women and Men in the Informal Economy: A Statistical Picture* (3rd edn, PRODOC of the ILO 2018) <https://www.ilo.org/sites/default/files/2024-04/Women_men_informal_economy_statistical_picture.pdf>

Kessler M 'Artikel 41' in H-U Vogt, D Oser, R Watter and CW Lüchinger (eds), *Basler Kommentar Obligationenrecht I* (Dike Verlag AG 2019)

Kirchschläger C, 'Articles 28/28a' in W Fischer and T Luterbacher (eds), *Kommentar zu den schweizerischen Haftpflichtbestimmungen* (Dike Publishing 2016)

Meili A, 'Article 28' in T Geiser and C Fountoulakis (eds), *Basler Kommentar Schweizerisches Zivilgesetzbuch I* (6th edn, Helbing Lichtenhahn Publishing 2022)

Richardson BJ, Le Bouthillier Y, McLeod-Kilmurray H and Wood S, 'Introduction: Climate Law and Developing Countries' in BJ Richardson, Y Le Bouthillier, H McLeod-Kilmurray and S Wood (eds), *Climate Law and Developing Countries: Legal and Policy Challenges for the World Economy* (Edward Elgar Publishing 2009)

## *Cases*

*Asmania et al. v Holcim* (2022) [case number], Justice of the Peace of the Canton of Zug (Switzerland) (*Asmania*)
*Lliuya v RWE* (2017) 2 O 285/15, Oberlandesgericht Hamm (Germany)
*Verein Klimaseniorinnen Schweiz et al. v Switzerland* (2024) 53600/20, European Court of Human Rights

## *Journal articles*

Amorim-Mai AT, Anguelovski I, Chu E and Connolly J, 'Intersectional Climate Justice: A Conceptual Pathway for Bridging Adaptation Planning, Transformative Action, and Social Equity' (2022) 41 *Urban Climate* <https://doi.org/10.1016/j.uclim.2021.101053> accessed 5 September 2024
Andrew RM, 'Global CO2 Emissions from Cement Production, 1928–2018' (2019) 11(4) *Earth System Science Data* 1675 <https://doi.org/10.5194/essd-11-1675-2019> accessed 2 September 2024
Andrijevic M, Crespo Cuaresma J, Lissner T, Thomas A and Schleussner C-F, 'Overcoming Gender Inequality for Climate Resilient Development' (2020) 11 *Nature Communications* 6261 <https://doi.org/10.1038/s41467-020-19856-w> accessed 7 September 2024
Callahan CW and Mankin JS, 'National Attribution of Historical Climate Damages' (2022) 172(3–4) *Climatic Change* 40 <http://dx.doi.org/10.1007/s10584-022-03387-y> accessed 7 September 2024
Cornwall A, 'Women's Empowerment: What Works?' (2016) 28(3) *Journal of International Development* 342 <https://doi.org/10.1002/jid.3210> accessed 5 September 2024
Djoudi H, Locatelli B, Vaast C, Asher K, Brockhaus M and Sijapati BB, 'Beyond Dichotomies: Gender and Intersecting Inequalities in Climate Change Studies' (2016) 45 *Ambio* 248 <https://doi.org/10.1007/s13280-016-0825-2> accessed 5 September 2024
Hefti A, 'Intersectional Victims as Agents of Change in International Human Rights-Based Climate Litigation' (2024) *Transnational Environmental Law* <https://doi.org/10.1017/S2047102524000128> accessed 5 September 2024
Kabeer N, 'Economic Pathways to Women's Empowerment and Active Citizenship: What Does The Evidence From Bangladesh Tell Us?' (2017) 53(5) *The Journal of Development Studies* 649 <https://doi.org/10.1080/00220388.2016.1205730> accessed 5 September 2024
Kaijser A and Kronsell A, 'Climate Change through the Lens of Intersectionality' (2014) 23(3) *Environmental Politics* 417 <https://doi.org/10.1080/09644016.2013.835203> accessed 5 September 2024
Karegar MA, Dixon TH, Malservisi R, Kusche J and Engelhart SE, 'Nuisance Flooding and Relative Sea-Level Rise: the Importance of Present-Day Land Motion' (2017) 7 *Scientific Reports* <https://doi.org/10.1038%2Fs41598-017-11544-y> accessed 2 September 2024
Martini, M and Lubis E, 'Analisis Yuridis Peralihan Tanah Girik Ke Hak Guna Usaha Berdasarkan Itikad Tidak Baik Di Pulau Pari Kepulauan Seribu DKI Jakarta' (2021) 7(1) *Veritas* <https://dx.doi.org/10.34005/veritas.v7i1.1253> accessed 6 September 2024
Mayaputri AP, Paramitha G and Isnaeni N, 'The Island's Call for Justice: NGO Advocacy in the Climate Litigation Case of Pari Island in Indonesia' (2024) 56 *Technium Social Sciences Journal* 282 <http://dx.doi.org/10.47577/tssj.v56i1.10818> accessed 2 September 2024
McClure J, Noy I, Kashima Y and Milfont T L, 'Attributions for Extreme Weather Events: Science and the People' (2022) 174(22) *Climatic Change* <https://doi.org/10.1007/s10584-022-03443-7> accessed 2 September 2024
Mikulewicz M, Caretta MA, Sultana F and Crawford NJW, 'Intersectionality and Climate Justice: A Call for Synergy in Climate Change Scholarship' (2023) 32(7)

*Environmental Politics* 1275 <https://doi.org/10.1080/09644016.2023.2172869> accessed 5 September 2024

Neumayer E and Plümper T, 'The Gendered Nature of Natural Disasters: The Impact of Catastrophic Events on the Gender Gap in Life Expectancy, 1981–2002' (2007) 97(3) *Annals of the Association of American Geographers* 551 <https://doi.org/10.1111/j.1467-8306.2007.00563.x> accessed 5 September 2024

Otto F, Minnerop P, Raju E, Harrington LJ, Stuart-Smith RF, Boyd E, James R, Jones R and Lauta KC, 'Causality and the Fate of Climate Litigation: The Role of the Social Superstructure Narrative' (2022) 13(5) *Global Policy* 736 <https://doi.org/10.1111/1758-5899.13113> accessed 2 September 2024

Peel J and Jolene L, 'Transnational Climate Litigation: The Contribution of the Global South' (2019) 113(3) *American Journal of International Law* <https://ssrn.com/abstract=3379155> accessed 6 September 2024

Pei X and Chib A 'Beyond the Gender (Dis)empowerment Dichotomy: The Mobile Phone as Social Catalyst for Gender Transformation in the Global South' (2020) 23(3) *New Media & Society* 578 <https://doi.org/10.1177/1461444820905295> accessed 7 September 2024

Rylander C, Øyvind Odland J and Manning Sandanger T, 'Climate Change and the Potential Effects on Maternal and Pregnancy Outcomes: An Assessment of the Most Vulnerable – the Mother, Fetus, and Newborn Child' (2013) 6(1) *Global Health Action* <https://doi.org/10.3402%2Fgha.v6i0.19538> accessed 7 September 2024

Shellae Versey H, 'Missing Pieces in the Discussion on Climate Change and Risk: Intersectionality and Compounded Vulnerability' (2021) 8(1) *Policy Insights from the Behavioral and Brain Sciences* 67 <https://doi.org/10.1177/2372732220982628> accessed 2 September 2024

Stuart-Smith RF, Otto F, Saad AI, Lisi G, Minnerop P, Cedervall Lauta K, van Zwieten K and Wetzer T, 'Filling the Evidentiary Gap in Climate Litigation' (2021) 11 *Nature Climate Change* 651 <https://doi.org/10.1038/s41558-021-01086-7> accessed 2 September 2024

Stuart-Smith RF, Saad A, Otto F, Lisi G, Lauta K, Minnerop P and Wether T, 'Attribution Science and Litigation: Facilitating Effective Legal Arguments and Strategies to Manage Climate Change Damages' (2021) <https://www.smithschool.ox.ac.uk/sites/default/files/2022-03/attribution-science-and-litigation.pdf> accessed 2 May 2024

Summers KH, Baird TD, Woodhouse E, Christie ME, McCabe JT, Terta F and Peter N, 'Mobile Phones and Women's Empowerment in Maasai Communities: How Men Shape Women's Social Relations and Access to Phones, Journal of Rural Studies' (2020) 77 *Journal of Rural Studies* 126 <http://dx.doi.org/10.1016/j.jrurstud.2020.04.013> accessed 7 September 2024

Tigre MA and Wewerinke-Singh M, 'Beyond the North-South Divide: Litigation's Role in Resolving Climate Change Loss and Damage Claims' (2023) 32(3) *Review of European, Comparative and International Environmental Law* 439 <https://doi.org/10.1111/reel.12517> accessed 2 September 2024

Urzola Gutiérrez N, 'Gender in Climate Litigation in latin America: Epistemic Justice Through a Feminist Lens' (2023) 16(1) *Journal of Human rights Practice* 208 <http://dx.doi.org/10.1093/jhuman/huad030> accessed 5 September 2024

Van Daalen K, Savić Kallesøe S, Davey F, Dada S, Jung L, Singh L, Issa R, Emilian CA, Kuhn I, Keygnaert I, Nilsson M, 'Extreme Events and Gender-Based Violence: A Mixed-Methods Systematic Review' (2022) 6(6) *The Lancet Planetary Health* E504 <https://doi.org/10.1016/s2542-5196(22)00088-2> accessed 5 September 2024

Vitousek S, Barnard PL, Fletcher CH, Frazer N, Erikson L and Storlazzi CD, 'Doubling of Coastal Flooding Frequency within Decades Due to Sea-Level Rise' (2017) 7 *Scientific Reports* 1399 <https://doi.org/10.1038/s41598-017-01362-7> accessed 2 September 2024

Walker-Crawford N, 'Climate Change in the Courtroom: An Anthropology of Neighbourly Relations' (2023) 23(1) *Anthropological Theory* 76 <https://doi.org/10.1177/14634996221138338> accessed 5 September 2024

## *Legislation and treaties*

Federal Act on the Amendment of the Swiss Civil Code (Switzerland) 1911
Federal Act on Private International Law (PILA) (Switzerland) 1987
Swiss Civil Code (CC) (Switzerland) 1907

## *Online sources*

Arlitta D, 'Ombudsman Temukan Maladministrasi dalam Penerbitan 62 SHM dan 14 SHGB di Pulau Pari' (*Ombudsman Republic Indonesia*, 10 April 2018) <https://ombudsman.go.id/artikel/r/artikel – press-release – ombudsman-temukan-maladministrasi-dalam-penerbitan-62-shm-dan-14-shgb-di-pulau-pari-> accessed 2 May 2024

Bern, 'Switzerland's Contribution to Recognising the Human Right to a Clean, Healthy and Sustainable Environment' (*The Federal Council, The Portal of the Swiss Government*, 28 July 2022) <https://www.admin.ch/gov/en/start/dokumentation/medienmitteilungen.msg-id–89824.html#:~:text=Back%20to%20overview-,Switzerland's%20contribution%20to%20recognising%20the%20human%20right,clean%2C%20healthy%20and%20sustainable%20environment&text=Bern%2C%2028.07.,environmental%20and%20human%20rights%20issues> accessed 8 September 2024

Donger E, 'Lessons on "Adaptation Litigation" from the Global South' (*Verfassungsblog*, 25 March 2022) <https://verfassungsblog.de/lessons-on-adaptation-litigation-from-the-global-south/> accessed 2 May 2024

Gaper F, 'Warga Pulau Pari Terdampak Banjir Rob, Holcim Digugat' (*KBR Indonesia*, 21 September 2022) <https://kbr.id/nasional/09-2022/warga-pulau-pari-terdampak-banjir-rob-holcim-digugat/109571.html> accessed 2 May 2024

Goldston JA, 'Climate Litigation through an Equality Lens' (*Open Global Rights*, 28 June 2020) <https://www.openglobalrights.org/climate-litigation-equality-lens> accessed 2 May 2024

HEKS, 'Call for Climate Justice' (*Call for Climate Justice*, 2022) <https://callforclimatejustice.org/en/the-case/> accessed 2 May 2024

HEKS, 'Asmanias Kampf für Klimagerechtigkeit' (*HEKS Blog*, 2023) <https://www.heks.ch/blog/asmanias-kampf-fuer-klimagerechtigkeit> accessed 2 May 2024

'Holcim Launches Its Strategy 2025 "Accelerating Green Growth"' (*Holcim*, 18 November 2021) <https://www.holcim.com/media/media-releases/holcim-launches-strategy-2025> accessed 7 September 2024

'Holcim unterzeichnet Net-Zero Pledge' (*Holcim*, 28 September 2020) <https://www.holcim.ch/de/lafargeholcim-unterzeichnet-net-zero-pledge#:~:text=Als%20erstes%20globales%20Baustoffunternehmen%20unterzeichnet,(SBTI)%20wissenschaftlich%20best%C3%A4tigt%20wurden.> accessed 30 October 2023

'Indonesian sue Swiss Firm Over Climate Change' (*Deutsche Welle News*, 2023) <https://www.youtube.com/watch?v=yJKXmPFz4a4> accessed 2 May 2024

Izzat F, 'Influence of Climate Change on Fisheries Resources in the Arab Region' (*Globefish*, 2015) <https://www.fao.org/in-action/globefish/market-reports/resource-detail/fr/c/338390/> accessed 2 May 2024

Jeung P, 'Four Indonesians Take Swiss Cement Giant to Court Over Climate' (*Al Jazeera*, 1 February 2023) <https://www.aljazeera.com/news/2023/2/1/four-indonesians-take-swiss-cement-giant-to-court-over-climate> accessed 2 May 2024

Müller M, 'Ein Paradies zerrt Holcim vor Gericht' Neue Zürcher Zeitung (*Zurich*, 2 February2023)<https://callforclimatejustice.org/wp-content/uploads/Seiten_22_23_Neue_Zuercher_Zeitung_2023-02-02.pdf> accessed 2 May 2024

'Perempuan Pulau Pari Mengeluh Sulitnya Menjaga Laut dan Pesisir' (*Bincang Perempuan*, 10 November 2023) <https://bincangperempuan.com/perempuan-pulau-pari-mengeluh-sulitnya-menjaga-laut-dan-pesisir/> accessed 2 May 2024

Reventlow NJ 'Building Systemic Justice: Reflections on Using the Master's Tools to Fight for Communities' Rights' (*Systemic Justice*, 18 May 2022) <https://www.nanijansen.org/blog/building-systemic-justice/> accessed 2 May 2024

Walker-Crawford N 'A Precedent-Setting Case' (*The Climate Case – Saúl vs. RWE*, 2023) <https://rwe.climatecase.org/en/legal#neighbourhood> accessed 2 May 2024

Weltspiegel, 'Indonesien: Inselbewohner verklagen Weltkonzern' (*ARD Media*, 24 September 2023) <https://www.ardmediathek.de/video/weltspiegel/indonesien-inselbewohner-verklagen-weltkonzern/das-erste/Y3JpZDovL2Rhc2Vyc3RlLmRlL3dlbHRzcGllZ2VsLzQyYWYwMzc3LTZjNDUtNDg0Zi1iODk1LWRjODQ0NDE3OGRmZQ#:~:text=Vier%20Bewohner%20der%20Insel%20Pari,f%C3%BCr%20den%20steigenden%20Meeresspiegel%20verantwortlich> accessed 2 May 2024

The World Bank Group, 'Indonesia, Climate Change Overview' (*World Bank Climate Change Knowledge Portal*, 2020) <https://climateknowledgeportal.worldbank.org/country/indonesia?fbclid=IwAR15fRpwkzJuhQ2nGZamVYiUofeEO5uN4KLp8v99a7XEaCQSAVBz4bMo90s> accessed 2 May 2024

## *Reports*

Bonnet F, Vanek J and Chen M, 'Women and Men in the Informal Economy – A Statistical Brief' (January 2019) <https://www.wiego.org/sites/default/files/publications/files/Women%20and%20Men%20in%20the%20Informal%20Economy%20-%20A%20Statistical%20Brief%20-%20for%20web.pdf> accessed 6 September 2024

Burger M and Tigre MA, 'Global Climate Litigation Report: 2023 Status Review' (July 2023) <https://scholarship.law.columbia.edu/sabin_climate_change/202/> accessed 2 September 2024

Griffin P, Heede R and van der Vlugt I, 'The Carbon Majors Database – Methodology Report 2017' (July 2017) <https://cdn.cdp.net/cdp-production/comfy/cms/files/files/000/000/979/original/Carbon-Majors-Database-2017-Method.pdf> accessed 2 September 2024

Habtezion S, 'Gender and Climate Change: Overview of Linkages between Gender and Climate Change' (April 2017) <https://reliefweb.int/report/world/gender-and-climate-change-overview-linkages-between-gender-and-climate-change> accessed 2 May 2024

Heede R, 'Carbon History of Holcim Ltd: Carbon Dioxide Emissions 1950–2021' (July 2022) <https://callforclimatejustice.org/wp-content/uploads/Heede-Report.pdf> accessed 2 May 2024

HEKS, 'Holcim's Climate Strategy: Too Little – Too Late' (January 2023) <https://callforclimatejustice.org/wp-content/uploads/HEKS-EPER_Climate-Analysis_Summary_EN_DEF.pdf> accessed 2 May 2024

Holcim, '2021 Sustainability Performance Report' (2022) <https://www.holcim.com/sites/holcim/files/2022-04/25022022-sustainability-performance_fy_2021_report-en.pdf> accessed 7 September 2024

Holcim, 'Climate Report 2021' (2022) <https://www.holcim.com/sites/holcim/files/2022-04/08042022-holcim-climate-report–2022.pdf> accessed 2 May 2024

IPCC, 'Chapter 12' in *Climate Change 2021: The Physical Science Basis* (August 2021) <https://www.ipcc.ch/report/ar6/wg1/downloads/report/IPCC_AR6_WGI_FullReport_small.pdf> accessed 2 September 2024

IPCC, 'Summary for Policymakers in Climate Change 2022 – Impacts, Adaptation and Vulnerability: Working Group II Contribution to the Sixth Assessment Report of the Intergovernmental Panel on Climate Change' in HO Pörtner et al. (eds), (2022) <https://www.ipcc.ch/report/ar6/wg2/downloads/report/IPCC_AR6_WGII_FullReport.pdf> accessed 21 November 2024

Picard M, 'Beyond Vulnerability to Gender Equality and Women's Empowerment and Leadership in Disaster Risk Reduction: Critical Actions for the United Nations System' (February 2021) <https://caribbean.eclac.org/publications/beyond-vulnerability-gender-equality-and-womens-empowerment-and-leadership-disaster> accessed 2 May 2024

Sellers S, 'Global Gender and Climate Alliance, Gender and Climate Change: A Closer Look at Existing Evidence' (November 2016) <http://wedo.org/wp-content/uploads/2016/11/GGCA-RP-FINAL.pdf> accessed 2 May 2024

Setzer J and Higham C, 'Global Trends in Climate Change Litigation: 2023 Snapshot' (*Grantham Research Institute on Climate Change and the Environment*, 2023) <https://www.lse.ac.uk/granthaminstitute/wp-content/uploads/2023/06/Global_trends_in_climate_change_litigation_2023_snapshot.pdf> accessed 1 September 2024

WALHI, 'The Impacts of Climate Change on the Island of Pari' (*NGO WALHI*, 2022)

The World Bank Group and Asian Development Bank, 'Climate Risk Profile: Indonesia' (2021) <https://www.adb.org/sites/default/files/publication/700411/climate-risk-country-profile-indonesia.pdf> accessed 8 September 2024

## *United Nations Reports*

CEDAW, 'General Recommendation No. 37 (2018) on the Gender-Related Dimensions of Disaster Risk Reduction in the Context of Climate Change' (CEDAW/C/GC/37, 2018)

ECOSOC, 'Report of the UN Secretary-General on Achieving Gender Equality and the Empowerment of All Women and Girls in the Context of Climate Change, Environmental and Disaster Risk Reduction Policies and Programmes, Presented to the Commission on the Status of Women' (UN doc E/CN.6/2022/3, 2022)

OHCHR, 'Analytical Study on Gender-Responsive Climate Action for the Full and Effective Enjoyment of the Rights of Women' (UN doc A/HRC/41/26, 2019)

UNFCCC, 'Differentiated Impacts of Climate Change on Women and Men; the Integration of Gender Considerations in Climate Policies, Plans and Actions; and Progress in Enhancing Gender Balance in National Climate Delegations: Synthesis Report by the Secretariat' (UN doc UNFCCC/SBI/2019/INF.8, 2019)

UNGA, 'The Human Right to a Clean, Healthy and Sustainable Environment' (UN doc A/76/L.75, 2022)

UNHRC, 'Summary of the Panel Discussion on Women's Rights and Climate Change: Climate Action, Good Practices and Lessons Learned: Report of the Office of the United Nations High Commissioner for Human Rights' (UN doc A/HRC/42/26, 2018)

UNHRC, 'Visit to Indonesia: Report of the Special Rapporteur on the Right to Food' (UN Doc A/HRC/40/56/Add.2, 2018)

UNHRC, 'Analytical Study on Gender-Responsive Climate Action for the Full and Effective Enjoyment of the Rights of Women: Report of the Office of United Nations High Commissioner for Human Rights' (UN doc A/HRC/41/26, 2019)

UNHRC, 'Report of the Office of the United Nations High Commissioner for Human Rights, Analytical Study on Gender-Responsive Climate Action for the Full and Effective Enjoyment of the Rights of Women to the human Rights Council' (UN doc A/HRC/41/26, 2019)

UNHRC, 'Report of the Special Rapporteur on Contemporary Forms of Racism, Racial Discrimination, Xenophobia and Related Intolerance: Ecological Crisis, Climate Justice and Racial Justice, E. Tendayi Achiume' (UN doc A/77/549, 2022)

UNHRC, 'Report of the Special Rapporteur on Violence Against Women and Girls, Its Causes and Consequences: In the Context of the Climate Crisis, Including Environmental Degradation and Related Disaster Risk Mitigation and Response, Reem Alsalem' (UN doc A/77/136, 2022)

UNHRC, 'Report of the Special Rapporteur on the Issue of Human Rights Obligations Relating to the Enjoyment of a Safe, Clean, Healthy and Sustainable Environment' (UN doc A/HRC/52/33, 2023)

## *Working papers*

Climate Accountability Institute, 'Carbon Major Database' (2023) <https://climateaccountability.org/pdf/SumRankingTo2017.pdf> accessed 2 May 2024

Hinkel J, Gussmann G, Lincke D and Völz V, 'Heutige und zukünftige Auswirkungen des Klimawandels und Meeresspiegelanstiegs auf der Insel Pari' (2023) *Global Climate Forum Working Paper 01/2023* <https://zenodo.org/record/7566046> accessed 2 May 2024

Chapter 6

# Forum shopping in climate litigation? Three cases involving the Torres Strait Islands[1]

*James Barrett*

## Introduction

Forum shopping, in a broad sense, is a practice by which parties in litigation seek to use the forum most advantageous to their aims.[2] Some consider it unscrupulous, whilst others consider it a rational exercise of agency by plaintiffs.[3] In the field of climate litigation, the positive attributes of forum shopping, particularly for vulnerable groups, are an important field of inquiry. This chapter focuses on three climate cases pursued by Torres Strait Islanders in three different fora, which offer a new perspective. The litigation challenges simplistic perspectives on Indigenous litigants as vulnerable minorities and advances a view of Indigenous litigants as sophisticated agents who are instrumentalising their rights and vulnerabilities strategically to achieve climate justice.

This chapter proceeds as follows: I briefly address my own position and methodology. I then address the meaning and usage of the phrase 'forum shopping'. With this context in place, I address the three climate cases involving Torres Strait Islanders by referencing their own statements and evidence. Having done this, I explain why I consider these cases to be positive instances of forum shopping, despite the potential counterarguments against this way of viewing the cases, and touch upon the role of lawyers and other representatives in the litigation. I also consider the motivations for and risks of forum shopping.

## My position and methodology

Although I have worked with First Nations peoples in my career as a lawyer, I am not a citizen of the Global South or any Indigenous group. A common view among Indigenous and non-Indigenous scholars from various fields appears to be that non-Indigenous peoples can and often do make a positive contribution to scholarship on Indigenous issues, as long as they engage respectfully, in good faith, and with an attitude of reflection with respect to their perspective on the subject matter.[4] That is what I seek to do. I describe the cases involving Torres Strait Islanders and their reasons for bringing those cases, in most part based on their own words or those of their representatives. This is not a complete or objective picture, to the

DOI: 10.4324/9781003470632-9

extent an objective view even exists. As Urzola Gutierrez has observed, even members of a single group experience the impacts of climate change differently, such that no one claimant or group of claimants can truly speak for their entire group.[5] Further, from an author's perspective, a degree of estrangement from one's subject matter is inevitable (unless they are writing about their own experiences, and even then, one's interpretation or reimagining of their experiences is influenced by their background and ideologies). As Sultana has said, based on her experience within feminist scholarship focused on the Global South, researchers from the Global South may find themselves set apart from other members of their group by social class, education, and other factors.[6] Reflecting on these matters need not be 'paralyz[ing]' or devolve into an exercise in 'navel-gazing'.[7] It seems clear enough to me that one's position does matter, but one can take steps to close the distance. I have sought to do this by drawing on the evidence given by Torres Strait Islanders, the submissions filed on their behalf, and their public statements. Before delving into the litigation, the concept of 'forum shopping' is unpacked next.

## 'Forum shopping': its meaning and usage

The first climate case involving the Torres Strait that came to my attention was *Pabai v Commonwealth of Australia* (*Pabai*),[8] also known as the *Australian Climate* case. This case was filed and heard in the Federal Court of Australia. I later learned that two other climate cases involving Torres Strait Islanders had been filed in different fora: one in the Human Rights Committee (*Billy v Australia*),[9] and another in the Land Court of Queensland (*Waratah Coal Pty Ltd v Youth Verdict Ltd et al. (No 6)*).[10] I thought of these three cases intuitively as an exercise in forum shopping. I assumed that the Torres Strait Islanders involved in each case had weighed the pros and cons of proceeding in different available fora and chose the forum they considered most likely to bring success, according to their view of what a successful outcome would be for them. I argue that this is the right way to view at least two of the cases (*Pabai* and *Billy*), although I should first set out what I mean by 'forum shopping', because it is an ambiguous term which people can use in different ways.

'Forum shopping' is often used as a colloquial or jargon term to describe a litigant's selection of one among two or more fora to pursue their case. Yet there appears to be 'no agreement on the exact meaning of the concept'.[11] In my view, there are a few different ways of using the term which fall along at least two axes.

The first axis has to do with the morality of forum shopping. Generally, people use the term 'forum shopping' to communicate one of three things, that (1) the litigant has necessarily done something unfair or otherwise morally reproachable (the 'immoral' sense) in choosing a particular forum; (2) the litigant has simply made a strategic choice about the forum to litigate their case, moral opinions aside (the 'amoral' sense); on (3) the litigant's lawyers have done the right thing by their client in steering them towards the forum which is most likely to secure their success (the 'moral' sense).[12] I use the term in the amoral sense, which, in my experience as a litigator and advisor, is the most commonly used sense of the term in legal practice. However, I recognise that there has been some scholarly debate over the term's meaning and usage, and I briefly address this.

The second axis has less to do with morality and more with what the litigant is trying to achieve. Along this axis, there are narrower and broader senses of 'forum shopping'. In its narrowest sense, *forum shopping* refers to a litigant seeking to have their case heard in the forum in which they are most likely to receive a favourable judgment on the merits of the case.[13] An intermediate sense is that a litigant simply seeks a forum where they will win the case, even if this is due to the application of 'jurisdictional or venue rules'.[14] In its broadest sense, *forum shopping* refers to a party seeking the most 'advantageous' forum,[15] which can mean the forum in which they are most likely to achieve their overall objectives, even if those objectives extend beyond the technical legal outcome of the litigation. Other objectives of litigation can include (1) increased pressure on government or increased publicity for a cause even if the forum cannot give mandatory orders and a monetary remedy does not prove to be forthcoming,[16] (2) the recognition of the strength of a case by a court even if that court's decision is likely to be overturned,[17] or (3) obtaining favourable comments from a tribunal on the merits of a legal argument even if the case is dismissed on other grounds.[18] It is the latter, the broadest sense of 'forum shopping', focused on overall objectives, that I employ in this chapter. So in summary, I am using the term 'forum shopping' in its amoral and broadest sense.

I acknowledge that there is a consensus in academic scholarship that the phrase 'forum shopping' is inherently ambiguous and poorly conceived.[19] At worst, the phrase wrongly implies that the practice is somehow immoral and anyone who employs it must be acting unscrupulously. Whilst, at best, the phrase fails to communicate properly that the practice itself is amoral, it can have negative or positive influences on the law and the quality of judicial decision-making depending on how it is employed.[20] Scholars have observed that some people utter the words 'forum shopping' if they consider that a party's conduct deserves reproach.[21] For all other cases, the term 'forum selection' is more appropriate.[22] From an academic perspective, I do not disagree with these views. However, even scholars readily admit that from a practical perspective, the term has 'been around for some time' and has stuck.[23] That the term can be used in different senses, or that the very same course of conduct might be described by some people as 'forum selection' and by others as 'forum shopping', depending on their perspectives or even their prejudices, is simply a fact about the rough-and-ready way in which language is used to communicate in the real world.

I invite and encourage the reader to critically dissect my usage of the word 'forum shopping' in this chapter. This would be for the best, because the concept of forum shopping would serve as a stage for debate over the extent to which Indigenous litigants have employed their rights strategically as rational agents in their fight to achieve climate justice. In fact, after considering the three climate cases involving the Torres Strait Islands next, I critically reflect upon my intuition that these were examples of forum shopping.

## The Torres Strait Island cases

The Torres Strait Islands (also known as *Zenadth Kes*) are on the dividing line between the Global North and the Global South, a dichotomy which does not easily apply to Indigenous groups within colonised territories.[24] The islands are located between the northern tip of Australia and Papua New Guinea. The population is almost entirely Indigenous. Yet because the islands are part of Australia, the Torres Strait Islanders can access Australian courts. A resident of the islands, Eddie Mabo, successfully fought for a declaration by the High Court of Australia that his people enjoyed native title and corresponding rights and interests.[25] This was the first time that such a declaration was issued by an Australian court. It was the most culturally significant case in modern Australian history and transformed the way many Australians thought about Australia's past and the relationship of First Nations peoples to their ancestral lands. The decision was followed, and codified to some degree, by the enactment of the Native Title Act 1993 (Cth). These domestic developments added to the rights afforded to Torres Strait Islanders under international law, including pursuant to Article 27 of the International Covenant on Civil and Political Rights (ICCPR), which protects the cultural, religious, and language rights of minorities. The Human Rights Committee (the treaty monitoring body for the ICCPR) has said that Article 27 'is directed towards ensuring the survival and continued development of the cultural, religious and social identity of the minorities concerned, thus enriching the fabric of society as a whole'.[26] Rights like these can help communities such as the Torres Strait Islanders protect their traditional lands and waters and their unique way of life, known as *Ailan Kastom* (island custom). This is demonstrated by three climate cases involving Torres Strait Islanders of different islands, language groups, genders, and ages. What unites them is that they are fighting to protect their islands and their unique, ancient culture from rising and warming seas. I explore those three cases chronologically by date of the final decision to compare and contrast how the Torres Strait Islanders involved instrumentalised their Indigenous rights[27] and vulnerabilities in different ways and different fora from the international level to the federal and state levels.

### *Billy v Australia*

*Billy v Australia* (also known as the *Torres Strait 8* case)[28] was the first of these three cases to be decided. Eight Torres Strait Islanders authored a communication to the Human Rights Committee under the Optional Protocol to the ICCPR which complained that Australia was violating certain articles of the ICCPR, including Article 27, concerning the right of minorities to enjoy their own culture.[29] Their primary complaints were that Australia had failed to take adequate measures to help them adapt to climate change by building infrastructure to protect their lives, way of life, homes, and culture from rising sea levels, and to mitigate climate change by putting in place sufficient emissions reduction targets and taking sufficient actions to meet those targets rather than promoting the utilisation of fossil fuels.[30] The authors were experiencing flooding and erosion, which endangered their homes, cultural sites, and plants and animals necessary for their subsistence and culture.[31] Burial sites were inundated. In a video filmed for the 23rd Biennale of Sydney, author Yessie Mosby recounted picking his ancestors' bones up off the beach 'like shells'.[32] He feared that his people would become refugees in their own country and his children's future would be lost.[33] The authors, as a group, complained that they would be forcibly displaced and their *Ailan Kastom* erased by climate change.[34] They sought remedies, including greater adaptation measures for coastal defence and resilience, amendments to law and policy as well as changed practices, and greater consultation concerning governmental decisions that have a major impact on greenhouse gases (GHGs) and adaptation measures in the Torres Strait.[35]

The Human Rights Committee found in favour of the Torres Strait Islanders and considered that Australia ought to provide them with compensation.[36] This was the first time an international treaty body issued a decision in favour of individual complainants on the merits in a climate-related case. A critical part of this decision was the Human Rights Committee's view that the case was admissible due to a lack of domestic remedies – even though the complainants had not sought domestic remedies, which is usually fatal to admissibility.[37] The Committee observed that the Australian government did not contest the authors' argument that the High Court of Australia had decided that a state organ has no duty of care to regulate potential environmental harm.[38] It referred to the case of *Graham Barclay Oysters v Ryan*,[39] in which the plaintiff unsuccessfully argued that a local council had a tortious duty to take reasonable care in the exercise of its statutory functions to prevent harm to consumers of oysters grown in a lake which had been polluted. The Australian government could have argued that the High Court's holding did not necessarily preclude climate cases based on a tortious duty of care,[40] although the government might have considered that this strategy would have opened it up to more climate cases in the long run. The authors also cited the lack of domestic human rights legislation incorporating the ICCPR. It was only later that the Human Rights Act 2019 (Qld) came into force in their state, and there is no such Act at the federal level. Since the authors filed their claim, two other groups of plaintiffs have relied on a tortious duty of care and the Human Rights Act 2019 (Qld), as discussed in the following passages.

Turning to the merits, the Committee upheld the authors' complaint that Australia had violated their right to enjoy their unique culture under Article 27. The Committee recalled that these minority rights are distinct from and additional to the rights held by all humans under the other articles of the ICCPR.[41] It focused on the effects of erosion and flooding of the islands; the inundation of burial sites, which are an essential part of the Torres Strait Islanders' communion with their ancestors; the loss of plants and animals critical to subsistence and the maintenance of their unique culture; and the risk of displacement.[42] It held that their culture was inherently tied to their island way of life and could not be recreated on mainland Australia if they were to be displaced.[43]

The Committee decided that Australia ought to pay compensation and stated that it wished to receive a letter from Australia within 180 days setting out what the country had done in response to the Committee's requests.[44] The government did submit this letter, but it did not mention compensation and stated that collaboration with locals and funding for programmes would be 'more appropriate'.[45] This response has been somewhat under-reported in comparison to the initial excitement around the decision that the government ought to pay compensation.[46] It is a stark reminder of the lack of power of most (but not all) international bodies to issue compulsory remedies. However, the government contributed to a new AUD 15 million sea wall and AUD 40 million coastal protection programme whilst the case was ongoing.[47] It is not self-evident that these projects were caused by the authors having filed their case. However, it would not be surprising if the case placed additional pressure on decision-makers in the government to take action (notwithstanding that the government did not comply with the Committee's preferred remedy).

### *Youth Verdict*

By way of contrast, *Waratah Coal Pty Ltd v Youth Verdict Ltd et al. (No 6)*[48] resulted in obvious and tangible success. In that case, several objectors sought and gained statutory recommendations from the Land Court of Queensland against the approval of a mining lease and environmental authority for a thermal coal mine in the Galilee Basin (also within Queensland, but relatively far from the Torres Strait Islands).

Although this was a climate-related case involving Torres Strait Islanders, there are two significant factors that set it apart from the other cases addressed in this chapter. First, no individual Torres Strait Islander was an active party in the case. The case was run by two organisations, Youth Verdict and the Bimblebox Alliance, in addition to individual objectors from the mainland. The Bimblebox Alliance does not claim to speak for Torres Strait Islanders; it is concerned with the health of the Bimblebox Nature Refuge within mainland Queensland. On the other hand, Youth Verdict describes itself as a group of 'young people in Queensland' who are 'fighting for First Nations people to have decision-making power over traditional lands and lead action on climate change to ensure all of our futures'.[49] Curiously, the court received no evidence of the actual membership of Youth Verdict,[50] although I have seen no reason to doubt Youth Verdict's mission statement. Additionally, Youth Verdict and the Bimblebox Alliance were represented by the same lawyers,[51] and the 'lion's share' of the evidence adduced by those lawyers related to the effects of mining on Bimblebox.[52] However, none of this should take away from the fact that individual Torres Strait Islanders played a crucial role in the case as witnesses by speaking for their country and culture and giving evidence on how these were already changing (which I will address shortly).[53]

Secondly, the task that Youth Verdict and the other objectors asked the court to undertake was quite different from that of the Human Rights Committee in *Billy* and the Federal Court of Australia in *Pabai*, discussed next. The court was not tasked with providing a view, or judicial decision, on whether the government had interfered with human rights or other obligations.[54] Instead, the court was tasked with carrying out an unusual administrative function of reviewing the merits of a decision to approve the development of a mine and making recommendations to the government. However, in carrying out this task, the court was obligated to consider human rights impacts and to make decisions compatible with human rights, pursuant to section 58(1) of the Human Rights Act 2019 (Qld).[55] According to section 28 of that Act, human rights include collective 'cultural rights' that inhere in Aboriginal and Torres Strait Islander peoples. These rights involve maintaining and enjoying culture, language, kinship ties, connection to country and the environment, and the right not to be assimilated or to have their culture destroyed.

Accordingly, Youth Verdict adduced evidence of the impact of coal mining and climate change on these rights, including on-country evidence from a family of Torres Strait Islanders called the Gutchens. Florence Gutchen described her island home of Poruma as her mother, who talks to her.[56] Kapua Gutchen said that on his island home of Erub, gardening culture is valued above the fisherman culture of the other islands because Erub has good soil and feeds the other islands.[57] They have garden ceremonies, which he would like to continue to share with his children and their children.[58] Lala Gutchen, Florence and Kapua's child, also described the garden ceremonies shared with her family members.[59] She described the obligation to look after the land and sea as something in her body that just takes over.[60] Yet the land and sea are threatened by factors such as erosion, rising sea levels, and inundation. These factors are also threatening the grave of Kapua's grandfather. Kapua said the grave would have originally been placed in the family's backyard rather than by the water. By now, the grave was at the high-water mark, and the water was eating away at the cement.[61]

The court found that sea level rise caused by climate change posed an existential threat to the culture of the Torres Strait Islands.[62] The court also considered 'principles of ecologically sustainable development in deciding what recommendation to make',[63] particularly the precautionary principle, and the intergenerational inequity that would be created by the disproportionate impact of emissions related to the mine on future generations.[64] The court's considerations demonstrate the powerful impact made by combining the voices of children (who would suffer intergenerational inequity) with those of Indigenous peoples (whose minority rights would be impacted). Lala Gutchen, for example, gave powerful evidence from her position at the intersection of these two categories: young and Indigenous. Taking these considerations into account, amongst other factors, the court recommended against approvals for the mine.[65] The government followed this recommendation.[66]

### *Pabai v Commonwealth of Australia*

The third case, which as of May 2024 was being litigated in the Federal Court of Australia, is *Pabai v Commonwealth of Australia*.[67] This case is a group action led by Pabai Pabai and Guy Paul Kabai, two men from the Guda Maluyligal Nation who hold native title rights and interests in their respective islands, Bouigu and Sabai.[68] They claim that the Australian government owes them a duty of care to take reasonable steps to protect Torres Strait Islanders, their traditional culture of *Ailan Kastom*, and their marine environment from the current and projected impacts of climate change.[69] Alternatively, the government owes them a duty of care to avoid causing property damage, loss of fulfilment of *Ailan Kastom*, loss of their native title rights, and injury, disease, or death by failing to take adequate adaptation measures.[70]

At one level, this can be considered a straightforward claim in the tort of negligence, rather than a claim that seeks to establish the existence of new statutory or constitutional rights or new causes of action. At another level, the duties of care for which the claimants are arguing are novel, and the establishment of those duties will be seriously complicated because the Australian government is being sued and the claim delves into matters of national public policy. These policy matters involve the weighing up of many factors that affect all Australians differently, which is squarely within the remit of the executive government and not of the judiciary: a point the government will no doubt rely upon in defeating the claim. The claimants argue that these novel duties arise in part due to their unique vulnerabilities.[71] They say that they cannot protect themselves and their culture alone, and they rely on the government for protection.[72] It is in their interests to instrumentalise their vulnerability in this way, because in Australian tort law, establishing a novel duty of care involves an analysis of the 'salient features' of the case, including the claimant's vulnerability to the exercise of a public authority's powers.[73] That is, *vulnerability* in the sense that the claimant could not reasonably be expected to adequately safeguard themselves from harm without the assistance of the authority.[74] This is, of course, not to say that the claimant is somehow inherently meek or disempowered, only that their circumstances make them vulnerable to harm. They can, of course, be fierce agents in their own cause, evidenced by their taking on litigation in the first place.

The claimants' statement of claim alleged that the government has again breached this duty of care by taking inadequate adaptation and mitigation measures, including failing to act according to the best available science and reducing emissions too slowly.[75] This has caused the loss of fulfilment of *Ailan Kastom* due to the erosion and inundation of cemeteries and sacred sites; the salinification of traditional gardens and changing seasonal patterns, which have disrupted gardening culture; and a loss of cultural connections to animals due to changed migratory patterns and populations of marine and terrestrial animals.[76]

A good deal of affidavit evidence in the case is publicly available on the Federal Court of Australia's website and tells the story in the words of the Torres Strait Islanders themselves. Fred Pabai lives in Brisbane but regularly travels back and forth to Boigu Island. He states how important the cemetery and sacred trees are to ceremonial life and recalls how sad he was to see that erosion had caused his great-grandfather's headstone, which was established long ago on dry land, to be washed out onto the beach.[77] Boggo Billy lives on Warraber Island. He gave evidence to the effect that the gardens are affected by saltwater and that all the signs about when to plant and harvest that ancestors passed down have changed recently.[78] As a result, it is much more difficult to grow crops, and fertiliser is now required (but even that does not help much).[79] Boggo also stated that he can't teach his children or grandchildren the old ways of gardening, because 'it's all different now'.[80] Jennifer Enosa now lives and works on Thursday Island, but her family is from Sabai. She recalls how the turtle mating season started and ended with the blooming of flowers, the first cracks of thunder, and the turning of the constellations.[81] Now there are fewer turtles, 'which has an impact on all aspects of culture, including hunting, traditional foods, male coming of age ceremonies, and totems'.[82] These accounts are, of course, just summaries of fragments in the rich and varied histories presented by Torres Strait Islanders in their affidavits, which are available to readers on the Federal Court of Australia's website.[83]

By way of remedies, the claimants seek declarations that the duty of care they contend for exists and is being breached, injunctions requiring the government to protect them and their *Ailan Kastom*, and compensation for loss and damage.[84] Because these orders would come from a domestic court, there is no real prospect that the Australian government would fail to obey them and argue that other remedies are more appropriate, as it did in its response to the *Billy* decision.

### *Observations on the three cases*

It is remarkable that these three claims have occurred in three different fora and were based on three different laws, even though they all involved Torres Strait Islanders voicing similar concerns about climate change. All three claims involved a complaint that erosion and inundation due to sea level rise would harm ancestral burial and other sacred sites, gardening, and hunting culture and cause property damage. The claims also included a complaint that the erosion and inundation may ultimately erase the unique culture of the Torres Strait Islanders, known as *Ailan Kastom*. And yet the first claim was based on the ICCPR and took place in the United Nations Human Rights Committee. The second was partly based on a state human rights statute, the Human Rights Act of 2019 (Qld), and took place in a state land court. The third, still being litigated as of May 2024, is based on the establishment of a novel, tortious duty of care and is taking place in the Federal Court of Australia.

It is evident that the Torres Strait Islanders involved in each case want to save their traditional lands, waters, and unique *Ailan Kastom*. They want their governments (which exist on local, state, and federal planes) to do more with respect to the adaptation and mitigation against the current and projected future impacts of climate change. There is also an aspect of each of their cases about setting global and national precedents and leading the fight against climate change. Yet they have used their minority rights and interests, as Torres Strait Islanders, in different ways and different fora to achieve the same fundamental aims. In my view, this represents tactically astute forum shopping with Indigenous rights and interests. In this instance, I mean 'forum shopping' in the broad sense that these litigants have acted strategically in airing similar factual concerns in different ways and different fora, according to what they think is most likely to achieve their distinct ambitions.[85] In a commercial context, it is often said that forum shopping is unfair to other parties[86] and has pejorative connotations.[87] But when those other parties are corporations or nation states that enjoy an asymmetry of power, this 'forum shopping' ought to be viewed as a positive way for climate litigants to engage with more powerful actors.

## Is this really 'forum shopping'?

One may question whether the fact that three different climate cases involving the Torres Strait Islands were litigated in three different fora is demonstrative of forum shopping or just 'forum selection' or 'fragmentation'. As alluded to earlier, this depends partly on one's operative definition of *forum shopping*. If one were only to use the term 'forum shopping' for litigants' decisions involving some moral turpitude beyond the ordinary strategic considerations made to advance one's case, then these cases cannot seriously be considered forum shopping. But that is not the sense in which I am using the term; rather, what the claimants in each of these three cases have done is use forum shopping as a rational, strategic exercise to advance Indigenous rights (or, in the *Youth Verdict* case, Indigenous rights amongst other matters, such as personal interests in the health of a nature reserve and broader social and economic interests). If one prefers to use the term 'forum selection' for a morally neutral or benevolent choice of forum, then that is very well as a semantic point, but it does not fundamentally change my view of the cases. Another semantic objection is that the claimants in each case are not really forum shopping but pursuing an overlapping but different set of objectives simultaneously in very different fora. Again, I do not disagree with these points substantively. I simply think that whether or not one characterises this kind of activity as 'forum shopping' depends largely on the breadth of one's usage of that term. I have used the term 'forum shopping' in an amoral and broad sense, meaning that the party is simply making a strategic choice according to what they believe is most likely to deliver successful outcomes (including but extending beyond just winning the litigation in a technical legal sense).

Semantics aside, two substantive points have been raised as potential objections during my discussions with others about these cases and whether they involve 'forum shopping'. I address these in turn. The first objection usually heeds the following lines: The cases are not actually run by the same litigants or centrally administered, so the 'Torres Strait Islanders' are not really 'forum shopping'. I think this objection rests on two false premises: First, it is not part of my argument that one plaintiff group called the 'Torres Strait Islanders' launched these cases or that the cases are centrally administered. The term 'Torres Strait Islanders' refers to First Nations peoples from the Torres Strait Islands. By using the words

'Torres Strait Islanders' in connection with all three cases, I do not mean to convey the impression that the cases are run by the very same individuals or centrally administered. Secondly, and in any event, the objection involves a misuse of terms. It seems to assume that 'forum shopping' involves the very same individuals or organisations launching cases in multiple fora, hoping that at least one will prove successful. But that is not what 'forum shopping' means. This objection seems more like 'parallel litigation',[88] a different phenomenon which I have made no claims about.

The second objection is stronger. It is along the following lines: The claimants in each case were not really forum shopping in the sense of picking and choosing between multiple available avenues. Instead, they were pursuing any litigation strategy they perceived to be available to them in circumstances where they had no good options: On the one hand, international treaty bodies have a more flexible approach to the merits of cases but cannot generally provide remedies; on the other hand, Australian courts can provide remedies, but they can only develop the law incrementally. Australia does not have a constitutional bill of rights or statutory framework of human rights law and has been late to develop any clear jurisprudence on climate change.

I would accept much of this objection, but not all of it. Australia has a rather piecemeal and developing framework of human rights legislation. Although it is no stranger to environmental litigation, it has hardly been a world leader regarding climate change jurisprudence. I can certainly see how, from the perspective of the *Billy* claimants, the litigants had no real choice but to seek justice in an international treaty body. The *Pabai* claimants are attempting to establish a duty of care unknown to Australian law. It is yet to be seen whether they will be successful and what remedies they will obtain, if any. In this context, what may appear to be 'forum shopping' could also be seen as an organic process of 'fragmentation' caused by different strategies pursued by different groups.

Notably, the groups involved in each case were also advised by different lawyers and funded and assisted by different organisations, all with their own professional opinions, experience, and skill sets. The *Billy* group was funded and supported by organisations including ClientEarth, a leading international non-governmental organisation (NGO) that did not have an office or operations in Australia (at least at that time), with support from barristers at Twenty Essex in London. The *Pabai* claimants, on the other hand, are represented by Australian solicitors and barristers and supported by the Grata Fund (which is based in Australia and includes Australian-educated lawyers in its governance structure). Meanwhile, the *Youth Verdict*'s case was run jointly with that of the Bimblebox Alliance (which is concerned with a nature reserve in mainland Queensland), and the same lawyers represented both organisations. Given this surrounding context, it is perhaps understandable that the different teams took different approaches, one international, one federal, and one state-based (none of which are inherently better or worse than the others). I am assuming that, in respect of the *Billy* and *Pabai* cases, the lead Torres Strait Islander claimants had the final say on the legal strategy and chosen forum;

this seems a fair assumption that one should ordinarily extend to any litigant and their lawyers, and I have not seen any evidence to the contrary.

However, I do not think that any of the points raised by the second objection change the fact that the *Billy* and *Pabai* claimants sought to have their claim heard in the forum they considered most likely to deliver on their objectives. These points simply give more context to why they might have chosen the forum they chose. On closer examination, the *Youth Verdict* case appears to stand apart from the other two cases, in that the Torres Strait Islanders involved were ostensibly only witnesses in a case run by other active parties and geared in large part towards protecting other First Nations groups and a nature reserve on the mainland. I do not intend the slightest suggestion that Torres Strait Islanders had no agency in the strategy employed, but given the different interest groups involved, it is less obvious that they played a determinative role in the selection of the forum.

## Motivations and risks of 'forum shopping'

The Torres Strait Islanders appear to share similar values and vulnerabilities, consistent with their shared cultural history and home environment. Their submissions and evidence in the three cases discussed earlier demonstrate that they are concerned that sea level rise and storm surges are endangering their burial sites and other sacred sites, their homes, the garden culture of some islands, and the plants on the islands. The populations of local wildlife that they rely on for sustenance and cultural practices are also threatened. Ultimately, they are concerned that they may have to relocate from the islands to survive, and with this, their connection to their traditional lands and waters and their unique *Ailan Kastom* will be lost.

This is not to say that all Torres Strait Islanders are the same or will experience the impacts of climate change in the same way. As Urzola Gutierrez has observed, it can be tempting to tell a story of a case brought on behalf of 'Indigenous people', but in reality, one claimant group cannot represent everyone remotely like them, and different individuals may have different priorities and strategies.[89] Urzola Gutierrez wrote that 'universalism should always be questioned since everyone suffers the impacts of climate change differently, even within the same social groups'.[90] The cases covered in this chapter demonstrate that even the different Torres Strait communities experience climate change in subtly different ways. Recall Kapua Gutchen's evidence in the *Youth Verdict* case; some islands have a garden culture, whilst others have a fishing culture, so the effects of climate change on culture are subtly different.

The cases also show that different individuals within the same broad group or groups may also hold different beliefs about the effectiveness of different fora. It appears that within the Torres Strait Islander groups, some individuals are more or less sceptical about the ability of domestic courts to protect their rights and interests. Whereas the *Billy* claimants argued that domestic courts could not provide an effective remedy, the claimants in *Pabai* in the Federal Court of Australia evidently hold a more optimistic view, because that is precisely what they are pursuing. These different approaches show that Indigenous communities, and even Indigenous peoples in the same communities, are not monolithic in their thoughts or actions.

The cases led by the Torres Strait Islanders are particularly interesting because these people hold the same rights and interests but the plaintiffs have chosen to rely upon and exercise their rights in different ways and different fora. The *Billy* claimants relied on their rights as human beings and members of a minority group in accordance with the ICCPR. The claimants in *Pabai* are relying on their rights as Torres Strait Islanders under national legislation, that is, the Native Title Act 1993 (Cth). Youth Verdict relied on state legislation, that is, the Human Rights Act 2019 (Qld). Although their stories and experiences were all similar, and their most fundamental aim of protecting their islands and traditional way of life from the consequences of climate change is essentially the same, the plaintiffs went about the cases in different ways, depending on the legal advice they received and what they wished to accomplish.

I would be remiss not to mention some typical risks of forum shopping and how they might impact Indigenous peoples pursuing climate change cases in different fora. The first risk is fragmentation: There may be a lack of 'decisional uniformity' between like cases, depending on the forum chosen for each case.[91] So far, this risk has been mitigated by what Barritt has called the 'consciously transnational' shape of climate litigation.[92] The trend appears to be towards decisional uniformity as courts or committees borrow from each other's jurisprudence. For example, in *Billy*, the Human Rights Committee cited seminal decisions in climate litigation from the Supreme Court of the Netherlands (i.e. *Urgenda Foundation v Netherlands*)[93] to the Inter-American Court of Human Rights (i.e. *Advisory Opinion 23*).[94] However, this is only a trend and does not guarantee similar results in every similar case. When deciding *Pabai*, the court will have to engage with the fact that two out of three climate cases involving the Torres Strait Islanders have already ended in victory for the claimants, including the *Billy* case, which is factually similar. Nonetheless, it can only decide the matter according to law based on the case pleaded, and the claimants are attempting to draw a very long bow by arguing that the Australian government has novel duties of care to them personally in the law of negligence when it makes national policy decisions on climate change. This is arguably inconsistent with precedents from the High Court of Australia, such as *Graham Barclay Oysters* (recall that the *Billy* claimants relied on this precedent to explain why they had not sought domestic remedies). At the very least, the precedent presents a tall hurdle. This being said, if the *Pabai* claimants fail domestically, they could still litigate internationally and achieve a similar result to the *Billy* claimants. Fragmentation, therefore, might not be as large of an issue as it appears.[95]

There are other risks of pursuing cases in international bodies rather than domestic courts. One is that an international body might find that the claimants have failed to exhaust domestic remedies, notwithstanding their case being at least *prima facie* meritorious. Several climate cases, such as *Sacchi v Argentina*[96] and *Agostinho v Portugal*,[97] have fallen afoul of this risk. Still, the *Billy* case demonstrates that a failure to seek domestic remedies will not bar all climate cases brought in international fora. Another is that a judgment for the plaintiff may not be enforceable in the jurisdiction where it really matters. In *Billy*, the Human Rights Committee decided that Australia ought to pay compensation, but Australia declined to do so. As Petsche has observed, a risk of forum shopping is that the focus by plaintiffs on other strategic considerations, including the procedural and substantive law of the forum, can distract them from the legal difficulties involved in enforcing a judgment should they be successful.[98]

## Conclusion

There is a tendency to think about climate change and Indigenous peoples as a story of vulnerable people in need of rescue from rising seas, extractive industries, or apathetic governments. The cases involving the Torres Strait Islanders reframe this narrative. The cases appear to be a positive manifestation of strategic 'forum shopping' in its broadest sense. But even if one disagrees with the perspective that the cases involved 'forum shopping', the essential point remains that these Indigenous groups are agents acting strategically in their own cause. Acknowledging that every Indigenous person and culture is unique and experiences the impacts of climate change in different ways, there are high-level similarities between their circumstances. Yet Indigenous groups have chosen to make claims in different fora, for different reasons. For instance, the Torres Strait Islanders have relied upon their minority rights and interests in slightly different ways and have instrumentalised their vulnerability in slightly different ways, depending on the forum. There are risks with forum shopping; only one climate case brought by Indigenous people in an international body has been successful on its merits, which is *Billy*. That case did not result in compensation being paid, although it did result in a world-first precedent and international attention from media, academia, and legal practitioners. It also coincided with tens of millions of dollars in funding for adaptation projects. Therefore, what 'success' means will differ for different plaintiffs, so climate litigants will continue to use different fora to achieve climate justice, depending on which would be most favourable to their aims. This should not be deprecated; rather, it is a rational exercise in strategy and agency.

## Notes

1 I thank the editors and anonymous reviewers for their helpful comments on drafts of this chapter. All errors are my own.
2 Markus Petsche, 'What's Wrong with Forum Shopping? An Attempt to Identify and Assess the Real Issues of a Controversial Practice' (2011) 25 *TIL* 1005, 1007–1008.
3 See Petsche (n 2) 1006–1007; Anthony Fitzsimmons, 'Forum Shopping: A Practitioner's Perspective' (2006) 31 *TGP* 314, 314.
4 For example, see Torjer Olsen, 'Privilege, Decentring and the Challenge of Being (Non-) Indigenous in the Study of Indigenous Issues' (2018) 27 *AJIE* 206; Mpoe Johannah Keikelame and Leslie Swartz, 'Decolonising Research Methodologies: Lessons from a Qualitative Research Project, Cape Town, South Africa' (2019) 12 *GHA* 1; Eivind Skille, 'Doing Research into Indigenous Issues Being Non-Indigenous' (2022) 22 *QR* 831.

5 Natalia Urzola Gutierrez, 'Gender in Climate Litigation in Latin America: Epistemic Justice Through a Feminist Lens' (2024) 16(1) *JHRP* 2, 8, 11, 16.
6 Farhana Sultana, 'Reflexivity, Positionality and Participatory Ethics: Negotiating Fieldwork Dilemmas in International Research' (2015) 6 *ACME* 374, 375.
7 Sultana (n 6) 375–376.
8 *Pabai v Commonwealth of Australia* (2022) VID622/2021, Federal Court of Australia (Australia) (undecided as at May 2024) (*Pabai*).
9 *Billy v Australia* (2022) CCPR/C/135/D/3624/2019 (*Billy*).
10 *Waratah Coal Pty Ltd v Youth Verdict Ltd et al. (No 6)* (2022) QLC 21, Land Court of Queensland (Australia) (*Youth Verdict*).
11 Petsche (n 2) 1007.
12 Petsche (n 2) 1007–1008. See also Fitzsimmons (n 3); Friedrich K Juenger, 'Forum Shopping, Domestic and International' (1989) 63 *Tu L Rev* 553.
13 In my experience, this sense is commonly used in practice, but not as often in academic scholarship.
14 Juenger (n 12) 553.
15 See Petsche (n 2) 1007–1008.
16 As occurred in *Billy* (n 9).
17 As occurred in *Minister for the Environment v Sharma* (2022) 291 FCR 311, Federal Court of Australia, Full Court (Australia) (*Sharma*).
18 As occurred in *Chiara Sacchi et al. v Argentina* (2019) CRC/C/88/D/105/2019, UN Committee on the Rights of the Child (*Sacchi*).
19 See Petsche (n 2); Fitzsimmons (n 3); Juenger (n 12).
20 Petsche (n 2); Fitzsimmons (n 3); Juenger (n 12).
21 Juenger (n 12) 553. See also Petsche (n 2) 1008.
22 Petsche (n 2) 1008.
23 Juenger (n 12) 553.
24 See Roberto Dainotto, 'South by Chance: Southern Questions on the Global South' (2017) 11 *The Global South* 39. See also Murcott, Tigre and Ann Samuel Introduction, n 7.
25 *Mabo v Queensland (No 2)* (1992) 175 CLR 1, High Court of Australia (Australia).
26 Human Rights Committee, General Comment 23 (1994) (HRI/GEN/1/Rev.1/38), [9].
27 By 'Indigenous rights' I mean rights that Indigenous peoples hold by virtue of the fact that they are Indigenous which they hold in addition to their 'human rights', that is, the rights they hold by virtue of the fact that they are human. A description of some of the Indigenous rights in international law can be found in Maria Antonia Tigre, 'Climate Change and Indigenous Groups: The Rise of Indigenous Voices in Climate Litigation' (2022) 9 *e-Publica* 214, 219–222. For further discussion on Indigenous peoples' rights, see Beckhauser and Broetto, Chapter 1.
28 *Billy* (n 9).
29 My focus is on how Indigenous peoples in the Torres Strait Islands have deployed their Indigenous rights. For an analysis of the other, general human rights–based arguments in the case and how they were treated, see, for example, Chhaya Bhardwaj, 'Adaptation and Human Rights: A Decision by the Human Rights Committee *Daniel Billy et al. v Australia* CCPR/C/135/D/3624/2019' (2023) 25 *ELR* 154; Maria Antonia Tigre, 'U.N. Human Rights Committee Finds That Australia is Violating Human Rights Obligations Towards Torres Strait Islanders for Climate Inaction' (*Climate Law*, 27 September 2022) <https://blogs.law.columbia.edu/climatechange/2022/09/27/u-n-human-rights-committee-finds-that-australia-is-violating-human-rights-obligations-towards-torres-strait-islanders-for-climate-inaction/> accessed 8 October 2023. For insights on the struggles of Indigenous peoples in Latin America, see Beckhauser and Broetto, Chapter 1, and for perspectives on the struggles of Indigenous peoples in India, see Garg and Hinduja, Chapter 2. For analysis on the ways in which people of the Pari

Islands, Indonesia, are disproportionately impacted by sea level rise and other climate change impacts, see Burri and Duarte Reyes, Chapter 5.

30 Communication No 3624/2019 under the Optional Protocol to the International Covenant on Civil and Political Rights (13 May 2019) [7]–[8].

31 Communication No 3624/2019 (n 30) [45(1)].

32 Biennale of Sydney, '23rd Biennale of Sydney Participant Interview – Torres Strait 8 – Yessie Mosby' (*YouTube*, 18 July 2020) <https://www.youtube.com/watch?v=qn0YqA2tkRM&t=245s> accessed 8 October 2023.

33 Biennale of Sydney, '23rd Biennale of Sydney Participant Interview – Torres Strait 8 – Yessie Mosby' (*YouTube*, 18 July 2020) <https://www.youtube.com/watch?v=qn0YqA2tkRM&t=245s> accessed 8 October 2023.

34 Communication No 3624/2019 (n 30), [30], [79], [198]; see *Mabo* (n 25).

35 Communication No 3624/2019 (n 30), [210]–[218].

36 *Billy* (n 9) [9]; see also Riccardo Luporini and Annalisa Savaresi, 'International Human Rights Bodies and Climate Litigation: Don't Look Up?' (2023) 32 *RECIEL* 267, 275; Tigre (n 27).

37 See, for example, *Sacchi* (n 18); *Agostinho v Portugal* (2024) European Court of Human Rights 39371/20.

38 *Billy* (n 9) [2.9].

39 *Graham Barclay Oysters v Ryan* (2002) 211 CLR 540, High Court of Australia (Australia).

40 *Sharma* (n 17) [348]–[351].

41 *Billy* (n 9) [8.13].

42 *Billy* (n 9) [5.2]–[5.3].

43 *Billy* (n 9) [8.14].

44 *Billy* (n 9) [12].

45 Australian Government, 'Response of Australia to the Views of the Human Rights Committee in Communication No 3624/2019 (Billy et al. v Australia)' (30 March 2023).

46 See ClientEarth, 'One Year on from Historic Torres Strait UN Climate Victory – No Compensation Despite Legal Finding' (*ClientEarth*, 25 September 2023) <https://www.clientearth.org/latest/press-office/press/one-year-on-from-historic-torres-strait-un-climate-victory-no-compensation-despite-legal-finding/#:~:text=One%20year%20on%20from%20the,finding%20to%20award%20them%20compensation> accessed 8 October 2023.

47 Queensland Department of Environment and Science, 'Case Study: Boigu Island Seawall' (18 May 2023) <https://www.des.qld.gov.au/climateaction/take-action/case-studies/boigu-island-seawall> accessed 8 October 2023.

48 *Youth Verdict* (n 10).

49 Youth Verdict <https://www.youthverdict.org.au/> accessed 4 June 2023.

50 *Youth Verdict* (n 10) [1579].

51 *Youth Verdict* (n 10) [51].

52 *Youth Verdict* (n 10) [141].

53 Youth Verdict, 'Meet the People Standing Up for Culture, Country and Climate' <https://www.youthverdict.org.au/culturevsclive> accessed 4 June 2023.

54 *Youth Verdict* (n 10) [544], [1290].

55 *Youth Verdict* (n 10) [46], [1289]–[1292].

56 *Youth Verdict* (n 10) [1552].

57 *Youth Verdict* (n 10) [1554].

58 *Youth Verdict* (n 10) [1554].

59 *Youth Verdict* (n 10) [1555].

60 *Youth Verdict* (n 10) [1559].

61 *Youth Verdict* (n 10) [1562].

62 *Youth Verdict* (n 10) [1568].

63 *Youth Verdict* (n 10) [1938].
64 *Youth Verdict* (n 10) [1938].
65 *Youth Verdict* (n 10) [1808]–[1809], [1941].
66 Queensland Department of Environment and Science, 'Waratah Galilee Coal Mine EA Refused' (3 April 2023) <https://www.des.qld.gov.au/our-department/news-media/mediareleases/waratah-galilee-coal-mine-ea-refused> accessed 4 June 2023.
67 *Pabai* (n 8).
68 Further Amended Statement of Claim, *Pabai v Commonwealth of Australia*, VID622/2021 (3 February 2023) [2]–[4].
69 Further Amended Statement of Claim (n 68) [81].
70 Further Amended Statement of Claim (n 68) [81A].
71 Further Amended Statement of Claim (n 68) Part IV.
72 Further Amended Statement of Claim (n 68) [63].
73 See *Caltex Refineries (Qld) Pty Limited v Stavar* (2009) 75 NSWLR 649, Supreme Court of New South Wales, Court of Appeal (Australia) [101]–[103] (Allsop P) (*Caltex*); *Hunter Area Health Service v Presland* (2005) 63 NSWLR 22, Supreme Court of New South Wales, Court of Appeal (Australia), [9] (Spigelman CJ) (*Presland*).
74 *Caltex* (n 73) [101], [103(d)]; *Presland* (n 73) [11]. For a detailed discussion on 'vulnerability', see Murcott, Tigre and Ann Samuel, 'Introduction', pp 1–3.
75 Further Amended Statement of Claim (n 68) Part V.
76 Further Amended Statement of Claim (n 68) Part VI.
77 Federal Court of Australia, Sworn Affidavit of Fred Pabai (stamped and redacted), VID622/2021 (13 December 2022) [53].
78 Federal Court of Australia, Sworn Affidavit of Boggo Billy (stamped and redacted), VID622/2021 (24 January 2022) [32]–[42].
79 Federal Court of Australia (n 78).
80 Federal Court of Australia (n 78).
81 Federal Court of Australia, Sworn Affidavit of Jennifer Enosa (stamped and redacted), VID622/2021 (22 January 2022) [29], [37].
82 Federal Court of Australia (n 81) [46].
83 Federal Court of Australia, 'Pabai Pabai v Commonwealth of Australia' <https://www.fedcourt.gov.au/services/access-to-files-and-transcripts/online-files/pabai-v-australia> accessed 14 May 2024.
84 Concise Statement, *Pabai v Commonwealth of Australia*, VID622/2021 (31 March 2022) [31]–[32].
85 Petsche (n 2) 1007–1008.
86 Petsche (n 2) 1010–1011.
87 Fitzsimmons (n 3) 314.
88 See James P George, 'Parallel Litigation' (1999) 51 *Baylor L Rev* 769.
89 Urzola Gutierrez (n 5) 8, 11, 16.
90 Urzola Gutierrez (n 5) 2. See also Danielle Johnson et al., 'Diversifying Indigenous Vulnerability and Adaptation: An Intersectional Reading of Māori Women's Experiences of Health, Wellbeing, and Climate Change' (2022) 14 *Sustainability* 5452.
91 Petsche (n 2) 1017–1018.
92 Emily Barritt, 'Consciously Transnational: Urgenda and the Shape of Climate Change Litigation: *The State of the Netherlands (Ministry of Economic Affairs and Climate Policy) v Urgenda Foundation*' (2020) 22 *ELR* 296.
93 *Billy* (n 9) [3.4], [4.7].
94 *Billy* (n 9) [3.4].
95 I thank one of the anonymous reviewers for this observation.
96 *Sacchi* (n 18).
97 *Agostinho* (n 37).
98 Petsche (n 2) 1016.

## Bibliography

### *Books and book chapters*

Abate Randall S and Kronk Elizabeth Ann (eds), *Climate Change and Indigenous Peoples: The Search for Legal Remedies* (Edward Elgar Publishing 2013)

Batros Ben and Khan Tessa, 'Thinking Strategically About Climate Litigation' in César Rodríguez-Garavito (ed), *Litigating the Climate Emergency* (CUP 2022)

### *Cases*

*Agostinho v Portugal* (2024) 39371/20, European Court of Human Rights

*Billy v Australia* (2022) CCPR/C/135/D/3624/2019 (*Billy*)

*Caltex Refineries (Qld) Pty Limited v Stavar* (2009) 75 NSWLR 649, Supreme Court of New South Wales, Court of Appeal (Australia) (*Caltex*)

*Graham Barclay Oysters v Ryan* (2002) 211 CLR 540, High Court of Australia (Australia)

*Human Rights Committee, General Comment* 23 (1994) (HRI/GEN/1/Rev.1/38)

*Hunter Area Health Service v Presland* (2005) 63 NSWLR 22, Supreme Court of New South Wales, Court of Appeal (Australia) (*Presland*)

*Mabo v Queensland* (No 2) (1992) 175 CLR 1, High Court of Australia (Australia)

*Minister for the Environment v Sharma* (2022) 291 FCR 311, Federal Court of Australia, Full Court (Australia) (*Sharma*)

*Pabai v Commonwealth of Australia* (2022) VID622/2021, Federal Court of Australia (Australia) (*Pabai*)

*Sacchi et al. v Argentina* (2019) CRC/C/88/D/105/2019, UN Committee on the Rights of the Child (*Sacchi*)

*Waratah Coal Pty Ltd v Youth Verdict Ltd et al.* (No 6) (2022) QLC 21, Land Court of Queensland (Australia) (*Youth Verdict*)

### *Journal articles*

Barritt Emily, 'Consciously Transnational: Urgenda and the Shape of Climate Change Litigation: *The State of the Netherlands (Ministry of Economic Affairs and Climate Policy) v Urgenda Foundation*' (2020) 22(4) *ELR* 296 <https://doi.org/10.1177/1461452920974493> accessed 1 September 2024

Bhardwaj Chhaya, 'Adaptation and Human Rights: A Decision by the Human Rights Committee Daniel Billy et al. v Australia CCPR/C/135/D/3624/2019' (2023) 25 *ELR* 154 <https://doi.org/10.1177/14614529231169544> accessed 1 September 2024

Dainotto Roberto, 'South by Chance: Southern Questions on the Global South' (2017) 11(2) *The Global South* <https://doi.org/10.2979/globalsouth.11.2.03> accessed 1 September 2024

Fitzsimmons Anthony, 'Forum Shopping: A Practitioner's Perspective' (2006) 31 *TGP* 314 <https://link.springer.com/article/10.1057/palgrave.gpp.2510076> accessed 1 September 2024

George James P, 'Parallel Litigation' (1999) 51 *Baylor L Rev* 769 <https://scholarship.law.tamu.edu/facscholar/427> accessed 1 September 2024

Gutierrez Natalia Urzola, 'Gender in Climate Litigation in Latin America: Epistemic Justice Through a Feminist Lens' 16(1) *JHRP* <https://doi.org/10.1093/jhuman/huad030> accessed 1 September 2024

Johnson Danielle et al., 'Diversifying Indigenous Vulnerability and Adaptation: An Intersectional Reading of Māori Women's Experiences of Health, Wellbeing, and Climate

Change' (2022) 14 *Sustainability* 5452 <https://doi.org/10.3390/su14095452> accessed 1 September 2024

Juenger Friedrich K, 'Forum Shopping, Domestic and International' (1989) 63 *Tu L Rev* 553 <https://www.tulanelawreview.org/pub/volume63/issue3/forum-shopping-domestic-and-international> accessed 1 September 2024

Keikelame Mpoe Johannah and Swartz Leslie, 'Decolonising Research Methodologies: Lessons from a Qualitative Research Project, Cape Town, South Africa' (2019) 12(1) *GHA* 1 <https://doi.org/10.1080/16549716.2018.1561175> accessed 1 September 2024

Luporini Riccardo and Savaresi Annalisa, 'International Human Rights Bodies and Climate Litigation: Don't Look Up?' (2023) 32 *RECIEL* 267 <https://doi.org/10.1111/reel.12491> accessed 1 September 2024

Olsen Torjer, 'Privilege, Decentring and the Challenge of Being (Non-) Indigenous in the Study of Indigenous Issues' (2018) 47(2) *AJIE* <https://www.researchgate.net/publication/318195530_Privilege_Decentring_and_the_Challenge_of_Being_Non-_Indigenous_in_the_Study_of_Indigenous_Issues> accessed 1 September 2024

Peel Jacqueline and Lin Jolene, 'Transnational Climate Litigation: The Contribution of the Global South' (2019) 113 *AJIL* 679 <https://doi.org/10.1017/ajil.2019.48> accessed 1 September 2024

Petsche Markus, 'What's Wrong with Forum Shopping? An Attempt to Identify and Assess the Real Issues of a Controversial Practice' (2011) 45(4) *TIL* 1005 <https://scholar.smu.edu/til/vol45/iss4/5> accessed 1 September 2024

Rodríguez-Garavito César, 'Human Rights: The Global South's Route to Climate Litigation' (2020) 114 *AJIL Unbound* 40 <https://doi.org/10.1017/aju.2020.4> accessed 1 September 2024

Skille Eivind, 'Doing Research into Indigenous Issues Being Non-Indigenous' (2022) 22 *QR* 831 <https://doi.org/10.1177/14687941211005947> accessed 1 September 2024

Sultana Farhana, 'Reflexivity, Positionality and Participatory Ethics: Negotiating Fieldwork Dilemmas in International Research' (2015) 6(3) *ACME* 374 <https://acme-journal.org/index.php/acme/article/view/786> accessed 1 September 2024

Tigre Maria Antonia, 'Climate Change and Indigenous Groups: The Rise of Indigenous Voices in Climate Litigation' (2022) 9 *e-Publica* 214 <https://scholarship.law.columbia.edu/sabin_climate_change/196> accessed 1 September 2024

Tigre Maria Antonia, 'U.N. Human Rights Committee Finds that Australia is Violating Human Rights Obligations Towards Torres Strait Islanders for Climate Inaction' (2022) *Climate Law* <https://blogs.law.columbia.edu/climatechange/2022/09/27/u-n-human-rights-committee-finds-that-australia-is-violating-human-rights-obligations-towards-torres-strait-islanders-for-climate-inaction/> accessed 8 October 2023

## *Legal submissions*

Australian Government, 'Response of Australia to the Views of the Human Rights Committee in Communication No 3624/2019 (Billy et al. v Australia)' (30 March 2023)

Communication No 105/2019 to the Committee on the Rights of the Child (23 September 2019)

Communication No 3624/2019 under the Optional Protocol to the International Covenant on Civil and Political Rights (13 May 2019)

Concise Statement, *Pabai v Commonwealth of Australia*, VID622/2021 (31 March 2022)

Federal Court of Australia, Sworn Affidavit of Fred Pabai (stamped and redacted), VID622/2021 (13 December 2022)

Federal Court of Australia, Sworn Affidavit of Jennifer Enosa (stamped and redacted), VID622/2021 (22 January 2022)

Federal of Australia, Sworn Affidavit of Boggo Billy (stamped and redacted), VID622/2021 (24 January 2022)

Further Amended Statement of Claim, *Pabai v Commonwealth of Australia*, VID622/2021 (3 February 2023)

## Legislation and treaties

Human Rights Act 2019 (Qld)

International Covenant on Civil and Political Rights

Native Title Act 1993 (Cth)

United Nations Declaration on the Rights of Indigenous Peoples

## Online sources

Biennale of Sydney, '23rd Biennale of Sydney Participant Interview – Torres Strait 8 – Yessie Mosby' (*YouTube*, 18 July 2020) <https://www.youtube.com/watch?v=qn0YqA2tkRM&t=245s> accessed 8 October 2023

ClientEarth, 'One Year on from Historic Torres Strait UN Climate Victory – No Compensation Despite Legal Finding' (*ClientEarth*, 25 September 2023) <https://www.clientearth.org/latest/press-office/press/one-year-on-from-historic-torres-strait-un-climate-victory-no-compensation-despite-legal-finding/#:~:text=One%20year%20on%20from%20the,finding%20to%20award%20them%20compensation> accessed 8 October 2023

climatecasechart.com

Federal Court of Australia, 'Pabai Pabai v Commonwealth of Australia' <https://www.fedcourt.gov.au/services/access-to-files-and-transcripts/online-files/pabai-v-australia> accessed 14 May 2024

Maria Antonia Tigre, 'U.N. Human Rights Committee Finds that Australia is Violating Human Rights Obligations Towards Torres Strait Islanders for Climate Inaction' (*Climate Law*, 27 September 2022) <https://blogs.law.columbia.edu/climatechange/2022/09/27/u-n-human-rights-committee-finds-that-australia-is-violating-human-rights-obligations-towards-torres-strait-islanders-for-climate-inaction/> accessed 8 October 2023

Queensland Department of Environment and Science, 'Waratah Galilee Coal Mine EA Refused' (*Queensland Government*, 3 April 2023) <https://www.des.qld.gov.au/our-department/news-media/mediareleases/waratah-galilee-coal-mine-ea-refused> accessed 4 June 2023

Queensland Department of Environment and Science, 'Case Study: Boigu Island Seawall' (*Queensland Government*, 18 May 2023) <https://www.des.qld.gov.au/climateaction/take-action/case-studies/boigu-island-seawall> accessed 8 October 2023

Sam Bookman, 'Indigenous Climate Litigation in Anglophone Settler-Colonial States: Contact, Cases and Caution' (*Voelkerrechtsblog*, 25 March 2022) <https://voelkerrechtsblog.org/indigenous-climate-litigation-in-anglophone-settler-colonial-states-context-cases-and-caution/> accessed 8 October 2023

www.business-humanrights.org

www.des.qld.gov.au

www.youthverdict.org.au

Chapter 7

# The need for child-led climate litigation in Bangladesh

## Lessons from India and Pakistan

*Preetkiran Kaur, S. Sathiabama and S. Vedavalli*

### Introduction

Children and future generations are exposed to climate change impacts and related risks, such as flooding, heat stress, water scarcity, poverty, and hunger, more than ever before. According to the Intergovernmental Panel for Climate Change (IPCC), children aged 10 years or younger in 2020 are expected to face nearly four to five times as many extreme events by 2100 compared with adults in 2020.[1] Children are more vulnerable to climate change impacts than adults because they require more food and water per unit of their body weight, are less able to survive extreme weather events, and are more susceptible to toxic chemicals, temperature changes, and diseases, among other factors.[2] Children's health, especially in the South Asian region, is vulnerable to climate change due to a unique combination of extreme weather, existing nutritional deficits, and a lack of access to sanitation.[3] Exposure to pollution is another concern. In 2016, around 4.2 million premature deaths worldwide were caused by ambient air pollution, with 91% occurring in low- and middle-income countries.[4] India, Pakistan, and Bangladesh experience higher burdens due to their high population density, their relatively high exposure levels to air pollution, and the proportion of people affected by chronic diseases.[5]

In 2021, the United Nations International Children's Emergency Fund (UNICEF) introduced the Children's Climate Risk Index (CCRI), the first comprehensive analysis of climate risk focused on children.[6] A country's ranking is based on children's exposure to climate and environmental shocks, such as cyclones and heatwaves, and their vulnerability to these shocks is determined by their access to essential services, such as water, sanitation, healthcare, and education.[7] Pakistan, Bangladesh, and India were ranked 14, 15, and 26, respectively, in the CCRI and were classified as 'extremely high-risk' among the South Asian states (SAS) for children's exposure to climate and environmental shocks.[8] The CCRI also reports that the three countries are 'extremely high risk',[9] despite emitting only 9.38% of global greenhouse gas (GHG) emissions.[10] The disproportionate exposure of SAS children, who have contributed very little to the problem,[11] to the impacts of climate change is illustrative of climate injustice.

DOI: 10.4324/9781003470632-10

Amongst SAS, Bangladesh is at the front line of climate change impacts. For instance, over the last two decades, it is reported to have been the seventh most affected country by extreme weather events.[12] It has exceptionally high exposure to flooding, including riverine, flash, and coastal, and high exposure to tropical cyclones and their associated hazards, as well as to drought.[13] Bangladesh is not only highly exposed to climate change but also ill-prepared to deal with its impacts, which is particularly concerning for children in the country.[14]

Against this background, there is a need to enhance the protection of children's rights and the agency of children amidst the climate crisis. Since around 2014, children have increasingly been involved in litigation to address environmental harm.[15] This chapter positions Bangladeshi children not merely as victims of climate change but also as agents who could seek legal redress through child-led climate litigation. The first section highlights the specific vulnerabilities of Bangladeshi children to climate change given biophysical and social factors. The second section frames the analysis, drawing on Fineman's vulnerability theory. This framing stresses the positive role of the state in building resilience for children. The third section critically discusses potential legal tools intended to protect Bangladeshi children from the impacts of climate change, highlighting its inadequacy. The fourth section proposes child-led climate change litigation as a tool to build climate resilience. Finally, drawing upon legal transplantation theory, the last section explores the potential of developing child-led climate litigation in Bangladesh through lessons from India and Pakistan.

## Vulnerability of Bangladeshi children to climate change

We use the term 'vulnerability' to refer to people's susceptibility to climate change and variability, influenced by biophysical and social factors.[16] Biophysical vulnerability arises from the impacts of a hazard event, often viewed in terms of the amount of damage experienced by a system because of an encounter with a hazard, whereas social factors relate to structures and systems in society and social conditions. As Cutter argues, an assessment of the interaction and intersection of both biophysical and social vulnerabilities is pertinent to gain a holistic understanding of how vulnerability is created.[17]

### *Biophysical vulnerability of Bangladesh*

Biophysical vulnerability theory focuses on environmental processes that create hazardous conditions and understands vulnerability as a pre-existing condition of human existence.[18] Experiences of vulnerability are inherently dynamic because every location has unique geographic characteristics. The 'hazards of place model' gives room to reflect on the uniqueness of each place, allowing for legitimising risk assessment and mitigation measures to be custom-framed.[19]

As a low-lying delta country in South Asia less than 15 ft above sea level,[20] Bangladesh is particularly vulnerable to climate change due to its geographical location, flat topography, dense population, and weak infrastructure exacerbating a range of climate-related challenges.[21] These challenges include cyclones, droughts, flash floods, salinity, sea level rise, and more. They have led to increased dengue outbreaks,[22] water shortages, disaster-related mortality, power disruptions, deeper poverty, and displacement.[23]

### *Vulnerability of Bangladeshi children*

Viewing vulnerability through an intersectional lens – inspired by Crenshaw[24] – invites analyses beyond a single frame,[25] encompassing intersecting factors that influence marginalisation and oppression, such as sex, race, class, and age.[26] Collocating Crenshaw's approach within the context of this chapter, it is apparent that the impacts of climate change are unevenly distributed, and that Bangladeshi children who live in poverty are a highly vulnerable group bearing significant impacts of climate change along multiple interlocking axes of oppression, despite contributing the least to the problem.[27] Indeed, research on the social vulnerability of children reveals that the climate change crisis is a child rights crisis.[28] In 2023, UNICEF warned that more than 19 million children in Bangladesh, from 20 of the country's 64 districts, are most vulnerable to the disastrous consequences of climate change.[29] Over 5 million children are under the age of 5, and the changing climate is already hindering the growth and development necessary for their lives and diminishing their prospects for a better future.[30]

Research shows that exposure to climate extremities in the early years of growth hampers the development of a child's immune system, leaving them prone to diseases and infections.[31] Among other issues, experiences and environmental influences on early health 'get under the skin' and interact with genetic predispositions.[32] Due to children's rapid growth and physiological and cognitive development, they are exposed and more vulnerable to biological, chemical, and physical environmental hazards compared to adults.[33] Children have lifelong outcomes in learning, behaviour, and both physical and mental well-being. For instance, early experiences build inside a child's body and create biological 'memories' that shape their development, for better or worse.[34] Additionally, constant stress affects the architecture of their developing brain, cardiovascular system, immune system, and metabolic regulatory controls.[35] Children have a lower capacity than adults to cope with temperature changes due to their different physiology and metabolism, including a higher surface-area-to-body mass ratio that leads to greater heat gain or loss, higher metabolic heat production during activities, and a lower sweat-producing capacity that reduces heat dissipation through evaporation.[36]

Reports indicate an increase in hospital admissions in Bangladesh for diarrheal diseases in children caused by increasing temperatures.[37] Studies conclude that extreme temperatures have a detrimental impact on the health of children, especially children under the age of 1, even causing heat-related deaths.[38] Extreme temperatures adversely impact the respiratory system of Bangladeshi children.[39] Researchers estimate that 31.3% of children's respiratory infections and 6.6% of asthma cases are due to climate change.[40] The global rise in temperature has led to longer summers, during which people use mosquito coils to keep them at bay. Mosquito coils release smoke, which leads to acute respiratory infections in children under the age of 5.[41] Low temperature also has a detrimental impact on children's health by causing skin irritability,[42] impairment of inflammatory and irritant dermatoses,[43] and eczema.[44] Climate-related displacement of vulnerable communities, such as farmer families in villages and coastal areas, often results in non-economic losses, including the disruption of social fabric, leading to loneliness, emotional regulation difficulties, and impaired cognitive development and academic performance among children.[45] All these factors warrant an exploration of the legal tools available to tackle the vulnerability of children to climate change in Bangladesh. We examine these tools with reference to Fineman's theory of vulnerability, and from the point of departure that the law ought to pursue substantive equality, recognising the innate vulnerability of all human beings, and the particular vulnerability of children in Bangladesh.

### *Formal vs substantive equality and vulnerability*

*Formal equality* is the application of laws to all persons equally, leaving each individual free to exercise their rights fully.[46] It is based on a negative concept of liberty, which adopts the view that equality can be achieved by granting autonomous individuals equal rights without state interference, and ignores structural barriers to the enjoyment of rights.[47] Formal equality empowers a liberal legal subject with a right to autonomy to govern his own life, while at the same time asserting his freedom from responding to the needs of others who should equally be independent and self-sufficient.[48] In contrast, *substantive equality* acknowledges that humans are not equally placed in society to enjoy rights fully. It rejects the idea of equality merely in terms of granting equal rights and acknowledges individual and structural barriers.[49] Substantive equality calls for positive measures to advance rights, particularly an active role played by the state to reduce barriers and level the playing field.[50]

Those who advance substantive equality argue that the depiction of an individual as a 'liberal legal subject' is flawed since vulnerability is innate, and every human being is a 'deeply dependent vulnerable subject'.[51] Leading this discourse, Fineman argues that a universal legal subject is vulnerable and prone to dependency (both chronic and episodic).[52] Therefore, the state has a corresponding obligation to reduce and compensate for that vulnerability by advancing substantive equality.[53] For Fineman, the condition of vulnerability is intrinsic to every human being and arises on account of the characteristics, experiences, or situations that are universal and define the human condition.[54] Fineman argues that since vulnerability is universal and intrinsic to human nature, discourse on vulnerability and rights cannot operate in silos. Yet she acknowledges different positions of individuals in terms of capacities and resources in society, which ultimately result in varying levels of vulnerability for human beings. Fineman further argues that vulnerability cannot be eradicated, and dependency cannot be brought to zero.[55] Ultimately, she proposes building resilience to mitigate vulnerability, where the state is an active regulator channelling its institutions towards resilience building for its subjects.

We agree that in the context of climate change, every individual is vulnerable, yet experiences of vulnerability vary due to the different physical and cognitive abilities,[56] developmental differences, and unique economic and institutional relationships they have with each other and with governments and state institutions.[57] To advance substantive equality amidst the biophysical vulnerability of Bangladesh, coupled with the particular vulnerability of Bangladeshi children to climate change, we argue that state intervention is crucial to build resilience.

According to Fineman, the state is entrusted with the responsibility to establish and monitor institutions that the human subject interacts with and build resilience.[58] However, it may be necessary for relationships with the state to be redefined to ensure sufficient resources and capabilities to respond in times of crisis. Fundamental rights have been granted under Part III of the Constitution of the People's Republic of Bangladesh (Constitution), along with the right of every citizen to enforce these fundamental rights.[59] Nevertheless, marginalised groups of society, such as women, people with disabilities, children, and unorganised labour sectors, remain handicapped by various structural barriers, such as poverty and illiteracy, and have either had no access to justice or have been denied justice.[60] Hence, the concept of public interest litigation (PIL) was introduced to permit public-spirited individuals to file litigation on behalf of the most vulnerable groups in the public interest. Contextualising this example in terms of vulnerability theory, fundamental rights were granted to individuals to build resilience, including because they were vulnerable to the state's abuse of power or implementation failures. However, even after rights have been granted, the relationship between the judiciary and individuals needs to be redefined to ensure access to justice for marginalised sections of society (i.e. 'more vulnerable groups').

Institutions such as the judiciary are brought into legal existence through state mechanisms,[61] and Fineman argues that they must work cumulatively and independently to provide or facilitate the acquisition of resources, namely, physical, human, social, ecological, or environmental.[62] These resources are necessary for building resilience in individuals.[63] For example, ecological resources refer to the positions we occupy concerning the physical, built, or natural environments in which we find ourselves; that is to say, the availability of ecological resources depends on our location and how we interact with the environment around us.[64] In the case of Bangladeshi children, climate change continuously destroys the ecology on which they depend, which, in turn, disproportionately affects their right to health. Vulnerability theory aids in recognising how the embedded institutional vulnerability of children to climate change intersects with the destruction of ecological resources. Children are disadvantageously positioned because they lack judicial recourse in cases concerning the violation of their rights due to climate change. Hence, the relationship between children and institutions needs to be redefined to grant them rights that will build their resilience against climate change.

Access to the resources referred to earlier must be monitored and regulated through legislation and the creation of agencies and commissions to protect the environment from further deterioration and advance the resilience of people.

### *Legal tools available to tackle the vulnerability of children to climate change*

This chapter proposes climate litigation for children in Bangladesh as a tool to build resilience against climate change. Additionally, the chapter proposes granting substantive rights coupled with an enforcing legal mechanism to ensure the justiciability of these rights. It is necessary to assess the legal tools available to tackle the vulnerability of children to climate change to test these proposals. The next section outlines relevant Bangladeshi laws that could be useful to children in the context of their health vulnerability amidst climate change. In our discussion of relevant laws, the term 'children' is used to refer to all persons up to the age of 18 years as defined under section 4 of the Bangladesh Children Act 2013.[65] This definition aligns with the United Nations Convention on the Rights of Child (CRC),[66] which defines a *child* as a human being below the age of 18 years unless, under the law applicable to the child, majority is attained earlier.[67] We begin by discussing procedural provisions, then turn to discuss substantive provisions, and finally make some observations.

#### *Procedural provisions*

Presently, Bangladeshi children are considered minors who cannot legally represent themselves in court. The Civil Procedure Code provides that

> any person who is of sound mind and has attained majority may act as next friend of a minor or as his guardian for the suit, provided that the interest of such person is not adverse to that of the minor and that he is not, in the case of a next friend, a defendant, or, in the case of a guardian for the suit, a plaintiff.[68]

Bangladeshi children have not yet utilised this provision to initiate child-led climate litigation. If they do, they would have to depend on public-spirited individuals and organisations to file PIL on their behalf, as a 'next friend'.[69] Article 102(1) of the Constitution deals with the enforcement of fundamental rights in courts (i.e. *locus standi*) and employs the term 'any person aggrieved' in delineating who can enforce fundamental rights in the courts. The scope of who has *locus standi* was clarified in *Mohiuddin Farooque v Bangladesh* (*FAP-20* case), which concerned a challenge to controlled flooding that would displace people and cause environmental degradation.[70] In this case, Bangladesh's apex court held that any person can approach the court under Article 102, where a violation of the rights of other members of the public has occurred. Thus, a person could initiate PIL on behalf of children or for children, which could be filed at the High Court Division of Bangladesh.

Under Article 102, a writ of mandamus can be issued by the courts to an authority to perform their legal duties properly. However, there are limitations to issuing a writ of mandamus. First, the writ can be issued only when the public functionary has a public duty under law and refuses to perform that duty.[71] Thus, the writ of mandamus is not an effective remedy in cases where the public authority has taken inadequate measures or the measures are ineffective. Second, in situations where the duty is based on the discretion of the public authority, the court cannot issue a mandamus to order the public authority to mandatorily exercise their discretion.[72] Third, in *Yunus Mia v Secretary Ministry of Public Works*,[73] the Supreme Court of Bangladesh held that a writ of mandamus could only be issued for the implementation of a decision and not for the implementation of its policies.[74] Hence, the plethora of policies framed by the government to curb climate change is directory in nature and not justiciable. Lastly, in *Dacca National Medical Institute v Province of East Pakistan*,[75] the court held that before petitioners file for a writ of mandamus, they must have made a demand for justice, and the same should have been refused. Arguably, this requirement makes the process of approaching the court to issue a directive to a public authority tedious and cumbersome.

Bangladesh, through the Environment Court Act 2010, has established environmental courts which exclusively deal with environmental conservation cases. Environmental courts have the jurisdiction to deal with all the offences under the Environment Conservation Act 1995 or any other Acts as notified by the government. However, the Act adopts a restrictive approach which allows the special magistrate court to take cognisance of an offence and the environmental court to receive any compensation claim, only on the written report of an inspector of the Department of Environment.[76] Nevertheless, direct cases from private persons without such prior authorisation can be admitted if the magistrate or the court is satisfied that the inspector has not taken the necessary steps within 60 days of the request made by the aggrieved person. Children would require effective legal representation to file their claims or complaints and to defend their cause. It is recommended that children be given direct access to the environmental courts and that the need for approval of the complaint by the inspector and legal representation should not be mandatory when seeking a judicial remedy in an environmental matter.

Under section 2(4) of the Children Act 2013, a child can approach the children's court if they were a victim or witness to any offence under any existing laws of Bangladesh. This raises the question whether the impacts of climate change could be considered an offence. No cases have been instituted yet concerning whether causing climate change harms amounts to an offence under environmental laws.[77]

### *Substantive provisions*

As mentioned earlier, fundamental rights are provided for in Part III of the Constitution. They include the right to the protection of law, guaranteed under Article 31, and the 'right to life and personal liberty', protected under Article 32, which have received judicial attention. For instance, *Mohiuddin Farooque v Bangladesh et al.* (*Radioactive Milk* case) concerned the consumption of food which contained radiation levels above the approved limit.[78] The Supreme Court extended the meaning of the right to life to include the protection of health, development of children, maintenance and improvement of public health by creating and sustaining conditions congenial to good health, and ensuring the quality of life consistent with human dignity.[79] The court further directed that the state has an obligation to protect the health and longevity of the people living in the country in terms of the right to life, guaranteed under Article 32, and the right to the protection of law, guaranteed under Article 31. The right to life can thus be invoked to protect people from any unjustified threat to their health and longevity.[80]

In the landmark *FAP-20 case*, the appellate division held that the right to life encompasses the right to protect the environment and to preserve its ecological balance within its ambit. Any act or omission concerning these rights is a violation of an individual's right to life. Justice BR Roy observed:

> Articles 31 and 32 of our Constitution protect right to life as Fundamental Right. It encompasses within its ambit, the protection and preservation of environment, ecological balance, free from pollution of air and water, sanitation without which life can hardly be enjoyed. Any act or omission contrary thereto will be violative of the said right to life.

Therefore, Bangladeshi children could argue that the state's duty to protect the climate system and their right to life has been violated by not reducing carbon and GHG emissions in Bangladesh.

In *Rabia Bhuiyan, MP v Ministry of Local Government and Rural Development et al.*,[81] a writ petition was filed to order the government to ensure clean and safe drinking water. In this case, the court upheld the state's duty to provide access to clean drinking water by linking environmental pollution to a violation of the right to life under the Constitution.[82]

Part II contains a set of 'fundamental principles of state policy', including Articles 15, 16, 18, and 21. Article 15 of the Constitution provides that the state has a duty to improve the standard of living of its citizens and provide necessities of life, such as food, shelter, housing, etc., along with public assistance in special circumstances, such as illness or unemployment. Article 16 stipulates the duty of the state to improve public health, especially in the rural population. Moreover, Article 18(1) of the Constitution mandates building physical resilience by raising the level of nutrition and improving the public health of its citizens. Further, Article 18A places a duty on the state to protect the environment and preserve biodiversity for present as well as future citizens. Lastly, Article 21 provides that 'every person in the service of the Republic has a duty to strive at all times to serve the people', which has been interpreted by the judiciary to advance the public trust doctrine.[83] As such, the government holds the nation's natural resources in public trust for the benefit of everyone.

Despite these provisions being described as directive principles that are not enforceable against the state, the interpretation thereof is closely linked to the 'equality clause' (Article 27) and the 'protection of the right to life and personal liberty' (Article 32).[84] In the *FAP-20 case*, it was held that the principles articulated in Articles 15, 16, and 18 form an integral component of the right to life, which implies a life of dignity and not mere animal existence and, hence, can be litigated in court.

To realise Article 18, Bangladesh enacted the Community Health Assessment Trust Act 2018. Section 4 of the Act states that community clinics shall be set up by the Community Clinic Health Care Trust with the prior approval of the government. In terms of section 10, it is the duty of the Trust established to provide uninterrupted integrated primary healthcare to village people through community clinics and to determine its extent and scope. Additionally, Bangladesh enacted the Communicable Diseases (Prevention, Control and Elimination) Act 2018 to raise awareness of, and prevent, control, and eliminate, infectious diseases, and to deal with public health emergencies and the reduction of public health risks. Section 5 of the Act lists the responsibilities and functions of a directorate to fulfil the goals set out in the preamble of the Act. Section 7 provides that an advisory committee shall be formed to assist the directorate in the fulfilment of the preambular goals. Section 25 creates sanctions to punish any person who obstructs the activities of the directorate.

Unfortunately, neither of the Acts discussed contains an accountability mechanism or grievance redress system if the state fails to fulfil its duties. For instance, the public is not afforded an avenue to complain about inadequate or ineffective measures taken by the advisory committee, directorate, or the Trust.

### *Observations*

Overall, the jurisprudence on protecting the health of children amidst climate change is scant and indirect. The apex court of Bangladesh has recognised the right to health as a subset of the right to life,[85] but the recourse that children have is limited. The vulnerability of the health of children due to climate change, combined with interlocking systems of oppression, is also not acknowledged in legislation.[86] Consequently, the appropriate remedies that children can seek to protect their right to health owing to climate change are limited. The state has been largely unresponsive by providing little to no legal remedy for children to protect their health amidst the climate crisis.

The National Children's Taskforce is a nationwide children's organisation established in Bangladesh to advance children's rights.[87] This organisation could be integrated with the environmental court to protect children's rights and the environment. To effectively tackle rising climate vulnerabilities amongst children in Bangladesh, it is recommended that the two bodies collaborate to explore the linkages between children's rights, climate change, and climate action to work towards achieving common goals. Further, the government should undertake initiatives to invest in research and development, enhance environmental awareness, and prioritise capacity building to address knowledge gaps, given that climate change litigation is a knowledge-intensive process. Dissemination of information will increase public participation and result in the government being better informed when drafting a legislation.[88]

For now, to successfully litigate public health issues, including those experienced by children due to climate change, the developed jurisprudence requires, first, that the petitioner meet the *locus standi* test of being 'an aggrieved person' and, second, that threats to children's health due to climate change violate the right to life. In the case of children, someone would need to litigate on their behalf.

If children no longer needed to rely on adults for legal representation and could raise their grievances independently, they would be more empowered to advance their claims in litigation. This development would embrace the shift from historical perceptions in the law that viewed children as 'objects' to one that recognises children as 'subjects' of law with their legal interests and rights.[89] It would require that the relationship between children and the judiciary in Bangladesh be redefined such that children have the right to initiate climate litigation claims in the court themselves as 'persons aggrieved', as opposed to with the support of a 'next friend' acting on their behalf. Their role in society would then no longer be restricted to being passive beneficiaries of policies and legislation framed by adults for them; instead, children would become active citizens who participate in the lawmaking process as stakeholders and joint decision-makers.

Endowing children with the right to raise their grievances would enhance their ability to shape the political discourse on climate change.[90] Children coming to the forefront to raise their grievances and demands from the government would change the power dynamics between the state and the citizens. States could become more conscious of their responsibility to protect the rights of children and take progressive measures to combat climate change.

Fineman argues that the collective reality of human vulnerability and the physical and social dependency that it inevitably generates should be a central concern of the state when defining the relationship between subjects and its institutions.[91] A genuinely responsive state would consider all interested parties and their competing vulnerabilities.[92] It is important for the state to develop legal mechanisms that ensure the enforcement of its existing responsibilities towards its citizens in building resilience by providing sufficient resources and capabilities. Child-led climate litigation is discussed in the next section as a potential mechanism to promote a more responsive state.

## *Child-led climate litigation*

Increasingly, people are pursuing judicial recourse to redress climate change issues through lawsuits or petitions referred to as 'climate change litigation',[93] including child-led strategic climate litigation. In strategic climate litigation, 'the claimants' motives go beyond the concerns of the individual litigant and aim at advancing climate policies, creating public awareness, or changing the behaviour of government or industry actors'.[94] Such litigation has the potential to transform children from being passive victims of climate change to agents advancing their rights. This form of litigation falls under the broader scope of youth-led climate change litigation. 'Youth-led litigation' includes cases involving plaintiffs who are (1) named children and young people, (2) a non-governmental organisation led by children and young people, or (3) a class of children and young people.[95]

The landmark case of *Neubauer et al. v Germany*[96] in the Constitutional Court of Germany is a prime example of how youth-led litigation has the potential to bring positive change and allow the younger generation to voice their concerns regarding climate change and its impact on their rights. A legal challenge to the Federal Climate Protection Act[97] was filed by young environmental activists stating that the provisions to mitigate climate change were inadequate and consequently violated fundamental rights guaranteed by the German Basic Law.[98] The court held in favour of the complainants and declared the challenged provisions unconstitutional because they did not sufficiently protect the younger generation against future infringements of their fundamental rights, especially in light of exacerbating the climate change crisis.[99] Children in the Global South have all the more reason for such litigation, considering their intensifying vulnerability.

### *Integrating children into the climate litigation process*

One way to integrate children into the climate litigation process in Bangladesh is through an existing environmental court that is mandated to provide speedy and effective remedies in cases of environmental violations. However, the mandatory requirement in the Environmental Courts Act that requires the court to take cognisance of the complaint or compensation application based on a written report by an inspector of the Department of Environment is a significant limitation.[100] It creates an obstacle by reducing direct contact between citizens and courts because the report is contingent on the discretion of the inspector.

In highly vulnerable countries like Bangladesh, climate litigation by and for children could be a breakthrough for redressing the violation of children's rights.[101] Climate litigation can be developed to build resilience by legal transplantation through the incorporation of legal rules from one jurisdiction to another.[102] Next, it is argued that the legal transplantation from India and Pakistan could advance children's climate litigation in Bangladesh.

India and Pakistan have faced only one climate case each, involving a child petitioner. In Pakistan, *Rabab Ali v Federation of Pakistan et al.* (*Ali*)[103] is a *pro bono* petition filed by a 7-year-old against the government's development of Thar coalfield. In India, a 9-year-old petitioner in *Ridhima Pandey v Union of India et al.* (*Pandey*) filed a case against the state for its inaction in mitigating climate change and for being directly affected by the adverse impacts of climate change and rising global temperatures.[104] In both cases, the petitioners sought directives to be issued to the respondents to reduce GHG emissions, among others, by invoking the violation of the children's right to a healthy environment encompassed within the right to life in their Constitutions. Several similarities can be identified in these two cases with respect to the questions of law raised, the grounds on which the violation of rights were established, and the final relief sought. Arguments were heard in *Ali* on 29 June 2016, and the case has not yet been heard on merits.[105] On the other hand, *Pandey* was dismissed. Despite this, the cases offer valuable lessons for child-led litigation in Bangladesh.

## Lessons from India and Pakistan

This section aims to draw lessons from India and Pakistan that could be helpful as an entry point for child-led climate litigation in Bangladesh. The legal systems of all three countries originate from the English common law as a result of the colonial history they share.[106] These states are considered to have characteristics of mixed legal systems with elements of civil law.[107] They are also dualist states that need to incorporate international law in their domestic legal systems to form binding obligations.[108] Bangladesh is known for its judicial transplantation from India and Pakistan.[109] Furthermore, a study shows that Bangladeshi courts frequently cite Indian judgments.[110] Since Bangladesh was a British colony, its legal system has been greatly influenced by common law traditions.[111] Considering that the three legal systems are similar, with similar legal historical legacies, legal transplantation in children's climate litigation from India and Pakistan serves as a potential tool for identifying climate action prospects for Bangladesh to address its vulnerabilities.

First, the section identifies the causes of action invoked in the two cases. Secondly, the section discusses admissibility and procedural criteria in India and Pakistan by analysing the legal standing of children and the jurisdiction of different courts for children to bring climate actions. Thirdly, the section examines the various remedies claimed in the two jurisdictions. In each discussion, lessons for child-led litigation in Bangladesh are considered.

### *Causes of action*

In *Ali*, it is argued that the respondents' development of the Thar coalfield will increase Pakistan's carbon dioxide ($CO_2$) emissions drastically, thus contributing to a destabilised climate system, while ignoring the renewable solar and wind energy technology.[112] Despite knowing Pakistan's vulnerability to climate change effects, the respondents have spent huge sums of money and resources to develop the Thar coalfield and various infrastructural projects for economic development since 2003. This was alleged to violate the doctrine of public trust and the fundamental rights of the Pakistanis. Additionally, it contravened the Paris Agreement and Pakistan's commitment to its intended nationally determined contribution (INDC) to 'promote and support low-carbon, climate-resilient development'.[113] The plaintiff, Rabab Ali, argued that she and the other children in Pakistan are adversely affected by the increasing level of $CO_2$ pollution in the atmosphere, which harms and continuously threatens their mental and physical health, quality of life, and well-being.[114] Depending on the outcome of this case, child-led climate litigation in Bangladesh could advance similar arguments or refine these arguments.

In *Pandey*, the plaintiff argued that she is vulnerable to climate change as a young person, that the government failed to take any effective science-based measure, and that there was a huge gap in the implementation of environmental legislation in India.[115] Without the government's action to reduce $CO_2$ and GHG emissions immediately, children and future generations would disproportionately suffer the dangers and catastrophic impacts of climate destabilisation and ocean acidification.[116] Additionally, the plaintiff alleged that the public trust doctrine and fundamental rights were violated.[117] Furthermore, the plaintiff noted that key environmental committees established by legislation had not discussed or issued specific directions concerning climate change, nor had they taken into account the various commitments made under the Paris Agreement and India's INDC.[118] The plaintiff showed that she was adversely and directly affected by the impacts of climate change.[119] However, in 2019, the National Green Tribunal found that climate change is already covered in the process of impact assessments and there was 'no reason to presume that the Paris Agreement and other international protocols are not reflected in the policies of the Government of India or are not taken into consideration in granting environment clearances'.[120] Given this finding, child-led climate litigation in Bangladesh would have to demonstrate to a court why a finding could be made that the Paris Agreement and other international protocols are not reflected in the policies of Bangladesh.

### *Procedural admissibility criteria*

The CRC provides that children have the right to be heard in any judicial and administrative proceedings affecting them.[121] Although children are largely recognised as legal persons, they cannot approach a court of law independently.[122] Children can only access a court of law through their guardian or a guardian appointed by the court.[123] In India and Pakistan, as in Bangladesh, a person who has not attained majority may institute proceedings in their own name by a person who is called the 'next friend' of the minor.[124] The procedural provisions are the same in all three jurisdictions. While they have been utilised to advance child-led climate litigation in India and Pakistan, this is not yet the case in Bangladesh.

To address the institution of legal proceedings by children against climate change, the issue of admissibility is examined next. That is to say, the legal standing of children and the jurisdiction of the various courts to admit cases while they are suing in special interest as aggrieved persons and in public interest litigation.

#### *Aggrieved person*

Generally, as defined by Judge James LJ in *Ex Parte Sidebotham*, standing is available only to an aggrieved person, 'who must be a man who has suffered a legal grievance, a man against whom a decision has been pronounced which has wrongfully deprived him of something or wrongfully refused him something or wrongfully affected his title to something'.[125] *Pandey* was filed under section 18, read with sections 14 and 15 of the National Green Tribunal Act 2010 on the ground that she was an 'aggrieved person'. Ridhima Pandey argued that she was directly affected by the adverse impacts of climate change and rising global temperatures, and that she belonged to the most vulnerable class of Indians affected by climate change.[126] In other words, the standing of the aggrieved person was invoked through a vulnerability lens. The National Green Tribunal did not make a finding on whether she had standing. The Supreme Court and lower courts have, however, granted standing to children in cases unrelated to the environment but concerning human rights.[127] By analogy, it is possible that Pandey would have been regarded as an 'aggrieved person' had she succeeded in relation to the merits of her claim.

### *Public interest litigation*

One of the clear exceptions to the aforementioned traditional rule is PIL, where no person or determinate class or group of persons is affected by a specific legal injury caused by an act or the omission of the state or any public authority.[128] Instead, injury is caused to the public interest.[129] PIL is a strong tool to address environmental harm.[130] In the context of climate litigation, it successfully breaks down barriers to legal standing for children. Instead of children relying on a 'next friend',[131] any person who is interested in the welfare of children can initiate a climate case to enforce children's constitutional rights.

*Ali* was a *pro bono* petition filed under Article 184(3) of the Pakistan Constitution, invoking the original constitutional jurisdiction of the apex court for environmental justice. She was represented by her father, who acted as her 'next friend'. The liberal approach for interpreting 'aggrieved persons' in the three countries facilitates PIL[132] as a legal mechanism for enforcing constitutionally guaranteed rights relating to the public interest.[133] Relevant rights include the right to live in a healthy environment, which falls within the ambit of the right to life in all the three countries.[134] In Pakistan, public interest relating to the climate system is integrated with the special interest that children are the most vulnerable to these impacts. Children could similarly file cases under Article 102 of the Bangladesh Constitution, provided they are represented by a next friend, such as a parent.

## ***Remedies***

The judiciary of the three countries follows an adversarial system that directs the judgment debtor to pay the winner's costs.[135] As enshrined in their Constitutions, the judiciary upholds the rule of law, the Constitution is the supreme law of the land, and the Supreme Court is the final interpreter of the law.[136] Access to justice in these countries has been liberalised through the creation of innovative orders and directives; widened standing provides people with access to the courts and the application of international environmental principles at the national level.[137] The most common remedies of these judiciaries include injunctions, directions, and civil and criminal damages.[138]

As at June 2023, children and youth-led climate litigation globally resulted in 42% of the remedies sought being declaratory relief, 37% being equitable relief, 18% of cases being litigated with strategic intention, and only 3% having asked for compensation.[139]

The relief sought by *Ali* and *Pandey* can be divided into three categories, namely, declaratory relief, equitable relief, and relief with strategic intention, which are discussed in turn in what follows, exposing lessons for child-led litigation in Bangladesh.

### *Declaratory relief*

In *Ali*, the plaintiff requested the court to grant remedies that were declaratory in nature. The plaintiff requested a declaration that the respondent had violated the doctrine of public trust and the fundamental rights to life, liberty, property, human dignity, information, and equal protection guaranteed by the Constitution of Pakistan.[140] The plaintiff argued that these guaranteed fundamental rights include in their ambit the inalienable right to a stable climate system.[141] The plaintiff argued that the violation occurred from not reducing dangerous levels of $CO_2$ in the atmosphere to below the maximum safe level of 350 ppm atmospheric $CO_2$ and by deliberately increasing Pakistan's $CO_2$ emissions through the development and promotion of coal. Furthermore, the plaintiff argued that the violation occurred by failing to develop quantifiable, state-wide targets for Pakistan to contribute its share in reducing atmospheric $CO_2$ to achieve global climate stabilisation, and by failing to develop and implement mitigation actions geared at achieving such a goal as part of the National Climate Change Policy and Pakistan's INDC.[142] Though *Pandey* argued the violation of the public trust doctrine and the right to live within a healthy environment, which falls within the ambit of the right to life, she did not request the court to make that declaration.[143]

Like India, Bangladesh has incorporated the public trust doctrine by interpreting Article 21 of the Constitution in four cases, where the Bangladesh Supreme Court transplanted the doctrine's usage from Indian cases.[144] The Indian Constitution does not explicitly refer to the doctrine; however, the doctrine has evolved through cases on environmental protection.[145] For instance, the Indian courts have held that natural and mineral resources are entitled to the protection of public trust and that the state's duty is akin to that of a trustee of a public trust; therefore, the state has a fiduciary duty to act as a protector.[146] In Bangladesh, the court has applied the doctrine to sea beaches and, interestingly, conferred the status of legal persons to all the rivers of Bangladesh.[147] Extending the application of the public trust doctrine in Bangladesh, and learning from *Pandey*, the climate could be considered a natural resource within the scope of the definition of 'environment' under section 2(d) of the Bangladesh Environment Act 1995. A declaratory order could be sought in Bangladeshi child-led climate litigation to the effect that the climate system must be held in public trust by the state.

### *Equitable relief*

The plaintiffs in *Ali* and *Pandey* requested a court order directing the state to prepare an inventory of every substantial source of GHG emissions within the state and to prepare quantifiable state-wide targets or a 'carbon budget'[148] for the total amount of $CO_2$ emissions that can be released until 2050. This would ensure that the state plays its part as a responsible member of the global community. The state would also have to assess climate-related issues while appraising projects for granting environmental clearance and undertake a realistic, holistic, and detailed assessment of every single case of forest diversion, including the impact on climate and not just the local factors. Bangladesh has ratified the Paris Agreement, and thus, children in Bangladesh could seek similar orders in future litigation.

### *Relief with strategic intention*

Some of the remedies requested by the plaintiffs in *Ali* and *Pandey* indicate the strategic intention of the child plaintiffs. These include requests to (1) re-write the National Climate Change Policy or Framework and the INDC to include a comprehensive national climate recovery plan; (2) adopt plans to immediately appropriate funds for producing alternative and renewable energy; (3) train all federal and provincial officials and experts on the pressing issue of climate change; and (4) translate relevant documents into the local languages. Similar relief could be sought in future child-led climate litigation in Bangladesh.

## Conclusion

The South Asian region continues to face the impacts of climate change with increasing temperatures and weather-related events. The climate change crisis is indeed a child rights crisis. Children form an extremely vulnerable group that suffers from the adverse effects of climate change that lead to furthering the displacement crisis that children face. Vulnerability theory advances substantive equality and active measures to build resilience among all people, recognising structural forms of oppression and people's varying levels of exposure and capabilities.

Cases like *Ali* and *Pandey* could be an entry point for child-led litigation in Bangladesh. They show that children can access courts and invoke wide-ranging remedies, including by relying on the public trust doctrine, as well as human rights arguments. In Bangladesh, such litigation could address violations of children's right to health and raise awareness of these issues that could be instrumental for the formulation of child-centric policies and extending access to justice for children. By learning lessons from successes and failures in child-led litigation in India and Pakistan, climate litigation claims could foster better responses from the government in its duties towards children, as well as greater autonomy for children to seek judicial redress to confront their vulnerability amidst the climate crisis.

## Notes

1 IPCC Working Group II – Impacts, Adaptation and Vulnerability, 'Overarching Frequently Asked Questions and Answers' (*IPCC*, June 2023) <https://www.ipcc.ch/report/ar6/wg2/about/frequently-asked-questions/keyfaq3/> accessed 21 November 2024.
2 United Nations Children's Fund (UNICEF) 'One Billion Children at "Extremely High Risk" of the Impacts of the Climate Crisis' (*UNICEF*, 19 August 2021) <https://www.unicef.org/press-releases/one-billion-children-extremely-high-risk-impacts-climate-crisis-unicef> accessed 24 December 2022.
3 Kathryn McMahon and Clark Gray, 'Climate Change, Social Vulnerability and Child Nutrition in South Asia' (2021) 71 *Global Environmental Change: Human and Policy Dimensions* 102414 <https://www.ncbi.nlm.nih.gov/pmc/articles/PMC8653856/> accessed 10 June 2023.
4 Ishwar Tiwari et al., 'Climate Change Impacts on the Health of South Asian Children and Women Subpopulations – A Scoping Review' (2022) 8 *Heliyon* e10811, 2.
5 Bhargav Krishna et al., 'Tackling the Health Burden of Air Pollution in South Asia' (2017) 359 *BMJ (Clinical Research Edition)* j5209.
6 UNICEF, 'The Climate Crisis is a Child Rights Crisis: Introducing the Children's Climate Risk Index' (*UNICEF*, 2021) <https://www.unicef.org/media/105376/file/UNICEF-climate-crisis-child-rights-crisis.pdf> accessed 2 November 2024.
7 UNICEF (n 6).
8 UNICEF (n 6) 79.
9 UNICEF (n 6) 120.
10 UNICEF (n 2).
11 UNICEF (n 2).
12 German Watch, 'Global Climate Risk Index 2021: Who Suffers Most from Extreme Weather Events? Weather-Related Loss Events in 2019 and 2000 to 2019' (*Germanwatch*, 2021) <https://germanwatch.org/en/19777> accessed 29 October 2023. See also: University of Notre Dame, 'Notre Dame Global Adaptation Initiative Country Index (ND-GAIN)' (2024) <https://gain.nd.edu/our-work/country-index/> accessed 16 September 2024; and European Commission, 'INFORM Risk Index 2025' (31 August 2024) <https://drmkc.jrc.ec.europa.eu/inform-index> accessed 16 September 2024, which ranks Bangladesh 26th out of 191 countries.
13 European Commission (n 12); M Golam Azad, 'Assessing Spatial Vulnerability of Bangladesh to Climate Change and Extremes: A Geographic Information System Approach' (2022) <https://doi.org/10.21203/rs.3.rs-887629/v1> accessed 29 October 2023.
14 University of Notre Dame (n 12); Azad (n 13).
15 Office of High Commissioner for Human Rights (OHCHR), 'Analytical Study on the Relationship between Climate Change and the Full and Effective Enjoyment of the Rights of the Child' (UN Doc. A/HRC/35/13, 4 May 2017).
16 Hans-Martin Füssel, 'Vulnerability: A Generally Applicable Conceptual Framework for Climate Change Research' (2007) 17 *Global Environmental Change* 155 <https://www.sciencedirect.com/science/article/pii/S0959378006000525> accessed 15 May 2024. For a detailed discussion on vulnerability see Murcott, Tigre and Ann Samuel Introduction, pp 1–3.
17 Susan L Cutter, 'Vulnerability to Environmental Hazards' (1996) 20(4) *Progress in Human Geography* 529.
18 Cutter (n 17).
19 Cutter (n 17) 533–537.

20 Robert Glenom, 'The Unfolding Tragedy of Climate Change in Bangladesh' (*Scientific American*, 2017) <https://blogs.scientificamerican.com/guest-blog/the-unfolding-tragedy-of-climate-change-in-bangladesh/> accessed 26 June 2023.

21 Garrett Kilroy, 'A Review of the Biophysical Impacts of Climate Change in Three Hotspot Regions in Africa and Asia' (2015) 15 *Regional Environmental Change* 771 <https://doi.org/10.1007/s10113-014-0709-6> accessed 26 February 2024.

22 Monir Hussain and Hosne Tilat Mahal, 'Revisit Child Health in the Face of Climate Change: A Study About Child Health as an Impact of Climate Change in Bangladesh' (*PAA 2022 Annual Meeting, Atlanta*, 2022).

23 Hussain and Mahal (n 22).

24 Kimberle Crenshaw, 'Demarginalizing the Intersection of Race and Sex: A Black Feminist Critique of Antidiscrimination Doctrine, Feminist Theory and Antiracist Politics' (1989) *University of Chicago Legal Forum* <http://chicagounbound.uchicago.edu/uclf/vol1989/iss1/8> accessed 29 October 2023. See also Murcott, Tigre and Ann Samuel Introduction, pp 3–5.

25 Crenshaw (n 24).

26 Crenshaw (n 24).

27 UNICEF, 'The Climate-Changed Child: A Children's Climate Risk Index Supplement' (*UNICEF*, November 2023).

28 UNICEF (n 6).

29 UNICEF Bangladesh, 'A Gathering Storm: Climate Change Clouds the Future of Children in Bangladesh' (April 2019) <https://www.unicef.org/rosa/media/3001/file/Report%20ClimateChange-Embargoed%20-%20UNICEF.pdf> accessed 26 June 2023.

30 UNICEF Bangladesh (n 29).

31 PE Sheffield and PJ Landrigan, 'Global Climate Change and Children's Health: Threats and Strategies for Prevention' (2011) 119(3) *Environ Health Perspect* <https://www.ncbi.nlm.nih.gov/pmc/articles/PMC3059989/> accessed 26 June 2023.

32 Centre on the Developing Child, Harvard University, Lifelong Health <https://developingchild.harvard.edu/science/deep-dives/lifelong-health/> accessed 29 October 2023.

33 Katherine Shea, 'Global Environmental Changes and Children's Health: Understanding the Challenges and Finding Solutions' (2003) 143 *The Journal of Pediatrics* <https://pubmed.ncbi.nlm.nih.gov/12970625/> accessed 29 April 2024.

34 Centre on the Developing Child (n 32).

35 Centre on the Developing Child (n 32).

36 Committee on Sports, Medicine and Fitness, 'Climatic Heat Stress and the Exercising Child and Adolescent' (2000) 106(1) *Pediatrics* <https://doi.org/10.1542/peds.106.1.158> accessed 26 June 2023.

37 A Gasparrini et al., 'Temporal Variation in Heat-Mortality Associations: A Multi-Country Study' (2015) 123 *Environment Health Perspective.*

38 Zhiwei Xu et al., 'Impact of Ambient Temperature on Children's Health: A Systematic Review' (2012) 117 *Environmental Research.*

39 Monir Hussain and Hosne Tilat Mahal, 'Revisit Child Health in the Face of Climate Change: A Study About Child Health as an Impact of Climate Change in Bangladesh' (*PAA 2022 Annual Meeting, Atlanta*, 2022).

40 Hussain and Mahal (n 39).

41 Hussain and Mahal (n 39).

42 W Uter, O Gefeller and HJ Schwanitz, 'An Epidemiological Study of the Influence of Season (Cold and Dry Air) on the Occurrence of Irritant Skin Changes of the Hands' (1998) 138 *Br J Dermatol.*

43 Uter, Gefeller and Schwanitz (n 42).

44 Ursula Krämer et al., 'Seasonality in Symptom Severity Influenced by Temperature or Grass Pollen: Results of a Panel Study in Children with Eczema' (2005) *Journal of Investigative Dermatology.*

45 Susie Burke, Ann Sanson and Judith Van Hoorn, 'The Psychological Effects of Climate Change on Children' (2018) 20 *Current Psychiatry Reports*. See also discussion on similar experiences of vulnerable farming communities in India, discussed in Garg and Hinduja, Chapter 2.
46 Philip Rich, 'What Can We Learn from Vulnerability Theory?' (2018) 352 *Honors Projects* <https://scholarworks.bgsu.edu/cgi/viewcontent.cgi?article=1461&context=honorsprojects> accessed 28 April 2024.
47 Rich (n 46).
48 Martha Fineman, 'Vulnerability Theory and the Role of Government' (2014) 26 *Yale Journal of Law and Feminism*.
49 Rich (n 46).
50 Rich (n 46).
51 Fineman (n 48).
52 Martha Fineman, 'The Vulnerable Subject: Anchoring Equality in the Human Condition' (2008) 20 *Yale Journal of Law and Feminism*.
53 Fineman (n 52).
54 Fineman (n 48).
55 Martha Fineman, 'The Vulnerable Subject: Anchoring Equality in the Human Condition' in Anne Bloom, David M Engel and Michael McCann (eds), *Wingspread Statement on the Precautionary Principle* (CUP 2018).
56 See LR Stanberry, MC Thomson and W James, 'Prioritizing the Needs of Children in a Changing Climate' (2018) 15(7) *PLoS Medicine* <https://doi.org/10.1371/journal.pmed.1002627> accessed 29 October 2023.
57 Rich (n 46); Martha Fineman, 'Vulnerability and Inevitable Inequality' (2017) 4(3) *Oslo Law Review* <https://web.gs.emory.edu/vulnerability/_includes/documents/Oslo-Review-Vulnerability-and-Inevitable-Inequality.pdf> accessed 28 April 2024.
58 Fineman (n 55).
59 Article 44 of the Constitution guarantees the right of every citizen to move the High Court Division in accordance with clause (1) of Article 102 for the enforcement of any of the fundamental rights conferred by Part III of the Constitution.
60 M Rafiqauzzaman, 'Public Interest Litigation in Bangladesh: A Case Study' (2002) 6(1) & (2) *Bangladesh Journal of Law* <https://www.biliabd.org/wp-content/uploads/2021/08/Muhd.-Refiquzzaman.pdf> accessed 29 April 2024.
61 Benjamin P Davis and Eric Aldieri, 'Precarity and Resistance: A Critique of Martha Fineman's Vulnerability Theory' (2021) 36 *Hypatia*.
62 Fineman (n 57).
63 Fineman (n 57).
64 Fineman (n 57).
65 This Act was enacted for the purpose of implementing the United Nations Convention on the Rights of the Child (CRC).
66 Article 1 CRC.
67 However, the meaning of *children* may vary in different laws of Bangladesh, where maturity may be attained earlier for specific purposes, like employment.
68 Rule 4, Order XXXII, CPC 1908 Bangladesh.
69 Najrana Imam, 'Justice for Children in Bangladesh: An Analysis of Recent Cases' (*Save the Children*, 2012).
70 *Mohiuddin Farooque v Bangladesh* (1997) 49 DLR (AD) 1, Supreme Court of Bangladesh (Bangladesh) (*FAP-20 case*).
71 Abdur Rob Howlader, 'Writ Jurisdiction of The Supreme Court of Bangladesh' (2006) 10 *Bangladesh Journal of Law* <https://www.biliabd.org/wp-content/uploads/2021/08/Abdur-Rob-Howlader.pdf> accessed 26 June 2023.
72 Howlader (n 71).

73 *Yunus Mia v Secretary Ministry of Public Works* (1993) 45 DLR, High Court Division of Bangladesh (Bangladesh).
74 *Yunus Mia* (n 73) [498].
75 *Dacca National Medical Institute v Province of East Pakistan* (1958) 10 DLR 343, Supreme Court of Bangladesh (Bangladesh).
76 Environment Court Act 2010, s 6(3) and s 7(4).
77 See 'Climate Change, Coming Soon to a Court Near You: Climate Litigation in Asia and the Pacific and Beyond' (*Asian Development Bank*) <https://www.adb.org/sites/default/files/publication/659631/climate-litigation-asia-pacific.pdf> accessed 1 May 2024.
78 *Mohiuddin Farooque v Bangladesh et al.* [1996] 48 DLR (HCD) 438, Supreme Court of Bangladesh (Bangladesh) (*Radioactive Milk case*).
79 *Mohiuddin Farooque* (n 78).
80 *Mohiuddin Farooque* (n 78).
81 *Rabia Bhuiyan MP v Ministry of Local Government and Rural Development et al.* (27 August 2007) 59 DLR (AD) (2007), Supreme Court of Bangladesh (Bangladesh).
82 *Rabia Bhuiyan MP* (n 81) [24].
83 The four cases are *Shah Abdul Hannan v Bangladesh* (2011) 16 BLC 386, *Faridul Alam v Bangladesh* (2010) 18 BLT 323, *Human Rights & Peace for Bangladesh v Bangladesh* (2010) 22 BLC 48, and *Human Rights & Peace for Bangladesh v Bangladesh* (2019) WP No 13989/2016.
84 Mohammad Badruzzaman and Nannu Mian, 'Right to Education in Bangladesh: An Appraisal for Constitutional Guarantee' (2015) 13 *Journal of Studies in Social Sciences* 1.
85 *Radioactive Milk case* (n 78).
86 'Climate Change Law of the World – Country: Bangladesh' (*Grantham Research Institute*) <https://climate-laws.org/geographies/bangladesh> accessed 26 April 2024.
87 'National Children's Taskforce, NCTFBD – National Children Taskforce' <https://www.nctfbd.org/> accessed 26 June 2023.
88 Ekawestri Widiati, 'Efficient Public Participation in the Local Law-Making Process' (2018) 33 *Yuridika* <https://doi.org/10.20473/ydk.v33i3.8914> accessed 10 May 2024.
89 Elizabeth Donger, 'Children and Youth in Strategic Climate Litigation: Advancing Rights through Legal Argument and Legal Mobilization' (2022) 11(2) *Transnational Environmental Law* 268.
90 L Parker et al., 'When the Kids Put Climate Change on Trial: Youth-Focused Rights-Based Climate Litigation Around the World' (2022) 13(1) *Journal of Human Rights and the Environment* 64 <https://doi.org/10.4337/jhre.2022.01.03> accessed 26 September 2024.
91 Martha Fineman, 'Vulnerability and Social Justice' (2019) 53(2) *Valparaiso University Law Review*.
92 Martha Fineman, 'The Vulnerable Subject and the Responsive State' (2010) 60 *Emory Law Journal* <https://scholarlycommons.law.emory.edu/elj/vol60/iss2/1> accessed 29 October 2023.
93 Marilyn Averill, 'Climate Litigation: Ethical Implication and Societal Impact' (2008) 85 *Denver University Law Review*.
94 Joana Setzer and Catherine Higham, 'Global Trends in Climate Change Litigation: 2022 Snapshot' (*Policy Report*, June 2022) 15.
95 Elizabeth Donger, 'Children and Youth in Strategic Climate Litigation: Advancing Rights through Legal Argument and Legal Mobilization' (2022) 11(2) *Transnational Environmental Law*.
96 *Neubauer et al. v Germany* (2020) Case No. BvR 2656/18/1, BvR78/20/1, BvR96/20/1, BvR288/20, German Federal Constitutional Court (Germany).
97 Federal Climate Protection Act, 2021.

98 Louis Kotze, 'Neubauer et al. Versus Germany: Planetary Climate Litigation for the Anthropocene?' (2021) *German Law Journal* <https://doi.org/10.1017/glj.2021.87> accessed 30 October 2023.

99 Kotze (n 98).

100 Environmental Courts Act 2010 s12.

101 Joana Setzer and Lisa Benjamin, 'Climate Litigation in the Global South: Constraints and Innovations' (2020) 9 *Transnational Environmental Law* 77.

102 William Ewald, 'Comparative Jurisprudence (II): The Logic of Legal Transplants' (1995) 43 *The American Journal of Comparative Law* 489 <https://doi.org/10.2307/840604> accessed 10 March 2024.

103 *Rabab Ali v Federation of Pakistan and another* (2016) Constitutional Petition No. ___ / I of 2016, Supreme Court of Pakistan (Pakistan) (*Ali*).

104 Petition in *Ridhima Pandey v Union of India et al.* (2019) 187/2017, National Green Tribunal (India) (*Pandey*). See also the discussion of *Pandey* in Dutta and Lofts, Chapter 4, pp 140–141.

105 'Pakistan' (*Our Children's Trust*) <https://www.ourchildrenstrust.org/pakistan-global-summary> accessed 17 June 2023.

106 '75 Years After Partition: These Maps Show How the British Split India' (*History*, 9 August 2022) <https://www.nationalgeographic.com/history/article/these-maps-show-how-the-british-split-india> accessed 6 November 2023. On the impacts of colonisation on India's legal system, see Garg and Hinduja, Chapter 2. For a Latin American perspective on the impact of colonisation on climate litigation, see Beckhauser and Broetto, Chapter 1.

107 Ashish Bhan and Mohit Rohatgi, 'Legal Systems in India: Overview' (*Thomson Reuters Practical Law*) <http://uk.practicallaw.thomsonreuters.com/w-017-5278?transitionType=Default&contextData=(sc.Default)&firstPage=true> accessed 10 June 2023; Martin Lau, 'Introduction to the Pakistani Legal System, with Special Reference to the Law of Contract' (1994) 1 *Yearbook of Islamic and Middle Eastern Law* 3; Bianca Karim and Tirza Theunissen, 'Bangladesh' in Dinah Shelton (ed), *International Law and Domestic Legal Systems: Incorporation, Transformation, and Persuasion* (Oxford University Press 2011).

108 Madelaine Chiam, 'Monism and Dualism in International Law' (*Oxford Bibliographies*, 27 June 2018) <https://www.oxfordbibliographies.com/display/document/obo-9780199796953/obo-9780199796953-0168.xml> accessed 10 June 2023.

109 See Sunil Khilnani, Vikram Raghavan and Arun K Thiruvengadam, 'Constitutionalism and the Judiciary in Bangladesh' in Sunil Khilnani, Vikram Raghavan and Arun K Thiruvengadam (eds), *Comparative Constitutionalism in South Asia* (Oxford University Press 2012) <https://academic.oup.com/book/25321/chapter/192329840> accessed 6 November 2023; see also Muhammad Ekramul Haque, 'Constitutional Borrowing and Transplants: Use of World Constitutions in the Making and Development of the Constitution of Bangladesh' (4 November 2022) <https://papers.ssrn.com/abstract=4267648> accessed 6 November 2023.

110 The Wire Staff, 'Sharp Fall in Citation of Supreme Court Judgments by Foreign Courts After 2014, Study Finds' (*The Wire*, 24 November 2020) <https://thewire.in/law/supreme-court-foreign-citations-study> accessed 10 June 2023.

111 See Azhar Uddin Bhuiyan, 'The Doctrine of Public Trust: Its Judicial Invocation in Bangladesh and the Future Potentials' (2021) IX *Jahangirnagar University Journal of Law* 89, 94; *See also* Mehadi Hasan and Nadim Zawad Akil, 'The Use of Foreign Judgment in the Legal System of Bangladesh' (*The Daily Star*, 27 November 2021) <https://www.thedailystar.net/law-our-rights/rights-advocacy/news/the-use-foreign-judgment-the-legal-system-bangladesh-2903861> accessed 6 November 2023.

112 *Ali* (n 103) [1].

113 *Ali* (n 103) [11].

114 *Ali* (n 103) [17].
115 *Pandey* (n 104) petition [1].
116 *Pandey* (n 104) petition [1].
117 *Pandey* (n 104) petition [III].
118 *Pandey* (n 104) petition [26].
119 *Pandey* (n 104) petition [49].
120 *Pandey* (n 104) order [3].
121 United Nations Convention on the Rights of the Child, (adopted 20 November 1989 UNGA Res 44/25) (CRC) Article 12.
122 Abdul Awal Khan, 'Social and Legal Barriers to Improving Human Rights of Climate Change Displaced People in Bangladesh' (2019) 2 *The Journal of Interrupted Studies* 103, 268.
123 Khan (n 122).
124 See rules 1 and 4, Order XXXII, CPC 1908 of India, Pakistan and Bangladesh.
125 *Ex Parte Sidebotham* (1880) 14 Ch. D. 458, 465.
126 *Pandey* (n 104) petition [1].
127 India has enacted child-centric laws to address systemic issues faced by children and to facilitate litigation of minors through next friend. The laws include the Protection of Children from Sexual Offences (POCSO) Act 2012, the Prohibition of Child Marriage Act (PCMA) 2006, the Child Labour (Prohibition & Regulation) Act 1986 (Amendment Act 2016), and the Right to Education (RTE) Act 2009. See, generally, *Hero Vinoth (Minor) v Seshammal* 2006 (5) SCC 545, *Vriddhi Minor (Through Next Friend) v Directorate of Education & Anr* W.P.(C) 9834/2024 (Delhi HC). Further, in *Nagaiah v Chowdamma (Dead) by LRs* Civil Appeal No 22969 of 2017 (SC, 8 January 2018), the agency of minors in litigation through 'next friend' is stressed.
128 RS Gupta, 'Widening the Rules of Locus Standi' (1984) 26 *Journal of the Indian Law Institute* 436.
129 Gupta (n 128).
130 Parvez Hassan and Azim Azfar, 'Securing Environmental Rights through Public Interest Litigation in South Asia Comment' (2003) 22 *Virginia Environmental Law Journal* 215 <https://heinonline.org/HOL/P?h=hein.journals/velj22&i=223> accessed 6 November 2023. See also Ladan and Maduekwe, Chapter 8, for a Nigerian perspective on PIL and climate litigation.
131 A *next friend* is a person who has attained legal majority and has the capacity to sue on behalf of minors, since they do not have capacity to sue. It can be guardians, parents, or any person with a legal relationship to the minor.
132 See Lavanya Rajamani, 'Public Interest Environmental Litigation in India: Exploring Issues of Access, Participation, Equity, Effectiveness and Sustainability' (2007) 19 *Journal of Environmental Law* 293 <https://doi.org/10.1093/jel/eqm020> accessed 6 November 2023. See also Dominic J Nardi Jr, 'Greening Environmental Rights: Separating Law and Morality in Environmental Public Interest Litigation in Pakistan' (2008) 38 *Environmental Law Reporter News & Analysis* 10029 <https://heinonline.org/HOL/P?h=hein.journals/elrna38&i=29> accessed 7 November 2023.
133 Hassan and Azfar (n 130).
134 Hassan and Azfar (n 130).
135 Jona Razzaque, 'Linking Human Rights, Development, and Environment: Experiences from Litigation in South Asia' (2007) 18 *Fordham Environmental Law Review* 587, 600.
136 Constitution of India Article 141; Constitution of Pakistan Article 189; Constitution of Bangladesh Article 111.
137 Hassan and Azfar (n 130).
138 See Jona Razzaque, *Public Interest Environmental Litigation in India, Bangladesh and Pakistan* (Eric C Orts & Kurt Deketelaere Series eds, Kluwer 2004) 35–47.

139 Maria Antonia Tigre, Romina Rodela, Asteropi Chatzinikola-Iliopoulos and S Sathiabama, 'The Significance and Transformative Potential of Youth-Led Litigation in the Context of Intra and Intergenerational Rights and Obligations' *Transnational Environmental Law* (Forthcoming 2024).
140 *Ali* (n 103) [37].
141 *Ali* (n 103) [37].
142 *Ali* (n 103) [38].
143 *Pandey* (n 104) petition, Prayer.
144 The four cases are *Shah Abdul Hannan v Bangladesh* (2011) 16 BLC 386; *Faridul Alam v Bangladesh* (2010) 18 BLT 323 [Court] (Country); *Human Rights & Peace for Bangladesh v Bangladesh* (2010) 22 BLC 48; and *Human Rights & Peace for Bangladesh v Bangladesh* (2019) WP No 13989/2016.
145 The first noted case of public trust doctrine was *MC Mehta v Kamal Nath* (1997) 1 SCC 388 (SC). See further, *T Majra Singh et al. v Indian Oil Corporation* et al., AIR (1999) J&K 81; *M I Builders Pvt Ltd v Radhey Shyam Sahu* et al., AIR 1999 SC 2468.
146 See Lavanyya Rajamani, 'Doctrine of Public Trust: A Tool to Ensure Effective State Management of Natural Resources' (1996) 38 *Journal of the Indian Law Institute* 72; Ivan, 'The Doctrine of Public Trust in India: Tracing the Development and Marking Out Future Requirements' (2011) 5 *Indian Journal of Human Development* 527; Paromita Goswami, 'Public Trust Doctrine: Implications For Democratisation of Water Governance' <https://nujslawreview.org/wp-content/uploads/2017/01/2016-9-1-2-Paromita-Goswami-Public-Trust-Doctrine-Implications-for-Democratisation-of-Water-Governance.pdf> accessed 26 September 2024.
147 *Human Rights and Peace for Bangladesh and others v Secretary of the Ministry of Shipping and others* (2016) Writ Petition No. 13989, Supreme Court of Bangladesh (Bangladesh) (*Turag River*) 275.
148 *Pandey* (n 104) Prayer.

## Bibliography

### *Books and book chapters*

Åstrand PO, Rodahl K, Dahl HA and Stromme SB, *Textbook of Work Physiology: Physiological Bases of Exercise* (4th edn, Human Kinetics 2003)
Chiam M, *Monism and Dualism in International Law* (Oxford Bibliographies 2018)
Jona Razzaque J, 'Public Interest Environmental Litigation in India, Pakistan and Bangladesh' in EC Orts and K Deketelaere (eds), *Public Interest Environmental Litigation in India, Pakistan and Bangladesh* (Kluwer 2004) <https://law-store.wolterskluwer.com/s/product/public-interest-environmental-litigation-in-india-pakistan/01t0f00000J3aztAAB?srsltid=AfmBOormQfKni0HVBXhJNKD0KSdLurnA2SpCvu6KhMLJEFtBZbZvzIad>
Karim B and Theunissen T, 'Bangladesh' in D Shelton (ed), *International Law and Domestic Legal Systems: Incorporation, Transformation, and Persuasion* (Oxford University Press 2011)
Khilnani S, Raghavan V and Thiruvengadam AK, 'Constitutionalism and the Judiciary in Bangladesh' in S Khilnani, V Raghavan and AK Thiruvengadam (eds), *Comparative Constitutionalism in South Asia* (Oxford University Press 2012)

### *Cases*

*Dacca National Medical Institute v Province of East Pakistan* (1958) 10 DLR 343, Supreme Court of Bangladesh (Bangladesh)

*Ex parte Sidebotham* [1879] CA14 (1880) ChD 458 Court of Appeal (England and Wales)
*Faridul Alam v Bangladesh* (2010) 18 BLT 323, Supreme Court of Bangladesh (Bangladesh)
*Farooque v Bangladesh* (1997) 49 DLR (AD) 1, Supreme Court of Bangladesh (Bangladesh)
*Farooque v Government of Bangladesh* (2001) WP 891 of 1994, Supreme Court of Bangladesh (Bangladesh)
*Hero Vinoth (Minor) vs Seshammal (2006)* (5) SCC 545 (India)
*Human Rights and Peace for Bangladesh et al. v Secretary of the Ministry of Shipping et al.* (2016) 13989, Supreme Court of Bangladesh (Bangladesh) (Turag River)
*M C Mehta v Kamal Nath* (1997) 1 SCC 388 (SC) (India)
*M I Builders Pvt Ltd v Radhey Shyam Sahu et al.*, AIR 1999 SC 2468 (India)
*Nagaiah v Chowdamma (Dead) by LRs* (2017) Civil Appeal No 22969 (India)
*Neubauer et al. v Germany* (2020) BvR 2656/18/1, BvR78/20/1, BvR96/20/1, BvR288/20, German Federal Constitutional Court (Germany)
*Rabab Ali v Federation of Pakistan and another* (2016) ___ / I of 2016, Supreme Court of Pakistan (Pakistan)
*Rabia Bhuiyan MP v Ministry of Local Government and Rural Development et al.* (2007) 59 DLR (AD) (2007), Supreme Court of Bangladesh (Bangladesh)
*Raj Behari Lal et al. v Mahabir Prasad et al.* (1955) AIR 1956 All 310, Allahabad High Court (India)
*Ridhima Pandey v Union of India and another* (2019) 187/2017, National Green Tribunal (India)
*Shah Abdul Hannan v Bangladesh* (2011) 16 BLC 386 (Bangladesh)
*Th Majra Singh et al., v Indian Oil Corporation et al.*, AIR (1999) J&K 81 (India)
*Vriddhi Minor (Through Next Friend) v Directorate of Education et al.*, W.P.(C) 9834/2024 (Delhi HC) (India)
*Yunus Mia v Secretary Ministry of Public Works* (1993) 45 (1993) DLR, High Court Division of Bangladesh (Bangladesh)

## Conventions

United Nations Convention on the Rights of the Child 1989 UNGA Res 44/25

## Journal articles

Averill M, 'Climate Litigation: Ethical Implications and Societal Impacts' (2008) 85 *Denver University Law Review* 899 <https://digitalcommons.du.edu/dlr/vol85/iss4/8> accessed 12 September 2024
Badruzzaman M and Mian N, 'Right to Education in Bangladesh: An Appraisal for Constitutional Guarantee' (2015) 13(1) *Journal of Studies in Social Sciences* 1 <https://www.researchgate.net/publication/281856081> accessed 12 September 2024
Bhuiyan AU, 'The Doctrine of Public Trust: Its Judicial Invocation in Bangladesh and the Future Potentials' (2021) 9(1) *Jahangirnagar University Journal of Law* 89 <https://ssrn.com/abstract=4026953> accessed 12 September 2024
Burger M, Wentz J and Horton R, 'The Law and Science of Climate Change Attribution' (2020) 45(1) *Columbia Journal of Environmental Law* 57 <https://doi.org/10.7916/cjel.v45i1.4730> accessed 12 September 2024
Burke S, Sanson AV and Van Hoorn J, 'The Psychological Effects of Climate Change on Children' (2018) 20(5) *Current Psychiatry Reports* 35 <https://doi.org/10.1007/s11920-018-0896-9> accessed 12 September 2024
Committee on Sports, Medicine and Fitness, 'Climatic Heat Stress and the Exercising Child and Adolescent' (2000) 106(1) *Pediatrics* 158 <https://doi.org/10.1542/peds.106.1.158> accessed 26 June 2023

Crenshaw K, 'Demarginalizing the Intersection of Race and Sex: A Black Feminist Critique of Antidiscrimination Doctrine, Feminist Theory and Antiracist Politics' (1989) *University of Chicago Legal Forum* <http://chicagounbound.uchicago.edu/uclf/vol1989/iss1/8> accessed 29 October 2023

Cutter SL, 'Vulnerability to Environmental Hazards' (1996) 20(4) *Progress in Human Geography* 529 <https://doi.org/10.1177/030913259602000407> accessed 10 September 2024

Davis BP and Aldieri E, 'Precarity and Resistance: A Critique of Martha Fineman's Vulnerability Theory' (2021) 36(2) *Hypatia* 321 <https://doi.org/10.1017/hyp.2021.25> accessed 12 September 2024

Donger E, 'Children and Youth in Strategic Climate Litigation: Advancing Rights through Legal Argument and Legal Mobilization' (2022) 11(2) *Transnational Environmental Law* 263 <https://doi.org/10.1017/S2047102522000218> accessed 12 September 2024

Ewald W, 'Comparative Jurisprudence (II): The Logic of Legal Transplants' (1995) 43(4) *The American Journal of Comparative Law* 489 <https://doi.org/10.2307/840604> accessed 10 March 2024

Fineman MA, 'The Vulnerable Subject: Anchoring Equality in the Human Condition' (2008) 20(1) *Yale Journal of Law & Feminism* 1 <https://ssrn.com/abstract=1131407> accessed 10 September 2024

Fineman MA, 'The Vulnerable Subject and the Responsive State' (2010) 60 *Emory Law Journal* <https://ssrn.com/abstract=1694740> accessed 29 October 2023

Fineman MA, 'Vulnerability Theory and the Role of Government' (2014) 26(1) *Yale Journal of Law & Feminism* <https://ssrn.com/abstract=2562737> accessed 10 September 2024

Fineman MA, 'Vulnerability and Inevitable Inequality' (2017) 4(3) *Oslo Law Review* 133 <https://ssrn.com/abstract=3087441> accessed 28 April 2024

Fineman MA, 'Vulnerability and Social Justice' (2019) 53 *Valparaiso University Law Review* 341 <https://dx.doi.org/10.2139/ssrn.3352825> accessed 12 September 2024

Funk CC and Brown ME, 'Declining Global Per Capita Agricultural Production and Warming Oceans Threaten Food Security' (2009) 1(3) *Springer* 271 <https://link.springer.com/article/10.1007/s12571-009-0026-y> accessed 30 October 2023

Füssel HM, 'Vulnerability: A Generally Applicable Conceptual Framework for Climate Change Research' (2007) 17(2) *Global Environmental Change* 155 <https://www.sciencedirect.com/science/article/pii/S0959378006000525> accessed 15 May 2024

Gasparrini A, Guo Y, Hashizume M, Kinney PL, Petkova EP, Lavigne E, Zanobetti A, Schwartz JD, Tobias A, Leone M, Tong S, Honda Y, Kom H and Armstrong BG, 'Temporal Variation in Heat-Mortality Associations: A Multi-Country Study' (2015) 123(11) *Environment Health Perspective* 1200 <https://doi.org/10.1289/ehp.1409070> accessed 11 September 2024

Goswami P, 'Public Trust Doctrine: Implications For Democratisation of Water Governance' <https://nujslawreview.org/wp-content/uploads/2017/01/2016-9-1-2-Paromita-Goswami-Public-Trust-Doctrine-Implications-for-Democratisation-of-Water-Governance.pdf> accessed 26 September 2024

Gupta RS, 'Widening the Rules of Locus Standi' (1984) 26 *Journal of the Indian Law Institute* 424 <http://hdl.handle.net/123456789/16902> accessed 12 September 2024

Hassan P and Azim Azfar A, 'Securing Environmental Rights through Public Interest Litigation in South Asia Comment' (2003) 22(3) *Virginia Environmental Law Journal* 215 <https://heinonline.org/HOL/P?h=hein.journals/velj22&i=223> accessed 6 November 2023

Howlader AR, 'Writ Jurisdiction of The Supreme Court of Bangladesh' (2006) 10 *Bangladesh Journal of Law* 21 <https://www.biliabd.org/wp-content/uploads/2021/08/Abdur-Rob-Howlader.pdf> accessed 26 June 2023

Ivan, 'The Doctrine of Public Trust in India: Tracing the Development and Marking out Future Requirements' (2011) 5 *Indian Journal of Human Development* 527

Khan AA, 'Social and Legal Barriers to Improving Human Rights of Climate Change Displaced People in Bangladesh' (2019) 2(1) *The Journal of Interrupted Studies* 103 <https://doi.org/10.1163/25430149-00201004> accessed 12 September 2024

Kilroy G, 'A Review of the Biophysical Impacts of Climate Change in Three Hotspot Regions in Africa and Asia' (2015) 15 *Regional Environmental Change* 771 <https://doi.org/10.1007/s10113-014-0709-6> accessed 10 September 2024

Kotzé LJ, 'Neubauer et al. versus Germany: Planetary Climate Litigation for the Anthropocene?' (2022) 22(8) *German Law Journal* 1423 <https://doi.org/10.1017/glj.2021.87> accessed 30 October 2023

Krämer U, Weidinger S, Darsow U, Möhrenschlager M, Ring J and Behrendt H, 'Seasonality in Symptom Severity Influenced by Temperature or Grass Pollen: Results of a Panel Study in Children with Eczema' (2005) 124(3) *Journal of Investigative Dermatology* 514 <https://doi.org/10.1111/j.0022-202X.2005.23625.x> accessed 11 September 2024

Krishna B, Balakrishnan K, Siddiqui AR, Begum BA, Bachani D and Brauer M, 'Tackling the Health Burden of Air Pollution in South Asia' (2017) *BMJ* 359 <https://doi.org/10.1136/bmj.j5209> accessed 10 September 2024

Lau M, 'Introduction to Pakistani Legal System, with Special Reference to the Law of Contract' (1994) 1(1) *Yearbook of Islamic and Middle Eastern Law Online* <https://doi.org/10.1163/221129895x00065> accessed 12 September 2024

McMahon K and Gray C, 'Climate Change, Social Vulnerability and Child Nutrition in South Asia' (2021) 71 *Global Environmental Change: Human and Policy Dimensions* 102414 <https://doi.org/10.1016/j.gloenvcha.2021.102414> accessed 10 June 2023

Nardi DJ, 'Greening Environmental Rights: Separating Law and Morality in Environmental Public Interest Litigation in Pakistan' (2008) 38 *Environmental Law Reporter News & Analysis* 10029 <https://heinonline.org/HOL/P?h=hein.journals/elrna38&i=29> accessed 7 November 2023

Parker L et al., 'When the Kids Put Climate Change on Trial: Youth-Focused Rights-Based Climate Litigation Around the World' (2022) 13(1) *Journal of Human Rights and the Environment* 64 <https://doi.org/10.4337/jhre.2022.01.03> accessed 26 September 2024

Priovashini C and Mallick B, 'A Bibliometric Review on the Drivers of Environmental Migration' (2021) 51(1) *Springer* <https://doi.org/10.1007/s13280-021-01543-9> accessed 15 May 2024

Rafiqauzzaman M, 'Public Interest Litigation in Bangladesh: A Case Study' (2002) 6(1–2) *Bangladesh Journal of Law* 127 <https://www.biliabd.org/wp-content/uploads/2021/08/Muhd.-Refiquzzaman.pdf> accessed 29 April 2024

Rajamani L, 'Doctrine of Public Trust: A Tool to Ensure Effective State Management of Natural Resources' (1996) 38 *Journal of the Indian Law Institute* 72

Rajamani L, 'Public Interest Environmental Litigation in India: Exploring Issues of Access, Participation, Equity, Effectiveness and Sustainability' (2007) 19(3) *Journal of Environmental Law* 293 <https://doi.org/10.1093/jel/eqm020> accessed 6 November 2023

Razzaque J, 'Linking Human Rights, Development, and Environment: Experiences from Litigation in South Asia' (2007) 18(3) *Fordham Environmental Law Review* 587 <https://www.jstor.org/stable/44175135> accessed 12 September 2024

Setzer J and Benjamin L, 'Climate Litigation in the Global South: Constraints and Innovations' (2020) 9(1) *Transnational Environmental Law* 77 <https://doi.org/10.1017/S2047102519000268> accessed 12 September 2024

Shea KM, 'Global Environmental Changes and Children's Health: Understanding the Challenges and Finding Solutions' (2003) 143(2) *The Journal of Pediatrics* 149 <https://pubmed.ncbi.nlm.nih.gov/12970625/> accessed 29 April 2024

Sheffield PE, Landrigan PJ, 'Global Climate Change and Children's Health: Threats and Strategies for Prevention' (2011) 119(3) *Environ Health Perspect* 291 <https://www.ncbi.nlm.nih.gov/pmc/articles/PMC3059989/> accessed 26 June

Stanberry LR, Thomson MC and James W, 'Prioritizing the Needs of Children in a Changing Climate' (2018) 15(7) *PLoS Medicine* <https://doi.org/10.1371/journal.pmed.1002627> accessed 29 October 2023

Tigre MA, Rodela R, Chatzinikola-Iliopoulos A and Sathiabama S, 'The Significance and Transformative Potential of Youth-Led Litigation in the Context of Intra and Intergenerational Rights and Obligations' *Transnational Environmental Law* (Forthcoming)

Tiwari I, Tilstra M, Campbell SM, Nielsen CC, Hodgins S, Vargas ARO, Whitfield K, Sapkota BP and Yamamoto SS, 'Climate Change Impacts on the Health of South Asian Children and Women Subpopulations – A Scoping Review' (2022) 28(8) *Heliyon* <https://doi.org/10.1016/j.heliyon.2022.e10811> accessed 10 September 2024

Uter W, Gefeller O and Schwanitz HJ, 'An Epidemiological Study of the Influence of Season (Cold and Dry Air) on the Occurrence of Irritant Skin Changes of the Hands' (1998) 138(2) *Br J Dermatol* 266 <https://doi.org/10.1046/j.1365-2133.1998.02072.x> accessed 11 September 2024

Widiati E, 'Efficient Public Participation in the Local Law-Making Process' (2018) 33(3) *Yuridika* 389 <http://dx.doi.org/10.20473/ydk.v33i3.8914> accessed 10 May 2024

Xu Z, Etzel RA, Su H, Yuang C, Guo Y and Tong S, 'Impact of Ambient Temperature on Children's Health: A Systematic Review' (2012) 117 *Environmental Research* 120 <https://doi.org/10.1016/j.envres.2012.07.002> accessed 11 September 2024

## Legislation

Bangladesh Climate Change Trust Act 2010

Child Labour (Prohibition & Regulation) Act 1986 (Amendment Act 2016) (India)

Communication Disease (Prevention, Control and Elimination) Act (Bangladesh) 2018

Community Health Assessment Trust Act (Bangladesh) 2018

The Constitution of the Islamic Republic of Pakistan, 1973

The Constitution of the People's Republic of Bangladesh, 1972

Environment Courts Act (Bangladesh) 2010

Prohibition of Child Marriage Act (PCMA) 2006 (India)

Protection of Children from Sexual Offences (POCSO) Act 2012 (India)

## Reports

Asian Development Bank, 'Climate Change, Coming Soon to a Court Near You: Climate Litigation in Asia and the Pacific and Beyond' (*Asian Development Bank*, 2020)

Hossain M, Mahal HT and Wagner B, 'Revisit Child Health in the Face of Climate Change: A Study About Child Health as an Impact of Climate Change in Bangladesh' (*PAA 2022 Annual Meeting, Atlanta*, July 2022) <https://www.researchgate.net/publication/362082935_Revisit_Child_Health_in_the_Face_of_Climate_Change_A_Study_About_Child_Health_as_an_Impact_of_Climate_Change_in_Bangladesh> accessed 11 September 2024

'Juvenile Justice Information Portfolio – Committee on the Rights of the Child – 3. State Party Reports: Pakistan' <https://www.unicef-irc.org/portfolios/documents/426_pakistan.htm>

OHCHR, 'Analytical Study on the Relationship between Climate Change and the Full and Effective Enjoyment of the Rights of the Child' (May 2017) <https://documents.un.org/doc/undoc/gen/g17/110/91/pdf/g1711091.pdf> accessed 10 September 2024

Rigaud Kanta K, de Sherbinin A, Jones B, Bergmann J, Clement V, Ober K, Schewe J, Adamo S, McCusker B, Heuser S and Midgley A, 'Groundswell: Preparing for Internal

Climate Migration' (*Washington*, March 2018) <https://hdl.handle.net/10986/29461> accessed 12 September 2024

Setzer Joana and Higham Catherine, 'Global Trends in Climate Change Litigation: 2022 Snapshot' (*Policy Report*, June 2022) 15

UNICEF, 'The Climate-Changed Child: A Children's Climate Risk Index Supplement' (November 2023) <https://www.unicef.org/media/147931/file/Theclimage-changedchild-ReportinEnglish.pdf> accessed 10 September 2024

UNICEF, 'The Climate Crisis is a Child Rights Crisis: Introducing the Children's Climate Risk Index' (August 2021) <https://www.unicef.org/media/105376/file/UNICEF-climate-crisis-child-rights-crisis.pdf> accessed 2 November 2023

Watts N, Amann M, Ayeb-Karlsson SA, Belesova K, Bouley T, Boykoff M et al., 'The Lancet Countdown on Health and Climate Change: From 25 Years of Inaction to a Global Transformation for Public Health' (2017) 391(10120) *The Lancet* P581 <https://doi.org/10.1016/S0140-6736(17)32464-9> accessed 11 September 2024

## Thesis

Philip Rich P, 'What Can We Learn from Vulnerability Theory?' (Honors Project, Bowling Green State University 2018)

## Online sources

'75 Years after Partition: These Maps Show How the British Split India' (*National Geographic*, 9 August 2022) <https://www.nationalgeographic.com/history/article/these-maps-show-how-the-british-split-india> accessed 6 November 2023

Arora Anshana, 'The Climate Crisis is a Child Rights Crisis: Introducing the Children's Climate Risk Index' (*UNICEF DATA*, 19 August 2021) https://data.unicef.org/resources/childrens-climate-risk-index-report/

'Bangladeshi Children Call on National Leaders to Address Climate Change as a Child Rights Issue' (*UNICEF Bangladesh*, 27 October 2021) <https://www.unicef.org/bangladesh/en/press-releases/bangladeshi-children-call-national-leaders-address-climate-change-child-rights-issue#:~:text=UNICEF's%20first%2Dever%20Children's%20Climate,risks%20and%20impacts%20on%20children> accessed 26 June 2023

Bhan A and Rohatgi M, 'Legal Systems in India: Overview' (*Thomson Reuters Practical Law*) <http://uk.practicallaw.thomsonreuters.com/w-017-5278?transitionType=Default&contextData=(sc.Default)&firstPage=true> accessed 10 June 2023

'Children in Four South Asian Countries at "Extremely High Risk" of the Impacts of the Climate Crisis – UNICEF' (*UNICEF*, 20 August 2021) <https://www.unicef.org/india/press-releases/children-four-south-asian-countries-extremely-high-risk-impacts-climate-crisis> accessed 10 June 2023

Glenom R, 'The Unfolding Tragedy of Climate Change in Bangladesh' (*Scientific American*, 21 April 2017) <https://blogs.scientificamerican.com/guest-blog/the-unfolding-tragedy-of-climate-change-in-bangladesh/> accessed 26 June 2023

Haque ME, 'Constitutional Borrowing and Transplants: Use of World Constitutions in the Making and Development of the Constitution of Bangladesh' (*The Daily Star*, 4 November 2022) <https://papers.ssrn.com/abstract=4267648> accessed 6 November 2023

Hasan M and Akil NZ, 'The Use of Foreign Judgment in the Legal System of Bangladesh' (*The Daily Star*, 27 November 2021) <https://www.thedailystar.net/law-our-rights/rights-advocacy/news/the-use-foreign-judgment-the-legal-system-bangladesh-2903861> accessed 6 November 2023

Hossain, M 'Climate Change Forcing Bangladeshi Children out of Schooling' (*World Economic Forum*, 11 May 2022) <https://www.weforum.org/agenda/2022/05/climate-disasters-bangladesh-children-work/> accessed 26 June 2023

IPCC Working Group II – Impacts, Adaptation and Vulnerability, 'Overarching Frequently Asked Questions and Answers' (*IPCC*, June 2023) <https://www.ipcc.ch/report/ar6/wg2/about/frequently-asked-questions/keyfaq3/> accessed 21 November 2024

Kagawa F, 'The Heat is On! Towards a Climate Resilient Education System in Bangladesh' (*UNICEF Regional Office for South Asia*, 2022)

'Lifelong Health' (*Harvard University Center on the Developing Child*) <https://developingchild.harvard.edu/science/deep-dives/lifelong-health/> accessed 29 October 2023

'Nutrition: Building a Foundation for Lifelong Health' <https://www.unicef.org/bangladesh/en/nutrition> accessed 29 March 2023

'One Billion Children at Extremely High Risk" of the Impacts of the Climate Crisis – UNICEF' (*UNICEF*, 19 August 2021) <https://www.unicef.org/press-releases/one-billion-children-extremely-high-risk-impacts-climate-crisis-unicef> accessed 24 December 2022

'Pakistan' (*Our Children's Trust*, 29 June 2016) <https://www.ourchildrenstrust.org/pakistan-global-summary> accessed 17 June 2023

Rojas D, 'How the Climate Crisis is Impacting Bangladesh?' (*The Climate Reality Project*, 9 December 2021) <https://www.climaterealityproject.org/blog/how-climate-crisis-impacting-bangladesh> accessed 26 June 2023

The Wire Staff, 'Sharp Fall in Citation of Supreme Court Judgments by Foreign Courts After 2014, Study Finds' (*The Wire*, 24 November 2020) <https://thewire.in/law/supreme-court-foreign-citations-study> accessed 10 June 2023

Chapter 8

# A human rights approach to environmental protection (HRAEP) as a tool for fostering climate resilience for the Nigerian woman

*Muhammed Tawfiq Ladan and Nkiruka Chidia Maduekwe*

## Introduction

As the global community grapples with the intense and devastating impacts of climate change (now termed the 'climate catastrophe'),[1,2] Nigeria is among the worst affected countries. The impacts of climate change are not proportionate to the greenhouse gas (GHG) emission contributions of countries in different regions, as regions that contributed the least are most vulnerable to its impacts, indicative of climate injustice.[3] Nigeria is situated in the West African region,[4] one of the global hotspots of high human vulnerability to the impacts of climate change.[5] The Sixth IPCC Synthesis Report found that exposure to climate vulnerability is 'higher in locations with poverty, governance challenges, limited access to basic services and resources, violent conflict, and high levels of climate-sensitive livelihoods, such as smallholder farmers, pastoralist, and fishing communities'.[6]

Like at the global level, the impacts of climate change within Nigeria are uneven, from the different geographical terrains[7] to various demographics (women, children, men, the disabled, and the elderly). Often, when discussing the different demographics with low resilience and high vulnerability to climate change impacts, women top the list.[8] This is because they have minimal ability to adapt and reduce exposure to the long-term stress or shock caused by climate change impacts.[9] For example, according to the United Nations, women constitute 80% of the persons displaced by climate change.[10] Notwithstanding, women play crucial roles, though often overlooked, in the functioning and flourishing of society, including in the home.

Although climate litigation is potentially a useful tool for women in Nigeria to foster climate resilience, at the time of writing, there is no case recorded before the Nigerian courts brought by women against the government, private companies, or individuals to advance mitigation of carbon emissions or strengthen resilience and adaptation efforts. Given Nigeria's pivotal position in sub-Saharan Africa, namely, economy and population, it is critical to address this gap. As such, this chapter interrogates the use of the human rights approach to environmental protection (HRAEP)

DOI: 10.4324/9781003470632-11

to effectively undertake climate litigation as a means for Nigerian women to build their resilience against climate change impacts.

The HRAEP practice and procedure discussed in this chapter are relevant to the women who seek to advance climate justice, in addition to the Nigerian and non-Nigerian legal practitioners who might be interested in supporting women's efforts to enhance their resilience through climate litigation in Nigeria. Also, this chapter is important to the judiciary, academia, and the public, in providing understanding and creating awareness on the proper procedure to effectively address climate change causes and impacts in Nigeria through a rights-based approach. This is particularly so because the chapter represents a first attempt to critically interrogate the practice and procedure of using Nigeria's Fundamental Rights (Enforcement Procedure) Rules 2009 as a tool for climate litigation, with a focus on the struggles of women in Nigeria.

The chapter is divided into seven sections and proceeds as follows: First, the chapter's introduction provides an overview of Nigeria's vulnerability to climate change. Second, the chapter takes a deeper dive into how this affects the Nigerian woman. Third, the chapter interrogates the HRAEP framework, its application, and the benefits. Fourth, the chapter discusses the challenges in utilising this approach. Fifth, the chapter proffers recommendations and next steps. Finally, the chapter presents the conclusion.

## Nigeria and climate vulnerability

Nigeria is situated in one of the global hotspots of high human vulnerability to climate change impacts.[11] According to Nigeria's updated nationally determined contribution, the country ranks as the tenth most vulnerable country in the world.[12] The impacts of climate change vary along the terrain.[13] They include droughts, rising temperatures, erosion, deforestation, flooding, desertification, and increasing sea levels.[14] With a population of over 220 million,[15] projected to reach over 400 million by the year 2050,[16] Nigeria is the most populated country in Africa.[17] Despite the seeming disadvantage this growing population might present, the positive aspect is that Nigeria has a youthful population, with 54% aged between 15 and 64 years and 43% between 0 and 14 years.[18] However, factors such as high rates of illiteracy, poverty, and inadequate health and education services remain a constant challenge.[19]

According to the Nigerian National Bureau of Statistics, 40.1% of the Nigerian population are poor, basically 82.9 million Nigerians.[20] Statistics show the impact of literacy on poverty rates, as males and females with no education or less than primary education have higher poverty rates than those with post-secondary education.[21] While the poverty rate in urban areas is 18%, rural areas record 52.1%.[22] A World Bank report finds that compared to 23.9% of households where the head engaged in wage work or 32.2% employed in non-farm enterprise, there was a 56.7% poverty rate in homes where the head engaged primarily in agriculture.[23] The report emphasised this disparity between the earnings by women and men, indicating that women earned less than men, especially in agriculture.[24]

Regarding essential services, such as water and electricity, as of 2020, only 55.4% of the Nigerian population had access to electricity, further broken down to 83.9% in the urban areas and 24.6% in the rural areas.[25] Also, as of 2019, only 14% of the Nigerian population is shown to have access to safe drinking water supply services,[26] 44% with access to essential sanitation services,[27] and 16% with access to vital hygiene services.[28]

With respect to security, Nigeria faces challenges such as terrorism, violent extremism, and conflicts between herders and farmers, which undermine governance, cause massive internal displacement, lead to property loss, drive migration, and disrupt economic activities and the normal functions of society.[29] The prolonged security threat, especially with the Boko Haram and herders and farmers conflict, is linked to Lake Chad's shrinkage[30] – estimated to be less than 10% of its area size in 1963.[31] As of 1963, Lake Chad was the fourth largest lake in Africa and provided water and livelihoods to over 30 million people, namely, fishing, animal husbandry, and agriculture.[32] The lake is bordered in the west by Nigeria, east by Chad, northwest by Niger, and south by Cameroon.[33] Presently, the lake has receded from the borders of Nigeria, with only minor water points remaining.[34]

The agriculture sector, which includes crop production, livestock, forestry, and fishing,[35] is the largest employer of labour in Nigeria, providing the primary source of livelihood for a significant number of the populace.[36] Around 87.6% of the sector's output stems from crop production, with 80% being small farm holders and accounting for 90% of the country's agricultural output.[37] According to the Food and Agriculture Organisation (FAO), Nigeria has a food insecurity challenge, with an estimated 25 million persons projected to face a food crisis or worse.[38] This crisis is influenced by a combination of the following factors: insurgency in the north, farmer and herders conflict, high international food and fuel prices, flooding, the sharp depreciation in the cost value of the Nigerian currency (naira: NGN), droughts, outdated methods of agriculture with reliance on rainfed production, use of hoes and cutlass, and rising production costs.[39]

Indeed, the challenges indicated further intensify Nigeria's high sensitivity and low adaptive capacity to climate change impacts, given exposure to violent conflict, governance challenges, limited access to basic services and resources, elevated poverty levels, and extreme dependence on climate-sensitive livelihoods. Although the general population is highly vulnerable, some groups are considered more vulnerable than others – specifically women.[40] For instance, in the Boko Haram situation, women and girls were, and are, primarily victims of the insurgency, leading to forced marriages, rape, and other human rights violations.[41] With the increase in food insecurity, as indicated earlier, pregnant and lactating women, and children below 5 years, face the risk of under/malnutrition and exposure to infectious diseases, among other social injustices.[42]

As shown in the NBS data mentioned previously, women suffer higher rates of poverty when compared to men. In addition, women generally shoulder the responsibility of having to sustain the family (mostly through sustenance farming, petty trading, and other forms of invisibilised and uncompensated labour). These women often lack rights to access farming lands (and are systemically prevented from being able to make decisions as to the use of the land), combined with burdens to care for older adults and the family, and are responsible for cooking, washing, and getting clean water for the family.[43] The next section explores how climate change impacts women in Nigeria.

## The Nigerian woman and climate change

Even though the impacts of climate change are global, its intensity and associated risks are influenced by demography, gender, community, and country, depending on the exposure, sensitivity, and capacity to adapt to the climate change stressors.[44] Within communities, the following are indicated as most vulnerable to suffering the adverse effects of climate change: the elderly, women, persons living with disabilities, and children.[45]

For women, historically entrenched patriarchy, cultural roles, and gender inequalities further reinforce their high vulnerability to environmental pollution, degradation, and impacts of climate change.[46] For instance, their vulnerability is informed by having to travel several miles in search of safe drinking water and being compelled to rely on harmful energy sources to cook the family food and for warmth; being excluded from decision-making processes about their lives and livelihoods and being deprived of leadership roles and decision-making powers; unequal access to and ownership of land; primary reliance on climate-sensitive incomes; limits to accessing finance; uneven responsibility of being a homemaker and a provider; and being exposed to gender-based violence.[47] According to Osman-Elasha, the vulnerability faced by women can be summed up as three-dimensional, namely, social, economic, and cultural.[48]

For the Nigerian woman, climate change generally further intensifies existing vulnerability to environmental pollution and degradation (in addition to the social impacts). This is felt most specifically by women who live in extractive industry communities, since the extractive industry in Nigeria is one of the biggest drivers of environmental degradation and pollution in Nigeria.[49] According to the nationally determined contribution (NDC) submitted by the Nigerian government in 2021, as of 2018, the energy sector was the largest carbon emitter, contributing 60% of the total carbon emissions in Nigeria.[50] The oil and gas sector contributed 36% of the total energy sector emissions.[51] Some of the impacts of the oil and gas sector are discussed next.

### *Gas flaring in Nigeria*

Gas flaring is a primary source of black carbon,[52] the second-highest global warming contributor, after carbon dioxide.[53] In addition to black carbon, gas flares produce up to 250 toxins,[54] which include carbon dioxide; polycyclic aromatic hydrocarbons; carbon monoxide; nitrogen oxide; aliphatic carbon oxide; hydrogen sulphide; sulphur dioxide; methane; volatile organic compounds, such as benzene, xylene, toluene; particulate matter;[55] and metals, such as 'barium, cyanide, selenium, cadmium, chromium, iron, manganese, lead, and copper'.[56] Gas flaring is one of the key sources of acid rain,[57] which in turn pollutes both surface and groundwater, proliferates water acidity, increases soil acidity, causes low crop yield, and generally leads to loss of biodiversity.[58] The Niger Delta has a higher concentration of acid rain compared to other parts of Nigeria because continuous gas flaring takes place.[59] The heat from gas flares destroys surrounding vegetation, 'exposes the crops to a semblance of continuous daylight',[60] increases soil temperature, and makes it hard, further decreasing its use for agricultural purposes.[61] In addition to air, water, and land pollution, gas flares create noise pollution, which scares wildlife away from the area.[62]

Gas flaring has been linked to high blood pressure; miscarriages; ectopic pregnancy; insomnia; respiratory illness, like chronic bronchitis, wheezing, and experiencing difficulty in breathing; skin-related illnesses, like persistent body itch and heat rash; deformity in children; impotency; endocrine disruption; neurological damage; gastrointestinal, cardiovascular-related, lung-related, and renal-related diseases; asthma; hypertension; prolonged coughing; excessive heat and discomfort; partial deafness from the noise of the flare; and cancer.[63] Also, pipeline explosions have caused loss of limbs, of hands, and ultimately, of life.[64]

### *Oil spillages in Nigeria*

Oil spillages affect the air that people breathe; pollute the ground and surface water people use to take their baths, cook, drink, wash clothes, and do domestic chores; kill fish in polluted creeks; and cause harm when people and animals touch or eat from contaminated soil or sediment.[65] According to a UNEP report on the Ogoni people, dermal exposure to oil spills has led to 'skin redness, oedema, dermatitis, rashes, blisters; inhalation exposure caused red, watery, and itchy eyes, coughing, and throat irritation, shortness of breath, headache, and confusion; while ingestion of hydrocarbon could lead to nausea and diarrhoea'.[66]

Daniel and Nna stress that contact with petroleum compounds can affect the human nervous system and 'produce a carcinogenic and mutagenic effect on humans'.[67] Nduka, Constance, and Obiakor state that hydrocarbon-contaminated water exposes 'the people to skin, lung, breasts, and abdominal cancer'.[68] Other health problems consist of 'enlarged liver, kidney, and spleen';[69] 'catarrh, cough, cholera, and diarrhoea';[70] 'gastroenteritis, respiratory and chromosomal damage, problems, skin irritation, high risk of miscarriage, stillbirth, birth deformities, headache, skin melanoma'.[71]

### *Social and economic costs*

Oil spills and gas flaring cause pollution and degradation of arable farmlands, creeks, and rivers; reduce access to wildlife; and destroy trees, all of which contribute to the economy.[72] Social and economic costs arise as a result, including because farmers, fishers, and hunters are forced to migrate to other communities.[73]

Another effect has been the addition of stress on already-limited resources, sometimes resulting in conflicts between the communities.[74] Also, the loss of fish has meant that communities which hitherto enjoyed and had access to fish from the rivers and creeks now have to buy imported frozen fish (informally known as iced or carton fish).[75] Their food sovereignty and security are thus undermined.

Further social strain is caused as many young men leave rural villages for the cities in search of non-existent employment,[76] leaving their wives and children behind.[77] According to Okoko, the practice of husbands leaving their wives in the villages to seek alternative employment in the cities has led to the prevalence of absentee husbands, emotional stress for the women, the burden of having to care for the children alone, and having to provide sustenance for the family.[78] The loss of means of livelihood further exacerbates poverty levels.[79]

Given that climate change is a consequence of anthropogenic actions primarily of industrialised nations and the harmful extractive practices of the corporations from these nations,[80] which are environmentally unsustainable, increasing the pollution and degradation of the environment, it is evident that addressing climate change cannot be undertaken without environmental protection and sustainability. Therefore, by demanding and holding individuals, governments, and private companies accountable for actions and inactions that pollute, degrade, and increase carbon emissions in the atmosphere, women are protecting their human rights to the environment and, in turn, protecting the environment. As espoused by Françoise D'Eaubonne in 1978,[81] there is an intricate nexus between protecting the woman and the environment;[82] thus, the salvation of one from abject male-driven destruction cannot be undertaken without the other – both must be saved simultaneously.[83]

Since women are among the most vulnerable to climate change impacts, they are critical to addressing this global challenge, and that is why there is the need to close the gender gap and for women to have access to opportunities to build the requisite skills, capacity, and ecosystem to effectively build climate resilience.[84] Given this need, the Nigerian government adopted the National Action Plan on Gender and Climate Change for Nigeria.[85] The NAP aims to mainstream gender considerations in Nigeria's efforts to address climate change.[86] Notwithstanding the NAP's laudable objectives, the Nigerian woman (especially those with climate-sensitive income) still grapples with the daily exacerbating risks and effects of climate change.[87]

The pertinent question, then, is, How can the Nigerian woman ensure that she thrives and acquires the capacity to overcome the impacts of climate change? The same is discussed in the next section. This chapter, therefore, proposes that a human rights approach to environmental protection (HRAEP) has the potential to operate as an effective tool for Nigerian women to ensure that the activities of individuals, private companies, and the government do not exacerbate climate change impacts and further increase vulnerability.

Note that within the context of this chapter, 'the Nigerian woman' is recognised as among a heterogeneous group of people with unique experiences. Yet she also identifies with a broader group of sub-Saharan African women, bearing in mind shared structural and systemic social, cultural, and economic challenges and experiences with environmental degradation and pollution, and access to energy, clean water, and sanitation. Indeed, the Nigerian woman's potential success story in climate litigation portends a replication of the same elsewhere in sub-Saharan Africa (of course, taking cognisance of jurisdictional peculiarities and heterogeneity within and among vulnerable groups). Indeed, other countries may be able to borrow a leaf from the Nigerian woman's experience and success. The next section interrogates the HRAEP approach and why it should be considered by the Nigerian woman and those seeking to support her struggles for climate justice as a potentially effective climate litigation tool.

## Why a human rights approach to environmental protection (HRAEP)?

The HRAEP refers to using human rights mechanisms to reduce, maintain, prevent, reverse, or restore the quality of air, water, land, animal, plant resources, and other natural resources by preventing or reducing the emission of pollution or polluting substances in the air, land, and water.[88] The concept of using HRAEP to address environmental degradation and pollution was largely unknown before the 1960s;[89] however, several events influenced the global embrace of using this concept to ensure environmental sustainability and protection. The events included the linkage of the right to life to enjoying a clean, safe, and healthy environment in the 1972 United Conference on the Human Environment, the preparation of the 1994 Draft Declaration of Principles on Human Rights and the Environment by Special Rapporteur Fatma Zohra Ksentini,[90] the inclusion of environmental rights in the African Charter on Human and Peoples' Rights in 1981,[91] the subsequent inclusion of environmental rights in the constitutional texts of over 180 countries,[92] and in June 2022, the recognition by the United Nations General Assembly of the right to a clean, healthy, and sustainable environment as a human right.[93]

Significantly, the 2022 IPCC Report recommends adaptation and mitigation actions that prioritise a rights-based approach to addressing climate change as one of the pathways to increase resilience and reduce sensitivity to climate change impacts.[94] The report emphasises that 'adaptation outcomes for the most vulnerable within and across countries and regions are enhanced through . . . focusing on . . . rights-based approaches'.[95] Within the context of this chapter, *HRAEP* is synonymous with *rights-based approaches* and part of the global phenomenon of environmental constitutionalism. Thus, appropriate adaptation and mitigation actions would be those that use human rights mechanisms to address climate change impacts. Of course, one means to enforce human rights is through judicial processes, which can entail engaging in climate change litigation.

According to Obani, climate change litigation presents an arduous challenge for women in Nigeria.[96] The author indicates three interventions that are crucial to ensuring women have access to justice and that the courts are more receptive to women's climate change claims, namely, the collection of data on women's and girl's climate change impact experience, the provision of legal aid for women to pursue these cases, and the enactment and enforcement of gender-sensitive legislation.[97] Olusegun and Oyelada reiterate Obani's position that the Nigerian woman finds it challenging to seek judicial redress.[98] In addition to identifying a lack of education and inadequate information on legal issues as one of the barriers for the Nigerian woman to access justice and obtain a legal remedy in the Nigerian courts,[99] Olusegun and Oyelada highlight a lack of employment, a lack of family members who could support them, and the burden of having to financially support their households as factors to hinder the Nigerian woman to meet cost for legal representation, cost of transportation, and filing fees.[100] These barriers positively emphasise the need for HRAEP as a tool for fostering climate resilience, because, as this chapter argues, HRAEP provides a platform for women to effectively pursue climate litigation cases, holding individuals, government, and private companies accountable for actions or inactions that drive climate change and, in the end, making women resilient to climate change impact.[101]

Before November 2021, there was minimal clarity regarding Nigeria's practice and procedure for seeking judicial redress of climate change impact.[102] However, on 17 November 2021, the then Nigerian president, Muhammed Buhari, assented to the Climate Change Act (CCA),[103] placing Nigeria as the second African country to have an explicit legal framework to govern and mainstream climate action in Nigeria.[104] According to Ladan, the CCA is the first comprehensive stand-alone climate change legislation in West Africa and 'provides a solid framework for climate action to achieve Nigeria's short-, medium-, and long-term goals on climate mitigation and adaptation'.[105]

Supplementing the myriad Nigerian legislations on protecting the environment, the Nigeria Climate Change Act 2021 is the first legislation that unequivocally provides for judicial redress against acts that negatively affect climate change mitigation and adaptation measures.[106] The Nigerian courts now have clear powers to adjudicate climate change or environmental matters.[107] The relevant provision – section 34 – lays to rest the argument of whether the Nigerian courts can adjudicate and enforce environmental rights matters. An environmental right is encapsulated in section 20 of the Nigerian 1999 Constitution (as amended).[108] In the past, it was argued that there was the absence of a clear legal framework to effectively pursue climate litigation in Nigeria, but the enactment of the Climate Change Act 2021 has changed the dynamics.[109] Additionally, given the recognition of the right to the environment as a fundamental right,[110] we assert that Nigeria envisages the utilisation of HRAEP as the means for enforcing the Act.

In Nigeria, fundamental human rights are enshrined and guaranteed by Chapter 4 of the 1999 Constitution (as amended) and the African Charter on Human and Peoples' Rights (Ratification and Enforcement) Act 1983.[111] In addition, section 20 of the 1999 Constitution (as amended) mandates the state to protect, improve, and safeguard the Nigerian environment, which is defined as including 'water, air, land, and all plants and human beings or animals living therein, and the inter-relationships which exist among these or any of them'.[112] The courts have held that in fulfilling this duty, the state is to 'protect the external surroundings of the people and ensure that they live in a safe and secure atmosphere free from any danger to their health or other conveniences'.[113] The right to a protected, improved, and safeguarded environment is further emphasised in Article 24, African Charter on Human and Peoples' Rights (Ratification and Enforcement) Act 1983,[114] which recognises and guarantees peoples' right to a generally satisfactory environment favourable to their environment.

Understanding how critical an effective enforcement mechanism is to ensure the protection of human rights, section 46 of the 1999 Constitution (as amended) gives the Chief Justice of Nigeria the power to make rules concerning the practice and procedure enabling the high court to efficiently provide redress to any person who alleges the infringement or likely infringement of the fundamental human rights. Presently, the Fundamental Rights (Enforcement Procedure) Rules 2009 (FREP Rules 2009)[115] is the enforcement mechanism for seeking redress for human rights infringement, and this has consistently been reiterated by the Nigerian courts.[116]

The Nigerian courts, through several cases, have emphasised the sacrosanct nature of these Rules, describing them as *sui generis*,[117] possessing constitutional flavour,[118] 'a special procedure designed for the enforcement of human rights, of which a departure or non-compliance would be fatal to enforcing the remedy',[119] and 'the only procedure through which an action can be brought to enforce rights'.[120] The provisions of the FREP Rules guide the conduct of the proceedings of all actions to enforce rights.

The FREP Rules aim to provide a simple and effective process for the enforcement of fundamental rights to avoid the cumbersome procedure and technicalities for their enforcement under the rules of common law or other statutory provisions.[121] Thus, by using a human rights approach in climate litigation, the Nigerian woman is adopting a reasonably simple process. In addition, section 46 of the 1999 Constitution (as amended) explicitly provides that financial aid be given to any indigent citizen to engage the services of a legal practitioner to enable redress for the infringement of fundamental rights. The Nigerian government has established a Legal Aids Council, with the mandate to provide this service.

One of the benefits of using HRAEP is that infringement of rights can be enforced against individuals, the government, and artificial persons (such as companies).[122] Also, an application for enforcing HRAEP is not affected by any statute of limitation, and this means that there is no time limit within which any person can bring an application to enforce HRAEP.[123] In addition, the FREP Rules 2009 stipulate the filing fees as 500 naira (NGN 500), 50 naira (NGN 50) for the affidavit, 100 naira (NGN 100) for a written address, and 100 naira (NGN 100) for other processes.[124] These filing fees are different from the legal fees of lawyers; however, they are relatively affordable in comparison to other types of claims.

Another benefit is that any person can approach the court seeking redress for infringement or likely infringement of rights, and this includes

> [a]nyone acting in his interest; anyone acting on behalf of another person; anyone acting as a member of, or in the interest of a group or class of persons; anyone acting in the public interest; and Association acting in the interest of its members or other individuals or groups.[125]

Therefore, unlike in other civil claims, restrictions on *locus standi* do not apply in human rights cases.[126] The courts are mandated to encourage and welcome public interest litigation in human rights enforcement applications.[127] Therefore, human rights activists, advocates, groups, and non-governmental organisations (NGOs) can institute human rights applications on behalf of any potential applicant.[128] Again, this addresses one of the intervention areas proposed by Obani, and that is legal aid. Through public interest litigation, climate litigation can be effectively undertaken by adopting the HRAEP approach on behalf of the Nigerian woman, as such dispelling the question of legal aid or lack of funds to seek redress before the courts.

A limitation of FREP Rules was discussed in *Kporharor v Yedi*, where the court held that an application to enforce a right under the FREP Rules cannot be filed by more than one person, as such application 'is incompetent and liable to be struck out'.[129] However, as provided for in paragraph 3 (e)(iii) FREP Rules 2009, 'anyone acting as a member of, or in the interest of a group or class of persons',[130] can apply to the court in the state to enforce the fundamental rights that have been, are being, or are likely to be infringed.[131] Thus, even though fundamental rights enforcement applications cannot be made by more than one person, an individual can do so in the interest of the public, a group, or a class of persons.[132] When acting in such a representative capacity, the applicant is mandated to include in the statement that he is acting on behalf of someone else.[133]

Concerning delay in accessing justice, once an application for enforcing human rights is filed, the FREP Rules mandate that it shall be heard within seven days from the date of filing.[134] Due to the urgent nature of applications under the FREP Rules, the hearing of an application can only be adjourned 'where extremely expedient; depending on the circumstances of each case; or upon such terms as the court may deem fit to make'.[135] Where a delay in hearing the application may cause exceptional hardship to the applicant and the court is satisfied that such is the case, the court may hear the applicant *ex parte*. An *ex parte* application must be supported by an affidavit stating sufficient grounds for why exceptional hardship would be caused to the applicant should the hearing of the application be delayed.[136] The next section discusses the challenges of using HRAEP.

## Challenges to effective HRAEP climate litigation

The previous section examined why HRAEP provides a potentially effective pathway for climate litigation and identified some of its benefits. Next, we consider factors that could reveal why the Nigerian woman has not yet brought climate change cases to hold governments, individuals, and private companies responsible for actions that exacerbate climate change causes and impacts.

Most environmental cases before the Nigerian courts have embraced a torts approach, invoking the private law remedy of damages, and not a human rights approach in seeking redress for environmental pollution and degradation.[137] However, the majority were unsuccessful because, in addition to having to overcome restrictive *locus standi* rules, it is often difficult to prove negligence, trespass, and public or private nuisance.[138] This has resulted in Nigerians pursuing redress for environmental harms in foreign jurisdictions, such as the United States of America (USA),[139] the United Kingdom (UK),[140] and the Netherlands.[141] Instead, they could adopt the HRAEP in the domestic jurisdiction and/or beyond.

Presently, there is an absence of cases adopting the HRAEP at the Nigerian Supreme Court or the Court of Appeal, where the enforcement of environmental rights as guaranteed by Article 24 of the Schedule to the ACHPR Act 1983 is addressed.[142] However, Orji identifies two unreported Federal High Court (FHC) cases where the applicants sought the enforcement of this provision.[143] They are *Gbemre v SPDC*[144] and *Okpara v SPDC*.[145] In each of the cases, the court gave conflicting decisions. On the one hand, in *Gbemre v SPDC*, Nwokorie J held that Article 24 of the Schedule to the ACHPR Act 1983 constituted a fundamental right to a healthy environment and that gas flaring violated that right.[146] On the other hand, in *Okpara v SPDC*, Nwodo J, refusing to be persuaded by the prior decision of his brother judge, held that the ACHPR Act 1983 did not constitute fundamental rights as contemplated by section 46(1) of the Constitution of the Federal Republic of Nigeria.[147]

The decision of the Supreme Court in *Okpara v SPDC* can be contested.[148] In *Abacha v Fawehinmi*, the Supreme Court unequivocally held that the incorporation of the Banjul Charter[149] into the Nigerian municipal laws made its provisions justiciable in the Nigerian courts,[150] and 'it would follow that the procedural provisions set out in the Fundamental Rights (Enforcement Procedure) Rules under Chapter 4 of the 1979 Constitution for enforcing fundamental rights . . . are applicable by extension, to the provisions of the African Charter'.[151]

It thus is settled law in Nigeria that (1) the Supreme Court is the apex and final court of appeal in Nigeria;[152] (2) based on the principle of precedent, or *stare decisis*, the decisions of superior courts are binding on lower courts when asked to determine the same issue;[153] and (3) the decision of the Supreme Court remains good law until it is set aside by that court.[154] Therefore, it is unclear why Nwodo J in *Okpara v SPDC* chose to ignore the decision of the superior court. In addition, before the case, which was decided in 2000, the Supreme Court, in *Ogugu v The State* – decided in 1994 – found that the provisions of the Schedule to the ACHPR Act 1983 are enforceable through the FREP Rules in the same manner as those of Chapter IV.[155] This makes it apparent that Nwodo J's decision failed to follow the good law made by the Supreme Court. To the extent of its inconsistency with the decision of the Supreme Court on this matter, we submit that Nwodo J's decision can be contested. In other words, *Okpara v SPDC* should not be viewed as an insurmountable obstacle to pursuing the HRAEP in future climate cases in Nigeria aimed at redressing human rights violations of the Nigerian woman.

Another reason the Nigerian woman may not yet have pursued HRAEP relates to the nature of the FREP Rules. Interestingly, the simplicity of the FREP Rules makes them challenging. The Nigerian courts have consistently held that where an application is brought under the FREP Rules, the court will only have jurisdiction in the matter where the enforcement or securing of the enforcement of fundamental rights is the principle or fundamental claim.[156] The facts relied upon must disclose that the basis of the claim is the infringement of the applicant's fundamental right.[157] Furthermore, a claim to enforce common-law rights or contractual rights is incompetent under the FREP Rules, as it is not meant to enforce such rights unless the 'contractual rights also infringe the Constitutional rights of the citizen'.[158]

Therefore, where (1) the enforcement or securing of the enforcement of fundamental rights constitutes an ancillary, accessory, or incidental claim to the substantive or principal claim; (2) where the alleged infringement 'of a fundamental right is ancillary or incidental to the substantive claim of the ordinary civil or common law nature';[159] and (3) where 'the claim shows a dispute under other areas of law',[160] such application would not succeed under the FREP Rules, because the court would become incompetent to properly invoke or exercise its jurisdiction,[161] resulting in the case being struck out for want of jurisdiction.[162] Nevertheless, should the court continue the proceedings without having jurisdiction over the matter, the whole proceedings and the resultant judgment would be null and void.[163]

The FREP Rules are such that any action founded on them is not subject to other rules of the court, including the Sheriff and Civil Process Act.[164] The FREP Rules are specially and specifically designed with their own distinctive rules by the 1999 Constitution with the sole purpose of speedy enforcement of Nigerian citizens' fundamental rights.[165] The courts have found that they do not provide 'for the importation of any other rule of court for the enforcement of such rights'.[166] However, 'where in the course of any Human Rights proceedings, any situation arises for which there is or appears to be no adequate provision in these Rules, the Civil Procedure Rules of the Court for the time being in force shall apply'.[167]

In bringing an application to enforce fundamental rights, the applicant has to demonstrate facts and circumstances which prove that the respondent has actually infringed, or is likely to infringe, on the rights.[168] The applicant also has the duty to 'place before the court all vital evidence regarding the infringement or breach of such rights'.[169] This is because the court would scrutinise and evaluate the facts as disclosed by the affidavit evidence to ascertain whether, as claimed, there has been an infringement of the fundamental rights.[170]

Furthermore, the onus is on the applicant to specify which of the fundamental rights, as guaranteed either in the 1999 Constitution and/or the ACHPR Act 1983, has been, is being, or is likely to be infringed.[171] The standard of proof will be that required to be discharged in civil cases, that is, on the balance of probabilities.[172] Although the infringement of fundamental rights might have elements of criminal acts, the standard of proof will remain on the balance of probabilities and not beyond reasonable doubt.[173] According to Tsammani JCA, notwithstanding that the allegations of breach of fundamental rights might have criminal connotations, it will not rise to the level of a criminal allegation, as that 'will defeat the purpose of section 46(1) of the 1999 Constitution of Nigeria, which seeks a simple, easy to attain and thus effective judicial process for the enforcement of fundamental rights available to citizens'.[174] The following section discusses the recommendations and next steps.

## Next steps

Human rights mechanisms are increasingly being utilised as a pathway to hold governments responsible for climate change causes and impacts. Examples are the ongoing climate litigation before the South Korean Constitutional Court[175] and a 2024 judgment by the European Court of Human Rights in *Verein Klimaseniorinnen Schweiz and Others v Switzerland (2024) ECHR (Application no. 53600/20).* The litigants in the South Korean case are young environmental activists and children, while for the ECHR case are elderly women. Such cases highlight two salient points, namely, that (1) the vulnerable groups are taking a proactive approach towards holding governments accountable for climate change actions and inactions, and (2) human rights mechanisms might be the most favourable pathway to achieving this.

Indeed, the benefit of HRAEP as a tool for the Nigerian woman to undertake climate litigation and ensure structures are put in place to strengthen resilience against the impacts of climate change cannot be overemphasised. This chapter proffers two salient factors that can ensure that this is realised, namely, increased awareness of and sensitisation to the impacts of climate change on women, particularly among government agencies, and an increase in public interest litigation. We elaborate on each of these briefly.

Addressing the challenge of a lack of awareness of the human rights impacts of climate change, particularly for women, agencies such as the National Orientation Agency (NOA), the Nigerian Institute of Advanced Legal Studies (NIALS), and the National Human Rights Commission (NHRC) have a critical role. They are empowered to ensure widespread awareness and sensitisation for women in urban and rural areas on their fundamental human rights and the impacts of climate change on their health and well-being. They should co-produce knowledge with women relating to the actions available. These agencies should take active steps in providing this service.

The Nigerian courts have defined *public interest litigation* as cases that concern 'the interest of Nigerian society or any segment of it in promoting human rights and advancing human rights law'.[176] Nigeria has numerous non-governmental organisations and civil society organisations focused on women and the girl child, such as the International Federation of Women Lawyers (FIDA), Women Environmental Programme (WEP), Women Initiative for Sustainable Environment (WISE), and others. Borrowing a leaf from *Klimaseniorinnen Schweiz and Others v Switzerland*, these NGOs and CSOs can proactively take the initiative to seek redress on behalf of the Nigerian woman. The FREP Rules 2009, as stated previously, encourage public interest litigation. Moreover, the Nigerian Bar Association has a Section on Public Interest Litigation (SPIDEL) equipped to undertake these cases.

More so, *pro bono* cases aimed at aiding women in effectively litigating against climate change might be considered mandatory when considering applications for the rank of Senior Advocate of Nigeria (SAN).

## Conclusion

Nigeria is one of the countries highly vulnerable to the impacts of climate change. Even though the entire Nigerian population is generally vulnerable, some groups, including women, have high sensitivity and low adaptive capacity to the shocks and stress wrought on by climate change. Taking active steps to address the climate crisis, in addition to being a party to several international and regional environmental legal instruments, including the Paris Agreement, Nigeria has municipal legislation aimed at, amongst others, providing a framework for mainstreaming climate change actions.

Understanding that addressing climate injustice and reducing the vulnerability of women to its impacts must transcend beyond the laws on paper to enforcement, one of the approaches recommended by the IPCC is adopting the rights-based approach. However, even though climate litigation is crucial to addressing the impacts of climate change on Nigerian women, unfortunately, for women in Nigeria, due to existing barriers to access to justice, climate change litigation is a challenge.

This chapter examined the HRAEP as a tool the Nigerian woman can utilise to overcome barriers to climate litigation. The chapter identified the challenges of using this approach. The chapter also proffered two factors that could promote the use of climate litigation by Nigerian women, empowering them to hold governments, individuals, and private companies responsible for actions that exacerbate climate change impacts and to enhance their resilience to these climate impacts. These factors are (1) awareness and sensitisation by NIALS, NOA, and NHRC and (2) public interest litigation by FIDA and other NGOs or CSOs that are established to foster the protection of women.

## Notes

1 United Nations Environmental Programme, 'Secretary-General on the launch of the Emissions Gap Report 2022' <www.unep.org/news-and-stories/video/secretary-general-launch-emissions-gap-report-2022> accessed 26 April 2024.
2 IPCC, 'Summary for Policymakers in Climate Change 2023: Synthesis Report, Contribution of Working Groups I, II and III to the Sixth Assessment Report of the Intergovernmental Panel on Climate Change' in Core Writing Team, H Lee and J Romero (eds), (2023) 1–34 <https://www.ipcc.ch/report/ar6/syr/downloads/report/IPCC_AR6_SYR_FullVolume.pdf> accessed 21 November 2024.
3 IPCC (n 2).
4 JF Ade Ajayi and others, 'Nigeria' (*Britannica*) <www.britannica.com/place/Nigeria> accessed 26 April 2024.
5 IPCC (n 2) 17.
6 IPCC (n 2) 17.

7 Namely, deforestation, droughts, desert encroachment, flooding, biodiversity loss, and others – see Hyellai Titus Pona et al., 'Environmental Health Situation in Nigeria: Current Status and Future Needs' (2021) 7 *Heliyon* 1.

8 See United Nations Women, 'Explainer: How Gender Inequality and Climate Change are Interconnected' (2022) <www.unwomen.org/en/news-stories/explainer/2022/02/explainer-how-gender-inequality-and-climate-change-are-interconnected> accessed 26 April 2024; United Nations Framework Convention for Climate Change, 'Five Reasons Why Climate Action Needs Women' (2023) <https://unfccc.int/news/five-reasons-why-climate-action-needs-women> accessed 26 April 2024; United Nations Framework Convention for Climate Change, 'Dimensions and Examples of the Gender-Differentiated Impacts of Climate Change, the Role of Women as Agents of Change and Opportunities for Women: Synthesis Report by the Secretariat' (2022) <https://unfccc.int/sites/default/files/resource/sbi2022_07.pdf> accessed 26 April 2024; Frank Ellis, 'Human Vulnerability and Food Security: Policy Implications' <https://odi.org/en/publications/human-vulnerability-and-food-insecurity-policy-implications/> accessed 26 April 2024; See also, Amy L Luers, 'The Surface of Vulnerability; An Analytical Framework for Examining Environmental Change' (2005) 15 *Global Environmental Change* 215, 218. See also Dutta and Lofts Chapter 4 and Burri and Duarte Reyes Chapter 5.

9 Luers (n 8).

10 United Nations Human Rights Office of the High Commissioner, 'Climate Change Exacerbates Violence Against Women and Girls' (2022) <www.ohchr.org/en/stories/2022/07/climate-change-exacerbates-violence-against-women-and-girls> accessed 26 April 2024.

11 IPCC (n 2) 17.

12 Federal Government of Nigeria, 'Nigeria's Nationally Determined Contribution – 2021 Update' <www4.unfccc.int/sites/NDCStaging/pages/Party.aspx?party=NGA> accessed 26 April 2024.

13 Pona et al. (n 7).

14 Pona et al. (n 7).

15 World Population Review, 'Nigeria Population 2023 (Live)' <https://worldpopulationreview.com/countries/nigeria-population> accessed 26 April 2024.

16 United Nations Population Fund, 'Executive Board of the United Nations Development Programme, the United Nations Population Fund and the United Nations Office for Project Services' (30 January to 3 February 2023) DP/FPA/CPD/NGA/9.

17 World Population Review (n 15).

18 United Nations Population Fund, 'World Population Dashboard Nigeria' <www.unfpa.org/data/world-population/NG> accessed 26 April 2024.

19 Federal Republic of Nigeria, 'National Security Strategy' (December 2019) 12–13 <https://ctc.gov.ng/national-security-strategy-2019/> accessed 26 April 2024.

20 National Bureau of Statistics, '2019 Poverty and Inequality in Nigeria: Executive Summary' <https://nigerianstat.gov.ng/elibrary/read/1092> accessed 26 April 2024.

21 National Bureau of Statistics (n 20).

22 National Bureau of Statistics (n 20).

23 World Bank, Nigeria Poverty Assessment 2022: A Better Future for all Nigerians (*World Bank* 2022) 21.

24 World Bank (n 23).

25 The World Bank, 'Access to Electricity (% of Population) – Nigeria' <https://data.worldbank.org/indicator/EG.ELC.ACCS.ZS?locations=NG> accessed 26 April 2024.

26 Federal Ministry of Water Resources (FMWR), Government of Nigeria, National Bureau of Statistics (NBS) and UNICEF, 'Water, Sanitation and Hygiene: National Outcome Routine Mapping (WASH NORM) 2019: A Report of Findings' (2020) <www.unicef.

org/nigeria/media/3576/file/WASH%20NORM%20Report%202019.pdf> accessed 26 April 2024.

27 FMWR (n 26).

28 FMWR (n 26).

29 Federal Republic of Nigeria (n 19).

30 Leon Usigbe, 'Silencing the Guns: Drying Lake Chad Basin gives rise to Crisis' (2019) <www.un.org/africarenewal/magazine/december-2019-march-2020/drying-lake-chad-basin-gives-rise-crisis> accessed 26 April 2024.

31 Zebulon Suifon Takwa, 'Addressing the Climate Change Insecurity Challenge in Nigeria and the Lake Chad Basin' <www.undp.org/sites/g/files/zskgke326/files/migration/oslo_governance_centre/89e8d11e6b388f1174e625ebf8790f2c84c7bd0cead6164b91887972950117e9.pdf> accessed 26 April 2024.

32 African Organization of Supreme Audit Institutions, 'Joint Environmental Audit on the Drying up of Lake Chad: Joint Audit Report' (*The European Union and the German Federal Ministry for Economic Cooperation and Development*, 2015).

33 African Organization of Supreme Audit Institutions (n 32).

34 African Organization of Supreme Audit Institutions (n 32).

35 Taiwo Oyaniran, 'Current State of Nigeria Agriculture and Agribusiness Sector' (*Paper Presented at the AfCFTA Workshop*, September 2020) <www.pwc.com/ng/en/assets/pdf/afcfta-agribusiness-current-state-nigeria-agriculture-sector.pdf> assessed 26 June 2023.

36 Federal Ministry of Agriculture and Rural Development, 'National Agricultural Technology and Innovation Policy (NATIP 2022–2027)' (*The Federal Ministry of Agriculture and Rural Development*, 2022) 10; World Bank (n 23) 49; Federal Ministry of Environment, 'National Climate Change Policy for Nigeria (2021–2030)' (*Department of Climate Change*) 18.

37 Oyaniran (n 35).

38 Food and Agriculture Organization of the United Nations (FAO), '25 Million Nigerian at High Risk of Food Insecurity in 2023' <www.fao.org/nigeria/news/detail-events/en/c/1630260/> accessed 26 April 2024.

39 Federal Republic of Nigeria (n 19); Oyaniran (n 35).

40 FAO (n 38).

41 Federal Republic of Nigeria (n 19).

42 FAO (n 38). For a discussion of intersectional climate justice, see also Murcott, Tigre and Ann Samuel, 'Introduction'.

43 See UN Women (n 8), UNFCCC (n 8).

44 See National Institute of Environmental Health Sciences, 'People Who are Vulnerable to Climate Change: Climate Change and Human Health' <www.niehs.nih.gov/research/programs/climatechange/health_impacts/vulnerable_people> accessed 26 April 2024; Milanika S Turner, 'Climate Change Hazards + Social Vulnerability = A Recipe for Disaster' (2022) 46(2) *Generations: Journal of the American Society on Aging*.

45 Turner (n 44).

46 UN Women (n 8); UNFCCC, 'Five Reasons why Climate Action Needs Women' (n 8); UNFCCC, 'Dimensions and Examples of the Gender-Differentiated Impacts of Climate Change' (n 8); Elllis (n 8); Luers (n 8). United Nations Environment Programme, 'Women and the Environment' (*UNEP*, 2004) [11]. Dutta and Lofts Chapter 4, pp 137–140; Burri and Duarte Reyes Chapter 5, pp 166–168.

47 See Turner (n 44); UN Women (n 8); UNFCCC (n 8); Chidiebere J Onwutuebe, 'Patriarchy and Women Vulnerability to Adverse Climate Change in Nigeria' (2019) 9 *Sage Open*; UN Women, 'UN Women and the World Bank Unveil New Data Analysis on Women and Poverty' (*UN Women*, 9 November 2017) <www.unwomen.org/en/news/stories/2017/11/news-un-women-and-the-world-bank-unveil-new-data-analysis-on-women-and-poverty> accessed 26 April 2024; Balgis Osman-Elasha, 'Women . . . In The Shadow of Climate Change' (2009) XLVI(3 & 4) *United Nations Chronicles Special*

*Climate Change Issue: To Protect Succeeding Generations* <www.un.org/en/chronicle/article/womenin-shadow-climate-change> accessed 26 April 2024; IPCC, 'Summary for Policymakers in Climate Change 2022 – Impacts, Adaptation and Vulnerability: Working Group II Contribution to the Sixth Assessment Report of the Intergovernmental Panel on Climate Change' in HO Pörtner et al. (eds), (2022) 3–33 <https://www.ipcc.ch/report/ar6/wg2/downloads/report/IPCC_AR6_WGII_FullReport.pdf> accessed 21 November 2024. C Owren, 'Women and the Environment' in J Aragon and M Miller (eds), *Global Women's Issues: Women in the World Today, Extended Version* (GPA Publications 2012) 171–175. Bureau of International Information Programs, United States Department of State.

48 Osman-Elasha (n 47).

49 Nkiruka Ugwuji Chidia Maduekwe, 'Achieving Environmental Sustainability in Nigeria's Extractive Industry: How Viable Is a Human Rights Approach to Environmental Protection?' (PhD thesis, University of Hull 2018) <https://hull-repository.worktribe.com/output/4429881> accessed 26 April 2024.

50 Federal Government of Nigeria (n 12).

51 Federal Government of Nigeria (n 12).

52 SO Giwa and others, 'Gas Flaring Attendant Impacts of Criteria and Particulate Pollutants: A Case for Niger Delta Region of Nigeria' (2017) *JKSU* 1; OG Fawole, XM Cai and AR MacKenzie, 'Gas Flaring and Resultant Air Pollution: A Review Focusing on Black Carbon' (2016) 216 *EP* 183, 187; Aniefiok E Ite, Udo John Ibok, U Margaret and Sunday W Petters, 'Petroleum Exploration and Production: Past and Present Environmental Issues in the Nigeria's Niger Delta' (2013) 1 *AJEP* 78, 82.

53 Fawole (n 52).

54 Imo J Ekpoh and Ajah E Obia, 'The Role of Gas Flaring in the Rapid Corrosion of Zinc Roofs in the Niger Delta Region of Nigeria' (2010) 30 *Environmentalist* 347, 348.

55 Earthworks, 'Think Again – Oil and Gas Air Pollution Fact Sheet' (2005) <https://earthworks.org/cms/assets/uploads/archive/files/publications/Airpollution.pdf> accessed 26 April 2024; AA Kadafa, 'Oil Exploration and Spillage in the Niger Delta of Nigeria' (2012) 2 *CER* 38, 45; AI Sodimu, VM Yilwa and GB Onwumere, 'The Impact of Gas Flaring from the Kaduna Refinery and Petrochemical Industry (KRPC) on Plant Diversity in Kaduna Northern Guinea Savanna Eco-Region of Nigeria' (2017) 69 *WSN* 168, 169; EI Seiyaboh and SC Izah, 'A Review of impacts of Gas Flaring on Vegetation and Water Resources in the Niger Delta Region of Nigeria' (2017) 2 *IJEEE* 48, 49; SO Giwa, OO Adama and OO Akinyemi, 'Baseline Black Carbon Emissions for Gas Flaring in the Niger Delta Region of Nigeria' (2014) 20 *JNGSE* 373; Ite et al. (n 52) 83; OCD Anejionu, PAN Ahiarammunnah and CJ Nri-Ezedi, 'Hydrocarbon Pollution in the Niger Delta: Geographies of Impacts and Appraisal of Lapses in Extant Legal Framework' (2015) 45 *RP* 65, 70.

56 Seiyaboh and Izah (n 55) 48, 49, 51.

57 SI Efe, 'Spatial Variation of Acid Rain and its Ecological Effect in Nigeria' (*Environmental Management Conference, Abeokuta*, September 2011) 383.

58 JK Nduka, FO Obumselu and NL Umedum, 'Crude Oil and Fractional Spillages Resulting from Exploration and Exploitation in Niger-Delta Region of Nigeria: A Review About the Environmental and Public Health Impact' in M Younes (ed), *Crude Oil Exploration in the World* (IT 2012) 62; United Nations Development Programme (UNDP) and Global Environment Facility (GEF), 'UNDP Project Document: Niger Delta Biodiversity Project' (2012) 35–36 <www.undp.org/content/dam/undp/documents/projects/NGA/Niger%20Delta%20Biodiversity_Prodoc.pdf> accessed 26 April 2024; EJ Dung, LS Bombom and TD Agusomu, 'The Effects of Gas Flaring on Crops in the Niger Delta, Nigeria' (2008) 73 *GJ* 297, 298; Ekpoh and Obia (n 54) 348; Anejionu, Ahiarammunnah and Nri-Ezedi (n 55); Giwa, Adama and Akinyemi (n 55) 374; Efe (n 57) 382 and 391.

59 Kadafa (n 55) 44.

60 Dung, Bombom and Agusomu (n 58) 304.
61 Kadafa (n 55) 45; Sodimu, Yilwa and Onwumere (n 55) 169; Seiyaboh and Izah (n 55) 49; Anejionu, Ahiarammunnah and Nri-ezedi (n 55) 72. Also see Dung, Bombom and Agusomu (n 58) for a detailed discussion on how gas flare heat affects different types of crops.
62 Seiyaboh and Izah (n 55) 49.
63 Sodimu, Yilwa and Onwumere (n 55) 170; Seiyaboh and Izah (n 55) 49; Ekpoh and Obia (n 54) 348; Nduka, Obumselu and Umedum (n 58) 64; Earthworks (n 55); Efe (n 57) 392; V Aigbokhaevbo and N Aniekwu, 'Environmental Abuses in Nigeria: Implications for Reproductive Health' (2013) XIX *ASICL* 233, 236–237 and 262.
64 FO Okorodudu, PO Okorodudu and EK Irikefe, 'A Model of Petroleum Pipeline Spillage Detection System for Use in the Niger Delta Region of Nigeria' (2016) 4 *IJRG* 1, 3; EO Omodanisi, AO Eludoyin and AT Salami, 'A Multi-Perspective View of the Effects of a Pipeline Explosion in Nigeria' (2014) 7 *IJDRR* 68, 185.
65 United Nations Environment Programme, 'Environmental Assessment of Ogoniland' (*UNEP*, 2011) 39; A Fentiman and N Zabbey, 'Environmental Degradation and Cultural Erosion in Ogoniland: A Case Study of the Oil Spills in Bodo' (2015) 2 *TEIS* 615, 618.
66 UNEP (n 65) 40.
67 IE Daniel and PJ Nna, 'Total Petroleum Hydrocarbon Concentration in Surface Water of Cross River Estuary, Niger Delta, Nigeria' (2016) *AJEE* 1, 2.
68 JKC Nduka, E Constance and E Obiakor, 'Selective Bioaccumulation of Metals by Different Parts of Some Fish Species from Crude Oil Polluted Water' (2006) 77 *BECT* 846; SO Osuide, 'Environmental Pollution in Nigeria' (1990) 14 *HI* 5, 8.
69 INE Onwurah et al., 'Crude Oil Spills in the Environment, Effects and Some Innovative Clean-Up Biotechnologies' (2007) 1 *IJER* 307, 310.
70 Samuel Aghalino and Bolade Eyinla, 'Oil Exploration and Marine Pollution: Evidence from the Niger Delta, Nigeria' (2009) 28 *JHE* 177, 179.
71 Kenneth Aroh et al., 'Oil Spill Incidents and Pipeline Vandalisation in Nigeria; Impact on Public Health and Negation to Attainment of Millennium Development Goal: The Ishiagu Example' (2010) 19 *DPM* 70, 80–81; Nenibarini Zabbey, Kabari Sam and Adugo T Onyebuchi, 'Remediation of Contaminated Lands in the Niger Delta, Nigeria: Prospects and Challenges' (2017) 586 *STE* 952, 955; Aigbokhaevbo and Aniekwu (n 63) 236–237, 262.
72 Bronwen Manby, 'The Price of Oil: Corporate Responsibility and Human Rights Violations in Nigeria's Oil Producing Communities' (*HRW*, 1999) 60; E Ugwu, 'FG Urged to Investigate Oil Spill in Abia Community' Thisday (*Umuahia*, 22 June 2016) <www.thisdaylive.com/index.php/2016/06/22/fg-urged-to-investigate-oil-spill-in-abia-community/> accessed 26 April 2024; Eno Okoko, 'Women and Environmental Change in the Niger Delta, Nigeria: Evidence from Ibeno' (1999) 6 *GPC* 373–375.
73 RE Egbe and D Thompson, 'Environmental Challenges of Oil Spillage for Families in Oil Producing Communities of the Niger Delta Region' (2010) 13 *JHER* 24, 26.
74 RE Egbe and D Thompson, 'Environmental Challenges of Oil Spillage for Families in Oil Producing Communities of the Niger Delta Region' (2010) 13 *JHER* 24, 2626; Zabbey, Sam and Onyebuchi (n 71) 956.
75 Egbe and Thompson (n 73) 29.
76 Egbe and Thompson (n 73) 29–30; Onyenekenwa Cyprian Eneh, 'Crippling Poverty Amidst Corporate Social Actions: A Critique of Peripheral Corporate Community Involvement in the Niger Delta Region of Nigeria' (2011) 1 *AJRD* 1, 7.
77 Okoko (n 72) 375.
78 Okoko (n 72) 377.
79 Angela N Nwachukwu and Joachim C Osuagwu, 'Effects of Oil Spillage on Groundwater Quality in Nigeria' (2014) *AJER* 271; EC Onwuka, 'Oil Extraction, Environmental Degradation and Poverty in the Niger Delta Region of Nigeria: a Viewpoint' (2005) 62 *IJES* 655.

80 IPCC (n 2).
81 François d'Eaubonne, 'Feminism-Ecology: Revolution or Mutation?' (1999) 4 *Ethics and the Environment* 175.
82 Maria Miles, 'Ecofeminism' (*Britannica*) <www.britannica.com/topic/ecofeminism> accessed 26 April 2024; Barbara T Gates, 'A Root of Ecofeminism: Ecoféminisme' (1996) 3 *Interdisciplinary Studies in Literature and Environment* 7, 9.
83 Miles (n 82).
84 United Nations, 'Climate Action: Why Women are Key to Climate Action' <www.un.org/en/climatechange/science/climate-issues/women> accessed 17 April 2024; United Nations Climate Change, 'Closing the Gap, Boosting Ambition: Investing in Women is Key to Climate Action' (March 2024) <https://unfccc.int/news/closing-the-gap-boosting-ambition-investing-in-women-is-key-to-climate-action> accessed 17 April 2024.
85 Federal Republic of Nigeria, 'National Action Plan on Gender and Climate Change for Nigeria' (2020) <https://climatechange.gov.ng/wp-content/uploads/2020/09/climate-change-and-gender-action-plan.pdf> accessed 26 April 2024.
86 Federal Republic of Nigeria (n 85).
87 Chukwuemeka Onyebuchi Onyimadu, 'Climate Change Adaptation and Wellbeing Among Smallholder Women Farmers in Gwagwalada and Kokona, Nigeria' (2023) 153 *Futures* 103238.
88 See Maduekwe (n 49).
89 David R Boyd, 'The Effectiveness of Constitutional Environmental Rights' (*Yale/UNITAR Workshop on Rights in Environmental Governance, New Haven*, 26–27 April 2013) 1 <https://environment.yale.edu/gem/events/yaleunitar-workshop-on-rights-in-environmental-governance/#gsc.tab=0> accessed 26 April 2024.
90 Currently named as Ms Fatma Zohra Ouhachi-Vasely; Earthjustice, 'Environmental Rights Report 2007: Human Rights and the Environment 1' <http://earthjustice.org/sites/default/files/library/references/2007-environmental-rights-report.pdf> accessed 26 April 2024.
91 African Charter on Human and Peoples' Rights (1982) 21 ILM 58.
92 David R Boyd, 'The Status of Constitutional Protection for the Environment in Other Nations' <https://davidsuzuki.org/wp-content/uploads/2013/11/status-constitutional-protection-environment-other-nations-SUMMARY.pdf> accessed 26 April 2024; David R Boyd, 'The Environmental Rights Revolution: A Global Study of Constitutions, Human Rights, and the Environment' (*UBCP*, 2012) 50.
93 UNGA, 'The Human Right to a Clean, Healthy and Sustainable Environment' (A/RES/76/300, 28 July 2022). See generally, Délton Winter de Carvalho and Rafaela Santos Martins da Rosa, 'Climate Constitutionalism as a Foundation for Climate Litigation in Latin America' (2024) 16(1) *Journal of Human Rights Practice* 71 <https://doi.org/10.1093/jhuman/huad055> accessed 7 September 2024, Melanie J Murcott and Clive Vinti, 'The Judge-Made "Duty" to Consider Climate Change in South Africa' (2024) 16(1) *Journal of Human Rights Practice* 125 <https://doi.org/10.1093/jhuman/huad069> accessed 7 September 2024.
94 IPCC (n 2) 66.
95 IPCC (n 2).
96 Pedi Obani, 'Women Battle When Trying to Take Climate Change Cases to Court – South Africa and Nigeria Study Shows' (7 March 2024) <https://theconversation.com/women-battle-when-trying-to-take-climate-change-cases-to-court-south-africa-and-nigeria-study-shows-why-224784> accessed 26 April 2024.
97 Obani (n 96).
98 Olaitan O Olusegun and Olatunji S Oyelade, 'Access to Justice for Nigerian Women: A Veritable Tool to Achieving Sustainable Development' (2022) 22 *International Journal of Discrimination and the Law* 4.
99 Olusegun and Oyelade (n 98) 20.

100 Olusegun and Oyelade (n 98) 17.
101 Obani (n 96).
102 See Uzuazo Etemire, 'Climate Change Litigation in Nigeria: Challenges and Opportunities' in Francesco Sindico and Makane Moïse Mbengue (eds), *Comparative Climate Change Litigation: Beyond the Usual Suspects* (Springer, 2021).
103 Soonest Nathaniel, 'President Buhari Signs Climate Change, AMCON Bills into Law' (*Channeltv*, 18 November 2021) <www.channelstv.com/2021/11/18/president-buhari-signs-climate-change-amcon-amendment-bills-into-law/> accessed 26 April 2024.
104 Jiata Ekele, 'Nigeria Climate Change Act: CSDevNet, Non-State Actors Strategise on Implementation' (*CSDevNet*) <https://csdevnet.org/nigeria-climate-change-act-csdevnet-non-state-actors-strategise-on-implementation/> accessed 26 April 2024.
105 Muhammed Tawfiq Ladan, 'A Review of Nigeria's 2021 Climate Change Act: Potential for Increased Climate Litigation' (*IUCN*, 28 March 2022) <www.iucn.org/news/commission-environmental-economic-and-social-policy/202203/a-review-nigerias-2021-climate-change-act-potential-increased-climate-litigation> accessed 26 April 2024.
106 Section 34 of the Climate Change Act (CCA) 2021.
107 Section 34(2) of the Climate Change Act (CCA) 2021.
108 See *Archbishop Anthony Olubunmi Okogie et al. v The Attorney-General of Lagos State* 1980 FNLR, Suit No FCA/L/74/80; *Attorney-General of Ondo State v the Attorney-General of the Federation et al.* (2002) LPELR-623 (SC); *Attorney-General of Lagos State v The Attorney-General of the Federation et al.* (2003) LPELR-620(SC), (2003) 838–1010 NSCQR Vol. 14.
109 See Ladan (n 105).
110 See Ord I r 2 Constitution of the Federal Republic of Nigeria, Fundamental Rights (Enforcement Procedure) Rules 2009 under Chapter IV of the Constitution, B1365 (FREP Rules 2009).
111 See *Alhaji Aliyu N Salihu v Suleiman Umar Gana et al.* (2014) LPELR-23069 (CA) 24, paras C-G; Ord I r 2 FREP Rules 2009 (n 110).
112 Section 37 National Environmental Standards and Regulations Enforcement Agency (Establishment) Act 2007 CAP 164 LFN 2007 (NESREA Act 2007).
113 See *Attorney-General of Lagos State v The Attorney-General of the Federation et al.* (2003) LPELR-620(SC), (2003) 919 NSCQR Vol. 14 (Nigeria) (*AG Lagos State v AG Federation*).
114 Article 24 African Charter on Human and Peoples' Rights (Ratification and Enforcement) Act 1983 CAP 10 LFN 1990 (ACHPR Act 1983).
115 FREP Rules 2009 (n 110).
116 *General Sani Abacha et al. v Chief Gani Fawehinmi* (2002) LPELR-14(SC) 185; *Rumugu Air and Space Nigeria Limited v Federal Airports Authority of Nigeria et al.* (2016) LPELR-41506 (CA) 14–15, paras F-E; *Nigeria Union of Teachers et al. v Conference of Secondary School Tutors (CSST) et al.* (2005) LPELR-5953 (CA) 26–27, paras D-D; *Solomon Ohakosim v Commissioner of Police Imo State et al.* (2009) LPELR-8874 (CA) 26–28, paras C-F, (2009) 11 NMLR 94 para 34; *Grace Jack v University of Agriculture Makurdi* (2004) 102 NSCQR Vol. 17; *Central Bank of Nigeria v Chief Daniel Obameneke Okemuo et al.* (2016) LPELR-41405 (CA) 6–8, paras E-A.
117 *Solomon Adekunle v Attorney-General of Ogun State* (2014) LPELR-22569 (CA) 23–24, paras B-C.
118 *Luke Loveday v The Comptroller of Prisons Federal Prisons Aba et al.* (2013) LPELR-22072 (CA) 34, paras F-G; *George Adumu v The Comptroller of Prisons Federal Prisons Aba et al.* (2013) LPELR-22069 (CA) 34, paras F-G.
119 *Raymond S Dongtoe v Civil Service Commission Plateau State* (2001) LPELR-959 (SC) 22, paras E-F.

120 *Mr Solomon Kporharor et al. v Mr Michael Yedi et al.* (2017) LPELR-42418 (CA) 8–13, paras F-A.
121 *Loveday v The Comptroller of Prisons Federal Prisons Aba* (n 89) 38–39, paras E-A; *George Adumu v The Comptroller of Prisons Federal Prisons Aba* (2013) LPELR-22069 (CA) 38–39, paras E-A. See also *Madam Ujueke Enemuo (Chairperson, Umuada-Umuchu) et al. v Alochukwu Ezeonyeka et al.* (2016) LPELR-40171 (CA) 21, paras A-C.
122 *Alhaji Lawwani Zakari v Inspector-General of Police et al.* (2000) LPELR-6780 (CA) 25–26, paras G-G; *The Nigerian Navy et al. v Lionel Okon Garrick* (2005) LPELR-7555 (CA) 50–52, paras A-C; *Alhaji Ibrahim Abdulhamid v Talal Akar et al.* (2006) 1449–1450 NSCQR Vol. 26; *Economic and Financial Crimes Commission v Ibrahim Suleiman et al.* (2016) LPELR-40790 (CA) 56–58, paras D-A.
123 See Ord III r 1 FREP Rules 2009 (n 110). See also *Mr James Olusegun Omoleye v Francis Oginni Olaniran et al.* (2010) 10 NMLR 460–461 para 11; *Mallam Nasir Ahmed El-Rufai v Senate of the National Assembly et al.* (2014) LPELR-231115 (CA) 47, paras B-E and 57–60, paras A-E; *Mrs Endurance Odubu v Lieutenant Olorunduyilemi Stephen et al.* (2012) LPELR-19792 (CA) 16–18, paras F-A.
124 Appendix A, FREP Rules 2009 (n 110).
125 Para 3 (e) (i-v) Preamble to the FREP Rules 2009 (n 110); *Mr Niyi Aluko et al. v Commissioner of Police et al.* (2016) LPELR-41342 (CA) 26–27 paras D-B; *Mrs Ganiat Amope Dilly v Inspector General of Police et al.* (2016) LPELR-41452 (CA) 9–10, paras F-F.
126 Para 3(e) Preamble to the FREP Rules 2009 (n 110); *Centre for Oil Pollution Watch v Nigerian National Petroleum Corporation* (2019) 5 NWLR [PT.1666] P.518; *Faith Okafor v Lagos State Government et al.* (2016) LPELR-41066 (CA) 13–14, paras A-B; *Ovai Ekpe Okon v Ovai Bassey Enem Enyiefem et al.* (2016) LPELR-41168 (CA) 14–16, paras E-A; *Dilly v Inspector General of Police* (n 125) 15–22, paras A-A; *Federal Road Safety Commission v Emmanuel A Ofoegbu* (2014) LPELR-24229 (CA).
127 Para 3(e) Preamble to the FREP Rules 2009 (n 110).
128 FREP Rules 2009 (n 110).
129 *Mr Solomon Kporharor et al. v Mr Michael Yedi et al.* (2017) LPELR-42418 (CA) 8–13, paras F-A. See also *Ikechukwu Okpara et al. v Shell Petroleum Development Company of Nigeria Limited & others* (2006) Unreported, suit no: FHC/PHC/C5/518/2005 of 29 September 2006, 21–22.
130 Para 3(e) (iii) Preamble to the FREP Rules 2009 (n 110).
131 Ord II r 1 FREP Rules 2009 (n 110).
132 *Okafor v Lagos State Government* (n 126) 13–14, paras A-B; *Okon v Enyiefem* (n 126) 14–16, paras E-A; *Dilly v Inspector General of Police* (n 125) 15–22, paras A-A; *Federal Road Safety Commission v Ofoegbu* (n 126).
133 *Aluko v Commissioner of Police* (n 125).
134 *Aluko v Commissioner of Police* (n 125), ord IV r 1.
135 *Aluko v Commissioner of Police* (n 125), ord IV r 2.
136 *Aluko v Commissioner of Police* (n 125), ord IV r 3.
137 See Jedrzej G Frynas, 'Oil in Nigeria: Conflict and Litigation between Oil Companies and Village Communities' (*LITVM*, 2000); OU Ndukwe, 'Elements of Nigerian Environmental Laws' (*UCP*, 2000) 112.
138 Ndukwe (n 137). For a discussion on the 'problem of proof', see Jamwal, Chapter 9.
139 Jad Mouawad, 'Shell to Pay $15.5 Million to Settle Nigerian Case' (*The New York Times*, 8 June 2009) <www.nytimes.com/2009/06/09/business/global/09shell.html?_r=2&ref=global> accessed 26 April 2024.
140 Business & Human Rights Resource Centre, 'Shell Lawsuit (Re Oil Spills & Bodo Community in Nigeria)' <http://business-humanrights.org/en/shell-lawsuit-re-oil-spills-bodo-community-in-nigeria> accessed 30 September 2018; J Vidal,

'Niger Delta Communities to Sue Shell in London for Oil Spill Compensation' (*The Guardian*, 7 January 2015) <www.theguardian.com/environment/2015/jan/07/niger-delta-communities-to-sue-shell-in-london-for-oil-spill-compensation> accessed 26 April 2024

141 Friends of the Earth Netherlands, 'Outcome Appeal Against Shell: Victory for the Environment and the Nigerian People – Friends of the Earth Netherlands' (*Friends of the Earth International*, 18 December 2015) <www.foei.org/news/outcome-appeal-shell-victory-environment-nigerian-people-friends-earth-netherlands> accessed 26 April 2024.

142 Edwin Egede, 'Human Rights and the Environment: Is There a Legally Enforceable Right to a Clean and Healthy Environment for the "Peoples" of the Niger Delta under the Framework of the 1999 Constitution of Nigeria?' (2007) 19 *SLJIL* 51, 76.

143 Uchenna J Orji, 'Right to a Clean Environment: Some Reflections' (2012) 42 *EPL* 285, 290.

144 *Mr Jonah Gbemre v Shell Petroleum Development Company Nigeria Ltd, Nigerian National Petroleum Corporation, Attorney General of the Federation* (2005) Unreported, suit no: FHC/B/CS/53/05 of 14 November 2005.

145 *Okpara v SPDC* (n 129).

146 *Gbemre v SPDC* (n 144) final order 2 of the court, 30.

147 *Okpara v SPDC* (n 129) 12–13.

148 Orji supports this position as well – see Orji (n 143) 290.

149 African Charter on Human and Peoples' Rights (adopted 27 June 1981, entered into force 21 October 1986) (1982) 21 ILM 58. Hereafter referred to as Banjul Charter.

150 *Abacha v Fawehinmi* (n 116) 12–13.

151 *Abacha v Fawehinmi* (n 116) 109.

152 Lanre Fagbohun, 'Introduction to Law: Nigerian Legal System' in DF Asaju (ed), *General Studies Book of Readings* (Vol. 2, LSUP 2006) 302; *Isaac Obiuweubi v Central Bank of Nigeria* (2011) LPELR-2185 (SC) 28–29, paras E-A, 86 NSCQR Vol. 45.

153 *Hon Chris Azubuogu v Hon (Dr) Harry N Oranezi et al.* (2017) LPELR-42669 (SC) 13–13, paras F-A.

154 *Abacha v Fawehinmi* (n 116) 98.

155 *Ogugu et al. v The State* (1994) 9 NWLR (Pt 366) 1, (1994) 10 Ilaw/sc.303/1990.

156 *Kporharor v Yedi* (n 120) 15–16, paras F-E; *Chief Francis Igwe et al. v Mr Godoy Ezeanochie et al.* (2009) LPELR-11885 (CA) 25–28, paras G-A; *The Federal Republic of Nigeria et al. v Lord Chief Udensi Ifegwu* (2003) LPELR-3173 (SC) 32, paras D-G; *Alhaji Tsoho Dan Amale v Sokoto Local Government et al.* (2012) LPELR-7842 (SC) 18–21, paras E-A; *University of Ilorin et al. v Idowu Oluwadare* (2006) 28–29 NSCQR Vol. 27; *Sea trucks Nigeria Limited v Panya Anigboro* (2001) 137–138 NSCQLR Vol. 5; *Rev Prof Paul Emeka v Rev Dr Chidi Okoroafor et al.* (2017) LPELR-417 (SC) 67–73, paras F-B; *Eze (Dr) Emma Umez Eronini et al. v Lady CA Eronini et al.* (2013) LPELR-20651 (CA); *Alhaji Abdulazeez Adefila et al. v His Royal Majesty-Oba James Adedapo Popoola (Oore of Otun-Ekiti) et al.* (2014) LPELR-22468 (CA) 14–15, paras F-B; *Federal Republic of Nigeria et al. v Alhaji Mohammed Sani Abacha et al.* (2014) (CA) 116–117, paras F-F; *Abdulhamid v Akar* (n 122) 1450–1451; *Abba v Joint Admissions and Matriculation Board & Anor* (2014) LPELR-CA/YL/7/2013, 20–21, paras C-A; *Alhaji Sheu Abdul Gafar v The Government of Kwara State et al.* (2007) LPELR-8073 (SC) 21–22, paras E-D; *Grace Jack v University of Agriculture Makurdi* (2004) LPELR-1587 (SC) 18, paras B-F; *Mrs Ganiat Amope Dilly v Inspector General of Police et al.* (2016) LPELR-41452 (CA) 23–24, paras E-B; *Mrs Ngozi Chile Oparaocha et al. v Barr Emeka A Obichere et al.* (2016) LPELR-40615 (CA) 64–65, paras D-B.

157 *Rumugu Air and Space Nigeria Limited v Federal Airports Authority of Nigeria* (n 116) 17–20, paras D-E; *Chief Francis Igwe et al. v Mr Godoy Ezeanochie et al.* (n 156) 25–28, paras G-A.
158 *Look Engine Parts Limited et al. v Ecobank Nigeria Plc et al.* (2014) LPELR-22522 (CA) 19–21, paras A-E.
159 *Rumugu Air and Space Nigeria Limited v Federal Airports Authority of Nigeria* (n 116) 24–27, paras F-B.
160 *Mr Silas Jumbo Essien v Chief Akpan Inyang et al.* (2011) LPELR-4125 (CA) 24, paras C-D.
161 See n 156.
162 *Mr IT Mbadike et al. v Lagos International Trade Fair Complex Management Board et al.* (2017) LPELR-41968 (CA) 34–35; *Omo Oba Adenire Adetona et al. v Economic and Financial Crimes Commission et al.* (2017) LPELR-42369 (CA) 33–35, paras B-C.
163 *Ziakade Patrick Akpobolokemi et al. v The Hon Captain Emmanuel Ihenacho et al.* (2016) LPELR-40563 (CA) 16; *Raymond S Dongtoe v Civil Service Commission Plateau State* (2001) LPELR-959 (SC) 18, paras B-E; *Mrs Ngozi Chile Oparaocha et al. v Barr Emeka A Obichere et al.* (2016) LPELR-40615 (CA) 54, paras C-D.
164 *Skye Bank Plc v Emerson Njoku et al.* (2016) LPELR-40447 (CA) 20–22, paras A-E.
165 *Skye Bank Plc v Njoku* (n 164).
166 *Skye Bank Plc v Njoku* (n 164) 23–24; *Oparaocha v Obichere* (n 163) 59, paras B-F; *Romanus Ihejiobi et al. v Mrs Grace Chinyere Ihejiobi et al.* (2013) LPELR-21957(CA) 21–22, paras F-A.
167 See Or XV r 4 FREP Rules 2009 (n 110); *Skye Bank Plc v Njoku* (n 164); *Abayomi Fabunmi v Commissioner of Police Osun State et al.* (2011) LPELR-8776 (CA) 10–11, paras C-A.
168 *Okafor v Lagos State Government* (n 126) 28 paras D-F; *Abbas Abdullhi Machika v Katsina State House of Assembly & Attorney General of Katsina State* (2010) 10 NMLR 404 para 57; *Stanley KC Okonkwo v Anthony Ezeonu et al.* (2017) LPELR-42785 (CA) 10, paras D-F.
169 *Mr Michael Nzekwesi Anekwe et al. v Mr Michael Aniekwensi (alias Morocco) et al.* (2009) 10 NMLR 24 para 30; *Edwin Onuba v Innocent Onuba et al.* (2010) 11 NMLR 339 para 50; *Blessing Chibunna Okpalaibekwe v Ebere Cyrian Okpalaibekwe* (201e0) 12 NMLR (Pt II) 99 para 15.
170 *Fort Royal Homes Limited et alv Economic and Financial Crimes Commission et al.* (2017) LPELR-42807 (CA) 29, paras D-F; *HRH Eze Sir JE Ukaobasi v Berthram Ezimora et al.* (2016) LPELR-40174 (CA) 31, paras B-E; *Barr Eric Chukwuemeka Igweokolo v Mr Marvel Akpoyibo et al.* (2017) LPELR-41882 (CA) 13–14, paras F-C.
171 *Okafor v Lagos State Government* (n 126) 28–29, paras F-C; *Federal Republic of Nigeria v Abacha* (n 156) 118, paras F-G; *Adekunle v AG Ogun State* (n 117) 42–43, paras E-G. See ss131–132 Evidence Act 2011.
172 *Adekunle v AG Ogun State* (n 117) 23–24, paras B-C. See s134 Evidence Act 2011.
173 *Adekunle v AG Ogun State* (n 117) 23–24, paras B-C. See s135 Evidence Act 2011.
174 *Adekunle v AG Ogun State* (n 117) 23–24, paras B-C. See s135 Evidence Act 2011.
175 Ju-min Park and Minwoo Park, 'South Korean Court Hears Children's Climate Change Case Against Government' (24 April 2024) *Reuters* <www.msn.com/en-us/news/world/south-korean-court-hears-children-s-climate-change-case-against-government/ar-AA1nAA5M> accessed 26 April 2024.
176 Park and Park (n 175); *Centre for Oil Pollution Watch v Nigerian National Petroleum Corporation* (n 126).

## Bibliography

### *Books and book chapters*

Boyd DR, *The Environmental Rights Revolution: A Global Study of Constitutions, Human Rights, and the Environment* (UBCP 2012)

Etemire U, 'Climate Change Litigation in Nigeria: Challenges and Opportunities' in F Sindico and MM Mbengue (eds), *Comparative Climate Change Litigation: Beyond the Usual Suspects* (Springer 2021)

Fagbohun L, 'Introduction to Law: Nigerian Legal System' in DF Asaju (ed), *General Studies Book of Readings* (Vol. 2, LSUP 2006)

Frynas JG, *Oil in Nigeria: Conflict and Litigation Between Oil Companies and Village Communities* (Transaction Publishers 2000)

Nduka JK, Obumselu FO and Umedum NL, 'Crude Oil and Fractional Spillages Resulting from Exploration and Exploitation in Niger-Delta Region of Nigeria: A Review About the Environmental and Public Health Impact' in M Younes (ed), *Crude Oil Exploration in the World* (IntechOpen 2012)

Ndukwe OU, *Elements of Nigerian Environmental Laws* (University of Calabar Press 2000)

Owren C, 'Women and the Environment' in J Aragon and M Miller (eds), *Global Women's Issues: Women in the World Today, Extended Version* (GPA Publications 2012)

### *Cases*

*Abacha et al. v Fawehinmi* (2002) LPELR-14, Supreme Court of Nigeria (Nigeria)

*Abayomi Fabunmi v Commissioner of Police Osun State et al.* (2011) LPELR-8776, Court of Appeal (Nigeria)

*Abbas Abdullhi Machika v Katsina State House of Assembly & Attorney General of Katsina State* (2010) 10 NMLR, Supreme Court of Nigeria (Nigeria)

*Adefila et al. v His Royal Majesty-Oba James Adedapo Popoola (Oore of Otun-Ekiti) et al.* (2014) LPELR-22468, Court of Appeal (Nigeria)

*Adumu v The Comptroller of Prisons Federal Prisons Aba et al.* (2013) LPELR-22069, Court of Appeal (Nigeria)

*Akpobolokemi et al. v The Hon Captain Emmanuel Ihenacho et al.* (2016) LPELR-40563, Court of Appeal (Nigeria)

*Alhaji Aliyu N Salihu v Suleiman Umar Gana et al.* (2014) LPELR-23069, Court of Appeal (Nigeria)

*Alhaji Ibrahim Abdulhamid v Talal Akar et al.* (2006) SC 240/2001, Supreme Court of Nigeria (Nigeria)

*Alhaji Lawwani Zakari v Inspector-General of Police et al.* (2000) LPELR-6780, Court of Appeal (Nigeria)

*Alhaji Sheu Abdul Gafar v The Government of Kwara State et al.* (2007) LPELR-8073, Supreme Court of Nigeria (Nigeria)

*Alhaji Tsoho Dan Amale v Sokoto Local Government et al.* (2012) LPELR-7842, Supreme Court of Nigeria (Nigeria)

*Archbishop Anthony Olubunmi Okogie et al. v The Attorney-General of Lagos State* (1980) FNLR FCA/L/74/80, Supreme Court of Nigeria (Nigeria)

*Attorney-General of Lagos State v The Attorney-General of the Federation et al.* (2003) LPELR-620(SC), (2003) 919 NSCQR Vol 14 (Nigeria)

*Attorney-General of Lagos State v The Attorney-General of the Federation et al.* (2004) SC 70/2004, Supreme Court of Nigeria (Nigeria)

*Attorney-General of Ondo State v The Attorney-General of the Federation et al.* (2002) LPELR-623, Supreme Court of Nigeria (Nigeria)

*Barr Eric Chukwuemeka Igweokolo v Mr Marvel Akpoyibo et al.* (2017) LPELR-41882, Court of Appeal (Nigeria)
*Blessing Chibunna Okpalaibekwe v Ebere Cyrian Okpalaibekwe* (2010) 12 NMLR (Pt II) 99 (Nigeria)
*Central Bank of Nigeria v Chief Daniel Obameneke Okemuo et al.* (2016) LPELR-41405 (CA) (Nigeria)
*Centre for Oil Pollution Watch v Nigerian National Petroleum Corporation* (2019) 5 NWLR [PT.1666] P.518, Supreme Court of Nigeria (Nigeria)
*Dongtoe v Civil Service Commission Plateau State* (2001) LPELR-959, Supreme Court of Nigeria (Nigeria)
*Economic and Financial Crimes Commission v Ibrahim Suleiman et al.* (2016) LPELR-40790 (CA) (Nigeria)
*Edwin Onuba v Innocent Onuba et al.* (2010) 11 NMLR 339 (Nigeria)
*Emeka v Okoroafor et al.* (2017) LPELR-417, Court of Appeal (Nigeria)
*Endurance Odubu v Lieutenant Olorunduyilemi Stephen et al.* (2012) LPELR-19792, Court of Appeal (Nigeria)
*Eze (Dr) Emma Umez Eronini et al. v Lady CA Eronini et al.* (2013) LPELR-20651, Court of Appeal (Nigeria)
*Faith Okafor v Lagos State Government et al.* (2016) LPELR-41066, Court of Appeal (Nigeria)
*Federal Republic of Nigeria et al. v Alhaji Mohammed Sani Abacha et al.* (2014), Court of Appeal (Nigeria)
*Federal Republic of Nigeria et al. v Lord Chief Udensi Ifegwu (*2003) LPELR-3173, Supreme Court of Nigeria (Nigeria)
*Federal Road Safety Commission v Ofoegbu* (2014) LPELR-24229, Court of Appeal (Nigeria)
*Fort Royal Homes Limited et al. v Economic and Financial Crimes Commission et al.* (2017) LPELR-42807, Court of Appeal (Nigeria)
*Ganiat Amope Dilly v Inspector General of Police et al.* (2016) LPELR-41452, Court of Appeal (Nigeria)
*Hon Chris Azubuogu v Hon (Dr) Harry N Oranezi et al.* (2017) LPELR-42669, Supreme Court of Nigeria (Nigeria)
*Igwe et al. v Ezeanochie et al.* (2009) LPELR-11885, Court of Appeal (Nigeria)
*Ikechukwu Okpara et al. v Shell Petroleum Development Company of Nigeria Limited et al.* (2006) FHC/PHC/C5/518/2005
*Jack v University of Agriculture Makurdi* (2004) 102 NSCQR LPELR-1587, Supreme Court of Nigeria (Nigeria)
*James Olusegun Omoleye v Olaniran et al.* (2010) 10 NMLR 460–461, Supreme Court of Nigeria (Nigeria)
*Jonah Gbemre v Shell Petroleum Development Company Nigeria Ltd, Nigerian National Petroleum Corporation, Attorney General of the Federation* (2005) FHC/B/CS/53/05, Federal High Court (Nigeria)
*Kporharor et al. v Yedi et al.* (2017) LPELR-42418, Court of Appeal (Nigeria)
*Look Engine Parts Limited et al. v Ecobank Nigeria Plc et al.* (2014) LPELR-22522, Court of Appeal (Nigeria)
*Loveday v The Comptroller of Prisons Federal Prisons Aba et al.* (2013) LPELR-22072, Court of Appeal (Nigeria)
*Madam Ujueke Enemuo (Chairperson, Umuada-Umuchu) et al. v Alochukwu Ezeonyeka et al.* (2016) LPELR-40171, Court of Appeal (Nigeria)
*Mallam Nasir Ahmed El-Rufai v Senate of the National Assembly et al.* (2014) LPELR-231115, Court of Appeal (Nigeria)
*Mbadike et al. v Lagos International Trade Fair Complex Management Board et al.* (2017) LPELR-41968, Court of Appeal (Nigeria)

*Ngozi Chile Oparaocha et al. v Barr Emeka A Obichere et al.* (2016) LPELR-40615, Court of Appeal (Nigeria)
*Nigeria Union of Teachers et al. v Conference of Secondary School Tutors (CSST) et al.* (2005) LPELR-5953, Court of Appeal (Nigeria)
*Nigerian Navy et al. v Lionel Okon Garrick* (2005) LPELR-7555, Court of Appeal (Nigeria)
*Niyi Aluko et al. v Commissioner of Police et al.* (2016) LPELR-41342, Court of Appeal (Nigeria)
*Nzekwesi Anekwe et al. v Aniekwensi (alias Morocco) et al.* (2009) 10 NMLR 24 –
*Ogugu et al. v The State* (1994) 9 NWLR (Pt 366) 1, (1994) 10 Ilaw/sc.303/1990
*Okonkwo v Ezeonu et al.* (2017) LPELR-42785, Court of Appeal (Nigeria)
*Omo Oba Adenire Adetona et al. v Economic and Financial Crimes Commission et al.* (2017) LPELR-42369, Court of Appeal (Nigeria)
*Ovai Ekpe Okon v Ovai Bassey Enem Enyiefem et al.* (2016) LPELR-41168, Court of Appeal (Nigeria)
*Romanus Ihejiobi et al. v Chinyere Ihejiobi et al.* (2013) LPELR-21957, Court of Appeal (Nigeria)
*Rumugu Air and Space Nigeria Limited v Federal Airports Authority of Nigeria et al.* (2016) LPELR-41506, Court of Appeal (Nigeria)
*Sea trucks Nigeria Limited v Panya Anigboro* (2001) 137–138 NSCQLR Vol 5
*Silas Jumbo Essien v Chief Akpan Inyang et al.* (2011) LPELR-4125, Court of Appeal (Nigeria)
*Skye Bank Plc v Emerson Njoku et al.* (2016) LPELR-40447, Court of Appeal (Nigeria)
*Solomon Adekunle v Attorney-General of Ogun State* (2014) LPELR-22569 (CA) (Nigeria)
*Solomon Ohakosim v Commissioner of Police Imo State et al.* (2009) LPELR-8874 (CA) (Nigeria)
*Ukaobasi v Berthram Ezimora et al.* (2016) LPELR-40174, Court of Appeal (Nigeria)
*University of Ilorin et al. v Idowu Oluwadare* (2006) 28–29 NSCQR Vol 27
*Verein Klimaseniorinnen Schweiz et al. v Switzerland* (2024) ECHR (Application no. 53600/20)
*Ziakade Patrick Akpobolokemi et al. v The Hon Captain Emmanuel Ihenacho et al.* (2016) LPELR-40563 (CA)

## *Journal articles*

Aghalino SO and Eyinla B, 'Oil Exploration and Marine Pollution: Evidence from the Niger Delta, Nigeria' (2009) 28 *Journal of Human Ecology* 178 <https://doi.org/10.1080/09709274.2009.11906236> accessed 15 September 2024
Aigbokhaevbo V and Aniekwu N, 'Environmental Abuses in Nigeria: Implications for Reproductive Health' (2013) 19(1) *Annual Survey of International & Comparative Law* 233 <https://digitalcommons.law.ggu.edu/annlsurvey/vol19/iss1/11> accessed 15 September 2024
Anejionu OCD, Ahiarammunnah PAN and CJ Nri-Ezedi, 'Hydrocarbon Pollution in the Niger Delta: Geographies of Impacts and Appraisal of Lapses in Extant Legal Framework' (2015) 45(C) *Resource Policy Eslevier* 65 <https://doi.org/10.1016/j.resourpol.2015.03.012> accessed 15 September 2024
Aroh KN, Ubong IU, Chibuogwu E and Harry IM, 'Oil Spill Incidents and Pipeline Vandalisation in Nigeria; Impact on Public Health and Negation to Attainment of Millennium Development Goal: The Ishiagu Example' (2010) 19(1) *Disaster Prevention and Management An International Journal* 70 <http://dx.doi.org/10.1108/09653561011022153> accessed 15 September 2024
Daniel IE and Nna PJ, 'Total Petroleum Hydrocarbon Concentration in Surface Water of Cross River Estuary, Niger Delta, Nigeria' (2016) 1(2) *Asian Journal of Environment & Ecology* 1 <https://doi.org/10.9734/AJEE/2016/31102> accessed 15 September 2024

De Carvalho DW and da Rosa RSM, 'Climate Constitutionalism as a Foundation for Climate Litigation in Latin America' (2024) 16(1) *Journal of Human Rights Practice* 71 <https://doi.org/10.1093/jhuman/huad055> accessed 7 September 2024

D'Eaubonne F, 'Feminism-Ecology: Revolution or Mutation?' (1999) 4(2) *Ethics and the Environment* 175 <https://www.jstor.org/stable/40338975> accessed 15 September 2024

Dung EJ, Bombom LS and Agusomu TD, 'The Effects of Gas Flaring on Crops in the Niger Delta, Nigeria' (2008) 73(4) *GeoJournal* 297 <http://dx.doi.org/10.1007/s10708-008-9207-z> accessed 15 September 2024

Efe SI, 'Spatial Variation of Acid Rain and Its Ecological Effect in Nigeria' 2 *COLERM Proceedings* <https://publications.funaab.edu.ng/index.php/COLERM/article/view/290> accessed 15 September 2024

Egbe RE and Thompson D, 'Environmental Challenges of Oil Spillage for Families in Oil Producing Communities of the Niger Delta Region' (2010) 13 *JHER* 24 <https://www.researchgate.net/publication/290786128_Environmental_Challenges_of_Oil_Spillage_for_Families_in_Oil_Producing_Communities_of_the_Niger_Delta_Region> accessed 15 September 2024

Ekpoh IJ and Obia AE, 'The Role of Gas Flaring in the Rapid Corrosion of Zinc Roofs in the Niger Delta Region of Nigeria' (2010) 30(4) *The Environmentalist* 347 <http://dx.doi.org/10.1007/s10669-010-9292-7> accessed 14 September 2024

Eneh OC, 'Crippling Poverty Amidst Corporate Social Actions: A Critique of Peripheral Corporate Community Involvement in the Niger Delta Region of Nigeria' (2011) 1(1) *Asian Journal of Rural Development* 1 <https://doi.org/10.3923/ajrd.2011.1.20> accessed 15 September 2024

Fawole OG, Cai XM and MacKenzie AR, 'Gas Flaring and Resultant Air Pollution: A Review Focusing on Black Carbon' (2016) 216 *Environmental Pollution* 182 <https://doi.org/10.1016/j.envpol.2016.05.075> accessed 14 September 2024

Fentiman A and Zabbey N, 'Environmental Degradation and Cultural Erosion in Ogoniland: A Case Study of the Oil Spills in Bodo' (2015) 2(4) *The Extractive Industries and Society* 615 <http://dx.doi.org/10.1016/j.exis.2015.05.008> accessed 15 September 2024

Gates BT, 'A Root of Ecofeminism: Ecoféminisme' (1996) 3(1) *Interdisciplinary Studies in Literature and Environment* 7 <https://doi.org/10.1093/isle/3.1.7> accessed 15 September 2024

Giwa SO, Adama OO and Akinyemi OO, 'Baseline Black Carbon Emissions for Gas Flaring in the Niger Delta Region of Nigeria' (2014) 20 *Journal of Natural Gas Science and Engineering* 373 <https://ui.adsabs.harvard.edu/link_gateway/2014JNGSE.20.373G/https://doi.org/10.1016/j.jngse.2014.07.026> accessed 15 September 2024

Ite AE, Ibok UJ, Ite MU and Petters SW, 'Petroleum Exploration and Production: Past and Present Environmental Issues in the Nigeria's Niger Delta' (2013) 1(4) *AJEP* 78 <https://doi.org/10.12691/env-1-4-2> accessed 14 September 2024

Kadafa AA, 'Oil Exploration and Spillage in the Niger Delta of Nigeria' (2012) 2(3) *CER* 38 <https://www.iiste.org/Journals/index.php/CER/article/view/1789/1868> accessed 14 September 2024

Luers AL, 'The Surface of Vulnerability: An Analytical Framework for Examining Environmental Change' (2005) 15(3) *Global Environmental Change* 214 <http://dx.doi.org/10.1016/j.gloenvcha.2005.04.003> accessed 14 September 2024

Murcott MJ and Vinti C, 'The Judge-Made "Duty" to Consider Climate Change in South Africa' (2024) 16(1) *Journal of Human Rights Practice* 125 <https://doi.org/10.1093/jhuman/huad069> accessed 7 September 2024

Nduka JKC, Constance E and Obiakor E, 'Selective Bioaccumulation of Metals by Different Parts of Some Fish Species from Crude Oil Polluted Water' (2006) 77(6) *BECT* 846 <https://doi.org/10.1007/s00128-006-1221-6> accessed 15 September 2024

Nwachukwu AN and Osuagwu JC, 'Effects of Oil Spillage on Groundwater Quality in Nigeria' (2014) 3(6) *Journal of Engineering Research* 271 <https://www.researchgate.net/

publication/330524890_Effects_of_Oil_Spillage_on_Groundwater_Quality_In_Nigeria> accessed 15 September 2024

Okoko E, Robson E, Jarosz L and Laurie N, 'Women and Environmental Change in the Niger Delta, Nigeria: Evidence from Ibeno' (1999) 6(4) *Gender, Place and Culture* 373 <https://www.proquest.com/scholarly-journals/women-environmental-change-niger-delta-nigeria/docview/211122764/se-2?accountid=14717> accessed 15 September 2024

Okorodudu FO, Okorodudu PO and Irikefe EK, 'A Model of Petroleum Pipeline Spillage Detection System for Use in the Niger Delta Region of Nigeria' (2016) 4 *IJRG* 1 <https://ssrn.com/abstract=4227171> accessed 15 September 2024

Olusegun OO and Oyelade OS, 'Access to Justice for Nigerian Women: A Veritable Tool to Achieving Sustainable Development' (2022) 22(1) *International Journal of Discrimination and the Law* 4 <https://doi.org/10.1177/13582291211043418> accessed 15 September 2024

Omodanisi EO, Eludoyin AO and Salami AT, 'A Multi-Perspective View of the Effects of a Pipeline Explosion in Nigeria' (2014) 7 *International Journal of Disaster Risk Reduction* 68 <https://doi.org/10.1016/j.ijdrr.2013.11.002> accessed 15 September 2024

Onwuka EC, 'Oil Extraction, Environmental Degradation and Poverty in the Niger Delta Region of Nigeria: A Viewpoint' (2005) 62(6) *IJES* 655 <http://dx.doi.org/10.1080/00207230500040823> accessed 15 September 2024

Onwurah INE, Ogugua V and Ochonogor Alfred, ''Crude Oil Spills in the Environment, Effects and Some Innovative Clean-Up Biotechnologies' (2007) 1(4) *IJER* 307 <https://www.researchgate.net/publication/27794350_Crude_Oils_Spills_in_the_Environment_Effects_and_Some_Innovative_Clean-Up_Biotechnologies> accessed 15 September 2024

Onwutuebe CJ, 'Patriarchy and Women Vulnerability to Adverse Climate Change in Nigeria' (2019) 9(1) *Sage Open* <https://doi.org/10.1177/2158244019825914> accessed 14 September 2024

Onyimadu CO, 'Climate Change Adaptation and Wellbeing Among Smallholder Women Farmers in Gwagwalada and Kokona, Nigeria' (2023) 153 *Futures* 103238 <https://doi.org/10.1016/j.futures.2023.103238> accessed 15 September 2024

Orji UJ, 'Right to a Clean Environment: Some Reflections' (2012) 42(4–5) *EPL* 285

Osuide SO, 'Environmental Pollution in Nigeria' (1990) 12(1) *Habitat International* 5 <https://www.ecolex.org/details/literature/environmental-pollution-in-nigeria-ana-044902/> accessed 15 September 2024

Pona HT, Xiaoli D, Ayantobo OO and Tetteh ND, 'Environmental Health Situation in Nigeria: Current Status and Future Needs' (2021) 7(3) *Heliyon* <https://doi.org/10.1016/j.heliyon.2021.e06330> accessed 14 September 2024

Seiyaboh EI and Izah SC, 'A Review of impacts of Gas Flaring on Vegetation and Water Resources in the Niger Delta Region of Nigeria' (2017) 2(4) *IJEEE* 48 <https://doi.org/10.11648/j.ijeee.20170204.11> accessed 15 September 2024

Sodimu AI, Yilwa VM and Onwumere GB, 'The Impact of Gas Flaring from the Kaduna Refinery and Petrochemical Industry (KRPC) on Plant Diversity in Kaduna Northern Guinea Savanna Eco-Region of Nigeria' (2017) 69 *WSN* 168 <https://worldscientificnews.com/the-impact-of-gas-flaring-from-the-kaduna-refinery-and-petrochemical-industry-krpc-on-plant-diversity-in-kaduna-northern-guinea-savanna-eco-region-of-nigeria/> accessed 15 September 2024

Solomon G, Nwaokocha C, Kuye S and Adama KO, 'Gas Flaring Attendant Impacts of Criteria and Particulate Pollutants: A Case for Niger Delta Region of Nigeria' (2017) 31(3) *JKSU* 209 <http://dx.doi.org/10.1016/j.jksues.2017.04.003> accessed 14 September 2024

Turner MS, 'Climate Change Hazards + Social Vulnerability = A Recipe for Disaster' (2022) 46(2) *Generations: Journal of the American Society on Aging* 1 <https://www.jstor.org/stable/48697096> accessed 14 September 2024

Zabbey N, Sam K and Onyebuchi AT, 'Remediation of Contaminated Lands in the Niger Delta, Nigeria: Prospects and Challenges' (2017) 15 *STE* 952 <https://doi.org/10.1016/j.scitotenv.2017.02.075> accessed 15 September 2024

## Legislation

Climate Change Act 2021
Constitution of the Federal Republic of Nigeria, Fundamental Rights (Enforcement Procedure) Rules 2009 under Chapter IV of the Constitution
Evidence Act 2011
National Environmental Standards and Regulations Enforcement Agency (Establishment) Act 2007 CAP 164 LFN 2007

## Online sources

'25 million Nigerian at High Risk of Food Insecurity in 2023' (*FOA of the UN*, 16 January 2023) <www.fao.org/nigeria/news/detail-events/en/c/1630260/> accessed 26 April 2024
'Access to Electricity (% of Population) – Nigeria' (*World Bank Group*, 2022) <https://data.worldbank.org/indicator/EG.ELC.ACCS.ZS?locations=NG> accessed 26 April 2024
Ajayi JFA and Falola TO, 'Nigeria' (*Britannica*, 15 September 2024) <www.britannica.com/place/Nigeria> accessed 26 April 2024
'Climate Change Exacerbates Violence Against Women and Girls' (*OHCHR*, 12 July 2022) <www.ohchr.org/en/stories/2022/07/climate-change-exacerbates-violence-against-women-and-girls> accessed 26 April 2024
'Closing the Gap, Boosting Ambition: Investing in Women is Key to Climate Action' (*United Nations Climate Change*, 8 March 2024) <https://unfccc.int/news/closing-the-gap-boosting-ambition-investing-in-women-is-key-to-climate-action> accessed 17 April 2024
Ekele J, 'Nigeria Climate Change Act: CSDevNet, Non-State Actors Strategise on Implementation' (*CSDevNet*) <https://csdevnet.org/nigeria-climate-change-act-csdevnet-non-state-actors-strategise-on-implementation/> accessed 26 April 2024
'Explainer: How Gender Inequality and Climate Change are Interconnected' (*United Nations Women*, 28 February 2022) <www.unwomen.org/en/news-stories/explainer/2022/02/explainer-how-gender-inequality-and-climate-change-are-interconnected> accessed 26 April 2024
FederalGovernment of Nigeria, 'Nigeria's Nationally Determined Contribution – 2021 Update' <www4.unfccc.int/sites/NDCStaging/pages/Party.aspx?party=NGA> accessed 26 April 2024
'FiveReasons Why Climate Action Needs Women' (*UN Climate Change News*, 8 March 2023) <https://unfccc.int/news/five-reasons-why-climate-action-needs-women> accessed 26 April 2024
Ladan MT, 'A Review of Nigeria's 2021 Climate Change Act: Potential for Increased Climate Litigation' (*IUCN*, 28 March 2022) <www.iucn.org/news/commission-environmental-economic-and-social-policy/202203/a-review-nigerias-2021-climate-change-act-potential-increased-climate-litigation> accessed 26 April 2024
Miles K, 'Ecofeminism: Sociology and Environmentalism' (*Encyclopedia Britannica*, 9 October 2018) <www.britannica.com/topic/ecofeminism> accessed 26 April 2024
Mouawad J, 'Shell to Pay $15.5 Million to Settle Nigerian Case' (*The New York Times*, 8 June 2009) <www.nytimes.com/2009/06/09/business/global/09shell.html?_r=2&ref=global> accessed 26 April 2024

Nathaniel S, 'President Buhari Signs Climate Change, AMCON Bills into Law' (*Channeltv*, 18 November 2021) <www.channelstv.com/2021/11/18/president-buhari-signs-climate-change-amcon-amendment-bills-into-law/> accessed 26 April 2024

'Nigeria Population 2023' (*World Population Review, Live*) <https://worldpopulationreview.com/countries/nigeria-population> accessed 26 April 2024

Obani P, 'Women Battle When Trying to Take Climate Change Cases to Court – South Africa and Nigeria Study Shows' (*The Conversation*, 7 March 2024) <https://theconversation.com/women-battle-when-trying-to-take-climate-change-cases-to-court-south-africa-and-nigeria-study-shows-why-224784> accessed 26 April 2024

'Outcome Appeal Against Shell: Victory for the Environment and the Nigerian People – Friends of the Earth Netherlands' (*Friends of the Earth International*, 18 December 2015) <www.foei.org/news/outcome-appeal-shell-victory-environment-nigerian-people-friends-earth-netherlands> accessed 26 April 2024

Park J and Park M, 'South Korean Court Hears Children's Climate Change Case Against Government' (*Reuters*, 24 April 2024) <https://www.reuters.com/business/environment/south-korean-court-hears-childrens-climate-change-case-against-government-2024-04-23/> accessed 26 April 2024

'People Who are Vulnerable to Climate Change: Climate Change and Human Health' (*National Institute of Environmental Health Sciences*, 30 August 2022) <www.niehs.nih.gov/research/programs/climatechange/health_impacts/vulnerable_people> accessed 26 April 2024

'Shell Lawsuit (Re Oil Spills & Bodo Community in Nigeria)' (*Business and Human Rights Resource Centre*) <http://business-humanrights.org/en/shell-lawsuit-re-oil-spills-bodo-community-in-nigeria> accessed 30 September 2018

Ugwu E, 'FG Urged to Investigate Oil Spill in Abia Community' (*This Day*, 22 June 2016) <www.thisdaylive.com/index.php/2016/06/22/fg-urged-to-investigate-oil-spill-in-abia-community/> accessed 26 April 2024

UNEnvironment Programme, 'António Guterres – Emissions Gap Report 2022 Message' (27 October 2022) <https://www.youtube.com/watch?v=mCkUcJUuCPE&ab_channel=UNEnvironmentProgramme> accessed 26 April 2024

'UN Women and the World Bank Unveil New Data Analysis on Women and Poverty' (*UN Women*, 9 November 2017) <www.unwomen.org/en/news/stories/2017/11/news-un-women-and-the-world-bank-unveil-new-data-analysis-on-women-and-poverty> accessed 26 April 2024

Usigbe L, 'Silencing the Guns: Drying Lake Chad Basin Gives Rise to Crisis' (*Africa Renewal*, 24 December 2019) <www.un.org/africarenewal/magazine/december-2019-march-2020/drying-lake-chad-basin-gives-rise-crisis> accessed 26 April 2024

Vida J, 'Niger Delta Communities to Sue Shell in Londong for Oil Spill Compensation' (*The Guardian*, 7 January 2024) <www.theguardian.com/environment/2015/jan/07/niger-delta-communities-to-sue-shell-in-london-for-oil-spill-compensation> accessed 26 April 2024

'Why Women are Key to Climate Action' (*United Nations Climate Action*) <www.un.org/en/climatechange/science/climate-issues/women> accessed 17 April 2024

'WorldPopulation Dashboard Nigeria' (*UN Population Fund*) <www.unfpa.org/data/world-population/NG> accessed 26 April 2024

## *Policies*

Federal Ministry of Agriculture and Rural Development, 'National Agricultural Technology and Innovation Policy (NATIP0 2022–2027' (2022) <https://agriculture.gov.ng/wp-content/uploads/2024/06/National-Agricultural-Technology-and-Innovation-Policy-NATIP-2022-2027.pdf> accessed 14 September 2024

Federal Ministry of Environment Department of Climate Change, 'National Climate Change Policy for Nigeria 2021–2030' (2021) <https://faolex.fao.org/docs/pdf/NIG209876.pdf> accessed 14 September 2024

FederalRepublic of Nigeria, 'National Security Strategy' (2019) <https://nctc.gov.ng/storage/2024/01/NSS–2019.pdf> accessed 26 April 2024

Federal Republic of Nigeria, 'National Action Plan on Gender and Climate Change for Nigeria' (2020) <https://climatechange.gov.ng/wp-content/uploads/2020/09/climate-change-and-gender-action-plan.pdf> accessed 26 April 2024

## *Reports*

'2019 Poverty and Inequality in Nigeria: Executive Summary' (*National Bureau of Statistics*, 2019) <https://nigerianstat.gov.ng/elibrary/read/1092> accessed 26 April 2024

African Organization of Supreme Audit Institutions, 'Joint Environmental Audit on the Drying up of Lake Chad: Joint Audit Report' (*Deutsche Gesellschaft für Internationale Zusammenarbeit (GIZ) GmbH*, May 2015) <https://www.giz.de/de/downloads/giz2015-en-joint-environmental-audit-report-lake-chad.pdf> accessed 14 September 2024

Boyd DR, 'The Status of Constitutional Protection for the Environment in other Nations' (*David Suzuki Foundation*, 2013) <https://davidsuzuki.org/wp-content/uploads/2013/11/status-constitutional-protection-environment-other-nations-SUMMARY.pdf> accessed 26 April 2024

'EnvironmentalAssessment of Ogoniland' (*UNEP*, 2011) <https://www.unep.org/resources/report/environmental-assessment-ogoniland#:~:text=A%20major%20new%20independent%20scientific,than%20many%20may%20have%20supposed> accessed 15 September 2024

'Environmental Rights Report' (*Earthjustice*, 2007) <https://earthjustice.org/library/references/2007-environmental-rights-report.pdf> accessed 15 September 2024

'Executive Board of the UN Development Programme, the UN Population Fund and the UN Office for Project Services, 'Decisions Adopted by the Executive Board in 2023' (*The World Bank*, 2023) <https://www.unfpa.org/sites/default/files/board-documents/main-document/ENG_Decisions%20adopted%20by%20the%20Executive%20Board%20during%202023.pdf> accessed 14 September 2024

FMWR, Government of Nigeria, NBS and UNICEF, 'Water, Sanitation and Hygiene: National Outcome Routine Mapping (WASH NORM) 2019: A Report of Findings' (November 2020) <www.unicef.org/nigeria/media/3576/file/WASH%20NORM%20Report%202019.pdf> accessed 26 April 2024

IPCC, 'Summary for Policymakers in Climate Change 2022 – Impacts, Adaptation and Vulnerability: Working Group II Contribution to the Sixth Assessment Report of the Intergovernmental Panel on Climate Change' in HO Pörtner et al. (eds), (2022) <https://www.ipcc.ch/report/ar6/wg2/downloads/report/IPCC_AR6_WGII_FullReport.pdf> accessed 21 November 2024

IPCC, 'Summary for Policymakers in Climate Change 2023: Synthesis Report, Contribution of Working Groups I, II and III to the Sixth Assessment Report of the Intergovernmental Panel on Climate Change' in Core Writing Team, H Lee and J Romero (eds), (2023) <https://www.ipcc.ch/report/ar6/syr/downloads/report/IPCC_AR6_SYR_FullVolume.pdf> accessed 21 November 2024

Lain JW and Vishwanath T, 'A Better Future for all Nigerians: Nigeria Poverty Assessment 2022' (Vol. 1, *World Bank*, 2022)

Manby B, 'The Price of Oil: Corporate Responsibility and Human Rights Violations in Nigeria's Oil Producing Communities' (*HRW*, 1999) <https://www.hrw.org/legacy/reports/1999/nigeria/nigeria0199.pdf> accessed 15 September 2024

Osman-Elasha B, 'Women . . . In The Shadow of Climate Change' (2009) 46 *United Nations Chronicles Special Climate Change Issue* <www.un.org/en/chronicle/article/womenin-shadow-climate-change> accessed 26 April 2024

Takwa ZS, 'Addressing the Climate Change Insecurity Challenge in Nigeria and the Lake Chad Basin' (*UNDP*, 2020) <www.undp.org/sites/g/files/zskgke326/files/migration/oslo_governance_centre/89e8d11e6b388f1174e625ebf8790f2c84c7bd0cead6164b91887972950117e9.pdf> accessed 26 April 2024

'UNDP Project Document: Niger Delta Biodiversity Project' (*UNDP and GEP*, 2012) <https://info.undp.org/docs/pdc/Documents/NGA/Niger%20Delta%20Biodiversity_Prodoc.pdf> accessed 15 September 2024

UNFCCC Secretariat, 'Dimensions and Examples of the Gender-Differentiated Impacts of Climate Change, the Role of Women as Agents of Change and Opportunities for Women: Synthesis Report by the Secretariat' (June 2022) <https://unfccc.int/sites/default/files/resource/sbi2022_07.pdf> accessed 26 April 2024

'Women and the Environment' (*UNEP*, 2004) <https://www.unep.org/resources/report/women-and-environment> accessed 14 September 2024

## *Thesis*

Maduekwe NUC, 'Achieving Environmental Sustainability in Nigeria's Extractive Industry: How Viable is a Human Rights Approach to Environmental Protection?' (PhD Thesis, University of Hull 2018)

## *Treaties*

African Charter on Human and Peoples' Rights (adopted 27 June 1981, entered into force 21 October 1986) (1982) 21 ILM 58

African Charter on Human and Peoples' Rights (Ratification and Enforcement) Act 1983 CAP 10 LFN 1990

## *Working paper*

Frank E, 'Human Vulnerability and Food Security: Policy Implications' (2003) *Forum for Food Security in Southern Africa* <https://odi.org/en/publications/human-vulnerability-and-food-insecurity-policy-implications/> accessed 26 April 2024

## *Other*

Boyd DR, 'The Effectiveness of Constitutional Environmental Rights' (*Yale/UNITAR Workshop on Rights in Environmental Governance, New Haven*, 26–27 April 2013) 1 <https://environment.yale.edu/gem/events/yaleunitar-workshop-on-rights-in-environmental-governance/#gsc.tab=0> accessed 26 April 2024

Earthworks, 'Think Again – Oil and Gas Air Pollution Fact Sheet' [2005] <https://earthworks.org/cms/assets/uploads/archive/files/publications/Airpollution.pdf> accessed 26 April 2024

Egede E, 'Human Rights and the Environment: Is There a Legally Enforceable Right to a Clean and Healthy Environment for the "Peoples" of the Niger Delta Under the Framework of the 1999 Constitution of Nigeria?' (2007) 19 *SLJIL* 51

Oyaniran T, 'Current State of Nigeria Agriculture and Agribusiness Sector' (*Paper Presented at the AfCFTA Workshop*, September 2020) <www.pwc.com/ng/en/assets/pdf/afcfta-agribusiness-current-state-nigeria-agriculture-sector.pdf> assessed 26 June 2023

UNGA, 'The Human Right to a Clean, Healthy and Sustainable Environment' A/RES/76/300 (28 July 2022)

Chapter 9

# A litigation strategy for vulnerable communities pursuing climate litigation

## The Indian iteration of the precautionary principle and the reversal of the burden of proof

*Kanika Jamwal*

### Introduction

This chapter begins with a story of a small river that flows through a water-scarce district in India's north-western province of Rajasthan.[1] The river supports agriculture, the primary economic activity in the 72 villages located in the river basin. Once full of water, the river had been gradually drying due to erratic, declining rainfall.[2] Consequently, the villages, largely populated by socio-economically marginalised groups,[3] witnessed a decline in agricultural productivity. This resulted in outward migration, an increase in pastoralism, and over-exploitation of groundwater. Residents attributed the drying of the river to warming temperatures and declining rainfall. This experience prompted a question for me: If the community were to litigate the drying of the river as a climate harm, would they be able to prove such a claim scientifically?

The sad reality is that the community's prospects of success are low because, like other forms of environmental litigation, climate litigation involves complex questions of science and law. In particular, failure-to-mitigate litigation (mitigation litigation) is riddled with such questions.[4] In mitigation litigation, the plaintiff must prove that an injury or risk of injury arises from global climate change and that the defendant's (in)action contributes to climate change.[5] However, this is inherently difficult to demonstrate, given the multiplicity of contributing factors and the non-linearity of causation. This is known as the problem of proof (the proof problem).[6] While there have been significant developments in attribution science, specific harms of climate change, especially in the Global South, have been relatively difficult to prove.[7] Climate litigants often have to grapple with scientific uncertainty.

Access to specialist scientific knowledge and adequate financial resources can be key to initiating and pursuing climate litigation.[8] Reportedly, the inadequate availability of these resources is a barrier to successful litigation for climate litigants in the Global South.[9] The lack of resources is particularly challenging when litigants belong to socially vulnerable communities or are protecting the interests of other

DOI: 10.4324/9781003470632-12

vulnerable entities, like the non-human environment. Given these challenges, this chapter provides a doctrinal response to these structural barriers climate litigants in the Global South face. It proposes a litigation strategy that employs the Indian Supreme Court's iteration of the precautionary principle (Indian iteration). While the strategy is useful for climate litigants in general, it is particularly instrumental for litigants from vulnerable communities and for those protecting the interests of the non-human environment.

Peel argues that the precautionary principle is useful in addressing the proof problem by allowing regulatory action even when there is scientific uncertainty.[10] She notes that 'the concept of precaution seeks to guide the development and application of international environmental law where there is scientific uncertainty', thus indicating that scientific uncertainty is at the core of all iterations of the principle.[11] However, that regulatory action can occur in the face of scientific uncertainty does not ease structural barriers to litigating climate mitigation and adaptation issues. While the precautionary principle lowers the standard of proof required to prove harm, the plaintiff continues to bear the burden of proving scientific uncertainty. Access to specialist scientific knowledge and adequate financial resources remains critical to discharging this burden. To address the proof problem, the Indian iteration goes a step further. It does this by unequivocally and unconditionally reversing the burden of proof.[12] This approach has been termed as the 'special burden of proof in environmental cases' by the Indian Supreme Court.[13] To satisfy this special burden of proof, the plaintiff is only required to establish scientific uncertainty and show a 'justified concern' or threat of harm. Once that is accomplished, the burden of proof is reversed. Accordingly, by relieving the plaintiff from shouldering the evidentiary burden, the Indian iteration eases structural barriers.

A few caveats to this argument must be explained pre-emptively. First, the Indian iteration of the principle suffers from inconsistent application. The judiciary has repeatedly conflated the precautionary principle with the principle of prevention, applying the former even when there is no scientific uncertainty. As a result, subordinate courts have conditioned their application to the provision of robust scientific evidence.[14] If this becomes the norm, it could defeat the utility of the Indian iteration of the principle for climate litigation.

Second, the chapter suggests that until attribution science and access to it improves,[15] a precautionary principle–driven strategy should be adopted. In other words, in cases where scientific evidence is inaccessible, unavailable, inadequate, or inconclusive, this strategy should be adopted. As explained below, such issues are commonplace in mitigation litigation initiated in the Global South and by vulnerable communities. Lastly, the structural barriers to litigating climate change are not specific to climate litigation or India. A lack of specialist scientific knowledge and adequate financial resources has been identified as the most widespread problem plaguing environmental litigation more generally in the Global South.[16] Therefore, the litigation strategy proposed in this chapter has relevance beyond India.

The chapter continues as follows: First, it outlines structural barriers faced by climate litigants in the Global South. Using vulnerability theory, it explains how these barriers are particularly significant for certain communities due to their pre-existing capacity constraints. Second, it briefly discusses existing institutional responses. Third, since the Indian iteration of the principle emerges from international law, the chapter discusses the internationally accepted iteration of the precautionary principle. It sheds light on different courts' iterations of the principle and their limited utility in addressing structural barriers. Fourth, it presents the central argument that the Indian iteration of the precautionary principle offers a useful litigation strategy for climate litigants. It explains the iteration and its utility in easing barriers. However, it acknowledges that this iteration suffers from an inconsistent judicial application. Finally, the chapter outlines the limitations of the argument and thereafter concludes.

## Structural barriers faced by climate litigants in Global South: a vulnerability framing

Environmental litigants in the Global South face several structural challenges that impede their access to justice.[17] Of these challenges, limited access to technical expertise and financial resources is particularly colossal in climate litigation.[18] Climate litigation suffers from a pre-existing problem, that is to say, the proof problem.[19]

Briefly, the proof problem requires the plaintiff to prove that the impugned harm is due to climate change, to which the defendant's emissions have contributed.[20] Proving the former requires access to impact attribution science, and the latter requires access to source attribution science. However, establishing this chain of causation can be the most difficult challenge faced by plaintiffs in climate litigation.[21] This challenge stems from gaps or uncertainties in climate science, particularly source attribution science.[22] Further, impact attribution studies have focused on ascertaining global or regional impacts of climate change instead of local impacts.[23] Moreover, generally, the Global South has received less scholarly attention from attribution scientists and suffers from inadequate studies.[24]

The lack of scientific evidence to prove particular harm is an obstacle to successful climate litigation in the Global South.[25] In fact, such a lack of evidence could be exploited by the defendants in denying liability for harm.[26] Access to specialist scientific knowledge and financial resources is crucial to addressing the proof problem.

The lack of specialist scientific knowledge and financial resources is particularly challenging for socially marginalised communities. First, social identities such as gender, class, caste, indigeneity, race, and age influence whether individuals face disproportionate impacts of climate change.[27] Thus, women, children, the elderly, and Indigenous peoples are often more vulnerable to climate change than others. In its latest guidance on the concept of climate risk,[28] the Intergovernmental Panel on Climate Change (IPCC) recognises that potential climate risk varies based on the vulnerability of the affected person.[29] Yet despite their disproportionate vulnerability, scientific knowledge of the specific impacts of climate change on vulnerable communities is inadequate.[30] Scientific studies have focused on human vulnerability to climate change in general, as opposed to studying the specific impacts of climate change on uniquely vulnerable groups, who experience intersectional injustice.[31] Vulnerable communities often sit at the intersection of social and economic injustice, further amplifying their marginalisation.[32] The Global Climate Litigation Report[33] notes that in these pre-existing circumstances of socio-economic marginalisation, a lack of adequate financial resources and scientific knowledge is a particularly high barrier to successful litigation.[34] Thus, while litigants in the Global South generally face these barriers, litigants from vulnerable communities are at a greater disadvantage.

Another entity disproportionately vulnerable to climate change is the non-human environment, which includes non-human animals, rivers, forests, and other life on Earth.[35] The IPCC echoes this by defining 'risk' as including potential adverse impacts on ecological systems and highlighting that 'risk management' must address the non-human environment too.[36] Despite this, non-human interests are perhaps the least represented in mainstream climate change discourse today.[37] Unsurprisingly, the impacts of climate change on the non-human environment have not been fully accounted for in attribution studies.[38] The limited available studies have focused primarily on impacts on biodiversity,[39] with 'little focus . . . given to individual animals and their flourishing or well-being'.[40] Accordingly, this may impede climate litigation for protecting more-than-human interests.

To ease the structural barriers discussed here, this chapter suggests a doctrinal response,[41] namely, the Indian iteration of the precautionary principle. This iteration is built upon the principle's international iterations and could be implemented to mitigate the barriers to litigating climate harms related to the 'proof problem'. A prerequisite to fully appreciating the Indian iteration of the principle is understanding the international iteration. The following section discusses the international iteration of the precautionary principle and its utility for litigants in the Global South.

## Internationally accepted iteration and its limited utility for climate litigants from vulnerable communities in the Global South

One of the most contested principles of environmental law, the precautionary principle, is anchored in several international legal instruments, including the Rio Declaration[42] and the United Nations Framework Convention on Climate Change (UNFCCC).[43] The most widely accepted iteration is contained in the Rio Declaration, which states:[44]

> In order to protect the environment, the precautionary approach shall be widely applied by States according to their capabilities. Where there are threats of serious or irreversible damage, lack of full scientific certainty shall not be used as a reason for postponing cost-effective measures to prevent environmental degradation.[45]

Though the principle has different iterations,[46] one element is common to all – that is, allowing regulatory measures to prevent potential harm to the environment and human health, even when scientific evidence regarding the harm is uncertain.[47] While the level of harm and the nature of risk vary in different iterations,[48] the principle allows regulatory action to preclude the activity if there is prevailing scientific uncertainty.

Drawing upon this common element, Peel and Omuko argue that the principle may be applied to deal with the proof problem in climate litigation.[49] Its application allows courts to lower the evidentiary standards concerning proof of harm.[50] Thus, where attribution science cannot provide conclusive evidence of climate harm, applying the precautionary principle will allow courts to regulate the impugned activity.

Arguably, for climate litigants in the Global South, this approach only alleviates part of the proof problem. That is, it lowers the standard of proof required by accepting proof that is not scientifically certain.[51] *However, the litigants still bear the burden of proving the threat and need to support it with a certain level of scientific evidence.*[52] In other words, they must prove the threat of harm through scientific evidence. Thus, the evidentiary burden still rests with the plaintiff. As noted earlier in the chapter, particularly in climate litigation, such evidence may not always be readily accessible or easily comprehensible. Accessing and comprehending it may require both financial resources and technical expertise. In such cases, the structural barriers faced by vulnerable communities in the Global South limit the utility of the internationally accepted iteration of the precautionary principle.

A few of the earlier iterations of the principle go a step ahead and reverse the burden of proof.[53] For example, the World Charter for Nature[54] states that when an activity poses a significant risk to nature, the project proponent shall demonstrate that the expected benefits of the activity outweigh the potential damage to nature.[55] The activity will not be allowed when there is scientific uncertainty regarding such impacts. Therefore, the Charter contains a clear mandate for reversing the burden of proof, requiring the proponent to alleviate the scientific uncertainty. If they fail to do so, a threat of harm is presumed, and the activity is not allowed. Similarly, applying the principle in the *Bluefin Tuna*[56] case, the International Tribunal for the Law and Sea (ITLOS) also reversed the burden of proof, though not in clear terms.[57] Here, the ITLOS passed an interim order precluding Japan from increasing its total allowable catch.[58] It did so on grounds of scientific uncertainty regarding the impact of an increased catch.[59]

Be that as it may, dominant international instruments do not ascribe to reversing the burden of proof.[60] Further, internationally, the approach toward reversing the burden of proof has been rather adverse from the perspective of vulnerable groups with limited resources. For example, in the context of the International Court of Justice (ICJ), the most recent explicit (in)application of the principle was in the *Pulp Mills* case.[61] Here, the Court unequivocally rejected the reversal of the burden of proof.[62] While noting that the precautionary approach may apply in interpreting the relevant treaty between the parties, it held that reversal of the burden of proof does not follow from such application.[63] In fact, it even refused to lower the standard of proof, requiring Argentina to provide 'convincing', 'clear', and 'conclusive' evidence that mills cause environmental damage.[64] Another example of an explicit rejection of reversing the burden of proof is demonstrated by the European Union. Despite being known for its proactive application of the principle, the European Commission has expressed strong reservations against reversing the burden of proof in all cases; the Commission limits the reversal of the burden of proof on a case-by-case basis.[65] In Australia, reversing the burden of proof is conditional on the litigant meeting a high threshold for establishing threat and scientific uncertainty.[66]

Accordingly, the internationally accepted iteration of the precautionary principle has limited utility in easing barriers to climate litigation arising from the proof problem. It addresses the proof problem by allowing regulatory action in the face of scientific uncertainty.[67] However, the plaintiff must still procure scientific evidence to prove harm, though such evidence may be inconclusive. Thus, while lowering the evidentiary standard, it does not shift the evidentiary burden. This is only partly useful for under-resourced litigants, such as vulnerable groups from the Global South, because they still need to secure access to scientific expertise and adequate financial resources to discharge the evidentiary burden. As elaborated in what follows, this is where the Indian iteration of the principle offers a glimmer of hope.

## Indian iteration of the precautionary principle: a systematic reversal of the burden of proof

The Indian Supreme Court's proactive approach in environmental cases has allowed it to lay down new legal principles and facilitate environmental justice through innovative methods.[68] Since India follows a common-law system, judicial decisions are a source of law, and the Supreme Court's decisions are binding on itself and all subordinate courts and tribunals.[69] Despite the contested status of the principle in international law, the Indian Supreme Court in *Vellore Citizens Welfare Forum v Union of India* (*Vellore*)[70] adopted the principle as a 'part of the environmental law of the country'.[71] Subsequently, in *A. P. Pollution Control Board v Prof MV Naidu* (*A. P. Pollution Control Board*),[72] the Supreme Court elaborated on the different elements of the principle.

While adopting the international law principle in *Vellore*, the court did not import it wholesale. Instead, it provided an iteration of the principle specific to the country's 'municipal law'.[73] Drawing upon different iterations,[74] it defined the principle as:

1. Environment measures by the state government and the statutory authorities must anticipate, prevent, and attack the causes of environmental degradation.
2. Where there are threats of serious and irreversible damage, lack of scientific certainty should not be used as a reason for postponing measures to prevent environmental degradation.

3. The '[o]nus of proof' is on the actor or the developer/industrialist to show that his action is environmentally benign.[75]

Thus, the Court identified four elements for the operation of the precautionary principle. First, the impugned activity must give rise to threats of serious and irreversible damage. Second, prevailing scientific evidence regarding such threats must be insufficient – that is, there must be scientific uncertainty regarding such threats. Third, any measures may be taken by the state to prevent such damage. Fourth, the burden of proof is reversed. That is, the project proponent or defendant must discharge the burden of proof that the activity is environmentally benign. It is the fourth element that, arguably, eases the structural barriers outlined.

Each element was elaborated by the Supreme Court in *A. P. Pollution Control Board*.[76] Judges have followed this seminal interpretation in subsequent decisions.[77] Regarding reversal of the burden of proof, the court indicated the need to fulfil certain preconditions. The litigant is required to prove three related elements regarding the impugned harm:[78] (1) There should be an identifiable risk of harm, (2) the impugned harm should be serious or irreversible, and (3) the risk of harm should be scientifically uncertain.

> Regarding the first element, the Supreme Court has not explicitly delineated what constitutes an 'identifiable risk'. However, the following jurisprudence indicates what it entails. 'The principle of precaution involves the *anticipation* of environmental harm and taking measures to avoid it or to choose the least environmentally harmful activity. . . . Precautionary duties must not only be triggered by the *suspicion* of concrete danger but also by *([j]ustified) concern* or risk potential.[79]

The Court set a low bar concerning the standard of risk which needs to be met to trigger the precautionary principle. Any *anticipatory* harm, *suspicion* of concrete danger, or even a *justified concern* may be enough to trigger the application of the principle. Therefore, arguably, to satisfy the first element of establishing an 'identifiable risk,' the litigant only needs to show that there is a 'justified concern' about the occurrence of the impugned harm.[80]

The second element is that the identifiable risk should relate to a serious or irreversible harm. The Court has not clarified what constitutes serious or irreversible harm. However, non-exhaustive illustrations have been provided, like the 'extinction of species, widespread toxic pollution in major threats to essential ecological processes'.[81] If a court were to consider whether the impacts of climate change would constitute 'serious or irreversible damage', it could interpret this by applying the principle of *ejusdem generis*.[82] On such interpretation, the impacts of climate change would readily meet this threshold.

Regarding the third element, there is no threshold prescribed for the level of scientific uncertainty to be proved.[83] Courts have applied the principle at various levels of 'scientific uncertainty.'[84] The principle has been applied from cases where the threat of harm is 'possible or worth researching' (scientific uncertainty) to cases where it is 'rigorously proven' (practically no scientific uncertainty).[85] In fact, the Supreme Court considers inadequate scientific evidence constituting scientific 'uncertainty' too.[86] Therefore, it deems scientific uncertainty as a spectrum or a sliding scale. Arguably, as long as the litigant can prove some level of scientific uncertainty, the standard will be met.

Therefore, as soon as the litigant can establish (1) the presence of scientifically uncertain and (2) justified concern(s) and (3) serious or irreversible harm, courts must presume the presence of non-negligible risk of harm. Consequently, the burden of proof automatically shifts to the defendant. The defendant must then prove the absence of non-negligible risk. In other words, the defendant must prove the absence of a 'reasonable ecological or medical concern'.[87]

The Indian iteration interprets the reversal of the burden of proof in a rather unique way. As noted earlier, elsewhere, courts have either refused to shift the burden, selectively shifted it, or set very high thresholds to trigger its shift. However, the Indian iteration sets a relatively low bar to trigger the reversal of the burden of proof. This low threshold does not require the plaintiff to provide robust scientific evidence of the risk of serious or irreversible harm; instead, the plaintiff is only required to show a justified concern of the threat of serious or irreversible harm and scientific uncertainty regarding it. Notably, the plaintiff is not required to show any particular level of scientific certainty, but rather some scientific uncertainty or even inadequacy of science. Thus, in India's iteration of the principle, a justified concern of harm, backed by conflicting scientific reports or even inadequate data, may trigger a reversal of the burden of proof.

In what ways does this iteration ease the structural barriers faced by climate litigants from vulnerable communities in the Global South? To answer this question, the following section explains the impacts of reversing the burden of proof and cases where it has been successfully done.

## The utility of the Indian iteration for climate litigants from vulnerable communities in the Global South

While the Indian iteration may facilitate climate litigation initiated by any litigant, it is particularly useful for climate litigants from vulnerable communities in the Global South. First, it directly eases the structural barriers faced by vulnerable communities. Second, it provides a level playing field for the parties by addressing information asymmetries. Third, enabled by the special tool of public interest litigation, this innovative iteration has been a judicial strategy to protect and future-proof underrepresented human and ecological interests.

### *Easing the structural barriers faced by vulnerable communities*

First, by systematically shifting the burden of proof in all cases, the Indian iteration of the principle relieves the plaintiff from shouldering the evidentiary burden. Second, such reversal is virtually unconditional, that is to say, it does not require the plaintiff to establish any high standard of threat or provide conclusive evidence of scientific uncertainty. Arguably, this may ease the pressure of acquiring access to specialist scientific expertise and evidence. Concomitantly, to some extent, it may also ease the financial constraints faced by under-resourced plaintiffs.

### *Providing a level playing field by addressing information asymmetries*

Reversal of the burden of proof is deemed to bear significant merit in cases where 'asymmetries exist between the information about risk available to different parties in a dispute'.[88] Such information asymmetries are inherent in climate litigation initiated by vulnerable communities in the Global South.

The need to address such information asymmetries and to provide a level playing field for vulnerable communities has been sufficient ground for the Indian Supreme Court to reverse the burden of proof. Its jurisprudence developed in cases where underrepresented interests were at stake, for example, where the interests of vulnerable communities and the environment were impacted.[89] In such cases, the court reasoned that it would be unfair to require the party seeking to preserve the environment in its prevailing state to shoulder the evidentiary burden.[90] Rather, the party seeking to undertake a potentially harmful activity should bear the burden.[91]

Understood in this context, the court's rationale for reversing the burden of proof is to address the power and information asymmetries between the parties.[92] In other words, it provides a level playing field to litigants from vulnerable communities.

### *Easing access to justice for vulnerable communities*

Through its innovative jurisprudence in developing the Indian iteration of the precautionary principle, the court has eased access to justice for vulnerable communities. To that end, by reversing the burden of proof, it has relieved the plaintiff from needing specific scientific expertise. To a certain extent, this eases the financial burden of litigation on the plaintiff.

Furthermore, the court has also futureproofed vulnerable communities against information asymmetries and procedural barriers they may face while litigating environmental or climate harm. The precautionary principle was developed in public interest litigation (PIL), a tool to ease access to justice for socio-economically marginalised communities.[93] Notably, PIL has been particularly instrumental in securing the environmental interests of vulnerable communities.[94] First, by relaxing the rule of *locus standi*, PIL allows a public-spirited individual to initiate litigation on behalf of communities to protect their interests.[95] Second, PIL has allowed Indian courts the flexibility to internalise and apply international environmental law principles even in the absence of legislative and executive action. Courts have used these opportunities to develop iterations which cater to protecting the underrepresented interests of vulnerable communities.[96] The successful transplant of the precautionary principle into the Indian environmental jurisprudence is a case in point. This can be replicated in other common-law jurisdictions to ease access to justice for vulnerable communities.

### *Examples of application of the principle and the reversal of the burden of proof*

This section discusses the cases in which the judiciary has operationalised the Indian iteration of the precautionary principle. Notably, the principle has been applied in several environmental cases by the Indian Supreme Court, the National Green Tribunal, and various provincial high courts. Three cases are discussed. They were selected with reference to four criteria.

First, only mitigation cases have been considered, because the proof problem is most evident in them. In these cases, the defendant's (in)action is challenged on the grounds that it contributes to climate change, causes injury, or poses the risk of injury to the petitioner. Thus, a link between the injury or risk of injury, climate change, and the defendant's (in)action must be proven.[97] Therefore, access to impact attribution and source attribution science is necessary to address the proof problem in such cases.[98]

Second, either the petitioner or the court raised climate-related impacts of an impugned activity in the cases, even if such discussion is at the periphery.[99] Over 59% of the cases in the Global South fall within this category.[100]

Third, and most importantly, the cases discussed include an application of the precautionary principle and reversal of the burden of proof. Fourth, the cases concern themselves with protecting the interests of vulnerable communities or entities.

Of the three cases discussed, two are squarely climate cases. These are *Karnataka Industrial Area Development Board v C Kenchappa* (*KIADB*)[101] and *Society For Protection of Environment and Biodiversity v Union of India* (*Construction Industry case*).[102] These cases have either been categorised as peripheral cases in existing literature[103] or listed in climate litigation databases.[104] In both cases, the concerned court discussed the potential climate impacts of the impugned activity. In these cases, the reversal of the burden of proof is implicit.

The third case, *T. N. Godavarman v Union of India* (*Godavarman*),[105] is an environmental case that only makes a passing reference to climate change. This case is significant because it consists of an explicit and exemplary application of the precautionary principle and the reversal of burden of proof.[106] Furthermore, it reflects the latest jurisprudence on the principle.

#### *Climate cases using the precautionary principle*

In the *Construction Industry* case, the issue before the National Green Tribunal was the 2016 Draft Environmental Impact Assessment Notification (Notification).[107] The Notification exempted building and construction projects from the requirement of procuring an environmental clearance.[108] In other words, it allowed these projects to be implemented without a comprehensive environmental impact assessment (EIA). The applicant argued that by exempting building and construction projects from an EIA, the Notification ignored the precautionary principle.[109] Further, they argued that unregulated construction activity would cause irreversible environmental damage and have serious repercussions for climate change.[110] In its decision, the Tribunal discussed the climate impacts of rampant construction activity.[111] It noted that construction activity consumes enormous resources and has a significant energy footprint;[112] it contributes 22% of the country's annual greenhouse gas (GHG) emissions.[113] Per the Tribunal, any provision allowing unregulated construction activity would violate India's international commitments under the Rio Declaration of 1992 and the Paris Agreement of 2015.[114]

Applying the precautionary principle, the Tribunal established scientific uncertainty and reversed the burden of proof, though not in clear terms. With respect to scientific uncertainty, it noted that allowing projects without impact assessments would be in derogation of the precautionary principle.[115] Arguably, its underlying rationale was that the absence of a comprehensive impact assessment indicated scientific uncertainty.[116] In other words, until detailed studies are conducted, impacts of a project on ecologically and environmentally vulnerable areas are invariably unknown and are therefore 'uncertain'.

The Tribunal also reversed the burden of proof. It highlighted that the defendant had not based its decision on any scientific studies.[117] According to the Tribunal, the relaxation of the EIA requirement was contingent on providing scientific proof that the said activity would improve the quality of the environment.[118] Since the defendant had failed to consider or present any such data, the exemption of building and construction activities from an EIA process could not be allowed.[119] Notably, the Tribunal did not require the applicant to prove the adverse impacts of unregulated construction on climate and ecology.[120] Rather, it placed the burden of proof on the defendant to prove that the activity was beneficial for all facets of the environment.[121] Since the defendant was unable to do so, the Tribunal quashed the impugned provisions of the Notification. Furthermore, the Tribunal's understanding and framing of vulnerability in this case included the non-human environment. While considering the impacts of the impugned activity, it took into account both ecology and the human environment.[122]

In the *KIADB* case, the Supreme Court was faced with the question of allowing the conversion of agricultural land for industrial use and the establishment of industries. The impugned lands were used for grazing cattle, agriculture, and residential purposes by rural communities in the area. The Karnataka Industrial Areas Development Board (KIADB) acquired these lands and sought to convert them for industrial use.

Agriculturalists from the affected villages petitioned in the high court of Karnataka, arguing that any such conversion would prevent them from grazing their cattle and that the establishment of industries would adversely affect the environment and ecology of the region. The high court quashed the allotment orders. Against this decision, KIADB appealed in the Supreme Court. In the Supreme Court, the respondent agriculturalists argued that the conversion of land without prior impact assessment could adversely impact the environment and ecology.[123] Arguably, the respondent agriculturalists highlighted a state of scientific uncertainty regarding the impact of the acquisition on the environment.[124]

The Supreme Court disallowed any further land acquisitions and conversion in the absence of scientific evidence ascertaining the ecological and climate impacts.[125] Notably, it placed this burden of proof on KIADB. It held that prior to acquiring and converting any land, KIADB must carry out the relevant impact assessments.[126] In reaching this conclusion, the court relied on the precautionary principle.[127] It explained the relationship between rampant development and industrialisation and global warming.[128] Thereafter, it extensively discussed the adverse impacts of climate change. Against this background, it expounded the key elements of the principle, that is, anticipatory regulatory action in the face of scientific uncertainty and reversing the onus of proof.

As in the *Construction Industry* case, the Court did not clearly establish scientific uncertainty. However, it was considered that the absence of a comprehensive impact assessment was equivalent to scientific uncertainty.[129] This is evident from the Court's extensive discussion regarding the adverse impacts of climate change, followed by a discussion on the precautionary principle.[130] Arguably, it appears that the Court sought to disallow any activity that could potentially contribute to climate change, unless proven otherwise through an EIA. In other words, scientific uncertainty regarding an activity's environmental and ecological impacts must be alleviated before it is allowed. It went further to mandate prior impact assessments and shifted the burden of proof onto KIADB.

Therefore, in both cases, as soon as the petitioner established a justified concern and prevailing scientific uncertainty, the courts applied the precautionary principle. In doing so, the courts presumed a threat of serious or irreversible harm and banned the impugned activity. By reversing the burden of proof, the courts required the defendant to procure scientific evidence to alleviate the scientific uncertainty and refute the presumption of harm.

### Godavarman: *The Supreme Court's 2022 jurisprudence on the precautionary principle*

In *Godavarman*, one of the petitioners, the Goa Foundation, was a voluntary organisation of environmentalists in the state of Goa. The Goa Foundation challenged the approval granted by the Standing Committee of National Board for Wildlife (NBWL) for doubling a railway line in Goa. The defendant project proponent was Rail Vikas Nigam Limited (RVNL). The proposed railway line passed through protected forests, non-protected forests, and a major tiger corridor.[131] The petitioners argued that doubling the line would lead to severe environmental degradation.[132] With respect to its climate impact, they argued that the project would cause massive deforestation, which would have an adverse impact on the climate and temperature of the protected areas.[133]

The Goa Foundation's primary claim was that the approval was granted without a comprehensive impact assessment of the project. This claim was supplemented by references to a preliminary report[134] that underlined the adverse impacts. Furthermore, the report also cast doubt on the veracity of the impact assessment that the project proponent had carried out.[135] For example, the petitioners contested the proponent's assessments based on which project had been proposed. Through their preliminary report, they argued that this assessment was unreasonable, unsound, and not based on facts.[136] Drawing on this, the Foundation called for more detailed impact assessments to be undertaken.[137]

Accordingly, it seems that the petitioners' primary strategy was to establish a state of scientific uncertainty regarding the impacts of the project by highlighting the absence of a comprehensive impact assessment. Further, they also established a likelihood or risk of harm. As noted earlier in this chapter, the absence of a comprehensive impact assessment itself indicates a state of scientific uncertainty.[138] In other words, until detailed studies are conducted, the impacts are 'uncertain'. Thus, by establishing an identifiable risk which is scientifically uncertain, the petitioner met the preconditions for applying the precautionary principle.

Noting the potentially adverse impacts of the project on the climate and temperature,[139] the Supreme Court relied on the precautionary principle to reach its decision.[140] The court took note of the scientific uncertainty regarding the harm and the presumed threat of harm and reversed the burden of proof. With respect to scientific uncertainty, the court noted the absence of comprehensive assessments and conflicting evidence in various instances. It noted that the actual loss of wildlife habitat was not accounted for.[141] Furthermore, it took note of the conflicting reports regarding the practicality of the proposed mitigation measures.[142] It also called for an independent assessment of the need for the project, given the contested nature of the assessments presented by the proponent.[143] Lastly, regarding the impacts of the project, the court held that a detailed assessment and analysis of the impacts of the project were required.[144] In light of this scientific uncertainty, it presumed a threat of harm and suspended the project until the defendant submitted new, detailed impact assessment studies. Thus, it reversed the burden of proof, requiring RVNL to alleviate the scientific uncertainty regarding the project.[145]

These positive examples of the application of the precautionary principle notwithstanding, as discussed next, its inconsistent application potentially impedes its utility in climate litigation.

## Limitations of the argument

In separate studies, Rajamani and Gill argue that courts have applied the precautionary principle even where there is no scientific uncertainty or where clear evidence of harm is available.[146] In such cases, instead of reversing the burden of proof, courts have engaged in a cost–benefit analysis based on the available scientific evidence.[147] Effectively, the burden of proof is shared by the parties, as opposed to it being reversed.[148] Normatively, by allowing the precautionary principle to operate even in cases of scientific certainty, the judiciary has conflated the precautionary principle with the principles of prevention and sustainable development.[149] Overall, this application is counterintuitive and dilutes the precautionary principle.

Further, when the very application of the principle is subjected to providing robust scientific evidence of the threat of harm, the burden of proof is not reversed. Instead, it is shared by the parties, therefore defeating the value of the principle as a tool for climate litigants from vulnerable communities. In that, by requiring them to provide robust scientific evidence and shouldering the evidentiary burden, it does not ease the structural barriers previously mentioned.

The possibility of introducing this precondition in the precautionary principle is not hypothetical. The National Green Tribunal has introduced the need for robust scientific evidence as a prerequisite to applying the precautionary principle.[150] However, insofar as the Indian Supreme Court is concerned, no such precondition has been introduced. Jurisprudentially, it has stayed firm on its commitment to applying the principle in instances of scientific uncertainty and reversing the burden of proof where applicable. In fact, as noted earlier, in *Godavarman*, it reinforced its long-standing position on the principle. That is, any justified concern of harm, even if scientifically uncertain, will trigger the application of the principle. In such cases, the burden of proof is reversed, and the defendant must prove that the activity is environmentally benign. As long as this interpretation is applied in its true spirit, the principle will serve as a useful strategy for vulnerable communities litigating climate harms in the Global South.

## Conclusion

As a strategy for climate litigation, the precautionary principle has been discussed in this chapter. Increasingly, with advancements in attribution science, the principle's value has been debated. However, for vulnerable communities in the Global South, attribution science is scant, and access to it is precarious. Accessibility hinges on the presence of specialist scientific knowledge and financial resources. Litigants in the Global South operate with limited availability of these resources. Often, such challenges impede them from successfully initiating and pursuing climate litigation.

In cases where scientific evidence is unavailable, inconclusive, or inaccessible, the Indian iteration of the precautionary principle is a useful litigation strategy. Unlike international counterparts, this iteration raises a presumption of harm and reverses the burden of proof. Such reversal hinges only on establishing a *prima facie* case, a requirement that is fulfilled by meeting a relatively low standard of proof. Thus, this iteration exempts the plaintiff from shouldering or discharging any evidentiary burden. In doing so, it eases the structural barriers and becomes a meritorious litigation strategy for climate litigants from vulnerable communities in the Global South. Given the utility of this iteration, its inconsistent application in the National Green Tribunal, subordinate courts, and the Supreme Court itself must be regularised by the Supreme Court. At the next opportunity, the Supreme Court must explicitly set aside the emerging practice of Indian courts requiring robust scientific evidence as a precondition to the principle's application.

## Notes

1 The story is from the author's doctoral fieldwork conducted in early 2024 in the various water-scarce regions of India.
2 In October 2024, the author was informed that the monsoon rainfall (in July–September 2024) was above average and the river is flowing again.
3 The dominant community populating these villages has been recognised as socio-economically disadvantaged and been accorded the status of 'Scheduled Tribes' by the Government of Rajasthan for targeted development.
4 See, generally, Mike Burger et al., 'Climate Science and Human Rights: Using Attribution Science to Frame Government Mitigation and Adaptation Obligations' in César Rodríguez-Garavito (ed), *Litigating the Climate Emergency* (CUP 2022). Burger et al. highlight the difference between the causation analysis in failure-to-mitigate cases and failure-to-adapt cases. They note that while the former require the plaintiff's access to both impact and source attribution science, the latter only requires access to impact attribution science.
5 Burger et al. (n 4).
6 'Proof problem' is another expression for the 'problem of proof', a term used by Lydia Akinyi Omuko, 'Applying the Precautionary Principle to Address the "Proof Problem" in Climate Change Litigation' (2016) 21(1) *Tilburg Law Review* 52.
7 Jacqueline Peel, 'Issues in Climate Litigation' (2011) 1 *CCLR* 17, 19 <https://doi.org/10.21552/CCLR/2011/1/162> accessed 18 September 2024.
8 Peel (n 7). See also Joana Setzer and Lisa Benjamin, 'Climate Litigation in the Global South: Constraints and Innovations' (2020) 9(1) *TEL* 77, 95–96 <https://doi.org/10.1017/S2047102519000268> accessed 18 September 2024; Patrick Toussaint, 'Loss and Damage and Climate Litigation: The Case for Greater Interlinkage' (2020) 30 *Review of European, Comparative and International Environmental Law* 16, 20 <https://doi.org/10.1111/reel.12335> accessed 18 September 2024. Toussiant cites the existence of robust scientific evidence as a precondition to successful litigation. See also the discussion of barriers in Beckhauser and Broetto Chapter 1, pp 51–53; Burri and Duarte Reyes Chapter 5, pp 174–175; and Ladan and Maduekwe Chapter 8, pp 245–247.
9 UN Environment Programme, 'Environmental Rule of Law: First Global Report' (*UN Environment Programme*, 2019) 185 <https://www.unep.org/resources/assessment/environmental-rule-law-first-global-report> accessed 18 September 2024; see also UN Environment Programme, 'Environmental Rule of Law: Tracking Progress and Charting Future Directions' (*UN Environment Programme*, 2023) 128 <https://wedocs.unep.org/bitstream/handle/20.500.11822/43943/Environmental_rule_of_law_progress.pdf> accessed 18 September 2024.
10 Jacqueline Peel, 'Precaution' in Lavanya Rajamani and Jacqueline Peel (eds), *Oxford Handbook of International Environmental Law* (2nd edn, OUP 2021) 304.
11 Peel (n 10).
12 See *Vellore Citizens Welfare Forum v Union of India* (1996) 1996 5 SCC 647, Indian Supreme Court (India) (*Vellore*). In this case, the Indian Supreme Court imported the precautionary principle and laid down its key elements.
13 *AP Pollution Control Board v Prof MV Naidu* (1992) 1992 2 SCC 718, Indian Supreme Court (India) (*AP Pollution Control Board*).
14 *AP Pollution Control Board* (n 13).
15 On attribution science, see L Delta Merner et al., 'Identifying Gaps in Climate-Litigation-Relevant Research: An Assessment from Interviews with Legal Scholars

and Practitioners' (*The Climate Social Science Network*, 2022) 6 <https://cssn.org/wp-content/uploads/2022/04/CSSN-Research-Report-2022_2-Identifying-Gaps-in-Climate-Litigation-Relevant-Research-An-Assessment-from-Interviews-with-Legal-Scholars-and-Practitioners.pdf> accessed 26 February 2024. Noting the inadequacy in attribution science in the Global South, authors call for an increased focus on the Global South.

16 See, for example, Gastón Medici-Colombo and Thays Ricarte, 'The Escazú Agreement Contribution to Environmental Justice in Latin America: An Exploratory Empirical Inquiry through the Lens of Climate Litigation' (2023) *Journal of Human Rights and Practice* 1, 8 <https://doi.org/10.1093/jhuman/huad029> accessed 18 September 2024. This article is part of a special issue, which provides a comprehensive review of procedural and structural barriers in environmental and climate litigation in the Global South generally. See Melanie Jean Murcott and Maria Antonia Tigre, 'Developments, Opportunities, and Complexities in Global South Climate Litigation' (2024) 16(1) *Journal of Human Rights Practice*.

17 UNEP (n 9). See also Beckhauser and Broetto Chapter 1, pp 51–53; Burri and Duarte Reyes Chapter 5, pp 174–175; and Ladan and Maduekwe Chapter 8, pp 245–247.

18 Setzer and Benjamin (n 8).

19 Setzer and Benjamin (n 8). They do not refer to the proof problem per se; however, note that climate litigation involves a policy–science nexus, and the lack of specialist knowledge to litigants in Global South poses a challenge.

20 Peel (n 7) 18–21.

21 Peel (n 7) 17, 19.

22 Burger et al. (n 4).

23 Merner et al. (n 15).

24 Ben Clarke et al., 'Extreme Weather Impacts of Climate Change: An Attribution Perspective' (2022) 1(1) *Environmental Research: Climate* 2, 15 <https://doi.org/10.1088/2752-5295/ac6e7d> accessed 18 September 2024; Jessica A Wentz et al., 'Research Priorities for Climate Litigation' (2022) 11(1) *Earth's Future* <https://doi.org/10.1029/2022EF002928> accessed 18 September 2024; Chloe Balhatchet, 'Can We Sue Our Way Out of the Climate Crisis?' (*Centre for Science and Policy, Cambridge University*, 8 December 2022) <https://www.csap.cam.ac.uk/news/article-can-we-sue-our-way-out-climate-crisis/> accessed 23 February 2024; Isabella Kaminski, 'How Geographical Gaps are Harming Climate Science' (*China Dialogue*, 15 August 2022) <https://chinadialogue.net/en/climate/how-geographical-gaps-are-harming-climate-science/> accessed 23 February 2024.

25 Peel (n 7).

26 Peel (n 10) 306. Peel notes that uncertainty may be caused by several reasons, including gaps in knowledge.

27 Vulnerability theory terms these as 'social and constructed vulnerability'. See, for example, Milka Sormunen, 'Rethinking Effective Remedies to the Climate Crisis: A Vulnerability Theory Approach' (2023) 24 *Human Rights Review* <https://doi.org/10.1007/s12142-023-00686-4> accessed 18 September 2024; IPCC, 'Summary for Policymakers in Climate Change 2022 – Impacts, Adaptation and Vulnerability: Working Group II Contribution to the Sixth Assessment Report of the Intergovernmental Panel on Climate Change' in HO Pörtner et al. (eds), (2022) 1467 <https://www.ipcc.ch/report/ar6/wg2/downloads/report/IPCC_AR6_WGII_FullReport.pdf> accessed 21 November 2024; Birsha Ohdedar, 'Climate Adaptation, Vulnerability and Rights-Based Litigation: Broadening the Scope of Climate Litigation Using Political Ecology' (2022) 13(1) *Journal of Human Rights and Environment* <https://doi.org/10.4337/jhre.2022.01.06> accessed 18 September 2024; Murcott, Tigre, and Ann Samuel, Introduction, pp 5–7.

28 Intergovernmental Panel on Climate Change (IPCC), 'The Concept of Risk in the IPCC Sixth Assessment Report: A Summary of Cross-Working Group Discussions' (*IPCC*, 4 September 2020) 5 <https://www.ipcc.ch/site/assets/uploads/2021/02/Risk-guidance-FINAL_15Feb2021.pdf> accessed 18 September 2024.

29 IPCC (n 28).

30 Sormunen (n 27). See also Jorge E Vinuales, 'Legal Techniques for Dealing with Scientific Uncertainty in Environmental Law' (2021) 43 *Vanderbilt Law Review* 500 <https://scholarship.law.vanderbilt.edu/vjtl/vol43/iss2/4> accessed 18 September 2024. Writing in the context of the Inuit petition, Vinuales provides an excerpt from the interview of the former chair of Inuit Circumpolar Conference, which points toward the gap in attribution science regarding the specific impacts of climate change on vulnerable communities.

31 IPCC (n 27) 1467–1468, the Report underlines the need for a more nuanced understanding and examination of vulnerable groups, including, women, poor, and disadvantaged, in vulnerability and risk assessment. See further Murcott, Tigre, and Ann Samuel, Introduction, pp 3–10, for a discussion on vulnerability and intersectionality.

32 Socio-economic class has been seen as an external factor contributing to increased social vulnerability. See I Otto et al., 'Social Vulnerability to Climate Change: A Review of Concepts and Evidence' (2017) 17(6) *Regional Environmental Change* <https://doi.org/10.1007/s10113-017-1105-9> accessed 18 September 2024.

33 UN Environmental Programme, 'Global Climate Litigation Report: 2023 Status Review' (*UN Environment Programme*, 2023) <https://wedocs.unep.org/bitstream/handle/20.500.11822/43008/global_climate_litigation_report_2023.pdf> accessed 18 September 2024.

34 UN Environmental Programme (n 33).

35 Sormunen (n 27).

36 IPCC (n 28) 6.

37 See, generally, Brian G Henninh and Zack Walsh (eds), *Climate Change Ethics and the Non-Human World* (Routledge 2020) 49; see also Nuria Almiron and Catia Faria, 'Climate Change Impacts on Free-Living Nonhuman Animals. Challenges for Media and Communication Ethics' (2019) 7(1) *Studies in Media and Communication* <https://core.ac.uk/download/pdf/228084307.pdf> accessed 3 May 2024.

38 Merner et al. (n 15).

39 See, for example, IPCC (n 27).

40 Rebekah Humphreys, 'Suffering, Sentientism, and Sustainability: An Analysis of a Non-Anthropocentric Moral Framework for Climate Ethics' in Brian G Henninh and Zack Walsh (eds), *Climate Change Ethics and the Non-Human World* (Routledge 2020) 49.

41 Institutional responses to these barriers have focused on providing litigants with financial, technical, and strategic support. Philanthropists have extended financial and technical expertise, while non-governmental organisations from the Global North have provided strategic support. For a detailed discussion, see Setzer and Benjamin (n 8) 96; Jacqueline Peel and Jolene Lin, 'Transnational Climate Litigation: The Contribution of the Global South' (2019) 113(4) *American Journal of International Law* 679 <https://doi.org/10.1017/ajil.2019.48> accessed 19 September 2024.

42 UNGA, 'Rio Declaration on Environment and Development' (12 August 1992) A/CONF.151/26 (Vol. I), principle 15.

43 United Nations Framework Convention on Climate Change (20 January 1994) A/RES/48/189, Article 3(3).

44 Several scholars refer to this version as the most widely accepted, cited, and uncontroversial. See, for example, Lavanya Rajamani, 'The Precautionary Principle' in Shibani Ghosh (ed), *Indian Environmental Law* (Orient Black Swan 2019).

45 UNGA (n 42).
46 For an overview of different versions, see Cass Sunstein, 'The Paralyzing Principle' (*Regulation*, Winter 2002–2003) 33 <https://www.cato.org/sites/cato.org/files/serials/files/regulation/2002/12/v25n4-9.pdf> accessed 22 June 2023.
47 Peel (n 10).
48 Sunstein (n 46).
49 Peel (n 7) 20; see also Omuko (n 6).
50 Peel (n 7) 20; see also Omuko (n 6). Both Peel and Omuko argue that the principle may allow the court to accept more general evidence of harm as probative of specific, local harm. Thus, arguably, it considerably lowers the standard of proof that must be met by the plaintiff.
51 See Peel (n 7) 20. Discussing versions of the principle that do not reverse burden of proof, Peel notes that they allow the court to accept probative evidence. Arguably, therefore, the onus to provide such evidence rests with the plaintiff.
52 See following text to n 61 to 64. In *Argentina v Uruguay (Pulp Mills on the River Uruguay)* (2006) ICJ Rep 113, 71, International Court of Justice (*Pulp Mills case)*, the ICJ refused to reverse the burden of proof and required the plaintiff to provide evidence of threat of harm.
53 See, for example, UNGA, 'World Charter for Nature' (1982) A/RES/37/7; 'Wingspread Statement on the Precautionary Principle' (*Wingspread Conference Centre, Racine, Wisconsin*, 1998) <http://www.gdrc.org/ugov/precaution–3.html> accessed 18 September 2024.
54 UNGA (n 53); 'Wingspread Statement on the Precautionary Principle' (n 53).
55 UNGA (n 53); 'Wingspread Statement on the Precautionary Principle' (n 53); UNGA (n 53) principle 11.
56 *New Zealand v Japan, Australia v Japan (Southern Bluefin Tuna)* (1999) International Tribunal for the Law of the Sea (*Bluefin Tuna case*) [89].
57 *Bluefin Tuna case* (n 56) [21] (Liang J). In a separate opinion, Liang J states that the Tribunal did not reverse the burden of proof per se. See also Daniel Kazhdan, 'Precautionary Pulp: Pulp Mills and the Evolving Dispute between International Tribunals Over the Reach of the Precautionary Principle' (2011) 38 *Ecology Law Quarterly* 527 <https://doi.org/10.15779/Z38084Q> accessed 18 September 2024.
58 Kazhdan (n 57) 533.
59 *Bluefin Tuna case* (n 56) [73], [74], and [80]. In two consecutive paras, the Tribunal takes note of conflicting scientific evidence provided by the parties. Subsequently, it indicates a situation of supervening scientific uncertainty, albeit not in these terms; it acknowledges that 'the Tribunal cannot conclusively assess the scientific evidence provided by the parties'.
60 See Rajamani (n 44).
61 *Pulp Mills* case (n 52). The court's current position on the reversal of the burden of proof seems to be the one expressed in *Pulp Mills*. See Peel (n 10) 317, where she considers the ICJ's position in international disputes as the one indicated in *Pulp Mills*.
62 See, generally, Kazhdan (n 57), who terms ICJ's interpretation of the principle as 'The New Precautionary Principle'.
63 *Pulp Mills* case (n 52).
64 Kazhdan (n 57) 545.
65 Commission of the European Communities, 'Communication on the Precautionary Principle' (Brussels, 2 February 2000) 20–21 <https://eur-lex.europa.eu/legal-content/EN/TXT/PDF/?uri=CELEX%3A52000DC0001&from=EN#:~:text=The%20precautionary%20principle%20should%20be,to%20the%20management%20of%20risk> accessed 18 September 2024. See also Sonia Boutillon, 'The Precautionary Principle: Development of an International Standard' (2002) 23 *Michigan Journal of International*

*Law* 429, 467. However, the European Court of Justice seems to be more relaxed in its application, although not as much as India. See Mehmat Suat Kayikci, 'The Burden of Proof within the Scope of the Precautionary Principle: International and European Perspectives' (2012) <http://dx.doi.org/10.2139/ssrn.2101613> accessed 22 June 2023.

66 See *Telstra Corporation Limited v Hornsby Shire Council* (2006) 146 LGERA 10, Land and Environment Court of New South Wales (Australia); Jacqueline Peel, 'When (Scientific) Rationality Rules: (Mis)Application of the Precautionary Principle in Australian Mobile Phone Tower Cases' (2007) 19(1) *Journal of Environmental Law* 103.

67 Peel (n 7) 20; see also Omuko (n 6).

68 Geetanjoy Sahu, 'Implications of Indian Supreme Court's Innovations for Environmental Jurisprudence' (2008) 4(1) *Law, Environment and Development Journal* 1. For insights on climate litigation in India more generally, see Garg and Hinduja, Chapter 2, and Dutta and Lofts, Chapter 4.

69 Constitution of India, Article 141.

70 *Vellore* (n 12).

71 *Vellore* (n 12) [13]–[14].

72 *AP Pollution Control Board* (n 13).

73 *Vellore* (n 12), [11].

74 The principle is a combination of the weak and strong versions. For further discussion, see Rajamani (n 44).

75 *Vellore* (n 12) [11].

76 *AP Pollution Control Board* (n 13) [27]–[41].

77 See, for examoplem, *Godavarman v Union of India et al.* (2022) LiveLaw SC 467, Indian Supreme Court (India) (*Godavarman*); *M/S Shri Radhey Stone Crusher v Rajasthan State Pollution Control* et al., 2010(4) RLW 3449 (Raj.); *Susetha v Union of India*, Write Petition No. 30725 of 2008 (Madras High Court).

78 *AP Pollution Control Board* (n 13) [38]–[39].

79 *AP Pollution Control Board* (n 13) [35].

80 One could argue, using the preceding excerpt, that 'identifiable risk' translates into establishing a 'non-negligible' risk. However, that would be incorrect. Non-negligibility is a standard that the court has set for the defendant. That is, the defendant must prove the *absence of a non-negligible risk* or a reasonable ecological or medicinal concern. The remaining text from the excerpt clarifies this. See *AP Pollution Control Board* (n 13) [39].

81 *AP Pollution Control Board* (n 13) [38].

82 The doctrine of *ejusdem generis* is a well-entrenched canon of interpretation often used by the Indian judiciary to interpret statutory provisions. To see an illustrative list of cases where the Indian judiciary has applied *ejusdem generis*, see *Parameswara Kurup v State of Kerala,* WP(C) (2021) 19429/2014, Kerela High Court (India). Notably, though the text at hand is an excerpt from a judicial decision, the text is 'legislative' in nature. In other words, the court is laying down law, not simply interpretating it. Thus, *ejusdem generis* could be applied in interpreting it.

83 In its exposition of each of the elements, the court does not prescribe a threshold for scientific uncertainty. See *AP Pollution Control Board* (n 13) [27]–[41].

84 For a comprehensive list of cases and analysis, see Gitanjali Gill, 'Precautionary Principle, Its Interpretation and Application by the Indian Judiciary: 'When I Use a Word It Means Just What I Choose It to Mean-Neither More nor Less' Humpty Dumpty' (2019) 21(4) *Environmental Law Review* 292 <https://doi.org/10.1177/1461452919890283> accessed 18 September 2024.

85 Gill (n 84).

86 See, generally, *AP Pollution Control Board* (n 13) [27]–[30]. While this interpretation has been critiqued by Rajamani (n 44), it may not be entirely incorrect. For example,

see Peel (n 10); note that scientific uncertainty may emerge from, inter alia, inaccurate or inadequate models, theories, and methods (methodological uncertainty).

87 *AP Pollution Control Board* (n 13) [39].

88 Carl F Cranor, 'Asymmetric Information, the Precautionary Principle, and Burdens of Proof' in Carolyn Raffensperger and Joel A Tickner (eds), *Protecting Public Health and the Environment: Implementing the Precautionary Principle* (Island Press 1999) 74.

89 For example, in both *Vellore* (n 12) and *AP Pollution Control Board* (n 13), the interest at stake was protecting water sources against potential industrial pollution. The water sources provided water to neighbouring villages and cities for domestic and other uses.

90 *AP Pollution Control Board* (n 13) [37].

91 *AP Pollution Control Board* (n 13) [37].

92 This conclusion is supported by the decision of the National Green Tribunal too, where the Tribunal noted the importance of reversing of burden of proof in environmental cases because it would be unfair to ask the 'common citizen' to provide scientific and technological information to preserve the status quo. See *Pandurang Sitaram Chalke and another v State of Maharashtra* (2013) 14/2012, National Green Tribunal, Western Zone Bench (India) (Pandurang); See also Rajamani (n 44) for her interpretation of the Pandurang case that supports this analysis.

93 Gitanjali Nain Gill, 'Human Rights and the Environment in India: Access through Public Interest Litigation' (2012) 14 *Environmental Law Review* 202 <https://doi.org/10.1350/enlr.2012.14.3.158> accessed 18 September 2024.

94 Gill (n 93).

95 UNEP (n 9) 185.

96 For a critical overview, see Aparna Chandra, 'India and International Law: Formal Dualism, Functional Monism' (2017) 57 *Indian Journal of International Law* 25–45; Lavanya Rajamani, 'International Law and the Constitutional Schema' in Sujit Choudhry et al. (eds), *The Oxford Handbook of the Indian Constitution* (OUP 2016).

97 Burger et al. (n 4).

98 Burger et al. (n 4).

99 Peel and Lin (n 41). Peripheral cases are those where 'climate issues are subsidiary to other arguments, or one of many arguments or issues raised in a dispute'.

100 Peel and Lin (n 41).

101 *Karnataka Industrial Area Development Board v Kenchappa* (2006) 2006 6 SCC 371, Indian Supreme Court (India) (*KIADB*).

102 *Society for Protection of Environment & Biodiversity v Union of India* (2016) 677/2016, National Green Tribunal (India) (*Construction Industry case*) <https://climatecasechart.com/wp-content/uploads/non-us-case-documents/2017/20171208_Application-No.-677of-2016-M.A.-No.-148-of-2017_decision.pdf> accessed 20 October 2024.

103 See, for example, Peel and Lin (n 41); Shibani Ghosh, 'Litigating Climate Claims in India' (2020) 114 *American Journal of International Law Unbound* 45–50 <https://doi.org/10.1017/aju.2020.5> accessed 18 September 2024.

104 Sabin Centre for Climate Change Law, 'Global Climate Litigation Database' <https://climatecasechart.com/non-us-jurisdiction/india/> accessed 13 May 2024.

105 *Godavarman* (n 77).

106 Kanika Jamwal and Aastha Kapoor, 'Resolving the Conundrum on the Precautionary Principle' (*Mongabay India*, 28 July 2022) <https://india.mongabay.com/2022/07/commentary-resolving-the-conundrum-on-the-precautionary-principle/> accessed 13 May 2024.

107 *Construction Industry case* (n 102) [1]–[4].

108 *Construction Industry case* (n 102) [2].

109 *Construction Industry case* (n 102) [4].
110 *Construction Industry case* (n 102) [2] and [5].
111 *Construction Industry case* (n 102) [5] and [27]. The court also made reference to and took note of the climate change arguments presented by the petitioner.
112 *Construction Industry case* (n 102) [27].
113 *Construction Industry case* (n 102) [27].
114 *Construction Industry case* (n 102) [48].
115 *Construction Industry case* (n 102) [20] and [48].
116 See Kanika Jamwal and Charu Sharma, 'The Curious Case of "Violation": Deconstructing the Procedure Under the Draft Environmental Impact Assessment Notification 2020', 6(1) *Indian Law Review*, 105 <https://doi.org/10.1080/24730580.2021.1992576> accessed 18 September 2024. The authors explain how the absence of a comprehensive impact assessment may constitute a situation of 'scientific uncertainty'. See also Peel (n 10), where it is noted that uncertainty may arise from, inter alia, 'gaps in knowledge (epistemic uncertainty), inaccurate or inadequate models, theories and methods (methodological uncertainty), or vagueness, context dependence, ambiguity, indeterminacy of theoretical terms, and under-specificity in natural and scientific language (linguistic uncertainty)'. Arguably, therefore, the absence of comprehensive EIA may result in epistemic uncertainty and methodological uncertainty both.
117 *Construction Industry case* (n 102) [25] and [26].
118 *Construction Industry case* (n 102) [25] and [26].
119 *Construction Industry case* (n 102) [25].
120 As noted in the preceding paragraph, in this case, the reversal of the burden of proof was implicit. Although the Tribunal did not explicitly reverse the burden of proof, it did so implicitly by quashing the Notification on the grounds that the defendant (as opposed to the plaintiff) was not able to prove that the activity was beneficial for all facets of the environment.
121 *Construction Industry case* (n 102) [26].
122 *Construction Industry case* (n 102) [26] and [48].
123 *KIADB* (n 101) [27]–[28].
124 See Jamwal and Kapoor (n 106).
125 *KIADB* (n 101) [100].
126 *KIADB* (n 101) [100].
127 *KIADB* (n 101) [77]–[79] and [99].
128 *KIADB* (n 101) [41]–[42].
129 This falls within the realm of epistemic uncertainty; see Peel (n 10).
130 *KIADB* (n 101) [41]–[65].
131 *Godavarman* (n 77) [21].
132 *Godavarman* (n 77) [14].
133 *Godavarman* (n 77) [14].
134 *Godavarman* (n 77) [9], [10], [11(vii)]. These references were made by the second petitioner, the Central Empowered Committee (CEC), a panel constituted by the Supreme Court of India to monitor compliance with the court's environmental law orders and place non-compliance cases before it. In this case, the CEC outlined the potential or likely threat of the project on the environment. Its report was preliminary in nature in that it referred to the need for detailed impact assessment studies to be carried out. One notes here that the CEC is outlining preliminary and 'likely' impacts simultaneously calling for independent and detailed impact assessments.
135 *Godavarman* (n 77) [9], [14].
136 *Godavarman* (n 77) [11(iv)] and [11(vii)].
137 *Godavarman* (n 77) [7] for contentions by Goa Foundation. See also, *Godavarman* (n 77) [10]. CEC's report was based on NTCA's report, which itself called for more detailed impact assessment to be undertaken.

138 See Jamwal and Kapoor (n 106).
139 *Godavarman* (n 77) [22].
140 *Godavarman* (n 77) [19].
141 *Godavarman* (n 77) [21].
142 *Godavarman* (n 77) [21].
143 *Godavarman* (n 77) [21].
144 *Godavarman* (n 77) [22].
145 *Godavarman* (n 77) [23].
146 See Rajamani (n 44); Gill's quantitative analysis in Gill 'Precautionary principle' (n 84).
147 Rajamani (n 44).
148 Rajamani (n 44). Though Rajamani does not, per se, argue that the burden of proof is shared, she highlights that the court engages in a cost–benefit analysis on the basis of available scientific evidence. Here, she highlights that the defendant is only expected to weigh in. Thus, arguably, both parties shoulder the evidentiary burden, not just the defendant.
149 See Rajamani (n 44).
150 See, for example, *M/s Sterlite Industries (India) Ltd Thoothukudi v The Chairman Tamil Nadu Pollution Control Board, Chennai* (2013) 22/2013 (SZ) and 23/2013 (SZ), National Green Tribunal, Principal Bench (India).

## Bibliography

### *Books and book chapters*

Burger M, Wentz J and Metzger D, 'Climate Science and Human Rights: Using Attribution Science to Frame Government Mitigation and Adaptation Obligations' in César Rodríguez-Garavito (ed), *Litigating the Climate Emergency* (Cambridge University Press 2022)

Cranor CF, 'Asymmetric Information, the Precautionary Principle, and Burdens of Proof' in Carolyn Raffensperger and Joel A Tickner (eds), *Protecting Public Health and the Environment: Implementing the Precautionary Principle* (Island Press 1999)

Intergovernmental Panel on Climate Change (IPCC), *Climate Change 2022 – Impacts, Adaptation and Vulnerability: Working Group II Contribution to the Sixth Assessment Report of the Intergovernmental Panel on Climate Change* (Cambridge University Press 2023)

Murcott MJ and Tigre MA (eds), *Developments, Opportunities, and Complexities in Global South Litigation* (Forthcoming 2024)

Peel J, 'Precaution' in L Rajamani and J Peel (eds), *Oxford Handbook of International Environmental Law* (2nd edn, OUP 2021)

Rajamani L, 'International Law and the Constitutional Schema' in Sujit Choudhry, Madhav Khosla and Pratap Bhanu Mehta (eds), *The Oxford Handbook of the Indian Constitution* (OUP 2016)

Rajamani L, 'The Precautionary Principle' in Shibani Ghosh (ed), *Indian Environmental Law* (Orient Black Swan, 2019)

### *Cases*

*AP Pollution Control Board v Prof MV Naidu* (1992) 1992 2 SCC 718, Indian Supreme Court (India)

*Argentina v Uruguay (Pulp Mills on the River Uruguay)* (2006) ICJ Rep 113, 71, International Court of Justice

*Godavarman v Union of India* (1996) WP(C)/202/1995, Indian Supreme Court (India)
*Karnataka Industrial Area Development Board v Kenchappa* (2006) 2006 6 SCC 371, Indian Supreme Court (India)
*M/S Shri Radhey Stone Crusher v Rajasthan State Pollution Control and Another* (2010) 2010(4) RLW 3449 (Raj.), Indian Supreme Court (India)
*M/s Sterlite Industries (India) Ltd Thoothukudi v The Chairman Tamil Nadu Pollution Control Board, Chennai* (2013) 22/2013 (SZ) and 23/2013 (SZ), National Green Tribunal, Principal Bench (India)
*New Zealand v Japan, Australia v Japan* (Southern Bluefin Tuna) (1999) International Tribunal for the Law of the Sea
*Pandurang Sitaram Chalke and another v State of Maharashtra* (2013) 14/2012, National Green Tribunal, Western Zone Bench (India) (Pandurang)
*Parameswara Kurup v State of Kerala*, WP(C) (2021) 19429/2014, Kerela High Court (India)
*Society for Protection of Environment & Biodiversity v Union of India* (2016) 677/2016, National Green Tribunal (India)
*Susetha v Union of India* Write Petition No. 30725 [2008] Madras High Court (2010)
*Telstra Corporation Limited v Hornsby Shire Council* (2006) 146 LGERA 10, Land and Environment Court of New South Wales (Australia)
*Vellore Citizens Welfare Forum v Union of India* (1996) 1996 5 SCC 647, Indian Supreme Court (India) (*Vellore*)

### *International instruments*

UNGA, 'World Charter for Nature' (1982) A/RES/37/7
UNGA, 'Rio Declaration on Environment and Development' (12 August 1992) A/CONF.151/26 (Vol. I) ('Rio Declaration')
United Nations Framework Convention on Climate Change (adopted 20 January 1994) A/RES/48/189 art 3(3)
'Wingspread Statement on the Precautionary Principle' (*Wingspread Conference Centre, Racine, Wisconsin*, 1998) <http://www.gdrc.org/ugov/precaution-3.html>

### *Journal articles*

Almiron N and Faria C, 'Climate Change Impacts on Free-Living Nonhuman Animals. Challenges for Media and Communication Ethics' (2019) 7(1) *Studies in Media and Communication* 37 <https://core.ac.uk/download/pdf/228084307.pdf> accessed 10 September 2024
Boutillon S, 'The Precautionary Principle: Development of an International Standard' (2002) 23(2) *Michigan Journal of International Law* 429 <https://ssrn.com/abstract=1564237> accessed 10 September 2024
Chandra A, 'India and International Law: Formal Dualism, Functional Monism' 57(1–2) *Indian Journal of International Law* 25 <http://dx.doi.org/10.1007/s40901-017-0069-0> accessed 10 September 2024
Clarke B, Otto F, Stuart-Smith Rupert and Harrington L, 'Extreme Weather Impacts of Climate Change: An Attribution Perspective' (2022) 1(1) *Environmental Research: Climate* 1 <https://doi.org/10.1088/2752-5295/ac6e7d> accessed 10 September 2024
Ghosh S, 'Litigating Climate Claims in India' (2020) 144 *AJIL Unbound* 45 <https://doi.org/10.1017/aju.2020.5> accessed 10 September 2024
Gill G, 'Human Rights and the Environment in India: Access through Public Interest Litigation' (2012) 14(3) *Environmental Law Review* 200 <https://doi.org/10.1350/enlr.2012.14.3.158> accessed 10 September 2024

Gill G, 'Precautionary Principle, Its Interpretation and Application by the Indian Judiciary: "When I Use a Word It Means Just What I Choose It to Mean-Neither More nor Less" Humpty Dumpty' (2019) 21(4) *Environmental Law Review* 292 <https://doi.org/10.1177/1461452919890283> accessed 10 September 2024

Jamwal K and Sharma C, 'The Curious Case of "Violation": Deconstructing the Procedure Under the Draft Environmental Impact Assessment Notification 2020' (2021) 6(1) *Indian Law Review* 96 <https://doi.org/10.1080/24730580.2021.1992576> accessed 10 September 2024

Kayikci S, 'The Burden of Proof within the Scope of the Precautionary Principle: International and European Perspectives' (2012) *SSRN Electronic Journal* <http://dx.doi.org/10.2139/ssrn.2101613> accessed 10 September 2024

Kazhdan D, 'Precautionary Pulp: Pulp Mills and the Evolving Dispute between International Tribunals Over the Reach of the Precautionary Principle' (2011) 38(2) *Ecology Law Quarterly* 527 <https://doi.org/10.15779/Z38084Q> accessed 10 September 2024

Medici-Colombo G and Ricarte T, 'The Escazú Agreement Contribution to Environmental Justice in Latin America: An Exploratory Empirical Inquiry through the Lens of Climate Litigation' (2023) 16(1) *Journal of Human Rights and Practice* 160 <https://doi.org/10.1093/jhuman/huad029> accessed 10 September 2024

Ohdedar B, 'Climate Adaptation, Vulnerability and Rights-Based Litigation: Broadening the Scope of Climate Litigation Using Political Ecology' (2022) 13(1) *Journal of Human Rights and Environment* 137 <https://doi.org/10.4337/jhre.2022.01.06> accessed 10 September

Omuko LA, 'Applying the Precautionary Principle to Address the "Proof Problem" in Climate Change Litigation' (2016) 21(1) *Tilburg Law Review* 52 <https://doi.org/10.1163/22112596-02101003> accessed 10 September 2024

Otto IM, Reckien D, Reyer CPO, Marcus R, Masson V, Jones L, Norton A and Serdeczny O, 'Social Vulnerability to Climate Change: A Review of Concepts and Evidence' (2017) 17(6) *Regional Environmental Change* 1651 <https://doi.org/10.1007/s10113-017-1105-9> accessed 10 September 2024

Peel J, 'When (Scientific) Rationality Rules: (Mis)Application of the Precautionary Principle in Australian Mobile Phone Tower Cases' (2007) 19(1) *Journal of Environmental Law* 103 <https://doi.org/10.1093/jel/eqm002> accessed 10 September 2024

Peel J, 'Issues in Climate Litigation' (2011) 5(1) *Carbon & Climate Law Review* <https://doi.org/10.21552/CCLR/2011/1/162> accessed 10 September 2024

Peel J and Lin J, 'Transnational Climate Litigation: The Contribution of the Global South' (2019) 113(4) *American Journal of International Law* 679 <https://doi.org/10.1017/ajil.2019.48> accessed 10 September 2024

Setzer J and Benjamin L, 'Climate Litigation in the Global South: Constraints and Innovations' (2020) 9(1) *Transnational Environmental Law* 77 <https://doi.org/10.1017/S2047102519000268> accessed 10 September 2024

Sormunen M, 'Rethinking Effective Remedies to the Climate Crisis: A Vulnerability Theory Approach' (2023) 24 *Human Rights Review* 171 <https://doi.org/10.1007/s12142-023-00686-4> accessed 10 September 2024

Sunstein C, 'The Paralyzing Principle' 25 *Regulation* 33 <https://www.cato.org/sites/cato.org/files/serials/files/regulation/2002/12/v25n4-9.pdf> accessed 22 June 2023

Toussaint P, 'Loss and Damage and Climate Litigation: The Case for Greater Interlinkage' (2020) 30(1) *Review of European, Comparative and International Environmental Law* 16 <https://doi.org/10.1111/reel.12335> accessed 10 September 2024

Vinuales JE, 'Legal Techniques for Dealing with Scientific Uncertainty in Environmental Law' (2021) 43(2) *Vanderbilt Law Review* 437 <https://scholarship.law.vanderbilt.edu/vjtl/vol43/iss2/4> accessed 10 September 2024

Wentz JA, Merner D, Franta B, Lehman A and Frumhoff PC, 'Research Priorities for Climate Litigation' (2022) 11(1) *Earth's Future* 1<https://doi.org/10.1029/2022EF002928> accessed 10 September 2024

## *Online sources*


Balhatchet C, 'Can We Sue Our Way Out of the Climate Crisis?' (*University of Cambridge Centre for Science and Policy*, 8 December 2022) <https://www.csap.cam.ac.uk/news/article-can-we-sue-our-way-out-climate-crisis/> accessed 10 September 2024

'GlobalClimate Litigation Database' (*Sabin Centre for Climate Change Law*) <https://climatecasechart.com/non-us-jurisdiction/india/> accessed 10 September 2024

Jamwal K and Kapoor A, 'Resolving the Conundrum on the Precautionary Principle' (*Mongabay*, 28 July 2022) <https://india.mongabay.com/2022/07/commentary-resolving-the-conundrum-on-the-precautionary-principle/> accessed 13 May 2024

Kaminski I, 'How Geographical Gaps are Harming Climate Science' (*Dialogue Earth*, 15 August 2022) <https://chinadialogue.net/en/climate/how-geographical-gaps-are-harming-climate-science/> accessed 23 February 2024


## *Reports*


IPCC, 'Summary for Policymakers in Climate Change 2022 – Impacts, Adaptation and Vulnerability: Working Group II Contribution to the Sixth Assessment Report of the Intergovernmental Panel on Climate Change' in HO Pörtner et al. (eds), (2022) <https://www.ipcc.ch/report/ar6/wg2/downloads/report/IPCC_AR6_WGII_FullReport.pdf> accessed 21 November 2024

Merner LD, Franta B and Frumhoff BP, 'Identifying Gaps in Climate-Litigation-Relevant Research: An Assessment from Interviews with Legal Scholars and Practitioners' (*The Climate Social Science Network*, April 2022) <https://cssn.org/wp-content/uploads/2022/04/CSSN-Research-Report-2022_2-Identifying-Gaps-in-Climate-Litigation-Relevant-Research-An-Assessment-from-Interviews-with-Legal-Scholars-and-Practitioners.pdf> accessed 26 February 2024

UNEnvironment Programme, 'Environmental Rule of Law: First Global Report' (*UN Environment Programme*, 2019) 185 <https://www.unep.org/resources/assessment/environmental-rule-law-first-global-report> accessed 18 September 2024

UN Environment Programme, 'Environmental Rule of Law: Tracking Progress and Charting Future Directions' (*UN Environment Programme*, 2023)

UN Environmental Programme, 'Global Climate Litigation Report: 2023 Status Review' (*UN Environment Programme*, 2023)


## *Blogs*


Jamwal K and Kapoor A, 'Resolving the Conundrum on the Precautionary Principle' (*Mongabay India*, 28 July 2022) <https://india.mongabay.com/2022/07/commentary-resolving-the-conundrum-on-the-precautionary-principle/>

Chapter 10

# Conclusion

## Key lessons and a future research agenda for climate litigation and vulnerabilities

*Maria Antonia Tigre, Melanie Jean Murcott, and Susan Ann Samuel*

### Introduction

This chapter synthesises the key lessons emerging from *Climate Litigation and Vulnerabilities: Global South Perspectives* and proposes directions for further research concerning climate litigation and vulnerabilities. Five main lessons are discussed. The first is the importance of addressing colonial legacies embedded in legal systems that shape climate litigation outcomes. The second lesson relates to the value of intersectionality in assessing vulnerabilities amidst the climate crisis. The third lesson emphasises the need for innovative legal strategies responsive to the distinct climate litigation challenges within the Global South. The fourth lesson concerns the need to overcome barriers to access to climate justice, including by virtue of structural challenges that impede marginalised communities from participating effectively in climate litigation. The last lesson relates to the facilitative role of courts in advancing intersectional climate justice. The chapter then sets out a future research agenda to build on the foundational work in this volume. The chapter proposes that future intersectional climate justice studies should broaden their focus beyond vulnerability experienced by relatively well-researched groups and focus, for instance, on LGBTQ+ communities, people with disabilities, people displaced by climate change, etc. Further, we argue that there remains a need to deepen engagement with intersectionality, a crucial lens. Additionally, new climate litigation research should delve into legal remedies that address the unique circumstances of vulnerable communities in the Global South, enhancing climate litigation's capacity to contribute meaningfully to global intersectional climate justice. Relatedly, research is required concerning how to ensure the implementation and enforcement of remedies and thus advance environmental rule of law. Lastly, the chapter identifies a need for more multidisciplinary studies, including in relation to climate litigation and political ecology, as well as local and international politics. In closing, the chapter proposes that climate litigation be envisioned as an imperfect but vital tool to recalibrate climate action.

DOI: 10.4324/9781003470632-13

## Climate litigation and vulnerabilities: key lessons

The chapters in this edited volume examined what it means to be vulnerable in a time of climate change, drawing on case studies from India, Bangladesh, Nigeria, the Pacific Islands, Indonesia, and Latin America. Authors delved into intersections among law, geography, science, philosophy, gender studies, history, and more to illustrate how litigation can be used to challenge systemic marginalisation and oppression linked to and heightened by the climate crisis. The work provides valuable insights into agency, resilience, and legal avenues available to women, children, and Indigenous peoples to confront the crisis. Emphasising the importance of including vulnerable communities in designing litigation strategies, chapters have explored the complexities of using legal systems to tackle both climate issues and ingrained social and economic inequalities. The volume collates overlapping and intersecting complex understandings of climate litigation in the Global South.

The key lessons from the volume include (1) the importance of identifying and being responsive to colonial legacies in the legal systems, (2) the value of recognising intersectionality when responding to vulnerability of populations amidst the climate crisis, (3) the need for innovative legal strategies suited to Global South contexts, (4) the need to overcome barriers to access to climate justice, and (5) the role of the courts in facilitating intersectional climate justice. These are briefly elaborated later. Notably, these lessons emerge in overlapping ways from the chapters. For instance, a chapter grappling with barriers to access to climate justice, in different ways, also highlights intersectionality, coloniality, the value in innovating legal strategies, and the role of courts in advancing intersectional climate justice. The five lessons, therefore, can be drawn from all the chapters, though they emerge in different constellations and with varying emphasis.

### *Identifying and overcoming colonial legacies in legal systems in the Global South*

Chapters in this volume demonstrate that several post-colonial legal systems in the Global South maintain an underlying colonial rationale or approach. Yet in order for climate litigation to tackle intersectional climate injustices, courts must be willing to engage with decolonial arguments and recognise knowledge of Indigenous peoples and other marginalised groups. Chapters 1 and 2 reflect on the ways in which judges can adjudicate climate change–relevant issues in ways that either maintain or challenge coloniality in legal systems. By analysing two climate cases from Ecuador and Colombia, in Chapter 1, Beckhauser and Broetto offer insight into the colonial nature of the interaction of the legal systems with Indigenous peoples' demands for climate justice in Latin America. They showcase ways in which judicial reasoning can depart from or uphold coloniality and advocate for the former approach. In a similar vein, Chapter 3, by Uehara, critiques formalistic legal traditions in Chile and Mexico that 'prevented judicial reasoning from extending beyond well-established national jurisprudence'[1] to address healthcare crises related to the climate crisis. She contrasts and presents as more conducive to climate justice more progressive approaches of judges in Colombia and Ecuador. Chapter 2, by Garg and Hinduja, explores how the legal system in India upholds colonial legacies that facilitate extractivist practices. Garg and Hinduja also challenge neocolonial extractivist 'solutions' for climate action that intensify marginalisation and oppression of the Adivasi people, highlighting the asymmetric social impacts of these so-called solutions. They advocate for anti-extractivist climate litigation that recognises the knowledge and experiences of, and livelihood impacts on, marginalised actors in relation to extractivist climate 'solutions'.

### *Comprehending intersectionality*

All chapters adopt an intersectional understanding of climate injustice and illustrate the ways in which geography – combined with inherent and socially construed conditions – informs vulnerability amidst the climate crisis.

From an Indian perspective, Chapter 2, by Garg and Hinduja, and Chapter 9, by Jamwal, highlight how socially marginalised communities in India experience barriers to access to climate justice, whilst also being particularly vulnerable to the causes and impacts of climate change.

From a Latin American perspective, Chapter 1, by Beckhauser and Broetto, speaks to the intersecting vulnerabilities of Indigenous peoples, while Chapter 3, by Uehara, emphasises how intersecting social and ecological challenges constitute health crises in Chile, Mexico, Ecuador, and Colombia. Uehara reveals how vulnerable people, due to their class, age, abilities, and other social factors, face significant barriers to healthcare access, which are heightened by the climate crisis. Concurrently, their healthcare challenges intersect with climate mitigation failures, such as greenhouse gas emissions that cause diseases and are worsening existing conditions. Chapter 3 thus calls for greater visibility of health crises in climate litigation.

Chapters 4, 5, and 8 draw attention to how the gendered impacts of climate change contribute to vulnerability, illustrating how interlinked contextual factors and power relations influence gendered vulnerability and must, in turn, influence climate litigation strategy. In Chapter 4, Dutta and Lofts highlight the absence of gender considerations in India's climate law and policy. They motivate for embedding gender-sensitive approaches through litigation. In Chapter 5, Burri and Duarte Reyes focus on how the struggles and agency of women of Pari Island, Indonesia, are influencing climate litigation against a carbon major, Holcim. In Chapter 8, Ladan and Maduekwe examine the Nigerian woman's vulnerability to climate change. These chapters highlight how, in different ways, women in India, Nigeria, and the Pari Islands are disproportionately impacted by climate change, including because they are disproportionately burdened with household responsibilities that become more onerous in the wake of disasters and extreme weather events.

Chapter 6, by Barrett, engages with the vulnerabilities of the Torres Strait Islanders. Barrett explains how Indigenous peoples, who are custodians of the land

and the sea, are experiencing existential threats as a result of biodiversity loss, erosion, rising sea levels, and inundation of burial sites essential for their communion with their ancestors.

Chapter 7, by Kaur et al., explores the particular vulnerabilities of children in Bangladesh. They illustrate that children's health in the South Asian region is particularly impacted by climate change due to extreme weather, existing nutritional deficits, and a lack of access to sanitation.

The overarching lesson emerging from these chapters is that litigation strategies in the Global South need to recognise and address intersectional vulnerabilities, rather than adopting a single-issue lens. Doing so requires lawyers to embrace the complex, legally disruptive nature of the climate crisis and engage with data from a variety of sources, emerging from multiple disciplines, that evidence these vulnerabilities. Crucially, climate litigation strategies must be co-produced with vulnerable groups, who are best placed to articulate how the climate crisis disproportionately impacts upon them.

### The value of innovative legal strategies

Chapter 5, by Burri and Duarte Reyes; Chapter 6, by Barrett; Chapter 7, by Kaur et al.; and Chapter 9, by Jamwal, present innovative approaches to litigation, such as including women in developing legal strategies (Chapters 5 and 8), instrumentalising vulnerability in multiple fora to confront the causes and impacts of climate change (Chapter 6), child-led litigation (Chapter 7), and applying the Indian iteration of the precautionary principle (Chapter 9). These chapters illustrate in various ways that strategic legal approaches can overcome some structural barriers, though they require supportive lawyers and legal frameworks and consistent application. Empowering marginalised groups to participate actively in litigation can transform it into a tool for intersectional climate justice that promotes agency. For instance, child-led climate litigation, discussed in Chapter 7, can encourage societies to question to what extent they live up to their duty of care for children and the limited agency afforded to children, despite burdening them with the legacy of ecological destabilisation. Further, Chapter 6 highlights how climate litigation can be a tool of political accountability and, hence, part of larger political transformation. As the chapter reveals, forum shopping allowed the Torres Strait Islanders to apply repeated political pressure on a government unwilling to act in response to climate change.

### Challenges of access and structural barriers

Chapter 8, by Ladan and Maduekwe, and Chapter 9, by Jamwal, address the significant barriers vulnerable communities face in litigating amidst the climate crisis, including a lack of financial resources, capacity, and technical expertise. For instance, Jamwal addresses the significant structural challenges faced by vulnerable communities in India when pursuing climate litigation, particularly to produce scientific evidence related to the causes and impacts of climate change. Overcoming these barriers requires systemic changes, such as regularising legal principles that ease the evidentiary burden (Chapter 9) and enhancing support through non-governmental organisations (NGOs) and advocacy (Chapter 8).

### *Facilitating climate justice through the role of courts*

Throughout the chapters, there is an acknowledgement of the courts' potential to contribute to climate justice, but also a recognition of their limitations. In particular, Chapters 1, 2, 3, 7, and 9 discuss the need for courts to adopt more progressive interpretations and consistent applications of principles that favour vulnerable people in climate litigation. Several chapters highlight instances where the courts have played this role.

Chapters illustrate the profound and disproportionate effects of climate change on vulnerable communities (including as a result of sea level rise, floods, droughts, hurricanes, and wildfires, which are increasing in frequency and intensity). The courts have an important role both in recognising, legitimising, and amplifying the concerns of people in the Global South and crafting appropriate remedies. This is particularly crucial in the Global South, where climate change is disproportionately devastating livelihoods, displacing communities, and exacerbating existing inequalities, and vulnerable populations – such as Indigenous groups, women, children, smallholder farmers, and rural communities – often lack the resources to recover from these events, compounding their vulnerability to future climate impacts.

## Climate litigation and vulnerabilities: a future research agenda

This volume represents a first step in investigating how climate litigation and vulnerabilities are connected. Yet much more research is needed to truly understand the connections between vulnerability and climate litigation in the Global South and beyond. A future research agenda must expand upon several underexplored areas. We have identified four areas, discussed in what follows. These are (1) the need to broaden inquiries about vulnerability in a time of climate crisis to include intersectional climate injustices not yet adequately addressed in literature and/or case law; (2) the need for intersectionality to permeate climate litigation and climate justice research; (3) research on legal remedies, enforcement, and environmental rule of law related to climate litigation; and (4) multidisciplinary research that engages political ecology and local and global politics.

### *Broadening the vulnerability inquiry*

While most climate litigation research – mirroring developments in courts and other tribunals worldwide – has rightly focused on women, children, and Indigenous groups, broader experiences of vulnerability and agency deserve greater attention to advance climate action and address intersectional climate injustice. This section briefly notes some of the non-exhaustive experiences of vulnerability and agency that could be explored in future intersectional climate justice research.

Climate migration is an increasingly urgent issue, as millions of people are displaced each year due to climate-related disasters, such as rising sea levels, droughts, and extreme weather events. Vulnerable populations, particularly in the Global South, are being forced to leave their homes in search of safer living conditions. Human (im)mobility creates a new set of legal challenges related to migratory status and the vulnerabilities of displaced communities. For instance, many climate migrants lack formal legal protections, as international law does not fully recognise them as refugees, leaving them in precarious situations where they face discrimination, poverty, and exclusion from essential services.

In this context, the intersection of climate migration and litigation is a growing area of focus. Legal claims may arise from the failure of governments to protect displaced communities, the violation of human rights due to inadequate housing or healthcare, or challenges to restrictive migration policies that ignore the realities of climate displacement. Future research should explore how climate litigation can address the specific vulnerabilities of climate migrants, ensuring that courts uphold their rights and that legal frameworks are developed to provide adequate protection for those displaced by climate change. The question of responsibility for displacement, whether by governments or corporations contributing to climate change, could also be pivotal in shaping future litigation strategies.

While some chapters briefly mention climate litigation as a means to address the vulnerability of the Earth and more-than-human life within her, further research is needed in this area. For instance, a key question relates to how climate litigation strategies can tackle the interrelated vulnerabilities of more-than-human life and human life in mutually reinforcing ways.

Although gender dimensions of vulnerability were explored in several chapters and cases they discussed, the analysis did not encompass the full spectrum of gender diversity, such as the experiences of gender-diverse communities often disproportionately affected by climate change but remaining marginalised in climate litigation. Future research could investigate how the intersection of gender, climate vulnerability, and access to justice plays out for these groups.

While Chapter 7 proposes avenues for child-led litigation, litigation on behalf of future generations (those not yet born) requires further inquiry. For example, the role of the Maastricht Principles on the Human Rights of Future Generations 2023 in future climate litigation is an area ripe for research.

Vulnerabilities linked to disabilities have not yet been adequately addressed in climate litigation research. People with disabilities are particularly vulnerable to climate impacts, facing barriers in accessing resources, justice, and protection during climate-related disasters and extreme weather events. Research is needed to understand how legal frameworks can better protect the rights of persons with disabilities amidst the climate crisis, including how courts can recognise their specific vulnerabilities when adjudicating cases.

Additionally, more climate litigation research is needed in relation to the struggles and agency of groups such as peasants, smallholder farmers, and coastal and rural communities. These groups are often on the front lines of climate change impacts yet often lack adequate legal protection or representation in climate litigation. The experiences of these groups in the Global South, where livelihoods are heavily dependent on the Earth's life support system, should be a key focus of legal strategies that acknowledge the unique challenges posed by climate change to food security, land rights, and rural livelihoods.

By expanding the focus to include a broader range of vulnerable populations and deepening the analysis of intersectionality and innovative legal remedies, future research can ensure that climate litigation more effectively responds to the diverse and pressing needs of those most at risk in the Global South.

### *Future research on intersectionality*

While intersectionality is a crucial lens throughout this volume, it deserves deeper examination in future climate litigation and climate justice research. Future research agendas should consider the intersecting impacts of race, class, caste, age, and other social determinants on climate vulnerability and resilience. Understanding the compounded vulnerabilities faced by women of colour, LGBTQ+ individuals and groups, migrants, and/or disabled persons in climate litigation can lead to more nuanced legal strategies and remedies that better address the needs of these people. These factors often amplify the severity of climate impacts for marginalised populations, who typically already face systemic discrimination and inadequate access to resources. Deepening analyses of how interlocking social conditions affect individuals and communities can foster understanding of complex, multi-layered vulnerabilities. Focusing on such intersections is essential for developing inclusive legal frameworks and policies that address the compounded risks and ensure equitable representation and protection in climate governance efforts.

For example, health is a critical yet often overlooked dimension of vulnerability in the context of climate change. Climate impacts – such as extreme heat, air pollution, vector-borne diseases, and natural disasters – disproportionately affect communities with pre-existing health vulnerabilities. Individuals with respiratory conditions or compromised immune systems face heightened risks during climate-related events. In the Global South, where healthcare infrastructure is often already under-resourced and some groups have limited access to healthcare, these risks are exacerbated, leaving the most vulnerable without adequate support or recourse. Addressing health vulnerabilities in climate litigation alongside other socially constructed vulnerabilities can emphasise the need for climate-responsive healthcare systems and legal protections that account for the public health implications of climate change, thereby promoting resilience and equity. This dynamic is even more crucial with the exacerbated effects of climate change. While Chapter 3 grappled with this topic in the Latin American context, further research is needed on how climate litigation in the Global South and beyond can address the health crises connected to the climate crisis.

### *Future research on legal remedies, enforcement, and environmental rule of law*

Future research must address the evolving legal remedies in climate litigation. As traditional remedies may no longer suffice to address the scale of climate harms, innovative judicial approaches must be developed that consider the long-term impacts on vulnerable groups. This could help secure climate litigation outcomes that advance restorative justice and preventive measures. Another critical area for future research in climate litigation is the enforcement of judicial decisions, as the gap between legal rulings and actual implementation is often wide. While courts may issue bold and groundbreaking decisions, a challenge is ensuring that these rulings are effectively enforced to bring about meaningful change. The political, economic, and institutional barriers to enforcement are significant and deserve in-depth examination. The question of implementation is also directly linked to remedies, yet further studies are crucial to understanding that connection.

In many cases, even when courts rule in favour of climate action, more adequate institutional capacity or political will is needed to implement these rulings and ensure progress. Research must explore how court decisions can be translated into tangible policy changes and how governments, companies, and other actors can be held accountable for compliance. Comparative studies on successful enforcement strategies from different jurisdictions could offer valuable insights, particularly in identifying mechanisms to ensure compliance with climate-related judicial decisions.

The role of civil society in monitoring and advocating for the enforcement of climate rulings is also crucial. Many climate judgments rely on public pressure and the work of NGOs and advocacy groups to push for implementation. Future research should consider how civil society can be better integrated into the enforcement process and how legal frameworks can empower these actors to take a more active role in ensuring compliance.

Moreover, there is a growing need to address the financial barriers to enforcement, particularly in countries with limited resources. Climate rulings often require significant investments in infrastructure, adaptation, or mitigation efforts, which may be beyond the capacity of the public or private sectors in some Global South countries. Research into funding mechanisms, such as international climate finance, climate funds, or penalties for non-compliance, could provide pathways for overcoming these barriers.

In addition, looking at how international mechanisms might support the enforcement of national climate rulings is essential. For example, the potential for international treaties or agreements to reinforce domestic court decisions could be explored. Crucially, the advisory opinions of the International Court of Justice and the Inter-American Court of Human Rights could further help. Additionally, the growing role of regional courts and human rights bodies in climate litigation, particularly in Latin America and Africa, opens up new avenues for ensuring that judicial decisions have cross-border effects and broader legal impact. These bodies could serve as a support structure for ensuring that national courts' climate rulings are respected and acted upon. By addressing the enforcement gap, future research can provide the tools to transform judicial victories in climate litigation into real-world climate action, ensuring that court decisions lead to effective and lasting outcomes for vulnerable populations.

Climate-related disasters expose deep gaps in the legal protection afforded to these groups, highlighting the urgent need for the law to address the disproportionate harm caused by climate change. Future research should examine how climate litigation can be used as a tool to protect vulnerable communities from the effects of such disasters. Legal action can compel governments and corporations to take preventive measures and improve disaster preparedness while ensuring that affected communities receive compensation and support in the aftermath of disasters. In this context, litigation serves not only as a tool for accountability but also as a means of promoting justice for those most impacted by climate change.

Lastly, the intersection of climate litigation with the environmental rule of law is becoming increasingly important. The environmental rule of law is the principle that legal frameworks should promote environmental sustainability, protect human rights, and ensure justice for all, especially in the face of environmental degradation. Climate litigation is crucial in strengthening the environmental rule of law by holding governments and corporations accountable for climate-related actions or inactions. As shown by examples worldwide, courts increasingly recognise the link between environmental protection and human rights, affirming that the failure to address climate change infringes on fundamental rights, such as the rights to a healthy environment, life, and dignity.

Integrating climate litigation into the environmental rule of law is especially important in the Global South, where legal systems may need to be developed or are under-resourced. Future research can help establish more robust legal frameworks that mitigate climate change and promote resilience and adaptive capacity in vulnerable populations. Among other legal interventions, just transition litigation can promote energy transitions that respect, promote, and fulfil human rights and avoid replicating colonial and extractivist approaches embedded in fossil fuel–driven energy. The need for a fast transition does not mean human rights should be overlooked.

Moreover, enforcing environmental laws through climate litigation can help address the systemic failures contributing to climate vulnerability, such as poor governance, weak regulatory frameworks, and corruption. This intersection underscores the broader role of the rule of law in addressing climate change, ensuring that laws are transparent, equitable, and enforceable, and that they serve the needs of those most affected by the climate crisis. Research in this area can provide critical insights into how courts and legal frameworks can better align with the principles of environmental rule of law to deliver meaningful, long-term protection for vulnerable communities facing climate-related disasters.

### *Future multidisciplinary research*

While we consolidated thoughts from the authors of chapters during a workshop at the University of Southampton on 3 October 2024, invaluable insights from three experts in disciplines outside of the law were revealed about the volume. These experts critically evaluated the position of climate litigation in the Global South and why it resonated for practices of climate action across the globe.

Firstly, Mushonga shared the crucial insight that more research on the political ecology of the courts is to be needed in the study of climate litigation.[2] Climate litigation faces critical tensions, especially in the Global South, where judicial reasoning often conflicts with the demands of Indigenous peoples. There is a disparity between what is desired – such as comprehensive environmental justice – and what is feasible within existing legal frameworks, many of which remain rooted in colonial legacies despite constitutional reforms that recognise Indigenous rights. These tensions, exacerbated by intersectional vulnerabilities, extend to issues of inclusion, highlighting who benefits from litigation and who is marginalised. While observing the evolution of climate cases can provide insights into these dynamics, interim solutions are needed to address immediate challenges. Political ecology offers a helpful framework by connecting law, power, and environmental justice, emphasising that vulnerabilities arise from political processes and that climate litigation is inherently political – and what comes through as a legal challenge is a result of what was politically made feasible for the law to thrive/function. Despite this, many analyses overlook applying a political ecology lens to court cases, missing opportunities to unravel underlying struggles. Additionally, the high costs of litigation create barriers for communities without financial means or assistance, further entrenching vulnerabilities within a system that often perpetuates capitalist interests. Addressing these challenges calls for a critical examination of legal systems within the broader socio-economic context, perhaps by engaging a 'political ecology of the courts' or 'legal political ecology' as frameworks with which to analyse court cases – to better understand and mitigate these tensions.

Secondly, Spaiser highlighted that climate litigation is part of larger political and societal transformation processes.[3] *Asmania et al. v Holcim* (Chapter 5) is a good example, as the transnational climate litigation case was accompanied by the *Call for Climate Justice* campaign in support of the litigation case. The campaign ensured broader public awareness and debate on climate justice. This is potentially beneficial not only to the case but also to the overall society where the case is being negotiated, facilitating solidarity with climate change–affected communities and shifts in attitudes that could result in political shifts, for example, through changed voting patterns. Chapters in this volume do not explore in any detail how climate litigation forms part of larger political and societal transformation processes, and this is an area ripe for future multidisciplinary inquiry.

Finally, Beardsworth argued that climate litigation is emerging as a strategy to rebalance Global North–South dynamics, where emerging legal strategies towards the most vulnerable in the South may offer examples of best practices for addressing the vulnerable in the North.[4] There is scope for comparative studies across North–South jurisdictions to explore this argument further.

Relatedly, Beardsworth argued that practices of litigation can operate as a powerful corrective of political inaction. For instance, Chapters 7 (the need for child-led litigation), 8 (a human rights approach to extreme vulnerability of the Nigerian woman), and 9 (the Indian iteration of the precautionary principle) show that climate litigation can create traction in national and international climate action and to address the struggles of vulnerable individuals and communities. This is at a time when the international politics of climate change is faced with multiple mitigation and adaptation challenges: most importantly, the deep mistrust between the North and the South. That said, the success of this approach will always depend on a robust legal framework within the state – one independent of political power and interest, where due process and the ability to access the courts are ensured and where legal sovereignty is maintained. The principle of equality before the law (and all that it facilitates) is, however, under strain at this historical juncture, including in large parts of Europe and the United States. Addressing climate action through litigation strategies for the most climate-vulnerable is vital in this context, for it not only confirms the importance of climate litigation for climate action in general but also points to how emerging legal strategies toward the most vulnerable in the South may offer examples of best practices for addressing the vulnerable in the North. The rebalancing of North–South dynamics through climate litigation would be an exciting consequence that the research outcomes of this volume could help facilitate.

## Closing remarks

The key lessons of and future research agenda emerging from this volume reveal that climate litigation is an imperfect but vital tool to recalibrate climate action, where innovative legal approaches addressing vulnerabilities in the Global South might inform best practices for safeguarding marginalised communities globally. The strategies, critiques, and insights articulated in this volume offer a promising start, but a great deal of further research and action is needed to respond to growing vulnerability amidst the climate crisis. The endeavour is undoubtedly overwhelming, but scholars, lawyers, activists, and others concerned about the planetary crisis should draw inspiration from the courageous refrain of climate justice activists in the Pacific Islands: 'We are not drowning; we are fighting.'

## Notes

1 See Uehara, Chapter 3, p 119.
2 Dr. Tafadzwa Mushonga, Lecturer in Environment, Society, and Political Ecology, University of Pretoria, spoke at the Southampton Workshop on 3 October 2024.
3 Dr. Viktoria Spaiser, Associate Professor in Sustainability Research and Computational Social Science, University of Leeds, School of Politics and International Studies.
4 Prof. Richard Beardsworth, Professor of International Politics and Head of School, University of Leeds, School of Politics and International Studies.

Appendix 1

# List of cases

## Domestic cases

### *Australia*

*Caltex Refineries (Qld) Pty Limited v Stavar* (2009) 75 NSWLR 649, Supreme Court of New South Wales, Court of Appeal (Australia)
*Graham Barclay Oysters v Ryan* (2002) 211 CLR 540, High Court of Australia (Australia)
*Hunter Area Health Service v Presland* (2005) 63 NSWLR 22, Supreme Court of New South Wales, Court of Appeal (Australia)
*Mabo v Queensland (No 2)* (1992) 175 CLR 1, High Court of Australia (Australia)
*Minister for the Environment v Sharma* (2022) 291 FCR 311, Federal Court of Australia, Full Court (Australia)
*Pabai v Commonwealth of Australia* (2022) VID622/2021, Federal Court of Australia (Australia)
*Telstra Corporation Limited v Hornsby Shire Council* (2006) 146 LGERA 10, Land and Environment Court of New South Wales (Australia)
*Waratah Coal Pty Ltd v Youth Verdict Ltd et al. (No 6*) (2022) QLC 21, Land Court of Queensland (Australia)

### *Bangladesh*

*Dacca National Medical Institute v Province of East Pakistan* (1958) 10 DLR 343, Supreme Court of Bangladesh (Bangladesh)
*Faridul Alam v Bangladesh* (2010) 18 BLT 323, Supreme Court of Bangladesh (Bangladesh)
*Farooque v Government of Bangladesh* (2001) WP 891 of 1994, Supreme Court of Bangladesh (Bangladesh)
*Human Rights & Peace for Bangladesh v Bangladesh* (2010) 22 BLC 48, Supreme Court of Bangladesh (Bangladesh)
*Human Rights & Peace for Bangladesh v Bangladesh* (2019) WP No. 13989/2016, Supreme Court of Bangladesh (Bangladesh)
*Human Rights and Peace for Bangladesh et al. v Secretary of the Ministry of Shipping et al.* (2016) 13989, Supreme Court of Bangladesh (Bangladesh)

*Mohiuddin Farooque v Bangladesh* (1997) 49 DLR (AD) 1, Supreme Court of Bangladesh (Bangladesh)
*Mohiuddin Farooque v Bangladesh et al.* (1996) 48 DLR (HCD) 438, Supreme Court of Bangladesh (Bangladesh)
*Rabia Bhuiyan MP v Ministry of Local Government and Rural Development et al.* (2007) 59 DLR (AD) (2007), Supreme Court of Bangladesh (Bangladesh)
*Shah Abdul Hannan v Bangladesh* (2011) 16 BLC 386, Supreme Court of Bangladesh (Bangladesh)
*Yunus Mia v Secretary Ministry of Public Works* (1993) 45 (1993) DLR, High Court Division of Bangladesh (Bangladesh)

## Brazil

*Conectas Direitos Humanos v BNDES and BNDESPar* (2022) ACP 1038657–42.2022.4.01.3400, Ninth Federal Civil Court of the Federal District (Brazil)
*ONG Costa Legal et al. v Municipality of Florianópolis et al.* (2021) No. 5012843–56.2021.4.04.7200, 6th Federal Court of Florianópolis, Santa Catarina (Brazil)

## Chile

*Mejillones Tourist Service Association et al. v Environmental Evaluation Service (SEA) of Antofagasta* (2021) 6930–2021 and 71.628–2021, Chilean Supreme Court of Justice (Chile)

## Colombia

*Center for Social Justice v Ministry of the Environment et al.* (2016) T-622/16, Colombia's Constitutional Court (Colombia)
*Future Generations v Ministry of the Environment et al.* (2018) 11001 22 03 000 2018 00319 00, Colombia's Supreme Court (Colombia)
*Osorio Palacio et al. v Colpatria EPS et al.* (2008) T-760/08, Colombia's Constitutional Court (Colombia)
*Pushaina et al. v Carbones del Cerrejón Limited et al.* (2017) SU698/17, Colombia's Constitutional Court (Colombia)
*Yánez González et al. v Alcaldía Municipal de Montería et al.* (2015) T-218/17, Colombia's Constitutional Court (Colombia)

## Ecuador

*Asanza Reyes et al. v Dr. Chiriboga and the Public Health Ministry of Ecuador* (2016) 074–16-SIS-CC, Ecuador's Constitutional Court (Ecuador)
*Baihua Caiga et al. v PetroOriental S.A* (2021) 22201202000469, Unidad Judicial de Familia, Mujer, Niñez y Adolescencia, Cantón Francisco de Orellana (Ecuador)

*Herrera Carrion et al. v Ministry of the Environment et al.* (2021) 21201202000170, Corte Provincial de Justicia de Sucumbíos (Ecuador)

### Germany

*Lliuya v RWE* (2017) 2 O 285/15, Oberlandesgericht Hamm (Germany)

*Neubauer et al. v Germany* (2020) BvR 2656/18/1, BvR78/20/1, BvR96/20/1, BvR288/20, German Federal Constitutional Court (Germany)

### India

*A.P. Pollution Control Board v Prof MV Naidu* (1992) 1992 2 SCC 718, Indian Supreme Court (India)

*Avas Vikas Parishad v Friends Co. Housing Society* (1996) AIR 1996 SC 114, Indian Supreme Court (India)

*Calcutta Electricity Supply Corporation (India) Ltd v Subhash Chandra Bose* (1992) AIR 1992 573, Indian Supreme Court (India)

*Charan Lal Sahu v Union of India* (1991) AIR 1991 SC 101, Indian Supreme Court (India)

*Chaudhary Laxmanbhai Parthibhai v State of Gujarat* (2012) /WPPIL/155/2011, Gujarat High Court (India)

*Coralie v Union Territory of Delhi* (1981) 1981 AIR 1981, Indian Supreme Court (India)

*Democratic Youth Federation v Union of India* (2011) MANU/SC/0653/2011, Indian Supreme Court (India)

*Gaurav Bansal v Union of India* (2014) 498/2014, National Green Tribunal (India)

*Godavarman v Union of India* (1996) WP(C)/202/1995, Indian Supreme Court (India)

*Godavarman v Union of India et al.* (2022) LiveLaw SC 467, Indian Supreme Court (India) (*Godavarman*)

*Hanuman Laxman Aroskar v Union of India* (2019) SC/0444/2019, Indian Supreme Court (India) (*Hanuman*)

*Karnataka Industrial Area Development Board v Kenchappa* (2006) 2006 6 SCC 371, Indian Supreme Court (India)

*Kasam Sidhiq Chuchiya v State of Gujarat* (2021) C/WPPIL/122/2018, Gujarat High Court (India)

*Lt. Col Nitisha v Union of India* (2021) W.P. 1109/2020, Indian Supreme Court (India) (*Nitisha*)

*Mahesh R. Desai v Union of India* (1988) W.P. 989, Indian Supreme Court (India)

*Maneka Gandhi v Union of India* (1978) 1978 AIR 597, Indian Supreme Court (India)

*Mehta v Kamal Nath* (1997) 1 SCC 388, Indian Supreme Court (India)

*M/S Shri Radhey Stone Crusher v Rajasthan State Pollution Control et al.* (2010) 2010(4) RLW 3449 (Raj.), Indian Supreme Court (India)

*M/s Sterlite Industries (India) Ltd Thoothukudi v The Chairman Tamil Nadu Pollution Control Board, Chennai* (2013) 22/2013 (SZ) and 23/2013 (SZ), National Green Tribunal, Principal Bench (India)

*Pandurang Sitaram Chalke et al. v State of Maharashtra* (2013) 14/2012, National Green Tribunal, Western Zone Bench (India) (*Pandurang*)

*Parameswara Kurup v State of Kerala, WP(C)* (2021) 19429/2014, Kerela High Court (India)

*Raj Behari Lal et al. v Mahabir Prasad et al.* (1955) AIR 1956 All 310, Allahabad High Court (India)

*Ranjitsinh et al. v Union of India* (2024) SC 2024 INC 280, Indian Supreme Court (India)

*Ridhima Pandey v Union of India et al.* (2019) 187/2017, National Green Tribunal (India)

*Sachidanand Pandey v State of West Bengal* (1987) AIR 1987 SC 1109, Indian Supreme Court (India)

*Shankarlal Gopalbhai Patel v Union of India* (2023) OA/06/2020, National Green Tribunal, Western Zone (India)

*Shri Dattatraya Kondaji Kale v Union of India* (2010) PIL/223/2010, Bombay High Court (India)

*Society for Protection of Environment & Biodiversity v Union of India* (2016) 677/2016, National Green Tribunal (India)

*State of Punjab v Chawla* (1997) AIR 1997 SC 1225, Indian Supreme Court (India)

*Subhash Kumar v The State of Bihar* (1991) 1991 AIR 420, Indian Supreme Court (India)

*Susetha v Union of India* (2008) W.P. 30725, Madras High Court (India)

*Suzlon Infrastructure Services Ltd v State of Kerala* (2010) W.P. (C) No. 34006/2010 Kerala High Court (India)

*Vellore Citizens Welfare Forum v Union of India* (1996) 1996 5 SCC 647, Indian Supreme Court (India)

## Kenya

*Environment and Land Court (ELC) of Iten, Legal Advice Centre T/A Kituo cha Sheria et al. v Attorney General et al.* (2022) ELC Petition No. 007 of 2022, The Environment and Land Court of Iten (Kenya)

## Mexico

*Greenpeace Mexico v Ministry of Energy et al.* (2020) 104/2020, Second District Court of Mexico (Mexico) (*Greenpeace Mexico*)

## Netherlands

*Urgenda Foundation v Netherlands* (2015) HAZA C/09/00456689, Supreme Court of the Netherlands (Netherlands)

## *Nigeria*

*Abayomi Fabunmi v Commissioner of Police Osun State et al.* (2011) LPELR-8776, Court of Appeal (Nigeria)

*Abbas Abdullhi Machika v Katsina State House of Assembly & Attorney General of Katsina State* (2010) 10 NMLR, Supreme Court of Nigeria (Nigeria)

*Alhaji Abdulazeez Adefila et al. v His Royal Majesty-Oba James Adedapo Popoola (Oore of Otun-Ekiti) et al.* (2014) LPELR-22468, Court of Appeal (Nigeria)

*Alhaji Aliyu N Salihu v Suleiman Umar Gana et al.* (2014) LPELR-23069, Court of Appeal (Nigeria)

*Alhaji Ibrahim Abdulhamid v Talal Akar et al.* (2006) SC 240/2001, Supreme Court of Nigeria (Nigeria)

*Alhaji Lawwani Zakari v Inspector-General of Police et al.* (2000) LPELR-6780, Court of Appeal (Nigeria)

*Alhaji Sheu Abdul Gafar v The Government of Kwara State et al.* (2007) LPELR-8073, Supreme Court of Nigeria (Nigeria)

*Alhaji Tsoho Dan Amale v Sokoto Local Government et al.* (2012) LPELR-7842, Supreme Court of Nigeria (Nigeria)

*Archbishop Anthony Olubunmi Okogie et al. v The Attorney-General of Lagos State* (1980) FNLR FCA/L/74/80, Supreme Court of Nigeria (Nigeria)

*Attorney-General of Lagos State v the Attorney-General of the Federation et al.* (2003) LPELR-620, (2003) 838–1010 NSCQR Vol 14, Supreme Court of Nigeria (Nigeria) ('*AG Lagos State v AG Federation*')

*Attorney-General of Ondo State v The Attorney-General of the Federation et al.* (2002) LPELR 623, Supreme Court of Nigeria (Nigeria)

*Barr Eric Chukwuemeka Igweokolo v Marvel Akpoyibo et al.* (2017) LPELR-41882, Court of Appeal (Nigeria)

*Blessing Chibunna Okpalaibekwe v Ebere Cyrian Okpalaibekwe* (2010) 12 NMLR (Pt II) 99, Supreme Court of Nigeria (Nigeria)

*Central Bank of Nigeria v Chief Daniel Obameneke Okemuo et al.* (2016) LPELR-41405, Court of Appeal (Nigeria)

*Centre for Oil Pollution Watch v Nigerian National Petroleum Corporation* (2019) 5 NWLR [PT.1666] P.518, Supreme Court of Nigeria (Nigeria)

*Chief Francis Igwe et al. v Ezeanochie et al.* (2009) LPELR-11885, Court of Appeal (Nigeria)

*Economic and Financial Crimes Commission v Ibrahim Suleiman et al.* (2016) LPELR-40790, Court of Appeal (Nigeria)

*Edwin Onuba v Innocent Onuba et al.* (2010) 11 NMLR 339, Supreme Court of Nigeria (Nigeria)

*Emeka v Okoroafor et al.* (2017) LPELR-417, Supreme Court of Nigeria (Nigeria)

*Endurance Odubu v Lieutenant Olorunduyilemi Stephen et al.* (2012) LPELR-19792, Court of Appeal (Nigeria)

*Eze Emma Umez Eronini et al. v Lady CA Eronini et al.* (2013) LPELR-20651, Court of Appeal (Nigeria)
*Faith Okafor v Lagos State Government et al.* (2016) LPELR-41066, Court of Appeal (Nigeria)
*Federal Republic of Nigeria et al. v Alhaji Mohammed Sani Abacha et al.* (2014) Court of Appeal (Nigeria)
*Federal Republic of Nigeria et al. v Lord Chief Udensi Ifegwu* (2003) LPELR-3173, Supreme Court of Nigeria (Nigeria)
*Federal Road Safety Commission v Ofoegbu* (2014) LPELR-24229, Court of Appeal (Nigeria)
*Fort Royal Homes Limited et al. v Economic and Financial Crimes Commission et al.* (2017) LPELR-42807, Court of Appeal (Nigeria)
*Ganiat Amope Dilly v Inspector General of Police et al.* (2016) LPELR-41452, Court of Appeal (Nigeria)
*General Sani Abacha et al. v Fawehinmi* (2002) LPELR-14, Supreme Court of Nigeria (Nigeria)
*George Adumu v The Comptroller of Prisons Federal Prisons Aba et al.* (2013) LPELR-22069, Court of Appeal (Nigeria)
*Grace Jack v University of Agriculture Makurdi* (2004) 102 NSCQR LPELR-1587, Supreme Court of Nigeria (Nigeria)
*Hon Chris Azubuogu v Hon Harry N Oranezi et al.* (2017) LPELR-42669, Supreme Court of Nigeria (Nigeria)
*HRH Eze Ukaobasi v Berthram Ezimora et al.* (2016) LPELR-40174, Court of Appeal (Nigeria)
*Ikechukwu Okpara et al. v Shell Petroleum Development Company of Nigeria Limited et al.* (2006) FHC/PHC/C5/518/2005, Federal High Court (Nigeria)
*Isaac Obiuweubi v Central Bank of Nigeria* (2011) LPELR-2185, Supreme Court of Nigeria (Nigeria)
*James Olosegun Omoleye v Olaniran et al.* (2010) 10 NMLR 460–461, Supreme Court of Nigeria (Nigeria)
*Jonah Gbemre v Shell Petroleum Development Company Nigeria Ltd, Nigerian National Petroleum Corporation, Attorney General of the Federation* (2005) FHC/B/CS/53/05, Federal High Court (Nigeria)
*Look Engine Parts Limited et al. v Ecobank Nigeria Plc et al.* (2014) LPELR-22522, Court of Appeal (Nigeria)
*Luke Loveday v The Comptroller of Prisons Federal Prisons Aba et al.* (2013) LPELR-22072, Court of Appeal (Nigeria)
*Mallam Nasir Ahmed El-Rufai v Senate of the National Assembly et al.* (2014) LPELR-231115, Court of Appeal (Nigeria)
*Mbadike et al. v Lagos International Trade Fair Complex Management Board et al.* (2017) LPELR-41968, Court of Appeal (Nigeria)
*Michael Nzekwesi Anekwe et al. v Aniekwensi (alias Morocco) et al.* (2009) 10 NMLR 24, Supreme Court of Nigeria (Nigeria)

*Ngozi Chile Oparaocha et al. v Barr Emeka A Obichere et al.* (2016) LPELR-40615, Court of Appeal (Nigeria)

*Nigeria Union of Teachers et al. v Conference of Secondary School Tutors (CSST) et al.* (2005) LPELR-5953, Court of Appeal (Nigeria)

*Nigerian Navy et al. v Lionel Okon Garrick* (2005) LPELR-7555, Court of Appeal (Nigeria)

*Niyi Aluko et al. v Commissioner of Police et al.* (2016) LPELR-41342, Court of Appeal (Nigeria)

*Ogugu et al. v The State* (1994) 9 NWLR (Pt 366) 1, (1994) 10 Ilaw/sc.303/1990, Supreme Court of Nigeria (Nigeria)

*Omo Oba Adenire Adetona et al. v Economic and Financial Crimes Commission et al.* (2017) LPELR-42369, Court of Appeal (Nigeria)

*Ovai Ekpe Okon v Ovai Bassey Enem Enyiefem et al.* (2016) LPELR-41168, Court of Appeal (Nigeria)

*Raymond Dongtoe v Civil Service Commission Plateau State* (2001) LPELR-959, Supreme Court of Nigeria (Nigeria)

*Romanus Ihejiobi et al. v Chinyere Ihejiobi et al.* (2013) LPELR-21957, Court of Appeal (Nigeria)

*Rumugu Air and Space Nigeria Limited v Federal Airports Authority of Nigeria et al.* (2016) LPELR-41506, Court of Appeal (Nigeria)

*Sea trucks Nigeria Limited v Panya Anigboro* (2001) 137–138 NSCQLR Vol 5, Supreme Court of Nigeria (Nigeria)

*Silas Jumbo Essien v Chief Akpan Inyang et al.* (2011) LPELR-4125, Court of Appeal (Nigeria)

*Skye Bank Plc v Emerson Njoku et al.* (2016) LPELR-40447, Court of Appeal (Nigeria)

*Solomon Adekunle v Attorney-General of Ogun State* (2014) LPELR-22569, Court of Appeal (Nigeria)

*Solomon Kporharor et al. v Michael Yedi et al.* (2017) LPELR-42418, Court of Appeal (Nigeria)

*Solomon Ohakosim v Commissioner of Police Imo State et al.* (2009) LPELR-8874, Court of Appeal (Nigeria)

*Stanley Okonkwo v Anthony Ezeonu et al.* (2017) LPELR-42785, Court of Appeal (Nigeria)

*Ujueke Enemuo (Chairperson, Umuada-Umuchu) et al. v Alochukwu Ezeonyeka et al.* (2016) LPELR-40171, Court of Appeal (Nigeria)

*University of Ilorin et al. v Idowu Oluwadare* (2006) 28–29 NSCQR Vol 27, Supreme Court of Nigeria (Nigeria)

*Ziakade Patrick Akpobolokemi et al. v The Hon Captain Emmanuel Ihenacho et al.* (2016) LPELR-40563, Court of Appeal (Nigeria)

## Pakistan

*Leghari v Federation of Pakistan* (2015) W.P. 25501/201, Lahore High Court (Pakistan)

*Rabab Ali v Federation of Pakistan et al.* (2016) ___ / I of 2016, Supreme Court of Pakistan (Pakistan) (*Ali*)

### Papua New Guinea

*Saonu and Morobe Provincial Government v Minister for Environment and Conservation and Climate Change et al.* (2021) OS (JR) 35 of 2021, Court of Justice at Waigani (Papua New Guinea)

### Philippines

*Global Legal Action on Climate Change v The Philippines Government* (2010) Philippines Supreme Court (Philippines)

*In Re Greenpeace Southeast Asia et al. v Chevron et al.* (2015) CHR-NI-2016–0001, Commission on Human Rights (Philippines)

### South Africa

*Minister of Mineral Resources and Energy et al. v Sustaining the Wild Coast NPC et al.* (2024) ZASCA 84, Supreme Court of Appeal (South Africa)

*Sustaining the Wild Coast NPC et al. v Minister of Mineral Resources et al.* (2022) ZAECMkHC 55, High Court (South Africa)

### Switzerland

*Asmania et al. v Holcim* (2023) A1 2023 9, Cantonal Court of the Canton of Zug (Switzerland) (*Asmania*)

### Uganda

*Mbabazi et al. v The Attorney General and National Environmental Management Authority* (2012) Civil Suit No. 283 of 2012, High Court of Kampala (Uganda)

### United Kingdom

*Ex parte Sidebotham* [1879] CA14 (1880) ChD 458, Court of Appeal (England and Wales)

## International and regional cases

### European Court of Human Rights

*Agostinho v Portugal* (2024) 39371/20, European Court of Human Rights

*Verein Klimaseniorinnen Schweiz et al. v Switzerland* (2024) 53600/20, European Court of Human Rights

### Inter-American Court of Human Rights

*Indigenous Communities of the Lhaka Honhat (Our Land) Association v Argentina* (2020) Serie C 400, Inter-American Court of Human Rights

*Kichwa Indigenous People of Sarayaku v Ecuador* (2012) Serie C 245, Inter-American Court of Human Rights

*Kuna Indigenous People of Madungandí and the Emberá Indigenous People of Bayano and their members v Panama* (2014) Serie C 284, Inter-American Court of Human Rights

*Lagos del Campo v Peru* (2017) Serie C 340, Inter-American Court of Human Rights

*Mayagna (Sumo) Awas Tingni Community v Nicaragua* (2001) Serie C 79, Inter-American Court of Human Rights

*Punta Piedra Garifuna Community and Its members v Honduras* (2015) Serie C 304, Inter-American Court of Human Rights

*Sawhoyamaxa Indigenous Community v Paraguay* (2006) Serie C 146, Inter-American Court of Human Rights

*Xakmok Kasek Indigenous Community v Paraguay* (2010) Serie C 214, Inter-American Court of Human Rights

*Yakye Axa Indigenous Community v Paraguay* (2005) Serie C 125, Inter-American Court of Human Rights

'Request for an Advisory Opinion on the Climate Emergency and Human Rights Submitted to the Inter-American Court of Human Rights by the Republic of Colombia and the Republic of Chile' (9 January 2023) <https://www.corteidh.or.cr/docs/opiniones/soc_1_2023_en.pdf> accessed 12 August 2024

### International Court of Justice

*Argentina v Uruguay (Pulp Mills on the River Uruguay)* (2006) ICJ Rep 113, 71, International Court of Justice

### International Tribunal for the Law of the Sea

*New Zealand v Japan, Australia v Japan (Southern Bluefin Tuna)* (1999) International Tribunal for the Law of the Sea

*Request for an Advisory Opinion submitted by the Commission of Small Island States on Climate Change and International Law* (Advisory Opinion of 21 May 2024) Case No. 31, available at <https://www.itlos.org/fileadmin/itlos/documents/cases/31/Advisory_Opinion/C31_Adv_Op_21.05.2024_orig.pdf>.

### UN Committee on the Rights of the Child

*Sacchi et al. v Argentina* (2019) CRC/C/88/D/105/2019, UN Committee on the Rights of the Child

### UN Human Rights Committee

*Billy v Australia* (2022) CCPR/C/135/D/3624/2019, UN Human Rights Committee

# Index